NILS **GOTTFRIES**
UPPSALA UNIVERSITY, SWEDEN

MACRO**ECONOMICS**

palgrave
macmillan

First published 2013 by
PALGRAVE MACMILLAN

Palgrave Macmillan in the UK is an imprint of Macmillan Publishers Limited,
registered in England, company number 785998, of Houndmills, Basingstoke,
Hampshire RG21 6XS.

Palgrave Macmillan in the US is a division of St Martin's Press LLC,
175 Fifth Avenue, New York, NY 10010.

Palgrave Macmillan is the global academic imprint of the above companies
and has companies and representatives throughout the world.

Palgrave® and Macmillan® are registered trademarks in the United States,
the United Kingdom, Europe and other countries.

ISBN 978–0–230–27597–3

This book is printed on paper suitable for recycling and made from fully
managed and sustained forest sources. Logging, pulping and manufacturing
processes are expected to conform to the environmental regulations of the
country of origin.

A catalogue record for this book is available from the British Library.

A catalog record for this book is available from the Library of Congress.

10   9   8   7   6   5   4   3   2   1
22   21   20   19   18   17   16   15   14   13

To Annika

BRIEF CONTENTS

CONTENTS

2 THE SHORT RUN

3 ECONOMIC POLICY

4 THE OPEN ECONOMY

5 BUSINESS CYCLES, POLICYMAKING, FINANCIAL MARKETS

LIST OF FIGURES

LIST OF TABLES

LIST OF VARIABLES

This list contains important variables which are used in this book. Variables are symbols representing economic quantities and prices and the notation is standard in macroeconomics. Each variable is explained as it is first introduced within the chapters, but this list will serve as a handy reference list.

A	real asset holdings measured in units of the domestically produced basket of goods
C	real consumption measured in units of the domestically produced basket of goods
D	real government debt; D/Y is the government debt ratio
E	indicator of technology (efficiency); EN is the effective number of workers
e	nominal exchange rate: the price of domestic currency in terms of foreign currency
e^e	expected future exchange rate, e^e_{t+1}
f	job-finding rate for employed workers
G	real government purchases: government consumption and investment, $G = C^G + I^G$
g	growth rate of technological efficiency (E) (sometimes g is used for growth of GDP)
I	real investment measured in units of the consumption basket
i	nominal interest rate as a share of the borrowed amount
i^*	foreign interest rate
IM	quantity of goods and services imported
K	real capital stock; K^d is the desired real capital stock
k	capital stock per effective worker: $k = K/(EN)$; k^* is the steady state level
L	labour force $L = N + U$
M	money supply
MC	marginal cost
MPC	marginal propensity to consume, the effect of income on consumption
MPK	marginal product of capital
MPL	marginal product of labour
n	growth rate of population
N	employment, the number of workers employed
N^n	natural level of employment

NX	net exports measured in units of domestically produced basket of goods
P	price level, a price index measuring the average price of all goods produced
P^*	foreign price level
$r \approx i - \pi$	real interest rate; $1 + r$ is the price of goods today in terms of goods next year
r^n	natural rate of interest
T	real taxes minus transfers; T^e is expected future real taxes minus transfers
Tr^F	net transfers from abroad
u	unemployment rate, $u = U/L$
U	number of workers unemployed, $U = L - N$
u^n	natural rate of unemployment
V	velocity of money, nominal production divided by the money supply $V = PY/M$
W	average nominal wage per worker in the economy; W^d is the firm's desired wage
W/P	real wage measured in how many units of the consumption basket you can buy
Y	real production; Y^e is expected future income
Y^*	foreign real production/income
Y^d	real disposable income, $Y^d = Y^\ell - T + rD + rF$
Y^ℓ	labour income plus pure profits which are distributed to households
Y^n	natural level of production
$\hat{Y}$	output gap, $\hat{Y} = (Y - Y^n)/Y^n$
Y^F	net primary income (wages, interest, dividends) from abroad
X	the quantity of goods and services exported
α	*alpha*, exponent for K in the Cobb–Douglas production function, measures the importance of capital for production
δ	*delta*, rate of depreciation
ε	*epsilon*, the real exchange rate, the price of domestically produced goods relative to foreign goods, $\varepsilon = eP/P^*$
η	*eta*, elasticity of demand for goods produced by a particular firm
λ	*lambda*, typically used to denote a fraction, used for different things in different places
μ	*mu*, mark-up as a proportion of marginal cost
π	*pi*, inflation rate, rate of price increase; π^* is inflation abroad
ρ	*rho*, subjective rate of discount

ABOUT THE AUTHOR

Nils Gottfries received his PhD at Stockholm University in 1985. He carried out research at the Institute for International Economic Studies until 1994, when he became Professor of Economics at Uppsala University. His main research areas are wage and price formation, and he published articles in the *Journal of Political Economy*, the *Quarterly Journal of Economics* and the *Economic Journal* amongst many journals. He has been Editor of the *Scandinavian Journal of Economics* and a member of the Swedish Government Commission on the euro (the Calmfors  Commission) and of the Economic Council of Sweden. He is the author of several government reports, and he has taught macroeconomics for many years at intermediate and graduate levels.

PREFACE

The process that led to the publication of this book started in the spring of 2008 when I decided to teach macroeconomics in a new way. I wanted to teach it in a way that was more thoroughly based on microeconomics and more internally consistent, while still emphasizing the market imperfections and rigidities that characterize real economies. Having taught PhD courses in macro and monetary economics at the universities of Stockholm and Uppsala for many years, I thought that it should be possible to teach undergraduate macro in a way that was closer to how we teach graduate macro yet without being overly technical. Late in 2008, I contacted the editors at Palgrave Macmillan and from then on the book project started to develop. After four years of experimentation, revision, rewriting, and reshuffling, here is the result.

What's different?

The combination of four characteristics makes this book different from other books at this level:

- *The book presents one consistent macroeconomic theory.* Such a theory is easier to understand and remember than a collection of loosely connected models. Students will leave this course with a good understanding of how the different parts of the economy fit together.
- *Macroeconomic theory is built up from microeconomics.* To analyse consumption, investment, prices, wages, unemployment, imports, exports, and international financial markets, we start from the microeconomic decisions of households and firms.
- *Although we start from microeconomics, we do not assume perfect markets and flexible prices.* From the beginning, we include important market imperfections and rigidities, which are central for how real economies function. Throughout the book, we assume that there is imperfect competition in the product market and unemployment in the labour market. When analysing the short run, we assume nominal wage rigidity.
- *The book has a distinct international perspective.* Instead of focusing on a few specific events in one particular country, we look at 50–60 years of data for several countries to see how well the theory matches the data.

While writing this book, my aim has been to find the middle ground between mainstream 'Keynesian' macro books, which present a set of interesting but rather loosely connected ideas, and 'classical' macro books, which present a precise and consistent macroeconomic theory that is rarely used for practical policy analysis or forecasting. The theory presented here is close to the mainstream macroeconomic theory that is used by central banks, government institutions, and in the financial markets. I have tried to present relevant macroeconomic theory as precisely as posible, yet without too much formal mathematics.

Level and prerequisites

The book is primarily designed for an intermediate course in macroeconomics. Ideally, students who use the book will be reasonably comfortable with elementary calculus and will have taken (or are simultaneously taking) a course in intermediate microeconomics.[1] The book could also be used, combined with additional material, for an advanced undergraduate course in macroeconomics. With its thorough treatment of international aspects, firms, and financial markets, it should be useful for master programmes in public policy, business administration, or finance.

The organization of the book

Introduction (Chapter 1)

In the introduction we explain the use of models in economics and key concepts in the national accounts.

The Long Run (Chapters 2–7)

In a market economy, most production is carried out by privately owned firms, so we start by analysing how firms produce and set prices. We assume that there is imperfect competition in the product market, so firms face limited demand for their products. We analyse how firms set prices to maximize profits and how the degree of competition affects the distribution of income.

Then we turn to the demand side. A thorough analysis of investment and consumption decisions gives us a deep understanding of what factors drive fluctuations in consumption and investment and the important role of expectations for aggregate demand. Throughout, we emphasize the role of the *real interest rate* as a key relative price that brings equality between supply and demand on the macroeconomic level.

To analyse long-run growth, we build on the microeconomic analysis of investment and savings decisions. This allows us to see clearly how market imperfections in product and labour markets, taxes on capital, and other factors affect the long-run level of income.[2]

---

1 Students should be reasonably familiar with functions, elementary rules of derivation, exponents and logs, simple equation systems and utility and profit maximization. The appendix to Chapter 1 reviews some basic mathematical concepts.

2 We use a 'Ramsey-style' model instead of the usual Solow growth model. One advantage is that this allows us to analyse long-run growth in the open economy, international borrowing, and foreign debt in a precise way (see below).

To analyse wage-setting and unemployment, we start from a model where firms set wages. Building on that model, we consider matching problems and union bargaining. We see how different factors affect the long-run level of employment and the real wage.

We bring money into the model and we analyse how inflation and interest rates are determined in the long run.

The Short Run (Chapters 8–9)

We analyse how shocks affect aggregate demand, production, and employment in the short run. The analysis of short-run wage adjustment and inflation builds explicitly on the theory of wage- and price-setting that is developed in the first part of the book, but the economy works in a different way in the short run because nominal wages and prices adjust slowly to shocks. This analysis gives us a clear understanding of the trade-off between inflation and unemployment. We see clearly the relation between the short and the long run.

Economic Policy (Chapters 10–11)

When analysing monetary policy we focus on the interest rate rather than the money supply. We use our macroeconomic theory (the *IS* curve and the Phillips curve) to analyse how the central bank should adjust the interest rate in response to several different shocks.

Our microeconomic analysis of consumption-savings decisions gives us a good basis for the analysis of fiscal policy. The sustainability of government finances and current fiscal imbalances are analysed thoroughly.

The Open Economy (Chapters 12–15)

We open up the economy for trade, allowing domestic and foreign consumers to choose between domestically produced and foreign goods. In international financial markets, investors can choose between lending in the home country and lending abroad. We look at the data to understand globalization in markets for goods and services and in the financial markets.

In open economies with integrated financial markets, savings may differ from investment. Our micro-based growth model allows us to analyse growth in the open economy, the current account and the long-run level of foreign debt.

We analyse the roles of monetary and fiscal policy in the open economy and we review the history of the exchange rate system and developments in the European Monetary Union.

Business Cycles, Institutions, Financial Markets (Chapters 16–18)

We examine the nature of business cycles, their causes, consequences, and costs.

We make policy endogenous and we analyse how institutions affect policymaking. This helps us to understand why many countries have made their central banks more independent.

A final chapter on financial markets explains the roles of the stock market and of banks and we try to understand financial crises. Again we start from microeconomics by considering the different roles of debt and equity as sources of finance for firms and financial institutions.

Additional features

- Each chapter ends with a summary of the main points in the chapter and an explanation of where we are going.
- There are exercises at the end of each chapter; answers to these exercises are available on the web page. These exercises have varying levels of difficulty, so the instructor may want to indicate which of the exercises the students should focus on primarily.
- Additional exercises, with answers, are available only to instructors (see below).
- Appendices contain additional material and some formal derivations. This material deepens the understanding but is not necessary for understanding the main points and the rest of the book. The instructor can choose which of this material to include in the course.

Companion website

The companion website contains the following material:
- Answers to all exercises in the book
- Multiple choice questions with answers
- Suggestions for further reading.

The following material is available for instructors:
- Power-point slides for lectures
- Additional exercises with answers that are not disclosed to students.

Alternative course designs

The core part of each chapter can be covered in a 90-minute lecture. Typically, a chapter starts with the core theory and continues with specific issues, applications, and data. The latter parts do not need to be covered in the lecture.

Because of the tight logical structure of the book, Chapters 1–14 are closely linked together. The analysis of the short run and policy in Chapters 8–11 builds on the analysis of production, price and wage-setting, investment and consumption decisions, which are presented in the preceding chapters. The tight structure brings obvious benefits to learners but a consequence is that one cannot omit a chapter, or change the order of Chapters 1–14, without creating confusion.

Chapters 15–18 are independent. This means that instructors can omit them, include only some of this material, or make these chapters extensive reading. Material from these chapters could be taught together with Chapters 1–14.

Chapter 15 on exchange rate systems and monetary union is an application of the theory of the open economy in the short run, which is presented in Chapter 14. Chapter 16 on business cycles could be taught together with Chapters 8–9 on the short run. Chapter 17 on institutions and policy could be taught together with Chapters 10–11 on monetary and fiscal policy. Chapter 18 on financial markets and crises could be taught after Chapter 10 on monetary policy.

More or less weight can be put on the mathematical derivations. Instructors who prefer a more formal presentation could make extensive use of the material in appendices.

Acknowledgements

During the development of this book I have benefited from close cooperation with the team at Palgrave Macmillan. Jaime Marshall initiated the project and has guided it through the various stages of the development process. Helen Bugler, as development editor, managed the content reviewing and market research process, and has given me detailed and very helpful feedback on the whole text.

I am grateful to:

Fredrik N. G. Andersson, Lund University, Sweden
Christian Groth, University of Copenhagen, Denmark
Martin van Tuijl, Tilburg University, the Netherlands
Gianluigi Vernasca, University of Essex, UK

and other external reviewers who read the manuscript carefully, pointing out weaknesses and forcing me to rethink and reorganize. Elizabeth Stone has polished the language meticulously. I also want to thank Aléta Bezuidenhout, Lucy Peers, and Jim Weaver.

Stefan Eriksson, Steinar Holden, Pecca Luukainen, and Erik Spector have read and given me very helpful comments on large parts of the manuscript.

I am also very grateful to the following who have read and commented on specific chapters: Irina Andone, Bengt Assarsson, Mikael Bask, Selva Bahar Baziki, Teodora Borota, Vesna Corbo, Pia Fromlet, Rob Hart, Bertil Holmlund, Glenn Mickelsson, Rachatar Nilavongse, Johan Söderberg, Karolina Stadin, Oskar Tysklind, and Jovan Zamac.

I want to thank my current and previous colleagues and students at Uppsala and Stockholm universities from whom I have learnt most of the things I know about macroeconomics. It was at the Institute for International Economic Studies in Stockholm that I learnt to play with small-scale micro-founded 'Mickey Mouse' models of the whole economy, and this way of thinking about macroeconomics permeates this book. In Uppsala I have learnt a lot about economics in general and the labour market in particular. I also want to thank generations of students at Uppsala University, who have suffered through my experiments with this course. Their questioning and feedback have been very useful.

Most of all I want to thank my family, my wife Annika, my daughter Cilla, and my sons Axel and Måns for their encouragement and patience with me during my writing of this book, but also before that. My mother Britt and my late father Arvid were always there to support and encourage me.

Nils Gottfries
Uppsala, December 2012

AUTHOR'S AND PUBLISHER'S ACKNOWLEDGEMENTS

The authors and publishers are grateful to the following for permission to reproduce figures, tables, and extracts of text:

Alan Heston, Robert Summers and Bettina Aten, for permission to use data from Penn World Table Version 6.1, Center for International Comparisons of Production, Income and Prices at the University of Pennsylvania, October 2002, in Figures 5.7, 5.8 and 5.9.

Bank of England for permission to use data in Figures 10.9 and 18.7.

The Conference Board Total Economy Database for permission to use data for Table 2.2 and Figure 2.9 from http://www.conference-board.org/data/economydatabase/.

De Nederlansche Bank for permission to use data in Table 12.1 from http://www.dnb.nl/en/home/index.jsp.

European Central Bank for permission to use data in Figures 10.1, 10.8. Data can be obtained via the ECB website free of charge at http://www.ecb.int/home/html/index.en.html.

Fromlet, P., for permission to use data from Fromlet, P., 2010, Rational Expectations and Inflation Targeting: An Analysis for Ten Countries, Working Paper 2010:17, Department of Economics, Uppsala University, in Table 15.1.

Harry Flam and Håkan Nordström, for permission to use data from Flam, H., and Nordstrom, H., Euro Effects on the Intensive and Extensive Margins of Trade, working paper, Stockholm University, 2007 in Figures 15.5 and 15.6.

Hilde Bjørnland, for permission to use data from Bjørnland, H., 2009, Monetary Policy and Exchange Rate Interactions in a Small Open Economy, *Scandinavian Journal of Economics*, 110, 197–221 and Bjørnland, H., 2008, Monetary Policy and Exchange Rate Overshooting: Dornbusch was Right After All, *Journal of International Economics*, 79, 64–77 in Figure 14.9.

The International Monetary Fund for permission to use data from International Financial Statistics in Figures 3.1, 7.3, 10.7, 12.6.

Lawrence Christiano, Mathias Trabandt and Karl Walentin for permission to use data from 'DSGE Models for Monetary Policy Analysis', 2011, Christiano, L. J., K. Walentin, and M. Trabandt, in *Handbook of Monetary Economics*, B. M. Friedman and M. Woodford (editors), Volume 3a, Chapter 7, pp. 285–367, Elsevier B.V., North-Holland in Figure 8.15.

Nathalie Girouard and Christophe André for permission to use data from Girouard, N. and C. André, 2005, Measuring Cyclically-adjusted Budget Balances for OECD Countries, *OECD Economics Department Working Papers*, No. 434 and OECD in Figure 11.6.

OECD for permission to use data in Figures 1.1, 1.3, 2.6, 3.2, 4.1, 6.1, 6.2, 6.3, 6.4, 6.5, 6.14, 6.15, 7.1, 7.2, 7.3, 9.8, 9.9, 9.10, 11.1, 11.2, 11.3, 11.4, 11.8, 12.1, 12.3, 12.4, 12.5, 12.7, 13.1, 13.5, 13.9, 15.2, 15.3, 15.7, 15.8, 16.1, 16.2, 16.3, 16.4, 16.5, 16.6, 16.7, 18.3, 18.4 and Tables 1.1, 1.2, 1.3, 1.4, 1.5, 7.1, 11.1, 11.2, 13.1, 13.2, 15.2, 15.3.

Pete Klenow and Chang-Tai Hsieh for permission to use data from Hsieh, C.-T., and P. J. Klenow, 2010, *American Economic Journal: Macroeconomics*, 2, 207–223 in Figures 5.7, 5.8 and 5.9.

Robert Barro and Jong-Wha Lee for permission to use data from Barro, R. and J.-W. Lee, 2001, International data on educational attainment: updates and implications, *Oxford Economic Papers*, 53, 541–563 in Figure 5.8 and 5.9.

Robert Shiller for permission to use stock market data in Figures 18.2, 18.3, 18.4 and 18.6 taken from Shiller, R., *Irrational Exuberance*, Princeton University Press, 2000, 2005.

The World Bank for permission to use data in Figures 5.10, 5.11, 5.12, 5.13, 5.14 and 5.15.

Every effort has been made to trace all the copyright holders but if any have been inadvertently overlooked the publishers will be pleased to make the necessary arrangements at the first opportunity.

1 INTRODUCTION

What is macroeconomics?
Why do we use models?
What data do we use?

Macroeconomics is the study of the economy as a whole. In macroeconomics we study production, employment, price increases, interest rates, and other economic developments in countries and even groups of countries.

Macroeconomic developments affect individuals and firms in many ways. The financial crisis that culminated in 2008–2009 is a good example. Some banks and other financial institutions made large losses, some even went bankrupt, and worries spread that other financial institutions might also go bankrupt. This led to a general lack of trust in the financial system and, as news about the financial crisis spread, firms and households became more pessimistic about the future. Firms postponed their purchases of new equipment and households reduced their consumption. Weak demand led to reduced hiring and increased layoffs of workers, increased unemployment, and a decrease in wage growth and inflation. The prices of most assets decreased dramatically.

In order to counteract the collapse of demand, central banks slashed interest rates to encourage borrowing and spending. Governments cut taxes and increased public expenditure so as to boost demand and, at the same time, the decline in production led to a sharp decrease in government tax revenue. As a consequence, budget deficits (the difference between government expenditure and tax revenue) increased.

Fig. 1.1 illustrates the effects of the financial crisis on the US, the UK, and the Eurozone. Production (gross domestic product, or GDP), private consumption, and investment are measured by indexes which are set to 100 for the year 2005. Unemployment is measured as a percentage of the labour force and the government balance is measured as a percentage of production (GDP). A negative government balance means a budget deficit. We see that investment declined by 15–20 percent while GDP declined by about 5 percent, there was a marked increase in unemployment, and the deficit increased in all three geographical areas.

The effects of the financial crisis were not confined to one sector of the economy alone. Every individual and every firm was affected in some way: firms lost orders, workers were laid off, pensioners saw their savings lose value, and house owners enjoyed lower interest payments on their mortgage loans. Economic developments on the national and global – that is, macroeconomic – level can have

1

Fig. 1.1 *The effects of the financial crisis*

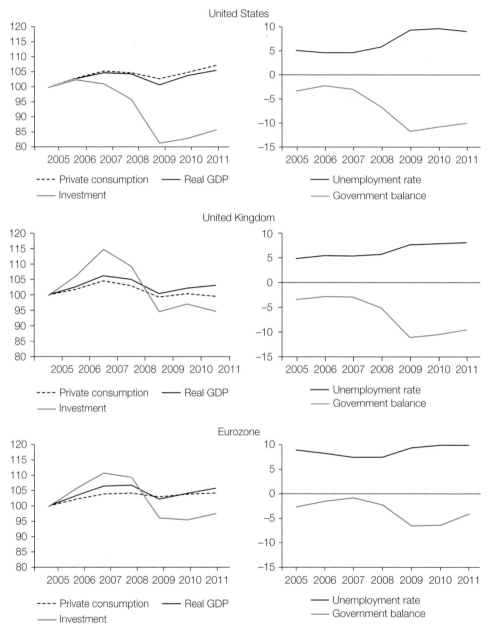

Note: The first diagram shows real production (GDP), investment and consumption where indexes are normalized to 100 in 2005. Unemployment is measured as a percentage of the labour force and the government balance is government net lending measured as a percentage of GDP.

Source: *OECD Economic Outlook*, OECD, 21 March 2012, http://www.oecd-ilibrary.org/statistics.

dramatic effects on us all. This is why it is so important to understand how the macroeconomy works.

Firms need to have a view of where the economy is going in order to make good decisions about investments and hiring. A multinational firm that decides where to allocate production, or to expand its sales organization, must consider the economic outlook for different countries carefully. The actors involved in financial markets watch economic developments closely because they know that new information has immediate effects on interest rates and asset prices. Consumers who are about to buy houses or cars may reconsider their decisions if they become afraid of losing their jobs because of an economic downturn.

As citizens in a democracy, we influence economic developments when we cast our votes. Different parties offer different suggestions as to how we should deal with unemployment, inflation, and large budget deficits. In order to take a stand on those proposals, we need to understand how the economy works.

The purpose of macroeconomics is to understand general economic developments in a given country and across the world. To analyse these developments, macroeconomists use *macroeconomic models*, which can be seen as simplified pictures of the whole economy. We begin this chapter by explaining why we need macroeconomic models. Then we give a brief overview of the contents of the book and we introduce the most important macroeconomic data used to describe macroeconomic developments. In the appendix we review some important mathematical concepts that are used throughout the book.

1.1 The big picture

In macroeconomics we try to understand the aggregate economy – that is, the sum of the activities of all the firms and the households in the economy. We try to understand what determines the level of production and income of a country, as well as fluctuations in unemployment, inflation, interest rates, and exchange rates. We also study how economic policy can affect the economy.

Clearly, these issues cannot be understood by looking at one part of the economy in isolation. We need to look at the whole picture. We need to have a complete theory of the whole economy. But such a theory is bound to be complicated. Macroeconomic developments are the results of billions of decisions taken by millions of households and thousands of firms, and all these households and firms face unique circumstances. To understand why a specific household buys a house or a car, we need to know a lot about that particular household. To understand the production, hiring and investment decisions of a specific firm, we need to know a lot about that particular firm. How could we then understand the decisions of *all* firms and households and the economy as a whole?

Macroeconomics is about the big picture, but economic theory can start only from the behaviour of individual households and firms. The approach taken in this book is to start from microeconomics. We will analyse macroeconomic problems using the standard tools of microeconomic analysis: rational choice and profit maximization, supply and demand. But to do that, we need to disregard much of the diversity across households and firms that we see in the real world. In order to analyse macroeconomic issues in a rigorous way, we need to make a simplified picture of how the economy works – we need to build a macroeconomic model.

A macroeconomic model with microeconomic foundations

A macroeconomic model is an extremely simplified imaginary economy – a 'toy economy' where firms and households behave in mechanical and predictable ways. The model that we present in this book gives a very simplified picture of the world, but our hope is that it will be able to capture the most central macroeconomic relationships and give us reasonably accurate answers to our questions.

Much of the time, we will use the language of mathematics to describe our model. We do this because mathematical symbols can be used to express economic relations in a very concise way. We describe the model economy in terms of a small number of *variables*. Variables are symbols representing economic quantities and prices. We will use Y for 'production', P for 'the price level', and i for 'the interest rate'. Y, P, and i are called variables because they represent quantities and prices that can take different numerical values in different situations.

The economic system is a system of *relations* between economic variables. How much a firm can produce depends on the quantities of inputs it uses; how much firms can sell in the export markets depends on the prices of exports and the income level abroad; and so on. We use mathematical *functions* to summarize those relations between different economic variables in a concise way.

In order to make our macroeconomic model manageable, we need to make some rather sweeping assumptions:

- *We analyse the decisions of households and firms as if all households and all firms were exactly identical.* This dramatically simplifies the problem. Rather than thinking about millions of consumers and firms, who all behave differently, we think of the *typical* consumer and the *typical* firm. Economists use the terms 'representative consumer' and 'representative firm'. The idea, of course, is that the typical consumer and the typical firm represent the *average* behaviour of all consumers and firms in the economy.
- *We assume that firms and households behave in a rational way and that they have simple objective functions.* When we say that firms and households are rational, we mean that they act in a consistent way so as to achieve a given objective. Firms invest, produce and set prices in order to maximize profits. The production possibilities available to the typical firm are described by a *production function*. Households make rational choices between consumption today and consumption in future periods, and between goods produced in the home country and imports from foreign countries. They have simple preferences which are described by a *utility function*.
- *We do not try to explain everything.* We limit our ambitions and take some variables as given in the analysis. Such variables are called *exogenous variables*. Exogenous variables are not constant, but we do not try to analyse how they are determined. Changes in exogenous variables are called *shocks*. Those variables that are determined within the model are called *endogenous variables*. For example, we take government expenditure as given (exogenous) in

most of our analysis, but the level of production is endogenously determined inside the model. Thus, we do not try to analyse how government expenditure is determined, but we do analyse how an exogenous change in government expenditure affects production in the short and the long run.

- *We use different versions of the model for different questions.* For example, there is considerable evidence that wages and prices adjust slowly to changing economic conditions. Therefore, we must use different models to analyse the effects of exogenous shocks in the short and the long run. When we analyse the *short-run effects* of changes in exogenous variables, we assume that wages and prices adjust slowly. When we analyse the *long-run effects* of the same shocks, we assume that wages and prices have time to adjust to the shock. The distinction between the long and the short run is further discussed below.

As a result of these assumptions, we have a stylized 'toy economy' which is sufficiently simple for us to understand how it works. Our basic macroeconomic model has *three markets*:

- a labour market
- a goods market
- a credit market (money market).

There are *three decision-makers*:

- the typical firm
- the typical household
- policymakers.

Policymakers are the country's central bank, which sets the interest rate (monetary policy), and the government, which decides about taxes and government expenditure (fiscal policy). In most of our analysis, monetary and fiscal policies are taken as exogenous, so we only model the decisions of the typical firm and the typical household. There are four important decisions that we need to understand in the basic model:[1]

1) price-setting
2) wage-setting
3) investment
4) consumption.

In our baseline model, the price-setting, wage-setting and investment decisions are made by the typical firm. We assume that there is monopolistic competition in the product market, so the typical firm sets a price and produces what is demanded at that price using the required amount of labour input. The consumption/savings decision is made by the typical consumer. Fig. 1.2 gives an overview of the model economy.

Later, in Chapters 12–15, we look at the *open economy* – that is, an economy which trades with the rest of the world. Then, we also need to analyse

---

1   These are not the only decisions but they are the ones we will focus on in our analysis.

Fig. 1.2 *Actors, markets, and flows in the model*

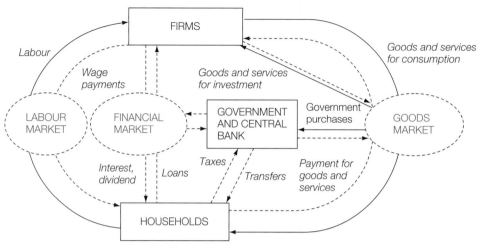

Note: Full arrows denote flows of goods and services or labour services. Dashed arrows denote money flows. The arrows between the government and the financial markets denote government borrowing and interest payments.

trade and international borrowing and lending; we need to analyse two more decisions:

5) the household's choice between goods produced at home and abroad
6) the foreign investor's choice between lending in different currencies.

We will spend a lot of effort analysing these decisions, and this analysis will give us the key economic relations of our macroeconomic model:

1) a price equation
2) a wage equation
3) an investment function
4) a consumption function
5) a net export function
6) an interest parity condition.[2]

Once we have derived our key economic relationships, we can use the results to analyse how the economy responds to shocks and economic policy in the short and the long run.

Why use an economic model when we can make the argument intuitively?

Economic arguments can be made in words, but developing a formal model helps us to clarify our arguments. There are several important advantages of a formal model:

---

2 The last equation says that the expected return should be the same on loans in different currencies.

- The model helps us to avoid errors of logic in our reasoning.
- The model helps us to see what assumptions we need to make in order to come to a certain conclusion. This is not always clear when we develop an argument verbally.
- Once we have set up and analysed a model, it is easier to see how alternative assumptions would affect the answer to the question under analysis.

Once we understand the logic of our model, we see much more clearly which assumptions are important for the conclusions and which are not. If two economists disagree on something, they can write down their models to clarify why they have come to different conclusions. Did the disagreement arise because one of them made an error of logic, or because the two economists have different views on how firms and consumers behave?

Having used a model to answer a specific question, we should always take a step back and ask ourselves what we have learned. Does the model capture the essential aspects of the problem? Are the results reasonable? Have we missed an important aspect of the problem?

You should try to think of the model not as a set of complicated mathematical expressions but as an imaginary economy. Apply your own common sense and try to envisage real consumers and firms interacting in the ways set out in the model. We should always try to explain intuitively what is going on and check whether the model makes intuitive sense.

Economists are often criticized by other social scientists for having too simplistic an understanding of human nature. Real consumers do not maximize very simple utility functions, and owners of firms may have other motives than to maximize profit. But in macroeconomics we are interested in rather limited aspects of human behaviour. We are trying to explain the broad developments in goods and labour markets. Although individual households and firms may have all kinds of specific motives for their behaviour, the hope is that our theory is able to capture average behaviour of firms and households in an approximate way. Whether it actually succeeds in doing that can be found out only by comparing the theoretical predictions with what we see in the data. Throughout this book, we will examine the relevant data in order to find out whether the data confirm or contradict our theory.

When studying an economic model, we should always keep in mind *what questions* we are trying to analyse. Why did we construct the model in the first place? A simplifying assumption that is reasonable for analysing one question may not be reasonable for analysing another question. A subtitle of each chapter in this book carries a question, or several questions, so that we can remind ourselves why we are doing the analysis in that chapter.

Using a model: an example

In order to illustrate the use of a formal model in economics, let us consider the following proposition:

> *'If we introduce government regulation that reduces working hours, firms need to hire more workers, which means that unemployment will fall.'*

This may appear obvious, but, as we will see, the proposition is based on some implicit assumptions. To see what these assumptions are, let us write down a simple economic model. Let Y be production, N be the number of workers employed, and H the number of hours per worker. Assume that workers produce E units per hour. Then production is the number of workers times hours per worker times how much they produce per hour:

$$Y = N \cdot H \cdot E.$$

Dividing by $H \cdot E$ on both sides, we can solve the equation for N:

$$N = \frac{Y}{H \cdot E}.$$

Finally, let us assume that there are L workers who are ready to work. Then the number of unemployed workers is $U = L - N$. Substituting the expression for N above into the definition of U we get

$$U = L - \frac{Y}{H \cdot E}.$$

Now, if H (hours worked) decreases, the last term, $Y/(H \cdot E)$, becomes larger (because Y is divided by a smaller number), and, since it has a negative sign, we are taking more and more away from L (available workers) and so U (unemployment) decreases. Thus we have proved the proposition above, that a reduction in work hours means that firms have to employ more workers, so unemployment falls.

But let us look once more at the equation above to see what implicit assumptions we made along the way. Implicitly, we assumed that L, E and Y remain constant, or at least that they do not change so much that the direct effect of H on U is counteracted. Effectively, we made a lot of implicit assumptions when we made the argument verbally. But how plausible are those assumptions?

Will L (the number of workers who want jobs) remain constant if working hours are reduced? Perhaps we can accept that as a first approximation. Will production per hour, E, remain the same? Probably not. If workers work a shorter length of time, they may be less exhausted and produce more per hour, so E will increase. We may nevertheless argue that this increase in productivity per hour is not enough to fully compensate for the decrease in hours; and so, for a given level of production, Y, firms will need more workers.

But what happens to production? There seems to be an implicit assumption in the argument made above that production remains constant. But to take production (Y) as constant when analysing the effects of a general reduction in working time is rather simplistic, and probably misleading. If we are talking about a general decrease in hours of work in the whole economy, it is very unlikely that production will remain constant. If wages per hour remain constant, firms may want to hire more workers. But it is unlikely that wages per hour remain constant. First, workers' total pay will decrease when work hours are reduced, in which case workers may ask for a higher wage per hour by way of compensation. Second, if firms hire more workers, a tighter labour market and upward pressure on wages will ensue. If wages increase, inflation increases, so the country's central bank will have to raise the interest rate, which will affect the overall level of demand in the economy, counteracting the increase in employment.

Clearly, it makes little sense to take production as given in the analysis. In order to analyse how a change in working hours affects unemployment, we need to understand how production is affected, and for that we need a complete macroeconomic model. This example reveals how, by writing down a model in mathematical terms, we see more clearly what assumptions are implicitly being made when we make the argument intuitively. In turn, this allows us to judge whether or not those assumptions are plausible. Once we see where the loose ends are, we can think of ways to make the analysis more complete and convincing. We can also look for empirical evidence that supports or contradicts our theory. We will return to this example in Chapter 6. Then we will analyse the consequences of reduced hours of work using a complete but simple macroeconomic model.

The short and the long run

As discussed above, macroeconomists may use different models to analyse different questions. In this book, we will use different versions of our macroeconomic model to analyse the short and the long run. The reason is simple: some assumptions, which are reasonable in the long run, are implausible in the short run. Most importantly, there is evidence that nominal wages and prices adjust slowly to shocks, and we need to take account of this when we analyse the short run.

In 1936 John Maynard Keynes published *General Theory of Employment, Interest, and Money*.[3] The theory presented by Keynes had a big influence on macroeconomics, and his ideas are still used to analyse business cycles and stabilization policy. A central assumption in Keynesian theory is that nominal wages are 'rigid' or 'sticky' – they may not adjust at all, or they adjust slowly, to changes in economic conditions. This is a key difference between *Keynesian theory* and *classical theory*, where wages and prices are assumed to continuously adjust so as to equate supply and demand in all markets at all times. Keynes argued that, when wages are rigid and there are unemployed resources, fiscal and monetary policy can be used to fight unemployment and to counteract shocks to the economy.

Following the publication of Keynes' book, economists tried to combine Keynesian and classical theory by assuming that, even if wages and prices are sticky in the short run, we expect them to respond to changes in economic conditions over the longer run. The view that wages and prices adjust slowly, so that the economy works in a *Keynesian* way in the short run and in a *classical* way in the long run, became a consensus among economists and policymakers. This consensus is called the *neoclassical synthesis* and it came to dominate macroeconomic thinking in the second half of the 20th century.[4] This is also the approach taken in this book, but our analysis will be influenced by more recent developments in macroeconomic research.

---

3 *General Theory of Employment, Interest, and Money* (London: Macmillan, 1936).
4 A leading proponent of this approach was the American economist Paul A. Samuelson. In 1970, Samuelson received the Sveriges Riksbank Prize in Economic Sciences in Memory of Alfred Nobel, more commonly known as the Nobel Prize in economics. The award was made: 'for the scientific work through which he has developed static and dynamic economic theory and actively contributed to raising the level of analysis in economic science'.

Towards the end of the 20th century, macroeconomic research became more classical again. The Keynesian view that policymakers should try to stabilize the economy was questioned. The modern version of classical macroeconomics is called *real business cycle theory*. Importantly, this theory claims that changes in production opportunities can be a significant cause of business cycle fluctuations. Such changes can arise, for example, because of the introduction of new technologies, crop failures, or structural change. Thus, the fluctuations that we observe may be completely rational adjustments to changes in production opportunities – if this is the case, it makes little sense for policymakers to try to stabilize those fluctuations. Today, there is wide consensus that changes in production opportunities are an important element in business fluctuations and such shocks will play an important role in our analysis. From a policy point of view, the key lesson is that policymakers need to try hard to distinguish between those fluctuations that should be stabilized and those that should not be stabilized.

1.2 Organization of this book

As discussed above, the existence of short-run wage and price rigidity means that we need to use different versions of the model for analysing the short and the long run. In this book, we first analyse the long run. We do this for three reasons:

1. Long-run changes in the level of income are much more important for general well-being than short-run fluctuations. Even if there is a downturn in the US economy, most Americans are still much better off than they were 50 years ago.
2. Short-run decisions about consumption and investment are driven by expectations about what will happen in the long run. To understand where those expectations come from, we first need to consider the long run.
3. It is hard to understand what stabilization policy can (and cannot) do without knowing where the economy is heading in the long run.

After the introduction, the book is divided into five parts that focus, in turn, on the long run, the short run, economic policy, the open economy and further topics. In the first four parts we build and extend our macroeconomic model and in the final part we go deeper into specific issues.

The long run (Chapters 2–7)

In the first part, we construct the building blocks of our macroeconomic model and we use these building blocks to analyse the long run. We first analyse the *supply side*: how firms produce goods and services using inputs of labour and capital (machines and buildings), how they set prices and sell their output in product markets. This analysis gives us an understanding of how the long-run level of production is determined and the distribution of income between labour and capital.

Then we consider the *demand side*. We analyse how firms decide about investment and how households chose between consumption and saving. We show that the *real interest rate* is an important determinant of demand for goods and services and we analyse how the real interest rate is determined in the long run.

Having understood what determines supply, demand and the real interest rate, we turn to *long-run growth*. We analyse how the long-run growth rate is related to capital accumulation, population growth and technological development. We try to understand why some countries are so much richer than others.

Then we turn to the *labour market*. We analyse why there is normally unemployment in a market economy and which factors determine the level of unemployment. The focus here is on the long-run level of unemployment rather than cyclical fluctuations.

The final step in the long-run analysis is to bring money into the picture and to analyse the relation between *money growth, inflation* and the *interest rate*.

The short run (Chapters 8–9)

As discussed above, the key difference between long- and short-run analysis is that wages and prices adjust slowly in the short run. We first analyse the demand side, taking prices as fixed, and this leads to the *IS-LM model*, which is a compact summary of Keynes' *General Theory*. With the *IS-LM* model we can analyse how a country's central bank can control the interest rate and the short-run effects of a whole range of macroeconomic shocks. Then we analyse wage and price adjustment in the short run. We derive a *Phillips curve* which shows how inflation is related to employment and production.

Economic policy (Chapters 10–11)

In the third part of the book, we use our model to analyse *monetary and fiscal policy*. First, we analyse how monetary policy should be conducted. How should a central bank react to various shocks? Next we introduce a government that spends money on public consumption and investment and finances this expenditure by taxing households and by borrowing. We first analyse the long run: the evolution of government debt and the sustainability of government finances. Then we consider the short run. We examine whether the government can help to stabilize aggregate demand by active fiscal policy – that is, by varying taxes and government expenditure so as to counteract business cycle fluctuations.

The open economy (Chapters 12–15)

Markets for goods and services and financial markets have become more and more integrated across countries. Exports and imports have increased relative to GDP, and financial markets allow countries to finance investment and consumption by borrowing abroad. Today, all countries are strongly affected by developments in other countries. The final step in the construction of our macroeconomic model is to open up the economy by allowing *foreign trade* in goods and services and borrowing and lending in *international financial markets*.

Once we have opened up our model to trade and international lending, we first analyse long-run *growth* and *foreign debt* in open economies. Then we turn to short-run analysis. Here we use the *Mundell–Fleming model*, which is an open economy version of the *IS-LM* model. We show that fiscal and monetary policy play very different roles depending on which exchange rate regime is in place. With a fixed exchange rate, the central bank has no control over the interest rate; with a floating exchange rate, monetary policy becomes very important. We use our model to analyse the advantages and disadvantages of alternative exchange rate regimes and of monetary union.

Business cycles, policymaking, and financial markets (Chapters 16–18)

In the final part of the book, we go deeper into some specific issues. We first study the *business cycle*: what it is and how it arises. Then we analyse how *policymaking institutions* influence how policy decisions are made. This will help us to understand why many countries have implemented reforms that have made central banks more independent. Finally, we analyse more deeply the role of *financial markets* and financial institutions, and we try to understand the mechanisms leading to *financial crises*.

1.3 Macroeconomic data

Every day, newspapers, TV, and the radio report a wealth of economic information that has been released by statistical bureaus around the world. In order to interpret this information, we need to understand the different concepts and definitions used when collecting and reporting economic data. In this section, we introduce some key definitions and data that are used to describe macroeconomic activity. Throughout the book, we examine macroeconomic data to evaluate how well they match our theory. It is therefore important that we understand the different concepts and definitions that are used when presenting economic data.

The most important source of information on economic activity is the *national accounts*. These are a system for bookkeeping for the whole country and the data are collected by official statistical agencies in the different countries.[5] The statistical conventions used in this system are a result of agreements made within the United Nations. National accounts data can be obtained from the web pages of national statistical agencies, and data for a large number of countries are available at the web pages of the European Union (EU), the International Monetary Fund (IMF), the Organisation for Economic Co-operation and Development

---

5 In 1984 the Nobel Prize in economics was awarded to the British economist Richard Stone 'for having made fundamental contributions to the development of systems of national accounts and hence greatly improved the basis for empirical economic analysis'.

(OECD), and the World Bank. In fact, most of the figures and tables in this book have been constructed using data from the OECD database *OECD Economic Outlook.*

In what follows we first introduce some important concepts in the national accounts. We use the classifications and terminology used by the OECD. Then we look at national accounts data for several countries. We examine which sectors contribute to production, how income is distributed, how production is used, and how much is saved and invested in different countries. Finally, we explain how GDP can be compared across countries and how we measure inflation and real growth of GDP.

National accounts

National accounts give us information that answers the following questions:

1. What is the value of all goods and services that are *produced* in a country and how much do different *production sectors* contribute to total production?
2. How large is the *income* of the country and how is it *distributed* between capital income (interest, dividends) and labour income (wages payments)?
3. Where do goods and services come from and how are they *used*? What fraction or production is used for consumption, investment and exports? How much is imported? What proportion of goods and services are used by the government and the private sector?
4. How much of the income is *saved and invested* in real and financial assets?

National accounts show *flows* of production, incomes, savings and investments during a particular period of time, typically a year or a quarter. Another source of information is *balance of payments statistics*, which shows flows of payments connected to exports, imports, international transfers and capital flows. Balance of payments statistics are closely related to national accounts, but some statistical discrepancies arise because data are collected from different sources.

Output, value added, and GDP

In order to measure the value of production, we can measure the sales of all firms and the value of production in the public sector and then add them up. This measure is called *output* in the national accounts system. But output is not a good measure of the amount of production that can be used for consumption and investment because a large share of output is used as input in other firms. One company may produce a screw, which is put into a motor, which is then put in the window lift of a car. If these different stages of production are carried out by different companies, the screw will be counted three times in the output measure. Thus we have a considerable amount of double counting.

Goods that are used as inputs in other firms are called *intermediate goods*. If we subtract the value of intermediate inputs from the value of output, we get *value added*. If a firm produces goods worth 10 million and the cost of intermediate inputs (raw materials, components, energy) is 4 million, the value added produced by that firm is 6 million. *Gross domestic product (GDP)* is the sum of all value added produced in the country. This distinction between output and value added is important; in developed countries, output is roughly twice as large as GDP because of extensive double counting. On average, each good and service is counted twice in the output measure.[6]

One billion is 1000 millions. Numbers in billions can be hard to grasp, but the value of GDP is a useful reference value in many contexts. If you know that number, you will be able to relate any number that you hear in the news to GDP in your country. It is therefore a good idea to learn the rough value of GDP in your country in billions. Table 1.2 below lists the values of GDP for different countries in billions in national currencies. For example, GDP in the UK was roughly 1500 billion pounds in 2008, so if the government decided to spend (or save) 15 billion pounds this would be roughly one percent of the total production of goods and services in the UK.[7]

Throughout this book, we express most magnitudes as fractions of GDP. Such fractions are much easier to interpret, and to remember, than values in billions. Also, comparisons between countries become meaningful when we look at fractions of GDP.

Some important concepts in the national accounts

All incomes come from production, but there are different measures of production and income which may be relevant, depending on what we want to measure. The following distinctions are important in the national accounts:

Market price and basic price

There is a difference between what consumers pay for a product and the income that the firm receives. The difference is *taxes less subsidies on products*. Taxes on products such as value added tax and sales taxes are called *indirect taxes*. Subsidies are money transfers from the government to firms, which may occur because the government wants to promote a certain type of production, for example. We can think of the *market price* as the price that the consumer pays and the *basic price* as the price that the producer gets after having paid indirect taxes and received subsidies related to production.[8]

When we say 'GDP' we usually mean GDP at market prices, the value in the market. GDP minus indirect taxes plus subsidies on products is called *gross value added at basic price*. Taxes less subsidies on products constitute around 10–15 percent of GDP, so gross value added at basic price is 10–15 percent lower than GDP. It is this latter income that is paid out as wages, interest and dividends. This

---

6 The other side of the coin is that roughly half the production costs of a typical firm are costs of intermediate inputs.

7 Of course, the value of GDP changes over time because of growth and inflation, so you will need to update this number now and then. With 2 percent inflation and 3 percent real growth, GDP increases about 5 percent per year in nominal terms.

8 The concepts 'producer price' and 'factor price' are similar, but not identical to 'basic price'.

means that, in order to examine the distribution of income between labour and capital, we need to look at value added at basic price.

Gross and net

The words 'gross' and 'net' mean different things in different contexts. In the national accounts, the terms 'net production' and 'net income' usually refer to production and income excluding *consumption of capital*, that is, depreciation. In developed countries, the overall depreciation rate of capital stock is about 7 percent, and capital stock is about twice as large as GDP, so consumption of capital is in the order of 14 percent of GDP (0.07 times 2).

Domestic product and national income

As already stated, all income comes from production, but income can come from production abroad. The word 'domestic' refers to the fact that GDP measures production by firms, government institutions, and self-employed individuals situated in the country. *National income* measures the income of those individuals who are *residents* in the country. Wages from working abroad, and interest and dividends from assets abroad, which go to residents of the country, are called *primary incomes from the rest of the world*. Net primary income from the rest of the world is primary income received by residents in the country from the rest of the world minus primary income generated in the country that goes to residents abroad. Net primary income from the rest of the world may be positive or negative and, for most countries, it constitutes only a couple of per cent of GDP. If we add net primary income from the rest of the world to GDP we get *gross national income* (*GNI*) at market prices.

Income and disposable income

The difference between primary income and disposable income is *taxes and transfers*, which are called *secondary incomes* in the national accounts. Households receive primary income in the form of wages, interest payments and dividends. Then they pay taxes to the government and they may also receive transfers from the government such as pension, sickness benefits and welfare. What remains is the households' *disposable income*.

When we consider the country as a whole, we have to add *net transfers from the rest of the world* to national income to obtain *national disposable income*. Examples of such transfers are foreign aid, transfers to and from the European Union, and remittances. Guest workers who live in a country for more than 12 months are counted as residents of the country where they are working. Any remittances sent by such workers to their relatives at home count as transfers between households in different countries, so they affect the disposable incomes of the countries involved. Needless to say, such remittances are measured with substantial measurement errors.

Many different measures of production and income

We can combine these concepts in many different ways, which means there is a whole range of different measures of production and income. Below are some examples:

> *GDP = gross domestic product at market price = the total value added produced*
> *GDP − taxes less subsidies on products = gross value added at basic price*
> *GDP − consumption of capital = net domestic product at market price*
> *GDP + net primary income from the rest of the world = gross national income at market price*
> *GDP + net primary income from the rest of the world − consumption of capital = net national income at market price*
> *GDP + net primary income and net transfers from the rest of the world − consumption of capital = net national disposable income at market price.*

Armed with these definitions, we can now address the questions posed at the beginning of this section: What proportion of GDP is *produced* in the various sectors? How is total income *distributed* between labour and capital income? What proportion of production is *used* for consumption, investment and exports? What proportion of GDP is *saved and invested*?

How much do different production sectors contribute to GDP?

We first look at the *production side* of the national accounts. Table 1.1 shows how production of gross value added is distributed across six different production sectors. You will note from the bottom of the table that the numbers are quite similar for the US and the Eurozone. Only 1–2 percent of value added is produced in agriculture. About one quarter of value added is produced in industry and construction and three quarters in the service industries. Services are divided into three groups: 'wholesale and retail trade, repairs, hotels, restaurants, and transport', 'financial intermediation, real estate, renting and business services', and 'other services'. Each of these service sectors constitutes about 20–30 percent of GDP, so each of these service sectors is similar in size to industry and construction taken together.

It is clear that, today, the service sectors dominate the economy. We should note, however, that many of these services are inputs into the production of goods. Industrial companies buy computer services, consulting, advertising and financial services, while the transport sector transports goods produced in industry. Industry is therefore more important than its share of GDP indicates.

Who gets the income?

Production generates income, which can be divided into labour income and capital income. Labour income consists primarily of wages and social security fees paid by employers. A substantial proportion of gross capital income is used to replace depreciated capital, and some of it is reinvested in the firms where it is generated (retained earnings); the rest is paid out as interest payments and dividends.

Table 1.1 *Gross value added by activity, percent of GDP, 2007*

	Agriculture, hunting and forestry; fishing	Industry, including energy	Construction	Wholesale and retail trade, repairs; hotels and restaurants; transport	Financial intermediation; real estate, renting and business activities	Other service activities
Australia	3	21	8	20	30	18
Austria	2	23	7	23	24	20
Belgium	1	19	5	23	29	23
Czech Republic	2	32	6	25	17	17
Denmark	1	20	6	21	25	26
Finland	3	26	6	22	21	21
France	2	14	6	19	33	25
Germany	1	26	4	17	29	22
Greece	4	14	6	34	19	24
Hungary	4	25	5	21	22	22
Ireland	2	24	10	18	28	19
Italy	2	21	6	23	27	21
Japan	1	23	6	19	27	24
Korea	3	30	7	18	22	20
Luxembourg	0	10	5	20	49	15
Mexico	3	28	7	28	20	13
Netherlands	2	19	6	22	28	24
Norway	1	38	5	17	18	20
Poland	4	25	7	27	19	19
Portugal	3	18	6	24	22	26
Slovak Republic	4	31	8	24	17	16
Spain	3	17	12	25	23	21
Sweden	1	23	5	19	25	26
Switzerland	1	22	5	22	24	25
Turkey	9	22	5	32	20	12
United Kingdom	1	17	6	21	32	23
United States	1	17	5	19	33	25
Eurozone	2	20	6	21	28	22

Source: *OECD National Accounts Statistics*, OECD, 5 January 2011, http://www.oecd-ilibrary.org/statistics.

To find out how total income is distributed between labour and capital, we consider the *income side* of the national accounts, which is shown in Table 1.2. As mentioned above, indirect taxes go straight to the government so they cannot be allocated between capital income and labour income. It is *gross value added at basic price* that is paid out as wages, interest and dividends, so when we examine the distribution of income, we relate labour income to this measure of income. *Compensation of employees* is the total remuneration, in cash or kind, payable by enterprises to employees in return for work. It includes the value of social contributions payable by employers to social security schemes or private social insurance schemes.

Table 1.2 *Gross domestic product, gross value added at basic prices, and the distribution of income, 2008, in national currencies, in billions*

	Gross domestic product	Taxes less subsidies on products		Gross value added at basic prices	Compensation of employees	
		Value	Percent of GDP		Value	Percent of gross value added at basic price
Australia	1253	89	7	1157	608	53
Austria	283	27	9	257	138	54
Belgium	345	37	11	308	177	57
Chile	89,263	7838	9	84,456	34,817	41
Czech Republic	3689	368	10	3321	1633	49
Denmark	1741	254	15	1486	982	66
Estonia	252	28	11	224	129	58
Finland	185	23	13	162	91	56
France	1949	198	10	1751	1005	57
Germany	2481	256	10	2225	1222	55
Greece	236	27	12	208	86	41
Hungary	26,754	3925	15	22,829	12,407	54
Iceland	1478	205	14	1273	816	64
Ireland	180	20	11	160	80	50
Israel	726	82	11	666	371	56
Italy	1568	159	10	1409	656	47
Japan	505,112	2335	0	515,897	263,822	51
Korea	1,026,452	106,764	10	919,688	474,954	52
Luxembourg	40	4	10	36	17	48
Mexico	12,092	309	3	12,002	3387	28
Netherlands	596	67	11	529	295	56
Norway	2517	256	10	2266	1079	48
Poland	1275	159	12	1116	476	43
Portugal	172	23	13	150	86	57
Slovak Republic	67	6	9	61	24	40
Slovenia	37	5	12	33	19	58
Spain	1088	92	8	996	531	53
Sweden	3204	394	12	2810	1725	61
Switzerland	544	31	6	513	333	65
United Kingdom	1446	150	10	1296	769	59
United States	14,369	994	7	13,376	8068	60
European Union (27 countries)	12,494	1314	11	11,180	6070	54

Source: *OECD National Accounts Statistics*, OECD, 30 December 2010, http://www.oecd-ilibrary.org/statistics.

As we see in the table, compensation of employees makes up 50–60 percent of gross value added at basic price in high-income countries. This percentage under-estimates the labour share of income in the economy, because compensation of employees does not include the income of the self-employed. The fee charged by a self-employed computer specialist for his services can be seen as a combined payment for his work and for the use of his office and his powerful computer. Thus it is a *mixed income*, consisting partly of labour and partly of capital income. One way to deal with this is to estimate the hypothetical wages of self-employed individuals and to use these to allocate the income of the self-employed between labour and capital income. When this is done, the result is that, in high-income countries, about 2/3 of gross income goes to labour and 1/3 goes to capital.

Note that these income shares are given in gross terms. If gross capital income is 1/3 of gross value added at basic price and the latter is 90 percent of GDP, gross capital income is 30 percent of GDP. With a capital stock twice as large as GDP and a depreciation rate of 7 percent, depreciation is 14 percent of GDP. Then *net* capital income is 16 percent of GDP (30 minus 14). Thus we see that roughly 50 percent of gross capital income is used to replace depreciated capital.

Where do goods and services come from and how are they used?

We now turn to the *user side* of the national accounts to see where the goods and services come from and how they are used. The available goods and services consist of domestic production (GDP) and imports. They are used for consump-tion and investment by the private sector (households and firms) and by the government, and some goods are exported. We can write this as follows:

$$Y + IM = C + I + C^G + I^G + X.$$

Y is GDP, IM is imports, C is private consumption, I is private investment, C^G is government consumption, I^G is government investment, and X is exports of goods and services.[9] We can rewrite this as

$$Y = C + I + C^G + I^G + NX$$

where NX is net exports, that is, exports minus imports. Table 1.3 shows the different components in percent of GDP at market prices.

In most countries, 50–60 percent of all goods and services are used for private consumption, while government consumption is around 20 percent. The US and the Scandinavian countries are the extremes. In the US, the private consumption share is 70 percent of GDP, while government consumption accounts for only 17 percent. In Sweden and Denmark, the private consumption share is around 50 percent and government consumption is nearly 30 percent of GDP. A large part of these differences arise because some services that are privately financed in some countries are tax-financed in others. In Sweden and Denmark, health care, educa-tion and child care are largely tax-financed. In the US, these services are privately

---

9 To be precise, this equality holds in nominal values. When we develop our theory, we will use *Y, IM*, and so on to denote real quantities, so the quantities must be multiplied by prices for the equation to hold. Here we disregard this by implicitly setting all prices to unity.

Table 1.3 *Consumption, investment, and net exports, percent of GDP, 2008*

	Private consumption	Government consumption	Investment	Private investment	Government investment	Exports	Imports	Net exports	Statist. discrep.
Australia	54	17	29	26	3	22	23	−1	0
Austria	53	19	22	21	1	58	53	5	−1
Belgium	52	23	22	21	2	86	85	1	−2
Canada	56	20	23	20	3	35	34	2	0
Czech Republic	50	20	24			77	72	5	−1
Denmark	49	27	21	19	2	55	52	3	−1
Estonia	55	19	29			71	76	−4	−1
Finland	52	23	22	19	2	47	43	4	0
France	57	23	22	19	3	27	29	−2	0
Germany	57	18	19	17	1	47	41	6	0
Greece	73	17	20	17	3	23	34	−10	0
Hungary	54	22	21			82	81	1	−2
Iceland	53	25	24	20	4	45	47	−3	0
Ireland	50	19	22	17	5	83	74	9	0
Israel	58	25	18			40	42	−1	0
Italy	59	20	21			29	29	−1	0
Japan	58	18	23	19	4	18	17	0	0
Korea	55	15	29	24	5	53	54	−1	−2
Luxembourg	32	15	20			178	146	33	0
Mexico	65	11	22			28	30	−2	−5
Netherlands	45	26	21	17	3	77	68	8	0
New Zealand	59	20	22	18	5	31	33	−2	−1
Norway	39	20	22	19	3	49	30	19	0
Poland	62	18	22			40	44	−4	−2
Portugal	67	20	22			32	43	−10	−1
Slovak Republic	57	17	25			83	85	−2	−3
Slovenia	53	18	29			67	70	−3	−3
Spain	57	20	29	25	4	26	32	−6	0
Sweden	47	26	20	17	3	53	46	7	0
Switzerland	57	11	21			56	45	11	0
Turkey	70	13	20	16	4	24	28	−4	−2
United Kingdom	64	22	17	14	2	29	32	−3	0
United States	70	17	18	15	3	13	18	−5	0

Source: *OECD Economic Outlook*, OECD, 29 December 2010, http://www.oecd-ilibrary.org/statistics.

financed to a much greater extent; so a substantial part of health and education expenditure count as private consumption in the US. Thus it is not necessarily the nature of the services that differs but the method of financing them.

Gross investment is 20–30 percent of GDP and most of this investment is made by the private sector. Government investments in roads, schools, and fighter jets constitute only a couple of percent of GDP.

Exports make up less than 20 percent of GDP in the US and the same is true for imports. In small countries, exports and imports make up a much bigger percentage of GDP. In fact, exports are almost equal to or even higher than GDP in some countries. This may appear strange: Does Belgium really export 86 percent of its production? What about Luxembourg, where exports constitute 178 percent of GDP? To understand these numbers, we must recall the difference between output and value added. Data for exports and imports are not really comparable to GDP because they are not in value added terms. They are measured as the total values of the goods and services exported and imported, including the intermediate inputs used to produce those goods and services, and a substantial share of these inputs are imported, especially in small countries.

Consider Sweden as an example, where exports constitute 53 percent of GDP. A car that is exported from Sweden contains a substantial amount of imported components: the whole car is not produced in Sweden. But GDP is measured in value added terms. To measure the importance of exports for the Swedish economy, we need to subtract imported inputs from the exports. The (direct and indirect) import content of exports can be calculated using so-called input–output tables, which show flows of intermediate goods between different production sectors.[10] Such calculations show that the import content of Swedish exports is 40 percent; so, in terms of value added, Swedish exports constitute 32 percent of GDP (0.6 times 53). One third of all goods and services produced in Sweden are exported. This is still a large proportion and reflects the globalization of the markets for goods and services.

Net exports can be positive or negative, depending on whether the country exports more than it imports, or conversely. In most countries, net exports constitute a few per cent of GDP, but there are some exceptions. In 2008, Greece and Portugal had large deficits in their trade of goods and services with other countries, while Norway and Switzerland had large surpluses.

Fig. 1.3 shows how the division between consumption, investment and net exports has changed since 1960 in some countries. In the US, the main changes are that private consumption has increased from about 60 to 70 percent of GDP, while net exports have decreased; the other shares are reasonably constant. In Sweden and the Netherlands there has been a substantial increase in public consumption, from below 20 to almost 30 percent of GDP, and corresponding declines in the proportion of private consumption and investment. Compared with 1960, the inhabitants of those countries pay a larger share of their incomes in taxes and

---

10 In 1973 the Nobel Prize in economics was awarded to the Russian economist Wassily Leontief 'for the development of the input–output method and for its application to important economic problems'.

Fig. 1.3 *Consumption, investment, and net exports, percent of GDP*

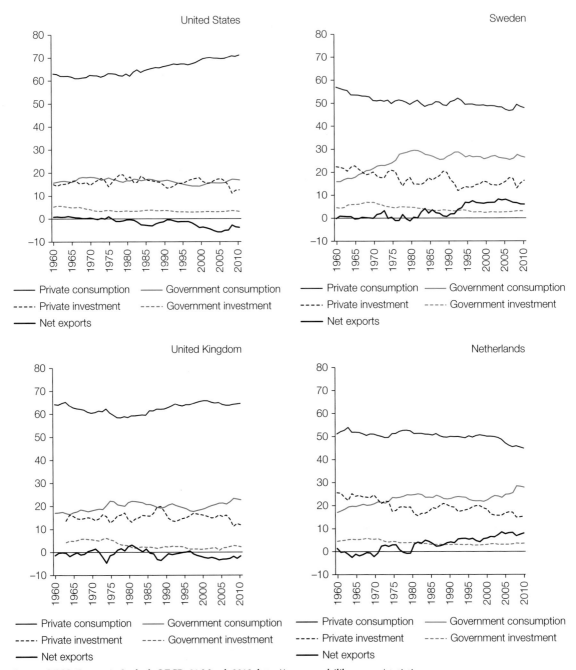

Source: *OECD Economic Outlook*, OECD, 21 March 2012, http://www.oecd-ilibrary.org/statistics.

the government provides a larger share of goods and services. Moreover, both countries have increased their net exports. In the UK, there is also some increase in government consumption relative to GDP, but the increase is smaller than in Sweden and the Netherlands.

Savings, investment, and the current account

The *current account balance* shows net payments to a country associated with trade in goods and services plus net primary income and net transfers from the rest of the world. Let Y^F denote net primary income from the rest of the world and let Tr^F be net transfers from the rest of the world. Then we have

$$Current\ account = net\ exports + net\ primary\ income + net\ transfers\ from$$
$$the\ rest\ of\ the\ world = NX + Y^F + Tr^F$$

where NX is net exports, namely, exports minus imports. If there is a surplus in the current account, payments to the country exceed payments from the country, and the surplus is used to accumulate claims on foreign countries or to pay off foreign debt.

To see how the current account is related to savings and investment, we start with income. All income comes from production, but income can come from production abroad. To obtain the *national income* we have to add net primary incomes from the rest of the world to GDP. To obtain *national disposable income* we also add net transfers from the rest of the world:

$$Gross\ national\ disposable\ income = Y + Y^F + Tr^F.$$

If we subtract private consumption, C, and government consumption, C^G, from gross national disposable income, we have the country's gross savings:

$$Gross\ savings = gross\ national\ disposable\ income - consumption$$
$$= Y + Y^F + Tr^F - C - C^G.$$

Savings can be used for *real investments* or for *net lending*, which includes lending and purchases of financial assets minus repayments of loans. Put differently, net lending is gross savings minus *real* investments:[11]

$$Net\ lending = gross\ savings - real\ investment$$
$$= Y + Y^F + Tr^F - C - C^G - I - I^G,$$

where I is private investment and I^G is government investment. Using the balance between sources and uses from the previous section, $Y = C + C^G + I + I^G + NX$, to substitute for Y we get

$$Net\ lending = \underbrace{C + C^G + I + I^G + NX}_{Y} + Y^F + Tr^F - C - C^G - I - I^G$$
$$= NX + Y^F + Tr^F = current\ account.$$

A country's net lending equals the *current account*, that is, exports minus imports plus net primary income and net current transfers from the rest of the world.

---

11 Another term for net lending is financial savings. Here, investment includes inventory investment. In the calculations we assume that income, savings, and investments are all measured in gross terms, but the same equations hold if we measure them in net terms, i.e. after subtracting capital depreciation.

A country's finances are analogous to those of an individual consumer. A consumer who consumes less than her income will save some of her income. She can use her savings to invest in real assets, such as a house, or put the money in the bank, buy some financial assets, or to pay back loans. Similarly, if a country's consumption and real investment are less than the income of the country, the inflow of payments exceeds the outflow of payments and the surplus is used to accumulate claims on foreign countries or to pay off foreign debt.

Table 1.4 shows income, savings, investment, and net lending as a percentage of GDP for different OECD countries in 2008. In most OECD countries, net primary income from abroad constituted only a few percent of GDP.

Net current transfers are negative and constitute 1–2 percent of GDP for most OECD countries; these include foreign aid and net payments to the EU and international organizations.

In most countries, gross savings are 20–25 percent of GDP and investments are of the same order, so the current account surplus or deficit is a few percent of GDP. Norway is an extreme case, with savings equal to 40 percent of GDP, while investments run at a more normal rate of 22 percent of GDP. As a result, the Norwegian current account shows a surplus equal to 18 percent of GDP. Norway saves a large part of its oil revenue but does not use it for investments in Norway. Instead, roughly half of Norway's gross savings is channelled to other countries in the form of lending and purchases of foreign assets.

Saving, investment, and net lending are carried out in both the private and the public sectors. The *private sector* consists of firms and households. Most production is carried out by firms. For statistical purposes, the *household sector* includes self-employed persons and non-profit organizations; so there is also some production in this sector. The household sector accounts for private consumption and a large part of the saving. *Firms*, by definition, do not consume, but they do save since a substantial portion of earnings (profits) are retained and reinvested. (In the end, this saving accrues to households since the households own the firms which increase in value when profits are reinvested.)

The *public sector* consists of *central government*, *local governments* and the *social insurance sector* (primarily the public pension system). In federal nations there is also a distinction between the federal government and the governments of the individual states that make up the federation. In statistical sources, there is often reference to the *consolidated public sector*. 'Consolidated' means that payments and claims between the different parts of the public sector are cancelled out in order to show the financial situation of the public sector as a whole.

To see clearly how private and public saving are related to national saving and the current account, let T denote taxes from the private sector to the government minus transfers from the government to the private sector (e.g. pensions). Let net government debt to the private sector be D and let the net interest payment on the debt be iD. We use use i to denote the interest rate expressed as a fraction of the debt so $i = 0.05$ means that the interest rate is 5 percent. Assume, for simplicity, that net primary income from the rest of the world (Y^F) accrues to the private sector and that net transfers from the rest of the world (Tr^F) go to the government.

Table 1.4 *Income, saving, investment, and net lending, percent of GDP, 2008*

	Gross domestic product	Net primary incomes from the rest of the world	Gross national income at market prices	Net current transfers from the rest of the world	Gross national disposable income	Final consumption expenditures	Gross saving	Gross investment	Net lending = current account (approx.)
Australia	100	−3	96	0	96	72	24	28	−3
Austria	100	−1	99	−1	98	71	27	23	4
Belgium	100	1	101	−1	100	75	25	24	1
Canada	100	−1	99	0	99	75	23	23	1
Chile	100	−8	92	2	94	71	23	25	−2
Czech Republic	100	−5	95	−1	95	70	24	25	0
Denmark	100	1	101	−2	99	75	25	22	3
Estonia	100	−5	95	1	95	75	21	29	−8
Finland	100	1	101	−1	99	74	25	22	3
France	100	1	101	−1	100	80	19	22	−3
Germany	100	2	102	−1	100	75	25	18	7
Greece	100	−3	97	0	96	92	4	21	−15
Hungary	100	−6	94	−1	93	76	17	24	−6
Iceland	100	−19	81	0	81	78	2	25	−22
Ireland	100	−13	87	−1	85	69	16	22	−6
Israel	100	−2	98	4	102	83	20	19	1
Italy	100	−2	98	−1	97	79	18	21	−3
Japan	100	3	103	0	103	76	25	24	3
Korea	100	1	101	0	101	70	31	31	0
Mexico	100	−2	98	2	101	75	25	27	−1
Netherlands	100	−2	98	−2	97	71	26	21	4
New Zealand	100	−7	93	0	93	79	15	22	−8
Norway	100	0	100	−1	99	59	40	22	18
Portugal	100	−3	97	1	98	87	11	23	−11
Slovak Republic	100	−3	97	−2	96	74	21	28	−6
Slovenia	100	−3	97	−1	96	71	25	32	−7
Spain	100	−3	97	−1	96	77	19	29	−9
Sweden	100	4	104	−1	102	73	29	20	9
Switzerland	100	−7	93	−2	91	67	24	21	2
United Kingdom	100	2	102	−1	101	86	15	17	−1
United States	100	1	100	−1	99	87	12	18	−6

Note: The numbers do not match perfectly because of rounding errors and because some minor details in the accounts have been omitted.
Source: *OECD National Accounts Statistics*, OECD, 3 January 2011, http://www.oecd-ilibrary.org/statistics.

Then we can decompose the country's net lending into private and public net lending:[12]

$$Net\ lending = Y + Y^F + Tr^F - C - C^G - I - I^G$$

$$= \underbrace{Y + Y^F + iD - T - C - I}_{private\ net\ lending} + \underbrace{T + Tr^F - iD - C^G - I^G}_{public\ net\ lending}.$$

Public net lending is also called the *general government financial balance*. If this is negative, there is a *budget deficit* for the public sector as a whole.

How can we compare incomes between countries?

In order to compare income levels between countries, we first need to measure income relative to the population, that is, income *per capita*. Thus we need a measure of the population of the country. The measure of population used by the OECD, for example, is based on residency; it includes persons who are *residents* in a country for one year or more, regardless of their citizenship.

We also need to take account of the fact that countries have different currencies and different price levels. One way to compare incomes is to convert incomes to the same currency using market exchange rates. This can be misleading, however, because the price levels in different countries are not the same. In a poor country, income is low in dollar terms, but a meal in a restaurant or a haircut is also much cheaper in dollar terms than it is in a rich country. Since price levels are lower in low-income countries, conversion of incomes using market exchange rates will lead us to exaggerate the income differentials between countries.

Purchasing power parities are conversion rates between currencies that reflect the purchasing powers of the currencies – that is, how much you can buy for each currency – *in the home country*. The rationale is that if one unit of currency X buys three times as many goods in its home country as one unit of currency Y in its home country, the rate of conversion should be one to three. Using conversion rates based on the purchasing power of different currencies we can compare income per capita in real terms, assuming that the money is spent in the home country. Therefore, the standard way to compare income levels is to use exchange rates based on purchasing power. Such conversion rates may coincide with market exchange rates, but most of the time they do not.

If we are interested in comparing standards of living, it would make more sense to compare disposable *income* per capita. This would mean that we would include net primary incomes and transfers from the rest of the world. A problem with this measure is that some transfers, such as remittances that workers living and working abroad send back to their families, are poorly measured. In practice, GDP per capita is the most common measure used to compare income levels in different countries. Yet we should be aware that GDP per capita measures

---

12 In this chapter, all variables are measured in nominal terms. When we construct our model we will use, for example, Y, C, and I to denote production and consumption in real terms, i.e., measured in units of goods.

production rather than income, so it will be a misleading measure of income when there are large primary incomes or transfers to or from the rest of the world.

Table 1.5 shows GDP per capita in 2008 for the OECD countries measured as an index with the OECD average equal to 100. Luxembourg is an outlier with extremely high GDP per capita, but this exaggerates the standard of living in Luxembourg. There are many non-resident workers who work and contribute

Table 1.5 *GDP per capita in the OECD countries, 2008*

Country	GDP per capita, OECD = 100, based on current PPPs	Purchasing power parities for GDP, US dollars per national currency	Exchange rates, US dollars per national currency	Purchasing power parities divided by exchange rates
Luxembourg	264	1.10	1.46	0.75
Norway	178	0.11	0.18	0.65
United States	138	1.00	1.00	1.00
Switzerland	134	0.65	0.93	0.70
Netherlands	126	1.18	1.46	0.81
Ireland	125	1.05	1.46	0.72
Austria	117	1.17	1.46	0.80
Denmark	116	0.12	0.20	0.64
Sweden	116	0.11	0.15	0.75
Australia	115	0.68	0.84	0.80
Iceland	115	0.01	0.01	0.74
Canada	114	0.81	0.93	0.87
Finland	111	1.09	1.46	0.74
Germany	109	1.23	1.46	0.84
Belgium	108	1.14	1.46	0.78
United Kingdom	108	1.56	1.84	0.85
Eurozone	103	1.24	1.46	0.85
France	101	1.13	1.46	0.77
Japan	100	0.01	0.01	0.88
Italy	98	1.27	1.46	0.87
Spain	98	1.39	1.46	0.95
Greece	88	1.43	1.46	0.97
New Zealand	86	0.67	0.70	0.95
Korea	79	0.00	0.00	1.40
Czech Republic	76	0.07	0.06	1.25
Portugal	73	1.54	1.46	1.05
Slovak Republic	68	1.88	1.41	1.33
Hungary	61	0.01	0.01	1.33
Poland	53	0.54	0.41	1.30
Mexico	45	0.13	0.09	1.49
Turkey	44	1.12	0.77	1.45

Source: *OECD National Accounts Statistics*, OECD, 12 March 2011, http://www.oecd-ilibrary.org/statistics.

to GDP in Luxembourg and those workers are not included in the population measure, making GDP per capita high.

As we see, the purchasing power parity (US dollars per national currency) is higher than the market exchange rate for poor countries, which reflects the relatively low price level in poor countries. Put differently, currencies of poor countries are worth more in terms of purchasing power than indicated by the market exchange rate. If we convert incomes using market exchange rates, we exaggerate the differences in the standard of living.

How do we measure real growth of production?

In most countries, prices increase with time, so the *nominal* value of *GDP* increases even if the quantities of goods and services produced remain unchanged. But a price increase does not increase the amount of goods available for consumption and investment. To measure the overall change in the *quantity* of goods and services produced, we use indexes of *real GDP*, also called *GDP in fixed prices*.

In a model economy with only one good, this is simple. Real GDP is simply the quantity of the good produced and nominal GDP is the value, or price times quantity. Using Y to denote production of the good, we measure the growth rate of real GDP from period t to period $t+1$ as

$$g_{t+1} = \frac{Y_{t+1}}{Y_t} - 1.$$

If, for example, $Y_{t+1}/Y_t = 1.03$ the real growth rate from period t to period $t+1$ is three hundredths, that is, 3 percent:

$$g_{t+1} = 0.03.$$

The situation becomes more complicated if more than one good is involved. Then we need to construct some *index* that summarizes the *average* growth of production across all the different goods and services produced in the economy. To do this, let us consider the case of two goods called A and B, with prices P^A and P^B, and quantities Y^A and Y^B. We first measure nominal GDP in year t:

$$GDP_t = P_t^A Y_t^A + P_t^B Y_t^B.$$

Then we measure *what nominal GDP would have been in year t+1 if prices had remained unchanged from the previous year:*[13]

$$P_t^A Y_{t+1}^A + P_t^B Y_{t+1}^B.$$

Dividing these two numbers and subtracting one we get a measure of real GDP growth:

$$g_{t+1} = \frac{P_t^A Y_{t+1}^A + P_t^B Y_{t+1}^B}{P_t^A Y_t^A + P_t^B Y_t^B} - 1.$$

If $g = 0.02$ we say that real GDP has increased by 2 percent. Effectively, we are measuring growth as a weighted average of the growth of the production of the two

---

13 Alternatively, the prices in year $t+1$ or the average of the prices in years t and $t+1$ can be used.

goods where goods with a higher price or quantity get a bigger weight.[14] We can see this more clearly by rewriting as follows:

$$g_{t+1} = \frac{P_t^A \, Y_{t+1}^A}{P_t^A \, Y_t^A + P_t^B Y_t^B} + \frac{P_t^B Y_{t+1}^B}{P_t^A \, Y_t^A + P_t^B Y_t^B} - 1$$

$$= \frac{P_t^A Y_t^A}{P_t^A \, Y_t^A + P_t^B Y_t^B} \frac{Y_{t+1}^A}{Y_t^A} + \frac{P_t^B Y_t^B}{P_t^A \, Y_t^A + P_t^B Y_t^B} \frac{Y_{t+1}^B}{Y_t^B} - 1.$$

In the second step we have multiplied and divided the first term by Y_t^A and the second term by Y_t^B. The last expression shows that real GDP growth is calculated as a weighted average of the growth of production of the two goods where the weights are the GDP shares of the goods in period t. This is reasonable since the GDP shares of the goods indicate how important the two goods are in production. Having done this calculation year by year we can construct a volume index of real GDP by starting from some base year where we set the index to 100, and then calculating an index for real GDP iteratively:

$$Y_{t+1} = \left(1 + g_{t+1}\right) Y_t.$$

An index calculated in this way is called a *chain index*. Note that the *level* of this index has no meaning; we can set it to 100 in some arbitrary year. What is interesting is how it *changes* over time.

How do we measure inflation?

Inflation is the change in the price level. One measure of the price level is the GDP deflator, which is calculated as

$$\text{GDP deflator} = \frac{\text{Nominal GDP}}{\text{Real GDP}}.$$

The GDP deflator is a measure of the price level of the goods and services produced. If nominal GDP increases relative to real GDP it must be because prices have increased. It is called 'deflator' because real GDP is obtained by dividing nominal GDP by the GDP deflator:

$$\text{Real GDP} = \frac{\text{Nominal GDP}}{\text{GDP deflator}}.$$

Another common measure of the price level is the *consumer price index* (CPI). To construct CPI, we measure inflation by how much more we must pay in order to consume the same consumption basket as the previous year:

$$\pi_{t+1} = \frac{P_{t+1}^A \, C_t^A + P_{t+1}^B C_t^B}{P_t^A \, C_t^A + P_t^B C_t^B} - 1.$$

We use the Greek letter π (pi) to denote inflation. If $\pi_t = 0.05$, consumer prices have increased by 5 percent compared with the previous year. This means that we

---

14 A *weighted average* is a sum of variables where the different variables have different weights. The average of X and Y is $(X + Y)/2 = 0.5X + 0.5Y$, with equal weight to X and Y. If, instead, we give X the weight $3/4$, we get a weighted average of $0.75X + 0.25Y$.

need to spend 5 percent more in order to buy the same combination (basket) of goods as last year. Again, we can rewrite this as a weighted average:

$$\pi_{t+1} = \frac{P_t^A \; C_t^A}{P_t^A \; C_t^A + P_t^B C_t^B} \frac{P_{t+1}^A}{P_t^A} + \frac{P_t^B C_t^B}{P_t^A \; C_t^A + P_t^B C_t^B} \frac{P_{t+1}^B}{P_t^B} - 1.$$

Inflation is measured as a weighted average of the price increases of the goods where the weights are the consumption shares in the previous year. Having calculated inflation in each year, CPI is then constructed as a chain index starting from an arbitrary base year where the index is set to an arbitrary number such as 100:

$$CPI_{t+1} = (1 + \pi_{t+1}) \; CPI_t.$$

The GDP deflator measures the price level of all goods and services produced in the country, while the CPI measures the price level of goods and services consumed in the country. The main difference is that the CPI excludes prices of goods used for investment, exports and by the government, and it includes a substantial proportion of imported goods. In practice, the correlation between changes in CPI and changes in the GDP deflator is very high in most countries because a large fraction of the goods and services that we consume are produced at home and export prices change along with domestic prices. In countries that produce goods with large fluctuations in prices, such as oil or other raw materials, changes in the GDP deflator may deviate substantially from inflation measured by CPI.

What have we learned?

A model is an imaginary toy economy with a few agents and a few markets. In our basic macro model there are three markets: the goods market, the labour market and the financial market. There are three decision-makers: firms, households and policymakers. Most of the time, we take policy as exogenous, so we focus on the behaviour of firms and households.

In the model, firms set wages and prices, and choose the inputs of capital (machines, buildings) and labour (workers) to maximize profits. Households choose between consuming today and saving for consumption in the future. In the open economy, households also choose between domestically produced and foreign goods and international investors choose between lending in different currencies. Thus we have six key economic decisions to analyse:

1) price-setting
2) wage-setting
3) investment
4) consumption
5) the household's choice between goods produced at home and imports
6) the foreign investor's choice between lending in different currencies.

We often use mathematics to describe and analyse a model. *Variables* are symbols representing economic quantities or prices, and they can take different values in different situations. *Functions* describe the relations between economic quantities and prices. *Endogenous* variables are determined within the model while *exogenous* variables are taken as given (unexplained) in the analysis.

The national accounts show how much is produced and in what sectors production takes place, how income is distributed and how goods are and services are used for consumption and investment by the private sector and the government.

The annual GDP is the sum of all *value added* produced in a given year.

The difference between *market price* and *basic price* is *taxes less subsidies on products*. Most of this difference is due to value added tax and sales taxes that are included in the market price but not in the basic price.

Net production usually refers to production minus consumption of capital (depreciation).

Wages from working abroad and capital income from assets abroad are called *primary incomes from the rest of the world*. If we add net primary incomes from the rest of the world to GDP we get *gross national income* (GNI) at market prices.

The difference between income and *disposable income* is *taxes and transfers* (secondary incomes). If we add net transfers from the rest of the world to national income we get *national disposable income.*

About three quarters of value added is produced in the service industries, a couple of percent in agriculture, and the rest in industry and construction.

About 2/3 of gross income goes to labour income (wages/salaries and social insurance fees) and about 1/3 goes to capital income. Roughly 50 percent of gross capital income is used to replace depreciated capital (about 15 percent of GDP) and the rest is paid out as interest and dividends, or kept as retained earnings and reinvested by the firms.

Production, Y, equals private consumption, C, plus private investment, I, plus government consumption, C^G and investment, I^G, plus net exports, NX (exports minus imports):

$$Y = C + I + C^G + I^G + NX.$$

In most OECD countries, 50–60 percent of all goods and services produced are used for private consumption, while government consumption constitutes 20–25 percent of GDP. Private investment accounts for about 20 percent of GDP, while government investment constitutes only a couple of percent of GDP.

The proportions of exports and imports as percentages of GDP vary substantially between countries, from below 20 percent in the US to above 50 percent in some small countries.

If we subtract consumption from national disposable income, we get savings. Savings can be used for *real investments* or for *net lending*. Put differently, net lending is savings minus *real* investments. If we let Y^F denote net primary income from the rest of the world and Tr^F denote net transfers from the rest of the world we have net lending of the country as a whole:

$$Net\ lending = savings - real\ investment = Y + Y^F + Tr^F - C - C^G - I - I^G.$$

Using the fact that $Y = C + C^G + I + I^G + NX$ we see that net lending of the country equals the *current account*:

$$Net\ lending = NX + Y^F + Tr^F = current\ account.$$

In order to compare standards of living between different countries we need to take account of differences in price levels. *Purchasing power parities* reflect how much you can buy of a given consumption basket for one unit of the currency in each country.

In order to measure growth in real GDP (GDP in fixed prices) we measure how much GDP would have increased if quantities had been what they actually were but prices had been the same as the previous year. In order to measure inflation, we measure how much more we would have to pay to buy the same consumption basket as the previous year.

The GDP deflator is equal to nominal GDP divided by real GDP.

Where do we go from here?

Having familiarized ourselves with some basic macroeconomic concepts and inspected some macroeconomic data, we now go on to build our macroeconomic model. Chapter 2 will focus on the supply side: production possibilities, factors of production, price-setting and the distribution of income. In Chapters 3 and 4 we examine the demand side: consumption and investment. In these three chapters we build a basic macroeconomic model that will be used in the rest of the book.

Exercises

1. What is the difference between exogenous and endogenous variables?

2. As explained in the chapter, firms make three important decisions in our macroeconomic model: price-setting, wage-setting and investment decisions. List any factors that you think could influence each of these decisions.

3. Households make two important decisions in our macroeconomic model: the choice between consumption and saving, and the choice between consuming domestically produced and imported goods. List any factors that could influence each of these decisions.

4. Foreign lenders make a choice between lending in different currencies. List some factors that could potentially influence this decision.

5. Data for Smalland can be found in Table 1.6. Use the data to calculate the following:
   a) GDP (*Hint: use the balance between sources and uses.*)
   b) Net domestic product at market price
   c) Net national disposable income at market price
   d) Labour income as a share of gross value added at basic price
   e) Gross and net capital income as a share of gross value added at basic price.

6. Let us assume that all primary income to and from the rest of the world goes to the private sector in Smalland and that net transfers from the rest of the world (RoW) go to the government. Use the data from Table 1.6 to

Table 1.6 *The economy of Smalland*

Private consumption	50	Government consumption	23
Private investment	20	Government investment	3
Exports	36	Imports	32
Primary income from RoW	5	Primary income to RoW	2
Taxes less subsidies on products	10	Net transfers from RoW	0
Capital stock	200	Depreciation rate	7.5 percent
Labour income	60		
Net interest payment from the government to private sector	1		
Government income from private sector (taxes etc.) minus transfers	24		

calculate the following numbers for Smalland:

a) Private gross saving and net lending
b) Government gross saving and net lending
c) The current account balance.

What is the relation between the numbers above?

7. Income in country A is 150 euros per day. Income in country B is 500 kirins per day. The exchange rate is 10 kirins per euro. A basket of consumption goods costs 30 euros in country A and 200 kirins in country B.

a) Express the income in country B as a fraction of income in country A using the market exchange rate.
b) Express the income in country B as a fraction of income in country A using the purchasing power of the two currencies.
c) Explain why the two numbers are not the same. (*Hint: express the cost of the basket in the two countries in euros.*)

8. Consumers buy three goods A, B, and C. We have price and quantity data for two years:

	P_t^A	Y_t^A	P_t^B	Y_t^B	P_t^C	Y_t^C
Year 1	10	8	20	5	5	4
Year 2	11	9	20	5	8	4

a) Calculate the percentage increase in nominal expenditure from year 1 to year 2.
b) Calculate inflation from year 1 to year 2.
c) Calculate an index of the real increase in consumption from year 1 to year 2 using the method described in the chapter to calculate real growth of GDP.
d) Compare the numbers in a, b and c and explain the relation between them.

Answers to the exercises can be found at: **www.palgrave.com/economics/gottfries.**

Appendix

Functions and derivatives

Macroeconomics is concerned with *relations* between different magnitudes such as production, investment, consumption, exports and the interest rate. It is convenient to use basic mathematical tools to describe such relations. Thus we use *variables* to represent various economic magnitudes and we use *functions* to summarize relations between different variables.

A *function* is a relation indicating that one thing depends on another. To take a simple example, most countries have a tax schedule that says that people with higher incomes must pay higher taxes. Instead of saying this in words we can use mathematical language:

$$T = T(Y).$$

T is the tax, Y is income and $T(Y)$ is a function saying that the tax depends in some way on the level of income. T and Y are *variables* that take different numerical values for different persons. Here, we have written the tax function in general terms, without specifying exactly how the tax depends on income. Therefore, we say that $T(Y)$ is a *general functional form*.

Now, we can be more specific and say that the tax increases, or stays constant, but does not decrease as income increases. In mathematical terms, this means that the *slope* of the function is positive. We say that the *derivative* of the tax function, which measures the slope of the function, is positive (or zero):

$$T'(Y) \geq 0.$$

The derivative of the tax function with respect to income is the *marginal tax* – how much *more* you pay in tax if you earn an additional euro (or pound). Note that the derivative of a function is itself a function of the explanatory variable. In many countries, the marginal tax is higher for higher incomes.

Typically, we will write down our models using *general functional forms*. This is a compact way of saying that there are some relations between certain economic quantities or prices. Sometimes we assume *specific functional forms*, however. Suppose, for example, that the tax schedule is such that you pay 30 per-cent on all income above a threshold of 1000 euros per year. This can be written in mathematical language:

$$T(Y) = 0 \qquad \text{if } Y < 1000$$
$$T(Y) = 0.30\,(Y - 1000) \qquad \text{if } Y > 1000.$$

One way to illustrate this function is to make a table such as Table 1.7, which shows taxes for different levels of income. Another is to draw the relation graphi-cally as in Fig. 1.4 where we have drawn the tax as a function of income. For every level of income on the horizontal axis we can read off the corresponding tax on the vertical axis. In this case the derivative (slope) of the tax function is zero for incomes below 1000 and 0.30 above this level. We see that the derivative (slope) of the tax function is itself a function of income.

Functions of several variables

The tax function above has one explanatory variable; the tax depends on the income and nothing else. But a function can have several explanatory variables. The amount a firm can produce depends not only on the number of workers

Table 1.7 *A tax schedule*

Y	500	1000	2000	3000	4000	5000
T	0	0	300	600	900	1200

Fig. 1.4 *A tax schedule*

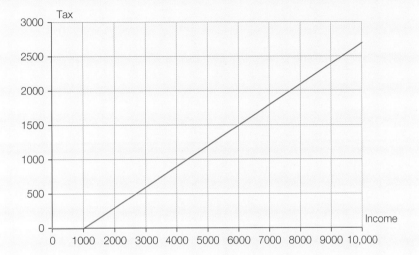

it has but also on the amount of capital (e.g. machines) it has. To say this in mathematical language we write

$$Y = F(K,N).$$

Here, Y is production and K is the capital stock, which we may think of as the number of machines, and N is the number of workers employed. This expression just says that there is *some* relation between the amount of inputs we put in and the amount we can produce.

Again, we can choose to be more specific and assume a specific function for the relationship. One example of a specific production function is

$$F(K,N) = 10\sqrt{KN}.$$

This production function says that if, for example, we have 6 machines and 6 workers, we can produce 60 units:

$$Y = 10\sqrt{6 \cdot 6} = 60.$$

We illustrate this function in Table 1.8, where we put the number of workers in the first row and the number of machines in the first column and where we have the amount of production for each combination of inputs in the table.

When there are several explanatory variables in the function, we cannot illustrate the whole function in one diagram, but we can illustrate it in different ways.

Table 1.8 *Inputs and production when* $F(K,N) = 10\sqrt{KN}$

	Workers		
Machines ↓	2	4	6
2	20	28	35
4	28	40	49
6	35	49	60

Fig. 1.5 *The relation between capital input and production for a given number of workers*

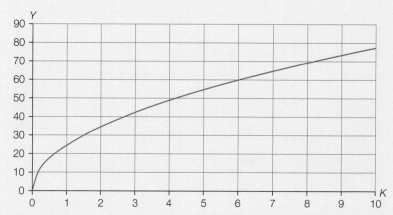

Note: The relation between capital input and production is drawn for the production function $Y = 10\sqrt{KN}$ and $N = 6$.

We can, for example, draw the relation between capital input and production *for a given number of workers*, as in Fig. 1.5.

When we have a function of several variables, we use *partial derivatives*. The partial derivative is again the slope of the function, but now it shows how much the value of the function increases *if we change one explanatory variable while holding the other variables constant*. In economic terms, the partial derivative of the production function with respect to capital is the *marginal product of capital*. It indicates how much production increases per unit increase in the capital stock when we keep labour input constant. The production function above can be written

$$F(K,N) = 10\sqrt{KN} = 10\,(KN)^{1/2} = 10K^{1/2}N^{1/2}.$$

To find the marginal product of capital, *MPK*, we take the derivative with respect to capital, treating N as if it were a constant:

$$MPK = 10 \cdot \frac{1}{2} \cdot K^{\frac{1}{2}-1} \cdot N^{\frac{1}{2}} = 5 \cdot K^{-\frac{1}{2}} \cdot N^{\frac{1}{2}} = 5\left(\frac{N}{K}\right)^{\frac{1}{2}} = 5\sqrt{\frac{N}{K}}.$$

Note that the marginal product of capital is itself a function of N and K. It is higher the more workers we have and lower the more capital we have for a given number of workers. That sounds plausible. An additional machine will be of less use if we already have a lot of machines and more useful if there are many workers who can use it. We will discuss the production function in more detail in Chapter 2.

Differentiation

Suppose Y depends on X according to some function F:

$$Y = F(X).$$

Let X_0 denote a particular value of X. Suppose now that starting from X_0 there is a small increase in X which we denote ΔX. How much will Y change as a result of the change in X?

Fig. 1.6 *The relation between changes in X and changes in Y*

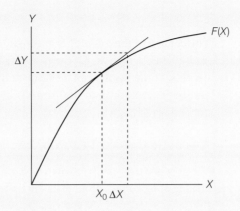

The exact answer is

$$\Delta Y = F\left(X_0 + \Delta X\right) - F\left(X_0\right).$$

An approximate answer is given by

$$\Delta Y \approx F'\left(X_0\right) \Delta X.$$

We get the approximate change in Y by multiplying ΔX by the derivative of the function F evaluated at $X = X_0$. This is illustrated graphically in Fig. 1.6. The change in Y that we obtain in this way is the change we get by moving along the *tangent* to the function F at $X = X_0$.

By looking at the figure we realize two things. First, this measure of the change in Y is an approximation of the true change in Y that we would get if we moved along the actual function F. The only case when we get exactly the right answer is if the function F is linear. Second, the approximation will be reasonably accurate if we are talking about a small change in X, but the bigger ΔX, the less accurate the approximation.

If we have several explanatory variables we calculate the change in Y in a similar way. We multiply the change in each explanatory variable with the corresponding derivative and add up the changes:

$$Y = F\left(X, Z\right) \quad \Rightarrow \quad \Delta Y \approx F_x\left(X_0, Z_0\right) \Delta X + F_z\left(X_0, Z_0\right) \Delta Z,$$

where $F_x\left(X_0, Z_0\right)$ and $F_z\left(X_0, Z_0\right)$ denote the partial derivatives with respect to X and Z, evaluated at the point $\left(X_0, Z_0\right)$.

The natural logarithm

The natural logarithm of a variable is a specific function of the variable. Let x be the natural logarithm of X: $x = \ln\left(X\right)$. Then, by definition,

$$X = e^x.$$

Differencing as described above, we get

$$\Delta X \approx e^x \Delta x$$

and thus

$$\Delta x \approx \frac{\Delta X}{X}.$$

The change in the log of X is approximately equal to the relative change in X, and multiplying by 100 we get the percentage change in X. It can be helpful to remember this. Some results can be easily derived by taking logs and then differentiating and remembering that (100 times) the change in the log is (approximately) the percentage change.

A practical rule of thumb

We now use the result above to derive a practical rule of thumb for the percentage change of a product or a ratio which we will use repeatedly in this book. To derive the rule, suppose that some variable Z is related to three other variables, X, Y and Q, in the following way:

$$Z = \frac{X \cdot Y}{Q}.$$

Taking natural logs on both sides we get

$$\ln Z = \ln X + \ln Y - \ln Q.$$

Now suppose there are some changes in the right-hand side variables. For the equality to hold before and after the change, the change in $\ln Z$ must be equal to the sum of the changes of the right-hand side variables:

$$\Delta \ln Z = \Delta \ln X + \Delta \ln Y - \Delta \ln Q.$$

Remembering that changes in logs are approximately equal to the relative (percentage) changes we get our rule of thumb:

$$\frac{\Delta Z}{Z} \approx \frac{\Delta X}{X} + \frac{\Delta Y}{Y} - \frac{\Delta Q}{Q}.$$

The percentage change in Z is the percentage change in X *plus* the percentage change in Y *minus* the percentage change in Q.

This is easy to remember, and very useful. It is also rather intuitive. We can think of the changes occurring one by one. Suppose first that X increases by 2 percent. This will increase XY/Q 2 percent. Suppose then Y increases 3 percent; this will increase XY/Q by a further 3 percent so the total change is now approximately 5 percent. But suppose then Q increases by 4 percent. When the denominator increases 4 percent, the whole ratio will fall by about 4 percent, so the net change is approximately one percent: $2 + 3 - 4 = +1$.

But this is an approximation. To check how accurate the approximation is we can calculate the exact change in Z. Denote the initial values X_0, Y_0, Q_0 so we have initially

$$Z_0 = X_0 Y_0 / Q_0.$$

The new values are $X_1 = 1.02 \cdot X_0$, $Y_1 = 1.03 \cdot Y_0$, $Q_1 = 1.04 \cdot Q_0$. The true value of Z after all the changes will therefore be

$$Z_1 = \frac{X_1 Y_1}{Q_1} = \frac{1.02 \cdot X_0 \cdot 1.03 \cdot Y_0}{1.04 \cdot Q_0} = \frac{1.02 \cdot 1.03}{1.04} \cdot \frac{X_0 \cdot Y_0}{Q_0} \approx 1.01019 \cdot Z_0.$$

Z increases 1.019 percent, so our rule of thumb gives a reasonably accurate approximation.

As an example of how this rule can be used, let Y be real production and let P be the price level. Then nominal GDP is P times Y and the growth rate of nominal GDP is the growth rate of real production *plus* the growth rate of the price level (inflation). If real GDP increases by 2 percent per year and inflation is 3 percent per year, nominal GDP will increase by approximately 5 percent per year.

As another example, let W be the wage per worker and let E be production per worker. Then the wage cost per unit of production is W/E and the growth rate of the wage cost per unit is the rate of wage increase *minus* the growth rate of productivity (E). If wages increase by 5 percent per year and productivity increases by 2 percent per year, wage costs per unit of production increase by about 3 percent per year.

Working with exponents

The expression x^n means x multiplied with itself n times. It follows that

$$x^n \cdot x^m = x^{n+m} \qquad \frac{x^n}{x^m} = x^{n-m}$$

$$(x^n)^m = x^{n \cdot m} \qquad \left(\frac{x^n}{y^m}\right)^k = \frac{x^{n \cdot k}}{y^{m \cdot k}}.$$

For example:

$$2^2 \cdot 2^3 = (2 \cdot 2) \cdot (2 \cdot 2 \cdot 2) = 2^5 \qquad \frac{2^2}{2^3} = \frac{2 \cdot 2}{2 \cdot 2 \cdot 2} = \frac{1}{2} = 2^{-1}$$

$$\left(2^2\right)^3 = (2 \cdot 2) \cdot (2 \cdot 2) \cdot (2 \cdot 2) = 2^6 \qquad \left(\frac{2^3}{3^2}\right)^3 = \frac{2^3}{3^2} \cdot \frac{2^3}{3^2} \cdot \frac{2^3}{3^2} = \frac{2^3 \cdot 2^3 \cdot 2^3}{3^2 \cdot 3^2 \cdot 3^2} = \frac{2^9}{3^6}.$$

The same principles apply when the exponents are numbers smaller than one, for example:

$$3^{1/2} \cdot 3^{1/2} = \sqrt{3} \cdot \sqrt{3} = 3.$$

PART 1 THE LONG RUN

2 PRODUCTION, PRICES, AND THE DISTRIBUTION OF INCOME

What determines the long-run level of income and its distribution?

In a market economy, most goods and services are produced by privately owned firms. These firms sell their products to consumers and to other firms, to be used as inputs into production or to increase production capacity. When we looked at the national accounts in Chapter 1, we saw that production generates income, and this income is divided between labour and capital income. But what determines the level of income and how it is distributed? These are the questions to be addressed in this chapter.

In order to produce, firms need qualified workers, buildings, equipment, energy, and raw materials. Such inputs are called *production factors*. As we will see, the level of income is determined by available production factors and the technology that is used in production. The main production factors are capital and labour and the technology is conveniently summarized by a *production function*. We will spend some time analysing the production function because it is a fundamental building block in our macroeconomic model.

The production function will help us to understand how production is determined for a given capital stock. Later (in Chapter 5) we will analyse how capital is accumulated over time and we will study the long-run growth of income.

The analysis in this chapter will help us to understand how income is distributed. There are three sources of income in our model: labour income (wages), interest payments, and profits that firms pay out to their owners. To understand the distribution of income, we need to understand how prices and wages are determined. As we will see, the share of income that goes to labour depends on the technology of production and the degree of competition in the product market. The more important labour is in production, the higher the share of income that goes to labour. The weaker the competition in the product market, the higher profits will be.

This chapter focuses on the *supply side* of the economy. In Chapters 3 and 4, we will analyse the *demand side* of the economy, consumption and investment, and we will also combine supply and demand into a macroeconomic model of the long run. Thus, we build a complete macroeconomic model in Chapters 2–4. These chapters will contain a lot of theory but this investment in theory will pay off in later chapters. We will constantly refer back to the results in Chapters 2–4 when we get to the more applied analysis in subsequent chapters.

In this chapter, we first introduce the production function, which describes the technology of production. Then we study how firms set prices and compete in the product market. Then we analyse what determines the level of production and income, and the real wage. Finally, we examine how income is distributed between workers and owners of firms and financial assets.

2.1　Production

The most fundamental economic conditions of a country are those that determine the opportunities to produce goods and services. In this section, we introduce the *production function*, which summarizes in compact form how production is related to the available factors of production. We also introduce a specific and very convenient production function, the *Cobb–Douglas* production function.

Production factors

The opportunities to produce goods and services depend on several factors. One factor is the input of *labour*. What matters is not only the number of workers available for production but also how many hours they work and the knowledge that they have. Workers' knowledge, which is accumulated through education and work experience, is called *human capital*.

Firms also use *intermediate goods*, which have been produced by other firms, as inputs in the production process, for example raw material, components, energy.

Another factor is *capital* – equipment in the form of machines, buildings, and other facilities that are used for production. Capital is a *stock* that is given at a point in time. As time goes by, capital is accumulated through *investment*, but there is also *depreciation*. Machines break down, roofs start to leak, painting needs to be renewed, and so on. Investment and depreciation add to and subtract from capital as time goes by, but, at a given time, the capital stock is given.

There are also *fixed factors*, such as land, which are available in limited supply and used for production. In order to produce agricultural products, for example, we need not only labour and capital, but also land. Machines and land are both given at a point in time, but while new machines can be produced and added to the stock as time goes by, land is available in (essentially) fixed supply.

Finally, the *technology* describes the available methods of production – how resources can be used to produce as much as possible. Better technology means that more can be produced with given inputs. A more efficient printing machine, for example, means that more books can be produced with a given input of labour.

The production function

Since we are interested in what determines GDP – namely, total value added in the economy – we disregard intermediate goods – that is, goods that are produced by one firm and used as inputs by other firms. Thus we assume that all firms produce final goods which are used for consumption and investment. Also, fixed factors play a small role in most industrialized economies. As we saw in Chapter 1, agricultural production constitutes only 1–3 percent of production in rich countries. We will therefore disregard fixed factors in our analysis.

To make things simple, we assume that employed workers work a fixed number of hours per year and we take the technology and the level of human capital as given.[1] Thus, the main factors of production are the capital stock and the number of workers employed. How much we can produce depends on how much capital and labour we use. We use a *production function* to describe the production possibilities in a compact way:

$$Y = F(K, N),$$

where Y is production, K is the capital stock, and N is the number of workers.

This production function says nothing more, or less, than what we have just said in words: how much we can produce depends on how much capital and labour we use. There is some *relation* between inputs and production. Put differently: in order to produce some given amount, we need a suitable combination of capital and labour. Note that, in theory, Y, K, and N are measured in *physical units*. Y measures how many units of the good the firm produces, K is the number of machines, and N is the number of workers employed by the firm. In macro data, Y and K are measured by indexes showing production and capital in fixed prices, as described in Chapter 1.

The mathematical expression $Y = F(K, N)$ is not at all specific about *how* production depends on capital and labour input. The expression does not tell us how important the two production factors are. It may be that one factor is very important while the other is of marginal importance. For this reason we call $Y = F(K, N)$ *a general functional form*.

We can be more specific, however, and say more precisely how production depends on the inputs. Here is a *specific production function*:

$$Y = 10\sqrt{KN}.$$

This production function says that if, for example, we have 30 machines and 30 workers, we can produce 300 units:

$$Y = 10\sqrt{30 \cdot 30} = 10 \cdot 30 = 300,$$

and if we have 10 machines and 40 workers we can produce 200 units:

$$Y = 10\sqrt{10 \cdot 40} = 10\sqrt{400} = 10 \cdot 20 = 200.$$

One way to illustrate this function is shown in Table 2.1, where we have the number of machines in the first row and the number of workers in the first column.

Table 2.1 *Production for different levels of inputs when $Y = 10\sqrt{KN}$*

Workers	Machines			
	10	20	30	40
10	**100**	141	173	200
20	141	**200**	245	283
30	173	245	**300**	346
40	200	283	346	**400**

Note: The numbers have been rounded off.

---

1 The importance of human capital for the long-run level of income is analysed in Chapter 4.

In the different cells of the table, we have the amount of production that results from each particular combination of capital and labour input.

Looking at this table, we see that this production function has three characteristics.

1. *Production is increasing in both factors.* If we assume, for example, that we have 40 workers employed, we look at the last line in the table. If we increase the number of machines from 10 to 40, production increases from 200 to 400. Similarly, if we fix the number of workers at 20, production increases from 141 to 283 as we increase the capital stock from 10 to 40. This seems reasonable. With more input of production factors, we should be able to produce more output.

2. *For a given labour input, the marginal product of capital decreases as we increase capital input.*[2] Again, assume that we have 40 workers employed. If we increase the number of machines from 10 to 20, production increases from 200 to 283 – that is, by 83 units. If we then add another 10 machines production increases from 283 to 346 – that is, by 63 units, and the next 10 machines give an increase in production of 54 units. Each additional 10 machines bring a smaller *increase* in production. Again, this seems reasonable. If we add capital without adding workers, each additional unit of capital brings a smaller increase in production than the previous one. If we have 40 carpenters employed, but only 20 hammers, 10 additional hammers will allow the carpenters to do much more work in a day. But if we already have 40 hammers, additional hammers may still be of use, but those hammers will add less to production compared to the first hammers.

3. *There are constant returns to scale.* If we go down along the diagonal in the table we see that production increases in proportion to the inputs. As the inputs double, production also doubles. Again this is reasonable in many situations. If there are no other production factors we should be able to double production by doubling the input of labour and capital. The basic idea is that if we have one factory, we can just put another one beside it, doubling both the inputs and the level of production.

In practice, there may be increasing returns to scale for an individual firm – that is, production increases more than proportionally as we increase the inputs. To produce cars you need at least one assembly line, and you need people to develop new models, which means that there are large *fixed costs* even if you produce a small number of cars. As you produce more cars, inputs will not increase in proportion to production. Thus there are substantial returns to scale in the car industry. On the other hand, a firm may run into decreasing returns to scale beyond a certain level of production because the firm becomes too big and difficult to organize. To simplify the analysis, we will disregard economies (and diseconomies) of scale and assume constant returns to scale.

---

2 The marginal product of capital measures how much production increases per unit increase of the capital stock for a given level of employment. Mathematically, it is the derivative of the production function with respect to capital.

In the following, we assume that production increases with increased inputs of capital and labour, that the marginal product of one factor is decreasing when the other is kept fixed, and that there are constant returns to scale.

The production function involves three variables, Y, K, and N. One way to illustrate the production function is to fix the number of workers and draw production as a function of the capital stock for a given number of workers. Fig. 2.1 shows the relation between capital input and production for the production function discussed above when labour input is fixed at 40 workers. For each level of capital on the K axis we can read off the level of production on the Y axis. If $K = 10$ we get $Y = 200$, if $K = 40$ we get $Y = 400$, and so on.

Fig. 2.1 illustrates the first property of the production function: the more we increase the capital input with a given number of workers, the more we produce. We also see the second property of the production function. As we increase the capital stock, the slope of the curve becomes flatter. For a given amount of labour, each new unit of capital gives us a smaller increase in production than the previous one.

An alternative way to illustrate the properties of the production function is to draw the *marginal product* of capital (MPK) as a function of capital input for a given number of workers. The marginal product of capital is the derivative (the slope) of the production function – that is, how much production increases when the stock of capital increases. To calculate the marginal product of capital, we treat N as if it were a constant, and take the *derivative* of the production function with respect to K as if K were the only variable in the production function. In this case, we can rewrite the production function:[3]

$$Y = 10\sqrt{KN} = 10\,(KN)^{1/2} = 10K^{1/2}N^{1/2}.$$

Fig. 2.1 *The relation between capital input (K) and production (Y) for a given number of workers (N = 40)*

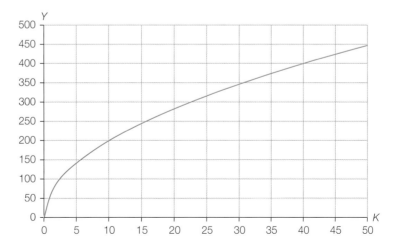

---

3 Here we use the facts that $\sqrt{x} = x^{1/2}$ and $(x \cdot y)^m = x^m \cdot y^m$.

Fig. 2.2 *The marginal product of capital (MPK) for given labour input (N = 40)*

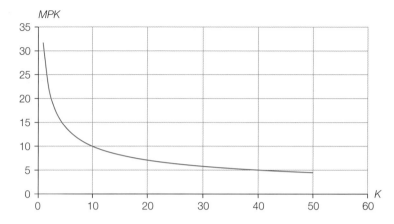

Taking the derivative with respect to K we get the marginal product of capital:[4]

$$MPK = 10 \cdot \frac{1}{2} \cdot K^{-1/2} \cdot N^{1/2} = 5\sqrt{\frac{N}{K}}.$$

The marginal product of capital is itself a function of the number of workers and the capital stock. Fig. 2.2 shows the marginal product of capital as a function of the capital stock when 40 workers are employed. We see that MPK is positive – that is, the curve is always above the x-axis. Also, it is decreasing: the *more* capital we have, the *less* production will *increase* if we add *another* unit of capital. If we increase the capital input from 10 to 11, production increases by about 10 units; if we increase capital from 40 to 41, production increases by about 5 units.

We can draw similar diagrams showing that, for a given amount of capital, the more workers we employ, the more we produce, but the more workers we add with a given capital stock, the less will production increase for each additional worker.

Technological development

So far we have considered the relation between inputs of capital and labour and production of goods for a given technology. But technological possibilities are not constant. Rather, technological progress is a key factor behind economic growth. In order to allow for technological change, we introduce another variable in our production function. We use the variable E to indicate the level of *technology* and write the production function:

$$Y = F(K, EN).$$

---

4 If we have a function $Y = ZX^n$ where Z is a constant, the derivative with respect to X is $dY/dX = ZnX^{n-1}$. If Z is a variable, the same rule applies but now we get the partial derivative with respect to X. Note that the derivative is itself a function of Z and X.

A better technology (higher E) means that more can be produced for a given input of capital and labour. Note that E multiplies the number of workers, N. This is a specific way to represent technological progress which implies that a 10 percent increase in E has the same effect on production as a 10 percent increase in the number of workers. We can think of E as the *efficiency* of the workforce. This specification will be convenient for our analysis of long-run growth in Chapter 5.

The Cobb–Douglas production function

A specific production function is the *Cobb–Douglas production function:*

$$Y = K^\alpha \, (EN)^{1-\alpha},$$

where α is a number between zero and one. This production function is often used in economics because it is simple and, as we shall see, it is broadly consistent with the facts about the distribution of income. If we set $E = 100$ and $\alpha = 1/2$ we get the production function that we discussed above.[5] As we will see later in this chapter, a value of α around 1/3 is more plausible, however.

Let us check that this production function has the three properties discussed above. The marginal product of capital is the derivative (the slope) of the production function – that is, how much production increases when the stock of capital increases. To calculate the marginal product of capital, we treat E and N as if they were constants, and take the *derivative* with respect to K as if K were the only variable in the production function. Doing this, we get the marginal product of capital:

$$MPK = \alpha K^{\alpha-1} \, (EN)^{1-\alpha}.$$

Since α is a positive number, the marginal product of capital is *positive*. Since $\alpha - 1 < 0$ the marginal product is *decreasing* in K: the higher K is, the lower is the marginal product of capital if E and N are kept fixed.

But what about constant returns to scale? Suppose we start with some specific levels of inputs K_0 and N_0 giving a specific level of production Y_0:

$$Y_0 = K_0^\alpha \, (EN_0)^{1-\alpha}.$$

Now double the inputs of capital and labour. How much production do we get?

$$Y = (2K_0)^\alpha \, (E \cdot 2N_0)^{1-\alpha} = 2^\alpha \cdot K_0^\alpha \cdot 2^{1-\alpha} \, (EN_0)^{1-\alpha} = 2K_0^\alpha \, (EN_0)^{1-\alpha} = 2Y_0.$$

Yes, production also doubles, so we have constant returns to scale. The Cobb–Douglas function has all the three properties discussed above: marginal products are positive and decreasing, and there are constant returns to scale. It is a reasonable production function.

The marginal product of labour

The marginal product of labour (MPL) measures how much production increases per additional worker for a given capital stock. As we will see, the marginal

---

5   $Y = K^{1/2} \, (EN)^{1/2} = K^{1/2} E^{1/2} N^{1/2} = E^{1/2} \, (KN)^{1/2} = \sqrt{100}\sqrt{KN} = 10\sqrt{KN}.$

Fig. 2.3 *The effect on the marginal product of labour (MPL) of an increase in E or K*

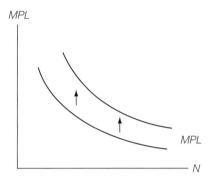

product of labour is the main determinant of the real wage, so it is interesting to ask how it is determined. Our analysis suggests the following:

- The better the *technology* we have, the *higher* is the marginal product of labour.
- The more *capital* we have per worker, the *higher* is the marginal product of labour.

We can use the Cobb–Douglas production to derive an explicit expression for the marginal product of labour. Since $(EN)^{1-\alpha} = E^{1-\alpha} N^{1-\alpha}$ we can write the production function as follows:

$$Y = K^{\alpha} E^{1-\alpha} N^{1-\alpha}.$$

To find the marginal product of labour, we now treat K and E as fixed and calculate the derivative with respect to N:

$$MPL = K^{\alpha} E^{1-\alpha} (1-\alpha) N^{-\alpha} = (1-\alpha) E^{1-\alpha} \left(\frac{K}{N} \right)^{\alpha}.$$

We see that if E or K increase, and N remains constant, the marginal product of labour increases. The effect of an increase in E or K on the marginal product of labour is illustrated in Fig. 2.3.

2.2 Goods markets and price-setting

In order to produce, firms need not only production factors and technological knowledge. There must also be demand for their products. In this section, we analyse demand and price-setting from the firm's point of view. We assume that the product market is characterized by *monopolistic competition*.[6]

Monopolistic competition

Monopolistic competition is a theoretical market structure which has similarities with both perfect competition and monopoly. It resembles perfect competition

---

6 You may find it helpful to review the chapter on monopolistic competition in your microeconomics textbook.

in that we assume a *large number of firms*, which compete with each other and produce similar products. But monopolistic competition differs from perfect competition in that goods produced by different firms are assumed to be *imperfect substitutes*. Each individual firm produces a good that is somewhat different from other goods in the market. This means that the firm faces a downward-sloping demand curve, which determines how much it can sell. If it raises its price by a few percent, it will sell less; if it cuts its price a little, it will sell more but it will not take over the whole market.

In a monopolistic market, firms have some *monopoly power*. They are not price takers in that they have at least some flexibility to set their own prices. Each firm faces a trade-off: if it raises the price, it gets more revenue per unit, but it also sells fewer units. As we will see, a monopolistic firm will set a price that is higher than the marginal cost of producing an additional unit. The price is set with a *mark-up* on marginal cost. Other important implications are that firms face limited demand for their products and that the demand for products produced by an individual firm depends on the overall level of demand in the economy as well as on the prices charged by the competitors. In this sense, firms are *demand-constrained*.

Because the number of firms is large, each individual firm takes the behaviour of the other firms as given when setting the price. This means that the firm disregards the reactions of the other firms when deciding about the price. Thus we abstract from tacit collusion, price wars and other types of strategic interactions between firms which are typical of oligopolistic markets with a small number of firms. The assumption that there are many competitors may be more or less realistic depending on which market we look at, but it certainly simplifies our analysis of firms' price-setting decisions.

In this book, we will assume that the product market is characterized by monopolistic competition because this is a more plausible market structure than perfect competition. In real life, there are hardly any firms that can sell an infinite amount at a given price, as they can under perfect competition, and most firms set their own prices instead of taking prices as given in the market.[7]

The price elasticity of demand

To understand price-setting, we consider the profit maximization problem of an individual firm. Let us denote the firms by numbers 1, 2, 3, and so on, and let i be the number of an individual firm. Thus, if there are 1000 firms in the economy we have $i = 1, 2, 3, \ldots, 999, 1000$. We can think of 1, 2, 3, and so forth as the *names* of the firms and their products. These names would be disastrous from a marketing point of view, but they suffice for a macroeconomic analysis.

To analyse competition in a market with many firms, we need to distinguish aggregate variables from firm-specific variables. We do this by putting the index

---

7 Exceptions are firms producing raw materials and agricultural products, which are sold in exchange markets with a large number of participants. In those markets, there is a real-life auctioneer (or at least a computer) who sets the price. Such markets resemble the theoretical idea of a competitive market. Obviously, an exchange market can only be organized if the good is completely homogenous.

i on variables that are firm-specific and letting variables without this index be the averages across firms. We assume that the demand for firm *i*'s production depends on its price relative to the average price and on aggregate income in the economy according to the following demand function:

$$Y_i = D(P_i/P)\,Y,$$

where Y_i is the production of firm *i*, P_i is the price charged by firm *i*, and *P* is the average price in the goods market, as measured by some price index, and *Y* is aver-age (aggregate) production/income as measured by some index. *D* is a decreasing function, so the higher the firm's price relative to the general price level, the less it sells. Put differently, the firm has to reduce the price in order to sell more. An increase in aggregate income shifts the demand curve out, as illustrated in Fig. 2.4.

The degree of competition in the market depends on whether buyers perceive the goods produced by different firms to be close substitutes. The closer the sub-stitutes that are available in the market, the more sales will be lost if the firm raises its price. A measure of the degree of competition is the *price elasticity* of the demand curve. It measures by how many percent demand will decrease if the firm's price is increased by one percent. We denote the price elasticity by η and it is defined as follows:

$$\eta = \frac{dY_i/Y_i}{dP_i/P_i} = \frac{dY_i}{dP_i}\frac{P_i}{Y_i}.$$

As we define it here, the price elasticity is a negative number because demand falls when the price is increased. If the elasticity is minus 5, for example, a one percent increase in the price leads to a reduction in sales by 5 percent. In a competitive market, the price elasticity is infinite because sales fall to zero as soon as the firm's price is raised above the market price. In a monopolistically competitive market the elasticity is lower, but we assume that it is larger than one in absolute value.[8]

Fig. 2.4 *The effect on demand of an increase in aggregate income*

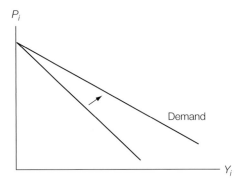

---

8   If the price elasticity is smaller than one in absolute value, a one percent price increase reduces sales by less than one percent, so total sales revenue increases when the firm raises its price. Since costs fall with reduced production, profits will increase. Therefore the firm will always have an incentive to raise the price in this case and we have no solution for the price. In most markets, competition is strong, so the elasticity is clearly above one.

The firm can choose to set a low price, and sell a lot, or a high price, and sell less. By setting a price, the firm picks a point on the demand curve, so choosing the price is the same as choosing how much to sell and produce.[9] Another way to view the demand function is to say that, in order to sell more, the firm has to reduce the price. Thus, we can view the price charged as a function of how much the firm plans to sell:

$$P_i = P(Y_i, P, Y).$$

This function is the *inverse demand function*. The elasticity of price with respect to quantity is the inverse of the price elasticity: if the price elasticity is minus 5, the firm must cut the price by 0.2 percent in order to sell 1 percent more.

The profit maximizing price

Profit is revenue minus costs. The *marginal cost* is the cost of producing an additional unit and it increases with the quantity produced when the capital stock is kept fixed. In a perfectly competitive market, a firm can sell as much as it wants to at a given market price, so if the market price is higher than the marginal cost, the firm can make more profit by producing and selling more. It is therefore optimal to increase production to the point where marginal cost equals the market price.

In a monopolistic market, a firm faces a downward-sloping demand function, so it has to reduce the price in order to sell more. If production is increased by one unit, the firm gets paid the price for that additional unit, but it has to reduce the price for all the units that it was selling before. As a consequence, the monopolistic firm will not increase production to the point where price is equal to marginal cost. Instead, it will produce less and set a price that exceeds the marginal cost. The price is set with a *mark-up* on marginal cost.

To see this more clearly, consider how the firm should choose price and quantity to maximize profits. Profit is revenue minus cost:

$$Profit = Revenue - Cost.$$

Revenue and cost both depend on how much the firm produces. Consider a production increase of one unit. If the increase in revenue from an additional unit sold is higher than the cost of producing that additional unit, it is profitable to increase production. To maximize profits, the firm should increase production to the point where the increase in revenue from an additional unit sold equals the cost of producing that additional unit. Put differently, the price should be set so that the *marginal revenue* from selling one more unit equals the *marginal cost* of producing it:

$$MR = MC.$$

Revenue is the quantity multiplied by the price, $Y_i \cdot P_i$, and, according to the inverse demand function above, the price is a function of how much you sell. Thus we have

$$Revenue = Y_i \cdot P(Y_i, P, Y).$$

---

9 We disregard inventories (stocks of goods to be sold) in this analysis.

To get the marginal revenue from an additional unit we take the derivative with respect to Y_i

$$MR = P_i + Y_i \cdot \frac{dP_i}{dY_i}.$$

The first term is positive and captures the fact that the firm sells an additional unit at the price P_i. The second term is negative and captures the decrease in revenue due to the reduction in price. These two terms together constitute the marginal increase in revenue from selling one more unit. Dividing and multiplying by P_i we get

$$MR = \left[1 + \frac{dP_i}{dY_i} \frac{Y_i}{P_i}\right] P_i.$$

Since

$$\frac{dP_i}{dY_i} \frac{Y_i}{P_i} = \frac{1}{\dfrac{dY_i}{dP_i} \dfrac{P_i}{Y_i}} = \frac{1}{\eta}$$

we have

$$MR = \left[1 + \frac{1}{\eta}\right] P_i.$$

Since we have assumed that the price elasticity is negative and larger than one in absolute value, $1/\eta$ must be a number between zero and minus one. Therefore, marginal revenue is positive, but smaller than the price. If, for example, the price elasticity is minus 5, marginal revenue is 80 percent of the price: $1 - 1/5 = 0.80$. To understand this, suppose a firm sells 100 units and decides to increase production by one unit. This is a one percent increase in production and in order to sell one percent more, the firm has to reduce the price on all the units it already sells by 1/5 of a per cent (1/500 times the price). Thus, the increase in revenue will be

$$P_i - \frac{1}{500} \cdot P_i \cdot 100 = P_i - 0.2P_i = 0.8P_i.$$

The firm has to choose a price–quantity combination along the demand curve. As discussed above, the optimal price–quantity combination is such that marginal revenue from selling one more unit equals marginal cost:

$$\left[1 + \frac{1}{\eta}\right] P_i = MC.$$

Fig. 2.5 illustrates profit maximization. We see that the marginal revenue curve is below the demand curve for every level of production and that the profit-maximizing price is above marginal cost.

We can also view this condition is as a condition determining the optimal price:

$$P_i = (1 + \mu) MC_i,$$

where μ is the mark-up expressed as a fraction of the marginal cost and where:

$$1 + \mu = \frac{1}{1 + 1/\eta}.$$

Fig. 2.5 *The profit-maximizing price and production level*

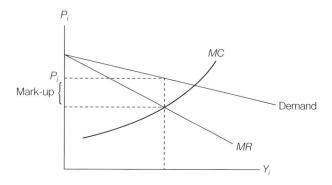

We see that the optimal price is equal to marginal cost times a *mark-up factor* $1 + \mu$ where the optimal mark-up μ depends on the price elasticity. If the price elasticity is minus 5 we get a mark-up of 25 percent:

$$1 + \mu = \frac{1}{1 - 1/5} = \frac{5}{5 - 1} = \frac{5}{4} = 1.25.$$

If the marginal cost is 200 euros, the firm will set the price at 250 euros.

If, instead, the elasticity is minus 11, the profit maximizing mark-up is only 10 percent. The price elasticity and the mark-up reflect the degree of competition in the product market. The more competition there is, the less monopoly power firms have, and the lower are the mark-ups and profits of the firms. Just like pure monopolies, monopolistic firms use their market power to raise prices, but their ability to do that depends on the price elasticity of demand.

The price elasticity and the mark-up reflect the degree of competition in the product market. In general, the mark-up may depend on various economic factors and change over time. To make the analysis as simple as possible, we will treat the mark-up as exogenous, however.[10] This notwithstanding, we will be able to analyse how the degree of competition affects the economic equilibrium, the distribution of income, and the long-run level of income.

But what determines marginal cost? This is easy to see. We assume that, in the short run, the capital stock is fixed, so in order to increase production, the firm has to hire more workers.[11] The cost of an additional worker is the wage and the increase in production from the marginal worker is the marginal product of

---

10   With the demand function assumed above, $Y_i = D(P_i/P)\, Y$, we have

$$\eta = \frac{dY_i}{dP_i} \frac{P_i}{Y_i} = D'\left(\frac{P_i}{P}\right) \frac{Y}{P} \frac{P_i}{D(P_i/P)\, Y} = D'\left(\frac{P_i}{P}\right) \frac{P_i/P}{D(P_i/P)},$$

Here we use the chain rule which says that the derivative of $D(P_i/P)$ with respect to P_i is D' times the derivative of P_i/P with respect to P_i. We see that, in general, the price elasticity depends on the relative price charged by the firm, but in most of our analysis we will consider a symmetric equilibrium where all firms charge the same price, so the price elasticity can be seen as a constant.

11   In the long run, the capital stock is variable. The determination of capital stock is analysed in Chapters 3 and 5.

labour. Thus the marginal cost for the additional units produced by an additional worker is the wage divided by the marginal product of labour:[12]

$$MC_i = \frac{W_i}{MPL_i},$$

where W_i is the wage per worker paid by firm i and MPL_i is the marginal product of labour in firm i. Suppose, for example, that the wage is 30 euros and that an additional worker increases production by 6 units. Then the price per unit for the additional units produced by the additional worker is 5 euros. Combining the equations above, we find that the profit-maximizing price of firm i is determined by

$$P_i = (1 + \mu) \frac{W_i}{MPL_i}.$$

To analyse price-setting under monopolistic competition, we have considered the decision problem of an individual firm. But from a macroeconomic perspective, we are interested in the average *price level* in the economy. To find out how the price level is determined, we use a trick that macroeconomists often use: we assume that all firms are *symmetric*. This means that they have the same production function, marginal cost, and symmetric demand functions. So, even though they produce different products, they face exactly symmetric decision problems. As a consequence, they will also set the same prices and wages. Thus we can omit the index i to get an equation for the price level in the economy:

$$P = (1 + \mu) \frac{W}{MPL}.$$

This price equation will play a central role in our macroeconomic analysis. We should think of P as the price set by the 'typical' firm and MPL as the marginal product of labour in the 'typical' firm. For now, we take nominal wage level as given; wage determination will be analysed in Chapters 6 and 9.

Price-setting in the Cobb–Douglas case

To see more clearly what determines the price level, we again use the Cobb–Douglas production function $Y = K^\alpha E^{1-\alpha} N^{1-\alpha}$. With this production function, the marginal product of labour is

$$MPL = K^\alpha E^{1-\alpha} (1 - \alpha) N^\alpha,$$

and substituting into the equation above we get an explicit expression for the price level:

$$P = \frac{1 + \mu}{1 - \alpha} \frac{W}{E^{1-\alpha}} \left(\frac{K}{N} \right)^{-\alpha}.$$

We see that the price level depends on four factors:

- a higher *mark-up* raises the price level

---

12 We put an index i on all variables because prices, wages, and marginal products may differ between firms. In equilibrium, they are the same for all firms, however.

- a higher *wage level* increases the price level because marginal costs increase
- better *technology* (higher E) reduces the price level because marginal costs fall
- more *capital per worker* reduces the price because the marginal product of the workers increases and this reduces marginal costs.

A simple pricing rule based on unit labour cost

With the Cobb–Douglas production function there is a simple relation between the marginal product of labour (MPL) and the average product of labour Y/N, that is, production per employed worker. To see this, we take the expression for MPL and multiply and divide by N:

$$MPL = K^\alpha E^{1-\alpha}(1-\alpha)N^{-\alpha} = (1-\alpha)\frac{K^\alpha E^{1-\alpha}N^{-\alpha}N}{N}$$

$$= (1-\alpha)\frac{K^\alpha E^{1-\alpha}N^{1-\alpha}}{N} = (1-\alpha)\frac{Y}{N}.$$

In the last step we used the production function $Y = K^\alpha E^{1-\alpha}N^{1-\alpha}$. The marginal product of labour is proportional to (but lower than) the average product of labour, Y/N. Thus we get a simple pricing rule:

$$P = (1+\mu)MC = (1+\mu)\frac{W}{MPL} = (1+\mu)\frac{W}{(1-\alpha)Y/N} = \frac{1+\mu}{1-\alpha} \times \frac{WN}{Y},$$

where WN/Y is *unit labour cost*, the wage cost per unit of production. We see that the price is proportional to unit labour cost: if the unit labour cost increases by 10 percent, prices increase by 10 percent. Although α and μ may also change over time, we would expect them to change slowly. Thus, our theory suggests that changes in the price level should be determined primarily by changes in unit labour costs. As we see in Fig. 2.6, there is indeed a close connection between changes in unit labour costs and changes in the price level as measured by the GDP deflator.

Fig. 2.6 *Increases in unit labour cost and inflation*

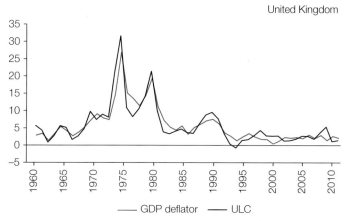

United Kingdom

— GDP deflator — ULC

(Figure continues over the page)

Fig. 2.6 *(Continued)*

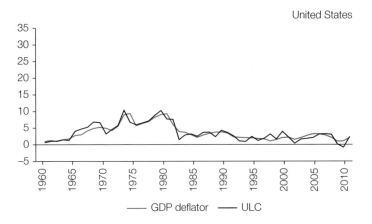

United States

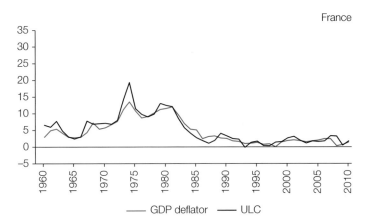

France

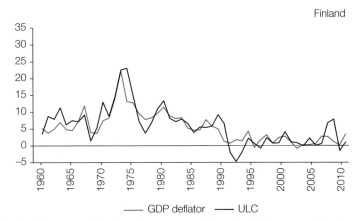

Finland

Note: ULC is unit labour cost for the total economy and the price level is measured by the GDP deflator. Both graphs show changes in percent.
Source: *OECD Economic Outlook*, OECD, 8 June 2012, http://www.oecd-ilibrary.org/statistics.

2.3   The natural level of production

We have analysed production and the price-setting of monopolistic firms. Now we consider the determinants of the level of production in the economy as a whole.

Production is determined by the capital stock, the number of workers employed, and the technology. At any point in time, the capital stock is given, determined by investments made in the past. The *labour force* consists of people who are either employed or looking for work – that is, unemployed. Those outside the labour force are children, students, pensioners, and people who, for some reason, do not work or look for work. We take the labour force as given and denote it by L.

Normally, there is some unemployment in a market economy. We use u to denote the *rate of unemployment*. It is measured as a fraction of the labour force. Using N to denote *employment* (the number of workers employed) we have:

$$N = (1-u)L.$$

If, for example, 6 percent of the labour force is unemployed and the labour force is 10 million, we have 9.4 million workers employed:

$$N = (1-u)L = (1-0.06) \cdot 10 \text{ million} = 9.4 \text{ million}.$$

We will analyse how unemployment is determined in Chapter 6. There, we will show that there is a 'normal' or 'long-run equilibrium' level of unemployment, which economists call the *natural rate of unemployment*. Actual unemployment fluctuates around this level, but, on average, unemployment will be at the natural level. For now, we take the natural rate of unemployment as given. We can also define the *natural level of employment* as the employment level that we will have when unemployment is at the natural level. Thus we have:

$$N^n = (1-u^n)L,$$

where N^n is the natural rate of employment and u^n is the natural level of unemployment.

We can also define the *natural level of production* as the level of production that we get for a given capital stock and a given labour force when employment is at the natural level, that is, when $N = (1-u^n)L$:

$$Y^n = F(K, E(1-u^n)L).$$

We see that the natural level of production depends on four factors:

- the stock of capital K
- the size of the labour force L
- the natural rate of unemployment u^n
- the technology E.

Fig. 2.7 illustrates the determination of the natural level of production for a given technology and capital stock.

When unemployment is at the natural level, production will be at the natural level. As the capital stock and technology change, the natural level of production will change: we will analyse such changes in Chapter 5. In the short run,

Fig. 2.7 *Determination of natural level of production for given technology and capital stock*

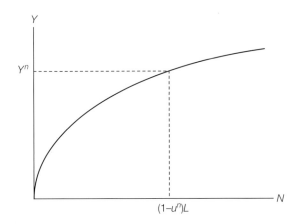

production and employment may deviate from their natural levels and we will analyse such fluctuations in Chapters 8–9. Although production is seldom exactly at the natural level, it is an important reference point because, according to our theory, employment and production will fluctuate around their natural levels.

2.4   The real wage and the distribution of income

In a closed economy, there are no incomes from abroad, so income equals production, and the level of production is determined by the factors listed in the previous section. But who gets the income? How much of the income will go to the workers and how much will go to capital income in the form of dividends and interest payments? In this section, we first analyse what determines the real wage and then we see how total income is distributed between labour income and capital income.

The real wage

Workers should not care about their nominal wage but about how much they can buy for their wage. The *real wage* is the wage expressed in terms of purchasing power, what quantity of goods and services you can buy for the wage. In our model, the *real wage* is obtained by dividing the nominal wage by the price level: W/P. The higher prices are, the less consumers can buy for a given nominal wage. As we saw above, the price level is equal to marginal cost multiplied by a mark-up factor, and the marginal cost is the wage divided by the marginal product of labour, so we have:

$$P = (1+\mu)\,MC = (1+\mu)\,\frac{W}{MPL}.$$

By rearranging this equation, we see immediately how the real wage is determined:

$$\frac{W}{P} = \frac{MPL}{1+\mu}.$$

Fig. 2.8 illustrates how the real wage is determined for a given capital stock. The marginal product of labour falls as employment increases. As we discussed above,

Fig. 2.8 *Determination of the real wage for given technology and capital stock*

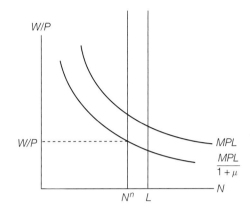

there is a natural level to which employment tends to converge in the long run. The real wage is equal to *MPL* at the natural level of employment divided by the mark-up factor.

If there were perfect competition, the mark-up would be zero ($\mu = 0$) and workers would be paid their marginal product. When firms have some monopoly power ($\mu > 0$), prices are higher and real wages are lower. To see this more clearly, consider the Cobb–Douglas case. In this case, the marginal product of labour is $MPL = (1 - \alpha) E^{1-\alpha} (K/N)^{\alpha}$, so when employment is at the natural level, the real wage is

$$\frac{W}{P} = \frac{1 - \alpha}{1 + \mu} E^{1-\alpha} \left(\frac{K}{N^n} \right)^{\alpha}.$$

We see that:

- the better the technology, the higher is the real wage
- the more capital we have per employed worker, the higher is the real wage
- better competition in the product market (lower μ) increases the real wage.

In the Cobb–Douglas case, there is a simple relation between the real wage and GDP per employed worker. To see this, we recall from Section 2.2 that $MPL = (1 - \alpha) Y/N$ and hence

$$P = (1 + \mu) \frac{W}{(1 - \alpha) Y/N}.$$

Solving for the real wage we see that it is proportional to GDP per capita:

$$\frac{W}{P} = \frac{1 - \alpha}{1 + \mu} \times \frac{Y}{N}.$$

The real wage is a fraction of real GDP per person employed. The more important labour is in production (lower α) and the lower the mark-up, μ, the higher is the real wage relative to GDP per employed worker.

The distribution of income

We assume that firms finance investments by borrowing from households, and paying interest to them. Since firms have monopoly power, they make profits, and we assume that those profits are handed out as dividends to the households that own the firms. Thus there are three sources of income in the model: wage income, interest, and pure profits.[13]

Multiplying both sides in the equation above by N/Y, we get the *labour share of income*:

$$\frac{WN}{PY} = \frac{1-\alpha}{1+\mu}.$$

The remaining income is non-labour income, which is used to replace depreciated capital and paid out in the form of interest and dividend payments. This share is one minus the labour share:

$$1 - \frac{1-\alpha}{1+\mu} = \frac{1+\mu}{1+\mu} - \frac{1-\alpha}{1+\mu} = \frac{1+\mu-1+\alpha}{1+\mu} = \frac{\alpha+\mu}{1+\mu}.$$

We see that there are two sources of non-labour income. First there is the return on capital as a production factor; with perfect competition, the capital share of income would be α. Then there are pure profits, which arise because firms have monopoly power, so that $\mu > 0$. We see that the distribution of income is determined by two factors:

- the coefficient α which measures the importance of capital in the production process
- the mark-up μ which reflects the degree of competition in the product market.

The more important capital is in production, the smaller is labour's share of income. Stronger competition reduces pure profits and raises labour's share of income.

Note that changes in the technology factor E, capital input, K, and the number of workers employed, N, leave the labour *share* constant. Of course, there is nothing that says that the parameters α and μ could not change over time. Nevertheless, when we compare developed countries, we would expect them to have access to similar technology and we would also expect the degree of competition in the product market to be similar. Hence, the labour share should be similar. So, how large is the labour share? Is it constant? Is it the same in all countries?

In Chapter 1, we saw that 'compensation of employees' typically constitutes 50–60 percent of gross value added at basic prices. The remaining fraction is 'gross operating surplus and mixed income', which includes income of self-employed.[14] Income of self-employed cannot easily be classified as either labour

---

13   Since we have not yet introduced the government there are no taxes and no government debt.
14   There is a small discrepancy because of indirect taxes.

Table 2.2 *Labour share (percent)*

	Austria	Belgium	Denmark	Finland	France	Germany	Ireland	Italy	Netherlands
1990	67.4	64.0	68.7	73.1	68.1	67.7	61.1	72.1	66.2
1995	66.7	65.1	65.7	66.8	66.4	68.2	63.0	66.9	67.1
2000	64.9	65.5	66.2	63.2	65.1	68.4	54.4	63.7	66.5
2005	62.8	69.4	67.7	65.3	65.4	65.0	56.0	64.5	65.3
2009	64.8	71.9	71.3	66.4	65.6	65.4	59.2	65.9	66.8
	Norway	Portugal	Spain	Sweden	Switzerland	United Kingdom	Canada	United States	Australia
1990	61.0	67.6	63.5	67.1	76.2	74.8	67.5	65.2	64.2
1995	59.5	65.3	63.3	64.9	76.8	71.2	65.2	64.2	62.8
2000	53.0	67.0	64.4	67.3	76.6	72.6	63.2	66.2	62.0
2005	50.5	67.6	60.9	67.1	76.6	72.1	62.1	63.9	59.4
2009	61.1	66.2	59.1	69.5	78.7	72.9	65.4	62.8	59.1

Note: The labour share is imputed by assigning a labour income to the self-employed.
Source: The Conference Board Total Economy Database, January 2011, http://www.conference-board.org/data/economydatabase/.

income or non-labour income. To come closer to the theoretical shares, one can impute some labour income to the self-employed by assigning them some reasonable wage, and classify the rest as return to capital and pure profits. Table 2.2 and Fig. 2.9 show labour shares imputed in this way. We see that the imputed labour share is around 2/3 and that it is fairly similar across countries. Furthermore, there have been relatively modest variations in the labour share over the last two decades. The Cobb–Douglas production function, which implies a constant labour share, is not completely at odds with reality. This is a reason why it is so popular among economists, and why we use it in this book.

Fig. 2.9 *The labour share in the United Kingdom, United States, Germany, and Sweden*

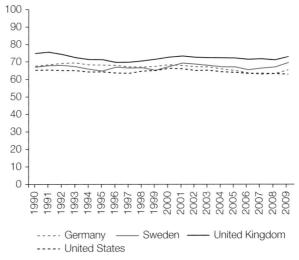

Source: The Conference Board Total Economy Database, January 2011, http://www.conference-board.org/data/economydatabase/.

The main conclusion from this analysis is that, in a market economy, the labour share of income is primarily determined by technological factors and the degree of competition in the product market. If capital is more important in production, a larger share of income will go to capital. With more competition in the product market, prices will be lower, and the labour share will increase. So, to what extent does the distribution of income depend on government policies?

Clearly, it is hard to influence the technology of production by using government policies, but political measures can be used to influence the degree of competition in the product market. In fact, many countries implement policies that reduce competition in product markets. When the government makes it hard to start new companies, this will raise monopoly profits and reduce the labour share of income. If, instead, the government encourages competition and polices anti-competitive behaviour (e.g. tacit collusion) by firms, this will raise real wages and the labour share of income. As we will see in Chapter 5, better competition also raises the return on investment, the capital stock, and the long-run level of income.

Finally, we should note that this theory applies to incomes before taxes. The government can, and often does, tax labour income and non-labour income at different rates. By shifting taxes from labour income to capital income, the government can influence the *after-tax* distribution of income, but as we will see in Chapter 5, this will have consequences for capital accumulation and the long run levels of capital and income.

What have we learned?

The production function shows that production, Y, depends on the input of production factors capital, K, and labour, N, and on the level of technology, E:

$$Y = F(K, EN).$$

We assume that the production function has three properties:

1. *Marginal products are positive.* More input gives more output.
2. *Marginal products are decreasing.* For a given labour input, each additional unit of capital increases production less than the previous one. For a given capital stock, each additional worker increases production less than the previous one.
3. There are *constant returns to scale.* If all factor inputs increase by x percent, production also increases by x percent.

We introduced a specific production function, the *Cobb–Douglas production function*:

$$Y'' = K^{\alpha} (EN)^{1-\alpha}.$$

The marginal products of capital and labour are found by taking derivatives with respect to K and N. An increase in labour input raises the marginal product of capital. An increase in capital input reduces the marginal product of capital. An improvement in technology, E, increases the marginal product of capital.

In a monopolistically competitive market, firms produce differentiated goods and face limited demand for their products. They cannot sell any amount they want at a given price. When the firm faces a downward-sloping demand curve, there is a trade-off between price and quantity, and choosing the price is equivalent to choosing the quantity. To maximize profits, firms produce at the point where marginal revenue equals marginal cost and they set the price with a mark-up over marginal cost. Marginal cost is equal to the wage, W, divided by the marginal product of labour, MPL, so we have:

$$P = (1 + \mu)\, MC = (1 + \mu)\, \frac{W}{MPL},$$

where μ is the mark-up expressed as a fraction of the marginal cost.

The price level depends on the mark-up, the wage, and the marginal product of labour. The latter depends on the technology and the amount of capital per worker.

The *natural rate of unemployment* is the long-run equilibrium rate of unemployment.

The natural (long-run equilibrium) level of production is determined by

$$Y^n = F(K, N^n) = F(K, E(1 - u^n)L).$$

The natural level of production depends on four factors:

1. the stock of capital K
2. the size of the labour force L
3. the natural rate of unemployment u^n
4. the technology E.

With the Cobb–Douglas production function $MPL = (1 - \alpha)\, Y/N$ and substituting into the price equation above we find that the price is proportional to the unit labour cost, WN/Y:

$$P = \frac{1 + \mu}{1 - \alpha} \times \frac{WN}{Y}.$$

The labour share of income is

$$\frac{WN}{PY} = \frac{1 - \alpha}{1 + \mu}.$$

The more important capital is in the production process (higher α) the lower is labour's share of income. Less competition in the product market leads to a higher mark-up and a lower labour share of income. In high-income countries the labour share of income is about 2/3.

Where do we go from here?

Having analysed the supply side, production and price-setting, we now turn to the demand side. Two main components of aggregate demand are investment and consumption. Much of Chapter 3 will be devoted to analysis of firms' investment decisions and Chapter 4 will focus on consumption decisions, which are made by households. Once we understand which factors determine aggregate demand, we will combine the supply and demand sides into a macroeconomic model of the whole economy. Then we will extend the model to analyse unemployment, inflation, the role of the government, foreign trade, and other issues.

Exercises

1. A firm faces the demand function

$$Y_i = \left(\frac{P_i}{P}\right)^{-\sigma} Y.$$

   a) Calculate the price elasticity of demand
      $$\frac{dY_i}{dP_i}\frac{P_i}{Y_i}.$$
   b) Derive the inverse demand function – that is, price as a function of Y_i, Y, and P.
   c) Calculate the elasticity of the inverse demand function $\frac{dP_i}{dY_i}\frac{Y_i}{P_i}$.
   d) The firm's revenue is $Y_i P_i$. Substitute the inverse demand function and calculate the marginal revenue: how much revenue increases if production increases one unit. Explain the result.

2. A firm has production function $Y_i = K_i^\alpha N_i^{1-\alpha}$. In a given period, the capital stock is given, so to produce more, the firm must increase labour input. The cost of labour is WN_i.
   a) What is the labour cost as a function of Y_i and K_i?
   b) Use the cost function to calculate an expression for the marginal cost.
   c) How does marginal cost depend on Y_i, K_i, and W? Explain your results in economic terms.

3. The price level is determined according to

$$P = (1+\mu)\frac{W}{MPL},$$

and production is determined by
$$Y = K^\alpha N^{1-\alpha}.$$
   a) Explain the price equation.
   b) Show that $MPL = (1-\alpha)APL$ where APL is the average product of labour.
   c) Find an expression for the labour share of income and calculate the labour share if $\alpha = 0.4$ and $\mu = 0.2$.
   d) Calculate the labour share if $\alpha = 0.28$ and $\mu = 0.08$. Explain the difference from the previous calculation.

4. A firm has profit $P_i Y_i - cY_i$ and the demand function is $Y_i = \kappa P_i^{-\sigma}$. Substitute for production in the profit function and maximize with respect to the price. Derive an expression for the optimal price.

5. Suppose that a political party wants to increase the labour share of income after tax. Analyse how the following measures might affect the labour share in a country:
   a) Limits on the number of firms that enter individual markets.
   b) Laws that increase the bargaining power of unions.
   c) Increased taxes on non-labour incomes such as dividends and interest and reduced taxes on wage income.
   d) A law stipulating reduced working hours.

6. A country has 10 percent unemployment. The production function is Cobb–Douglas with $\alpha = 0.3$.

a) By how much will production increase if unemployment is reduced to 5 percent while the capital stock, the labour force, and technology are unchanged? Explain your result.

b) If unemployment remains permanently on the lower level, is it likely that the capital stock will remain unchanged?

Answers to the exercises can be found at: **www.palgrave.com/economics/gottfries.**

Appendix

Isoquants and constant returns to scale

The production function shows how production, Y, depends on the input of production factors capital, K, and labour, N. In the main text we illustrated the production function by drawing Y as a function of K for given N. Another way to illustrate the production function is shown in Fig. 2.10, where we have the factor inputs on the main axes and draw *isoquants* for different levels of production. Each isoquant corresponds to a certain level of production. The points along an isoquant show *combinations* of capital and labour input that give the same level of production.

Isoquants are like level curves on a map where the level of production corresponds to the height of the mountain. As we increase capital and labour input, we move up to the right, reaching higher levels of production.

Fig. 2.10 *Isoquants and constant returns to scale*

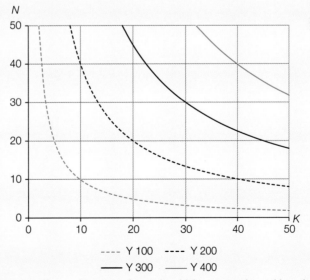

Note: The curves show the combinations of capital and labour input that yield production equal to 100, 200, 300, and 400.

Again we can see the three properties of the production function:

i) The marginal product of capital is positive: if we fix labour input at some level, more capital moves us up to a higher isoquant.

ii) The marginal product is decreasing: if we fix labour input and increase capital input we need more and more capital to reach the next isoquant.

iii) Constant returns to scale: as we double the inputs we reach an isoquant with twice as much production.

What factors determine investment?

In Chapter 2 we analysed the supply side of the economy. We saw that production possibilities are determined by available technology and factors of production. But for production to take place it is not enough that we have production factors and the knowledge to produce. There must also be demand for the goods and services that are produced. This is true on the microeconomic level – for the individual firm – but also on the macroeconomic level.

So where does demand come from? As we saw in Chapter 1, goods and services are used for private consumption and investment, government consumption and investment, and exports. In this and the following chapter we will explore the demand side of the economy. Since we have not yet introduced a government, or trade with other countries, aggregate demand in our model consists of private consumption and investment. We will study the investment decision of the typical firm and the consumption/savings choice of the typical consumer. This will help us to understand which factors can cause changes in investment, consumption, and aggregate demand. The government and trade with foreign countries will be added to the model in Chapters 11 and 12.

Consumption and investment decisions involve allocation of resources over time. Consumption gives satisfaction right away while investment increases production capacity in the future. A consumer who abstains from consumption today, and saves some income, can consume more in the future. When firms invest, they buy machines today that are used to produce more goods and services in the future. Economists call such choices *intertemporal choices.*

Firms finance a large proportion of their investments by borrowing money, and they pay interest on their debt. Consumers who deposit savings in a bank will earn interest on them. Therefore, the interest rate is an important factor that determines investment, consumption, and aggregate demand. The interest rate in monetary terms is called the *nominal interest rate.* As we will see, it is the *real interest rate* – the interest rate measured in terms of goods – that matters for consumption and investment decisions.

This chapter starts with an analysis of the relation between nominal and real interest rates. Then we analyse the investment decisions made by firms. In Chapter 4, we study the consumption decisions made by households and we combine aggregate demand (consumption and investment) with the supply side from Chapter 2 to find out how the real interest rate is determined in the long run. In this way, we build a basic macroeconomic model of the whole economy. This will require hard work, but work that will pay off. The theory developed in

Chapters 2–4 will be used throughout the rest of the book to analyse growth, business cycles, economic policy, and other issues.

3.1   Nominal and real interest rates, and discounting

In this section we show that the interest rate can be seen as an *intertemporal price* – a price that is relevant for transactions over time. We explain the difference between the nominal and the real interest rate and we show that the real interest rate is approximately equal to the nominal interest rate minus inflation.

The price of money

Suppose a consumer borrows one unit of currency today and pays back next year with interest. The consumer gets one currency unit to spend today, but has to pay back with interest next year. Put differently, the interest rate is the additional amount you have to pay next year to obtain one unit of money today. The higher the nominal interest rate, the more expensive it is to get money today. In this sense, the nominal interest rate is the price of money.

Let i_t denote the *nominal interest rate* from period t to $t+1$. We can take the period to be one year. Here, the interest rate is measured as a *fraction* of the amount borrowed, so $i_t = 0.05$ means that the interest rate is 5 percent. If you borrow one unit of money today, you must pay $1 + i_t$ units of money next year. Therefore, one plus the interest rate is *the price of money* today in terms of money next year.

But a relative price can be measured in two ways. We could also ask: what is the price of money next year in terms of money today? Put differently: how much do I have to save today to get one unit of money next year? This price is the inverse – that is, $1/(1+i_t)$. In order to get one unit of money next year, I need to put $1/(1+i_t)$ units in the bank today. If I do that I will have one unit of money next year because

$$\frac{1}{1+i_t} \cdot (1+i_t) = 1.$$

The price of money next year in terms of money today, $1/(1+i_t)$, is called the *discount factor*. The discount factor tells us how to value future incomes in terms of money today. Normally, the nominal interest rate is positive, so money in the future is less valuable than money today. The reason why money today is more valuable is that money today can be put in the bank to get interest on it. Therefore, we have to discount future values when we evaluate a stream of future incomes or expenditures. We will see several examples of this when we study investment and consumption decisions.

In practice, there is more than one interest rate in the economy. Different borrowers and lenders face different interest rates depending on the risk associated with the loan and other factors. A stable company can borrow at a lower rate than a company with uncertain prospects, and households get a lower rate on their deposits than the rate they pay when they borrow from the bank. In the following, we simplify our macroeconomic analysis by assuming that there is only one interest rate in the credit market at which all firms and households can borrow and lend. When we study financial markets in more depth in Chapter 18, we will have more to say about different interest rates.

The price of goods today in terms of goods next year

Consider a consumer who makes a choice between buying one unit of consumption in period t or buying one unit of consumption in period $t+1$. P_t is the price of one unit of consumption in period t and P_{t+1} is the price of one unit of consumption in period $t+1$.[1] But these prices are not directly comparable. A consumer who saves and consumes tomorrow will earn interest in the meantime. In order to compare the prices of goods consumed in different periods we must somehow convert the prices to the same period.

One way to do this is to compare the cost *in terms of money today* of consuming one unit today or in the next period. The cost of consuming one unit in period t is clearly P_t. In order to consume one unit in period $t+1$, the consumer has to save $P_{t+1}/(1+i_t)$ in period t. By saving this amount in period t, the consumer has just enough money to buy one unit in the next period because $(1+i_t)P_{t+1}/(1+i_t) = P_{t+1}$. Therefore, the price of consumption today in terms of consumption in the next period is

$$\frac{P_t}{P_{t+1}/(1+i_t)} = \frac{1+i_t}{P_{t+1}/P_t}.$$

This relative price between consumption in period t and consumption in period $t+1$ is an *intertemporal relative price*. It shows the price, in terms of consumption in the next period, of consuming one more unit today. To see how this relative price is related to inflation, recall that inflation is the rate of change of prices:

$$\pi_t = \frac{P_t - P_{t-1}}{P_{t-1}}.$$

Note that the ratio P_{t+1}/P_t is one plus the inflation rate in period $t+1$. This can be seen by adding and subtracting P_t in the numerator:

$$\frac{P_{t+1}}{P_t} = \frac{P_t + P_{t+1} - P_t}{P_t} = \frac{P_t}{P_t} + \frac{P_{t+1}-P_t}{P_t} = 1 + \frac{P_{t+1}-P_t}{P_t} = 1 + \pi_{t+1}.$$

Thus we can write the price of goods today in terms of goods next year as

$$\frac{1+i_t}{1+\pi_{t+1}}.$$

If there is no inflation, so $P_{t+1} = P_t$, and the interest rate is 5 per cent, this relative price is 1.05, so you have to give up 1.05 units next year in order to consume one more unit today. If the interest rate is 5 per cent and inflation in the next period is

---

1 Consumption is measured in terms of units of a consumption basket consisting of all the different goods produced by different monopolistic firms.

3 per cent we get

$$\frac{1+i_t}{1+\pi_{t+1}} = \frac{1.05}{1.03} \approx 1.02.$$

In this case you have to give up approximately 1.02 units next year in order to consume one more unit today.

Normally, the interest rate is higher than inflation, so the relative price of goods today is larger than unity. This means that you get more than one unit of consumption in the next period if you abstain from consuming one unit today. The *real* interest rate measures *how much more* you get. We define the real interest rate by the following equation:

$$1+r_{t+1} = \frac{1+i_t}{1+\pi_{t+1}},$$

or equivalently

$$r_{t+1} = \frac{1+i_t}{1+\pi_{t+1}} - 1.$$

We use r_{t+1} to denote the real interest rate between period t and $t+1$ because it is the real return you *get in period* $t+1$ after taking account of inflation.[2] We can think of the real interest rate as the *inflation-adjusted interest rate*. If we save, we get interest on our savings, but if prices increase, goods next year become more expensive. The net return is the real interest rate.

A higher nominal interest rate implies a higher real interest rate as the return on savings increases. A higher inflation rate reduces the real interest rate because inflation reduces the value of our savings. If there is no inflation, the real interest rate is equal to the nominal interest rate. If inflation is positive, the real interest rate is lower than the nominal rate.

An approximate measure of the real interest rate

For reasonably small values of the nominal interest rate and the inflation rate we can use an approximation:

$$1+r_{t+1} = \frac{1+i_t}{1+\pi_{t+1}} \approx 1 + i_t - \pi_{t+1}$$

and thus

$$r_{t+1} \approx i_t - \pi_{t+1}.$$

The real interest rate is approximately equal to the nominal interest rate minus the inflation rate. To check how well this approximation works, assume that the interest rate is 10 percent and the inflation rate is 8 percent. Then we get

$$r_{t+1} = \frac{1+i_t}{1+\pi_{t+1}} - 1 = \frac{1.10}{1.08} - 1 \approx 1.0185 - 1 \approx 0.02.$$

---

2 The nominal interest rate between period t and $t+1$ is denoted i_t because it is the interest rate agreed on in the loan contract in period t and $t+1$, and when we say that the one year interest rate is 5 percent we mean that the interest rate on a loan over the coming year is 5 percent.

This is just an application of a rule of thumb for growth rates, which was derived in the appendix to Chapter 1. The rule of thumb says that the growth rate of a ratio is approximately equal to the growth rate of the numerator minus the growth rate of the denominator. If you save a nominal amount X this corresponds to X/P consumption units. Your savings in money terms, X, grow at a rate determined by the nominal interest rate and the price level grows with inflation. In real terms, your assets grow at the rate $i_t - \pi_{t+1}$; inflation eats up some of the nominal return that we get on our savings.

1

Nominal and real interest rates in the last 60 years

In Fig. 3.1 we see the short-term interest rate and inflation for some countries. Most of the time, the interest rate was higher than inflation, so the real interest rate was positive, and the nominal interest rate was positively correlated with

Fig. 3.1 *Inflation and the interest rate*

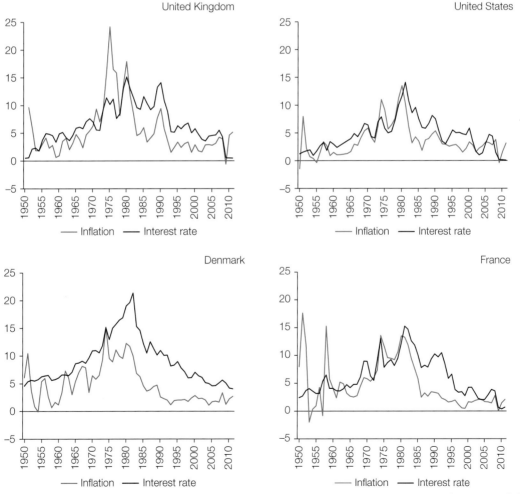

Note: Interest rate and inflation are both shown in percentage units. Interest rates are short term: money market, Treasury bills or short-term bonds. Inflation is measured by retail price index for the UK, CPI for all items for other countries.
Source: International Financial Statistics, IMF.

inflation, so the nominal interest rate tended to compensate for inflation. The real interest rate was nevertheless far from constant. In the 1970s, inflation was high and nominal interest rates were also high, but not sufficiently so to compensate for inflation. As a result, the real interest rate was close to zero and even negative some of the time. As we will see in the rest of this chapter, the real interest rate is an important variable which influences investment, consumption, and aggregate demand.

3.2   Investment

As we saw in Chapter 2, capital is an important production factor and the capital stock affects the long-run level of income. At a given point in time, the capital stock is fixed, determined by investments that were made in the past, but as time goes by the capital stock changes. The capital stock changes for two reasons:

- *Investment* adds new buildings and machines to the capital stock.
- *Depreciation* reduces the capital stock as machines break down or become obsolete, buildings have to be torn down or repaired, and so on.

The change of the capital stock from one year to the next is determined by the difference between investment and depreciation, which is called *net investment*. In many rich countries, the capital stock is more than twice as large as production during one year (GDP). Gross investment may be about 10 percent of the capital stock (20–30 percent of GDP) and depreciation is about 7 percent, so the capital stock grows at the rate of 2–3 percent per year, roughly in line with GDP.

In the short run, investment is an important and volatile component of aggregate demand. As we saw in Chapter 1, about 20–30 percent of GDP is used for investment. Fig. 3.2 shows that investment is closely correlated with GDP, rising in booms and falling in recessions, but much more volatile than GDP. Most of the time, the growth rate of GDP is between zero and 5 percent, while the growth of investment often varies between minus 5 and plus 10 percent. Because of this high volatility, fluctuations in investment play a very important role in the business cycle.

The desired capital stock and investment

Investment is made to increase the capital stock, so in order to understand investment we need to understand what level of capital firms want to have.

Let K_t denote the capital stock *at the beginning of period t*. Again we take the period to be one year. We assume that this stock can be used for production in period t but that any capital that is added during period t can only be used for production in period $t+1$. We also assume that the capital stock depreciates at a constant rate, δ. A plausible number is $\delta = 0.07$: each year 7 percent of the capital stock is eaten by ants, or it depreciates in some other way.

The following equation shows how the capital stock changes over time:

$$K_{t+1} - K_t = \underbrace{I_t - \delta K_t}_{net\ investment} \ .$$

Fig. 3.2 *Growth rates for private investment and GDP*

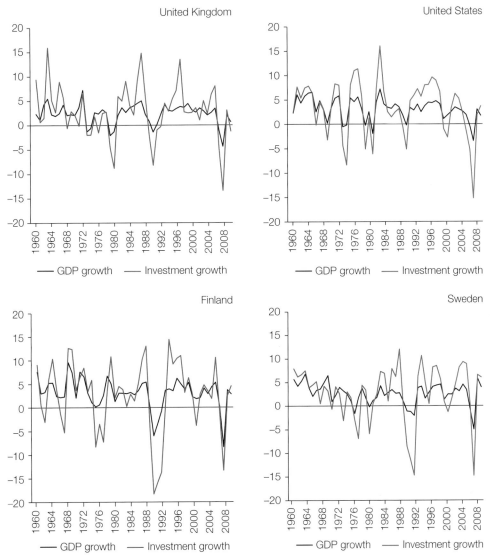

Note: Figure shows growth rates in percent for GDP and investment (gross fixed capital formation) in fixed prices.
Source: *OECD Economic Outlook*, OECD, 10 July 2012, http://www.oecd-ilibrary.org/statistics.

The change in the capital stock is gross investment made in period t minus the depreciation of the capital stock during period t. Put differently, the capital stock at the beginning of period $t+1$ is equal to the capital stock at the beginning of period t plus net investment during period t.

Let K^d_{t+1} denote the *desired capital stock* in period $t+1$ and assume that investment in period t is made so as to reach the desired level of capital in period $t+1$. Then investment will be

$$I_t = K^d_{t+1} - K_t + \delta K_t.$$

We see that investment is made for two reasons: to increase the capital stock $(K_{t+1}^d - K_t)$ and to replace depreciated capital (δK_t). In order to understand investment we need to understand how the desired capital stock is determined. In the following, we first analyse demand for capital in the long run. Then we consider demand for capital in the short run.

The long-run demand for capital

In our macroeconomic model, we do not distinguish consumption goods, such as food and clothing, from capital goods, such as machines and buildings. We assume that there is a basket of goods with price P_t that can be used for consumption as well as for investment. At any point in time, capital can be bought and sold at the price P_t. We assume that the capital stock is owned by the firms and that firms finance all their investments by borrowing from the households in the credit market. In each period, firms pay out all their profits as dividends to households. Thus we leave out equity finance – that is, financing of investment by issuing shares and reinvestment of profits (retained earnings).[3]

In order to determine the desired capital stock consider a firm that buys one unit of capital in year t, uses it for production in year $t + 1$, sells what remains of the capital and pays back the loan at the end of that period. What is the effect on the profits of the firm?

In period t, the firm borrows the amount P_t and uses the money to buy the machine, but since the new machine does not contribute to production in that period, profits in period t are unaffected. Profits in periods after $t + 1$ are also unaffected because we assume that the firm sells the machine at the end of period $t + 1$. In period $t + 1$, profits are affected in three different ways:

1. The additional unit of capital brings in additional revenue equal to the *marginal revenue product* –that is, the marginal product of capital times marginal revenue: $MPK_{t+1} \cdot MR_{t+1}$.
2. What remains of the capital after depreciation can be sold in the product market and the receipt from this sale is $(1 - \delta) P_{t+1}$.
3. The loan has to be paid back with interest: $P_t + i_t P_t$.

Therefore the effect of one extra unit of investment in year t on profits in year $t + 1$ is[4]

$$MPK_{t+1} \cdot MR_{t+1} + (1 - \delta) P_{t+1} - (1 + i_t) P_t.$$

For a low level of planned capital in period $t + 1$, MPK is high, the sum of the three terms is positive, and profits can be increased by investing more. For a large planned capital stock, MPK is low, the sum is negative, and profits can be increased by reducing investments. When the capital stock is chosen optimally, the sum of the three terms should be equal to zero.

---

3 Equity exists in the model since households own the firms and get dividends when firms make profits, but share ownership is taken as given. Financing issues are analysed in Chapter 18.
4 In practice, firms do not know what the future price level or marginal revenue will be, so this would hold in terms of expectations.

We know from our analysis of price-setting in Chapter 2 that marginal revenue is $MR_{t+1} = P_{t+1} / (1 + \mu)$. Substituting for MR_{t+1} and dividing through by P_{t+1} we get

$$\frac{MPK_{t+1}}{1 + \mu} + 1 - \delta - \frac{1 + i_t}{P_{t+1}/P_t} = 0.$$

Since $(1 + i_t) / (P_{t+1}/P_t)$ is one plus the real interest rate, we can write the condition determining the desired capital stock as

$$\frac{MPK_{t+1}}{1 + \mu} - \delta = r_{t+1},$$

where r_{t+1} is the real interest rate from period t to $t + 1$.[5] This is a very important equation that shows how the capital stock is determined in the long run. We will use it extensively in Chapters 5 and 13 in order to study capital accumulation and growth. The left-hand side is the *net* real revenue that the typical firm gets from the additional unit of capital: the marginal revenue product in real terms minus the depreciation. The right-hand side is the real interest rate. In order to finance the investment the firm has to borrow money and the *real* cost of this is the real interest rate. When the capital stock is optimally chosen, the marginal revenue product minus depreciation is equal to the real interest rate.[6]

As we saw in Chapter 2, the marginal product of capital depends on the number of workers employed. The more workers that are employed and using the capital stock, the higher is the marginal product of capital. When looking at the whole economy in the long run, we take employment as given, assuming that employment is at the natural level, N^n, determined by $N^n = (1 - u^n) L$. So when we analyse the demand for capital in the long run, MPK in the above expression should be interpreted as the marginal product of capital when employment is on its natural level. If the production function is $F(K, EN)$ and we use $F_K(K, EN)$ to denote the partial derivative with respect to K, we have the following condition determining the long-run demand for capital:

$$\frac{F_K(K, EN^n)}{1 + \mu} - \delta = r.$$

For simplicity, we have omitted the time index. The determination of the capital stock is illustrated in Fig. 3.3. As the capital stock increases, the marginal product of capital decreases and at some point it is no longer profitable to increase the capital stock. If there were perfect competition, firms would invest until the marginal product minus depreciation was equal to the real interest rate. When firms have monopoly power, they raise prices and produce less. As a consequence, they also invest less in capital for a given real interest rate.

---

5 We are reasoning as if the firm knew the future with certainty. In practice, it is the *expected* real interest rate from t to $t + 1$ and the expected marginal revenue product that determine investment.

6 Alternatively we can write $\dfrac{MPK}{1 + \mu} = r + \delta$ where the right-hand side is called the *user cost of capital*. It is the real cost for a firm for using a unit of capital in production.

Fig. 3.3 *The long-run demand for capital when employment is on the natural level*

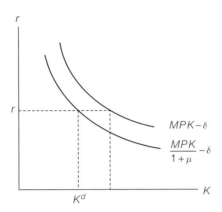

To see more concretely how different factors affect the long-run demand for capital, we can use the Cobb–Douglas production function. With this production function $MPK = \alpha K^{\alpha-1} (EN)^{1-\alpha}$ so the condition determining optimal capital stock is

$$\frac{\alpha K^{\alpha-1} (EN)^{1-\alpha}}{1+\mu} = r + \delta.$$

From this equation, we can solve for the optimal capital stock when employment is at the natural level $N = N^n$:[7]

$$K = \left[\frac{\alpha}{(r+\delta)(1+\mu)} \right]^{\frac{1}{1-\alpha}} EN^n.$$

We see that the demand for capital depends on the real interest rate, the depreciation rate, the mark-up, the technology, and the level of employment. A higher real interest rate has a negative effect on the demand for capital because this raises the cost of financing investment. A higher depreciation rate reduces the desired capital stock because it reduces the net return on investments. A higher mark-up reduces the demand for capital because firms use their monopoly power to raise prices and reduce their production. An improvement in technology increases the demand for capital because production becomes more profitable for a given labour input and real interest rate.

With more workers employed, it is optimal to increase the capital stock. Note that the demand for capital is proportional to the natural level of employment. If a country has twice as many workers as another country, the optimal capital stock is twice as high. This is a consequence of constant returns to scale.

---

7   To solve for the capital stock, we first multiply both sides by $K^{1-\alpha}$ and divide by $(r+\delta)$:

$$\frac{\alpha}{(r+\delta)(1+\mu)} (EN^n)^{1-\alpha} = K^{1-\alpha}.$$

Then we raise both sides to $1/(1-\alpha)$ and switch the left- and the right-hand sides.

The short-run demand for capital

So far, we have analysed the long-run demand for capital, assuming that employment is at the natural level. We derived a condition that determines the long-run demand for capital and we will use this condition to analyse long-run growth in Chapters 5 and 13. When we come to the analysis of short-run fluctuations in Chapters 8–9, we will need to understand short-run fluctuations in investment. As a preparation for the short-run analysis, we now consider what factors influence investment in the short run.

In the short run, employment and production can be above or below the natural levels, depending on the level of demand. Suppose that firms expect aggregate demand in the next period to be Y^e. How much will they invest? To find out, we again use the condition that the net marginal return on capital should be equal to the real interest rate:

$$\frac{MPK_{t+1}}{1+\mu} - \delta = r_{t+1}.$$

Now we use the fact that, for the Cobb–Douglas production function, the marginal product of capital is equal to $\alpha Y/K$.[8] Substituting into the equation above, we get

$$\frac{\alpha}{1+\mu}\frac{Y_{t+1}}{K_{t+1}} = r_{t+1} + \delta.$$

Solving for the capital stock, and setting $Y = Y^e$, we get the desired capital stock for a given level of demand and a given real interest rate:[9]

$$K^d = \frac{\alpha}{(1+\mu)(r+\delta)}Y^e.$$

Again we see that the desired capital stock depends on the (expected) real interest rate, the mark-up, and the depreciation rate. The main difference compared with the long-run demand for capital is that the expected level of demand affects the desired capital stock. In fact, the demand for capital is proportional to the expected level of demand. This follows from constant returns to scale. If firms expect 2 percent higher demand in the next period, they want a 2 percent higher capital stock in order to produce and satisfy that demand.

The investment function

Assuming that investors make enough investment to achieve the desired capital stock, as seen from period t, we get investment as

$$I = K^d - K + \delta K = \frac{\alpha}{(1+\mu)(r+\delta)}Y^e - (1-\delta)K.$$

---

8   As we saw in Chapter 2, $MPK = \alpha K^{\alpha-1}(EN)^{1-\alpha} = \alpha K^{\alpha}(EN)^{1-\alpha}/K = \alpha Y/K$.
9   To solve for the capital stock, multiply by K_{t+1} and divide by $r_t + \delta$.

We see that investment is driven by *three factors*:

1. the *real interest rate, r*, which determines the *required return* on the investment
2. *expected aggregate demand next period, Y^e*, which determines how much capital is needed
3. the *stock of capital at the beginning of the period, K*, because the more capital we have the smaller is the need to make additional investments.[10]

For future use, we summarize what we have learnt about investment by writing down an *investment function* with these three factors as explanatory variables:

$$I = I(r, Y^e, K).$$

Fig. 3.4 illustrates how investment depends on the interest rate. The function is downward-sloping because a lower interest rate will increase investment. An increase in aggregate demand increases investment for a given interest rate so the schedule shifts out. We will use this investment function when we study short-run fluctuations. We can also use it for the long run provided that we interpret Y^e as the expected future natural level of production.

Fig. 3.4 *The effect on investment of an increase in aggregate demand*

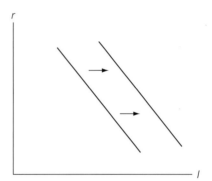

3.3   The accelerator effect and the volatility of investment

As we saw above, investment fluctuates a lot over the business cycle. The analysis above helps us to understand this high volatility of investment. Assume that $\alpha = 1/3$, $\delta = 0.07$, $\mu = 0.10$ and $r = 0.05$. Then the desired level of the capital stock is roughly 2.5 times expected production:

$$K^d = \frac{\alpha}{(1+\mu)(r+\delta)} Y^e = \frac{1/3}{1.10\,(0.05+0.07)} Y^e \approx 2.5 \cdot Y^e.$$

But how do firms form expectations about future demand? A simple assumption is that firms form their expectations about future demand based on the current level of demand: $Y^e_{t+1} = Y_t$. Assuming that they always make sufficient investment to reach the desired capital stock, we have

---

10 Depreciation and the mark-up also affect investment, but we would expect those factors to be rather constant over time and that is why they are not listed explicitly as explanatory variables in the investment function.

$$K_{t+1} = K^d_{t+1} = 2.5 \cdot Y_t.$$

Then, investment is

$$I_t = K^d_{t+1} - K_t + \delta K_t = 2.5 \cdot Y_t - 2.5 \cdot Y_{t-1} + 0.07 \cdot 2.5 \cdot Y_{t-1}.$$

And dividing by Y_{t-1} we get

$$\frac{I_t}{Y_{t-1}} = 2.5 \cdot \frac{\Delta Y_t}{Y_{t-1}} + 0.175,$$

where $\Delta Y_t / Y_{t-1}$ is the growth rate of GDP from period $t - 1$ to period t. We see that investment is very sensitive to the growth rate. According to this investment function, a one percent increase in the growth rate should increase investment by about 2.5 percent of GDP.

Suppose that the growth rate is initially steady at 2 percent per year. Then investment is 22.5 percent of lagged GDP. Of this, replacement investment constitutes 17.5 percent and net investment constitutes 5 percent of GDP in the previous period ($2.5 \cdot 0.02 = 0.05$). Suppose now that there is a recession so that growth stops completely in one year. According to the expression above, investment should decrease to 17.5 percent of GDP. This means a reduction in aggregate demand equal to 5 percent of GDP and a decrease in investment of more than 20 percent, from 22.5 to 17.5 percent of GDP. The reason why investment is so volatile is that the desired capital stock is more than twice as large as GDP and that firms want to keep a certain relation between production and the capital stock. If expected demand increases by 2 percent, the desired capital stock also increases by about 2 percent, but this corresponds to 5 percent of aggregate demand.

The dependency of investment on the growth of demand is called the *accelerator effect* and it helps to explain the high volatility of investment that we discussed at the beginning of this section. Investment is sensitive to expected fluctuations in demand and, at the same time, fluctuations in investment contribute in an important way to fluctuations in demand. Therefore, investment fluctuations play a very important role in the business cycle.

The above calculation exaggerates the volatility of investment, however, and this is for two reasons. First, investment takes time and there are various decision lags and adjustment costs that slow down investment responses to changes in aggregate demand. Second, investors may form expectations in more sophisticated ways. If they think that the change in demand is temporary, they will make smaller revisions of their investment plans. Nonetheless, our analysis helps us to understand why investment is such a volatile component of aggregate demand.

3.4   Inventory and housing investment

So far, we have only discussed firms' investment in capital goods used for production, such as machines and buildings. Such investment is called *business fixed investment* and it is divided into *equipment* (machines) and *structures* (buildings). These two components are of roughly equal magnitude, and machines and buildings play similar roles in the production process. The depreciation rates differ, however. While equipment depreciates at a rate of about 12 percent per year, buildings depreciate at a rate of around 3–4 percent per year. The average depreciation rate for business capital is about 7 percent per year.

Firms have yet another form of capital: inventories. Inventories can be divided into three categories. *Finished goods* are goods held in inventory by the firms that have produced the goods. Inventories of *raw materials* are of stocks of inputs held by the firms. *Goods in process* are half-finished goods which, at a point in time, are stored by the firm. The change in the stocks of inventories is called *inventory investment* and it can be either positive – that is, inventories increase – or negative, so that inventories decrease.

How should we think about fluctuations in the stock of inventories? It is quite useful to think of inventories as a form of productive capital, similar to machines and buildings. In order to sell goods, the firm has to have finished goods to sell.[11] In order to produce, it must hold stocks of half-finished goods and inputs. As a consequence, the desire to hold inventories is closely related to the level of production and there is a strong accelerator effect on the demand for inventories. When demand increases, firms want to increase their inventory stocks, and this gives a further boost to aggregate demand.

One specific aspect of inventory investment is that it is sometimes negative – that is, the stock of inventories decreases. As a consequence, inventory investment can either add to or subtract from aggregate demand. Inventory investment is a small and sometimes negative part of aggregate demand, but it fluctuates a good deal, so inventory investments play an important role in the business cycle.

Residential investment is investment in houses for people to live in. Such investments can be made by firms and by individual households. Property is a form of productive capital: it is used to produce housing services which are part of GDP. This is most obvious in the case where a firm invests in the house and rents out apartments. Even if it is a household that buys the house, we can think of this as an investment in capital that is used to produce housing services for the owner. In fact, this is how it is treated in the national accounts: the stock of owner-occupied houses is included in the capital stock of the country and imputed rents for those houses are included in GDP. If you have a house, you are contributing to GDP just by living in it, although there is no money changing hands.

The demand for housing depends on income, so as people become richer they demand more housing services. A larger stock of housing is needed to produce those housing services. Again we have the accelerator effect. Like other forms of investment, housing investment is high when incomes are growing, and investment cycles in real estate sometimes contribute to very strong booms and recessions. As we will discuss in Chapter 18, such cycles sometimes lead to financial crises because a large part of the investment is financed by loans via the banking system. When the housing market collapses, some banks also collapse.

Thus we can conclude that business investment in buildings and equipment, inventory investment, and investment in housing are all affected by strong accelerator effects. Hence they are volatile components of aggregate demand.

---

11 This will not be the case if production is carried out after orders have been received.

What have we learned?

One plus the nominal interest rate, i_t, is the price of money today in terms of money next year. If you spend one dollar more today you have $1 + i_t$ less dollars to spend next year.

One divided by one plus the nominal interest rate, the *discount factor*, is the price of money next year in terms of money today. To get one dollar next year you must save $1/(1 + i_t)$ dollars today.

One plus the *real interest rate* is the price of goods today in terms of goods next year. Put differently, the real interest rate measures how much more you can consume in the next period if you abstain from one unit of consumption today. It is the 'inflation corrected' interest rate.

The price of goods today is P_t and the discounted price of goods next year is $P_{t+1}/(1 + i_t)$, so the relative price of goods today is

$$1 + r_{t+1} = \frac{P_t}{P_{t+1}/(1 + i_t)} = \frac{1 + i_t}{P_{t+1}/P_t} = \frac{1 + i_t}{1 + \pi_{t+1}} \approx 1 + i_t - \pi_{t+1}.$$

The real interest rate is approximately equal to the nominal interest minus inflation:

$$r_{t+1} \approx i_t - \pi_{t+1}.$$

Investment constitutes about 20 percent of aggregate demand in high-income countries and the share is higher in fast-growing countries. It is a very volatile component of aggregate demand.

The change in the capital stock is gross investment minus the depreciation of the capital stock:

$$K_{t+1} - K_t = I_t - \delta K_t.$$

Firms invest for two reasons: to increase the capital stock and to replace depreciating capital:

$$I_t = K_{t+t}^d - K_t + \delta K_t.$$

The desired capital stock is chosen by the firm so that the real marginal revenue product of capital minus the depreciation rate equals the real interest rate:

$$\frac{MPK_{t+1}}{1 + \mu} - \delta = r_{t+1}.$$

According to the *investment function*

$$I = I(r, Y^e, K),$$

investment depends on three factors:

1. A higher expected real interest rate has a negative effect on investment
2. Higher expected future demand increases investment
3. A higher capital stock at the beginning of the period reduces investment.

When demand and production grow fast, firms want to increase their capital stocks so that investment will be high. The high volatility of investment is due to the fact that net investment is driven by changes in the desired capital stock and the capital stock is large relative to production. The relation between demand growth and investment is called the *accelerator effect*.

Where do we go from here?

In the next chapter, we continue our analysis of the demand side by studying the largest component of aggregate demand: private consumption. We explore the consumption/savings decision of the typical consumer and show how consumption depends on income, wealth, expected future income, and the real interest rate. Then we combine the supply and demand sides of the economy into a complete macroeconomic model of the whole economy. This analysis will help us to understand how production, consumption, investment, and the real interest rate are determined in the long run.

Exercises

1. This year, Karl's favourite hamburger costs 4 euros. Next year, it is expected to cost 4 euros and 10 cents. The interest rate on savings is 4.5 per cent.
   a) How many more hamburgers can Karl eat next year if he abstains from one hamburger per week (52 hamburgers) this year?
   b) Use the answer to calculate the real interest rate in terms of hamburgers.
   c) What is the inflation rate in terms of hamburgers?
   d) Calculate the real interest rate in terms of hamburgers using the formula $r = i - \pi$. Do you get the same answer? Explain your result.

2. In the text, we derived an equation for the long-run demand for capital:

$$K = \left[\frac{\alpha}{(r+\delta)(1+\mu)} \right]^{\frac{1}{1-\alpha}} EN^n.$$

Explain how each parameter and variable in this equation affects the long-run demand for capital.

3. Investment is much more volatile than GDP. Why?

4. Analyse how each of the following events might affect investment:

   a) Inflation increases and the central bank does not seem to care.
   b) Inflation increases and the central bank reacts by raising the interest rate more than the increase in the inflation rate.
   c) A tax reform induces more workers to enter the labour market.
   d) Computers become cheaper and more powerful.
   e) A pension reform leads to increased savings as people realize that their pensions will be lower.

5. Consider an economy where firms lease capital (machines) from leasing firms. The rental price per unit of capital is R. Capital can be bought at the price P, the nominal interest rate is i and there is no inflation. Capital depreciates at the rate δ.
   a) The production function is $Y = \sqrt{KN}$. The product market is competitive and profit is $PY - WN - RK$. Calculate the desired capital stock for given N.
   b) The rental market is competitive. At what rental price will the rental firms break even?
   c) Combine the results in a) and b) to find the long-run capital stock.

Answers to the exercises can be found at:
www.palgrave.com/economics/gottfries.

Appendix

Investment of the firm and aggregate investment

To see more clearly how firms' investment decisions relate to aggregate investment, note that we can write the marginal product for an individual firm i as

$$MPK_i = \alpha K_i^{\alpha-1} E^{1-\alpha} N_i^{1-\alpha} = \alpha \frac{K_i^{\alpha} E^{1-\alpha} N_i^{1-\alpha}}{K_i} = \alpha \frac{Y_i}{K_i}.$$

The optimal choice of capital input for firm i is characterized by the following condition:

$$\frac{\alpha Y_i / K_i}{1+\mu} = r + \delta.$$

Solving for the capital stock and substituting the demand function $Y_i = D(P_i/P) Y$ we get the desired amount of capital of firm i for a given level of aggregate demand and for given prices:

$$K_i^d = \frac{\alpha}{(1+\mu)(r+\delta)} D\left(\frac{P_i}{P}\right) Y.$$

Investments made this year can only be used next year, so when deciding how much to invest, firms look ahead to expected aggregate demand, which we denote Y^e, and prices next year. The capital stock and the firm's price are both chosen by the individual firm, but we consider a macroeconomic equilibrium where all firms set the same price, and choose the same capital stock. We assume that $D(1) = 1$, so this gives us the aggregate demand for capital

$$K^d = \frac{\alpha}{(1+\mu)(r+\delta)} Y^e.$$

Adjustment costs and investment

In our analysis above, we assumed that it is always possible to buy new machines at the price P and that capital becomes productive after one period. But it is costly to instal new machines, workers need to be hired and trained to run the new machines, and production may have to be reorganized. Therefore, investment is associated with lags and adjustment costs that slow down adjustment of the capital stock. One way to think about this is to assume that only a proportion λ of the gap between the desired and the actual capital stock can be closed in a particular year. Then we have

$$I_t = \lambda \left(K^d - K\right) + \delta K = \frac{\lambda \alpha}{(1+\mu)(r+\delta)} Y^e - (\lambda - \delta) K.$$

This investment function implies more sluggish investment, and a weaker accelerator effect, but the main determinants of investment are still the same: the real interest rate, expected future aggregate demand, and the capital stock at the beginning of the period.

4 CONSUMPTION AND THE NATURAL RATE OF INTEREST

What factors determine consumption and the real interest rate?

In this chapter we continue our exploration of the demand side of the economy by studying private consumption. Consumption is the ultimate purpose of production. The main reason why people work, produce, and invest is that they want to consume, today and in the future. Individuals receive income in the form of wages, interest, and dividends, and, whether they think about it or not, they make a decision every period of their lives about how much of this income to consume and how much to save.

As we saw in Chapter 1, saving is income minus consumption. The main reason to save is to consume in the future, so the saving decision is really a choice between consuming today and consuming in the future. Saving is deferred consumption. In a closed economy, savings equals investment, so savings determine investment, the long-run stock of capital, and the long-run level of production. In an open economy, savings decisions affect a country's current account and the long-run level of foreign debt.[1]

From a business cycle perspective, private consumption is important because it is the largest component of aggregate demand. As we saw in Chapter 1, consumption makes up 50–60 percent of GDP in most countries. Although less volatile than investment, it plays an important role in the business cycle because of its sheer size. As seen in Fig. 4.1, consumption growth is closely correlated with GDP growth, and the volatility of consumption is of similar magnitude to that of GDP.

In this chapter, we analyse the consumption/savings decision starting from microeconomic theory. We assume that households make a rational choice between consumption today and consumption in the future, taking account of the interest rate and expectations about future income. This analysis may appear very theoretical at first sight. In practice, we don't know what will happen in the future, so it seems rather meaningless to make detailed plans for future consumption. Few, if any, consumers make the detailed calculations that we make here.[2] Yet it makes intuitive sense that the choice between consuming today and saving for the future depends on our outlook for the future. A consumer who thinks he will lose his job tomorrow will not consume as much as a consumer who has

---

1 Long-run accumulation of capital and foreign debt are analysed in Chapters 5 and 13.
2 The readers of this book will be able to make more intelligent consumption/savings decisions after reading this chapter, and as more people read the book consumers will start to behave more in line with the theory presented here.

Fig. 4.1 *Consumption and GDP growth*

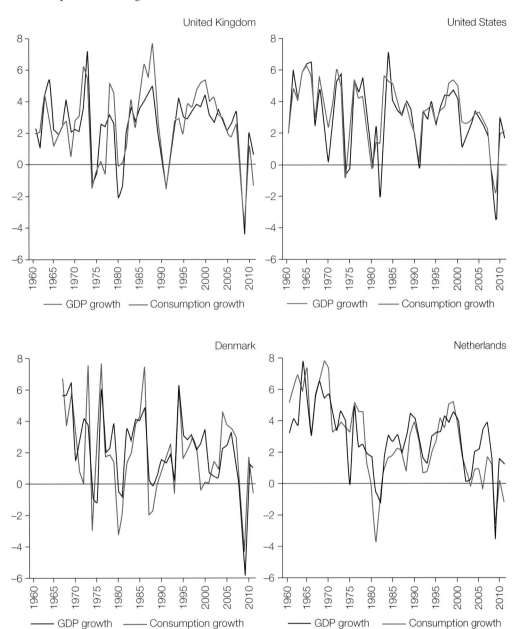

Note: The figure shows growth rates in percent for GDP and private consumption in fixed prices.
Source: *OECD Economic Outlook*, OECD, 10 July 2012, http://www.oecd-ilibrary.org/statistics.

bright expectations about his future career. As we will see, our analysis will give us clear insights about the importance of different factors for consumption. The analysis is rather complicated, but the results are simple, intuitive, and plausible.

The end result of our analysis will be a *consumption function* that relates private consumption to the following factors:

- current income
- expected future income
- the interest rate
- assets (wealth).

Our analysis will help us to understand how important these different factors are for consumption and the consumption function will play an important role in our macroeconomic analysis.

Adding consumption and investment, which we studied in Chapter 3, we get aggregate demand – that is, demand for goods and services in the economy as a whole. In the long run, aggregate demand must be equal to the natural level of production, which we studied in Chapter 2. But for demand to be equal to supply there must be a price that adjusts so as to equalize demand and supply. What price is that? As we will see, it is the *real interest rate* that brings about equilibrium between demand and supply for the economy as a whole. We define the *natural rate of interest* as the real interest rate that makes aggregate demand equal to the natural level of production.

We first analyse the consumption decisions made by households. Then we combine the supply side from Chapter 2 with the demand side analysed in this and the previous chapter into a complete macroeconomic model that shows how production, consumption, investment, and the real interest rate are determined in the long run.

4.1 Consumption in a two-period model

To analyse what economic theory can tell us about consumption behaviour, we start by considering a consumer who lives for only two periods, so the savings decision is a choice between consumption today and consumption in the next period. Then we consider another extreme case: a consumer who lives forever. Neither case is particularly realistic, but these two cases are simpler to analyse than the case of a consumer who has a finite and uncertain lifetime. As we will see, a lot of insight can be obtained by analysing these extreme cases.

The lifetime budget constraint

Consider a consumer who knows for certain that she will live for two periods and that she will have real labour income Y_1^{ℓ} and Y_2^{ℓ} in the two periods. By real income we mean income expressed in units of consumption. The consumer has no assets initially and she does not intend to leave any bequest when she dies. Let i be the interest rate from period t to period $t+1$ and let C_1 and C_2 denote consumption in the two periods. Income in the first period can be used for consumption in that period, or it can be saved. Savings in period 1 are

$$P_1 Y_1^{\ell} - P_1 C_1.$$

In the second period, the consumer again gets her labour income, and she also has her assets, which give a nominal return, i. Since she does not leave any bequests, she will consume everything she has in period 2, so her consumption expenditure in period 2 will be her labour income plus her assets and the return on the assets:

$$P_2 C_2 = P_2 Y_2^\ell + (1 + i)\left(P_1 Y_1^\ell - P_1 C_1\right).$$

Dividing by P_2 we get

$$C_2 = Y_2^\ell + \frac{1+i}{P_2}P_1\left(Y_1^\ell - C_1\right) = Y_2^\ell + \frac{1+i}{P_2/P_1}\left(Y_1^\ell - C_1\right) = Y_2^\ell + (1+r)\left(Y_1^\ell - C_1\right).$$

Here we have used the definition of the real interest rate: $1 + r = (1 + i)/(P_2/P_1)$.

We see immediately that if C_1 increases by one unit, C_2 will decrease by $1 + r$ units. As we showed in Chapter 3, $1 + r$ is the price of consumption today in terms of future consumption. Conversely, if we reduce consumption by one unit today, we can increase consumption by $1 + r$ units next period. The real interest rate is the premium for waiting.

Dividing by $1 + r$ and collecting the consumption terms on the left-hand side we can write the expression above in another way:

$$C_1 + \frac{C_2}{1+r} = Y_1^\ell + \frac{Y_2^\ell}{1+r}.$$

The left-hand side is the present value of lifetime consumption and the right-hand side is the present value of lifetime labour income, $1/(1+r)$ being the discount factor. We call this expression the *lifetime budget constraint*. It says that the present value of lifetime consumption must be equal to the present value of lifetime income. This budget constraint is illustrated in Fig. 4.2. Incomes in the two periods are given by the point A. This point is a feasible consumption choice because the consumer could always choose to consume her labour income in each period. But other choices are also attainable by moving along the budget line. If the consumer abstains from one unit of consumption in period 1, consumption in

Fig. 4.2 *The lifetime budget constraint*

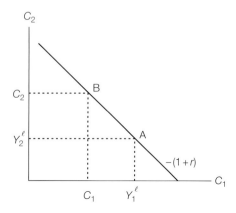

period 2 can be increased by $1 + r$ units. Therefore, the budget line has a slope of minus $(1 + r)$.

Suppose, for example, that the consumer decides to consume at point B. This means that consumption is lower than income in period 1, so the consumer saves some of her labour income in period 1. Consequently, consumption in period 2 is bigger than labour income in that period. Since the slope of the budget line is minus $(1 + r)$, we see in the figure that the distance $C_2 - Y_2^\ell$ is $1 + r$ times the distance $Y_1^\ell - C_1$, that is,

$$C_2 - Y_2^\ell = (1 + r)\left[Y_1^\ell - C_1\right].$$

If we divide by $1 + r$ we see that this is just another way of writing the lifetime budget constraint.

We see that the choice between consumption in two periods is very similar to the choice between consumption of apples and oranges with a given budget. Instead of choosing between different goods in the same period, we chose between consumption in the two periods and the relative price is one plus the real interest rate.

Intertemporal preferences

But how does the consumer choose between consumption in different periods? To analyse this, we need to specify the preferences of the typical consumer. We assume that the total utility over the lifetime can be written as a sum of the utilities obtained in the different periods:

$$U = u\left(C_1\right) + \frac{u\left(C_2\right)}{1 + \rho}.$$

The utility function $u\left(C_1\right)$ shows the utility the consumer gets from consumption in period 1. As illustrated in Fig. 4.3, the utility function is an increasing function because the consumer gets increased utility from consuming more. Also, we assume that marginal utility is decreasing: the more one consumes the less utility one gets from an *additional* unit of consumption. This is also seen in the figure because the slope of the function becomes flatter as consumption increases. Mathematically we write this $u'\left(C_1\right) > 0$ and $u''\left(C_1\right) \leq 0$.

Fig. 4.3 *The utility function*

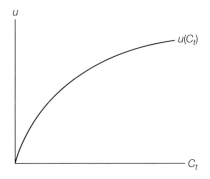

An important consequence of decreasing marginal utility is that the consumer prefers an even flow of consumption to an uneven one. To consume 500 units every year is better than consuming 450 in even years and 550 in odd years because the consumption increase from 500 to 550 gives a smaller increase in utility than the reduction in utility when consumption is decreased from 500 to 450.

Note that the lifetime utility specified above is seen from the perspective of period t when the savings decision is made. We assume that the utility obtained in period $t+1$ is given by the same utility function divided by $1 + \rho$ where $\rho > 0$. The parameter ρ shows how consumption in the future is valued compared with consumption today. The higher ρ is, the less the consumer cares about future consumption. Put differently, ρ is a measure of the *degree of impatience* and when ρ is positive the consumer values consumption in the future less than consumption today. The parameter ρ is called the *subjective discount rate*. Note that it is not an observable market rate but a parameter describing the preferences of the typical consumer.

Since marginal utility is decreasing in consumption in the two periods, we can illustrate preferences in another way, by drawing indifference curves in a diagram with consumption in the two periods on the axes. Just like the isoquants for the production function, these curves can be seen as level curves on a map. This time, the levels indicated by the curves are the levels of utility reached by the consumer and curves further up and to the right are associated with higher utility. Each curve is associated with a given level of lifetime utility. An expression for the slope of a difference curve can be obtained by assuming that we have some levels of consumption in the two periods giving a lifetime utility U^0:

$$U^0 = u(C_1) + \frac{u(C_2)}{1+\rho}.$$

Assume now that we change consumption in the two periods in such a way that lifetime utility is kept constant. Then we must have:

$$u'(C_1) \Delta C_1 + \frac{u'(C_2)}{1+\rho} \Delta C_2 = 0,$$

where ΔC_1 and ΔC_2 denote small changes in consumption in the two periods. Hence the slope of the indifference curve is

$$\frac{\Delta C_2}{\Delta C_1} = -\frac{u'(C_1)}{u'(C_2)/(1+\rho)}.$$

The slope of the indifference curve is the *marginal rate of substitution* between consumption in the two periods. It is the ratio of the marginal utilities of consumption in the two periods, as seen from period 1.

The interest rate and the planned consumption path

The optimal consumption choice is illustrated in Fig. 4.4. The optimal consumption choice is given by point B where an indifference curve is tangent to the budget line. This is the optimal consumption choice because the consumer reaches the highest attainable indifference curve and hence the highest possible lifetime utility. In the case illustrated here, consumption is lower than income

Fig. 4.4 *The choice between consumption today and consumption in the next period*

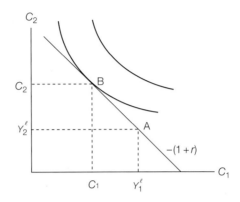

in period 1, so the consumer saves some of his labour income in period 1 and consumes more than his labour income in period 2. If, instead, the tangency point is to the right of point A, the consumer borrows money in period 1 and pays back the loan in period 2. The point of tangency depends on the preferences of the consumer. A consumer who is more impatient has a higher ρ and steeper indifference curves, so the tangency point will be further to the right – that is, the impatient consumer consumes more today than the more patient consumer.

At the optimum, the marginal rate of substitution between consumption in the two periods should be equal to the price of consumption today in terms of consumption next period – that is, $1 + r$. Thus the optimal consumption/savings decision is characterized by the following condition:

$$\frac{u'(C_1)}{u'(C_2)/(1+\rho)} = 1+r.$$

In order to see the implications of this condition, it is useful to divide by $1 + \rho$ on both sides:

$$\frac{u'(C_1)}{u'(C_2)} = \frac{1+r}{1+\rho}.$$

If the subjective discount rate is equal to the market rate of interest, the right-hand side is equal to unity, which means that the left-hand side must also be equal to unity. This can only be true if consumption is equal in the two periods. Thus we see that, if the subjective discount rate is equal to the market rate of interest, the consumer will plan for consumption to be constant over time. This is a consequence of the preference for smooth consumption. Independent of how much income the individual gets in different periods, she wants to save (or borrow) so as to smooth consumption over time. This is illustrated in Fig. 4.5 where the tangency points illustrate optimal consumption choice for two consumers with different incomes in the two periods. Two different consumers with different incomes in the two periods, here given by points A and B, will consume different amounts, but both will consume the same amount in both periods.

Fig. 4.5 *Consumption choice when the subjective rate of discount equals the real interest rate*

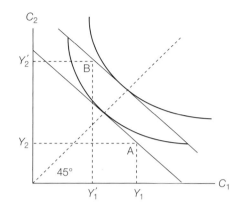

But suppose the consumer is more impatient than the market, so he discounts the future more – that is, $\rho > r$. In this case, the right-hand side is smaller than one and, since marginal utility is a decreasing function of consumption, this must imply that the consumer will consume more today than tomorrow. This makes sense: a more impatient consumer will consume more today than tomorrow and his consumption will decrease over time.

The effect of the real interest rate on consumption

Suppose now that the interest rate increases. How will this affect consumption in period 1? An increase in the interest rate makes the budget line steeper – that is, the slope becomes more negative, as illustrated by the dotted line in Fig. 4.6. The consumer can always choose to consume her labour income in each period, so the budget line must still pass through point A. Hence, the budget line pivots around point A as the real interest rate changes.

What happens to consumption in period 1? We see from Fig. 4.6 that the tangency point is at a point where C_1 is the same as before the increase in the

Fig. 4.6 *The effect of an increase in the real interest rate on consumption*

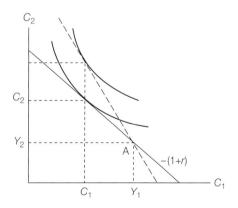

interest rate. This is not necessarily the case, however. In general, consumption in the first period can either decrease or increase, depending on the exact shape of the indifference curves. This can be understood in terms of substitution and income effects. The change in the relative price makes consumption in the current period more expensive in terms of foregone future consumption, and this induces a shift from current consumption to future consumption – a *substitution effect*. But there is also an income effect. Since this consumer was initially a saver, the increase in the real interest rate benefits the consumer. He is better off when he gets a higher return on his savings, so there is a positive *income effect* on consumption.

For consumers who plan to bring assets into the future, substitution and income effects on current consumption go in different directions. The substitution effect is negative and the income effect is positive, so the interest rate has an ambiguous effect on current consumption and saving, and the net effect on consumption may very well be small. Since the capital stock is about twice as large as GDP, most consumers have positive wealth, so we would expect substitution and income effects to go in different directions for the typical consumer. In fact, most empirical studies find rather small effects of the interest rate on consumption.

How is consumption in period 2 affected by the increase in the interest rate? We see in Fig. 4.6 that future consumption increases. The substitution and the income effect both raise future consumption, so future consumption will increase.[3]

Note that if a consumer is a borrower, substitution and income effects on consumption in period 1 go in the same direction: consumption becomes more expensive today compared with the next period and the borrower is made worse off by a higher interest rate. Therefore, a net borrower will reduce her consumption when the interest rate increases.

4.2   Consumption in an infinite horizon model

Above we analysed the consumption decision of a consumer who lives for two periods. Now we go to the opposite extreme and consider a consumer who lives forever. We assume that lifetime utility as seen from period t is a discounted sum of utilities from consumption in current and all future periods given by

$$U_t = u\,(C_t) + \frac{u\,(C_{t+1})}{1+\rho} + \frac{u\,(C_{t+2})}{(1+\rho)^2} + \dots$$

As before, ρ represents the degree of impatience, and future utilities are discounted with the discount factor $1/\,(1+\rho)$. To simplify, we assume that future incomes, real interest rates, and so forth, are known with certainty. The consumer makes a plan for his consumption in all future periods so as to maximize the discounted sum of utilities obtained in all future periods.

---

3   We assume that current and future consumption are both normal goods, so income effects are positive.

To analyse the consumer's problem we need to specify the budget constraint. As before, we use Y_t^ℓ to denote real labour income and we let A_t denote *real* asset holdings brought into period t. This stock changes over time according to the following equation:

$$A_{t+1} = Y_t^\ell + (1 + r_t) A_t - C_t.$$

The stock of wealth brought into the next period is equal to labour income plus the assets at the beginning of the current period and the real return received on those assets minus consumption.[4]

As concerns the optimal consumption path over time, the argument made in the two-period model still holds. Consumption should be planned so that the marginal rate of substitution is equal to one plus the real rate of interest. Therefore, the first-order condition is the same as in the two-period case:

$$\frac{u'(C_t)}{u'(C_{t+1})/(1+\rho)} = 1 + r_{t+1}.$$

Now, this condition applies to any two periods t and $t+1$.

Sustainable consumption

To analyse consumption in the infinite horizon case, we first consider the case when real labour income and the real interest rate are expected to be constant for all future periods at the levels Y^ℓ and r. We assume that the subjective rate of discount equals the market interest rate. Then, the first-order condition says that the consumer should plan for a constant level of consumption for all future periods. The question, then, is what level of consumption is sustainable in the long run. The answer is simple: in order to keep consumption constant for all future periods consumption has to be such that the real stock of assets is held constant:

$$A_t = A_{t+1} = A_{t+2} = \ldots.$$

If the consumer consumes more, assets will decrease, and sooner or later she will have to reduce consumption. Therefore, the *sustainable level of consumption* can be found by substituting $A_{t+1} = A_t$ in the budget constraint:

$$A_t = Y^\ell + A_t + rA_t - C_t.$$

This gives us the sustainable level of consumption as

$$C_t = Y^\ell + rA_t.$$

---

4 To see how this equation can be expressed in terms of nominal asset holdings and interest rates, let X_t be the nominal stock of assets that the consumer has at the beginning of period t. The stock of assets changes over time according to the following equation:

$$X_{t+1} = P_t Y_t^\ell + X_t + i_{t-1} X_t - P_t C_t.$$

Now define A_{t+1} as the *real* asset holdings brought into period $t+1$: $A_{t+1} = X_{t+1}/P_t$. Then we have

$$A_{t+1} = \frac{X_{t+1}}{P_t} = Y_t^\ell + \frac{1 + i_{t-1}}{P_t/P_{t-1}} \frac{X_t}{P_{t-1}} - C_t = Y_t^\ell + (1 + r_t) A_t - C_t.$$

This result is intuitive. *The sustainable level of consumption is equal to the (constant) labour income plus the real return on the assets.* Note that the sustainable level of consumption depends on the stock of assets, and the stock of assets depends on how much the consumer saved in the past, but whatever assets the consumer has, the optimal plan is to consume the real return on those assets and maintain the asset holdings at their current level.

This sustainable level of consumption is the optimal choice for a consumer when her subjective rate of discount equals the market interest rate. Clearly, a more impatient consumer will consume more than this, which means that her assets will decrease over time. As assets decrease, she will also have to reduce consumption. Eventually, she will become very poor. Conversely, a consumer who has a value of ρ which is lower than the market real interest rate will consume less than her sustainable level of consumption and accumulate assets over time.

The consumption function

Above, we have assumed that the consumer's expected labour income is constant. But consumers may expect future income to be different from current income, and the interest rate varies over time. More generally, we would expect consumption to depend on four factors:

- higher current income should lead to an increase in consumption
- higher expected future labour income should lead to higher consumption
- a higher real interest rate, r, may have a negative effect on consumption, although this is not certain because there are substitutions and income effects
- with a higher stock of assets consumption should increase.

Therefore we specify a *consumption function* relating consumption to these four factors:

$$C = C(Y, Y^e, r, A).$$

Y is current income, Y^e is expected future labour income, r is the real interest rate, and A is the stock of assets. We will use this consumption function in our macroeconomic analysis. But how important are these different factors for consumption? To analyse this, it is useful to consider a specific consumption function.

A specific consumption function

To derive a specific consumption, we need to make some simplifying assumptions. We assume that, from period $t + 1$ onwards, labour income is expected to be constant and equal to Y^e_{t+1} and the real interest rate is expected to be constant and equal to ρ: $\bar{r} = \rho$. We also assume that the utility function is the natural log function $u(C_t) = \ln(C_t)$. With these assumptions, we can derive a specific consumption function:

$$C_t = \frac{\bar{r}[Y_t + A_t] + Y^e_{t+1}}{\frac{1 + r_{t+1}}{1 + \rho} + \bar{r}},$$

where Y_t is total real income of the consumer – that is, labour income plus the real return on the assets: $Y_t = Y_t^\ell + r_t A_t$. This equation is derived in the appendix to this chapter. We see that consumption depends on the four factors mentioned above: current income, expected future labour income, the real interest rate, and the stock of assets (wealth). The equation looks a bit complicated, but the advantage of this specific consumption function is that it allows us to evaluate how important different factors are for consumption. Let us consider each of the four factors.

Current income affects consumption, but the effect is small. If, for example, the real interest rate and the subjective rate of discount are both 3 percent, consumption is equal to

$$C = \frac{0.03\,[Y+A] + Y^e}{1.03} \approx 0.03\,[Y+A] + 0.97 \cdot Y^e.$$

Suppose that there is a *temporary* increase in income: current income increases by 100 units without any change in expected future income. In this case, consumption should increase by only three units. Roughly speaking, the consumer should consume only the real interest on any temporary income. The reason, of course, is that the consumer prefers a smooth flow of consumption to an uneven one. It is better to consume a little more today and in all future periods than to consume a lot today and then go back to the old level of consumption when the party is over. If you win 1000 euros in a lottery and the real interest rate is 3 percent, you should consume only 30 euros this year. This conclusion is really boring, but wise. No wonder they call economics 'the dismal science'!

The long-run level of labour income, Y^e, is much more important for consumption. If expected future labour income increases by 100, consumption will increase by about 97 units – that is, roughly in line with income. The reason, of course, is that this income is expected every period so the sustainable level of consumption increases by roughly the same amount. If current and expected future income both increase by the same amount, consumption will increase in line with income.

The interest rate, r, is in the denominator in the consumption function above, so an increase in the interest rate has a negative effect on consumption. According to this consumption function, an increase in the real interest rate by *one percentage unit* – for example, from 0.02 to 0.03 – should reduce consumption by about *one percent.*[5] However, most empirical studies indicate that the effect of the interest rate on consumption is smaller than this.

The effect of the *stock of assets* on consumption is easy to interpret. If $r_{t+1} = \bar{r} = \rho$ the derivative of the consumption function with respect to wealth is $r/(1+r)$, which is approximately equal to r.[6] If wealth increases, for example because of an unexpected capital gain, the increase in consumption should be roughly equal to the real interest rate on the increase in wealth. In order to smooth consumption over time, the optimal solution is to consume the real interest rate on the assets, independent of how much assets you have.

---

5 Since the denominator increases about one percent the ratio decreases about one percent.
6 This follows from the fact that r and $\bar{r}$ are both small numbers and can be checked by putting numbers into the consumption function.

Comparing the different factors that affect consumption, we see that, unless the consumer has a very high level of wealth, expected future labour income is the main determinant of consumption. This can be seen by considering a numerical example. Suppose a consumer has labour income equal to 100 today and in the future, and that her wealth is twice her yearly labour income, namely 200.[7] Assume that the real interest rate and the subjective rate of discount are both 3 percent. Then our consumption function says that consumption is equal to

$$C = \frac{0.03\,[100 + 200] + 100}{1 + 0.03} = \frac{3 + 6 + 100}{1.03} \approx 3 + 6 + 97 = 106.$$

Consumption is 106 units – labour income (100) plus the real return on assets (0.03 times 200). Of this consumption, 97 units reflect expectations about future labour income, 3 units reflect current labour income, and 6 units are due to income from assets.

We see that, like investment, consumption is an expectations-driven variable: expected future income is the main determinant of consumption. Other factors such as current income, interest rate and assets play a role too, but they are less important. Consumers' expectations – often referred to as *consumer confidence* – are very important for consumption. Therefore, policymakers and business cycle analysts keep a close eye on indicators of consumer confidence when making business cycle forecasts.

Expectations about future income

According to our theory, expected future income is the most important determinant of consumption. This leads to the question how consumers form expectations about future incomes. Suppose, for example, that there is an increase in current income. How will this affect expectations about future income? Here we can think of two special cases. One is that the increase in income is perceived as *transitory*, so income in the next period is unaffected. In this case, our theory says that the consumer will only consume the interest on the additional income. Another possibility is that the increase in income is perceived as *permanent* – that is, income is expected to remain on the new level. In that case, consumption should increase roughly in line with the increase in income.

The distinction between transitory and permanent income changes is emphasized in *the permanent income theory of consumption* which was developed by the American economist Milton Friedman in the 1950s. Friedman hypothesized that we can decompose income into a permanent and a transitory part and he argued that consumption will depend only on the permanent part of income. As we have seen above, this is essentially true according to the theory developed here: transitory changes in income will have very small effects on consumption.[8]

---

7 In rich countries, the capital stock is about twice as large as GDP so a number of this order is realistic as an average. In the real economy, wealth is very unevenly distributed, however.

8 Milton Friedman was awarded the Nobel Prize in 1976 'for his achievements in the fields of consumption analysis, monetary history and theory and for his demonstration of the complexity of stabilization policy'.

The question, then, is whether a change in income is perceived as transitory or permanent. Surely, consumers' expectations will depend on what caused the change in income. A consumer who gains a large sum of money on a lottery will not (unless he is an extreme optimist) think that he will win again in each future period. A lottery gain should be perceived as temporary, so our theory predicts that consumers should save a large part of the gain. Similarly, a farmer or a campsite owner, whose income is subject to wide seasonal variation, will not vary his consumption month by month with current income, but try to smooth consumption over the year.

But most changes in income are not of this character. On the individual level, the typical change in real income will arise because of a wage change or because a consumer price change affects real income. Typically, a wage or a price increase is not reversed in the next period, so such changes would typically be perceived as relatively persistent. Other important sources of income changes are job losses, or that a previously unemployed individual finds a job. Again, such changes will be perceived as relatively permanent. Thus we conclude that, on the individual level, most, but not all changes in income would probably be perceived as fairly permanent.

On the macroeconomic level we know that, in the end, all income goes to the consumers, so one could argue that, to a first approximation, what matters for aggregate consumption is the level of aggregate income. So, how persistent are changes in aggregate income? To address this question, let us look again at the time series for GDP growth in Fig. 4.1. If changes in GDP were purely temporary, we would expect that a large increase in GDP is followed by an equally large decrease in GDP so there would be negative serial correlation in the growth rates. If, on the other hand, changes in income were permanent, we would expect changes in GDP to be uncorrelated over time. If there were a big increase in GDP this year, this would not help us to predict how much GDP would change next year. Looking carefully at the data, we see that there is no sign that an increase in income is immediately reversed. On the contrary, periods with high income growth are typically followed by more growth, and declines in income are often followed by further declines. If GDP increases at an unusually high rate this year it will, most likely, increase at a relatively high rate also in the coming year. Thus it seems that changes in income are in fact very persistent. We will discuss business cycles further in Chapter 16.

So, if changes in income are highly persistent, what does this imply for consumption? Suppose that expected future labour income is equal to current labour income and that the real interest rate is constant and equal to the subjective rate of discount. Then our consumption theory implies that consumption is equal to income.[9] This theory explains the two main facts that we see when we look at the data: that consumption is closely correlated with income and that the volatility

---

9 To be more precise, the relevant income measure is net disposable income after tax and depreciation. Thus we need to subtract depreciation and taxes minus transfers from GDP. As we will see in Chapter 5, it is more realistic to assume that the real interest rate is somewhat higher than the subjective rate of discount. These modifications do not fundamentally change our analysis.

of consumption is roughly similar to that of income. Of course, there is two-way causation between income and consumption. Higher income raises consumption but higher consumption raises aggregate demand and production in the short run. Thus, the close correlation between income and consumption cannot be seen as a definite proof that our theory is correct, but we can conclude that the theory is broadly consistent with the data.

The marginal propensity to consume

Keynes introduced the concept *marginal propensity to consume (MPC)* by which he meant the marginal effect of an increase in income on consumption. We see that one key determinant of the marginal propensity to consume is whether consumers perceive the increase in income as permanent or transitory. Another factor is the extent to which consumers are liquidity-constrained, as will be discussed below.

4.3   Liquidity constraints, demographics, durable goods

In this section we consider some specific factors that were omitted in the analysis above.

Liquidity-constrained consumers

All consumers may not have such forward-looking plans for future consumption as described above. One reason may be that consumers do not always have access to credit. For example, a student who has low income today but expects a high income in the future may want to consume more than her current income today, but the bank may be unwilling to lend to her. There may also be 'myopic' (short-sighted) consumers who do not care much about the future and who would like to borrow and spend as much as possible today; again banks will probably be unwilling to lend to such consumers. Constraints on the availability of credit are called 'liquidity constraints'. If a substantial proportion of consumers are liquidity-constrained, current labour income will be more important for consumption because the liquidity-constrained consumers will simply spend whatever labour income they have.

Some researchers have tried to estimate the proportion of liquidity-constrained consumers. The estimates vary, but most estimates are somewhere between 30 and 60 percent. This would suggest that the marginal propensity to consume out of temporary changes in income is somewhere around one half. If the change in income is perceived as permanent, the marginal propensity to consume should be close to unity.

Demographic effects on consumption and saving

To analyse the macro economy as if there were one typical consumer helps us to think clearly about what determines consumption. But of course, we omit important aspects of reality when we do this. One omitted aspect is the effect of demography on consumption and saving.

So, what effects should we expect of demography on savings? Young people have relatively weak incentives to save because they have relatively low incomes and most of them expect their income to increase in the future. Retired people also have weak incentives to save because many of them have substantial assets relative to their pension and they have less time left to consume their savings. Therefore, we expect middle-aged individuals to save the most. They have relatively high incomes and they can look forward to a period as retirees with substantially lower incomes. Countries with a large share of population in middle age should have high savings relative to income.

The theory of how consumption varies over the life cycle is called the *life cycle theory of consumption* and it is primarily associated with the Italian economist Franco Modigliani (active in the US) who received the Nobel Prize in 1985.[10]

Durable goods

At the beginning of this chapter, we stated that consumption gives satisfaction right away while investment increases production capacity in the future. But some types of consumption goods have more of an investment good character. *Durable goods* such as cars, refrigerators, furniture, and home computers last for a considerable time and yield services to the consumer during that time. The purchase of such an item can be seen as an investment made by the consumer that yields a stream of utility for several years. The *expenditure* on such a good is registered when the good is purchased, but it gives satisfaction over a longer period.

As with other investment, there is a form of accelerator effect that affects the demand for durable goods and, for this reason, purchases of durable goods are more volatile than other components of private consumption expenditure. Consumers with higher incomes want more cars per family, or cars of better quality. Suppose, for simplicity, that the demand for cars is proportional to income, so a 3 percent increase in income increases the desired stock of cars by 3 percent, and assume that cars depreciate at a rate of 10 percent. Then the demand for cars is closely related to the growth of income. To see this, note that if income is constant and the stock of cars is at the desired level, the demand for cars arises only because cars depreciate and have to be replaced. In such a situation, purchases of new cars correspond to 10 percent of the stock. But if income increases by 3 percent in a year, car purchases increase by an amount corresponding to 3 percent of the stock. This is a 30 percent increase in the demand for new cars.

In fact, purchases of durable goods contribute a great deal to fluctuations in aggregate consumption. Demand for food is a much more stable component of aggregate demand.

---

10 The Nobel Price was awarded to Franco Modigliani in 1985 'for his pioneering analyses of saving and of financial markets'.

4.4 Aggregate demand and the natural rate of interest

In Chapter 2, we analysed how production is related to the input of production factors according to the production function $Y^n = F(K, EN)$. We assumed that, in the long run, employment is at the natural level, so the long-run equilibrium (natural) level of production is determined by

$$Y^n = F(K, E(1 - u^n)L).$$

But firms do not produce if there is no demand for their products. At any point in time, actual production is determined by aggregate demand, which consists of consumption and investment:

$$Y = C(Y, Y^e, r, A) + I(r, Y^e, K).$$

This means that, for production to be at the natural level, the real interest rate has to be such that aggregate demand equals the natural level of production. The real interest rate that brings about this equality is called the *natural rate of interest*.

The determination of the natural rate of interest is illustrated in Fig. 4.7. We can think of this as a standard diagram of a market, showing supply and demand as functions of the price. Recall that one plus the real interest rate is the price of goods today in terms of goods in the future. What the diagram says is that, for production to be at its natural level, the *intertemporal relative price* has to be such that demand for goods *today* equals supply of goods *today*.

In the long run, we expect production to be at the natural level, so the real interest rate must be equal to the natural rate of interest. But who sets the interest rate? Who makes sure that the real interest rate is at the right level?

One way to think of this is that the central bank in the country sets the interest rate. If the real interest rate is below the natural rate of interest, production will be above the natural level and employment will also be above the natural level. In such a situation, wages rise and inflation is high, so the central bank will raise the interest rate.[11] A higher real interest rate reduces aggregate demand so we

Fig. 4.7 *Aggregate demand, long-run aggregate supply, and the natural rate of interest*

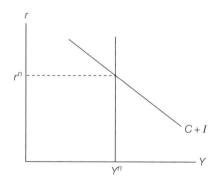

---

11 According to the *Taylor Rule*, which is discussed in Chapter 10, the central bank will react to an increase in inflation by raising the interest rate more than the increase in inflation, so the real interest rate increases.

approach the natural level of production. Conversely, if the real interest rate is above the natural level, production will be below the natural level, inflation will be low, and the central bank will reduce the interest rate. We will analyse this adjustment in more detail when we study monetary policy in Chapter 10.

The notion of a natural rate of interest was first introduced by the Swedish economist Knut Wicksell, who was active around 1900. Wicksell argued that the objective of monetary policy should be price stability and that, at any point in time, there is a natural rate of interest which depends on the expected return on investment. If the interest rate is kept below the natural rate, there will be inflation, and the converse also applies. He suggested a norm for policy: monetary policy should stabilize prices by keeping the interest rate equal to the natural rate of interest. As we will see in Chapter 10, this is pretty much how central banks think about monetary policy today.

An alternative way to look at the long-run equilibrium is to define the savings function:

$$S(Y,Y^e,r,A) \equiv Y - C(Y,Y^e,r,A).$$

We can then write the long equilibrium condition

$$S(Y^n,Y^e,r,A) = I(r,Y^e,K).$$

Thus, another way to define the natural rate of interest is as the real interest rate that makes desired savings equal to desired investment when production is at its natural level. If the interest rate is too high, consumers want to save more than they invest and there is excess supply of credit, which leads to downward pressure on the interest rate. If the interest rate is too low, there is excess demand for loans to finance investments and the interest rate will increase. The equality between savings and investment is illustrated in Fig. 4.8.

If, for example, there is an increase in firms' willingness to invest because of innovations or improved expectations about future growth, the investment curve will shift outwards and the natural rate of interest will increase. The effect of such a shock is illustrated in Fig. 4.8 and Fig. 4.9. Note that the increase in investment will be smaller than the shift in the investment function because the increase in the interest rate counteracts the shock to investment demand. If the real interest rate had remained unchanged, investment would have increased from

Fig. 4.8 *Savings, investment, and the natural rate of interest*

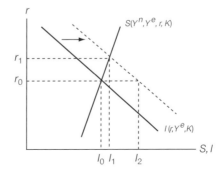

Fig. 4.9 *The effect of optimism on the natural rate of interest*

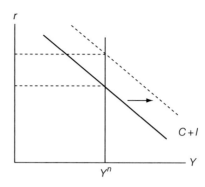

I_0 to I_2, but because of the increase in the interest rate, investment will increase only to I_1.

4.5 The Fisher equation

The equation

$$i = r + \pi$$

is called the *Fisher equation* after the American economist Irwin Fisher. This equation can be interpreted in several different ways. As we saw in Chapter 3, it can be seen as a *definition*, saying that the real interest rate is (approximately) equal to the nominal interest rate minus inflation:

$$r = i - \pi.$$

This definition of the real interest rate can be applied both to *expected* and *realized* values. The *expected* real interest rate over the next 12 months equals the one-year nominal interest rate minus the expected inflation rate over the next 12 months. The *realized* real interest rate is the nominal interest rate minus the actual inflation over the same period.

We can also see the Fisher equation as a *causal* statement saying that the nominal interest rate is determined by the real interest rate and inflation. Such an interpretation makes sense in the long run. According to the theory presented in this chapter, the natural rate of interest is determined by the willingness to save and invest. It is determined by real factors and independent of the rate of inflation, so when inflation increases, the nominal interest rate must increase to compensate for inflation. An increase in inflation by one percentage unit should increase the nominal interest rate by one percentage unit if other factors remain unchanged. This result comes from the fact that both savers and investors react to the *real* interest rates – that is, the relative price of goods today compared with goods in the next period.

Looking again at Fig. 3.1, we see that there is quite a close correlation between inflation and the nominal interest rate. In periods of high inflation, the nominal interest rate is typically high too. The relation is far from perfect, however, and movements from year to year in inflation and the nominal interest rate are not closely related. There was a period in the 1970s when the interest rate was lower than inflation. Theoretically, there are several reasons why there is no exact one-to-one relation between inflation and the nominal interest rate:

1. The natural rate of interest is not a constant. It is defined as the real interest rate that brings equality between savings and investments when production is on its natural level, so that real shocks, which affect the willingness to save and invest, will affect the natural rate of interest. Technological progress that opens up possibilities to make new and profitable investments will raise investment and the natural rate of interest. If consumers become more worried about the future, this will increase savings and reduce the natural rate of interest.

2. What matters for savings and investment decisions is the *expected* inflation. But variations in inflation are not always expected. Unexpected variations in inflation will not affect the nominal interest rate. This is one reason why the short-run relation between inflation and the interest rate is weaker than the long-run relation.

3. The real rate of interest can deviate from the natural level in the short run because of monetary policy and regulations of credit markets. As we will see, the central bank controls the level of the nominal interest rate in the short run, so what happens to the real rate in the short run depends on how monetary policy is conducted. As inflation increased in the early 1970s, central banks raised their interest rates less than inflation, so real interest rates became very low. Also, financial markets were quite heavily regulated in this period, and interest rates in many countries were kept below the level that would have prevailed in an unregulated market. When we analyse the short run and monetary policy in Chapters 8–10, we will have more to say about short-run fluctuations in the interest rate.[12]

What have we learned?

Private consumption constitutes 50–70 percent of GDP in most high-income countries. It is about as volatile as GDP and highly correlated with GDP.

The *lifetime budget constraint* says that the present value of lifetime consumption must be equal to the present value of lifetime income. In a two-period model, the lifetime budget constraint is

$$C_1 + \frac{C_2}{1+r} = Y_1^{\ell} + \frac{Y_2^{\ell}}{1+r}.$$

---

12 For analyses of how real and nominal interest rates have evolved, see Olivier J. Blanchard and Laurence H. Summers, 'Perspectives on high world real interest rates', *Brookings Papers on Economic Activity* (1984:2), 273–334; Robert. J. Barro and Xavier Sala-i-Martin, 'World real interest rates', *NBER Macroeconomics Annual*, 5 (1990), 15–61; Jagjit S. Chadha and Nicholas H. Dimsdale, 'A long view of real interest rates', *Oxford Review of Economic Policy*, 15 (1999), 17–45.

The consumer's subjective rate of discount, ρ, shows how consumption in the next period is valued compared with consumption today.

To maximize lifetime utility, consumption should be chosen so that the marginal rate of substitution between consumption today and consumption in the next period is equal to the price of goods today relative to the (discounted) price of goods next year – that is, one plus the real interest rate:

$$\frac{u'(C_t)}{u'(C_{t+1})/(1+\rho)} = \frac{P_t}{P_{t+1}/(1+i_t)} = 1 + r_{t+1}.$$

According to the *consumption function*

$$C = C(Y, Y^e, r, A)$$

consumption depends on four factors:

1. Higher current income, Y, leads to an increase in consumption.
2. Higher expected future labour income, Y^e, leads to higher consumption.
3. We assume that a higher real interest rate, r, has a negative effect on consumption.
4. With a higher stock of assets, A, consumption will increase.

For a typical consumer, expected future labour income is the most important factor determining consumption.

In order to smooth consumption over time, a forward-looking consumer will only consume the real interest rate on a temporary increase in income.

The *marginal propensity to consume* (the effect of income on consumption) depends on whether the increase in income is perceived as temporary or permanent, and on the degree to which consumers are credit-rationed.

In practice, changes in production and income are quite persistent so we would expect consumers to spend a substantial proportion of an increase in income.

Private consumption is highly correlated with GDP because of two-way causality: income affects consumption and consumption is the largest component of aggregate demand.

If the real interest rate increases, the substitution effects reduces current consumption. If the consumer is a net saver, there is also a positive income effect of higher interest income so the net effect on current consumption and savings is ambiguous.

If the consumer's subjective rate of discount, ρ, is equal to the real interest rate, r, the consumer will plan for a constant consumption over time. This follows from the first-order condition above. With a constant labour income and constant real interest rate, the sustainable level of consumption is

$$C_t = Y^\ell + rA_t.$$

A consumer, who wants to smooth consumption over time, should consume labour income plus the real interest rate on the assets, thus maintaining the real stock of assets unchanged. Consumers who are more impatient will consume more than their income so that their assets decrease over time.

The *natural rate of interest* is the real interest rate that makes aggregate demand equal to the natural level of production. Equivalently, the natural rate of interest makes desired saving equal to desired investment when production is at the natural level.

If the real interest rate is higher than the natural rate, production will be below the natural level and unemployment will be above the natural level.

In the long run, we can see the *Fisher equation*

$$i = r + \pi$$

as a causal statement saying that the nominal interest rate is determined by the real interest rate and inflation. The real interest rate is determined by real factors that affect supply and demand while inflation is determined by monetary policy. When inflation increases, the nominal interest rate must increase in order to compensate for inflation.

Where do we go from here?

In Chapters 2–4 we have analysed the supply and demand sides of the economy, and we have combined them into a macroeconomic model of the whole economy. In the next chapter, we use this model to analyse long-run growth. Then, in Chapter 6, we study the labour market in depth in order to understand why there is always unemployment in a market economy. Chapter 7 introduces money into the model, and in Chapters 8–11 we use our model to analyse short-run fluctuations and the roles of fiscal and monetary policy.

Exercises

1. A consumer lives for two periods. She maximizes lifetime utility

$$U = \ln(C_1) + \frac{\ln(C_2)}{1 + \rho}.$$

The budget constraint is

$$C_1 + \frac{C_2}{1+r} = A_1 + Y_1^\ell + \frac{Y_2^\ell}{1+r},$$

where A_1 is initial wealth.
a) What is the first-order condition for consumption in this case?
b) Use the first-order condition to substitute for C_2 in the budget constraint, and solve for C_1.
c) Set $\rho = 0$ and investigate how Y_1^ℓ, A_1, Y_2^ℓ and r affect consumption. Interpret the results.

d) Suppose that $A_1 = Y_1 = Y_2 = 100$ and $\rho = r = 0$. What is consumption in period 1?
e) Suppose that $A_1 = Y_1 = Y_2 = 100$, $r = 0$ and $\rho = 0.10$. What is consumption in period 1? Explain the difference compared with the previous case.

2. Anna lives for two periods, 1 and 2. Her consumption in the two periods is determined by the tangency point between the indifference curve (I) and the budget line in Fig. 4.10.
a) Is Anna saving or borrowing in period 1?
b) Suppose the real interest rate falls. Draw the new budget line so that it is tangent to the indifference curve $\tilde{I}$. How is Anna's

Fig. 4.10 *The real interest rate on consumption with negative saving*

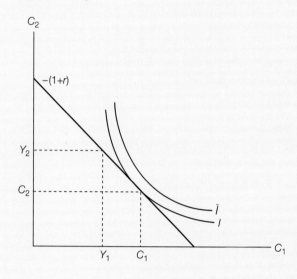

consumption in period 1 affected by the decrease in the interest rate?

c) What happens to savings (borrowing) in period 1?

d) How is Anna's consumption in period 2 affected by the decrease in the interest rate?

e) Try to explain the results in terms of income and substitution effects.

Answers to the exercises can be found at:
www.palgrave.com/economics/gottfries.

Appendix

An alternative explanation of the condition for optimal consumption

An alternative way of explaining the first-order condition is as follows. Assume that the consumer can invest his savings in period t at the nominal interest rate i_t. Suppose that the consumer has chosen a plan for consumption today and in the future. Then consider a deviation from this plan where the consumer saves an additional small amount X in period t and increases his expenditure in period $t+1$ by X plus the interest he has earned on the additional savings.[13] What is the effect on total expected utility?

If the consumer saves an extra small amount X in period t he will reduce his consumption by X/P_t units of consumption. If, for example, he saves 100 and the price of one unit of the consumption basket is 20, he must reduce his consumption in period t by 5 units. This decreases utility in period t by

$$\frac{X}{P_t}u'(C_t).$$

In the next period, the consumer can spend what he saved plus the interest he earned – that is, $X + i_t X$, and this gives a utility increase equal to

$$\frac{(1+i_t)X}{P_{t+1}}\frac{u'(C_{t+1})}{1+\rho}.$$

---

13 Note that this change of plan will leave the wealth that he brings into period $t+2$ unchanged, so utility from period $t+2$ onwards is unaffected.

Note that we look at the utility from the perspective of period t, when the consumer makes his savings decision, so utility in period $t+1$ is discounted by $1/(1+\rho)$. If the original consumption plan was optimal, this modification of the plan should not increase or decrease total utility, so for the plan to be optimal we must have

$$\frac{X}{P_t} u'(C_t) - \frac{(1+i_t)X}{P_{t+1}} \frac{u'(C_{t+1})}{1+\rho} = 0,$$

which can be rewritten

$$\frac{u'(C_t)}{u'(C_{t+1})/(1+\rho)} = \frac{1+i_t}{P_{t+1}/P_t}.$$

The left-hand side is the marginal rate of substitution between consumption today and next year and the right-hand side is one plus the real interest rate.

A specific consumption function

In order to see more exactly how important different factors are for consumption, it is useful to derive a specific consumption function. In order to do that we need to make some simplifying assumptions. We assume that, from period $t+1$ onwards, labour income is expected to be constant and equal to Y^e and the real interest rate is expected to be constant and equal to ρ: $\bar{r} = \rho$. This means that consumption from the next period onwards is expected to be on the sustainable level

$$C_{t+1} = Y^e_{t+1} + \bar{r} A_{t+1}.$$

Let Y_t be the total real income of the consumer $Y_t = Y^\ell_t + r_t A_t$. With this notation, we can write the budget constraint

$$A_{t+1} = Y_t + A_t - C_t.$$

Using this to substitute for A_{t+1} above we get

$$C_{t+1} = Y^e_{t+1} + \bar{r}[Y_t + A_t - C_t].$$

Let us also assume that the utility function is the natural log function:

$$u(C_t) = \ln(C_t).$$

With this utility function, the marginal utility is simply one divided by consumption:

$$u'(C_t) = \frac{d\ln(C_t)}{dC_t} = \frac{1}{C_t}.$$

If we put this in the condition for optimal consumption we get

$$\frac{C_{t+1}}{C_t} = \frac{1+r_{t+1}}{1+\rho}.$$

Using this equation to substitute for C_{t+1} above we get

$$\frac{1+r_{t+1}}{1+\rho}C_t = Y^e_{t+1} + \bar{r}[Y_t + A_t - C_t].$$

To solve for current consumption, we add $\bar{r}C_t$ on both sides and solve for C_t:

$$\frac{1+r_{t+1}}{1+\rho}C_t + \bar{r}C_t = \bar{r}[Y_t + A_t] + Y^e_{t+1}$$

$$\left[\frac{1+r_{t+1}}{1+\rho} + \bar{r}\right]C_t = \bar{r}[Y_t + A_t] + Y^e_{t+1}.$$

Dividing by the parenthesis on the left, we get the consumption function

$$C_t = \frac{\bar{r}[Y_t + A_t] + Y^e_{t+1}}{\dfrac{1+r_{t+1}}{1+\rho} + \bar{r}}.$$

The savings ratio

Often, consumption behaviour is discussed in terms of the savings ratio – that is, how large a proportion of their income that consumers save. Our consumption function can be rewritten as an equation for savings. In real terms, savings as a proportion of income are given by

$$\frac{Y - C}{Y} = 1 - \frac{C}{Y} = 1 - \frac{\bar{r}[1 + A/Y] + Y^e/Y}{\dfrac{1+r}{1+\rho} + \bar{r}}.$$

The higher wealth is relative to current income and the higher expected future income growth is, the lower is the savings ratio. Put differently, the savings ratio will be low when people are optimistic about the future.

Liquidity-constrained consumers

A simple way to capture the idea that some consumers simply consume whatever income they have is to assume that a proportion λ (lambda) of the consumers have no wealth and just consume their current labour income. The other consumers hold all the assets and behave in line with the forward-looking consumption theory described above. Assuming that both groups have the same labour income per capita, the total labour income of the myopic consumers is λY^ℓ and the total labour income of the forward-looking consumers is $(1 - \lambda)Y^\ell$. Then we get the total consumption of the myopic consumers:

$$C^m = \lambda Y^\ell,$$

and of the forward-looking consumers, setting $\rho = r$ for simplicity,

$$C^f = \frac{r\left[(1-\lambda)Y^\ell + rA + A\right] + (1-\lambda)Y^e}{1+r}.$$

Then total consumption is

$$C = C^m + C^f = \lambda Y^\ell + \frac{r}{1+r}(1-\lambda)Y^\ell + \frac{1-\lambda}{1+r}Y^e + rA.$$

The factors determining consumption are the same as in the case without myopic consumers but the difference is that current labour income is more important for consumption in this case. Taking the derivative of consumption with respect to current labour income in the above equation we get

$$\frac{dC}{dY^\ell} = \lambda + \frac{r}{1+r}(1-\lambda).$$

The higher λ is, the bigger is the effect of current income on consumption.

5 CAPITAL ACCUMULATION AND GROWTH

Why are some countries richer than others?

Incomes in the rich countries have grown steadily, decade after decade, and income per capita in the rich countries is many times higher than it was 100 years ago. At the same time, there are extremely large income differentials between the richest and the poorest countries in the world. Income per capita in the poorest countries is one twentieth of income per capita in the US, or even lower. What generates long-run growth and what determines the long-run level of income in a country? Why are the income differentials between countries so large and persistent?

One factor that determines production possibilities is the capital stock that the country has. In Chapter 2, we analysed how production is determined *for a given level of capital*. The capital stock in a country changes slowly, so taking it as given makes sense if we look at a period of a few years, but as time goes by the capital stock will change. To understand income differentials between countries, we need to analyse long-run capital accumulation and growth.

The growth of the capital stock depends on how much is saved and invested, and on depreciation, which reduces the capital stock. In rich countries, gross savings and investment are about 20 percent of GDP (see Chapter 1) and the capital stock is just over twice as large as yearly GDP (see Table 5.1 below). With a depreciation rate of around 7 percent, depreciation is about 15 percent of GDP, so net investment is about 5 percent of GDP. This means that the capital stock grows by about 2.5 percent per year, roughly in line with GDP.

In this chapter we analyse how the capital stock and production in a country are determined in the very long run. The time perspective is decades rather than years. To clearly see how different factors are related, we analyse growth in two steps. We first analyse capital accumulation and growth in an economy with a given population and a given technology. We show that a country that starts with a low level of capital will accumulate capital and production will increase. Eventually, the capital stock will reach a long-run equilibrium level, and growth will stop. Capital accumulation in itself is not sufficient to generate growth in the very long run because the marginal product of capital falls as we add more capital with a given number of workers and a given technology. Then we introduce a growing population and technological development. We show that these factors can generate long-run growth of GDP.

The model that we analyse here was first presented by F. P. Ramsey in 1928 and further developed by David Cass and Tjalling Coopmans in the 1960s. For short, we will call it the Ramsey model. An alternative model of growth, with largely similar implications is the Solow growth model, which was developed by Robert Solow and T. H. Swan in the mid-1950s. This model is presented in the appendix to this chapter.

Our theory will give us some ideas about what factors may cause the large income differentials that we observe. Some of these factors are hard to measure, however. As we will see, observed differences in capital stocks and education take us only part of the way towards an understanding of income differentials between countries. Law and order and other institutional and political factors seem to play important roles in the determination of the long-run level of income.

We first analyse capital accumulation for given population and technology and we examine under what conditions countries will converge to the same level of income. Then we introduce growth in population and technological change. Having developed the theory, we use it to try to explain income differences between countries. We also examine whether poor countries are catching up with the rich countries. Finally, we briefly discuss how technological development is determined.

5.1 Long-run adjustment of the capital stock for given population and technology

In order to understand capital accumulation and growth, we use the production function from Chapter 2:

$$Y = F(K, EN).$$

We first consider an economy with a given technology, E, and a constant population. We assume that a constant fraction of the population is working, so employment, N, is also constant. For given technology and number of workers, the level of production depends on the capital stock.

As we saw in Chapter 3, the profit-maximizing choice of capital stock is such that the marginal revenue product of capital minus depreciation is equal to the required return – that is, the real interest rate. Let us assume that, in the long run, the real interest rate is constant and equal to $\bar{r}$. Then the long-run level of the capital stock is determined by the condition

$$\frac{MPK}{1+\mu} - \delta = \bar{r}.$$

The marginal product of capital falls as we add more capital for a given number of workers and given technology. Therefore, there is only one level of capital for which this condition holds for a given real interest rate. We use K^* to denote this long-run equilibrium level of the capital stock and we call it the *steady state* level of the capital stock. (The term 'steady state' will be explained in Section 5.3.) The determination of the capital stock in the very long run is illustrated in Fig. 5.1.

The incentive to save and invest depends on the level of the capital stock. If $K <$ K^*, the marginal return on investment is high, so the incentive to save and invest is high, and the capital stock will grow. If $K > K^*$, an additional unit of capital

Fig. 5.1 *The long-run adjustment of capital for constant population and technology*

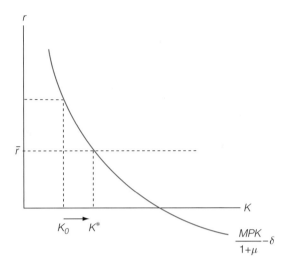

brings a low return, so investment will be low, and the capital stock will shrink. An economy with constant population and technology will eventually end up in a situation with a constant level of capital. With a constant level of capital, population and technology, production will also be constant, so there is no long-run growth.

But what determines the long-run level of the real interest rate? To find this out, we use the theory of consumption/savings choice discussed in Chapter 4. The optimality condition for the consumer's saving decision is that the marginal rate of substitution between consumption today and consumption next year should be equal to the relative price between goods in the two periods – that is, one plus the real interest rate:

$$\frac{U'(C_t)}{U'(C_{t+1})/(1+\rho)} = 1 + r_{t+1},$$

where ρ is the subjective discount rate. If there is no growth, consumption must be constant, so the marginal utility is the same in all periods. In that case, the only way this condition can be fulfilled is that the real interest rate be equal to the consumer's subjective rate of discount:

$$\bar{r} = \rho.$$

We see that the real interest rate is determined by the degree of impatience. Intuitively, r has to be equal to ρ for consumers to be satisfied with a constant level of consumption. If the real interest rate exceeds the subjective rate of discount, consumers prefer to save so as to consume more in the future than they consume today. If the real interest rate is smaller than the subjective rate of discount, consumers prefer to borrow and consume more today. Therefore, the only interest rate that is consistent with a constant level of consumption is a real interest rate that is equal to the subjective rate of discount.

Having determined the long-run level of the real interest rate, we can conclude that, in the long run, the capital stock reaches an equilibrium level which is determined by the condition

$$\frac{MPK}{1+\mu} - \delta = \rho.$$

But what happens if we start with a capital stock that is lower than K^*? Since we have a low level of capital relative to the population, the marginal return on capital is high and firms have strong incentives to invest. With a high desire to invest there is high demand for loans and a high real interest rate. We know from our analysis of consumption that if $r > \rho$ consumers will consume less than their income and accumulate assets. In this simple economy, the only asset available to households is loans to firms that invest in the capital stock, so asset accumulation takes the form of lending to firms, which accumulate real capital. Hence, the capital stock will increase towards K^*.[1]

This long-run adjustment of the capital stock is illustrated in Fig. 5.1. Starting from a low level of capital, K_0, the natural interest rate is high and there is a period of capital accumulation and growth. As the capital stock increases, the marginal product of capital decreases, and we reach a point where firms no longer want to increase the capital stock. At this point capital accumulation stops, and so does the growth of production.

We can illustrate the same adjustment in the investment–savings diagram that we introduced in Chapter 4. When capital is at the steady state level K^*, production is at the steady state level Y^* determined by

$$Y^* = F(K^*, EN^n)$$

and the real interest rate is equal to ρ. The unbroken lines in Fig. 5.2 show investments and savings as functions of the interest rate when $K = K^*$ and $Y = Y^*$. But

Fig. 5.2 *The effect of capital accumulation on investment, saving, and the real rate of interest*

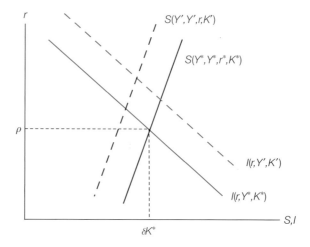

---

1 We have assumed that the capital stock is owned by the firms and financed by borrowing from the households, so households have claims on firms which correspond to the value of the capital stock. In practice, a substantial part of firms' investments is financed by retained earnings (profits), so the capital stock is indirectly owned by the households who own the firms. In practice, households also own some of the capital stock directly, e.g. in the form of private houses.

suppose instead that we start from lower levels of capital and production K' and Y'. Such a situation is illustrated by the dashed lines. Since we have less capital, the return on investment is higher, so the investment schedule is further to the right. Since income is lower, savings are lower for a given interest rate, so the savings schedule is further to the left. Thus we see that the real interest rate will be higher than ρ in this situation. Then we know, from our theory of consumption in Chapter 4, that households will save some of their income, so the capital stock will grow towards the steady state level.[2]

Patience – a virtue?

Patience is said to be one of the seven heavenly virtues. Is it advantageous to be patient in our model? To analyse this question, suppose we start in a steady state with $\rho = \rho_1$ and $K = K_1$, as illustrated in Fig. 5.3.

Suppose that consumers start to care more about the future, so ρ falls to ρ_2. At the initial level of capital, the marginal return on capital and the real interest rate exceed ρ_2 so households start to save more and their savings are channelled into investments. There is a period with high growth, and eventually the capital stock ends up at the higher level K_2. With more capital, there will also be a higher level of production and income. The path of capital accumulation and production growth is illustrated in Fig. 5.4.

We see that, if consumers start to care more about the future, savings and investments will increase and the long level of the capital stock will also increase. The more patient we are, the higher will the long-run level of income be. Patience, indeed, is a virtue. But again the capital stock will stop growing at some point. More saving will raise the long levels of capital and income, but cannot, by itself, generate long-run growth. An increase in savings generates a transition period

Fig. 5.3 *The long-run effect of a lower subjective discount rate*

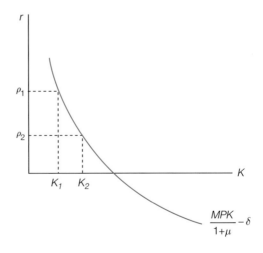

---

2 Note that investment may very well be lower than the steady state level but since the initial capital stock is smaller, depreciation is smaller too, so the capital stock increases.

Fig. 5.4 *The effect of a decrease in the subjective discount rate at time t_0*

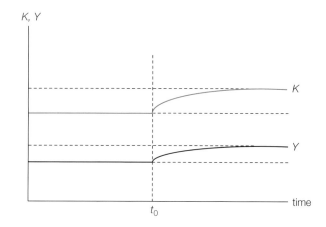

with high growth, but eventually the capital stock and production will stabilize on a higher level.

The key reason why capital accumulation cannot bring growth in the very long run is the decreasing marginal product of capital (see Chapter 2). For a given number of workers and a given technology, each marginal unit of capital brings less additional production. At the same time, it is costly to use capital because the capital stock depreciates and has to be replaced. With a very high capital stock, the marginal product of capital will be lower than the rate of depreciation. Therefore, it does not make sense to accumulate capital forever if the labour force and technology are constant.

If the population grows, or technology improves with time, the marginal product of capital will rise, giving firms incentives to increase the capital stock. The effects of technological change and population growth will be analysed in Section 5.3, but before doing that we examine the implications of constant returns to scale.

5.2 Convergence

To further characterize the steady state, we make use of our assumption of *constant returns to scale*. As we discussed in Chapter 2, constant returns to scale means that if we double the inputs of both capital and labour we double production. Let us investigate what this implies for the production function. Suppose, for example, that 20 machines and 100 workers can produce 1000 units of the good. We can write this using the production function

$$F(20, 100) = 1000.$$

If the production function has the property of constant returns to scale, 40 machines and 200 workers should be able to produce 2000 units of the good:

$$F(2 \cdot 20, 2 \cdot 100) = 2 \cdot 1000.$$

Similarly, if we increase all inputs 10 percent, production should also increase 10 percent:

$$F(1.1 \cdot 20, 1.1 \cdot 100) = 1.1 \cdot 1000.$$

More generally, if we multiply the inputs by some arbitrary factor, z, production should also be multiplied by the same factor z. Furthermore, this should be the case for *any* initial values of K and N that we start with. Thus we define constant returns to scale as follows:

A production function has the property of constant returns to scale if the following is true: if $F(K,EN) = Y$ for some numbers K,N,E,Y, then for any number z

$$F(zK, zEN) = zY.$$

Example: $z = 2$ If $F(K,EN) = Y$ then $F(2K, E2N) = 2Y$.

Note that we have written the production function so that a 10 percent increase in E has the same effect on production as a 10 percent increase in N. In order to analyse what happens to production when E and N change over time, or between countries, it is useful to think of EN as the *effective* number of workers. If we choose $z = \frac{1}{EN}$ we get an expression relating production per effective worker to the capital stock per effective worker:

$$F\left(\frac{1}{EN}K, \frac{1}{EN}EN\right) = \frac{1}{EN}Y,$$

that is,

$$\frac{Y}{EN} = F\left(\frac{K}{EN}, 1\right).$$

Production *per effective worker* is a function of the capital stock *per effective worker*. With constant returns to scale, the size of the economy does not matter. Countries with the same technology E and the same capital per worker K/N will have the same GDP per worker independent of their size. This seems reasonable, at least as a rough approximation.[3] To simplify notation, we use lower case k to denote the capital stock per worker:

$$k = \frac{K}{EN}$$

and we also use the simplified notation

$$f(k) = F\left(\frac{K}{EN}, 1\right).$$

Note that $f'(k)$ is the marginal product of capital: $f'(k) = F_K(k,1)$. We see that the marginal product of capital depends on how much capital there is per effective worker. With this notation, the steady state capital stock per effective worker, k^*, is determined by the following condition:

$$\frac{f'(k^*)}{1+\mu} - \delta = \bar{r}.$$

---

3   A small country that does not trade with other countries will be unable to exploit all gains from specialization: this effect is not included in our model. Effectively, we assume that the country, or trade area, is sufficiently large to reap gains from specialization.

Fig. 5.5 *The long-run adjustment of capital stock per effective worker*

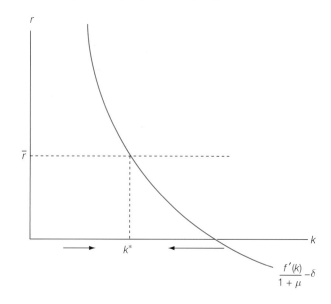

The determination of k is illustrated in Fig. 5.5. You will notice that this is the same diagram as Fig. 5.1. The only difference is that we now have capital per effective worker on the horizontal axis. If the stock of capital per effective worker is low, the return to investment is high, and the capital stock per effective worker will increase towards the steady state level. If the stock of capital per effective worker is high, the return to investment is low, and the capital stock per effective worker will decrease.

In the steady state we have

$$\frac{K}{EN} = k^* \quad \text{and} \quad \frac{Y}{EN} = f(k^*),$$

or, alternatively,

$$K^* = k^* EN$$

and

$$Y^* = f(k^*) EN.$$

The long-run levels of capital and output are proportional to employment. Because of constant returns to scale, production per capita in the steady state is independent of the size of the population.

Let us sum up what we have learnt. In the long run, and for a given number of workers and a given technology:

- the capital stock and production will eventually reach steady state levels
- investment cannot generate permanent growth because the marginal product of capital falls as we add more capital with a given number of workers
- the subjective discount rate determines the long-run required return on capital and thus the long-run levels of capital and income
- if consumers care more about the future, the required return on capital decreases and the long-run levels of capital and production increase

- for a given subjective discount rate and technology, production and the capital stock will be proportional to the number of workers
- the long-run level of production per capita will be the same in all countries which have access to the same technology, independent of the size of the country and the initial capital stock.

Thus our theory predicts that, under certain conditions, all countries will *converge* to the same level of capital and income per capita, independent of the initial level of capital. What is required for convergence is that all countries have access to the same production technology, that this technology is characterized by constant returns to scale, and that the required return on investment and employment relative to population are the same in all countries.

5.3 Population growth and technological development

So far we have developed a theory about growth in transition periods. If a country starts with a low level of capital, the capital stock and production will grow until the capital stock reaches the steady state level. This transition period may be very long. The capital is large relative to GDP and net investment is typically 2–3 percent of the capital stock, so adjustment takes time. Eventually, however, growth will stop. Without growth of the population or technological improvements, we cannot have growth going on for a century. For production to grow over very long periods there must be population growth and/or technological change.

In order to analyse the effects of population growth and technological change, we consider an economy where the number of employed workers grows continuously at the rate n and where the efficiency factor, E, grows continuously at the rate g:

$$\frac{\Delta N}{N} = n \quad \text{and} \quad \frac{\Delta E}{E} = g.$$

In order to simplify the analysis, we assume that these growth rates are constant. As we will show below, this economy will have a constant real interest rate in steady state, which we denote by $\bar{r}$. Given this long-run real interest rate, the steady state level of capital per effective worker is determined by the same condition as before:

$$\frac{f'(k^*)}{1+\mu} - \delta = \bar{r}.$$

We see that, if $\bar{r}$, δ and μ are constant, capital per effective worker must also be constant. With a constant capital per effective worker we have

$$K = k^* EN \quad \text{and} \quad Y = f(k^*) EN.$$

Applying our rule of thumb for growth rates we find that[4]

$$\frac{\Delta K}{K} = \frac{\Delta Y}{Y} = g + n.$$

---

4 The rule of thumb for growth rates was introduced in the appendix to Chapter 1. It says that the growth rate of a product is the sum of the growth rates of the two variables in the product.

The capital stock and production both grow at the rate $g + n$ so that capital and production per effective worker is kept constant. Also, the capital–output ratio, K/Y, is constant in steady state:

$$\frac{K}{Y} = \frac{k^* EN}{f(k^*) EN} = \frac{k^*}{f(k^*)}.$$

The term *steady state* is used to describe this stable growth path. It is a long-run equilibrium situation, but not in the sense that everything is constant. The economy is growing, but production and the capital stock grow at the same constant rate. The *ratios* of capital per effective worker and capital to production are constant.

In most rich countries, population growth is close to zero and the GDP growth rate is about 2.5 percent. The capital stock is about twice as large as (yearly) GDP and it grows at about the same rate as GDP, so the ratio of capital to GDP is roughly constant. This suggests that the economy is close to a steady state growth path where

$$n \approx 0, \qquad \frac{\Delta Y}{Y} = \frac{\Delta K}{K} = g \approx 0.025, \qquad \frac{K}{Y} \approx 2.$$

We can conclude that the 2–3 percent growth that we observe in rich countries is fundamentally driven by technical change. The capital stock increases in line with production, but the ultimate engine of long-run growth is technical change.

The long-run rate of return in a growing economy

Above, we analysed the steady state for a given real interest rate, but we have not yet found out how this long-run real interest rate is determined in a growing economy. To find this interest rate, we use again the condition for optimal consumption whereby the marginal rate of substitution over time is equal to one plus the real interest rate:

$$\frac{U'(C_t)}{U'(C_{t+1})/(1+\rho)} = 1 + r_t.$$

We also assume a specific utility function, the natural log function:

$$U(C_t) = \ln C_t.$$

With this utility function, the marginal utility of consumption is simply $1/C_t$ and the first-order condition for optimal consumption choice is

$$\frac{C_{t+1}}{C_t} = \frac{1+r_t}{1+\rho}.$$

In a closed economy with constant growth, consumption per capita must grow at the same rate as GDP per capita.[5] Thus we have $C_{t+1}/C_t = 1 + g$ and consequently

$$1 + g = \frac{1+\bar{r}}{1+\rho}.$$

---

5 If consumption grew faster than income it would eventually become larger than income. If consumption grew more slowly than income, the consumption as a share of income would fall to zero.

Here, the right-hand side is approximately $1 + \bar{r} - \rho$. Therefore, the real interest rate in the steady state must be approximately equal to the subjective discount rate plus the growth of production per worker:

$$\bar{r} \approx \rho + g.$$

This equation determines the long-run real interest rate in a growing economy. An economy with high growth should have a high real interest rate. Why is this? The reason can be found in the theory of consumption. In a growing economy, consumers expect to have higher income in the future than today. If the real interest rate were equal to the subjective discount rate, consumers would prefer to consume the same amount in every period. In a growing economy, this would mean that they would take loans based on their expected future incomes so as to consume more than their income today. But in a closed economy there is nobody else you can borrow from. All consumers behave in the same way. Therefore, the real interest rate has to be such that consumers are satisfied with consuming less today than next year. Consumption must grow at the same pace as income, and this requires a real interest rate that is higher than the subjective rate of discount.

Thus we see that an economy with high growth should have a high real interest rate and a high real return on investment. The capital stock per effective worker is determined by

$$\frac{f'(k^*)}{1 + \mu} = \rho + g + \delta.$$

This conclusion will be modified when we allow for international lending because international capital flows may equalize real interest rates and real returns on investment. Consumers in a growing economy may be able to borrow in the international credit market based on their high future incomes and financial capital should flow to where the return on investment is highest. But international financial capital flows are limited by various barriers, so we would not expect real returns to be completely equalized. Therefore, we should still expect higher real returns in a growing economy. We will return to these issues once we have opened up our economy for international trade and borrowing and lending in international financial markets in Chapter 12.

Explicit solutions for the long-run levels of capital and GDP

In order to make this analysis more concrete, let us try to find explicit solutions for the long-run levels of capital and GDP. Again, we use the Cobb-Douglas production function, $F(K, EN) = K^\alpha (EN)^{1-\alpha}$ which gives us

$$MPK = \alpha K^{\alpha-1} (EN)^{1-\alpha} = \alpha \left(\frac{K}{EN} \right)^{\alpha-1} = \alpha k^{\alpha-1}.$$

We substitute into the profit maximization condition for optimal choice of capital stock $MPK / (1 + \mu) - \delta = \bar{r}$,

$$\frac{\alpha k^{\alpha-1}}{1 + \mu} = \bar{r} + \delta,$$

and multiply on both sides by $(1+\mu)/\alpha$,

$$k^{\alpha-1} = \frac{(\bar{r}+\delta)(1+\mu)}{\alpha}.$$

Since $\alpha - 1$ is a negative number we invert both sides:

$$k^{1-\alpha} = \frac{\alpha}{(1+\mu)(\bar{r}+\delta)}.$$

Finally, we raise both sides to the power $1/(1-\alpha)$ we get the steady state level of capital per effective worker:

$$k^* = \left(\frac{\alpha}{(1+\mu)(\bar{r}+\delta)}\right)^{\frac{1}{1-\alpha}}.$$

Using the production function and assuming that employment is on its natural level we get an expression for GDP:

$$Y = K^\alpha (EN)^{1-\alpha} = \left(\frac{K}{EN}\right)^\alpha EN = (k^*)^\alpha EN = \left(\frac{\alpha}{(1+\mu)(\bar{r}+\delta)}\right)^{\frac{\alpha}{1-\alpha}} EN.$$

Dividing by L we get GDP per worker in the labour force:

$$\frac{Y}{L} = \left(\frac{\alpha}{(1+\mu)(\bar{r}+\delta)}\right)^{\frac{\alpha}{1-\alpha}} E(1-u),$$

where u is the unemployment rate. Here, we have used the fact that

$$\frac{N}{L} = \frac{L-U}{L} = 1 - \frac{U}{L} = 1-u.$$

We know that the capital share is about 1/3, and setting $\alpha = 1/3$ the exponent in this expression becomes one half, so we have

$$\frac{Y}{L} = E(1-u)\sqrt{\frac{1/3}{(1+\mu)(\bar{r}+\delta)}}.$$

We see that production increases if technology improves or unemployment decreases. A higher mark-up and a higher required return on investment will reduce the steady state levels of capital and income.

We can use this equation to investigate how important different factors are for the long-run level of production. To do this, we need to put in some reasonable numbers. Estimates suggest that the mark-up is fairly small, so let us set the mark-up to 5 percent, $\mu = 0.05$. In the model, there is no stock market and the real return is the same on all loans. In practice, different borrowers face different interest rates. Firms borrow at higher interest rates than the government and they also finance investments by issuing shares. The long-term real return in the stock markets has been around 7 percent. We therefore set the required return on investments to 7 percent: $\bar{r} = 0.07$, and the depreciation rate is also assumed to be 7 percent. Let us assume that the unemployment rate is 5 percent. The value of E depends on units of measurement for GDP. Here we just treat E as an arbitrary index and set $E = 100$. Thus we have:

$$\alpha = 1/3, \ \mu = 0.05, \ \bar{r} = 0.07, \ \delta = 0.07, \ u = 0.05, \ E = 100.$$

With these numbers, we get:

$$\frac{Y}{L} = 100 \cdot (1 - 0.05) \sqrt{\frac{1/3}{(1+0.05)\,(0.07+0.07)}} \approx 143.1.$$

This number is just an index number that depends on the choice to set $E = 100$, but we can use the equation to investigate how much production *changes* if we change certain parameters:

- If technology improves by 10 percent, we have $E = 110$: this will increase steady state production by 10 percent to 157.4.
- If unemployment increases from 5 to 10 percent, production will decrease to 135.5, a decrease of 5.3 percent.
- If there is less competition in the product market, the mark-up increases from 5 to 10 percent, production falls to 139.8 – a decrease of 2.3 percent.
- If the required real return on investment increases from 7 to 10 percent production falls to 129.8 – a decrease of 9 percent.

The ratio of capital to production and the savings rate

Using the baseline numbers above, we can also calculate the ratio of capital to production on the steady state growth path:

$$\frac{K}{Y} = \frac{K/(EN)}{Y/(EN)} = \frac{k^*}{y^*} = \frac{k^*}{(k^*)^\alpha} = (k^*)^{1-\alpha}$$

$$= \frac{\alpha}{(1+\mu)\,(\bar{r}+\delta)} \approx \frac{1/3}{1.05 \cdot (0.07+0.07)} \approx 2.3.$$

Our theory predicts that the capital stock will be about twice as large as yearly GDP. This is not too far off from the numbers observed for rich countries (see Table 5.1 below). Poor countries have less capital relative to production. This is also consistent with our theory: one reason why poor countries have lower production per capita is that they have less capital per worker.

How large a share of income is saved on the steady state growth path? Gross savings equals investment, which is the increase in the capital stock plus depreciation:

$$\frac{\Delta K + \delta K}{Y} = \frac{(n+g)\,K+\delta K}{Y} = (n+g+\delta)\frac{K}{Y} = (0.03+0.07)\cdot 2.3 = 0.23,$$

where we have assumed that GDP growth $(g+n)$ is 3 percent. This savings ratio is roughly in line with the savings and investment shares reported in Table 1.4.

5.4   The Golden Rule

We have assumed that the marginal product is always positive, so a country with a bigger capital stock in steady state will have higher production. But will an economy with more capital also have higher consumption? Not necessarily. To maintain a high capital stock is costly. Each year, a fraction of the capital stock depreciates and has to be replaced. Also, in order to keep the capital stock per effective worker constant we have to make investments so that the capital stock grows at the rate $g + n$. Therefore, maintaining a very high capital stock will be costly in terms of consumption. There is some level of capital that maximizes consumption in steady state. To find this level of capital, note that on a steady state growth path, the capital stock grows at the rate $g + n$, so the necessary investment is

$$I = \Delta K + \delta K = \frac{\Delta K}{K} K + \delta K = (n+g) K + \delta K = (n+g+\delta) K.$$

Therefore, consumption per effective worker is

$$\frac{Y}{EN} - \frac{I}{EN} = f(k) - (n+g+\delta) k.$$

The first term is the production obtained from the capital stock and the second is the gross investment needed in order to maintain that level of capital per effective worker. The capital stock that maximizes steady state consumption is found by taking the derivative with respect to k. This gives us

$$f'(k) = n + g + \delta.$$

To maximize steady state consumption, the capital stock should be increased until the marginal product of capital is equal to the sum of the population and technological growth rates and the depreciation rate. This rule is called the *Golden Rule*. Increasing the capital stock beyond this level will not increase consumption because the investment necessary to maintain additional units of capital per effective worker will exceed the additional production obtained from the higher capital stock.

The golden rule capital stock can be compared with the steady state capital stock that we will have in long-run equilibrium. It is determined by

$$\frac{f'(k)}{1+\mu} = \bar{r} + \delta,$$

where $\bar{r} = \rho + g$. Is this capital stock larger or smaller than the Golden Rule capital stock? If we set the mark-up to zero, we see that this depends on whether real return on capital, r, is larger or smaller than the real growth rate, $g + n$. Realistic numbers for rich countries may be that the real return on capital is 5–7 percent while the real growth rate is 2–3 percent. This means that the right-hand side is bigger in the market equilibrium, so the marginal product of capital is also higher. Since the marginal product falls as the capital stock increases, the capital stock must be smaller in the market equilibrium than it should be according to the Golden Rule. This conclusion is reinforced if we have a positive mark-up.

Thus we see that the capital stock is below the level which would maximize steady state consumption. Why? Don't we want to maximize long-run consumption? The answer is that consumers are impatient, so they discount future utility. Therefore, they do not save enough to reach the Golden Rule capital stock.

5.5   Why are some countries richer than others?

We now have a theory about the long-run level of income. Let us use it to try to understand income differences between countries. The column marked 'GDP per capita' in Table 5.1 shows real GDP per capita in a number of countries. The index is chosen so that GDP per capita in the US is equal to one. Put differently, the table shows GDP per capita *relative to the United States*. In the poorest countries, GDP per capita is only 2–6 percent of what it is in the US. For example, GDP per capita in Bangladesh is 5 percent of that in the US. This means that GDP per capita in the US is *20 times* higher than that of Bangladesh.

Considering the theory that we have just presented, the surprising thing is that income differentials between countries are so large and so persistent. After all, our theory tells us that, if a country has a small stock of capital initially, the marginal product of capital is high, so the incentives to invest and save are strong, and the country will grow quickly. If a country has a large capital stock initially, the return on investment is low, and less investment should be made. Hence, we would expect to see poor countries catching up with the rich countries. We should see a *convergence* of incomes.

As we will see in Chapter 12, the argument for convergence is even stronger when countries can borrow and lend from each other in international financial markets. Poor countries should be able to grow quickly, financing some of their investment by borrowing abroad. Investments in poor countries should be profitable since the return to investment should be high in countries with little capital per worker. But income differentials between different countries are enormous, and they have been large for a long time.

So why are there so large and persistent income differentials between countries? Let us look at the model again to see which factors can cause income differences in the long run. According to our model, the steady state levels of income per capita will differ between countries if there are differences in:

- the depreciation rate δ
- the degree of impatience ρ
- the degree of competition and mark-up μ
- the natural rate of unemployment u^n
- technology.

So, could differences in these parameters explain the long-run differences in incomes between countries?

It is hard to believe that depreciation rates or degrees of impatience differ greatly between countries. The degree of competition and the natural level of unemployment differ between countries, but the differences are too small to explain why the richest countries have 20 times higher income per capita than the poorest countries. This leaves 'technology' as the main explanation for income differentials. This conclusion is not very helpful, however, because E is just a factor capturing everything beyond capital and labour that may affect production possibilities.

Table 5.1 *Capital and GDP per capita*

Country	GDP per capita	Capital per capita	Schooling (years)	Predicted GDP/capita based on K	Predicted GDP/capita based on K and S	Capital Relative to GDP
USA	1.00	1.80	12.05	1.00	1.00	1.80
Norway	0.90	2.34	11.85	1.09	1.08	2.61
Canada	0.81	1.69	11.62	0.98	0.96	2.10
Denmark	0.80	1.71	9.66	0.98	0.84	2.14
Switzerland	0.79	2.19	10.48	1.07	0.96	2.76
Hong Kong	0.78	1.60	9.41	0.96	0.81	2.05
Ireland	0.76	0.98	9.35	0.82	0.68	1.29
Australia	0.76	1.58	10.92	0.96	0.89	2.06
Iceland	0.76	1.60	8.83	0.96	0.78	2.11
Japan	0.73	2.23	9.47	1.07	0.91	3.07
Netherlands	0.72	1.47	9.36	0.94	0.78	2.04
Belgium	0.70	1.53	9.34	0.95	0.79	2.18
Austria	0.70	1.65	8.35	0.97	0.76	2.37
Sweden	0.69	1.38	11.41	0.92	0.88	2.00
Finland	0.69	1.45	9.99	0.93	0.81	2.12
United Kingdom	0.68	1.19	9.42	0.87	0.73	1.75
Germany	0.67	1.56	10.20	0.95	0.85	2.32
France	0.66	1.52	7.86	0.94	0.72	2.29
Italy	0.64	1.40	7.18	0.92	0.67	2.17
New Zealand	0.56	1.15	11.74	0.86	0.85	2.04
Israel	0.54	1.17	9.60	0.87	0.74	2.17
Spain	0.53	1.16	7.28	0.86	0.63	2.16
Barbados	0.49	0.38	8.73	0.60	0.48	0.78
Portugal	0.48	0.96	5.87	0.81	0.54	1.99
Greece	0.44	0.91	8.67	0.80	0.64	2.08
Korea, Republic of	0.42	1.03	10.84	0.83	0.77	2.46
Mauritius	0.40	0.37	6.00	0.59	0.39	0.90
Trinidad &Tobago	0.39	0.36	7.76	0.58	0.44	0.93
Argentina	0.33	0.52	8.83	0.66	0.53	1.57
Hungary	0.31	0.62	9.13	0.70	0.58	1.99
Chile	0.29	0.43	7.55	0.62	0.46	1.49
Uruguay	0.29	0.33	7.56	0.57	0.42	1.14
Mexico	0.27	0.43	7.23	0.62	0.45	1.58
Poland	0.27	0.52	9.84	0.66	0.57	1.93
Malaysia	0.26	0.47	6.80	0.64	0.45	1.79
South Africa	0.23	0.20	6.14	0.48	0.33	0.90
Brazil	0.22	0.35	4.88	0.58	0.36	1.63
Turkey	0.21	0.33	5.29	0.57	0.36	1.56
Venezuela	0.20	0.32	6.64	0.56	0.39	1.58
Iran	0.20	0.28	5.31	0.54	0.35	1.41
Tunisia	0.20	0.22	5.02	0.50	0.31	1.09
Thailand	0.19	0.49	6.50	0.65	0.45	2.58
Panama	0.19	0.36	8.55	0.58	0.46	1.92
Algeria	0.17	0.25	5.37	0.52	0.33	1.43

(Table continues over the page)

Table 5.1 *(Continued)*

Country	GDP per capita	Capital per capita	Schooling (years)	Predicted GDP/capita based on K	Predicted GDP/capita based on K and S	Capital Relative to GDP
Costa Rica	0.16	0.22	6.05	0.49	0.33	1.32
Colombia	0.16	0.18	5.27	0.46	0.30	1.11
Dominican Republic	0.16	0.15	4.93	0.43	0.27	0.93
Romania	0.14	0.33	9.51	0.57	0.48	2.30
Paraguay	0.13	0.15	6.18	0.44	0.30	1.14
Peru	0.13	0.24	7.58	0.51	0.38	1.81
El Salvador	0.13	0.09	5.15	0.37	0.24	0.72
Egypt	0.12	0.06	5.51	0.32	0.21	0.48
Syria	0.12	0.10	5.78	0.38	0.25	0.80
Guatemala	0.12	0.08	3.49	0.36	0.20	0.69
Jordan	0.12	0.15	6.91	0.44	0.31	1.24
Philippines	0.11	0.15	8.21	0.44	0.34	1.32
Indonesia	0.11	0.16	4.99	0.45	0.28	1.43
China	0.11	0.14	6.36	0.43	0.29	1.31
Sri Lanka	0.11	0.11	6.87	0.40	0.28	1.03
Ecuador	0.10	0.18	6.41	0.46	0.32	1.72
Jamaica	0.10	0.19	5.26	0.47	0.30	1.95
Bolivia	0.08	0.08	5.58	0.35	0.23	0.92
India	0.08	0.07	5.06	0.33	0.21	0.88
Zimbabwe	0.07	0.11	5.35	0.39	0.25	1.46
Congo, Republic of	0.07	0.06	5.15	0.33	0.21	0.87
Cameroon	0.06	0.04	3.54	0.29	0.16	0.67
Honduras	0.06	0.08	4.80	0.36	0.22	1.37
Pakistan	0.06	0.05	3.88	0.31	0.18	0.89
Bangladesh	0.05	0.04	2.58	0.28	0.15	0.82
Senegal	0.05	0.03	2.55	0.25	0.13	0.60
Nepal	0.04	0.05	2.43	0.31	0.16	1.20
Lesotho	0.04	0.10	4.23	0.38	0.23	2.41
Ghana	0.04	0.02	3.89	0.23	0.14	0.58
Gambia, The	0.04	0.02	2.31	0.24	0.12	0.65
Kenya	0.04	0.03	4.20	0.25	0.15	0.78
Benin	0.03	0.02	2.34	0.23	0.12	0.60
Mozambique	0.03	0.01	1.11	0.17	0.08	0.30
Uganda	0.03	0.01	3.51	0.15	0.09	0.22
Mali	0.03	0.02	0.88	0.21	0.10	0.63
Rwanda	0.03	0.01	2.56	0.18	0.10	0.39
Togo	0.03	0.02	3.33	0.24	0.13	0.93
Niger	0.03	0.01	1.02	0.19	0.09	0.51
Zambia	0.02	0.03	5.46	0.25	0.16	1.24
Malawi	0.02	0.02	3.20	0.21	0.12	0.70
Guinea-Bissau	0.02	0.03	0.84	0.27	0.13	1.63
Tanzania	0.01	0.02	2.71	0.23	0.12	1.63

Sources: PWT 6.1, Alan Heston, Robert Summers, and Bettina Aten, Penn World Table Version 6.1, Center for International Comparisons of Production, Income and Prices at the University of Pennsylvania, October 2002, and Chang.-Tai Hsieh and Peter J. Klenow, 'Development accounting', *American Economic Journal: Macroeconomics*, 2 (2010), 207–223.

We can think of a number of additional factors that have not been explicitly included in the model:

- taxes on capital, law and order, and other factors that affect the return on investments
- the role of government in providing infrastructure that is complementary to private investment
- the level of education and experience of the workforce (human capital)
- access to technology
- natural resources and population density
- the efficiency of the economic and social system, which affects the way resources are utilized.

Can these factors help to explain the income differentials that we observe?

Differences in physical capital input

As we have seen, capital accumulation is a central aspect of growth. Could the large and persistent income differentials that we see between countries reflect differences in the incentives to accumulate capital?

In order to discuss this question, we need to ask what kinds of assets constitute the capital stock of a country. So far, we have thought of capital as machines, but what else should be included in the capital stock? When considering this issue, note that 'capital' in our model has the following characteristics:

- it is a *stock* that *contributes to production* of goods and services
- it is *produced* and can be increased by saving and investing
- it *depreciates*.

In our model we only have one homogenous capital stock, which is owned by the firms, but in practice there are many kinds of capital. Machines are clearly a good example, and so are industrial buildings and offices. Apartment buildings are part of the capital stock since they are needed to produce housing services, which are included in GDP. Privately owned houses are also part of the capital stock and an estimate of the hypothetical rent on such houses is included in GDP. Schools, hospitals, roads, railways, and telecommunication networks are also part of the capital stock.

Typically, different types of capital are *complements* to one another in production, so an increase in one type of capital will raise the marginal return on other types of capital. Improvements in communication systems, roads, and railways, for example, will raise the return on private investment and stimulate private capital accumulation. In most countries, the government plays a major role in the provision of communication systems, education, and health care.

Many factors can affect the incentives to accumulate capital. Taxes on capital income reduce the net return on investment and the long-run capital stock. Many poor countries suffer from corruption and lawlessness, so investors face substantial risk that the return on their investments will be appropriated by the government or the mafia. Such costs can be seen as a tax on investment,

Fig. 5.6 *The effect of higher capital taxes on the long-run capital stock*

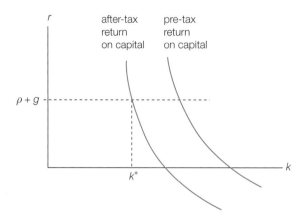

which reduces the long-run capital stock and the level of income in the country. The effect of capital taxation on the long-run capital stock is illustrated in Fig. 5.6. Differences in the incentives to accumulate capital might explain some of the long-run differences in capital stocks and incomes.

What proportion of the differences in GDP per capita across countries can be explained by differences in capital stocks? Let us use the Cobb–Douglas production function to examine this question. Production per worker is given by

$$\frac{Y}{N} = \frac{K^\alpha E^{1-\alpha} N^{1-\alpha}}{N} = K^\alpha E^{1-\alpha} N^{-\alpha} = \frac{K^\alpha}{N^\alpha} E^{1-\alpha} = \left(\frac{K}{N}\right)^\alpha E^{1-\alpha}.$$

Can this theory help us to understand why GDP per capita in India is 8 percent of what it is in the US? To see what our theory says, we apply the production function to the US and to India:

$$\frac{Y_{US}}{N_{US}} = \left(\frac{K_{US}}{N_{US}}\right)^\alpha E_{US}^{1-\alpha} \qquad \frac{Y_{India}}{N_{India}} = \left(\frac{K_{India}}{N_{India}}\right)^\alpha E_{India}^{1-\alpha}.$$

Here we have two equations – expressions where the left-hand side is equal to the right-hand side. This means that the ratio of the left-hand sides must be equal to the ratio of the right-hand sides of these two equations:

$$\frac{Y_{India}/N_{India}}{Y_{US}/N_{US}} = \frac{(K_{India}/N_{India})^\alpha \, E_{India}^{1-\alpha}}{(K_{US}/N_{US})^\alpha \, E_{US}^{1-\alpha}} = \left(\frac{K_{India}/N_{India}}{K_{US}/N_{US}}\right)^\alpha \left(\frac{E_{India}}{E_{US}}\right)^{1-\alpha}.$$

Differences in production per worker are explained by differences in capital per worker and differences in 'technology' E that reflect various unobserved factors. Let us see how large a part of the income difference between the US and India can be explained by differences in capital per worker. To simplify, we disregard variations in employment rates and assume that the number of workers is proportional to the population. We set $\alpha = 1/3$ in line with evidence that the capital share of income is around one third. The capital stock in the US is 1.8, or 1.8 times US GDP. The capital stock per capita India is 0.07 – about 4 percent of that in the US. Armed with these numbers we can calculate what GDP in India would have been if the only difference between the US and India had been that India has a lower capital stock per capita:

$$\frac{Y_{India}/N_{India}}{Y_{US}/N_{US}} = 0.04^{1/3} = 0.34.$$

GDP per capita in India would have been 34 percent of that in the US. As we see in Table 5.1, GDP per capita in India is about 8 percent of what it is in the US. Thus, the difference in capital input explains only part of the income differential between the US and India. Clearly, there must be other factors that are important; E is not the same for all countries.

The same problem occurs if we try to explain income differentials between other rich and poor countries. Column five in Table 5.1 shows the predicted level of GDP per capita according to the equation above for all the countries when we set E to match the numbers for the US. Fig. 5.7 illustrates how well this model explains the data. The curve shows predicted GDP per capita and the dots show the actual values for the different countries. The dot with K/N equal to 1.8 and Y/N equal to 1 is the observation for the US. Since we have chosen E to fit the US data, this observation is on the curve.

We see that there is a clear positive relation between the capital stock per capita and GDP per capita. Differences in capital stocks do account for some of the differences in production per capita. Yet most observations are far below the curve. Most countries are much poorer relative to the US than can be explained by differences in capital stocks per capita. Statistical analysis shows that differences in capital per worker can account for about 20 percent of the income differences between countries.[6]

Fig. 5.7 *Capital stock and GDP per capita*

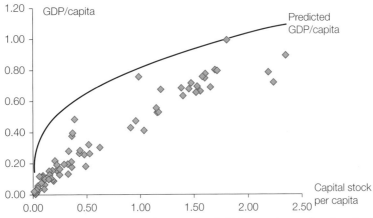

Note: GDP per capita in the US is set to 1.00. The curve shows predicted GDP per capita as a function of capital per capita with the technology factor set to match data for the US. The dots show actual data for different countries.

Sources: PWT 6.1, Alan Heston, Robert Summers, and Bettina Aten, Penn World Table Version 6.1, Center for International Comparisons of Production, Income and Prices at the University of Pennsylvania, October 2002, and Chang.-Tai Hsieh and Peter J. Klenow, 'Development accounting', *American Economic Journal: Macroeconomics*, 2 (2010), 207–223; and R. Barro and J-W. Lee, 2001, 'International data on educational attainment: updates and implications', *Oxford Economic Papers*, 53 (2001), 541–563.

---

6 See Chang-Tai Hsieh and Peter J. Klenow, 'Development accounting', *American Economic Journal: Macroeconomics*, 2 (2010), 207–223.

Differences in human capital[7]

Above, we discussed what it is that characterizes the capital stock. We noted that it is a stock that contributes to production, that is produced and can be increased by saving and investing, and that it also depreciates.

Education is not included in our standard measure of the capital stock, but in economic terms, education has many similarities with physical capital. Knowledge that workers have acquired contributes to production, and at any point in time this stock of knowledge is what it is. The level of education can be raised over time, but this requires input of labour and capital. Investments must be made in schools and universities, teachers must be hired, and students must spend long hours in the classroom and the library. Also, education depreciates as it becomes obsolete and people die taking with them the knowledge that they accumulated during their lifetimes.

Because of the strong similarity between physical capital and education, economists often use the term *human capital* to denote the level of education and experience in the labour force. Human capital is accumulated not only by formal education but also at home and at the workplace – so-called 'learning by doing'. Health care can also be seen as a form of investment in human capital. If the labour force is kept healthy, it will produce more than if many workers are handicapped by illness.

The part of human capital on which we have the best data is schooling. The column marked *schooling* in Table 5.1 shows estimates of the average years of schooling of the adult population in different countries. Fig. 5.8 shows the relation between schooling and GDP per capita. Again we see a positive relation. Differences in education can account for some of the income differentials between countries.

Let us try to take account of education in our theoretical model. We define the *productivity-adjusted labour force* as Nh where h is the human capital per worker. Suppose further that human capital is determined by

$$h = e^{\gamma S},$$

where S is schooling. The derivative of this function with respect to S is[8]

$$\frac{dh}{dS} = \gamma e^{\gamma S} = \gamma h,$$

so we have

$$\frac{dh/h}{dS} = \gamma.$$

---

7 This section is partly based on Peter J. Klenow and Andres Rodrigues-Claire, 'The neoclassical revival in growth economics: Has it gone too far?', *NBER Macroeconomics Annual* 12 (1997), 73–103; Robert E. Hall and Charles I. Jones, 'Why do some countries produce so much more output per worker than others?', *Quarterly Journal of Economics*, 114 (1999), 83–116; and David Romer, *Advanced Macroeconomics*, 4th ed. (Boston: McGraw Hill, 2012), Section 3.8.

8 Here we use the chain rule and the fact that the derivative of e^x is e^x.

Fig. 5.8 *Schooling attainment and GDP per capita*

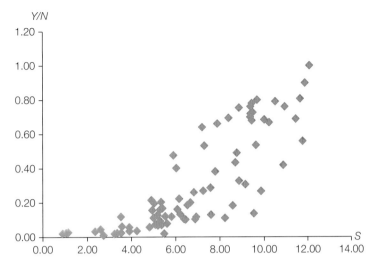

Sources: PWT 6.1, Alan Heston, Robert Summers, and Bettina Aten, Penn World Table Version 6.1, Center for International Comparisons of Production, Income and Prices at the University of Pennsylvania, October 2002, and Chang.-Tai Hsieh and Peter J. Klenow, 'Development accounting', *American Economic Journal: Macroeconomics*, 2 (2010), 207–223; and R. Barro and J-W. Lee, 2001, 'International data on educational attainment: updates and implications', *Oxford Economic Papers*, 53 (2001), 541–563.

We see that γ measures by how many percent an additional year of schooling increases the productivity of the typical worker. Economists have estimated the returns to schooling by comparing income levels of workers with different levels of schooling. The result is that an additional year of schooling raises productivity by about 10 percent. Based on such estimates we set $\gamma = 0.10$.[9] As before, we set $\alpha = 1/3$. We now have the production function

$$Y = K^{1/3} \left(ENe^{0.10S} \right)^{2/3}.$$

Average schooling in the US is 12 years and average schooling in India is 5 years. Following the same steps as above, we can obtain an expression for what GDP per capita would have been if E had been the same in India as in the US:

$$\frac{Y_{India}/N_{India}}{Y_{US}/N_{US}} = \left(\frac{K_{India}/N_{India}}{K_{US}/N_{US}} \right)^{1/3} e^{0.10(S_{India}-S_{US})2/3} = 0.04^{1/3} e^{0.10(5-12)2/3} \approx 0.21.$$

When we take account of differences in both physical and human capital we get the prediction that GDP per capita in India should be one fifth of what it is in the US. We have come closer to the 8 percent that we see in the data but there is still a large part that is unexplained.

9　If we assume that workers are paid in proportion to their marginal product, we can estimate the return to schooling by comparing wages of workers with different levels of education.

Fig. 5.9 *Predicted and actual GDP per capita based on capital and schooling*

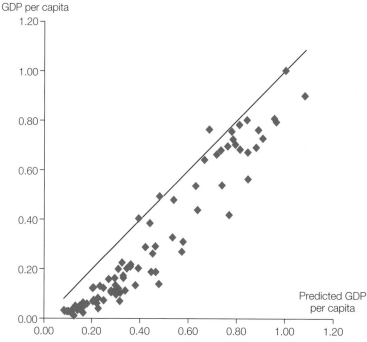

Sources: PWT 6.1, Alan Heston, Robert Summers, and Bettina Aten, Penn World Table Version 6.1, Center for International Comparisons of Production, Income and Prices at the University of Pennsylvania, October 2002, and Chang.-Tai Hsieh and Peter J. Klenow, 'Development accounting', *American Economic Journal: Macroeconomics*, 2 (2010), 207–223; and R. Barro and J-W. Lee, 2001, 'International data on educational attainment: updates and implications', *Oxford Economic Papers*, 53 (2001), 541–563.

Column 6 in Table 5.1 shows predicted GDP per capita using this equation. These numbers show how well our production function explains income differentials when we take account of differences in both physical and human capital. In Fig. 5.9 we have the predicted GDP per capita on the horizontal axis and actual GDP per capita on the vertical axis. If the model explained income differences perfectly, all dots would be on the 45-degree line. Almost all dots are below the line, however. The poorest countries, in particular, are far below the line: the poor countries are much poorer than one would predict based on differences in physical capital and schooling.

Calculations along these lines have led researchers to the conclusion that about 20 percent of the income differences that we observe between countries can be explained by differences in physical capital and another 10–30 percent can be explained by differences in human capital. Taken together, observed differences in physical capital and human capital explain at most 50 percent of income differentials.[10] Our theory takes us some way towards an understanding of income differentials, but clearly there are other factors that are important.

10 For a review of the literature, see Chiang-Tai Hsieh and Peter J. Klenow, 'Development accounting', *American Economic Journal: Macroeconomics*, 2 (2010), 207–223.

With the production function above, a substantial part of the income differentials that we see must be attributed to differences in 'technology', E. In fact, E is a residual representing everything that we cannot observe. It may be technology, but also other factors that we have omitted in our theory.

Access to technology

If we interpret E in a narrow way as technology the question arises why not all countries have access to the same technology. One can argue that technological knowledge should be easy to transfer between countries. The blueprints (recipes) for how you produce many goods are generally available. But of course there are also barriers that limit the transfer of knowledge. In order to use modern technological knowledge, workers and managers need to have adequate education. Also, a lot of know-how is transferred from one employee to another in an informal way. New technological knowledge may be protected by patents, or kept secret within companies. Firms in poor countries may not have access to such know-how.

On the other hand, even if technological know-how is kept private, the company with that know-how could still profit from the lower level of wages in a poor country by moving production to a subsidiary in the poor country. In fact, multinational companies do this to a great extent, but there are costs of setting up production abroad and companies may worry that their intellectual property rights will not be respected if the judicial system functions poorly. Thus, poor countries may not have access to the same technological possibilities as rich countries.

Natural resources

One argument, which is sometimes made, is that poor countries are poor because they are overpopulated. This argument makes no sense in our model because the production function has constant returns to scale in capital and labour. In the long run, the capital stock will adjust to the size of the population so that all countries have the same capital stock, and the same production, per worker.

To make sense of the overpopulation argument, we must introduce some natural resource such as land into the production function. Suppose that we have the following production function:

$$Y = K^\alpha Z^\lambda (EN)^{1-\alpha-\lambda},$$

where Z is land, which we take as a fixed factor which, contrary to capital, cannot be produced. Dividing by N we get production per capita:

$$\frac{Y}{N} = \left(\frac{K}{N}\right)^\alpha \left(\frac{Z}{N}\right)^\lambda E^{1-\alpha-\lambda},$$

where $\lambda > 0$. Now, production per capita depends not only on the capital stock but also on the amount of land per capita. A country with little land per capita will be poorer and a country with much land will be richer.

In practice, however, agriculture constitutes a small share of the economy in rich countries. As we saw in Chapter 1, production in agriculture constitutes only 1–3 percent of GDP in the richest countries. Also, differences in population density help very little in explaining differences in income per capita. Argentina, Brazil, Kenya, and Zaire have 10–25 persons per square kilometre, while Belgium, Japan, and Holland have 320–360 persons per square kilometre. Clearly, the high incomes of the latter cannot be explained by abundant access to land.[11]

The same argument applies to other natural resources. They play a small role in most rich countries. The dominating sectors in modern economies are industry and services. Raw materials are needed to produce goods, but raw materials can be transported between countries. Japan and most European countries have few natural resources. Many countries in Africa are poor although they are rich in natural resources. Natural resources help to explain why *some* countries are rich, particularly some oil-producing countries, but they contribute little in explaining the overall picture of income differentials across the world.

'Institutions'

So far, we have largely discussed income differentials in terms of differences in resources and production possibilities, assuming that available resources are always used in the most efficient way. We have assumed that firms always produce as much as they can with the amount of capital and labour that they have. But the real world is much more complicated than our simple model, with many different goods and services being produced and complicated relations between firms producing inputs and final products. Another source of income differentials between countries is that resources are used more or less efficiently in different countries because of differences in economic systems.

Economists use the term *institutions* as a summary term for the political and social structures that constitute the framework for economic decision-making. These 'institutions' include laws, political systems, organizations, and less formal rules of behaviour in a society. The perfectly competitive market is an institution which, under certain conditions, leads to a socially efficient outcome, but real economic systems are far from this idealized model. There are many factors that may lead individuals to pursue activities, which are privately profitable but socially inefficient. Economists use the term *rent-seeking* for such activities.

We have already discussed some examples of rent-seeking. Firms in our model have monopoly power and exploit this power by raising prices above the marginal cost. As we have seen, monopoly power reduces the return to investment in physical capital and the long-run level of production. The socially efficient solution would be to set the price equal to marginal cost. Many poor countries suffer from heavy regulation, which limits competition. This means that a large part of income goes to pure profits and the return on investment is reduced.

Similar inefficiency may arise in the labour market. When unions compete with each other, trying to raise the wages of their members more than other unions,

---

11 This argument follows Mancur Olson, 'Big bills left on the sidewalk: Why some countries are rich and others poor', *Journal of Economic Perspectives*, 10:2 (1996), 3–24.

the result is a high natural rate of unemployment. This reduces production both directly, because fewer persons work, and indirectly, since the long-run capital stock will also be lower. The labour market will be analysed in depth in Chapter 6.

Other sources of inefficiency are crime, corruption, and lawlessness. As we discussed above, these factors impose a form of tax on investment. If there is a substantial risk that someone will steal your assets, or it is necessary to pay bribes, this reduces the expected return on investments. Investment will be lower and the long-run level of the capital stock will be lower. We may think of these factors as raising the required return on investment by adding a margin to the subjective rate of discount. Equally important, crime and corruption will lead to *inefficient* investment since individuals prefer to save in assets that are easy to hide and protect, even if they are not very productive. Money that is saved may be used to buy gold or put in a foreign bank account.

Government policies are very important for growth. Law and order and a judicial system that enforces contracts in an impartial way are central prerequisites for a well-functioning market economy. Investments in transport and communication systems are complementary to private investment. If the government does not make those investments, the return on private investment will be lower, so there will also be less private investment, and it will be invested in a less efficient way than it could have been.

Also, the government typically plays an important role in organizing and financing education, especially for younger children. One reason is that children cannot finance their educational investments on their own. Not all children have rich parents who can pay for education, so it is often necessary that the state provides the education, or gives loans to students, so as to achieve an efficient level of investment in human capital.

Unfortunately, government policies can also be detrimental to growth. If government regulation makes it difficult to start new firms, or to enter new markets, this will reduce competition. Heavy taxes on capital income deter investment. In many countries, the government is a rent-seeker itself. Dictators and corrupted bureaucrats grab what they can from private investors in the form of bribes, fees, and taxes. But the expectation that this will happen stalls investment and the investment that does take place is channelled abroad or into assets with a low social return.

In practice it is hard to measure and identify the effects of the above discussed 'institutional' factors, but much research is currently being carried out on this. Two striking examples, which prove that institutional differences can be very important, are Germany and Korea. Both these countries were divided into two parts in the mid-20th century. One part introduced a socialist planned economy and the other had a capitalist market economy. Background factors such as the educational level, natural resources, culture, and historical background were very similar for the two parts. The results of these 'experiments' were clear and striking: income increased much faster in the part that had a market economy. This difference cannot be explained by differences in investments in physical and human capital. In fact, socialist economies had very high investment ratios and they were rather successful in raising the level of education. Yet GDP per capita lagged far behind in those countries. These examples are extreme but they do point to the important role of institutional factors.[12]

5.6   Are poor countries catching up?

We have seen that there are large income differences between rich and poor countries and we have discussed factors that could explain those differences. But are those income differentials increasing or decreasing? Are we in a transitory phase where poor countries are catching up with the rich countries or are the poor countries lagging further behind? The answer is that some poor countries are catching up while others are doing very poorly.

Fig. 5.10 shows PPP-adjusted GDP per capita in 1980–2009 for European market economies – we have excluded countries such as Poland and Hungary, which were socialist planned economies during part of the period.[13] We have also excluded countries with less than 3 million inhabitants in year 2000 and those with missing data. From this figure, it is not easy to see whether income levels are converging or diverging.

Fig. 5.10 *GDP per capita in 1980–2009, 17 European market economies*

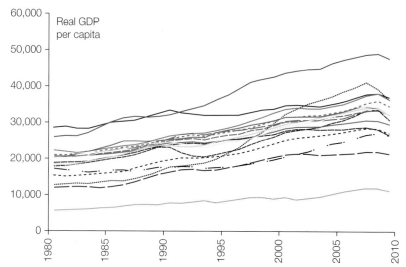

Note: GDP, PPP (constant 2005 international $). PPP GDP is gross domestic product converted to international dollars using purchasing power parity rates. An international dollar has the same purchasing power over GDP as the US dollar has in the United States. Data are in constant 2005 international dollars.
Source: World Bank, International Comparison Program database.

---

12   Mancur Olson points to this example in 'Big bills left on the sidewalk: Why some countries are rich and others poor', *Journal of Economic Perspectives*, 10:2 (1996), 3–24.

13   Socialist planned economies are excluded because the theory presented in this book is a theory of a market economy. We would expect the growth process to be quite different in a planned economy. Also, data are missing in many cases, and when data are available the comparison is less reliable.

Fig. 5.11 *GDP per capita in 1980 and growth 1980–2009, European market economies*

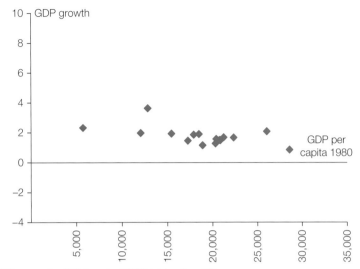

Note: GDP per capita, PPP (constant 2005 international $).
Source: World Bank, International Comparison Program database.

A better way to see if poor countries are catching up is to plot average growth rates in 1980–2009 against GDP per capita in 1980, as is done in Fig. 5.11. We have put GDP per capita 1980 on the horizontal axis and the average growth rate in 1980–2009 on the vertical axis. If countries that initially had a high level of income grew relatively slowly between 1980 and 2009, the dots further to the right should be lower down than the dots further to the left. In fact, we see some indications of convergence among European market economies. Turkey, Portugal, and Ireland, which were relatively poor in 1980, have had relatively high growth rates in the period 1980–2009. Switzerland, which was the richest country in 1980, had relatively low growth.

Fig. 5.12 shows very clearly that the Asian countries are catching up. Many Asian countries were very poor in 1980 but they have had high growth rates since. So when we look at the data for European market economies and for Asia, we see clear indications that poor countries are catching up.

Fig. 5.13 shows a similar diagram for the Americas. The income difference between the US and Canada and the other countries is very big and there are no obvious signs that the gap is diminishing. Some Latin American countries have been catching up but others have had a poor growth performance.

Most African countries were also very poor in 1980, but with respect to growth we see a very mixed picture in Fig. 5.14. In some African countries, GDP per capita has grown 2–4 percent per year, but others have had very low and even negative growth – some of the countries in Africa have become poorer rather than richer. On the whole, there are no clear signs that poor African countries were catching up in this period.

Looking across the world, we see that some poor countries have been catching up, but many have remained poor. In Fig. 5.15, we have included data for all

Fig. 5.12 *GDP per capita in 1980 and growth 1980–2009, Asia and Australia*

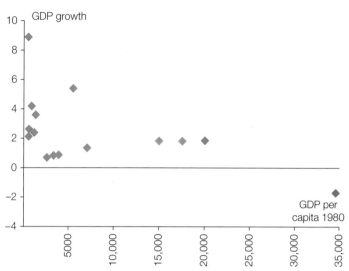

Note: GDP per capita, PPP (constant 2005 international $).
Source: World Bank, International Comparison Program database.

Fig. 5.13 *GDP per capita in 1980 and growth 1980–2009, North and South America*

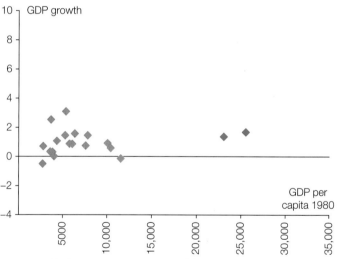

Note: GDP per capita, PPP (constant 2005 international $).
Source: World Bank, International Comparison Program database.

the countries included in Figs. 5.10–5.14 above. A striking feature of Fig. 5.15 is that all countries which had more than 3 percent growth in GDP per capita were countries which started with a relatively low level of income. This observation supports the idea that poor countries have the potential to catch up, but that only some countries are able to utilize this potential.[14]

---

14 See Mancur Olson, 'Big bills left on the sidewalk: Why some countries are rich and others poor', *Journal of Economic Perspectives*, 10:2 (1996), 3–24, for an argument along these lines.

Fig. 5.14 *GDP per capita in 1980 and growth 1980–2009, Africa*

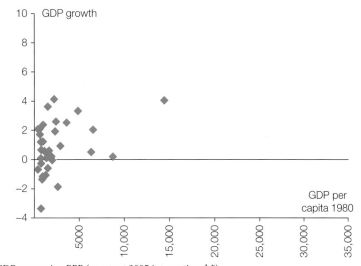

Note: GDP per capita, PPP (constant 2005 international $).
Source: World Bank, International Comparison Program database.

Fig. 5.15 *GDP per capita in 1980 and growth 1980–2009, all countries*

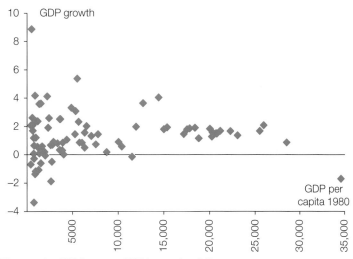

Note: GDP per capita, PPP (constant 2005 international $).
Source: World Bank, International Comparison Program database.

5.7   What determines technological development?

According to the theory presented here, accumulation of physical capital will, sooner or later, run into diminishing returns, and there is a limit to how much schooling can be increased. Therefore, the long-run growth of per capita income is primarily determined by the growth of the technology factor (E). So far, we have taken the growth rate of technological knowledge as exogenous. But what determines the speed of technological development? One line of research tries to understand the nature of technological progress. Sometimes, this strand of research is called *endogenous growth theory* because it tries to make long-run growth endogenously determined.[15]

Let us think of E as knowledge. The development of new knowledge requires labour and other resources. A simple way to make the growth of knowledge endogenous is to introduce a sector for research and development (R&D) in the model. Assume, for simplicity, that this sector uses only labour and that the role of the R&D sector is to increase the technology factor according to the following 'production function':

$$\Delta E = a N_R^v E^\theta.$$

N_R is the number of workers employed in the R&D sector. The parameter a reflects the productivity of the R&D sector and we assume that the parameters v and θ are positive. The parameter θ measures how useful existing knowledge is when producing new knowledge. The basic idea here is that we use labour and knowledge to produce new knowledge, so the more knowledge we have, the more easily we can produce new knowledge. It is hard to imagine someone inventing the car before the engine had been invented, or the laptop being invented before the mainframe computer.

A key characteristic of knowledge is that it is a *non-rival* good. Many firms can use the same knowledge at the same time. In the model just outlined, E is used both in the production of goods and services and in the production of new knowledge. Also, technological knowledge can be transferred between countries. Therefore, it does not make sense to think of the production of knowledge as occurring separately in different countries, isolated from each other. Instead, we may think of the production function above as describing the production of knowledge in the world as a whole.

To simplify our analysis, we assume that the world population is constant and that a fraction λ of the workers in the world work in the R&D sector. Then, the growth rate of E is

$$g = \frac{\Delta E}{E} = a (\lambda N)^v E^{\theta-1}.$$

Here we see that if $\theta = 1$ the growth rate of E is constant and equal to

$$g = a (\lambda N)^v.$$

Production in this economy is determined by the same production function as before, with a fraction $1 - \lambda$ of the workers producing goods and services, so on the steady state growth path we have

$$Y = f(k^*) E (1 - \lambda) N.$$

Since k^* is constant and determined by the same condition as above, income will also grow at the rate g.

---

15 Models of endogenous growth were developed by Paul Romer, Robert Lucas, Gene Grossman and Elhanan Helpman, and Phillippe Aghion and Peter Howitt in papers published around 1990. See references in note 16 below for more thorough overviews of this literature.

The basic lesson from this model is that the more people we assign to do R&D, the higher the growth rate will be – forever! Long-run growth is truly endogenous and can be affected by policy. A subsidy, or tax advantage, that is given to R&D activity will raise the share of the workers working in R&D and the long-run growth rate.

In this model, knowledge, E, is *produced* just as physical capital, K, is produced, but there is a fundamental difference between the stock of knowledge and the stock of physical capital. Investment in physical capital cannot, by itself, generate long-run growth because of diminishing returns when labour input is fixed. If a large share of the workers produce machines, this will raise the long-run *level* of production, but for a given technology, growth will stop at some point because there won't be any workers to use additional machines. But if $\theta = 1$, the production of knowledge is characterized by *constant returns in terms of knowledge itself.* The production of new ideas does not run into diminishing returns. Therefore, more resources to R&D can raise the growth rate forever.

This model says that any policy that promotes R&D will raise the rate of growth forever. This conclusion is based on the assumption that θ is exactly equal to unity. But how plausible is that? Is there any reason to believe that θ is equal to unity? Recall that our basic argument for constant returns to scale in the production of goods and services was the idea of replication. If we have a factory that produces a certain number of cars with a certain number of workers and machines, we should be able to put up an identical factory beside it. This would lead to a doubling of both inputs and output. But there is no similar argument for why θ should be exactly unity. In fact, this is very unlikely.

So what happens if θ differs from unity? If $\theta > 1$, growth is explosive: the more knowledge we have, the more quickly the economy will grow for a given input of labour in R&D. Explosive growth is not what we see in the data.

The more plausible case is that $\theta < 1$ – that is, it becomes progressively harder to increase the stock of knowledge when all the easy inventions have already been made. Then, for a constant λ and N, growth will eventually slow down. Put differently, more and more workers must be put into R&D if E is to increase at a constant rate. In fact, this case is more in line with what we observe. The fraction of resources that is put into R&D has been increasing over time, yet the growth rate has been fairly constant in advanced economies. Apparently, growth is becoming more and more expensive in terms of real resources. Expenditure on R&D is a small fraction of GDP, so it may continue to grow, but it cannot grow forever. Therefore, we should expect growth to eventually slow down.

But one factor counteracts this tendency. In the analysis above we assumed a constant population. With a growing population, the *number* of workers doing research will increase even if the proportion of workers doing research remains constant. Because of the growing number of researchers, there will be some growth even if $\theta < 1$. What we see in the world today is that more and more countries are participating in research and development. A growing number of researchers help to extend the technological frontier, and this should help to maintain worldwide growth.

In this section, we have only touched very briefly on theory that makes technological development and growth endogenous. There has been much interesting research on growth in recent decades and we could easily spend the rest of the book covering growth theory. We will not do that but leave growth and move on to other topics. There are several books which cover growth in much more depth than we have been able to do here.[16]

What have we learned?

In high-income countries, gross investment is about 20 percent of GDP. The capital stock is just over twice as large as yearly GDP and the depreciation rate is around 7 percent, so depreciation is about 15 percent of GDP. This means that net investment is about 5 percent of GDP and that the capital stock grows about 2.5 percent per year, roughly in line with GDP.

The *effective number of workers* is the number of workers, N, multiplied by the technology factor, E. With constant returns to scale, production per effective worker is a function of capital per effective worker:

$$\frac{Y}{EN} = F\left(\frac{K}{EN}, 1\right) = f(k) \qquad \text{where} \qquad k = \frac{K}{EN}.$$

The *steady state* is a situation where the economy grows but capital per effective worker and production per effective worker are both constant, so

$$K = k^* EN \qquad \text{and} \qquad Y = f(k^*) EN.$$

Using the rule of thumb for growth rates, we see that the capital stock and GDP grow at a rate equal to the population growth rate plus the rate at which technology improves:

$$\frac{\Delta K}{K} = \frac{\Delta Y}{Y} = n + g.$$

On the steady state growth path, the capital stock per effective worker is such that the real marginal revenue product of capital minus the depreciation rate equals the real interest rate:

$$\frac{f'(k^*)}{1+\mu} - \delta = \bar{r}.$$

The real interest rate is equal to the subjective rate of discount plus the growth of production per worker:

$$\bar{r} = \rho + g.$$

A higher willingness to save and invest (a lower subjective rate of discount) leads to higher long-run levels of capital and production in the country but

---

16 For a more thorough analysis of the issues that we have touched upon here, see David N. Weil, *Economic Growth* (Boston: Pearson, 2012); C. Jones, *Introduction to Economic Growth* (New York: Norton, 2002); or Romer, *Advanced Macroeconomics*. A general discussion is found in Gregory Mankiw, 'The growth of nations', *Brookings Papers on Economic Activity*, 1 (1995), 275–326.

saving alone cannot generate long-run growth because the marginal product of capital decreases as we add more capital with a given number of workers. For GDP to grow in the long run we need population growth and/or technological development.

The *Golden Rule* says that, to maximize steady state consumption, the capital stock should be increased until the marginal product of capital is equal to the sum of the population and technological growth rates and the depreciation rate:

$$f'(k) = n + g + \delta.$$

Increasing the capital stock beyond this level will not increase consumption because the investment necessary to maintain additional units of capital per effective worker will exceed the additional production obtained from the higher capital stock. In practice, the capital stock is below the golden rule level.

Observed differences in physical capital and education (human capital) can explain about 50 percent of the income differentials between countries, but income differences are much larger than can be explained by these factors alone. Other factors such as political and social structures clearly play important roles. Examples of such 'institutions' are tax systems, law and order, and the degree of corruption.

Since 1980, some poor countries have been catching up, with high growth rates, but many others have remained poor.

If it becomes progressively harder to improve the technology, more and more workers must be put into R&D if technology is to improve at a constant rate. In fact, there has been fairly constant growth of GDP per capita around 2 percent in the most advanced economies, but the cost of growth has increased as a larger proportion of the resources have been put into research and development.

Where do we go from here?

As we have seen in this chapter, the level of employment is an important determinant of income. If fewer persons work, the level of income will be lower. Also, unemployment is an important social problem. So far, we have taken the rate of unemployment as given. In the next chapter we try to understand why there is unemployment in a market economy and what factors affect the level of unemployment.

Exercises

1. Consider the production function:
   $Y = \sqrt{KN}$.
   a) What will production be if $K = 10$ and $N = 40$?
   b) What will production be if $K = 20$ and $N = 80$?

   c) Compare the results above and explain the relation between production in the two cases.

2. Consider a country that has no population growth and where there is no technological development. The capital stock is on the

steady state level. Then a substantial part of the capital stock is destroyed by an earthquake. Fortunately, very few people die in the earthquake.

a) Illustrate what happens in a diagram with the capital stock on the horizontal axis and the real rate of return on the vertical axis.

b) Draw diagrams with time on the horizontal axis to illustrate what happens over time with the capital stock, investment, the real interest rate, and production.

3. Do the same analysis as above assuming that 15 percent of the capital stock is destroyed and 5 percent of the working-age population dies.

a) Illustrate what happens in a diagram with the capital stock on the horizontal axis and the real rate of return on the vertical axis. What is the long-run effect on the capital stock and production?

b) Draw diagrams with time on the horizontal axis to illustrate what happens over time with the capital stock, investment, the real interest rate, and production.

4. Let us add working time to the model and assume that the production function is

$$Y = F(K, EHN)$$

where H is working time.

a) What is now the condition determining the steady state capital stock per effective worker?

b) Suppose a law is passed that reduces working time by 5 percent. How does this affect the steady state capital stock if the natural rate of unemployment remains unchanged?

c) Consider a country that has no population growth and where there is no technological development. The capital stock is on the steady state level. Draw diagrams with time on the horizontal axis to illustrate what happens over time with the capital stock, investment, the real interest rate, and production after the reduction in working time.

5. The theory presented in this chapter predicts that, under certain conditions, GDP per capita should converge. In the long run, all countries should have the same GDP per capita. Explain the intuition behind this result.

6. What, in your judgement, is the most important reason why countries have not converged to the same level of income per capita?

7. According to the theory presented here, there should be a higher real return on loans in a growing economy. Explain this result.

8. Should the government subsidise research and development (R&D)? (*Hint: Are there any externalities or other market failures?*)

9. Should the government subsidise education?

10. Suppose that there was no depreciation of capital. How would this affect

a) the levels of the capital stock and production?

b) the growth rates of the capital stock and production?

11. Suppose the tax on capital is raised. Illustrate the effects on the capital stock and production in the long and the short run.

12. The first-order condition (Euler equation) for consumption is

$$\frac{U'(C_t)}{U'(C_{t+1})/(1+\rho)} = 1 + r_{t+1}.$$

a) Explain this condition.

b) Find an expression for the long-run real interest rate if the utility function is the natural log function $U(C_t) = \ln C_t$ and if technology grows at the rate g. What will the real interest rate be if $\rho = 0.03$ and $g = 0.03$?

c) Suppose that the real (net) return is taxed at the rate τ. How will this affect the required return on investment? What will the real interest rate be if $\rho = 0.03$, $g = 0.03$ and $\tau = 0.3$?

d) Suppose that the mafia extracts a fraction λ of the *gross* real return on investments. How will this affect the required return on investment? What will the required return on investment be if $\rho = 0.03$, $g = 0.03$ and $\lambda = 0.10$?

13. In this chapter we found an expression for the steady state level of production per person in the labour force:

$$\frac{Y}{L} = \sqrt{\frac{1/3}{(1+\mu)(\bar{r}+\delta)}} \cdot 1000 \cdot (1-u).$$

Assume that $\mu = 0.10$, $\delta = 0.06$, $u = 0.10$, and $E = 1000$. Calculate steady state production for the three levels of the required return that you calculated in the previous exercise. Explain the result.

14. In view of the above analysis, is it a good idea to tax capital income?

15. An intensive training program makes the workers 5 percent more efficient. How will this affect GDP in the short and the long run?

16. Sudden immigration increases the labour force by 5 percent. How will this affect the capital stock and production in the short and the long run?

Answers to the exercises can be found at:
www.palgrave.com/economics/gottfries.

Appendix

Growth accounting

When we look at the growth experience of different countries, we may ask what it was that generated growth and why growth has differed between countries. We can use the production function to analyse this question. A simple accounting exercise allows us to decompose growth into three parts, generated by growth of capital, growth of labour input, and improved technology. We start from the Cobb–Douglas production function

$$Y = K^\alpha E^{1-\alpha} N^{1-\alpha}$$

and take natural logarithms on both sides

$$\ln Y = \alpha \ln K + (1-\alpha)\ln E + (1-\alpha)\ln N.$$

Suppose now that K, E, and N change over time. Then the change in log production will be

$$\Delta \ln Y = \alpha \Delta \ln K + (1-\alpha)\Delta \ln E + (1-\alpha)\Delta \ln N.$$

Since changes in natural logs are approximately equal to relative (percentage) changes we get

$$\frac{\Delta Y}{Y} \approx \alpha \frac{\Delta K}{K} + (1-\alpha)\frac{\Delta E}{E} + (1-\alpha)\frac{\Delta N}{N}.$$

The growth of output, capital, and labour input can all be observed. The growth in E cannot be observed, but if we believe in the production function, we can calculate the contribution of technology to economic growth:

$$(1-\alpha)\frac{\Delta E}{E} = \frac{\Delta Y}{Y} - \alpha\frac{\Delta K}{K} - (1-\alpha)\frac{\Delta N}{N}.$$

The effect of changes in 'technology' is calculated as a residual, known as the *Solow residual*. The Solow residual is a catch-all residual which captures all income growth that is not due to increases in capital and labour. For a typical rich country, GDP and the capital stock may increase 2.4 percent per year, and there is close to zero population growth. Setting $\alpha = 1/3$ we get

$$Solow\ residual = 0.024 - \frac{1}{3} \cdot 0.024 = 0.024 - 0.008 = 0.016 = 1.6\ \text{percent}.$$

Of the 2.4 percent growth that we observe from one year to the next, 1.6 percent is due to improved technology and 0.8 percent is due to capital accumulation. As we saw in our analysis of steady state growth, capital accumulation is ultimately driven by technological progress, however.

The Solow growth model

In the mid 1950s the American economist Robert Solow analysed growth in a somewhat different model.[17] He made the simplifying assumption that *consumers always save a constant fraction s of their income*:

$$C = (1-s)\,Y.$$

Consumption is assumed to be independent of the interest rate, and the effects of asset holdings and expectations about future incomes are also disregarded. The assumption of a constant savings rate was inspired by observations made by the Belarussian economist Simon Kuznets (active in the US) who had gathered national accounts data for long periods and many countries. Kuznets had found that savings were a relatively stable share of income.[18]

Solow considered an economy which cannot borrow from the rest of the world, so investment is equal to savings:

$$I = Y - C = Y - (1-s)\,Y = sY = sF\,(K, EN)\,.$$

Fig. 5.16 *The consumption function when savings are a constant share of income*

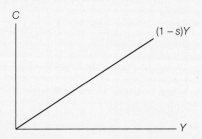

17 Robert M. Solow received the Nobel Prize in 1987 'for his contributions to the theory of economic growth'.
18 Simon Kuznets received the Nobel Prize in 1971 'for his empirically founded interpretation of economic growth which has led to new and deepened insight into the economic and social structure and process of development'.

Fig. 5.17 *Convergence to steady state in the Solow growth model*

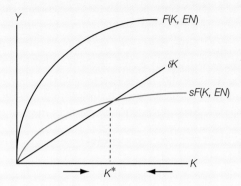

If population (employment) and technology are constant, the capital stock will change over time according to

$$\Delta K = sF(K, EN) - \delta K.$$

The first term on the right-hand side is gross investment (saving) and δK is the investment required to maintain the capital stock. If we start with a low level of capital, savings will be higher than depreciation so the capital stock increases. If we start from a high level of capital, depreciation will exceed savings and the capital stock will decrease. In the long run, the economy converges to long-run equilibrium where the capital stock does not grow, $\Delta K = 0$, and where savings are just sufficient to cover depreciation:

$$sF(K, EN) = \delta K.$$

We get convergence to a long-run equilibrium, or 'steady state', just as in the Ramsey model presented in the main text. The reasoning is somewhat different, however. Rather than focusing on the marginal return on investment and the real interest rate, as we did in the Ramsey model, we now focus on the quantities *savings* and *depreciation*. If we start with a low capital stock, the capital stock will increase because savings exceed depreciation. There will be growth in the transition period, but in the long run we end up with a constant capital stock and zero growth. Like the Ramsey model, the Solow growth model also predicts that, with constant returns, the long-run capital stock will be proportional to the number of workers in the country.

We can analyse an increase in savings in the Solow model. If consumers start to save a larger part of their income, the curve $sF(K, EN)$ will shift up and we see immediately that the steady state capital stock will increase. So we end up with the same conclusion as before. An increase in the propensity to save (thrift) will lead to a period of growth and the economy will end up with a higher capital stock and higher income per capita, but growth will stop eventually. The reason is the same as in the Ramsey model: the marginal product of capital decreases for a given amount of labour. To get long-run growth, we must have population growth and/or a continuous improvement in technology.

One reason why we focus on the Ramsey model in the main text is that it is easier to apply to the open economy. As we saw in Chapter 1, firms and households in the open economy can borrow from and lend to the rest of the world, so savings need not be equal to investment. As we will see in Chapter 13, savings often differ substantially from investment in open economies.

6 WAGE–SETTING AND UNEMPLOYMENT

Why is there always unemployment in a market economy?

Unemployment seems to be an unavoidable characteristic of a market economy. The problem of unemployment is a matter of constant concern and debate. High unemployment means that fewer individuals are working, so production is lower than it could be. Unemployment is a source of poverty and inequality. Why is there always unemployment in a market economy? Why is unemployment higher in some countries and lower in other countries? Why is unemployment so much higher today than it was in the 1960s?

In this chapter we study some reasons why there is normally excess supply of workers – that is, more workers who want to work than there are jobs available. The theory presented here is a theory of the average rate of unemployment over the business cycle. Economists usually call this rate the 'long-run equilibrium' rate of unemployment or the 'natural' rate of unemployment. In the short run, unemployment may be higher or lower than this level; such deviations are called 'cyclical' unemployment. Cyclical unemployment will be discussed when we look at the analysis of short-run fluctuations in Chapters 8 and 9.

We start by showing some descriptive labour market statistics and explaining the relations between stocks and flows in the labour market. Then we formulate a simple model of worker turnover and wage-setting and we show that it may be efficient for firms to set wages above the market clearing level, so that demand for workers is lower than supply. This theory is a version of the so-called the *efficiency wage theory* of unemployment.

Then we discuss the *matching* process whereby workers and firms find suitable matches. We show that the willingness and ability of unemployed workers to compete for jobs affects the equilibrium rate of unemployment in the economy. We also analyse the roles of *unions*, *minimum wages*, and *skill-biased technical change*. We ask why unemployment differs between countries and why, in most countries, unemployment is higher today than it was in the 1960s. We end with a look at data for flows in and out of unemployment and long-term unemployment.

The problem of unemployment is not simple to analyse. The labour market is a complicated market and different parts of the labour market work in different ways. However, economic theory can give us some understanding of why there is normally unemployment in a market economy, and which factors can affect the level of unemployment.

6.1   Stocks and flows in the labour market

Many of the data for the labour market come from *labour force surveys.* In these surveys a random sample of individuals are asked if they worked at least one hour in the previous week. If they did, they are counted as *employed.* The self-employed, people on holiday or on sick leave from their current job are also counted as employed, as well as members of the armed forces. If the individual did not work, is currently available for work, and is seeking work, the person is counted as *unemployed.* 'Seeking work' means that the person took specific steps to seek work, such registering at an employment office, applying for work, contacting employers, or answering newspaper advertisements. Individuals preparing to become self-employed, students seeking work, and individuals who have found a job but not yet started on it are also counted as unemployed.

Employed and unemployed workers taken together constitute the *labour force.* People who do not work and also do not actively seek work are counted as *outside the labour force.* These individuals may be studying, retired, or taking care of the home or children. Some are unable to work because of health problems. Some workers say that they want a job but do not actively seek work. Such workers are called *discouraged workers.* Since they do not search actively, these workers do not count as unemployed; hence they are outside the labour force.

At any point in time, a person is employed, unemployed, or outside the labour force. Employment, unemployment, and the number of workers outside the labour force are the key *stock variables*, which describe the state of the labour market. But it is not the same persons who are employed, unemployed, or outside the labour force all the time. Instead, there are large *flows of workers* between the different states. There are not only flows between employment and unemployment, but also turnover between jobs and flows in and out of the labour force. In order to understand how the labour market functions, it is important to understand these flows. We start this chapter with a quick look at some data describing stocks and flows in the labour market.

Employed, unemployed, and outside the labour force

Fig. 6.1 shows shares of the whole population of men, 15–64 years old, who were *unemployed, outside the labour force,* and the sum of those, which we will call *not employed.* These stocks are all measured in percent of all men in this age group, so the sum of the share that is outside the labour force and the share that is unemployed is the share that is not employed. In 2008, the share of men that was not employed was 12 percent in Iceland and 37 percent in Hungary. In most countries, between 20 and 30 percent of the men were not employed. Of those not employed, the great majority are outside the labour force – that is, they are not actively seeking work.

As seen in Fig. 6.2, the share of men aged 15–64 that do not work has increased over time. A primary reason why fewer men aged 15–64 work today is the increased length of time spent in education.

If we look at the data for the US, we see that the share outside the labour force follows a relatively stable trend. Most of the short-run fluctuations in employment

Fig. 6.1 *Not employed, not in the labour force, and unemployed, percent of the population of men aged 15–64, 2008*

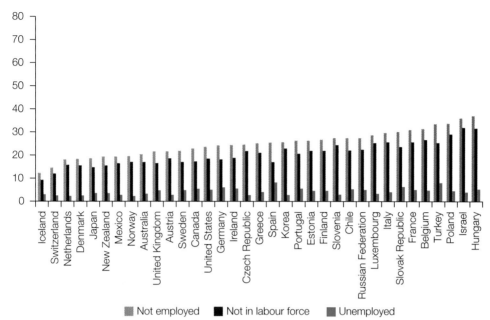

Source: *OECD Employment and Labour Market Statistics*, OECD, 4 April 2011, http://www.oecd-ilibrary.org/statistics.

are associated with fluctuations in unemployment rather than with variations in the numbers outside the labour force. In the recessions in 1975, 1982, 1992, 2002, and 2008, the share of men not working increased, and most of this increase was due to an increase in unemployment rather than workers leaving the labour force. Workers who actively seek work are more likely to remain unemployed when there is low demand for workers. The cycles in employment are associated with movements between employment and unemployment rather than movements between employment and being outside the labour force.

Looking at the data for the other countries included in Fig. 6.2 we see again that fluctuations in employment are primarily associated with movements of workers between employment and unemployment. Sharp increases in employment mean falling unemployment, but in those countries we also see some cyclical variation in labour force participation. When unemployment increases, some individuals leave the labour force – they stop actively looking for work. This was particularly clear in connection with the Swedish and Finnish financial crisis in 1991–1993. When the labour market was weak, some individuals chose to study instead of looking for jobs. Some workers gave up looking for jobs when there were few jobs available and became *discouraged workers*. Another factor that may contribute to this pattern, especially in Sweden, is active labour market policy, which has meant that some of those who lose jobs in a recession go into retraining programmes. This means that they are counted as outside the labour force.

Fig. 6.3 shows that labour force participation by women differs much more between countries. The share not employed varies from 20 percent in Iceland to

Fig. 6.2 *Not employed, not in the labour force, and unemployed, percent of the population of men aged 15–64*

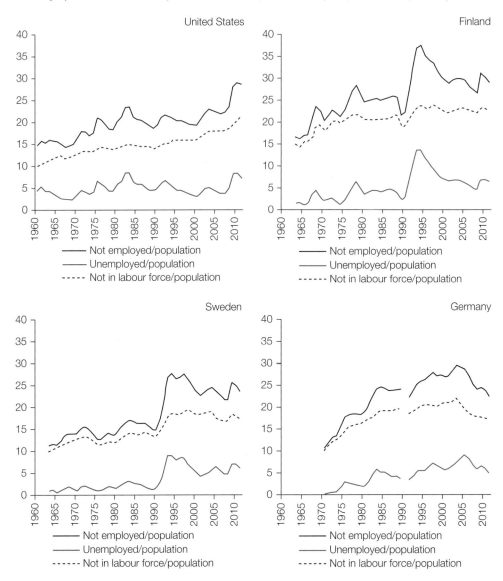

77 percent in Turkey. The great majority of women who do not work are outside the labour force – that is, they are not actively seeking work.

Fig. 6.4 shows that women in the countries shown work to a much greater extent than they did some decades ago. In Sweden and Finland, however, this trend was reversed as financial crises hit these countries in the early 1990s.

Many of the differences in labour force participation have to do with the length of education, whether students work while they are studying, retirement ages and pension systems, and whether women participate in the labour market or concentrate on household work. These are interesting issues to study, but we will not do so in the present chapter. Thus we shall not analyse workers' decisions whether

Fig. 6.2 *(Continued)*

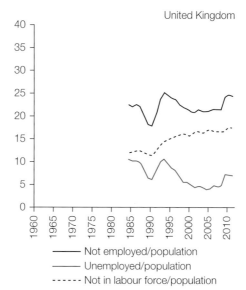

Note: The data for Germany before 1990 is data for West Germany.
Source: *OECD Employment and Labour Market Statistics*, OECD, 10 July 2012, http://www.oecd-ilibrary.org/statistics.

Fig. 6.3 *Not employed, not in the labour force, and unemployed, percent of the population of women aged 15–64, 2008*

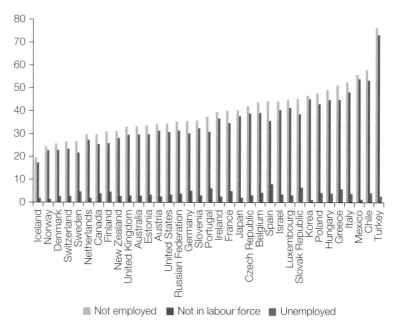

Source: *OECD Employment and Labour Market Statistics*, OECD, 4 April 2011, http://www.oecd-ilibrary.org/statistics.

Fig. 6.4 *Not employed, not in the labour force, and unemployed, percent of the population of women aged 15–64*

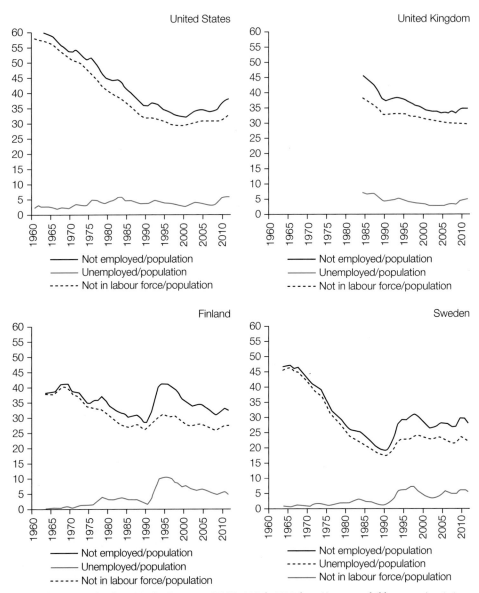

Source: *OECD Employment and Labour Market Statistics*, OECD, 10 July 2011, http://www.oecd-ilibrary.org/statistics.

or not to seek work. Instead, we will take the labour force as exogenous and focus on wage formation and unemployment. Why are workers who actively seek work sometimes unable to find a job? To understand this, it is important to understand the relations between stocks and flows in the labour market.

Unemployment as a percentage of the labour force

Normally, unemployment is measured as a percentage of the labour force, and that is what we will do in this book. The following notation will be used:

N employment, the number of persons who work

U unemployment

$L = N + U$ the labour force

$u = \dfrac{U}{L} = \dfrac{L-N}{L}$ unemployment as a share of the labour force

For the UK, for example, data for 2008 for all persons aged 15–64 were as follows:

$$L = 30.4 \text{ million}, \quad N = 28.8 \text{ million}, \quad U = L - N = 1.6 \text{ million}$$

$$u = \frac{U}{L} = \frac{1.6}{30.4} = 0.054 = 5.4 \text{ percent.}$$

Thus, the unemployment *rate* in the UK was 5.4 percent. Fig. 6.5 shows unemployment rates for men and women as a percentage of the labour force for different countries in 2008. There are large differences. Unemployment rates were above 10 percent in Spain and Turkey, while Switzerland and Denmark had unemployment rates between 2 and 4 percent. In most countries, unemployment as a share of the labour force was somewhat higher for women than for men, but in most cases the difference is not dramatic.

Flows

In most countries, between 4 and 8 percent of individuals in the labour force are unemployed, but it is not the same people who are out of work all the time. Instead, there is substantial turnover in the labour market. There are not only

Fig. 6.5 *Unemployment, percent of the labour force, men and women aged 15–64*

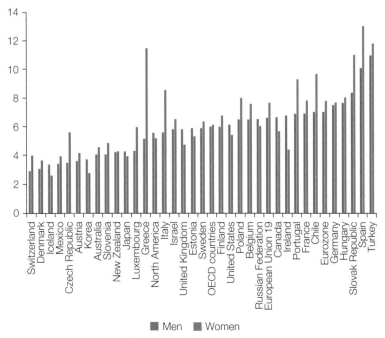

■ Men ■ Women

Source: *OECD Employment and Labour Market Statistics*, OECD, 18 April 2011, http://www.oecd-ilibrary.org/statistics.

Fig. 6.6 *Labour market flows*

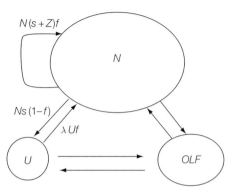

Note: The notation is explained in Section 6.2. N is employment, U is unemployment and OLF is the stock of workers outside the labour force. The probability to find a job is f for an employed job seeker is and λf for an unemployed job seeker. A share Z of the employed workers seek another job and switch if they find one. A fraction s of the employed workers leave their jobs for exogenous reasons and seek another job. Thus the flow from unemployment to employment is $\lambda U f$, the turnover between jobs is $N(s+Z)f$, and the flow from employment to unemployment is $Ns(1-f)$.

flows between employment and unemployment, but also directly between jobs and in and out of the labour force. Some employed workers are involuntarily laid off, but more often workers leave their jobs voluntarily, often going directly to another job. Fig. 6.6 illustrates the flows between the different stocks in the labour market. The notation for the different flows will be explained in the next section.

The magnitudes of these flows vary between countries. In the US, the flows are large. Estimates suggest that, each month, 2.6 percent of employed workers switch directly from one job to another without going through a period in unemployment and 1.5 percent of the employed workers become unemployed.[1] Also, about 2 percent of the employed workers leave the labour force and a similar number enter the labour force, going directly into jobs. This means that about 6 percent of employed workers leave their jobs each month $(2.6+1.5+2=6.1)$.

The flow from unemployment to employment is similar to the flow in the reverse direction – 1.5 percent of employment. With an unemployment rate that is normally around 6 percent in the US, this means that each month about a quarter of the unemployed workers find jobs.[2] Another 12 percent of the unemployed workers leave the labour force, that is, they stop seeking work, so the exit rate from unemployment is about 37 percent $(25+12$ percent$)$.

In most European countries, the flows are smaller. For Germany, Michael Burda and Charles Wyplosz (1994) report flows that imply that 0.3 percent of the employed workers switch directly from one job to another, 0.8 percent

---

1 These numbers for the US are taken from Olivier J. Blanchard and Peter A. Diamond, 'The cyclical behavior of the gross flows of US workers', *Brookings Papers on Economic Activity*, 2 (1990), 85–143 and Eran Yashiv, 'Labor search and matching in macroeconomics', *European Economic Review*, 51 (2007), 1859–1895.

2 $\dfrac{0.015 \cdot N}{0.06 \cdot L} = \dfrac{0.015}{0.06} \cdot \dfrac{N}{L} = \dfrac{0.015}{0.06} \cdot 0.94 \approx \dfrac{1}{4}.$

become unemployed, and 0.6 percent leave the labour force each month.[3] Thus about 1.7 percent of employed German workers leave their jobs each month $(0.3 + 0.8 + 0.6 = 1.7)$. The chance that an unemployed worker finds a job is 8 percent, and 4 percent of the unemployed workers leave the labour force each month, giving an exit rate from unemployment of only 12 percent. Because of differences in data collection methods, these numbers are not perfectly comparable to the numbers for the US, but they do suggest much smaller flows in Germany.

The flows in the UK are in-between those for Germany and the US. For example, Simon Burgess and Helene Turon report an exit rate from unemployment equal to 19 percent.[4]

6.2 A model of turnover and the job-finding rate

In our theory of turnover and wage-setting, we disregard flows in and out of the labour force.[5] To capture the flows between jobs and between employment and unemployment in a simple way, we assume that, each month, a share s of the employed workers leave their jobs for exogenous reasons, for example because they were laid off for some reason or the worker decided to quit because he became tired of the job. We assume that these workers apply for another job and if they do not get one, they become unemployed.

As we have just seen, there are substantial flows of workers between jobs, and to capture this we assume that a share Z of the employed workers look for another job, and quit if they get another job. Thus we have:

s the share of employed workers who apply for other jobs and leave, independently of whether or not they find another job

Z the share of employed workers who apply for other jobs and quit if they find one.

With these assumptions, what is the chance that an unemployed worker gets a job? To analyse this in a simple way, let us consider a situation where employment and the labour force are constant. Assume that employed and unemployed job seekers have the same chance of getting a job, and denote this probability by f. To see what determines this probability we need to know the number of job openings and the number of job seekers.

- How many job openings are there each month? The number of job openings left by those who leave for exogenous reasons is $N \cdot s$. The number of job openings left by those who quit only if they get another job is $N \cdot Z \cdot f$. Thus, the total number of job openings is $Ns + NZf$.

3   Michael Burda and Charles Wyplosz, 'Gross worker and job flows in Europe', *European Economic Review*, 38 (1994), 1287–1315.
4   Simon Burgess and Helene Turon, 'Unemployment dynamics in Britain', *Economic Journal*, 115 (2005), 423–448.
5   Inclusion of those flows does not change the analysis if the flows in and out of the labour force are treated as exogenous. Then it just means that some employed and unemployed workers are exogenously replaced by workers from outside the labour force.

● How many workers are seeking a job? The workers seeking work consist of the workers unemployed at the beginning of the month, U, plus those who quit exogenously, $N \cdot s$, plus those searching on the job, $N \cdot Z$. Thus, the total number of workers seeking a job is $U + sN + NZ$.

The chance that a job seeker finds a job is the number of job openings divided by the number of job seekers:

$$f = \frac{Ns + NZf}{U + Ns + NZ}.$$

If we multiply by $(U + sN + NZ)$ on both sides and multiply f into the parenthesis we see that the term $N \cdot Z \cdot f$ cancels out and we get $fU + fNs = Ns$. Thus we get

$$f = \frac{Ns}{U + Ns}.$$

The share Z disappeared from the expression because every employed worker who switches jobs leaves one job opening and takes another. Turnover between jobs does not leave any job openings for unemployed workers. The expression for f can be approximated as follows:

$$f = \frac{Ns}{U + Ns} = \frac{s}{\frac{U}{N} + s} = \frac{s}{\frac{U}{L}\frac{L}{N} + s} \approx \frac{s}{u + s},$$

where u is the unemployment rate U/L. This approximation holds because L/N is a number close to unity. We use the approximation because it is intuitive and easy to remember. The chance of getting a job is equal to the share of jobs being left by those who leave their jobs for exogenous reasons divided by the share of job seekers – that is, the unemployed plus those who leave their jobs for exogenous reasons. The chance of getting a job decreases if unemployment increases and increases if there is higher turnover. If, for example, s is 2 percent and u is 6 percent, the chance of getting a job within a month is approximately 25 percent ($0.02/(0.02 + 0.06)$). If, instead, s is 1 percent and u is 9 percent, the chance of finding a job within a month is only about 10 percent ($0.01/(0.09 + 0.01)$).

We have shown a relatively obvious result: the higher the unemployment rate, the lower is the chance to find a job – for unemployed workers and for workers searching on the job. To complete our theory of the labour market, we need to examine the relation between unemployment and wage formation.

6.3 A model of wage-setting and unemployment

So far, we have presented data and a model of turnover and the job-finding rate. These relations say nothing about how the level of unemployment is determined. In order to analyse this, we need to analyse wage-setting and labour demand. We first consider a situation without unions or government regulation, in which firms are free to set wages as they want.

So how do firms set wages? One may think that firms would always want wages to be as low as possible, but firms compete with other firms for workers. As we have just discussed, there is high turnover in the labour market. Many workers quit their jobs each year, and firms want to keep their good workers. Turnover is costly for firms for several reasons. Workers' leaving can cause disruptions in production, and firms have to recruit and train new workers when experienced workers quit. Also, new and inexperienced workers may make mistakes and this is also costly for the firm.

Workers' decisions whether or not to look for alternative jobs depend on many factors. There are many personal factors that affect an individual worker's decision to switch jobs, but the wage is an important factor. A firm that sets a very low wage will lose a lot of workers because the workers will look for other jobs and leave as soon as better opportunities arise. For this reason, it is not optimal for the firm to set a very low wage compared with what other firms offer. This would lead to very high turnover and costly disruptions in production. The firm has to balance the cost savings from a lower wage against the increase in turnover cost that comes with a lower wage.

For this reason, it may not be desirable for the firm to cut the wage even if there are unemployed workers outside the factory gate ready to work for a lower wage. A wage above the market clearing level can be efficient from the firm's point of view. This so-called *efficiency wage theory* explains why there is always unemployment in a market economy.[6]

To analyse this more rigorously, we first analyse the wage-setting problem of the firm. Then we show that when firms set wages so as to maximize profits, there will be excess supply in the labour market – that is, unemployment. We rely on graphic exposition; a mathematical formulation can be found in the appendix to this chapter.

On-the-job search, turnover of workers, and wage-setting

As was mentioned above, we assume that a share Z of the workers want to switch jobs and are looking for another job, but they only quit if they find another job. To capture the idea that turnover depends on the wage, we assume that this share depends on the wage that the firm pays relative to the average wage in the economy. This is captured by the following function:

$$Z_i = Z\left(\frac{W_i}{W}\right).$$

Z_i is the share of workers in firm i searching on the job, W_i is the wage in firm i and W is the average wage level in the economy. In this analysis, we can take the period to be one month so Z_i is the share of workers searching on the job in a particular month and W_i is the monthly wage. Working time per worker is taken to be exogenous.

The function Z is a decreasing function, so the higher the wage, the lower the share of the workers that want to switch jobs. This function is illustrated in Fig. 6.7.

---

6 Here we focus on the relation between wages and turnover but there are also other versions of efficiency wage theory, which are discussed below. The labour turnover model was developed by Joseph Stiglitz, Ekkehart Schlicht and Steven Salop in the 1970s.

Fig. 6.7 *The share of workers looking for another job*

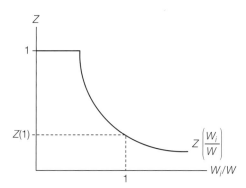

If the firm sets as a very low wage, all the workers will look for another job so $Z(W_i/W) = 1$. As the wage increases, the share of workers looking for another job falls and the function flattens out because the share cannot go below zero.

Implicit in this function is an idea that workers are heterogeneous. Some may like the job at a particular firm better than others. If the firm sets a high wage, only those workers who are very dissatisfied will look for another job. Another implicit assumption is that the firm cannot observe the degree of satisfaction of individual workers and adjust the wage so as to keep each individual worker that it wants to keep.

Now consider the wage-setting problem of the firm. We use N_i for the number of workers employed in firm i. The direct wage cost is $W_i \cdot N_i$. We assume that there is also a *hiring and training cost* $h \cdot W$ which the firm has to pay if it hires a worker. This cost is assumed to be proportional to the general wage level in the economy. If, for example, $h = 3$, the hiring cost corresponds to three times the average monthly wage.

We now consider long-run equilibrium with constant employment for each firm, so the firm replaces all workers who leave. This means that the firm has a turnover cost equal to

$$TC_i = h \cdot W \cdot \left[s + Z(W_i/W) \cdot f \right] \cdot N_i.$$

As before, s is the share of employees leaving their job for exogenous reasons and f is the probability of getting a new job for those searching on the job. We see that if the firm pays a higher wage, this will reduce turnover costs because fewer workers will look for another job. If the general wage level increases, more workers will look for other jobs and the turnover cost increases. Finally, if the chance of getting a job increases, this will mean that more workers will quit, so turnover costs increase.

The firm's cost per worker is the direct wage cost plus the turnover cost per worker:

$$W_i + h \cdot W \cdot \left[s + Z(W_i/W) \cdot f \right].$$

Independent of how many workers the firm employs, the firm should set the wage that *minimizes* the total labour cost for having those workers employed. A higher wage has two effects on the total labour cost. On the one hand, a one dollar wage increase raises the direct wage cost per worker by one dollar. On the other hand, a higher wage reduces turnover and the costs associated with the recruitment and training of new workers. A very low wage will lead to extremely large turnover costs. A very high wage will make the wage bill very high. The firm has to set a wage that strikes a balance between minimizing wage costs and minimizing turnover costs.

This problem is illustrated in Fig. 6.8. The horizontal axis measures the wage set by the individual firm i and the vertical axis measures wage and turnover costs per worker. The direct wage cost is simply the wage and represented by the upward-sloping line. The turnover costs TC_i decrease with the wage. If the wage is very high, workers are very happy to stay, and only few workers quit and have to be replaced. The total labour cost is the sum of these two costs and it is shown as a u-shaped curve. The firm's optimal wage is the wage that *minimizes* the total cost per worker.

This theory shows why wages need not fall even if there is unemployment. Although there are unemployed workers ready to work for a lower wage, the firm may not find it profitable to reduce the wage. If the firm were to do that, then the increase in turnover costs would be larger than the amount saved by reducing the wage.

Now consider an improvement in the labour market situation – that is, a decrease in unemployment. As we saw in the previous section, $f \approx s/(u+s)$ so if unemployment falls, it becomes easier to find a job. An increase in the chance of finding a job increases turnover costs, so the TC curve shifts up. As we see in Fig. 6.9, this will increase the firm's optimal wage: now the wage that minimizes the total labour cost is further to the right.

Fig. 6.8 *The labour cost per worker*

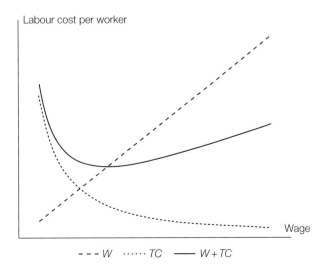

Labour cost per worker

Wage

$---W$ $\cdots\cdots TC$ $\longrightarrow W+TC$

Fig. 6.9 *The effect of a higher job-finding rate on the labour cost per worker*

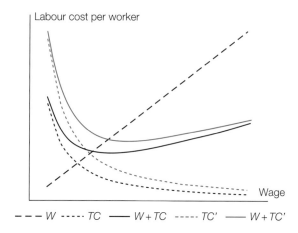

Fig. 6.10 *The equilibrium rate of unemployment*

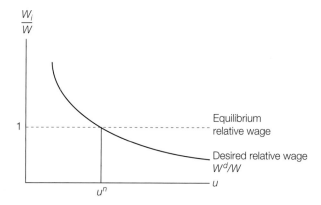

Fig. 6.10 shows the desired relative wage as a function of unemployment. The higher unemployment is, the lower is the firm's desired relative wage. If there is high unemployment, the firm is less worried about losing good workers, and hence it will set a lower wage. If unemployment falls to a low level, firms want to raise their wages so as to retain their workers.

The natural rate of unemployment

To determine the equilibrium level of unemployment we use the idea of the 'typical' firm. We assume that all firms have the same turnover costs. If there is high unemployment, all firms want to reduce their relative wages, so wages fall. If unemployment is low, all firms want to raise their relative wages, so wages increase. In long-run equilibrium, the level of unemployment must be such that the typical firm has no incentive to overbid or underbid the others – that is, the desired relative wage is unity. The only level of unemployment where firms are satisfied with their relative wage is the unemployment rate denoted u^n in Fig. 6.10.

This equilibrium rate of unemployment is called the *natural rate of unemployment*. It is an equilibrium level because no firm has incentive to change its relative wage when unemployment is on this level.

The notion of a natural or long-run equilibrium rate of unemployment was developed by the US economists Edmund Phelps and Milton Friedman in the late 1960s. The name 'natural rate' alludes to Knut Wicksell's notion of a natural rate of interest.[7]

The wage-setting equation

We can summarize this theory of unemployment and wage-setting in the form of a *wage-setting equation* relating the desired wage, W^d, to unemployment, u, and the average wage level W:

$$W^d = (1 + a - bu) W,$$

where a and b are constants with positive values. This equation says that if unemployment is high (so that bu is bigger than a) firms want to set a wage below the average wage level, and if there is low unemployment, firms want to raise wages above the average wage level. If unemployment is zero, for example, firms want to set the wage $(1 + a) W$. In the long-run equilibrium, the desired wage must be equal to the average wage and for this to be the case unemployment must be at the natural level. Setting $W^d = W$ and solving for unemployment we find an expression for the natural rate of unemployment:[8]

$$u^n = \frac{a}{b}.$$

Any factor that shifts up the wage-setting equation will increase the coefficient a and the natural rate of unemployment. We can rewrite the wage-setting equation in a more intuitive way:

$$W^d = (1 + a - bu) W = W - b \left(u - \frac{a}{b} \right) W = W - b (u - u^n) W.$$

This equation shows that, if unemployment is above the natural rate, firms desire to set a wage below the average wage level, and if unemployment is below the natural rate, firms desire to set a wage above the average wage level. We can also formulate this as a dynamic wage equation showing desired wage increases over time. To do this we write the wage equation

$$W^d_t = W_t - b (u_t - u^n) W_{t-1}.$$

The reason why we multiply the last term in this equation by the wage level in the previous period rather than the current wage level is just for mathematical

---

7 Another name is 'structural unemployment'. Milton Friedman received the Nobel Prize in 1976 'for his achievements in the fields of consumption analysis, monetary history and theory and for his demonstration of the complexity of stabilization policy'. Edmund S. Phelps received the Nobel Prize in 2006 'for his analysis of intertemporal tradeoffs in macroeconomic policy'. A classic paper is Milton Friedman, 'The role of monetary policy', *American Economic Review*, 58 (1968), 1–17.

8 Setting $W^d = W$ and dividing by W we get $1 = 1 + a - bu$. Subtracting 1, adding bu on both sides and dividing by b we get the result.

convenience. It does not affect our qualitative conclusions. Subtracting W_{t-1} on both sides and dividing by W_{t-1} we get an equation for the desired wage increase:

$$\frac{\Delta W_t^d}{W_{t-1}} = \frac{\Delta W_t}{W_{t-1}} - b(u_t - u^n).$$

Here $\Delta W_t^d / W_{t-1}$ is the desired wage increase and $\Delta W_t / W_{t-1}$ is the average wage increase. This equation says that if unemployment is higher than the natural level, firms want to raise wages less than the average wage increase. For the desired wage increase to be equal to the average wage increase, unemployment must be at the natural level. We will use this equation when we study short-run wage adjustment and inflation in Chapter 9.

The natural level of employment and the real wage

The relation between unemployment and employment is found as follows:

$$N = L - U = \left(1 - \frac{U}{L}\right)L = (1 - u)L.$$

Thus we can define the *natural level of employment* as

$$N^n = (1 - u^n)L.$$

When employment is higher than N^n it is easy to find a job, turnover is high, and firms have the incentive to raise wages more than other firms. In the short run, nominal wages are rigid, but, over time, wage inflation will increase and employment will fall. Conversely, if employment is below the natural rate, unemployment is high, wages tend to rise less quickly, and employment increases. Therefore, the only employment level which is consistent with constant wage increases is the natural level of employment N^n.

Why do high wage increases lead to lower employment? We will study the mechanism in more detail when we come to the short-run analysis in Chapters 8–9 and 14. In an economy with a floating exchange rate, the basic mechanism is that higher wage increases lead to higher inflation, so the central bank of the country will raise the interest rate in order to counteract inflation. A high interest rate has a negative effect on consumption, investment, and aggregate demand and production, so firms hire fewer workers.

In a country that is a member of a monetary union, high wage increases compared with wage increases abroad lead to loss of competitiveness and a reduction in exports. Either way, high wage increases will have negative effects on employment. If employment is above the natural level, wages will increase until employment is brought back to the natural level and wage increases are stabilized at an appropriate level.

But how is the real wage determined? To find the real wage, recall the price-setting equation that we derived in Chapter 2:

$$P = (1 + \mu)\frac{W}{MPL}.$$

Fig. 6.11 *Supply and demand in the labour market*

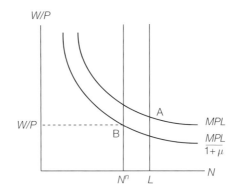

From this equation we get the real wage

$$\frac{W}{P} = \frac{MPL}{1+\mu}.$$

Fig. 6.11 illustrates the determination of employment and the real wage for a given capital stock. With perfect competition in goods and labour markets, we would have full employment and the real wage would be equal to the marginal product of labour at full employment. This means that we would be at point A. Since there is monopolistic competition in the product market, and unemployment in the labour market, we are instead at point B. The real wage is lower because firms price with a mark-up over marginal cost and employment is lower because a higher level of employment would lead to wage inflation.[9]

This analysis suggests a number of factors that influence the long-run level of unemployment. Any factor that tends to increase wages will raise the level of unemployment. If hiring and training becomes more costly (h increases) unemployment will increase. High exogenous quits (s) and high on-the-job job search (S) also increase the level of unemployment.

The theory presented here is a version of the *efficiency wage theory* of unemployment. This theory explains why there will always be some unemployment in a free market economy even if firms are free to set wages as they please. Although there are unemployed workers willing to work, firms will not cut wages to the point where there is no unemployment and workers are indifferent between having and not having the job because this would lead to high turnover.

There are other versions of efficiency wage theory, with similar implications. One version puts emphasis on workers' effort, pointing to the fact that an employer's surveillance of their employees' work is less than perfect. This means that workers can shirk, putting in less effort than is expected of them. If the firm pays a good wage, workers have the incentive to do a good job so as to keep the job rather than running the risk of losing it if they are discovered to be shirking.

---

9 The vertical line at the natural level of employment can be seen as a 'wage-setting line'. To the left of this line, there is downward pressure on wages, and to the right of the line, wages will rise. The curve showing $MPL/(1+\mu)$ can be seen as a price-setting curve. It shows the real wage that follows from the price-setting behaviour of firms.

Another reason to pay good wages is to be able to recruit and retain good workers. When workers differ in productivity, a low wage will make it hard for the firm to recruit and retain the best workers. In the words of Richard Layard, Stephen Nickell, and Richard Jackman, the idea of efficiency wage theory is that firms choose a wage policy so as to 'recruit, retain and motivate' the workers.[10] Some economists have tried to 'test' theories of the labour market by asking managers what arguments are relevant to their wage-setting. Such surveys have generally found strong support for various versions of the efficiency wage theory.[11]

The efficiency wage theory gives us one explanation of why the labour market is in disequilibrium, with more workers wanting to work than there are jobs available. There are several other factors that affect wage-setting and unemployment. In the following sections we discuss *matching problems, unions, minimum wages,* and *skill-biased technical change.*

6.4   Matching problems and search incentives

So far, we have discussed the labour market as if all workers had the same productivity in all jobs and there were no costs involved for the employee in searching for jobs. In practice, there is a lot of heterogeneity in the labour market. Each job has its specific characteristics and requirements, and each worker has his specific education and experience. Workers and firms may fit together more or less well – the *match* between an individual worker and a specific job may be more or less good. Also, workers have imperfect information about which jobs are available and firms have imperfect information about what workers are available. For these reasons, it takes time for workers to locate jobs and for firms to make contact with workers. There is a complicated *matching process* going on in the labour market where firms try to find suitable workers and workers try to find suitable jobs.

Once we think about this matching process, we realize that unemployed workers play an active role in this process and that their behaviour will affect their chances of getting a job. Unemployed workers do not just sit there, waiting for a job, nor do they apply for every available job opening. Rather than applying for any available job anywhere in the country, unemployed workers will wait for a suitable job opportunity which is not too far away from home and where they can use their competence and get an acceptable wage. The decision as to which jobs to apply for will be affected by economic incentives. An important factor here is the level of unemployment benefits. With generous unemployment benefits, workers can afford to wait for a good opportunity to arise. If unemployment benefits are low,

10 For reviews and discussions of efficiency wage models, see Richard Layard, Stephen Nickell, and Richard Jackman, *Unemployment: Macroeconomic Performance and the Labour Market* (Oxford: Oxford University Press, 1991), ch. 3; George A. Akerlof and Janet L. Yellen (eds.), *Efficiency Wage Models of the Labor Market* (Cambridge: Cambridge University Press, 1986), and David Romer *Advanced Macroeconomics*, 4th ed. (New York: McGraw Hill Irwin, 2012).

11 See, for example, Jonas Agell and Per Lundborg, 1995, 'Theories of pay and unemployment: survey evidence from Swedish manufacturing firms', *Scandinavian Journal of Economics*, 97 (1995), 295–307, and Carl. M. Campbell and Kunal S. Kamlani, 'The reasons for wage rigidity: evidence from a survey of firms', *Quarterly Journal of Economics*, 112 (1997), 759–789.

unemployed workers who have no funds of their own may have to take the first job that they can get.

A simple way to include this in our model of the labour market is to assume that, effectively, a proportion λ of the unemployed workers search for jobs. This proportion can represent several things:

1. It can represent *search effort*. If unemployed workers spend little time searching, the effective number of unemployed workers searching is low.
2. It may represent the *choosiness* of the unemployed workers. If the unemployed workers apply for fewer jobs, the chances of their getting a job are lower.
3. Also, it can capture the *ability* of unemployed workers to compete for jobs. Some of the unemployed workers may have lost skills so they cannot effectively compete for some of the jobs.

In short, we can think of λ as representing the *willingness and ability* of the unemployed workers to compete for the jobs. When a proportion λ of the unemployed workers search effectively for jobs, the chance for an employed worker of finding a job is

$$f = \frac{s}{\lambda u + s}$$

and the chance for an unemployed worker of finding a job is λf. If λ decreases because unemployed workers become less willing, or able, to compete for the jobs, this will raise the chance that a worker searching on the job actually finds a job. This, in turn, puts upward pressure on wages, so the wage-setting schedule in Fig. 6.10 is shifted upwards, and the natural rate of unemployment increases.

As mentioned above, one factor that may affect λ is the *unemployment benefit system*. A more generous unemployment benefit system may make unemployed workers choosier and reduce their incentives to search for available jobs. In fact, the theory developed here has a very clear quantitative implication. It says that if the unemployment benefit system changes in such a way that unemployed workers become more choosy and apply for 10 percent fewer jobs, unemployment will increase by about 10 percent. If unemployment was originally 5 percent of the labour force, it will rise to 5.5 percent of the labour force.[12] Thus, we can find out the long-run macroeconomic effects of a change in unemployment benefits by studying how the job search behaviour of individual workers is affected. To understand this, note that it is the competition from unemployed workers that prevents wages from increasing. If, for some reason, the unemployed do not compete effectively for jobs, there will be more upward pressure on wages and the only way that this wage pressure can be contained is if the level of unemployment increases.

The long-run level of employment depends not only on search incentives but also on the *ability* of unemployed workers to compete for jobs. If there is a *mismatch* between worker skills and labour demand, firms will compete for the workers with the right skills and wages will rise although there are many workers unemployed. For this reason, a well-functioning education system is important for the labour market. If the education system is not working well,

---

12 This is shown in the appendix to this chapter.

there will be shortages of certain skills and upward pressure on wages even though unemployment is high.

Also, labour market policy could potentially play an important role in the matching process. Employment agencies can help workers and firms to find each other and labour market programmes can help workers to acquire the skills that are in demand in the labour market. The efficiency of education systems and labour market policies are hard to measure, but we realize that they may play important roles in the functioning of the labour market.

Matching problems and job search behaviour have been studied extensively in *search and matching theory*. The American economists Peter Diamond and Dale Mortensen and the Cypriot economist Christopher Pissarides (working in the UK) are leading contributors to this theory; they received the Nobel Prize for this work in 2010.[13]

6.5 Wage bargaining and unions

Another factor that affects wages and unemployment is that workers have bargaining power. Workers can threaten to strike, or to take some other action which is costly for the firm. When workers have the option to act collectively in this way, they can force the firm to bargain with them and push up the wage above the level that the firm would prefer to set.[14] The workers' bargaining power may be enhanced by a union that can organize collective action and act as a representative of the workers in the bargain. Therefore it may be in the workers' interest to organize a union. In many European countries, union contracts cover 70–80 percent of the wages in the economy. Unions play a less important role in the US and in the UK.[15]

To see the consequences of unions in our model, let us simplify by assuming that all workers are organized in identical unions which bargain with the individual firms. Since the wage that comes out of a bargain is higher than the wage that the firm would like to set, we can think of worker unions as adding a *union mark-up* to the wage. This implies that the wage-setting schedule is shifted up, as illustrated in Fig. 6.12. For each level of unemployment on the horizontal axis, the relative wage that comes out of the bargain with an individual firm is higher. But in

---

13 The Nobel Prize 2010 was awarded jointly to Peter A. Diamond, Dale T. Mortensen and Christopher A. Pissarides 'for their analysis of markets with search frictions'. The basic search-matching model is presented in Christopher Pissarides, *Equilibrium Unemployment Theory*, 2nd ed. (Cambridge, MA: The MIT Press, 2000).

14 One prerequisite for workers to have bargaining power is that there are labour turnover costs which make it costly for firms to replace employed workers (insiders) with other workers taken from the unemployment pool (outsiders). For an introduction to the literature on insiders and outsiders, see Assar Lindbeck and Dennis Snower, 'Insiders versus outsiders', *Journal of Economic Perspectives*, 15 (2001), 165–188.

15 In some countries, e.g. France, union membership is fairly low, but union contracts extend also to workers who are not members of the union. Therefore unions in France are much more important than their membership indicates; see Richard Layard, Stephen Nickell, and Richard Jackman, *Unemployment: Macroeconomic Performance and the Labour Market* (Oxford: Oxford University Press, 1991), chs 1 and 2.

Fig. 6.12 *The effect of bargaining on the equilibrium rate of unemployment*

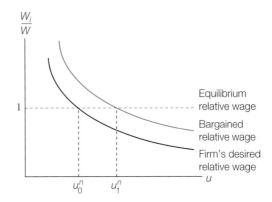

equilibrium, no union can raise its relative wage above unity. The end result is that the natural rate of unemployment must increase. Unions add to wage pressure, and to prevent wages from rising faster and faster, the increased wage pressure must be countered by higher unemployment.

With stronger unions, there will be lower employment in the long run. Unions may see lower employment as an acceptable price to pay if they can raise the real wages of their members, so what happens to the real wage? As we know from Chapter 2, the real wage is equal to the marginal product of labour divided by the mark-up factor. With the Cobb–Douglas production function we have $MPL = K^{\alpha}E^{1-\alpha}(1-\alpha)N^{-\alpha}$ so the real wage is

$$\frac{W}{P} = \frac{MPL}{1+\mu} = \frac{1-\alpha}{1+\mu}E\left(\frac{K}{EN}\right)^{\alpha}.$$

For a given level of capital, a lower level of employment means that each employed worker has more capital to work with, so the marginal product and the real wage will increase. Thus it is true that unions can raise the real wage at the price of lower employment.

Note that this holds only in the short run, however. In the long run, we cannot take the capital stock as constant. In Chapter 5 we showed that, in the long run, the capital stock *per effective worker, K/(EN),* will reach a steady state value k^*. This steady state value depends on the technology and the required return on capital, but it is independent of union bargaining power, so, in the long run, the real wage is also independent of union bargaining power. In the long run, wage increases are passed on into prices, leaving real wages unchanged. With 10 percent higher wages, prices will also be 10 percent higher, so workers' real incomes do not change. Thus, unions may be able to raise real wages in the short run but in the long run they only increase unemployment.

Obviously, this simple macroeconomic analysis misses many important aspects of unions. Unions play a bigger role in some sectors than in others so they influence *relative* wages of different types of workers. They tend to be strong in traditional industries such as the steel, car, and transport industries, where there are many workers doing similar jobs and production is capital-intensive, so that interruptions in the production process are very costly for the firms. They are strong also in some parts of the public sector. Often, unions represent workers who have little bargaining power if they act on their own.

Unions also play other roles. As representatives of the workers, they negotiate with the firm to achieve mutually beneficial agreements about working conditions, organization of work, pension systems and other conditions. Rather than negotiating with each individual worker, the firm can negotiate with union leaders who represent the interests of the workers. Thus, unions have important tasks which are not captured in our simple macroeconomic model.[16]

Nevertheless, our analysis points to a fundamental problem. Each individual union has an incentive to try to raise the real wage of its members, but when all unions do this, they do not achieve any increase in the real wage, at least not in the long run. The only result is higher unemployment. Although the members of each individual union would benefit if only they could raise their wage, the outcome when all unions try to raise wages is harmful for everyone.

We can illustrate this problem in the form of a game between two unions. Suppose that the economy consists of two sectors, A and B, producing two different products. There are two unions organizing workers in the two sectors. In each sector, a worker produces 10 units and we set the mark-up to zero so the price of the product produced in a sector is the wage in the sector divided by 10. Assume also that employment in each sector is 10,000 divided by the wage.[17] Furthermore, we let the consumer price index be[18]

$$P = \sqrt{P_A P_B} = \sqrt{\frac{W_A}{10} \frac{W_B}{10}}.$$

To make it simple, we assume that each union can choose between two different wages, 100 and 110. This game is illustrated in Table 6.1. We assume that the two unions set wages simultaneously without any communication between them.

To analyse what will happen in this game, note that if both unions set the wage 100, both prices are 10, the price level is 10, the real wage is 10, and employment is 100 for both unions. Consider now the situation from the perspective of union A. If union A raises its wage to 110, the price in sector A increases to 11, so the price level increases to 10.5 and union A raises its real wage to 110/10.5, which is roughly equal to 10.5. Since the price level increases less than union A's

---

16 An interesting book that emphasizes this point is *What Do Unions Do?* by Richard B. Freeman and James L. Medoff (New York: Basic Books, 1984).

17 To motivate this, let total expenditure be MV where M is the money supply and V is velocity, and both are taken as exogenous. Suppose further that consumers direct half their expenditure to sector A. Then employment in sector A will be

$$N_A = \frac{Y_A}{10} = \frac{MV/2}{10P_A} = \frac{MV/2}{W_A}.$$

If we set $MV = 20{,}000$ we get the labour demand function assumed in the text. The assumption that money supply is exogenous is unrealistic but we get similar conclusions if we assume that the central bank has an inflation target as in Chapter 10.

18 Since $\sqrt{P_A P_B} = P_A^{0.5} P_B^{0.5}$ this price index is a *geometric average* of the prices. Under certain conditions, this is the appropriate price index. A similar price index is used for domestic and foreign goods in the appendix to Chapter 12. For the present argument, the exact form of the price index is not important, however.

Table 6.1 *A game between two unions*

	$W_B = 100$	$W_B = 110$
$W_A = 100$	$P = \sqrt{\dfrac{W_A}{10}\dfrac{W_B}{10}} = \sqrt{\dfrac{100}{10}\dfrac{100}{10}} = 10$ $\dfrac{W_A}{P} = \dfrac{100}{10} = 10, \ \dfrac{W_B}{P} = \dfrac{100}{10} = 10$ $N_A = \dfrac{10000}{100} = 100, \ N_B = \dfrac{10000}{100} = 100$	$P = \sqrt{\dfrac{W_A}{10}\dfrac{W_B}{10}} = \sqrt{\dfrac{100}{10}\dfrac{110}{10}} \approx 10.5$ $\dfrac{W_A}{P} \approx \dfrac{100}{10.5} \approx 9.5, \ \dfrac{W_B}{P} \approx \dfrac{110}{10.5} \approx 10.5$ $N_A = \dfrac{10000}{100} = 100, \ N_B = \dfrac{10000}{110} \approx 91$
$W_A = 110$	$P = \sqrt{\dfrac{W_A}{10}\dfrac{W_B}{10}} = \sqrt{\dfrac{110}{10}\dfrac{100}{10}} \approx 10.5$ $\dfrac{W_A}{P} \approx 10.5, \ \dfrac{W_B}{P} \approx 9.5$ $N_A = \dfrac{10000}{110} \approx 91, \ N_B = \dfrac{10000}{100} = 100$	$P = \sqrt{\dfrac{W_A}{10}\dfrac{W_B}{10}} = \sqrt{\dfrac{110}{10}\dfrac{110}{10}} = 11$ $\dfrac{W_A}{P} = 10, \ \dfrac{W_B}{P} = 10$ $N_A = \dfrac{10000}{110} \approx 91, \ N_B = \dfrac{10000}{110} \approx 91$

wage, union A gets a real wage increase. This real wage increase comes at the cost of reduced employment, so the union faces a trade-off. If the union does not want to raise the wage, and the same applies to union B, the wage 100 is the equilibrium wage in the sense that neither union wants to deviate from this equilibrium.

But union A may consider that lower employment is a reasonable price to pay for a higher real wage. So union A may prefer to set the wage at 110, and union B may think the same way. In such a case, a situation where both unions set the wage, 100 is not an equilibrium situation because both unions have incentives to deviate from this equilibrium and set a higher wage.

So what happens if both unions raise their wages to 110? This is seen in the lower right box of Table 6.1. Wages are 10 percent higher but prices are also 10 percent higher, so there is no change in the real wage compared with the case when wages were 100. The only thing that has been achieved by the higher wages is a lower level of employment.

Unions would have been better off if wages had been 100 than they are when wages are 110, but if unions act in an uncoordinated way, each union has an incentive to raise the wage to 110 and the equilibrium is where both unions set this wage. In effect, each union tries to set a higher wage than the other union but neither union succeeds in doing this.[19]

To avoid this outcome, unions have incentives to try to coordinate their bargaining so as to prevent the general wage level being pushed too high. In fact, there is a considerable amount of coordination in many bargaining systems. Such coordination can take the form of central agreements between associations of employers and unions. In many cases, the coordination is achieved in

---

19 Those who have studied game theory will recognize this problem as the *Prisoner's Dilemma*.

Fig. 6.13 *The Calmfors–Driffill curve*

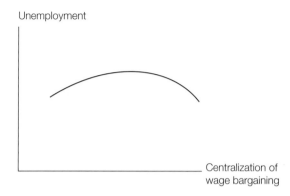

a less formal way by so-called *pattern bargaining*, which means that one group of unions and employers first strike a bargain and there is an implicit or explicit understanding that the other unions and employers will follow with wage contracts on the same level. By coordinating, unions and employers can avoid a situation where the race for higher wages leads to an unsatisfactory outcome for everyone.

Lars Calmfors and John Driffill have argued that the degree of coordination of wage bargaining matters for unemployment.[20] Unemployment will be highest if the bargaining takes place on the branch level, without coordination. The reason is that branch level unions are strong enough to push up wages but not so large that they take responsibility for the macroeconomic consequences of their actions. As explained above, each union tries to get a higher wage than the others and the result is that all wages are raised until unemployment has increased to a high level. Highly centralised (or coordinated) unions realize that there is no point in pushing up the general wage level too high, so they hold back wages. If, on the other hand, wage negotiations take place on the firm level, the competition between firms helps to hold back wages. Thus there is a nonlinear relation between the degree of centralization and unemployment, with unemployment first increasing as we go from firm level bargaining to branch level unions, and falling again as we go to full centralization. This relation between centralization and unemployment is shown in Fig. 6.13.

6.6 Minimum wages and skill-biased technical change

Above, we considered a situation where unions were symmetric and there were no minimum wages. In practice, different parts of the labour market work in quite different ways. Unions play a more important role in markets for workers

---

20 Lars Calmfors and John Driffill, 'Centralisation of wage bargaining and macroeconomic performance', *Economic Policy*, 6 (1988), 13–61. For a review of this literature, see Lars Calmfors, 'Centralisation of wage bargaining and macroeconomic performance – a survey', *OECD Economic Studies*, 21 (1993).

Fig. 6.14 *Minimum wages and the effect on unemployment amongst highly educated and less educated workers*

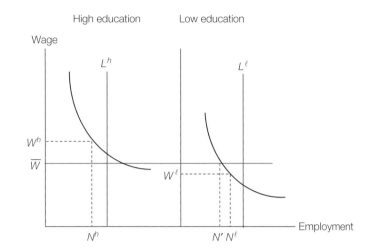

with a relatively low level of education. Also, many countries have minimum wages which are set by the government, or in union contracts. Unions and government regulations are less important in the markets for highly educated workers.

To illustrate this, we can think of an economy with two separate labour markets, one for highly educated and one for workers with a low level education. Fig. 6.14 illustrates supply and demand in the two labour markets. Labour supply in the two markets is L^h and L^ℓ. Suppose that, in an unregulated market, wages are set at the levels W^h and W^ℓ and the employment levels are N^h and N^ℓ so there is some unemployment in both markets. If the minimum wage sets a floor for wages at the level $\bar{W}$, employment of less educated will be lower: N' instead of N^ℓ. This illustrates that a rigid wage structure can be yet another cause of unemployment.

A factor that has received a lot of attention recently is *skill-biased technical change*. Such technical change tends to increase demand for highly educated workers at the same time as demand for less educated workers falls when their jobs are replaced by machines. In terms of Fig. 6.14, the demand curve for highly educated workers shifts to the right while the demand curve for less educated workers shifts to the left and unemployment increases among the unskilled.

Skill-biased technical change is nothing new. Since the middle of the 19th century, demand for educated workers has increased and this demand has been satisfied by a continuous increase in the share of each cohort of workers who get higher education. But the process seems to have speeded up and changed character in recent decades, leading to a substantial fall in the demand for less skilled workers and increasing differences in the wages firms are ready to pay for different workers.

Around 1900, the emergence of large-scale industry, with machines and assembly lines, benefited educated workers, but also workers with low or modest skills. By moving from a small farm or from handicraft to the assembly line or the manufacturing workshop, a worker with modest skills could suddenly produce much more. Today, automatization means that fewer manual workers are needed, while very specific skills are required to operate advanced machines. Many service sectors such as IT services and financial services also require workers with high education and very specific skills. Thus it appears that demand for less educated workers has fallen more quickly than supply.

In a market economy, a firm will hire a worker only if the value of what the worker produces exceeds the wage. If wages do not reflect the productivity differences between workers, workers with low productivity will have difficulties finding a job. To the extent that rising unemployment is due to excess supply of unskilled workers, this creates a difficult dilemma for unions and policy makers. Either there has to be an acceptance of bigger wage differences between skilled and unskilled workers, or there will be high unemployment among less skilled workers. Governments can alleviate these problems by reducing taxes on low incomes. Several countries have introduced a so-called *earned income tax credit* which is a reduction in the tax on low labour income. The purpose is to make it desirable to work and possible to live on the wage even if you earn a low wage. For the longer term, skill-biased technical change raises questions about how the education system should be designed in order to make the great majority of workers employable at reasonable wages.

6.7   Persistent high unemployment

In 2008, before the global financial crisis had really affected the labour market, the average unemployment rate in the Eurozone was 7.7 percent, but as we saw in Fig. 6.5, unemployment rates differed substantially between countries. There are also long-term trends in unemployment. In most countries, unemployment is higher today than it was in the 1960s. Why are there such large variations in unemployment across time and between countries? We do not have a definite answer, but our theory gives some possible reasons.

Why do unemployment rates differ between countries?

According to the theories presented above, various *institutional factors* affect the natural rate of unemployment. Differences with respect to those underlying factors may help to explain differences in unemployment rates between countries. The following factors may be important:

- Hiring costs raise unemployment as firms become more anxious to keep the workers they have, which puts upward pressure on wages.
- Generous unemployment benefits may make workers more selective in their job search and raise unemployment.
- Mismatch between worker skills and labour demand means that unemployed workers have difficulties competing for jobs, which will raise the level of unemployment.
- A well-functioning education system and active labour market policy could potentially reduce mismatch and unemployment.

- Strong unions raise wages, which has a negative effect on employment, but coordination of wage bargaining may counter this effect.
- A rigid wage structure that does not reflect productivity differences between workers will create unemployment among less skilled workers.

There has been much research trying to identify the causes of high unemployment.[21] One line of research is *cross-country studies* which try to explain unemployment differences between countries by institutional differences.[22] Statistical analysis gives some support for the theory. Countries with generous unemployment benefits tend to have higher unemployment rates, especially if there is no time limit for how long benefits can be received. Strong unions also seem to raise unemployment, but this effect is counteracted if bargaining is coordinated.

Job security legislation is legislation that limits the employer's freedom to fire workers. It is often argued that such legislation is bad for employment, but in cross-country comparisons, one does not find clear effects of job security legislation on unemployment. Some researchers have found that active labour market policy tends to reduce unemployment.

The results of cross-country studies should be interpreted with caution, however. Institutional factors are difficult to measure and to compare across countries. Also, there are a limited number of countries for which we have data, so there is a considerable risk that omitted factors lead to 'spurious' correlations – that is, accidental correlations which do not reflect causal relations between the variables.

For these reasons, most modern research uses microeconomic data instead, where employment histories of individuals can be tracked. Researchers try to isolate the effects of the unemployment benefit system by following workers over time and comparing different groups of workers where one group was affected by a change of the benefit system and one was not. Most such studies find that unemployment benefits do affect job search, supporting the view that generous benefits lead to higher unemployment. Also, the length of the period for which unemployed workers are eligible for unemployment benefits seems to be important.

How large are these effects? Estimates vary considerably, but most estimates give an elasticity of unemployment duration with respect to the level of benefits between 0.1 and 1.0.[23] To see what this means, suppose the elasticity is 0.5. Then

---

21 A good review of this research is Richard Layard, Stephen Nickell, and Richard Jackman, *Unemployment: Macroeconomic Performance and the Labour Market* (Oxford: Oxford University Press, 1991), reprinted with new introduction 2005. Reviews can also be found in textbooks in labour economics, e.g. Pierre Cahuc and André Zylberberg, *Labor Economics* (Cambridge, MA: The MIT Press, 2004).

22 One example is Stephen Nickell and Richard Layard, 'Labour market institutions and economic performance', in Orley Ashenfelter and David Card (eds.), *Handbook of Labor Economics*, vol. 3 (Amsterdam: Elsevier, 1999).

23 For reviews of such studies, see Bertil Holmlund, 1998, 'Unemployment insurance in theory and practice', *Scandinavian Journal of Economics*, 100 (1998), 113–141; Pierre Cahuc and André Zylberberg, *Labor Economics* (Cambridge, MA: The MIT Press, 2004); and Rafael Lalive, Jan van Ours, and Josef Zweimuller, Josef, 'How changes in financial incentives affect the duration of unemployment', *Review of Economic Studies*, 73 (2006), 1009–1038.

a 10 percent increase in benefits (e.g. from 50 to 55 percent of the previous wage) will increase the average duration of unemployment by 5 percent – that is, on average workers will be unemployed for 5 percent longer. This corresponds to an increase in the unemployment rate from, for example, 6 percent to 6.3 percent. The elasticity with respect to the duration of benefits is of similar magnitude, so an increase in the time unemployed workers are eligible for benefits by 10 percent, say from 10 to 11 months, will also increase the duration of unemployment about 5 percent, for example, from 20 to 21 weeks. These numbers are quite uncertain, however.

Why is unemployment so much higher than it was in the 1960s?

Fig. 6.15 shows how unemployment has evolved over time. Unemployment fluctuates from year to year and there are also some longer-term trends.

In the US, there is no clear trend: before the financial crisis in 2008, it was not far above the level in the 1960s. Looking at Fig. 6.15, we may conclude that the natural rate of unemployment is around 6 percent in the US.

In other countries, there have been long-term trends, however. Many European countries had unemployment rates around 2–4 percent in the 1960s, but unemployment increased substantially in the 1970s, peaked around 1982, and remained high until the middle of the 1990s. Sweden and Finland managed to keep unemployment at low levels until 1991 when severe banking crises brought dramatic increases in unemployment. In the decade from the late 1990s until the global financial crisis started in 2008, unemployment decreased in most countries.

According to the theory presented above, there is a long-run equilibrium ('natural') rate of unemployment which depends on how well the labour market works. Supply and demand shocks may temporarily bring unemployment away from this level, but after some time, unemployment will return to the natural level. Therefore, a large and persistent increase in unemployment can only be explained by an increase in the natural rate of unemployment. Such a change may be explained by changes in the 'institutional' factors discussed above. Can we identify any such changes?

There were institutional changes in the labour market in the late 1960s and early 1970s that may have contributed to a higher natural rate of unemployment. Many countries raised their unemployment benefits in the late 1960s and early 1970s and there were also new laws and regulations of the labour market which may have affected the natural rate of unemployment. Unions were generally strong in the 1970s. The rise in unemployment in the mid-1970s may be a delayed effect of such changes. Mismatch is hard to measure, but there are no strong indications that the pace of restructuring was higher after 1970 than it was in the 1960s.

Although much research has been done on the causes of high unemployment, we have no simple answer as to why unemployment is so much higher than it was in the 1960s. Our theory suggests many factors that may play a role and some of them are hard to measure. Many economists and politicians have drawn the conclusion that labour markets need to be deregulated; in other words that there should be less government involvement in the labour market. Benefit systems have become less generous and job security legislation has been weakened. Laws that benefit unions have been changed and unions are weaker today than they were in

Fig. 6.15 *Unemployment in percent of the labour force*

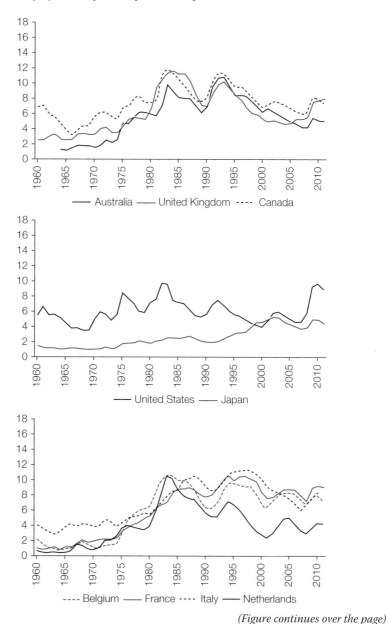

(Figure continues over the page)

Fig. 6.15 *(Continued)*

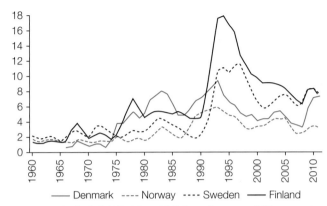

Source: *OECD Economic Outlook*, OECD, 9 June 2012, http://www.oecd-ilibrary.org/statistics.

the 1970s. In most countries unemployment declined after the mid-1990s, but it is still above the level of the 1960s.

Do temporary shocks have persistent effects on employment?

For some countries, the graph for unemployment looks like a staircase. Sometimes, there is an increase in unemployment as a result of a major crisis, and after that, unemployment remains high for many years. Some countries had major recessions in the 1970s, which raised unemployment. In the UK, the inflation-fighting policies of the Thatcher government around 1980 led to an increase in unemployment and then it remained high for many years. Finland and Sweden kept unemployment low until severe banking crises in 1991–1992, which led to large and very persistent increases in unemployment. Thus it seems that temporary shocks can have very persistent effects on employment.

One reason why temporary shocks can have persistent effects on employment is that workers who lose their jobs in a downturn lose skills, and this makes it hard for them to get a new job. Yet few workers are truly unemployable and most workers who lose their jobs in a downturn do get new jobs, so this cannot, by itself, explain the high persistence of unemployment that we see on the macroeconomic level.

The wage formation process plays an important role. If a negative shock puts many workers out of work, some adjustment is needed to get those workers back to work. According to the theory described above, high unemployment should put downward pressure on wages, and when inflation falls we would also expect the central bank to reduce interest rates so as to stimulate aggregate demand. But wages respond sluggishly to an increase in unemployment, so this process may take a long time.

One important factor here is that wages are set in negotiations between firms and unions representing primarily the employed workers, the *insiders*, who are little affected by high unemployment. As a result, unemployment may have a weak effect on wages. If insiders continue to demand high wage increases even when unemployment is high, inflation continues and there is little room for the central bank of the country to reduce the interest rate.[24]

The exchange rate system also plays a role. As we will see later, the exchange rate system affects the ability of a central bank to react to shocks. With a fixed exchange rate, the central bank is unable to respond to shocks by changing interest rates. In such a situation, slow wage adjustment implies that shocks will have persistent effects on employment. We will discuss this further when we analyse fiscal and monetary policy in the open economy in Chapters 14–15.

6.8   Long-term unemployment

There is no question that high unemployment is a major social problem, but zero unemployment is neither feasible nor a desirable objective for policy. After all, it is natural and acceptable that some workers are unemployed in the transition between different jobs. Also, it is rational for a worker not to take the first job she can get but to wait for a job where she can use her specific competence and be rewarded for this with a reasonable wage. If workers are occasionally unemployed for a few weeks between jobs, this is not necessarily a big social problem. The really serious social problem occurs when workers are stuck in unemployment for many months or even years.

So how long will a typical worker be unemployed? To see what determines the expected *duration* of unemployment, assume for simplicity that workers who find a job in a particular month start working at the end of that month so that all workers who become unemployed remain unemployed for at least one month. Let x be the exit rate from unemployment. It is equal to the job-finding rate for the unemployed, λf, plus the rate at which unemployed workers leave the labour force. We denote the latter rate by v. It represents workers leaving for exogenous reasons and discouraged workers who give up searching. Then the exit rate is

$$x = \lambda f + v.$$

If the probability of leaving unemployment is x, the probability of remaining unemployed the second month is $1 - x$, the probability of remaining unemployed the third month is $(1 - x)(1 - x)$, and so on. The expected duration of unemployment is the probability of being unemployed at least one month times 1, plus the probability of being unemployed the second month times 1, plus the probability of

24 For reviews of research on these issues, see Olivier J. Blanchard, 'Wage bargaining and unemployment persistence', *Journal of Money, Credit and Banking*, 23 (1991), 277–292; Charles R. Bean, 'European unemployment: a survey', *Journal of Economic Literature*, 32 (1994), 573–619; Assar Lindbeck and Dennis Snower, 'Insiders versus outsiders', *Journal of Economic Perspectives*, 15 (2001), 165–188.

being unemployed the third month times 1, and so on. Thus we get the duration of unemployment as

$$1 + (1-x) \cdot 1 + (1-x)^2 \cdot 1 + (1-x)^3 \cdot 1 + \ldots = \frac{1}{1-(1-x)} = \frac{1}{x}$$

$$= \frac{1}{\lambda f + v} = \frac{1}{\dfrac{\lambda s}{\lambda u + s} + v},$$

where we have used the fact that $f = s/(\lambda u + s)$. The duration of unemployment depends on three factors:

- A higher rate of unemployment means that there are more workers competing for available jobs and less chance to find a job, which leads to a longer duration of unemployment.
- A high rate of separations (people leaving jobs) means that there are more job openings, so the duration of unemployment decreases.
- A high rate of exit from the labour force also reduces the duration of unemployment, as more workers end their unemployment spell by dropping out of the labour force.

How high is the exit rate from unemployment? A simple way to estimate this is to note that, if unemployment is constant, the inflow into unemployment must be equal to the outflow. If we assume that all workers who enter unemployment remain unemployed for at least one month, we can calculate the inflow during a month as the number of unemployed workers who have been unemployed less than one month. The monthly inflow rate is then calculated as the share of all unemployed workers who been unemployed less than one month at the time of the survey.[25] In a long-run equilibrium, this is also the outflow rate from unemployment.

Fig. 6.16 shows that there are very large differences between the labour markets in different countries. In the US, the inflow (and outflow) measured as the share of the unemployed workers who have been unemployed less than one month, is 37 percent, implying a duration of unemployment of about 3 months ($1/0.37 = 2.7$). In Germany, France, and Italy, this flow is around 5 percent of the stock of unemployment, implying a duration of 20 months ($1/0.05 = 20$). Partly this difference reflects the higher unemployment rates in the latter countries, but the main difference is the rate of turnover. Workers in the US leave their jobs at a much higher rate, and this creates openings for unemployed workers to find jobs more quickly. The Scandinavian countries also have relatively high turnover in the labour market.

The standard measure of long-term unemployment is the number of workers who have been unemployed for more than 12 months. The higher the exit rate, the fewer workers will end up in long-term unemployment. As seen in Fig. 6.16, there

---

25 Since some workers remain unemployed less than a month, this number will underestimate the exit and entry rates, but it can serve as a rough measure of the entry and exit rates.

Fig. 6.16 *Short-term and long-term unemployment, percent of the unemployed*

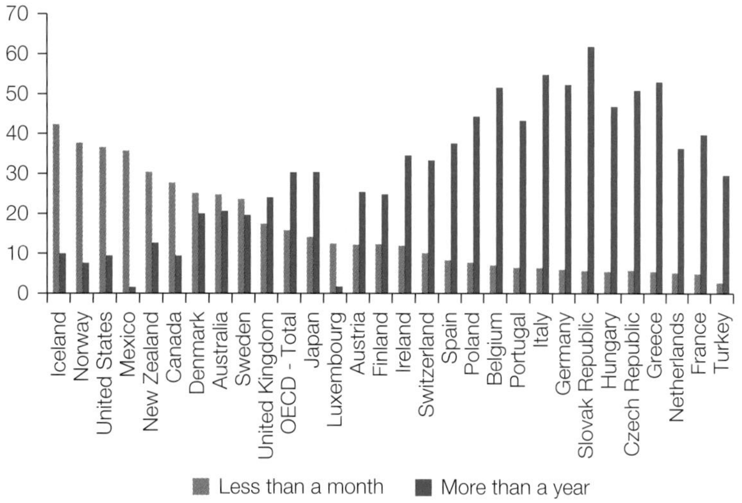

Note: The figure shows workers who have been unemployed less than a month and more than one year as shares of total unemployment, average 1999–2008.
Source: *OECD Employment and Labour Market Statistics*, OECD, 27 April 2011, http://www.oecd-ilibrary.org/statistics.

are substantial differences between countries. In the high turnover countries, about 10 percent of unemployment is long term. In the low turnover countries, 30–60 percent of the unemployed have been out of jobs for more than a year.[26]

What have we learned?

Workers are either employed, unemployed, or outside the labour force. To count as unemployed, a worker must be actively seeking work or waiting to start a job.

We use L to denote the labour force, N to denote employment and U to denote unemployment, so $L = N + U$ and unemployment as a share of the labour force is

$$u = \frac{U}{L} = \frac{L - N}{L}.$$

The *natural rate of unemployment*, u^n, is the long-run equilibrium rate of unemployment. Short-run deviations from the natural rate are called *cyclical unemployment*.

In a simple model of turnover, the job-finding rate is approximately $s/(\lambda u + s)$ where u is the unemployment rate, λ measures the willingness and ability of the

---

26 A good summary of research on unemployment and wage formation can be found in Richard Layard, Stephen Nickell, and Richard Jackman, *Unemployment: Macroeconomic Performance and the Labour Market* (Oxford: Oxford University Press, 1991), reprinted with new introduction 2005. The *OECD Employment Outlook* describes labour markets in the OECD countries.

unemployed to compete for the jobs, and s is the rate of exogenous job separations. The job-finding rate increases if turnover is higher and decreases with
higher unemployment.

Turnover is costly for firms, so when setting wages firms have to balance the
cost savings from reduced wages against the increased risk of losing workers. As a
result, they may not want to reduce the wage although there are unemployed
workers waiting for jobs.

A higher wage increases the direct wage cost but it also reduces turnover.
If unemployment falls, it becomes easier to find a job and turnover increases. Then
firms have incentives to raise wages so as to reduce turnover.

In the efficiency wage model, the natural rate of unemployment is the level
of unemployment which is such that firms do not have incentives to overbid or underbid each other in their wage-setting. Put differently, the natural
level of unemployment is such that the typical firm's desired relative wage is
unity.

Since nominal wages are rigid, an increase in aggregate demand may raise
employment in the short run, but as unemployment falls below the natural
rate, there will be high wage increases and high inflation. When inflation is
high, the central bank will raise interest rates, aggregate demand will fall and
unemployment will increase.

The efficiency wage model implies that high hiring costs tend to increase unemployment because firms raise wages to reduce turnover costs. High exogenous
quitting of jobs into unemployment and high on-the-job job search also raise
unemployment because they increase turnover costs.

We can summarize the theory of unemployment and wage-setting in the form
of a wage-setting equation relating the desired wage, W^d, to unemployment, u,
and the average wage level, W:

$$W^d = (1 + a - bu)\, W,$$

where a and b are constants with positive values. Setting $W^d = W$ and solving for
unemployment we find an expression for the natural rate of unemployment:

$$u^n = \frac{a}{b}.$$

Any factor that shifts up the wage-setting equation will increase the coefficient a
and the natural rate of unemployment. We can also formulate this as a dynamic
wage equation showing desired wage increases over time:

$$\frac{\Delta W_t^d}{W_{t-1}} = \frac{\Delta W_t}{W_{t-1}} - b\,(u_t - u^n).$$

This equation says that if unemployment is higher than the natural level, firms
want to raise wages less than the average wage increase. We will use this equation
when we study short-run wage adjustment and inflation in Chapter 9.

Since $N = L - U = (1 - U/L)\,L = (1 - u)\,L$ we can define the *natural level of
employment* as

$$N^n = (1 - u^n)\,L.$$

Jobs and workers are heterogeneous, and firms and job seekers are engaged in a matching process where they try to find good matches between workers and jobs. Unemployed workers play an important role in this process. If unemployed workers search less intensively for jobs or if they are less willing or able to compete for the jobs, unemployment will have a weaker effect on wage pressure and the natural rate of unemployment will increase.

Unions with strong bargaining power put upward pressure on wages and, to compensate, the long-run level of unemployment must increase. The real wage increases in the short run but in the long run there is a required return on capital, so the real wage cannot increase. Coordination of the wage bargaining may help to avoid a situation where competing wage demands lead to a low long-run level of employment.

Minimum wages may raise unemployment among low skilled workers, and this problem is made worse by skill-biased technical change.

In many countries, unemployment increased in the 1970s and stayed on a high level for a couple of decades. In the decade before the financial crisis in 2008, unemployment decreased in many countries but it was still much higher than it was in the 1960s. There is some evidence that the rise in unemployment in the 1970s was due to institutional changes such as a more generous unemployment benefit system, but the exact causes are not clear.

It appears that shocks to unemployment can have persistent effects. Unemployment has often increased in connection with a major crisis, or inflation-fighting policies, and then it has remained high for a long time. One reason may be that workers who remain unemployed for some time lose skills and find it difficult to compete for the jobs. Another may be that wages are set in negotiations between firms and insiders, who are not much affected by unemployment, so wages respond slowly to high unemployment.

The expected duration of unemployment is the inverse of the exit rate from unemployment. There are big differences in exit rates and long-term unemployment between countries. In the US, the monthly exit rate is about 1/3 and the expected duration is about three months. In Germany and France, the exit rates are below 10 percent and the expected duration is more than a year. Partly this is due to differences in unemployment rates, but the main difference is that turnover is much higher in the US labour market.

Where do we go from here?

So far, we have concentrated on the real side of the macro economy: production, consumption, investment, the real interest rate, and employment. Now it is time to introduce money and to analyse how the price level and inflation are determined. In the next chapter, we analyse the relation between money and inflation in the long run. Then, in Chapters 8 and 9, we study the short run. The key difference between the long and the short run is that nominal wages and prices are sticky in the short run.

Exercises

1. In a certain economy there are one million men and one million women of working age (15–64). Of the men, 740,000 are employed and 200,000 are outside the labour force. Of the women, 640,000 are employed and 300,000 are outside the labour force.
   a) What are the employment rates (of the population) for men and women?
   b) What are the unemployment rates (of the labour force) for men and women?

2. We have found that the monthly job-finding rate for an employed job seeker is approximately

   $$f \approx \frac{s}{\lambda u + s},$$

   where s is the number of workers exogenously leaving jobs, u is the unemployment rate, and λ measures the ability and willingness of the unemployed job seekers to compete for the jobs. We assume that $\lambda = 1$.
   a) Calculate the job-finding rate for the different values below and fill in the table.

	$u = 0.04$	$u = 0.08$
$s = 0.01$		
$s = 0.02$		

   b) Assume that 10 percent of the unemployed workers leave the labour force each month. What is the duration of unemployment in each case?

	$u = 0.04$	$u = 0.08$
$s = 0.01$		
$s = 0.02$		

3. If an unemployed worker has difficulty finding a job, what is typically the problem?
   a) There are very few job openings available.
   b) The worker is not spending enough effort finding jobs.
   c) The worker is too choosy and does not accept the jobs he could get.

   d) The worker has trouble competing for the jobs which are available.
   In your view, which of these is the most common problem? Which is the least common problem? Explain why you come to this conclusion. (The answer is a subjective evaluation so there is no correct answer.)

4. Suppose that we have two types of worker, those with high skills and those with low skills. Labour demand shifts substantially in such a way that, for given wages, demand for skilled workers increases and demand for unskilled workers falls. In which ways can society deal with this situation? What can the government do? What can the unions do?

5. Suppose that there is rapid productivity growth because of technological innovations – that is, E increases.
   a) What is the effect on labour demand for a given real wage?
   b) According to the theory presented here, what is the effect on employment and real wages if the unemployment benefit is a constant share of the pre-unemployment wage?
   c) According to the theory presented here, what is the effect on employment and real wages if the unemployment benefit is kept constant in real terms?

6. Suppose we pass a law that working hours must be shortened. According to the theory presented here, what is the effect on employment and real wages? Consider two cases:
   a) The unemployment benefit is a constant share of the pre-unemployment wage.
   b) The unemployment benefit is kept constant in real terms.

7. In the efficiency wage model, the labour cost per worker is the direct wage cost plus the turnover cost
   $$W_i + h \cdot W \cdot [s + Z(W_i/W) \cdot f].$$

a) When the wage is set so that this cost is minimized, the derivative with respect to the wage is zero. Derive this condition. *(Hint: Note that according to the 'chain rule' the derivative of $Z(W_i/W)$ with respect to W_i is $Z'(W_i/W)/W$.)*

b) Consider a situation where all firms set the same wage, use $f = \dfrac{s}{\lambda u + s}$ to

substitute for f and solve for the natural rate of unemployment.

c) According to this theory, what factors influence the natural rate of unemployment and why?

Answers to the exercises can be found at: **www.palgrave.com/economics/gottfries**.

Appendix

Gross flows in the labour market

Let us see what our model of turnover implies for the *gross flows* in the labour market. Consider first the flow from unemployment to employment. Although the chance of getting a job falls when more workers are unemployed, there are more unemployed workers applying for the available jobs, so the flow into employment increases. Therefore, high unemployment means that there is a high flow out of unemployment measured in *numbers* of workers. In our simple model of turnover, the *number* of unemployed workers getting jobs is equal to U times λf:

$$U\lambda f = uL\lambda \frac{s}{\lambda u + s} = L\frac{\lambda s}{\lambda + s/u}.$$

We see that the number of workers flowing out of unemployment increases with the unemployment rate because there are more unemployed workers competing for available job openings.

The other side of the coin is that, when there are more unemployed workers competing for jobs, a larger share of job leavers become unemployed because they are unable to find another job immediately. The flow from employment to unemployment is the number of job leavers times the chance of not finding a job – that is, $Ns(1-f)$, which is also higher if unemployment is high. Thus we see that, in absolute terms, there will be larger flows in and out of unemployment when unemployment is high, but the chance of getting a job is still low.

Two more reasons why flows in and out of unemployment are high when unemployment is high are the discouraged worker effect, which means that some unemployed workers temporarily leave the labour force, and the use of temporary layoffs and recalls as a way to adjust employment when demand is low. These aspects are not included in the model analysed here.

An explicit solution for the optimal wage and the natural rate of unemployment

In order to find an explicit solution for the optimal wage, we assume a specific function determining the share of employed workers searching on the job:

$$Z = S\left(\frac{W_i}{W}\right)^{-\sigma},$$

where S is a constant between zero and one, W_i is the wage set by firm i, W is the average wage, and where σ is a positive constant. If the firm sets the same wage as other firms, $W_i = W$, the share looking for another job is S. A plausible number for S may be $S = 0.05$ – that is, 5 percent of the employed workers look for other jobs when the firm's wage is on the same level as other wages.[27]

The total cost per worker is the direct wage cost plus the turnover cost:

$$W_i + hW \left(s + S \left(W_i/W\right)^{-\sigma} f\right) = W_i + hWs + hWSW_i^{-\sigma} W^\sigma f.$$

Taking the derivative with respect to W_i we get the first-order condition

$$1 - hWS\sigma W_i^{-\sigma-1} W^\sigma f = 0.$$

Solving this equation, we get the firm's optimal wage, which we denote as W^d:[28]

$$W^d = \left(h\sigma Sf\right)^{1/(1+\sigma)} W.$$

The firm's optimal wage increases if it is easier to find a job. The easier it is for workers to find jobs, the more costly is the turnover and the more anxious the firm is to reduce turnover. Also, a higher average wage level in the economy implies that the individual firm will also set a higher wage. If it does not raise its wage in line with the general wage level, it will lose workers.

In order to relate the chances of finding a job to unemployment, we use $f \approx s/(\lambda u + s)$. Substituting into the expression for the wage we get the desired relative wage:

$$\frac{W^d}{W} = \left(\frac{h\sigma Ss}{\lambda u + s}\right)^{1/(1+\sigma)}.$$

When unemployment increases, the firm's desired relative wage decreases.

The long-run equilibrium level of unemployment is the level of unemployment at which the *desired relative wage* is equal to one:

$$1 = \left(\frac{h\sigma Ss}{\lambda u + s}\right)^{1/(1+\sigma)}.$$

Raising both sides to $1 + \sigma$, multiplying by $\lambda u + s$ and subtracting s on both sides we get the natural (equilibrium) rate of unemployment:

$$u^n = \frac{h\sigma Ss - s}{\lambda} = \frac{s}{\lambda}\left(h\sigma S - 1\right).$$

We see that if s, S or h increase, or λ decreases, the natural level of unemployment will increase.

---

27 Since the share looking for another job cannot be above one, this function can only hold if W_i is not too far below the average wage. In long-run equilibrium, all firms set the same wage.

28 To solve the equation we multiply by $W_i^{1+\sigma}$ to get

$$W_i^{1+\sigma} - hS\sigma W^{1+\sigma} f = 0.$$

Then we add $hS\sigma W^{1+\sigma} f$ on both sides and raise both sides to the power $1/(1+\sigma)$.

7 MONEY AND INFLATION IN THE LONG RUN

What determines the long-run rate of inflation?

A general increase in the price level from one year to the next is called *inflation*. Very high inflation causes economic costs because the price system works less efficiently. High inflation makes it hard to keep track of and to compare prices, and fluctuations in inflation lead to random gains and losses for borrowers and lenders. To maintain a low and stable rate of inflation is the primary goal of most central banks. So which factors determine the rate of inflation?

In this chapter we show that the central bank of a country (or a monetary union) can control the long-run rate of inflation because it can control the quantity of money in circulation (the money supply). Money is the unit of account, so prices of goods and services are expressed in terms of money. If there is more money 'chasing' available goods and services, the price level will increase. The relation between money growth and inflation is far from stable, but, *ceteris paribus* (all else being equal), the central bank can reduce or increase the rate of inflation by reducing or increasing the rate of money growth.

By 'money', we do not mean wealth in general but money that is used to make payments. In our theoretical model, money is the *medium of exchange* – that is, payments for goods and services and wage payments are made with money, and money is the *unit of account* – prices and wages are set in terms of money. Also, money is an asset that *does not yield interest*, so the interest rate is the opportunity cost of holding money. In our theoretical model, we assume that the quantity of money in circulation is *controlled by the central bank*. Based on these assumptions, we formulate a theory of the relation between money growth, inflation, and the interest rate in the *long run*.

When we look at the real world, it is not obvious which assets should count as money. The most obvious example of money is notes and coins, but there are other assets that may be used to make payments. As we will see, there are several different empirical definitions of money.

In this chapter, we first discuss the functions of money and the relation between money growth and inflation in the long run. Then we consider alternative empirical definitions of money and the empirical relation between money growth and inflation. We analyse how money holdings relate to inflation and the role of money creation as a source of income for the government. Finally, we analyse whether it is important to keep inflation on a low level. Should we always dislike inflation or can some inflation be good for the economy?

The focus here is on average inflation over a period of many years. In Chapters 8–10, we study how monetary policy affects interest rates, economic activity, and inflation in the short run.

7.1 The functions of money

The most obvious example of money is currency – notes and coins. Currency is an asset with certain specific characteristics:

1. Currency can be used as a *medium of exchange*. It is accepted as payment for most goods and services. Many transactions are carried out with currency, and the more transactions there are, the more currency is needed to carry out those transactions.

2. Currency is the *unit of account*. Normally, prices and wages are specified in units of home currency, not in kilos of potatoes, for example, or in foreign currency. Also, debt contracts are normally specified in terms of money – that is, the loan contract stipulates that the borrower has to repay the amount of money that was borrowed with interest.

3. Currency is a *store of value that does not yield interest*. To put money under the mattress is one way to save but not a very good one since you earn no interest on your savings under the mattress. Therefore, the interest rate is the *opportunity cost* of holding money, the income that you forego by holding currency instead of an asset that pays interest.

In our theoretical model we assume that there is an asset called 'money' which has these three characteristics and we also assume that the central bank can control the quantity of money:

1. Money is the medium of exchange in the model economy. The more transactions there are, the more money is needed to carry out those transactions.

2. Money is the unit of account: prices, wages, and debt contracts are specified in terms of money.

3. Money is a store of value that does not yield interest, so the opportunity cost of holding money is the interest foregone.

4. The central bank can control the quantity of money.

Different assets match this description more or less accurately. We can initially think of the quantity of money as the total amount of currency (notes and coins) in circulation. In Section 7.3 we discuss what other assets than currency might be included in our measure of the quantity of money.

7.2 Money and inflation in the long run

Money is the unit of account, so prices are quoted as the amount of money one has to pay for a loaf of bread or a kilo of tomatoes. Therefore, we would expect that, if the quantity of money in circulation increases, prices will also increase. If all individuals suddenly discover that the notes in their pockets have mated and produced new little coins, they will either spend the money or lend it so someone who wants to spend it, so demand for goods will increase. With more money 'chasing' the available goods and services, prices will increase.

A simple theory of the relation between money and inflation can be obtained by assuming that money has an exogenously fixed *velocity of circulation* – that it travels around the circular flow of income a certain number of times per year (see Fig. 1.2). Suppose, as a stylized example, that firms pay out wages, interest, and dividends to households in cash every month, and that households use all that cash to purchase goods from the firms during the month. The amount of cash needed to carry out these transactions corresponds to the value of one month's production and the cash circulates through firms and households 12 times per year. If we measure income on a yearly basis, velocity is equal to 12, and the money needed to carry out all transactions is 1/12 of nominal GDP.

If we denote the velocity by V and the quantity of money is M, the following equality must hold:

$$M \cdot V = P \cdot Y,$$

where P is the price level, Y is real production, and $P \cdot Y$ is the nominal value of production (GDP). The quantity of money times velocity is equal to the nominal value of GDP.

The equation above contains four variables. In the long run, production is at its natural level. If we assume that the central bank controls the money supply and if we take velocity as exogenous, we get a simple theory of the price level. It is found by setting production equal to the natural level of production, $Y = Y^n$, and dividing both sides by Y^n:

$$P = \frac{M \cdot V}{Y^n}.$$

For given levels of production and velocity, the price level is proportional to the money supply. If the money supply increases by 10 percent, so does the price level.

It may appear strange that we derive an equation for the price level here when we have already derived an equation for the price level in Chapter 2:

$$P = (1 + \mu) \frac{W}{MPL}.$$

Note, however, that both equations can hold if wages change together with prices. We assume that wages and prices adjust in the long run, so if the money supply increases by 10 percent, wages and prices also increase by 10 percent. Then the equality above will still hold.

Inflation is the rate of growth of the price level: $\pi = \Delta P/P$. We can use our rule of thumb for growth rates to calculate the inflation rate as[1]

$$\pi = \frac{\Delta M}{M} + \frac{\Delta V}{V} - \frac{\Delta Y^n}{Y^n}.$$

---

1   The rule of thumb for growth rates is that the growth rate of $X \cdot Y/Z$ is the growth rate of X plus the growth rate of Y minus the growth rate of Z; see the appendix to Chapter 1.

The faster the quantity of money increases, the higher is inflation, *ceteris paribus* – that is, if everything else is constant. If velocity is constant, inflation is the rate of money growth minus real growth of GDP. In reality, everything else is not constant, however, so money growth is not the only determinant of inflation. For a given rate of money growth, changes in velocity and production will also affect inflation. But we see that money growth is an important determinant of inflation.

But what is the effect of money growth on real variables such as production, employment, the real wage, and the real interest rate? We have already answered this question in Chapters 2–6. As we saw there, we can understand how the real variables are determined without saying anything about the supply of money or the price level. This result comes from the fact that what consumers and firms care about is real things. Production depends on the available real factors of production, and savings and investment decisions depend on real income and the real rate of interest. Therefore, we could analyse how production and the real interest rate are determined in the long run without knowing anything about the supply of money. Changes in the quantity of money affect the price level but do not affect real variables. We say that *money is neutral* with respect to the real economy.

7.3   Alternative definitions of money

The key implication of our analysis is that the rate of money growth is an important determinant of the rate of inflation. But what assets should count as 'money'? In a modern economy, we do not always pay with cash. At the end of the month, wages are transferred electronically to our accounts and we often pay for consumption goods with debit cards, credit cards, or cheques. What medium of exchange is used in those transactions?

Monetary base

To understand what assets serve as money in a modern economy, note that when a consumer with an account in Bank A uses his debit card to pay in a shop that has an account in Bank B, the money is transferred from Bank A to Bank B. But this transaction is not made by sending someone with a bag of cash from Bank A to Bank B. Instead, banks have accounts in an electronic payment system that is managed by the central bank and which handles payments between the banks. The money is transferred electronically from the account of Bank A to the account of Bank B. The accounts in this payment system are claims that the banks have on the central bank and, in order to make the payment, Bank A must have the money in its account to transfer to Bank B.[2]

If the consumer uses a credit card instead, the only difference is that it is the credit card company that pays the shop from its bank account. Again, there is a

---

2   To be precise, the balance may be positive or negative during the day, but if the bank has a deficit at the end of the day, it must borrow from the central bank and pay interest on the loan. We will analyse this in more detail in Chapter 10.

transfer of money between the bank of the credit card company and the bank of the shop.

Thus, when a consumer pays with a debit or credit card, or a cheque, the money on some bank's account in the payment system is used to carry out the payment. Furthermore, banks can draw money from their accounts as cash to put in their cash machines, thus converting electronic money to physical money. Therefore, the amount of coins and notes in circulation plus the claims that the banks have on the central bank are the ultimate *mediums of exchange* in a modern economy The sum of cash in circulation and banks' claims on the central bank are called the *monetary base*, or *high-powered money*:

> *Monetary base = notes and coins in circulation + banks' claims on the central bank*

The central bank can control the monetary base. The primary way in which it does so is by *open market operations* where the central bank buys and sells government securities (treasury bills or bonds). If the central bank buys government bonds from a bank, it pays by transferring the money to the bank's account in the payment system and thus increasing the monetary base.

A modern version of open market operations is *repurchase agreements* where the central bank buys government securities with a contract that the transaction will be reversed in a short time, such as one week. Another way in which the central bank can increase the monetary base is by *overnight lending* to banks. In Chapter 10 we will discuss in more detail how the central bank controls the monetary base.

Thus we see that the monetary base has all the four characteristics discussed above:

1. The monetary base is used to carry out transactions. In fact, *all payments are ultimately made with monetary base.*
2. Prices and wages are set in units of the monetary base.
3. Cash does not yield interest. In many countries, banks get interest on their accounts in the central bank, but this interest is lower than the market rate.
4. The central bank can control the monetary base by various forms of open market operations and lending to banks.

We see that the monetary base corresponds closely to our theoretical notion of money. The relation between the volume of transactions and the need for monetary base is not simple, however, because it depends on how payments are made. Money in the accounts of the payment system can be transferred back and forth very quickly, so the money in these accounts can be used to make a large number of payments in a single day. Coins and notes circulate at a slower rate. Changes in payment habits may lead to large changes in the velocity of the monetary base. If, for example, consumers increase their use of their debit cards and make fewer payments with cash, less monetary base will be needed for a given amount of purchases. Therefore, the relation between the volume of transactions and the demand for monetary base can be quite unstable. The relation between payments habits and velocity is further analysed in the appendix to this chapter.

M1

An alternative way to think about the definition of money is to ask what assets an individual consumer or firm can use to make payments. From the point of view of a consumer we may view cash and certain kinds of bank deposits as mediums of exchange. Accounts from which we can make payments using debit cards or by writing cheques can be seen as mediums of exchange for consumers and firms. One measure of money is called M1 and it is defined as follows:

$$M1 = notes\ and\ coins\ in\ circulation + demand\ deposits.$$

Demand deposits are accounts from which money can be withdrawn at any time without notice. In the US and some other countries, there is a fairly clear distinction between demand deposits and other kinds of deposits, but in many countries the distinction is less clear. There are accounts with different conditions and it is not obvious which accounts should count as 'money'. Another problem with the M1 definition is that M1 is not directly controlled by the central bank. Individuals can easily transfer money between different accounts, thereby changing M1.

Broad money aggregates

There are also broader definitions of money that are sometimes used. One measure, M2, includes savings deposits and time deposits below a certain total value. These are deposits that yield interest and which may be costly to withdraw at short notice. An even broader measure, M3, also includes large time deposits and some money market funds. These monetary aggregates are not controlled by the central bank, and savings and time deposits cannot be used to make payments. To make a payment, the owner has to transfer the money to a demand deposit account or go to the bank to withdraw cash. Therefore, savings and time deposits are not mediums of exchange but forms of financial savings. Furthermore, these assets yield interest while a key characteristic of money in our theory is that money does not yield interest. Therefore, the monetary base and M1 are the empirical measures of the stock of money, which most closely correspond to our theoretical notion of money as we have defined it above.[3]

7.4 Does money growth explain inflation?

The theory presented above points to money growth as an important determinant of inflation. It does not, however, say that money is the only cause of inflation. For a given rate of money growth, variations in velocity and growth of real GDP also lead to variations in inflation. So how well does money growth explain inflation? Table 7.1 and Fig. 7.1 show average growth in M1 and consumer price inflation for the period 1990–2010 for some OECD countries. For countries with high money growth rates, the correlation is relatively strong. There is clearly a relation between money growth and inflation if we look at countries with very large

---

3 Banks and financial intermediation will be discussed in Chapter 18.

Table 7.1 *Money growth and inflation, 1990–2010*

	Money growth	Inflation
United States	4	2
New Zealand	5	2
Japan	6	0
Switzerland	6	1
Denmark	7	2
Canada	8	2
Australia	9	2
United Kingdom	9	2
Korea	12	4
Israel	15	5
Iceland	16	4
Chile	17	6
Poland	20	14
Mexico	20	11
Turkey	47	41

Note: The table shows yearly M1 growth and consumer price
inflation for the OECD countries where data is available.
Source: *OECD Economic Outlook*, OECD, 17 April 2012,
http://www.oecd-ilibrary.org/statistics.

Fig. 7.1 *Money growth and inflation, 1990–2010, percent*

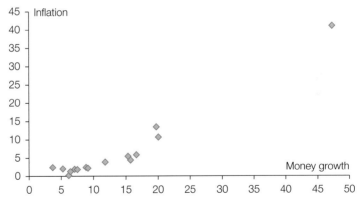

Note: The figure shows yearly M1 growth and consumer price inflation for the OECD countries where
data is available.
Source: *OECD Economic Outlook*, OECD, 17 April 2012, http://www.oecd-ilibrary.org/statistics.

differences in money growth. If we look at countries with low money growth
rates, there is no relation, however. The first eight countries in the table had
money growth rates between 4 and 9 percent, yet all had inflation rates below
3 percent. Clearly, there were also differences in real growth and changes in
velocity that affected the relation between money growth and inflation in this
period.

  If we look at changes from year to year for an individual country, the connection
between money growth and inflation is very weak. As we see in Fig. 7.2, money

Fig. 7.2 *Money growth and inflation*

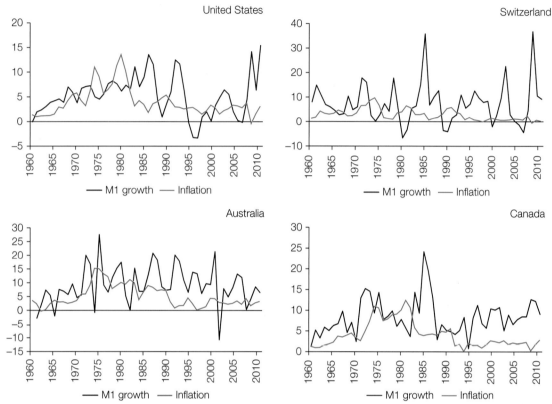

Note: Money growth is measured by the growth rate of M1. Inflation is measured by the growth rate of the consumer price index.
Source: *OECD Economic Outlook*, OECD, 19 April 2012, http://www.oecd-ilibrary.org/statistics.

growth does not help much to explain changes in inflation. Clearly, the velocity of money is far from constant.

Fig. 7.3 shows two measures of velocity. We see that there are large variations in velocity from one year to the next.

Should we conclude that money growth is unimportant for inflation? No. Higher money growth will lead to higher inflation, *ceteris paribus*. By changing money growth, the central bank can control inflation seen over a longer period, but to do that it has to take account of changes in real production and changes in velocity. In practice, however, central banks control inflation by setting the interest rate. We will see how the central bank can control the interest rate when we analyse monetary policy in the short run in Chapters 8–10.

7.5   Money demand

The interest rate and money demand

One of the factors that may affect velocity is the interest rate. The nominal interest rate is the opportunity cost of holding money – cash that does not yield interest –

Fig. 7.3 *Velocity*

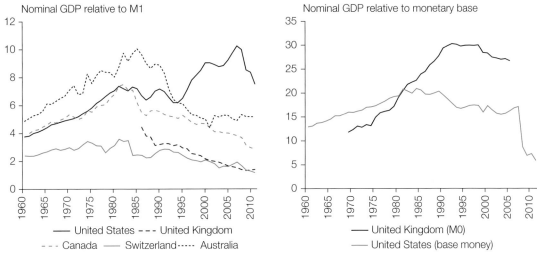

Nominal GDP relative to M1

Nominal GDP relative to monetary base

— United States --- United Kingdom
--- Canada — Switzerland ····· Australia

— United Kingdom (M0)
— United States (base money)

Source: International Financial Statistics, IMF, 27 June 2012. International Financial Statistics, IMF, 17 June 2012.

so if the interest rate is high it is plausible that people will be less willing to hold money. This means that money will circulate at a faster rate, so the velocity of money is an increasing function of the interest rate:

$$V = V(i).$$

Then we can rewrite the equation $MV = PY$ as

$$\frac{M}{P} = \frac{Y}{V(i)}.$$

Here, we can think of the right-hand side as the real *demand for money* – that is, the amount of money that households, firms, and banks want to have to carry out their transactions. The equation says that the available supply of money, measured in real terms, must be equal to the demand for money. We see that demand for money increases with a higher level of production and decreases if the interest rate increases.[4] The interest rate is the opportunity cost of holding money so if the interest rate increases, demand for money will decrease.

Inflation and real money holdings

We know from our analysis of savings and investment that, in the long run, the *real* interest rate is equal to the natural rate of interest, which is independent of monetary policy. Since the real interest rate is the nominal interest rate minus inflation, $r = i - \pi$, the nominal interest rate must be equal to the natural (real) rate of interest plus inflation:

$$i = r^n + \pi.$$

---

4 If the interest rate increases, V increases, so Y/V decreases.

In the long run, the nominal interest rate compensates for inflation, which erodes the value of the money that is lent. Thus we have

$$\frac{M}{P} = \frac{Y^n}{V(r^n + \pi)}.$$

From this equation we see that higher inflation leads to a *decrease* in the real money holdings. Since money growth increases inflation, this may appear paradoxical. The *faster* the nominal money supply increases, the *lower* is the real money supply. But recall that inflation raises the nominal rate of interest, which is the opportunity cost of holding money, and this is why real money balances decrease.

The connection between inflation and real money holdings is most obvious in an economy with hyperinflation. In such an economy, money loses value very quickly and the nominal rate of interest is high to compensate for inflation. As a result, people are very unwilling to hold money. As soon as they get their wage, they will buy something that is more likely to keep its real value, or try to lend their money at the high interest rate. Hence, the price level will be so high that real money holdings are reduced. The price level is determined by

$$P = \frac{MV(r^n + \pi)}{Y^n}.$$

When money supply grows fast, the nominal money supply is high, but the price level is even higher. This is illustrated in Fig. 7.4, where we illustrate the path of money supply and the price level for an economy which first has a constant money supply and price level and then a constantly growing money supply and price level from time τ onwards. We assume here that the increase in money growth is unexpected but perfectly foreseen after time τ. Production is at the natural level, assumed to be constant. We consider the natural logs of prices and money because a constant change in the log of P corresponds to a constant percentage change – that is, constant inflation. When money growth and inflation increase, the nominal interest rate will increase and real demand for money balances decreases. Hence there is a jump in the price level and a downward jump in real balances. After that, money and prices grow at the same rate. Inflation is a tax on holding money and the higher the inflation tax on money, the less people want to hold of it, in real terms.

Fig. 7.4 *An unexpected and permanent increase in the money growth rate at time τ*

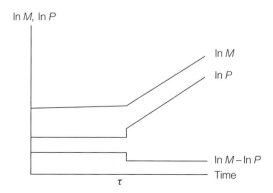

To sum up, the relation between money and interest rates is a complicated relationship. Over the long run, high growth of money raises inflation and the nominal interest rate while not affecting the real interest rate. A high nominal interest rate increases the opportunity cost of holding money so real money demand falls (velocity increases). Therefore, a high rate of money growth reduces the real quantity of money.

7.6   Seignorage

As we discussed above, the central bank can control the monetary base. It can create as much monetary base as it wants. The monetary base needs to increase if the volume of transactions increases over time and in order to increase the monetary base, the central bank lends money to the government and to the private sector. When the central bank buys government bonds, it is effectively lending to the government. This is most obvious if the central bank buys the bond directly from the government, but even if it buys the bond from a private bank, we can think of it as an indirect loan to the government. The only difference is that the bond has passed through the hands of the private bank.

   To sell bonds to the central bank – directly or indirectly – is one way in which a government can finance a deficit. The revenue from money creation is called *seignorage*. But how much expenditure can be financed in this way? This is easy to find out. If the increase of the monetary base is ΔM, seignorage as a proportion of GDP is

$$\frac{\Delta M}{PY}.$$

Assume that real GDP increases at the rate $g + n$ where g is the rate of improvement of technology and n is the population growth rate. If we use M to denote the monetary base we have $M = P \cdot Y/V$. Using the rule of thumb for growth rates and assuming that velocity is constant we have

$$\frac{\Delta M}{M} = \pi + g + n.$$

The monetary base must increase at the same rate as nominal GDP – at the rate $\pi + g + n$. Using this to substitute for ΔM in the expression above we get

$$\frac{\Delta M}{PY} = (\pi + g + n)\frac{M}{PY} = \frac{\pi + g + n}{V}.$$

Suppose, for example, that inflation is 2 percent and the real growth rate is 3 percent – then the growth rate of nominal GDP is 5 percent. Suppose, further, that the monetary base is 1/20 of GDP – the velocity of the monetary base is 20. Then seignorage is a quarter of a percent of GDP ($0.05/20 = 0.0025$). A government deficit in this order can be financed by seignorage.

   Note that seignorage arises for two reasons. First, real growth increases the demand for monetary base. Second, inflation reduces the real value of the monetary base so the monetary base has to increases in nominal terms. The latter part of the seignorage can be seen as an *inflation tax*. Expressed as a fraction of GDP it is the inflation rate divided by the velocity of the monetary base, π/V. In our numerical example, it is one promille of GDP (0.02/20).

7.7 Should we dislike inflation?

The primary goal of most central banks is 'price stability', which is typically interpreted as low inflation. But why is it important to have low inflation and what level of inflation is a reasonable target? Should we aim at 2, 3, 5, or zero percent inflation?

One might argue that low inflation is important because high inflation erodes the value of our wages. When prices rise, we can buy less with a given nominal wage, so we all become poorer. But recall that, according to the theory in Chapter 2, the real wage is determined by the marginal product of labour and the mark-up, both of which are independent of inflation:

$$\frac{W}{P} = \frac{MPL}{1+\mu}.$$

Inflation implies a general increase in *all* prices including the price of labour. If all prices and wages increase by 10 per cent the real wage is unchanged. Thus we would not expect inflation to have any major effect on real wages. The main argument against inflation must be a different one.

With high inflation, firms need to change prices more often. Restaurants, for example, need to print new menus more frequently. These so-called 'menu costs' are a concrete but probably a minor cost of inflation.

A more important consequence of high inflation is that the *price system* functions less well. One effect of inflation is that, since firms change prices at different points in time, relative prices change back and forth. A firm that has not changed its price for a while will have a relatively low price and a firm that has recently changed its price will have a relatively high price. Such relative price changes lead to inefficient reallocation of consumption because relative price changes occur which do not reflect differences in the marginal costs of production.

Another effect is that it becomes harder to remember and compare prices. In order to compare prices when there is high inflation, you need to remember not only *what* the price was last time you observed the price of an individual good. In order to adjust for the general increase in the price level you must also remember *when* you observed the price. This information problem distorts consumption choices. An individual may abstain from buying a good which is perceived as relatively expensive when in fact it is not because all prices have increased.

The functioning of the price system is important for economic efficiency. More efficient firms can offer lower prices and attract more sales, thereby raising the welfare of the consumers. If relative prices are distorted or consumers find it hard to compare prices because of high inflation, this can have substantial negative effects on welfare.

Another aspect is that *tax and benefit systems* are typically specified in nominal terms – that is, in terms of money. For given rules in the tax and benefit systems, inflation changes the real levels of taxes and benefits. For a given tax schedule, a general increase in prices and wages means that individuals are moved to higher tax brackets. During a period when benefits remain constant in nominal terms, their real values are eroded by inflation.

The costs described above will arise even if inflation is stable and foreseen by households and firms. In practice, however, countries with high inflation also tend to have more *variable* inflation rates. This means that inflation is sometimes higher than expected and sometimes lower than expected. *Unexpected inflation* redistributes income and wealth in unpredictable ways. If wages are set in one-year wage contracts, unexpectedly high inflation will reduce real wages below the level that was expected when the contracts were written. Also, unexpected inflation reduces the real value of outstanding loans. Put differently, the realized real interest rate becomes lower than what was expected when the loan was made. This uncertainty complicates decision-making and planning for lenders as well as for borrowers.

Clearly, these costs will be substantial if inflation is very high and variable, and this motivates a monetary policy that aims for low and reasonably stable inflation. But how low? Should we try to get inflation down to zero? There are some arguments against having such a low inflation target:

1. The costs of inflation, which we have discussed above, are probably not very large for low or moderate inflation rates. It is probably not necessary to bring inflation down to zero in order to make these costs small.

2. Another argument against a very low inflation target has to do with nominal wage rigidity. The labour market is segmented into many different submarkets and there are shocks that shift supply and demand in different labour markets. Relative wage movements are needed in order to adjust to these shocks. If inflation is very low, some of these relative wage adjustments may require nominal wages to fall but there is evidence that firms seldom reduce the nominal wages of their workers. This may be because of social conventions or union contracts. In some countries there are laws saying that mutual agreement is needed in order to implement a wage cut. Such *downward nominal wage rigidity* may prevent some relative wage adjustments which are necessary in order to maintain high employment. With low inflation, it is more likely that downward rigidity prevents wage adjustment.[5]

3. Another argument for having an inflation target above zero has to do with the fact that there is a *zero lower bound* on the interest rate. Nobody wants to lend at a rate below zero because it is better to keep the money under the mattress than to lend at a negative interest rate. Suppose that we have a very low inflation rate and, as a consequence, a very low nominal interest rate. Now, suppose there is a negative demand shock so that a reduction in the real

5 For an analysis of the consequences of downward nominal wage rigidity, see Steinar Holden, 'The cost of price stability: downward nominal wage rigidity in Europe', *Economica*, 71 (2004), 183–208. See also William Dickens, Lorenz Götte, Erika Groshen, Steinar Holden, Julian Messina, Mark Schweitzer, Jarkko Turunen, and Melanie Ward-Warmedinger, 'How wages change: micro evidence from the International Wage Flexibility Project', *Journal of Economic Perspectives*, 21 (2007), 195–214.

interest rate is needed in order to prop up aggregate demand. But if the nominal interest rate is already low, the central bank may be unable to reduce the interest rate sufficiently to counteract the effect of the demand shock. We may then find ourselves in a situation where inflation is low or even negative, and the interest rate has reached the lower bound. In order to give the central bank scope to counteract negative demand shocks, it is better to keep a positive rate of inflation in normal times.

Thus we can conclude that very high inflation is clearly undesirable, and zero inflation is probably too low. Whether 2 percent inflation is better than 4 percent inflation is hard to know, however. In practice, most countries have decided to aim for a low but positive rate of inflation. Many central banks have inflation targets in the range 2–3 percent.

What have we learned?

In our theory we assume that money is:
- a medium of exchange
- a unit of account
- a store of value that does not yield interest
- a stock that is controlled by the central bank.

The prime example of money is currency (cash), but other assets can fulfil similar roles.

Velocity V is defined by

$$M \cdot V = P \cdot Y.$$

If we take velocity as exogenous, the money supply to be controlled by the central bank, and production to be at its natural level, the price level is determined by

$$P = \frac{M \cdot V}{Y^n}.$$

Inflation is the rate of change of the price level, so the rule of thumb for growth rates gives

$$\pi = \frac{\Delta M}{M} + \frac{\Delta V}{V} - \frac{\Delta Y^n}{Y^n}.$$

The *monetary base* is currency in circulation plus banks' claims on the central bank. The monetary base corresponds closely to our concept of money because all payments involve the use of monetary base and the central bank can control the monetary base by open market operations and lending to banks.

M1 is another definition of money; it includes currency plus demand deposits. It is typically larger than the monetary base because banks need to hold only a fraction of their demand deposits as reserves. It is less tightly controlled by the central bank than the monetary base.

There are broader 'money' aggregates, which include interest-bearing assets that cannot be used directly as a medium of exchange. These are more general measures of liquid assets and financial intermediation.

Countries with very high money growth rates typically have high inflation rates, but from year to year there is not much correlation between money growth and inflation in low-inflation countries. Velocity is far from constant.

Demand for money increases with the volume of transactions. Since money yields zero or low interest, the interest is the opportunity cost of holding money – that is, the income you forego if you hold money. Therefore, the velocity of money is an increasing function of the interest rate. Put differently, money demand decreases with the rate of interest rate. We have the equilibrium condition saying that real money supply should be equal to money demand:

$$\frac{M}{P} = \frac{Y}{V(i)}.$$

Seignorage is the revenue that the central bank gets from increasing the supply of monetary base. With normal growth and inflation rates it is a fraction of a percent of GDP.

High inflation leads to costs of changing prices and distortions of the price system. Unexpected inflation leads to random redistribution since wages, nominal interest rates, and tax and benefits systems are specified in nominal terms. Very low inflation and deflation may also be problematic because there are impediments to nominal wage cuts and there is a zero lower bound for the interest rate. Many central banks have inflation targets between 2 and 4 percent.

Where do we go from here?

In this chapter, we introduced money into our model, and we analysed the relation between money, inflation, and interest rates in the long run. This completes our analysis of the long run and we now turn to analysis of how the macro economy functions in the short run. We will use the same basic model to analyse short-run fluctuations, but there is an important difference. In the short run, wages and prices adjust slowly. As we will see, this has important consequences for how the economy responds to exogenous shocks.

Exercises

1. Discuss whether the following items qualify as 'money' in the sense that they have the four characteristics that money has in our theory:
   a) Gold
   b) Dollar bills
   c) Money on a savings account
   d) A credit card
   e) Foreign currency
   f) Banks' claims in the payment system (reserves).

2. Discuss how the following eventualities may affect the demand for monetary base:
   a) Because of high inflation, people start to use foreign currency for large payments.
   b) Summer comes and people go on holiday.
   c) Because of financial uncertainty, banks start to hold more money in their accounts in the payment system.
   d) It becomes possible to pay with credit card on buses and trains.

3. Suppose that money grows at a rate of 10 percent per year, GDP grows at a rate of 3 percent per year, and velocity is constant. What is the inflation rate?

4. Suppose that inflation is 3 percent, GDP grows 2 percent per year and velocity is constant. What is the growth rate of the money supply?

5. 'High inflation is a tax on people who save.' Is this true or false?

6. 'The inflation tax is an alternative to explicit taxation of income.' Is this true or false?

7. 'Higher expected inflation in the future will raise inflation today.' Is this true or false? If true, clarify the conditions under which the statement may be true.

8. In 2004 GDP in the US was 11,876 billion dollars and in 2005 it was 12,718 billion dollars. The monetary base was 759 billion in 2004 and 787 billion in 2005.
   a) Calculate the velocity for the monetary base in 2004 and 2005.
   b) Calculate seignorage relative to GDP ($\Delta M/(PY)$) in 2005.
   c) Use the equation in Section 7.6 to calculate what seignorage would have been if velocity had remained unchanged between 2004 and 2005.
   d) Explain the difference between the results in b) and c).

9. Suppose that the velocity of the monetary base is 20, real GDP grows 3 percent per year and inflation is 2 percent.
   a) Use the equation derived in this chapter to calculate seignorage relative to GDP.

b) Calculate seignorage relative to GDP if the real growth rate is instead 8 percent and velocity remains unchanged.

c) Calculate seignorage relative to GDP if inflation is instead 7 percent and velocity remains unchanged.

d) Would you expect velocity to be the same in cases b) and c) as in a)? Consider both the short and the long run.

e) Is the result in c) an over- or underestimation of the increase in seignorage?

10. Assume that velocity is determined by the function

$$V = V^0 e^{bi}.$$

The nominal interest rate is determined by $i = r^n + \pi$ where the natural (real) rate of interest, r^n, is taken as given.
   a) Write down an expression for seinorage as a fraction of GDP. We assume that there is no population growth ($n = 0$).
   b) Calculate an expression for the rate of inflation that maximizes seignorage. How does the result depend on the parameters b and g? Explain the result.
   c) What inflation rate maximizes seignorage if $b = 0.5$ and $g = 0.02$?
   d) Assume that $b = 0.5$, $g = 0.02$, $r^n = 0.03$, and $V^0 = 19.6$. Calculate money growth and seignorage as a fraction of GDP when inflation is 2 and 6 percent. Explain the results.
   e) Calculate seignorage relative to GDP when inflation is 100, 200 and 300 percent. Explain the result.

Answers to the exercises can be found at: **www.palgrave.com/economics/gottfries**.

Appendix

Transaction habits, demand for money, and the money multiplier

To understand how the demand for monetary base is related to the volume of transactions, let us use nominal GDP as a measure of transactions and assume that a fraction λ of the transactions is made with cash and a fraction $1 - \lambda$ is made by debit cards and cheques drawing on demand deposits. Suppose that currency has velocity v_c – that is, each unit of currency is used for v_c transactions during a year. Then currency holdings are equal to $\lambda PY / v_c$. Similarly we assume that each unit of demand deposits is used for v_d transactions during a year, so holdings of demand deposits are $(1 - \lambda) PY / v_d$. Finally, assume that banks, on average, hold reserves in the central bank equal to a fraction rr of their demand deposits, where rr is a number smaller than unity. Then the monetary base (H) needed to carry out all these transactions is

$$H = \frac{\lambda PY}{v_c} + rr \frac{(1 - \lambda) PY}{v_d} = \left[\frac{\lambda}{v_c} + rr \frac{1 - \lambda}{v_d} \right] PY.$$

Thus we have

$$HV = PY \qquad \text{where} \qquad V = \left[\frac{\lambda}{v_c} + rr \frac{1 - \lambda}{v_d} \right]^{-1}.$$

The velocity of the monetary base depends on payment habits. Suppose, for example that $v_c = v_d$. Then, if people start to use their debit cards more, the velocity of circulation of the monetary base will increase. Less monetary base will be needed per transaction because banks hold only a fraction of their demand deposits in the form of monetary base.

With the assumptions made above, M1 is

$$M1 = \frac{\lambda PY}{v_c} + \frac{(1 - \lambda) PY}{v_d} = \left[\frac{\lambda}{v_c} + \frac{1 - \lambda}{v_d} \right] PY.$$

Using the relation between PY and H above we can find the relation between M1 and the monetary base:

$$M1 = \frac{\dfrac{\lambda}{v_c} + \dfrac{1 - \lambda}{v_d}}{\dfrac{\lambda}{v_c} + rr \dfrac{1 - \lambda}{v_d}} H.$$

Dividing by $(1 - \lambda) / v_d$ in the numerator and the denominator, we can rewrite this as

$$M1 = \frac{cr + 1}{cr + rr} H; \qquad \text{where} \qquad cr = \frac{\lambda / v_c}{(1 - \lambda) / v_d}.$$

Here, cr is the ratio of cash to demand deposits. For given rr and cr, M1 is proportional to H and since the ratio of reserves to deposits is smaller than one, M1 is larger than H. For given cr and rr, M1 is equal to a multiplier times the monetary base.

PART 2 THE SHORT RUN

THE INTEREST RATE AND PRODUCTION IN THE SHORT RUN

What causes short-run fluctuations in production and employment?

In the previous chapter we saw that there is a clear distinction between real and nominal variables. In the long run, real variables such as production, the real wage, and the real interest rate are independent of the money supply. Production is determined by the available production factors, the level of technology, and the natural rate of unemployment. The real wage is determined by the marginal product of labour and the mark-up factor, and the real rate of interest is determined so as to make desired savings equal to desired investment when production is at the natural level.

With the real variables determined in this way, the level of the money supply determines the nominal variables – that is, variables expressed in monetary units. These include the price level and the nominal wage. The growth rate of the money supply determines the inflation rate and the nominal interest rate. Thus, we have a *recursive* system when we look at the economy in the long run: we can analyse the real variables first and then the nominal ones. This is how we proceeded in Chapters 2–7.

There are two fundamental reasons behind this division between real and nominal variables:

1. *The neutrality of money.* Standard economic theory says that people care about real things. Workers and firms care about real income, the real wage, and the real interest rate. If the money supply and all prices and wages increase by 10 percent, real consumption, utility, and profits stay the same. In theory, nobody should care if one litre of milk costs one, two, or three euros if wages and all other prices rise in the same proportion.
2. *Flexible wages and prices.* When analysing the long run, we assumed that prices and wages adjusted to any changes in the exogenous variables that may occur. In fact, this is the *definition* of the long run; the long-run effect of a change in an exogenous variable is the effect on the economy after enough time has passed for wages and prices to adjust to the shock.

The forces behind wage and price adjustment were analysed in Chapter 6. Whenever employment is above the natural level, all firms want to raise their relative wages, so there is upward pressure on wages. Conversely, when employment is low, firms have incentives to reduce their relative wages. Therefore, the only possible long-run equilibrium is where employment and production are at their natural levels.

This analysis is relevant for the long run, but wages and prices do not adjust from one day to the next. Numerous studies have documented that wages and prices change infrequently.[1] The evidence shows that wages change about once per year, but wage contracts are often longer than that. Union wage contracts typically cover periods of one, two or three years. This means that the wage that is paid out in a particular month may be determined in a contract that was agreed on three years ago. Studies of price-setting practices show that prices change once or twice per year. Hence we know that wages and prices adjust slowly to shocks; they are 'sticky'. As we will see at the end of this chapter, there is also evidence on the macroeconomic level showing that wages and prices respond very slowly to shocks.

Slow wage and price adjustment implies that the economy functions very differently in the short run compared with the long run. In the short run, aggregate demand for goods and services may be higher or lower than the natural level of production. Firms produce what they can sell and hire the workers they need to satisfy demand, so employment may also be above or below the natural level.[2] When production is above the natural level employment will also be above the natural level and unemployment will be below the natural level. This leads to upward pressure on wages and prices. In this chapter, we take the price level as given, however.

As a result of slow wage and price adjustment, the short-run effect of a specific exogenous shock is different from the long-run effect of the same shock. Consider, for example, a change in the pension system that reduces expected future pensions. To compensate for this, people start to save more. We know from the national accounts that, in a closed economy, investment is equal to savings, so in the long run higher savings should increase the capital stock, leading to a *higher* level of production. But in the short run, higher savings means a decrease in aggregate demand, which may very well lead to *lower* production. Thus, we need to make a clear distinction between the short and the long run when analysing how exogenous shocks affect the economy.

Another important consequence of slow wage and price adjustment is that monetary policy can affect real variables. In the long run, a 2 percent increase in the money supply will increase the price level by 2 percent and leave the real money supply, M/P, and other real variables unchanged. But with slow price adjustment in the short run, a change in the nominal money supply, M, affects the real money supply, M/P. As a consequence, monetary policy can affect real variables such as the real interest rate and production. Therefore, we must analyse

1 Reviews of such studies can be found in John Taylor, 'Staggered price and wage setting in macroeconomics', in Michael Woodford and John Taylor (eds.), *Handbook of Monetary Economics*, 1B (Amsterdam: North-Holland, 1999); Luis Álvarez *et al.*, 'Sticky prices in the Eurozone: A summary of new micro evidence', *Journal of the European Economic Association*, 4 (2006), 575–584; and Peter Klenow and Benjamin Malin, *Microeconomic Evidence on Price-setting*, NBER working paper 15826, Cambridge, MA, 2010.
2 Since markets are monopolistic, prices are set higher than (expected) marginal cost. If there is an unexpected increase in demand after prices have been set, firms have incentives to satisfy that increase in demand by increasing their production.

the determination of real and nominal variables simultaneously when we consider the short run. We no longer have a recursive structure, where real variables are determined independent of the nominal price level and the money supply.

The theory of the short run will help us to understand short-run fluctuations – business cycles – and why countries sometimes end up in depression, with production and employment far below the natural level. To analyse the short run, we use the *IS-LM model*, which summarizes the theory that John Maynard Keynes developed in the 1930s.[3] The *IS-LM* model shows how the nominal interest rate and production are determined for a given level of prices. The *IS-LM* model consists of two equations. One equation, *IS*, says that production must be equal to aggregate demand. The other equation, *LM*, says that money demand must be equal to money supply. We have already seen these equations when we analysed the long run. The difference is that we now take prices as given. As we will see, this makes a big difference.

In reality, wages and prices are not completely rigid but they adjust to some extent to shocks, even in the short run. The adjustment is slow, however, so we simplify by keeping prices exogenous in this chapter. Short-run wage and price adjustment is analysed in Chapter 9.

In the following, we first analyse the market for goods and services and we derive the *IS curve* which shows how the level of production depends on the interest rate. Then we analyse the money market and derive the *LM curve*, which shows how the interest rate depends on the level of production for a given money supply. Combining the *IS* and *LM* curves, we have the *IS-LM* model, which we will use to analyse the short-run effects of shocks and economic policy. At the end of the chapter we look at some empirical evidence on the effects of monetary policy.

8.1   Goods market equilibrium and the multiplier effect

We first analyse the goods market. This will help us to see how aggregate production is determined in the short run. Aggregate demand consists of private consumption and private investment. Adding consumption and investment we get an equation determining aggregate demand:

$$Y = C(Y, Y^e, r, A) + I(r, Y^e, K).$$

As before, Y denotes real production (and income), C is private consumption, Y^e is expected future income, r is the expected real interest rate, A is the asset holdings (wealth) of the consumer, and K is the capital stock at the beginning of the period. $Y, C,$ and I are measured in units of the consumption basket. $C(Y, Y^e, r, A)$ and $I(r, Y^e, K)$ are consumption and investment functions which we derived in Chapters 3 and 4, and which represent the behaviour of consumers and firms.

---

3 John Maynard Keynes presented his theory in *General Theory of Employment, Interest, and Money* (London, Macmillan, 1936). John Hicks and Alvin Hansen formalized his theory and called this formalization the *IS-LM* model.

In Chapters 11 and 12 we will add a government and exports and imports. This will affect our analysis of aggregate demand but we start with the simpler case of a closed economy without a government sector.

The equation above is not new. In the long-run analysis, we used it to determine the real rate of interest, assuming that production was at the natural level. Our motivation was that, if production would be above the natural level, employment would be above the natural level, and there would be upward pressure on wages. Similarly, production below the natural level would imply downward pressure on wages. But in the short run, wages and prices adjust slowly, so aggregate demand can be higher or lower than the natural level of production. At any point in time, firms produce in order to satisfy demand, so the equation above determines the level of production in the short run for a given interest rate.

The determination of demand and production is illustrated in Fig. 8.1. We have the level of production (and income) on the horizontal axis and aggregate demand on the vertical axis. The line with a 45-degree slope shows points where aggregate demand is equal to production. We have also drawn the consumption function, which shows that consumption increases with income. It is drawn for a given real interest rate, given expectations about future income, and a given level of assets. Adding consumption and investment we get a line, denoted $C + I$, that shows aggregate demand as a function of income. We can call this line the *aggregate demand schedule.* Since consumption increases with income, so does aggregate demand. The slope of the aggregate demand schedule is determined by the marginal propensity to consume – that is, the derivative of the consumption function with respect to income. Provided that consumers save a share of any additional income that they receive, the marginal propensity to consume out of income is below unity, so the slope is smaller than unity. Note that the aggregate demand schedule is drawn for a given interest rate, wealth, capital stock, and taking other variables that influence consumption and investment as given.

Production is determined by aggregate demand, so the short-run equilibrium level of production is Y_0 where the aggregate demand schedule intersects the 45-degree line. If production is below this level, demand exceeds production, so firms will increase production. Conversely, if production is above Y_0, firms are unable to sell what they produce, so production will fall. Therefore the short-run equilibrium level of production is Y_0.

Note that this short-run equilibrium level of production may be above or below the natural level. In Fig. 8.1, the short-run equilibrium is below the natural level of production. This means that employment will also be below the natural level, so unemployment is above the natural level.

Suppose now that firms become more optimistic about the future, so investment increases by an amount equal to ΔI units of production. Such a shock will shift the aggregate demand schedule up by an amount ΔI. Again, we can find the new equilibrium level of production at the intersection with the 45-degree line. As we see in Fig. 8.2, the increase in production from Y_0 to Y_2 is *larger* than the original upward shift in the aggregate demand schedule, which was due to the exogenous shock. Why is this? The reason is that an exogenous increase in investment raises demand and leads to a corresponding increase in production,

Fig. 8.1 *Short-run equilibrium in the product market*

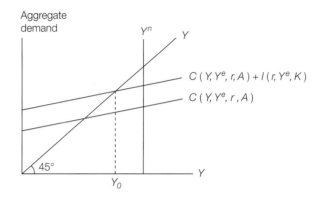

Fig. 8.2 *The multiplier effect*

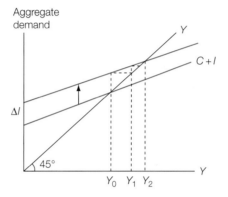

but as income increases there will be a further increase in consumption, leading to a further increase in demand and production, and so on. The initial effect is that production increases to Y_1, which is equal to $Y_0 + \Delta I$, but Y_1 is not an equilibrium because at that level of production aggregate demand $(C + I)$ is higher than production. Therefore, production must increase further – and this process continues until a new equilibrium is reached.

How large is the total increase in production? To understand this, suppose that the original shock increased investment by 1000 euros and that the marginal propensity to consume out of current income is 0.6. Then the direct effect of the shock is an increase in production by 1000 euros. But production generates income and that income goes to the consumers in the form of wages, interest payments, and dividends, so consumers' incomes also increase by 1000 euros. They will therefore increase their consumption by 600 euros and this increases demand and production by a further 600 euros. This is still not an equilibrium situation, however, because the additional 600 euros of production also go to the consumers as added income and increases their consumption by another 360 euros (0.6 times 600), and so on. The total effect on production is

$$1000 + 0.6 \cdot 1000 + 0.6 \cdot 0.6 \cdot 1000 + \ldots = 1000 + 600 + 360 + \ldots = 2500.$$

We see that production increases more than the initial shock to demand. In this case, the final effect on production is 2.5 times as large as the original demand shock. The general formula is that if the marginal propensity to consume is c and the original demand shock is ΔI, the total increase in production is determined by the infinite sum[4]

$$\Delta Y = \Delta I + c\Delta I + c^2\Delta I + c^3\Delta I + \ldots = \left(1 + c + c^2 + c^3 + \ldots\right)\Delta I = \frac{1}{1-c}\Delta I.$$

The total effect of a demand shock is equal to the shock multiplied by a factor which is greater than one. If $c=0.6$ the multiplier is 2.5 as $1/(1-0.6)=1/0.4=2.5$. The higher the marginal propensity to consume out of current income, the larger is the total effect. This amplification of the initial effect of a shock is called the *multiplier effect*.

In Chapters 11–14, we will make the model more realistic by including a government and trade with foreign countries. As we will see, this will reduce the size of the multiplier because the government taxes away some of the additional income and part of the increase in demand is directed towards goods produced abroad.

8.2 How the interest rate affects demand and production

As we saw in Chapters 3 and 4, the real interest rate is an important determinant of aggregate demand. What determines consumption and investment decisions is the expected real interest rate, the nominal interest rate minus expected inflation:

$$r = i - \pi^e.$$

Here, i is the nominal interest rate from this year to the next and π^e is expected inflation from this year to the next. As we will see later in this chapter, the central bank can control the nominal interest rate. In order to see how the nominal interest rate affects aggregate demand, we substitute the expression for the expected real interest rate in our equation for aggregate demand:

$$Y = C\left(Y, Y^e, i - \pi^e, A\right) + I\left(i - \pi^e, Y^e, K\right).$$

In the short-run analysis we take expected inflation as exogenous. This means that an increase in the nominal interest rate increases the expected real interest rate, so consumption and investment will decrease. The effect on production is illustrated in Fig. 8.3. The increase in the interest rate shifts the aggregate demand schedule

---

4 This can be proved simply. Let the value of the sum inside the brackets be S:

$$S = 1 + c + c^2 + c^3 + \ldots$$

Then we can write

$$S = 1 + c + c^2 + c^3 + \ldots = 1 + c\left(1 + c + c^2 + c^3 + \ldots\right) = 1 + cS.$$

Subtracting cS on both sides we get $S - cS = 1$, $(1-c)S = 1$ and $S = 1/(1-c)$.

Fig. 8.3 *The effect on production of an increase in the interest rate*

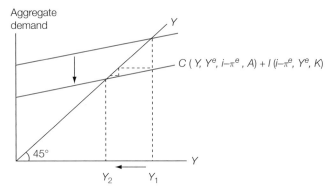

down. As demand falls, production and income decrease, and this leads to a further decrease in consumption. Again, we have a multiplier effect, so the decrease in production will be larger than the direct effect on consumption and investment. The total effect of an increase in the interest rate on production depends on how sensitive consumption and investment are to the interest rate, and the size of the multiplier effect.

The *IS* curve

The relation between the interest rate and production is shown in Fig. 8.4. We have the interest rate on the vertical axis and production on the horizontal axis. We see that there is a negative relation between the interest rate and production. If the interest rate increases from i_1 to i_2, production will decrease from Y_1 to Y_2. This relation is called the *IS curve*. It shows the short-run equilibrium level of production for each level of the interest rate.

Alternatively, we can say that the *IS* curve shows, for a given level of the interest rate, the level of production at which desired savings equals desired investment:

$$Y - C(Y, Y^e, i - \pi^e, A) = I(i - \pi^e, Y^e, K).$$

Here, the left-hand side is aggregate savings and the right-hand side is investment. This is why it is called the *IS curve*.

Fig. 8.4 *The IS curve*

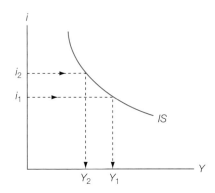

In the national accounts, savings are always equal to investment in a closed economy. But the way this equality is brought about differs between the short and the long run. In the long-run analysis we assumed that production was at the natural level and the real interest rate adjusted in order to equalize savings and investment. In the short run, production adjusts so that savings equals investments for a given interest rate. If there is an increase in the interest rate, investment decreases, and production must fall until savings have fallen by the same amount.[5]

Changes in exogenous variables shift the *IS* curve. If consumers become more optimistic about future income, they will increase their consumption, so aggregate demand and production increase for a given interest rate. The *IS* curve shifts to the right.

Let us sum up what we have learnt about the *IS* curve:

- The *IS* curve shows *what production will be in the goods market for a given interest rate.*
- Changes in the interest rate imply movements *along* the *IS* curve.
- *IS slopes downward* because a higher interest rate has a negative effect on consumption, investment, and aggregate demand.
- The *IS* curve will *shift* if there are changes in exogenous variables (shocks) which affect consumption or investment.

We will use the *IS* curve to analyse the effects of shocks and policy on the macro economy. To do this, it is very important to understand the difference between movements *along* the *IS* curve and *shifts* in the *IS* curve. Changes in the interest rate and production imply movements along the *IS* curve. Shocks to other variables that affect consumption and investment imply shifts of the *IS* curve.

The multiplier and the slope of the *IS* curve

To see more precisely how production is determined we may assume specific functional forms for the consumption and investment functions. Let us assume linear functions:

$$C = a_0 + a_1 Y + a_2 Y^e - a_3 (i - \pi^e) + a_4 A$$

$$I = b_0 - b_1 (i - \pi^e) + b_2 Y^e - b_3 K.$$

The coefficients a_1, a_2, a_3, a_4, b_1, b_2 and b_3 are all positive numbers. Substituting into the goods market equilibrium condition we get

$$Y = a_0 + a_1 Y + a_2 Y^e - a_3 (i - \pi^e) + a_4 A + b_0 - b_1 (i - \pi^e) + b_2 Y^e - b_3 K.$$

To solve for equilibrium production, we subtract $a_1 Y$ on both sides:

$$Y - a_1 Y = a_0 + b_0 - (a_3 + b_1) (i - \pi^e) + (a_2 + b_2) Y^e + a_4 A - b_3 K$$

---

5 To the extent that production is storable, there may be unplanned (undesired) investments during the adjustment process. If firms produce more than they can sell, inventories accumulate, which leads to unplanned inventory investment. But as firms see inventories accumulate, they will reduce production.

and rewrite the left-hand side:

$$Y(1-a_1) = a_0 + b_0 - (a_3 + b_1)(i - \pi^e) + (a_2 + b_2)Y^e + a_4 A - b_3 K.$$

Dividing by $1 - a_1$ on both sides we get

$$Y = \frac{a_0 + b_0}{1-a_1} - \frac{a_3 + b_1}{1-a_1}i + \frac{a_3 + b_1}{1-a_1}\pi^e + \frac{a_2 + b_2}{1-a_1}Y^e + \frac{a_4}{1-a_1}A - \frac{b_3}{1-a_1}K.$$

This shows what production will be for a given interest rate. It is the equation for the *IS* curve. Suppose, for example, that consumers and firms become more optimistic about the future. The effect on production is found by differentiating with respect to Y^e:

$$\Delta Y = \frac{a_2 + b_2}{1-a_1}\Delta Y^e.$$

The direct effect of Y^e on consumption and investment is $a_2 + b_2$ and then there is a multiplier effect, so the total effect is $1/(1-a_1)$ times as large. Note that the coefficient a_1 is the marginal propensity to consume out of current income.

Similarly, the effect of the interest rate on production is found by differentiating with respect to i:

$$\Delta Y = -\frac{a_3 + b_1}{1-a_1}\Delta i.$$

The effect of the interest rate on production is negative. It depends on a_3 and b_1, which measure how sensitive consumption and investment are to the interest rate. Also, the bigger is the marginal propensity to consume out of the current income (a_1), the bigger is the multiplier effect and the total effect of the interest rate on production. The bigger these effects are, the more a change in the interest rate affects production and the flatter will the *IS* curve be.[6]

The *IS* curve and the natural rate of interest

Roughly speaking, we can think of the *IS* curve as a standard microeconomic demand function. As was explained in Chapter 3, one plus the real interest rate is the price of goods today in terms of goods next year. Consumers choose between consuming today and consuming next year. Investors use goods today to increase the capital stock and future production. If the real interest rate increases, investment and consumption today become more expensive in terms of goods next period, so demand for goods today will decrease. This is why the *IS* curve has a negative slope.

The *IS* curve is not quite a standard microeconomic demand function, however, because of the multiplier effect. This effect amplifies the effect of the interest rate on demand because lower demand means lower production and income, and a further decrease in consumption. Hence the slope of the *IS* curve depends not only on how sensitive consumption and investment are to the interest rate but also on the size of the multiplier effect.

---

6 Note that production depends on the interest rate, so when we draw the *IS* curve we have the explanatory variable on the vertical axis and the dependent variable on the horizontal axis.

Fig. 8.5 *The IS curve and the natural rate of interest*

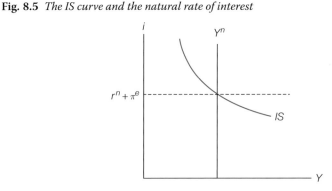

The long-run level of supply is given by the natural level of production. Fig. 8.5 combines the *IS* curve with a line showing the natural level of production. The *IS* curve intersects this line when the nominal interest rate is equal to the natural (real) rate plus expected inflation. This follows from the definition of the natural interest rate as the real interest rate that makes aggregate demand equal to the natural level of production.

This completes our analysis of short-run equilibrium in the goods market. We have derived the *IS* curve, which shows how production depends on the interest rate. The next step is to analyse how the central bank can control the interest rate.

8.3   The money market and the interest rate

Now and then we hear on the news that the central bank has decided to change – or not to change – the interest rate. To see how the central bank can control the interest rate, we need to analyse the market for short-term loans, which is called the *money market.*

In our model economy, households have their savings in three kinds of assets. They own *shares* of the firms which give them dividend payments, they hold *currency* for transaction purposes, and they make *loans* to firms. For the moment we disregard the stock market, assuming simply that the households hold on to their shares in the firms. (We will analyse the stock market in Chapter 18.) This means that households choose between keeping their savings in the form of currency and lending the money to the firms in the money market.[7] If households generally have too much cash compared with what they need for their transactions, they will lend their money, increasing the supply of loans, and the interest rate will fall. Conversely, if there is too little cash, all households want their loans to be paid back, and the interest rate will increase in the money market. For the money market to be in equilibrium, households must be satisfied with their cash balances.

---

7   In practice, the household will often deposit the money in a bank, which then lends the money to a firm or another household, but to keep things simple, we have no banks in our model. Banks are analysed in Chapter 18.

Therefore, we can analyse determination of the interest rate by considering the demand and supply of money. If demand and supply of money balance each other, the demand for and supply of loans must also balance. Therefore, we assume that the interest rate adjusts so that money supply equals money demand:

$$\frac{M}{P} = \frac{Y}{V(i)}.$$

This is the *LM* equation. The right-hand side is money demand which we introduced in Chapter 7. Money demand increases with production because transactions increase, and decreases with a higher interest rate because the interest rate is the opportunity cost of holding money. The money supply, *M*, is determined by the central bank and we take the price level, *P*, as exogenous here. For given levels of money and production, this equation determines the interest rate in the money market. Fig. 8.6 illustrates how the interest rate is determined so that money demand equals money supply.

Suppose now that the central bank wants to reduce the interest rate. Fig. 8.7 shows that the central bank can do that by increasing the money supply. If the central bank buys government bonds from banks, the money supply increases and the interest rate falls. In practice, central banks use repurchase agreements to control the interest rate. For now, we can think of repurchase agreements as short-term

Fig. 8.6 *Money market equilibrium*

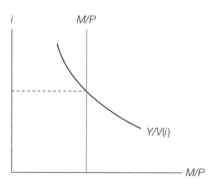

Fig. 8.7 *The effect of an increase in the money supply on the interest rate*

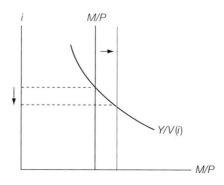

loans to banks, which increase the monetary base. The details of central bank operations will be discussed in Chapter 10.

The *LM* curve

The demand for money depends on the level of production, so changes in production affect the money market. Consider an increase in production and assume that the central bank holds the money supply constant. Increased production implies more transactions and higher demand for money for a given interest rate. As illustrated in Fig. 8.8, the money demand curve shifts out. People need more money for transactions, so they are less willing to lend and the interest rate increases in the money market. If the supply of money does not change, the interest rate must increase until demand for money is again equal to the (unchanged) supply of money.

The relation between production and the interest rate for a given money supply can be illustrated in a diagram with production on the horizontal axis and the interest rate on the vertical axis as in Fig. 8.9. The *LM* curve shows what the interest rate will be in the money market for a given level of production. We call it the *LM* curve because Keynes used the term 'liquidity preference' for money demand. Like the *IS* curve, the *LM* curve gives us a relation between production and the interest rate. This time, the causal relation goes the other way, however. An increase in production leads to a higher volume of transactions and more

Fig. 8.8 *The effect of an increase in production on the interest rate*

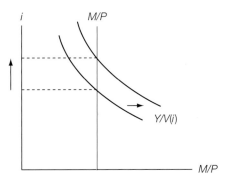

Fig. 8.9 *The LM curve*

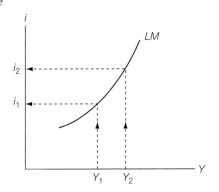

demand for cash, so people become less willing to lend money and the interest rate increases. If production increases from Y_1 to Y_2 the interest rate will increase from i_1 to i_2. This is a movement *along* the *LM* curve. The slope of the *LM* curve depends on how production affects money demand and on the interest elasticity of money demand.

Exogenous shocks that affect the demand and supply of money will shift the *LM* curve. An increase in the money supply will shift the *LM* curve down since a lower interest rate is required for people to hold a larger money stock for a given level of production. An increase in the price level will shift the *LM* curve up since the real money supply decreases so that a higher interest rate is required for the money market to be in equilibrium.

Let us sum up what we know about the *LM* curve:

- The *LM* curve shows *what the interest rate will be in the money market for each level of production* for a given money supply and price level.
- Changes in production imply movements *along* the *LM* curve.
- *LM slopes upward* because higher production leads to a higher volume of transactions and more demand for cash, so people become less willing to lend money and the interest rate increases.
- An increase in the money supply or a decrease in the price level *shifts* the *LM* curve downwards.

8.4 Equilibrium in the goods and money markets

To determine the equilibrium levels of the interest rate and production, we combine the equilibrium conditions for the goods and money markets. This gives us the *IS-LM* model. If we write out the equations for consumption and investment separately we have four equations determining four variables:

$Y = C + I$	Goods market equilibrium
$C = C(Y, Y^e, i - \pi^e, A)$	Consumption function
$I = I(i - \pi^e, Y^e, K)$	Investment function
$\dfrac{M}{P} = \dfrac{Y}{V(i)}.$	Money market equilibrium

Fig. 8.10 illustrates the logical structure of the *IS-LM* model. The endogenous variables are inside the oval and the exogenous variables are outside. There are four endogenous variables in the model, Y, C, I, and i, corresponding to the four equations above. Each arrow shows an influence of one variable on another. For example, production affects the interest rate via money demand. We see that there are quite a few interdependencies in the model. It is a good idea to consider each arrow and think about what it represents.

The first three equations above give us the *IS* curve and the last gives us the *LM* curve. Fig. 8.11 illustrates the short-run macroeconomic equilibrium for a given money supply and price level. The only levels of interest and income where goods and money markets are both in equilibrium are the levels Y_1 and i_1, determined by the intersection of the *IS* and *LM* curves at point A. To see why, consider for example the point B where production is Y_2 and the interest rate is i_2. Since this

Fig. 8.10 *Exogenous and endogenous variables in the* IS-LM *model with exogenous money supply*

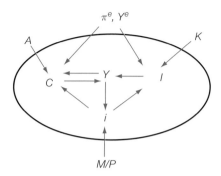

Fig. 8.11 *Short-run equilibrium in goods and money markets*

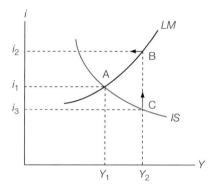

point is on the *LM* curve, the money market is in equilibrium. Households are satisfied with the cash they have. But the goods market is not in equilibrium. The *IS* curve shows the equilibrium level of demand and production for a given interest rate, so if the interest rate is i_2 the level of demand is lower than Y_2. Firms are unable to sell what they produce at point A and they will reduce their production as indicated by the arrow pointing to the left. As production falls, money demand will decrease, and the interest rate will fall, bringing the economy towards the equilibrium point A.

What about point C where production is Y_2 and the interest rate is i_3? This point is on the *IS* curve, so the goods market is in equilibrium. Production equals demand for goods. But the money market is not in equilibrium. Recall that the *LM* curve shows the equilibrium rate of interest for a given level of production. At production Y_2 the interest rate i_3 is too low for the money market to be in equilibrium, so there is excess demand for money. At this low interest rate, households want to hold more cash, so they want to reduce their lending and this puts upward pressure on the interest rate, as indicated by the arrow pointing upwards. As the interest rate increases, investment and consumption will decrease and production will fall.

Therefore, neither point B nor point C are equilibrium situations. In both cases, there is imbalance in some market, setting off a change in one market which in turn affects the other market. Only at the point of intersection of the *IS* and *LM* curves do we have equilibrium in both markets.

Note that the equilibrium in the *IS-LM* model is a short-run equilibrium for a given price level where production is determined by aggregate demand. So, what happened to the production function? Is it no longer relevant? Yes, it is still there, but in the background. In the short run the role of the production function is to determine employment. For a given level of aggregate demand, firms hire the number of workers they need, and that number depends on the production function. The resulting level of employment may be above or below the natural level.

8.5 Effects of exogenous shocks and policy in the *IS-LM* model

We can use the *IS-LM* model to analyse the short-run effects of exogenous shocks and alternative policy responses to those shocks. To analyse how changes in the exogenous variables affect the macroeconomy, we proceed in four steps:

1. *Look at the IS and LM equations to figure out how the IS and LM curves shift.* Which way do they shift and why? Are both curves affected or only one?
2. *See in the IS-LM diagram how equilibrium production and the interest rate are affected.* Is production higher or lower at the new intersection point? Has the interest rate increased or decreased?
3. *Explain in words what is happening in the goods and the money markets as a consequence of the shock.* We start with the direct effect of the shock on the goods or the money market. Then we follow the indirect effects and end up with conclusions about how the interest rate and production are affected by the shock. This should help us to understand the directions of the effects that we found in the graphic analysis in step 2.
4. *Consider how employment, consumption, and investment are affected by the shock.* Once we have found out how production and the interest rate are affected we can use the consumption and investment functions to work out how these variables are affected.

We can also consider alternative policy responses to a given shock. As we will see below, the effect of an exogenous shock will be different if the central bank keeps the interest rate constant compared to the case when it keeps the money supply constant.

An increase in the money supply

Let us use this scheme to analyse the effects of a change in monetary policy. Suppose that the central bank wants to reduce the interest rate. To do that it has to increase the money supply:

1. *Which curves shift and why?* Looking at the *IS* and *LM* equations, we see that money supply affects the *LM* equation but not the *IS* equation. An increase

Fig. 8.12 *The short-run effect of an increase in the money supply*

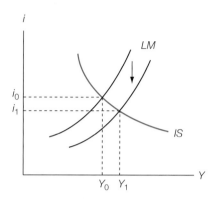

in the money supply shifts the *LM* curve down, as shown in Fig. 8.12, because there will be a lower interest rate for any given level of production. The *IS* curve is unchanged.

2. *What is the effect on production and the interest rate?* The interest rate falls from i_0 to i_1 and production increases from Y_0 to Y_1.

3. *What is the economic explanation?* In order to reduce the interest rate, the central bank buys government securities, or lends to banks, thereby increasing the monetary base and reducing the interest rate. As the interest rate decreases, consumption and investment increase. Firms produce whatever is demanded, so production also increases.

4. *What happens to other variables?* The decrease in the interest rate leads to increases in consumption and investment. As production and income increase, this leads to a further increase in consumption. Since production increases, employment must also increase.

We see that the short-run effect of an increase in the money supply is very different from the long-run effect. In the long run, the supply of money affects the price level, but the real money supply and production are unaffected. But because of slow price adjustment, monetary policy can change the real money supply and the real interest rate in the short run. By changing the real interest rate, monetary policy can affect aggregate demand and production. In this way, monetary policy affects the real side of the economy and monetary policy can potentially be used to stabilize the economy.

When analysing the effect of an increase in the money supply, we treated prices as exogenous and constant. Note, however, that even if there is some adjustment of prices, the central bank will still be able to control the interest rate by adjusting the money supply. What is needed for monetary policy to have effects on real variables is that prices are 'sticky' so that they do not change *in proportion* to the money supply.

A shock to aggregate demand with constant money supply

Let us use the scheme above to analyse what happens if consumers and investors become more optimistic about future income, so expected future income, Y^e, increases. As we will see, the effect of the shock will depend on how the central bank reacts to the shock. Let us first assume that the central bank holds the money supply constant, so we treat M as exogenous while the interest rate is endogenously determined.

1. *Which curves shift and why?* Looking at the IS and LM equations, we see that Y^e enters the IS equation. Demand will be higher for a given interest rate, so the IS curve *shifts to the right* as seen in Fig. 8.13. At the original interest rate, i_0, the equilibrium level of production would be Y_2. The LM curve does not shift because expected future income does not have any direct effect on money demand or money supply.

2. *What is the effect on production and the interest rate?* As we see in Fig. 8.13, the new equilibrium point is further up to the right. Production and the interest rate both increase, from Y_0 and i_0 to Y_1 and i_1.

3. *What is the economic explanation?* As consumers become more optimistic about future incomes, they feel richer and spend more. As investors become more optimistic about future demand they invest to increase their capital stocks. This increases demand, and firms produce more to satisfy demand. As production increases, income increases, and consumers spend even more. The multiplier effect leads to a further increase in production.

   As production increases, transactions increase and this leads to increased demand for money. People become less willing to lend and this leads to an increase in the interest rate until money demand is equal to the (unchanged) money supply. The increase in the interest rate *counteracts* the increase in consumption and investment. Without the increase in the interest rate, production would have increased to Y_2, but because of the increase in the interest rate, production increases only to Y_1.

4. *What happens to other variables?* Since production increases, employment must increase. To understand what happens to consumption and investment, we look at the consumption and investment functions. The direct effect of an increase in expected future income is that consumption and investment both increase. This leads to an increase in production and income, which leads to a further increase consumption. There is also an increase in the interest rate, which counteracts the increase in consumption and investment.

We see that an aggregate demand shock, which is due to a change of expectations, will affect production, income, and employment in the short run. When the money supply is kept constant, the interest rate will increase. Depending on the

Fig. 8.13 *The short-run effect of increased optimism*

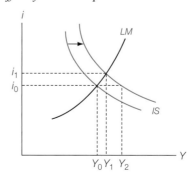

initial situation and the size of the shock, production may end up above or below its natural level.

A shock to aggregate demand with constant interest rate

Above, we analysed the effect of a shock to aggregate demand, assuming that the money supply was kept constant. In practice, it is unlikely that the money supply will remain constant, however. As we will see in Chapter 10, central banks typically set a target for the interest rate and keep the interest rate on that level. If the central bank wants to keep the interest rate unchanged at i_0, it has to increase the money supply so that LM shifts out together with IS. In that case, the increase in production will be larger as production will increase to Y_2 instead.

Thus we see that the effect of the demand shock will depend on the reaction of the central bank. Typically, the central bank would keep neither the money supply nor the interest rate constant. In Chapter 10 we will analyse in depth how the central bank should react to different types of shocks.

8.6 Does monetary policy really matter?

The main lessons that we learn from the IS-LM model are that, because of slow wage and price adjustment, demand side shocks can lead to deviations of production from the natural level of production and monetary policy can affect production in the short run. Once we put a government into our model, we will see that the same applies to fiscal policy – that is, changes in government expenditure and taxes. This implies that monetary and fiscal policy could potentially play a stabilizing role, easing the adjustment to various shocks.

This 'Keynesian' view of the world came to dominate after Keynes wrote his *General Theory* and it is still an approach that is widely used for macroeconomic forecasting and applied policy analysis at central banks, ministries of finance, forecasting institutes, and international organizations. The key difference between the IS-LM model and the classical long-run analysis presented in Chapters 2–7 is that the price level is taken as exogenous in the IS-LM model. But do we know if this view is correct? How important is wage and price rigidity? How quickly do wages and prices adjust? Does monetary policy really affect real economic activity or is money neutral – as implied by the classical analysis?

As discussed in the introduction to this chapter, we know that wages and prices change infrequently and that wage contracts typically have a length of one to three years. Thus we know from microeconomic evidence that there is price and wage rigidity. But what if we look at macroeconomic data? Do macroeconomic data support the IS-LM model? Is it true that an expansion of the money supply, which reduces the interest rate, leads to an expansion of output and that prices respond slowly?

One may think that a simple way to test this would be to examine the *correlation* between changes in the interest rate and changes in production, to see if production increased when interest rates were lowered. Such an investigation can

Fig. 8.14 *A negative demand shock counteracted by the central bank*

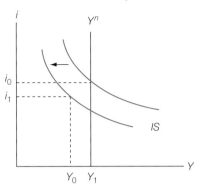

easily give us the wrong answer, however. To see why, suppose that the *IS-LM* model is a perfect description of the world we live in. When will the interest rate be reduced? Clearly, interest rate will be reduced when there is a negative demand shock – when the *IS* curve is shifting to the left (see Fig. 8.14). This will be the case if the central bank keeps the money supply constant and, more generally, if the central bank adjusts interest rates so as to keep production near the natural level. As a result, we see a reduction in the interest rate associated with a lower level of production. So if we only look at the correlation we will conclude that lower interest rates lead to *lower* production – just the opposite of what the *IS-LM* model predicts!

A good example from the real world is what happened when the financial crisis broke out in 2008. As the crisis spread, firms and consumers became more pessimistic about the future, demand and production decreased, and central banks reduced their interest rates to counteract the fall in demand.

The problem is that there are *many variables* that affect the macroeconomic equilibrium, and some of these variables are *not observable*. In the case of the financial crisis, there were problems in the financial sector that led to a change in consumers' and firms' expectations, and this led to a fall in aggregate demand and a change in monetary policy. The example points at the key problem that we face when we try to test macroeconomic theories. If we see two variables X and Y increase or decrease together, it may be because X has a positive effect on Y, because Y has a positive effect on X, or because there is some unobserved variable Z in the background which affects both X and Y. In the case of the financial crisis, Z was the change in expectations, which affected both aggregate demand and monetary policy.

In a theoretical model, we may very well take some variables as exogenous for the sake of analysing a specific problem. We can ask *what happens if* the central bank increases the money supply and all other exogenous variables remain constant. This is what we did when we analysed the effect of monetary policy in the *IS-LM* model. But in practice, policymakers react to what is happening in the economy. The economists at the central bank spend most of their time analysing what is happening and how the central bank should react to new information.

We do not employ hundreds of economists at our central banks in order for them to sit in a black box and make random experiments with monetary policy.

But to *test* whether the theory is right, we would like to do just that: change the interest rate in random ways in different countries so that we are sure that the changes are *not* reactions to what happens in the economy. Such controlled experiments would allow us to find out how monetary policy affects the economy.

Unfortunately, we have not yet been allowed to do random experiments with monetary policy. No country has offered to be a laboratory for such experiments. Instead, we must try to learn from the data that we have – that is, from historical experience.

The empirical strategy, then, is to try to separate *exogenous policy shocks* from *policy reactions* to what happens in the economy. One way in which economists approach this question is by estimating a *policy rule* and then interpreting the residuals in such a regression as the truly exogenous policy shocks. In this way, they hope to isolate reasonably exogenous policy shocks. To illustrate this method, consider the following statistical (econometric) model:

$$y_t = a_{10} + a_{11}\pi_{t-1} + a_{12}y_{t-1} + a_{13}i_{t-1} + e_t$$

$$\pi_t = a_{20} + a_{21}\pi_{t-1} + a_{22}y_{t-1} + a_{23}i_{t-1} + a_{24}e_t + \varepsilon_t$$

$$i_t = a_{30} + a_{31}\pi_{t-1} + a_{32}y_{t-1} + a_{33}i_{t-1} + a_{34}\varepsilon_t + a_{35}\varepsilon_t + \eta_t.$$

The first two equations describe the dynamics of inflation and output, and e_t and ε_t are unobserved shocks arising in the private sector. The last equation is the assumed *monetary policy rule*. We see that monetary policy can react to data from the previous period and to the shocks to production and inflation in the current period. The shock η_t is the monetary policy shock.

If we assume that the three shocks are uncorrelated, it is possible to estimate this model and work out the dynamic effects of a monetary policy shock to see how it affects production and inflation. A model such as the one above is called a *vector autoregressive (VAR) model*.[8] This empirical methodology was developed by the American economist Christopher Sims, who received the Nobel Prize in 2011.[9] Different versions of the VAR methodology have been used in the empirical literature that tries to identify the effects of monetary policy shocks on the macroeconomy.

Fig. 8.15 shows the effects of a US monetary policy shock on various macroeconomic variables in a recent study that uses the VAR method. The figure shows the effects on the interest rate, production, employment, and inflation one, two, three and more quarters after the shock. A typical monetary policy shock raises the interest rate 0.6 percentage points and reduces real GDP by about 0.3 percentage points. The maximum effect occurs after about six quarters, reflecting lags in the response of investment and consumption to changes in the interest rate.

---

8 Here, it is assumed that monetary policy can react to the shocks to production and inflation in the same period but production and inflation react with a lag to monetary policy. Some assumption of this type is necessary in order to separate policy shocks from other shocks. When such identifying assumptions are imposed the model is called a Structural VAR (SVAR) model.

9 The 2011 Nobel Prize in economics was awarded jointly to Thomas J. Sargent and Christopher A. Sims 'for their empirical research on cause and effect in the macroeconomy'.

Fig. 8.15 *Effects of a monetary policy shock in the United States*

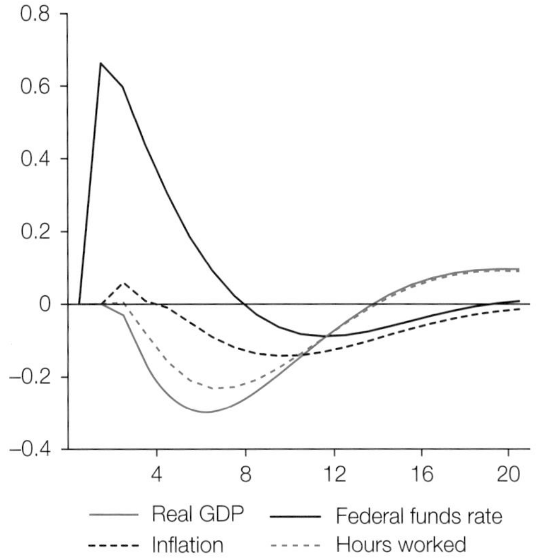

Note: The figure shows the response of GDP, hours worked, and inflation to a typical monetary policy shock. The interest rate and inflation are measured in percentage points, while GDP is measured in percent deviations from the steady state.
Source: Lawrence J. Christiano, Karl Walentin, and Mathias Trabandt, 'DSGE models for monetary policy analysis', in *Handbook of Monetary Economics*, ed. Benjamin M. Friedman and Michael Woodford (Amsterdam: North-Holland, 2011), vol. 3a, ch. 7, pp. 285–367.

We see that inflation responds very sluggishly to the monetary policy shock. Inflation starts to decrease after one year and the maximum effect occurs after two to three years.[10] These estimates support the view that prices adjust very slowly and that monetary policy does have effects on real economic activity.

The main problem with this approach to estimating real effects of policy shocks is that, in order to correctly identify policy shocks, we have to have the correctly specified monetary policy rule in the model. If, for example, the central bank is reacting to some leading indicator which we do not include in our econometric model, our estimates will be biased. When a leading indicator predicts an increase in GDP, the central bank will raise the interest rate so as to counteract the shock, so we see an increase in the interest rate followed by an *increase* in GDP. We may then incorrectly interpret this as showing that an increase in the interest rate has a positive effect on GDP.

In order to correctly estimate of the effects of policy we need, in principle, to include all relevant economic information that the central bank reacts to when we estimate the policy rule. If we do not, we have not fully isolated truly exogenous monetary policy shocks. Obviously, this is not practically possible, so in general we would expect the real effects of monetary policy to be underestimated in a VAR model. Yet this remains the main way in which economists try to estimate the effects of monetary policy.

---

10 In fact, inflation first increases when the interest rate has been increased. One reason may be that interest payments are a cost for firms so there is an initial 'cost–push' effect of the interest rate. For more discussion of this, see Chapter 10.

What have we learned?

The *IS-LM* model is a theory of economic activity in the short run. The price level is taken as given and production is determined by aggregate demand. The *IS-LM* model shows how the goods market and the money market together determine the level of production and the interest rate. For given wages and prices, demand shocks can move production away from the natural level, and monetary policy can affect the level of economic activity.

There are two equilibrium conditions. Goods market equilibrium requires production to be equal to aggregate demand (*IS*) and money market equilibrium requires real money supply to be equal to real money demand (*LM*):

$$Y = C(Y, Y^e, i - \pi^e, A) + I(i - \pi^e, Y^e, K), \qquad\qquad IS$$

$$\frac{M}{P} = \frac{Y}{V(i)}. \qquad\qquad LM$$

Production is determined by aggregate demand, which consists of consumption and investment. The *multiplier effect* implies that any exogenous change in demand will raise production more than the initial increase in demand. The multiplier is bigger than unity because an increase in demand increases production and income and this leads to a further increases in consumption and income. The size of the multiplier effect depends on the marginal propensity to consume (*MPC*).

The *IS-LM* model can be illustrated in a diagram with production on the horizontal axis and the interest rate on the vertical axis. The *IS curve* shows how the interest rate affects the level of production. It slopes downward because an increase in the interest rate has a negative effect on aggregate demand and production. The effect of the interest rate on demand depends on the interest sensitivity of investment and consumption, and on the size of the multiplier effect. Changes in the interest rate imply movements *along* the *IS* curve. Changes in exogenous variables which directly affect consumption and investment will *shift* the *IS* curve.

The *LM curve* shows what the interest rate will be in the money market for each level of production for a given money supply. It slopes upward because higher production leads to a higher interest rate in the money market. As production increases, transactions increase, demand for money increases, and the interest rate must rise to keep money demand equal to the unchanged money supply. An increase in the money supply or a decrease in the price level will shift the *LM* curve downward.

An expansion of the money supply shifts the *LM* curve down, leading to a new equilibrium with lower interest rate and higher production. As the central bank buys government bonds, or lends to banks, the interest rate is reduced, and this has a positive effect on consumption and investment. As aggregate demand increases, production increases to satisfy the additional demand. As incomes increase, there are further increases in consumption and aggregate demand.

Increased consumer optimism shifts the *IS* curve to the right. For a given money supply, this leads to a new equilibrium with higher production and a higher interest rate. Higher demand leads to higher production, more transactions, and higher demand for money. People are less willing to lend their money, so the interest rate increases, and this counteracts the increase in production.

If the central bank wants to hold the interest rate constant when there is an increase in demand it has to increase the money supply so that *LM* shifts out together with *IS*. In that case, the increase in production will be larger. In practice, it is very unlikely that the money supply or the interest rate will remain constant because the central bank will react to the shock in the way it finds appropriate (see Chapter 10).

Empirical evidence from statistical VAR models suggests that an increase in the interest rate has a negative effect on production and employment with the maximum effect occurring after six quarters. Inflation falls but only after a considerable lag, and the maximum effect on inflation occurs after about two years.

Where do we go from here?

In this chapter we analysed how aggregate demand and production are determined in the short run. We have seen that the interest rate is an important determinant of aggregate demand, and that the central bank can control the interest rate by adjusting the money supply so that the interest rate is on the desired level. In this chapter, we simplified by keeping prices exogenous. But wages and prices are not completely rigid. In the next chapter, we analyse wage and price adjustment and we derive the *Phillips curve*, which shows how production, employment, and inflation are related in the short run.

Exercises

1. We have the following model:

(1) $Y = C + I$ production = demand

(2) $C = C^0 + bY$ consumption
    $C^0 > 0, \quad 0 < b < 1$ function

(3) $I = I^0 - di$ investment
    $I^0, d > 0$ function

(4) $\dfrac{M}{P} = eY - fi$ money market
    $e, f > 0$ equilibrium

$Y = $ real production, $C = $ consumption, $I = $ investment, $i = $ interest rate, $M = $ money supply, $P = $ price level.

a) Illustrate the consumption function in a diagram with production on the horizontal axis and consumption on the vertical axis. Interpret the parameters C^0 and b.

b) Illustrate the investment function in a diagram with the interest rate on the vertical axis and investment on the horizontal axis. Interpret the parameters I^0 and d.

c) Suppose that the central bank holds the interest rate constant. Use equations (1)–(3) to solve for production for a given interest rate. Illustrate this relation in a diagram with production on the horizontal axis and the interest rate on the vertical axis. What is the name of this relation?

d) Use the result in c) to calculate the effect on production of an increased willingness to invest represented by $\Delta I^0 > 0$.

e) Use the result in c) to calculate the effect of an increase in the interest rate on production and interpret the result. How does the effect depend on the parameters d and b? Explain.

f) What is the role of equation (4) when the central bank sets the interest rate at some target level?

2. Use the same model as in the previous exercise but now assume that the central bank keeps the money supply constant. Then the endogenous variables are Y, C, I, and i.

a) Rewrite equation (4) with the interest rate on the left-hand side. How does the interest rate depend on production according to equation (4)? Illustrate this relation in a diagram with production on the horizontal axis and the interest rate on the vertical axis. What is the name of this relation?

b) Use the result in a) to substitute for the interest rate in the investment function. Then use the result and (2) to substitute for I and C in equation (1) and solve for production for a given money supply.

c) Use the result to calculate the effect of an increased willingness to invest represented by $\Delta I_0 > 0$.

d) Compare the result to the case in exercise 1 when the central bank keeps the interest rate constant. In which case do we get the biggest effect on production? Why? Illustrate the difference using the IS and LM curves.

e) How do the parameters e and f affect the result above? Explain.

3. We now introduce taxes and government demand for goods and services. We assume that the tax increases with income. We

assume that the central bank holds the interest rate constant.

(1)	$Y = C + I + G$	production = demand
(2)	$C = C^0 + b(Y - T)$ $0 < b < 1$	consumption function
(3)	$T = -T^0 + tY$ $0 < t < 1$	tax schedule
(4)	$I = I^0 - di$ $I^0, d > 0$	investment function

a) Use the equations to find the level of production for a given interest rate.

b) Assume that the government starts to demand more goods and services so that $\Delta G > 0$. Use the result in a) to calculate the effect on production. How does the effect depend on the marginal tax? Explain.

c) Suppose that the government reduces taxes by increasing T^0. What happens to the tax schedule? Use the result in a) to calculate the effect on production. How does the effect depend on the marginal tax? Explain.

4. Suppose that labour income increases by 100 million. Among the consumers, 20 percent have no assets and just consume their current labour income. The other 80 percent behave in accordance with the consumption theory presented in Chapter 4. Of the increase in income, 50 percent is perceived as a permanent increase in real income and 50 percent as a temporary increase which will be reversed next year. Make a rough calculation of the effect on consumption.

5. Suppose that production is initially at the natural level, then a new technology is discovered, which makes it possible to produce much more fuel-efficient engines for cars.

a) How will this affect investment, consumption, and the IS curve? (*Hint: How are the variables in the investment and consumption functions affected?*)

b) What happens to production and the interest rate if the central bank keeps the money supply constant?

c) The central bank can adjust the money supply so as to control the interest rate.

What do you think that the central bank should do with the interest rate?

Answers to the exercises can be found at: **www.palgrave.com/economics/ gottfries**.

Appendix

The slope of the *LM* curve

To be able to calculate the interest rate as function of production and money supply, we assume that velocity is a linear function of the interest rate:

$$V = v_0 + v_1 i.$$

Here, v_1 measures how velocity changes with the interest rate. A higher v_1 means that velocity increases a lot when the interest rate increases. Now the money market equilibrium condition is

$$M(v_0 + v_1 i) = PY.$$

Dividing by M on both sides and subtracting v_0 on both sides we get

$$v_1 i = \frac{PY}{M} - v_0.$$

Dividing by v_1 we get the interest rate:

$$i = \frac{1}{v_1} \frac{Y}{M/P} - \frac{v_0}{v_1}.$$

This is the equation for the *LM* curve. The effect of production on the interest rate is found by differentiating with respect to Y:

$$\Delta i = \frac{1}{v_1} \frac{\Delta Y}{M/P}.$$

The slope of the *LM* curve is positive. If production increases, the interest rate must increase for the money market to be in equilibrium. The slope depends on how much production affects the demand for money and the interest sensitivity of money demand. The weaker the effect of the interest rate on the velocity, the more will the interest rate increase and the steeper is the *LM* curve. In the special case when velocity is independent of the interest rate, $v_1 = 0$, we have

$$Y = v_0 \frac{M}{P}.$$

In this case, the equation for the *LM* curve is vertical, so the level of production is independent of the position of the *IS* curve.

An increase in the money supply will reduce the interest rate for a given level of production and an increase in the price level has the opposite effect. Exogenous factors may also shift the demand for money and the *LM* curve. If, for example, people start to use credit cards to a greater extent, the need for cash to make transactions will be reduced. Formally, we can think of this as an increase in v_0 and this will shift the *LM* curve downwards. People are more willing to lend money now that they do not need so much cash, so if the money supply is unchanged, the interest rate will fall.

9 ECONOMIC ACTIVITY AND INFLATION IN THE SHORT RUN

Is there a choice between low inflation and low unemployment?

As we saw in Chapter 8, changes in the money supply and other exogenous variables have very different effects in the short run compared with the long run. The reason for this difference is that nominal wages and prices adjust slowly. The price level was taken as exogenous in the analysis in Chapter 8. In this chapter we tie the short and the long run together by asking how the economy moves from the short run, where wages and prices are sticky, to the long run, where wages and prices adjust fully to any shocks that occur. To understand this adjustment, we need to understand how wages and prices are set.

The evidence shows that nominal wages are more rigid than prices. Therefore, we base our theory on the assumption that nominal wages adjust slowly. To simplify, we ignore price rigidity and assume that prices are completely flexible. To introduce wage rigidity in a simple way, we start from the wage-setting equation that we formulated in Chapter 6. We take the period to be one year and we assume that some wages are set the year before, while other wages are flexible and adjust immediately to changing conditions in the labour market. This means that, if employment rises above the natural level, some wages will react within the same year, while other wages respond with a lag.

Our analysis leads to the *Phillips curve*, which shows how inflation is related to employment and production. The Phillips curve is a key relation that links the short run and the long run in our macroeconomic analysis.

High unemployment means a waste of resources and high inflation disrupts the price system. Therefore, low unemployment and low inflation are two important goals of economic policy. Our theory of wage and price adjustment will allow us to analyse whether there is a choice between inflation and unemployment, in the short and the long run. The theory of the wage and price adjustment which we develop here will be the basis for our analysis of monetary policy in Chapter 10.

We will derive three versions of the Phillips curve in this chapter. We first derive a Phillips curve relating wage increases to unemployment. Then we relate price inflation to wage increases so we have a Phillips curve in terms of unemployment and price inflation. Finally, we derive a Phillips curve in terms of the deviation of production from its natural level (the output gap) and inflation. This latter version of the Phillips curve will be useful when we analyse monetary policy in Chapter 10. Having derived different versions of the Phillips curve, we then analyse the relation between inflation and unemployment in the short and in the long run. Finally, we look at data to see if the data are consistent with our theory.

9.1 Unemployment and wage inflation

To understand wage adjustment, we start from the efficiency wage theory of wage-setting that we presented in Chapter 6. If we would add search frictions and unions, the results would be very similar. Recall that we defined the natural rate of unemployment, u^n, as the level of unemployment at which no firm wants to change its relative wage. If unemployment is lower than the natural level, turnover is high, and all firms want to raise their *relative* wages to keep their workers. If unemployment is higher than the natural level, each firm wants to reduce its relative wage. Based on this theory, we derived an equation for the desired wage change:

$$\frac{\Delta W_t^d}{W_{t-1}} = \frac{\Delta W_t}{W_{t-1}} - b\left(u_t - u^n\right).$$

This wage-setting equation says that if unemployment is at the natural level, each individual firm wants to raise its wage in line with average wage growth in the labour market. If unemployment is above the natural level, each firm wants to raise its wage less than the average wage growth. The coefficient b shows how sensitive desired wages are to variations in unemployment. This wage-setting rule is illustrated in Fig. 9.1.

In order to introduce nominal wage rigidity in the simplest possible way, we assume that a fraction $1 - \lambda$ of the firms set wages at the end of the previous year. We can imagine that they announce their wage contracts in December of the previous year. We call the wage set by those firms the 'rigid wage' and denote it by W^r. The rigid-wage firms have to set their wages based on the *expected* wage and unemployment levels in the coming period. A fraction λ of the firms have completely flexible wages and the wage set by those firms, the 'flexible wage', is denoted W^x. From a macro perspective, we are interested in the average wage increase, which is a weighted average of the rates of change of the two wages:

$$\frac{\Delta W_t}{W_{t-1}} = \lambda \frac{\Delta W_t^x}{W_{t-1}} + (1 - \lambda)\frac{\Delta W_t^r}{W_{t-1}}.$$

Fig. 9.1 *The wage-setting rule*

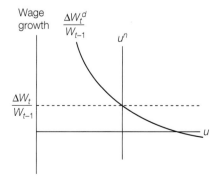

To solve the model, we first note that the flexible wage is set according to the wage-setting rule above:

$$\frac{\Delta W_t^x}{W_{t-1}} = \frac{\Delta W_t}{W_{t-1}} - b\left(u_t - u^n\right).$$

But what about the rigid wage? To find it, we need to realize one thing: the increase in the rigid wage will be set equal to the *expected* average wage increase as seen from the end of the previous year:

$$\frac{\Delta W_t^r}{W_{t-1}} = \frac{\Delta W_t^e}{W_{t-1}}.$$

This is shown formally in the appendix to this chapter, but the result can be explained intuitively. The expected wage level is a weighted average of the rigid wage and the expected flexible wage. If the expected wage level was higher than the rigid wage, this would mean that the expected flexible wage would be higher than the rigid wage. But since the flexible wage is set optimally, based on actual conditions, there would be an incentive for the rigid-wage firms to raise their wages. Therefore, it can never be optimal for rigid-wage firms to set a wage below the expected average wage level.

Substituting the equations above for the flexible and the rigid wage into the equation for the average wage change we get

$$\frac{\Delta W_t}{W_{t-1}} = \lambda \left[\frac{\Delta W_t}{W_{t-1}} - b\left(u_t - u^n\right) \right] + (1-\lambda)\frac{\Delta W_t^e}{W_{t-1}}.$$

Now we can solve for the average wage change to get

$$\frac{\Delta W_t}{W_{t-1}} = \frac{\Delta W_t^e}{W_{t-1}} - \hat{b}\left(u_t - u^n\right) \qquad \text{where} \quad \hat{b} = \frac{\lambda b}{1-\lambda}.$$

This relation between wage inflation and unemployment is called the *Phillips curve*. The Phillips curve is named after the economist A. W. H. Phillips (from New Zeeland but active in the UK) who documented the empirical relation between unemployment and wage growth in 1958.[1]

The Phillips curve is illustrated in Fig. 9.2. It is drawn for a given expected average wage increase. It slopes downward because higher unemployment means that the flexible-wage firms will set lower wages. The slope of the Phillips curve depends on two parameters. The parameter b comes from the wage-setting rule in Chapter 6 and reflects how unemployment affects the desired relative wage of the firm. The more individual firms want to respond to unemployment in their wage-setting, the steeper is the Phillips curve. The parameter λ is the fraction of firms with flexible wages. If many firms have flexible wages, the parameter λ has a high value, so the Phillips curve is steep.

Note that if almost all firms set wages at the end of the previous period, λ is very low and he Phillips curve is almost flat. In this case, there is almost complete

---

1   A. W. H. Phillips, 'The relationship between unemployment and the rate of change of money wages in the United Kingdom 1861–1957', *Economica*, 25 (1958), 283–299. We call it a curve, and draw it as a curve, although it is formally a line according to our simplified equations.

Fig. 9.2 *The Phillips curve in terms of unemployment and wage inflation*

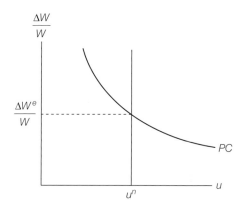

wage rigidity in the short run. The parameter λ can be seen as a measure of wage flexibility in this simple model.

The more firms expect wages to increase, the more they will raise wages for a given level of unemployment. If unemployment is at the natural level, wages will rise in line with expectations. Therefore, the Phillips curve intersects the vertical line indicating the natural rate of unemployment at a wage increase that is equal to the expected wage increase.

9.2   Unemployment and price inflation

As we saw in Chapter 1, a general increase in the price level is called *inflation*. In our model economy, P is the price of the consumption basket and we measure inflation as the relative increase in the price level from the previous year:

$$\pi_t = \frac{P_t - P_{t-1}}{P_{t-1}} = \frac{\Delta P_t}{P_{t-1}}.$$

If $\pi = 0.10$ inflation is 10 percent.

To analyse the relation between wage and price changes as simply as possible, we use a simplified production function for our short-run analysis. The simplification is that we omit capital so that labour is the only input. Thus we write the production function as follows:

$$Y = EN,$$

where N is employment and E is labour productivity. This is equivalent to setting $\alpha = 0$ in the Cobb–Douglas production function. This assumption simplifies our analysis of short-run wage and price adjustment without fundamentally changing the conclusions. With this production function, E is both the marginal and the average product of labour and the cost of production is simply

$$WN = W\frac{Y}{E} = \frac{W}{E} \cdot Y.$$

Marginal (and average) cost is simply the wage divided by productivity, W/E. As in Chapter 2, we assume that prices are set with a mark-up on marginal cost:

$$P = (1 + \mu)\,\frac{W}{E},$$

where $(1 + \mu)$ is a constant mark-up factor. If $\mu = 0.20$ for example, the price is equal to marginal cost plus 20 percent. Using the rule of thumb for percentage changes, we see that inflation is equal to wage growth minus labour productivity growth:[2]

$$\pi = \frac{\Delta W}{W} - \frac{\Delta E}{E}.$$

Suppose, for example, that wages increase by 5 percent and productivity increases by 3 percent. Then, in order to keep an unchanged mark-up, firms will raise prices by 2 percent. Productivity growth is taken as exogenous in our analysis of wage and price dynamics.

If the above equation holds for actual wage and productivity changes, it should hold also for expected changes, so expected inflation is determined by expected changes in wages and productivity:

$$\pi^e = \frac{\Delta W^e}{W} - \frac{\Delta E^e}{E}.$$

In order to find out how inflation is determined, we first substitute the expression for the average wage increase from Section 9.1 into the expression for inflation above:

$$\pi = \frac{\Delta W^e}{W} - \hat{b}\,(u - u^n) - \frac{\Delta E}{E}.$$

Using the equation for expected inflation above to substitute for the expected wage change we get a second version of the Phillips curve relating inflation to unemployment:

$$\pi = \pi^e + \frac{\Delta E^e}{E} - \hat{b}\,(u - u^n) - \frac{\Delta E}{E} = \pi^e - \hat{b}\,(u - u^n) - \left(\frac{\Delta E}{E} - \frac{\Delta E^e}{E}\right).$$

We see that inflation depends on three factors:

- expected inflation
- unemployment
- unexpected changes in productivity.

An *unexpected* increase in productivity will reduce inflation because it reduces firms' marginal costs after the rigid wages have been set. *Expected* productivity growth does not have the same effect because wage setters take account of expected productivity growth when they set their wages.

In practice, other factors can affect inflation after wages have been set. Firms have other costs than wage costs, and these may change unexpectedly. Prices of oil and other raw materials raise firms' costs and firms pass those costs on to prices. Unexpected oil price increases have direct effects on the price level via the price of petrol. An unexpected increase in the value added tax will raise prices more

---

2 The rule of thumb was presented in the appendix to Chapter 1.

or less immediately. Such factors have roughly similar effects as unexpectedly low productivity growth. We will use the term *cost–push shocks* as a summary term for all these shocks to inflation and denote them by z. Thus we have a Phillips curve:

$$\pi = \pi^e - \hat{b}\,(u - u^n) + z.$$

9.3 Inflation and the output gap

In order to discuss stabilization policy, it is useful to see how inflation is related to production. Therefore, we now derive a third version of the Phillips curve relating inflation to the level of production. Higher production means higher employment and lower unemployment, so there is a close relation between the deviation of unemployment from its natural level and the deviation of production from its natural level. To find the exact relation between unemployment and production, we use the definition of the unemployment rate $u = (L - N)/L$, where L is the labour force, and our simplified production function from the previous section $Y = EN$:

$$u - u^n = \frac{L - N}{L} - \frac{L - N^n}{L} = -\frac{N - N^n}{L} = -\frac{Y/E - Y^n/E}{L} = -\frac{Y^n}{EL}\frac{Y - Y^n}{Y^n}.$$

Note that EL is what production would be if there was full employment and that $Y^n/(EL)$ is a number close to unity. $\hat{Y}$ is the percentage deviation of production from the natural level, which we call the *output gap*:

$$\hat{Y} = \frac{Y - Y^n}{Y^n}.$$

The equation above has a simple message: when production is above the natural level, unemployment is below the natural level, and when production is below the natural level, unemployment is above the natural level. Substituting into the Phillips curve we can express the Phillips curve in terms of inflation and the output gap:

$$\pi = \pi^e + \beta\hat{Y} + z,$$

where $\beta = \hat{b}\dfrac{Y^n}{EL} = \dfrac{\lambda b}{1 - \lambda}\dfrac{Y^n}{EL}$.

This is another version of the Phillips curve and the one we will use to analyse monetary policy in Chapter 10. We see that inflation depends on three factors:

- A higher *expected inflation rate* raises inflation because it implies higher expected wage increases, and firms match expected wage increases in order to keep their workers.
- A positive *output gap* increases inflation because firms will raise their wages more when production and employment are above their natural levels.
- *Cost–push shocks* such as unexpected increases in oil prices and negative productivity shocks raise inflation for given wages.

This Phillips curve is illustrated in Fig. 9.3. It cuts the line showing the natural level of production at the expected inflation rate. If wage setters expect a higher

Fig. 9.3 *The Phillips curve in terms of production and inflation*

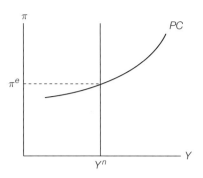

inflation rate, the Phillips curve shifts up. The slope of the Phillips curve depends on the degree of wage rigidity (λ) and on how sensitive firms' desired wages are to unemployment (b).

9.4 Information delays, contracts, and staggered wages

The theory of wage and price adjustment which we have presented here is very simplified. The key assumption is that a substantial proportion of the wages are set the year before in nominal terms – that is, in terms of money. Of course, the real world is more complicated than our simple model. In practice, we can think of several other factors that contribute to slow wage and price adjustment:

- *Wage and price setters have imperfect information.* It takes time for workers and firms to discover that the situation has changed and to adjust to shocks.
- *Many wage contracts cover periods longer than one year.* Union wage contracts often fix wages for two or three years.
- *Wage and price changes are not fully synchronized.* Firms change wages and prices at different points in time.

To understand the last point, consider again the efficiency wage model in Chapter 6 and assume that all firms change wages once per year but that they do not change their wages at the same time. Let us assume that 1/12 of the firms change their wages in a given month. Suppose that the labour market is over-heated, so each individual firm has an incentive to raise its relative wage in order to reduce the turnover among its workers. Since only 1/12 of the firms change their wages in a given month, the firms that do change their wages must take account of the fact that 11/12 of the firms do *not* change their wages at the same time. They only need to raise their wages a little in order to offer a high relative wage. Therefore, those firms that can change their wages will change wages less than they would have done if all firms had changed their wages at the same time. As a result, wage adjustment is slowed down. Although all firms change their wages once a year, it will take more than one year for the full wage adjustment to occur after a shock.

Consequences of unsynchronized wage and price adjustment were analysed in the late 1970s and early 1980s.[3] Today, unsynchronized wage and price adjustment is a key feature of so-called 'New Keynesian' models which are used by central banks all over the world to analyse monetary policy.[4]

We can conclude that the slope of the Phillips curve (β) depends not only on the wage-setting rule and the fraction of wages that are rigid, but also on how quickly wage and price setters learn about the state of the economy, the length of wage contracts, and the degree of synchronization of wage and price changes. To bring those aspects into the model is quite complicated, however, so we will stick to our simple assumption that a proportion of the wages are set in advance.

9.5   Is there a choice between low inflation and low unemployment?

Low inflation and low unemployment are two important goals of economic policy. The Phillips curve shows that unemployment and inflation are negatively related in the short run, so there seems to be a short-run *trade-off* between inflation and unemployment. In the short run, we can buy higher employment (and production) at the price of higher inflation. At the same time, our analysis warns us that this trade-off may not be stable. The position of the Phillips curve depends on the expected inflation rate, which may not be constant. In order to see how the trade-off between inflation and unemployment changes over time, we need to understand how wage setters form expectations about inflation.

How do people form expectations about future inflation? Presumably, they look at past inflation rates and monetary policy. If prices have been stable, people may expect them to remain stable. If inflation has been high, people will probably expect inflation to continue. If the central bank has a clear and credible inflation target, people may expect inflation to be close to the target.

In the following, we consider three different assumptions about the expected rate of inflation which may be reasonable in different situations:

1. The price level is expected to remain the same as it was last year.
2. Inflation is expected to be the same as it was last year.
3. Inflation is expected to be equal to the inflation target of the central bank.

In each case, we ask the following question:

Is there a choice between low inflation and low unemployment?

---

3 Models of asynchronized wage-setting were developed by John Taylor and Guillermo Calvo. Related models of overlapping wage contracts and wage indexation were developed by Stanley Fischer and Jo Anna Gray.

4 Macroeconomic models with unsynchronized wage and price adjustment are more realistic but also more complicated to analyse than the model presented here. Presentations of New Keynesian models can be found in Richard Clarida, Jordi Gali, and Mark Gertler, 'The science of monetary policy: a new keynesian perspective', *Journal of Economic Literature*, 37 (1999), 1661–1707, and Jordi Gali, *Monetary Policy, Inflation, and the Business Cycle* (Princeton: Princeton University Press, 2008).

Assumption 1: The price level is expected to remain unchanged

In an economy with a stable price level, wage setters may expect the price level to remain constant. In this case, expected inflation is zero and the Phillips curve is simply

$$\pi = \beta \hat{Y} + z.$$

As we saw in Chapter 8, expansionary monetary policy can raise production and employment in the short run, but the Phillips curve tells us that there is a cost in terms of higher inflation. From a policy perspective, this Phillips curve represents a *trade-off* between inflation and unemployment, as illustrated in Fig. 9.4.

One may argue that raising employment is more important than keeping low inflation, so it is reasonable to accept some inflation in order to keep employment on a high level. Thus we may prefer to raise production to Y_1 although this increases inflation to π_1.

There is a problem with this reasoning, however. It is likely that wage setters form their expectations about future inflation by looking at what the inflation rate has been in the past. If the central bank keeps production above the natural level, wage setters will, sooner or later, discover that prices increase in every period. Then they will no longer expect zero inflation, so the Phillips curve will shift upwards. Therefore, the situation with production above the natural level is not a long-run equilibrium.

Fig. 9.4 *The Phillips curve when prices are expected to remain constant*

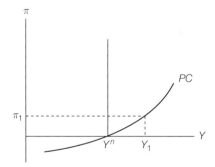

Assumption 2: Wage setters expect inflation to continue

In a situation when inflation is high and variable, a more plausible assumption is that wage setters form their expectations about inflation based on what inflation has been in the past. How will this affect the trade-off between inflation and unemployment? To analyse this as simply as possible, suppose that wage setters expect inflation to be the same as it was in the previous year:

$$\pi^e = \pi_{-1}.$$

Now we get the Phillips curve

$$\pi = \pi_{-1} + \beta \hat{Y} + z.$$

Fig. 9.5 *The Phillips curve when expected inflation equals inflation in the previous period*

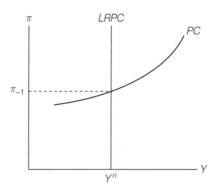

Fig. 9.6 *The effect of a period of expansionary monetary policy when $\pi_t^e = \pi_{t-1}$*

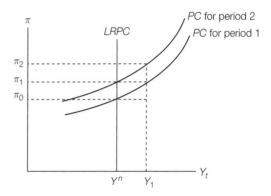

In this case, the position of the Phillips curve is determined by inflation in the previous year, as illustrated in Fig. 9.5. The trade-off between inflation and unemployment is no longer stable because the Phillips curve will shift depending on what happens to inflation.

Fig. 9.6 illustrates the effect of expansionary monetary policy. Suppose that inflation was π_0 in period zero and production in period 1 is Y_1. Expected inflation is π_0 but since production is above the natural level, inflation will increase to π_1. In the next period, the expected inflation rate is π_1 so the Phillips curve shifts up. What happens to production depends on the policy. By sufficiently expansionary monetary policy (low interest rate and increasing money supply) the central bank can keep production at Y_1 but then inflation will increase to π_2. This will shift the Phillips curve even further up in period 3, and so on. We see that production can be kept above the natural level, but only at the cost of *accelerating* inflation.

Alternatively, suppose that the central bank pursues a less expansionary monetary policy, so production returns to the natural level from period 2 onwards. Then inflation will remain at π_1 in period 2. We are back to the original level of production, but with a *higher* inflation rate. Inflation remains high simply because wage setters expect inflation to continue. We see that a policy that temporarily raises the level of production can lead to a permanent increase in inflation.

We can rewrite this Phillips curve in a different way by subtracting lagged inflation on both sides in the equation above:

$$\Delta \pi = \beta \hat{Y} + z.$$

This equation shows that if production is above the natural level, inflation accelerates, and if production is below the natural level, inflation falls. For this reason, the natural rate of unemployment is sometimes called *NAIRU – the non-accelerating-inflation rate of unemployment*. Further, the vertical line at the natural level of production is sometimes called *the long-run Phillips curve (LRPC)* because it is only along this curve that inflation will remain stable.

The conclusion is that production cannot be kept permanently above the natural level because inflation would eventually reach astronomic levels. In the long run, there is not a choice between inflation and unemployment. Instead, there is the possibility of achieving *temporarily* higher production and employment at the cost of *permanently* higher inflation.

If we accept this view of the world, the policy conclusions are clear:

1. It is quite costly to keep production above the natural level. By doing that we raise the level of inflation and then inflation will remain high even if production returns to the natural level. As we discussed in Chapter 7, high inflation is costly because it makes the price system work less efficiently.
2. If inflation is high it may be worthwhile to bring it down. Although there will be a period with low production and employment, we get a permanent reduction in inflation. If we care enough about the future, a temporary cost in terms of production and employment may be worth paying for a permanent gain in terms of lower inflation.

These are the policy lessons that Margaret Thatcher, prime minister in the UK, and Paul Volker, chairman of the Federal Reserve Board (the central bank of the USA), drew in the late 1970s, and which led them to the decision to bring down inflation. In both countries, interest rates were raised and inflation was brought down to a low level in the early 1980s, and inflation has remained low since then. A few years later, many other countries followed the same path.

Assumption 3: A strict and credible inflation target

In the last two decades, many central banks have adopted *inflation targets*, and they have managed to keep inflation reasonably close to their targets. With a strict and credible inflation target, it is plausible that the inflation target itself affects the expected inflation rate. After all, the target rate is the inflation rate that the central bank tries to achieve and the central bank has more information about the economic situation than have most wage and price setters. If we believe that the central bank does its best to reach its target, the best prediction may be that inflation will be equal to the target. With such expectations, we get the Phillips curve

$$\pi = \pi^{\otimes} + \beta \hat{Y} + z,$$

where $\pi^{\otimes}$ is the inflation target. This Phillips curve is illustrated in Fig. 9.7.

Fig. 9.7 *The Phillips curve when the expected inflation rate equals the inflation target*

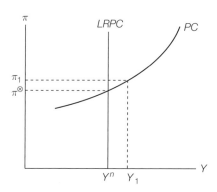

Now suppose there is a demand shock that raises production above the natural level. This raises inflation above target, but in this case the expected rate of inflation does not change. The inflation target 'anchors' the expected rate of inflation and the Phillips curve remains stable. With a clear and credible inflation target, there is less risk that high inflation perpetuates just because people expect high inflation.

Does this mean that, once we have established a credible inflation target, we have a stable trade-off between inflation and unemployment, so we can buy higher employment at the price of higher inflation? Clearly, this is not possible. If the central bank tries to keep production systematically above the natural level, inflation will be higher than the target, and the credibility of the inflation target will be gradually undermined. In order to maintain credibility of the target, the central bank must try to keep inflation close to the target on average.

9.6   What does the data say?

If the expected inflation rate were constant over time, the Phillips curve should be stable. We should see a negative correlation between inflation and unemployment. But as we see in Fig. 9.8, there is no clear relation between inflation and unemployment. Sometimes inflation and unemployment have moved in opposite directions, sometimes they have not. If we look carefully, we see that in most cases when unemployment increased rapidly inflation came down, but over the longer run the two variables are not closely related.

In fact, inflation was trending upwards in the late 1960s and much of the 1970s although unemployment was higher in the 1970s than it was in the 1960s. This unpleasant combination of increasing inflation and increasing unemployment was called *stagflation*, and it posed a difficult dilemma for policymakers. In the beginning of the 1980s, many policymakers decided to bring inflation down. They succeeded in this, but at the price of further increases in unemployment. From the early 1980s, central banks have kept inflation low but unemployment has evolved in different ways in different countries.

Fig. 9.8 *Unemployment and inflation, percent*

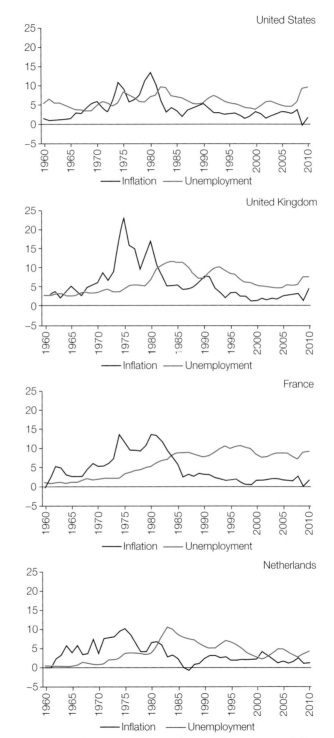

Source: *OECD Economic Outlook*, OECD, 24 November 2011, http://www.oecd-ilibrary.org/statistics.

We see that there is no stable Phillips curve relating inflation to unemployment. Our theory suggests two reasons why the Phillips curve may have shifted:

1. *High inflation tends to persist.* If wage setters see that inflation is high, they will expect high inflation, so wages increase at a rapid rate and inflation continues even if unemployment is at the natural level. If people expect inflation to continue at the rate observed in the past, there is a relation between unemployment and the *change* in inflation, not between the *levels* of unemployment and inflation. In this view, the rising inflation in the late 1960s and early 1970s was a sign that unemployment was below the natural level in this period. Later in the 1970s, high inflation continued simply because people expected high inflation. Similarly, the low-inflation policies of the central banks in the 1980s reduced the expected rate of inflation and brought about a permanent reduction in the inflation rate.

2. *The natural level of unemployment may not be constant.* As we discussed in Chapter 6, the natural level of unemployment may change because of structural changes in the labour market. Many economists argue that stricter labour market regulation and more generous unemployment benefits raised the natural level of unemployment in the 1970s, and that the reversal of those policies led to a decrease in the natural level of unemployment in the 1990s.

In order to address the two problems above, let us examine the evidence for the 'accelerationist' Phillips curve, which relates the *change* in inflation to the output gap:[5]

$$\Delta \pi = \beta \hat{Y} + z.$$

To do this, we need a measure of the output gap. A simple way to take account of changes in the natural level of production is to assume that the natural level of production can be modelled as a smooth trend. The *Hodrick–Prescott filter* is a method for constructing a smooth trend and we use this trend as a measure of the natural level of production. The *output gap* is then measured as the deviation from the trend. The decomposition of GDP into trend and cycle is done with the natural log of real GDP so the output gap is approximately equal to the relative (percent) deviation from trend. Fig. 9.9 illustrates the decomposition into trend and cycle for the US.[6]

Fig. 9.10 shows the relation between the *output gap*, measured as the deviation of log GDP from trend, and the *change* in inflation. We see that there is a clear positive relation between the two variables, especially in the 1970s when inflation was high and variable. The data give quite strong support for the hypothesis that inflation accelerates when there is a positive output gap, as predicted by the Phillips curve with expected inflation equal to past inflation (Assumption 2 above). Of course, the relation is not perfect because there are other factors that affect inflation. For example, there were large increases in oil prices in 1973 and 1979 and a large oil price decrease in 1986, and we see that, in some of the

---

5 Alternatively, we could examine the relation between the change in inflation and cyclical unemployment, but the result would be similar.

6 The Hodrick–Prescott filter and alternative ways of decomposing production into trend and cycle are discussed in Chapter 16. As discussed there, the trend deviation in production measures the output gap only if the natural level of production follows a smooth trend.

Fig. 9.9 *GDP and trend for the United States (log of GDP)*

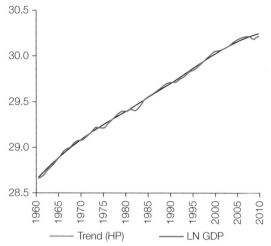

Source: *OECD Economic Outlook*, OECD, 24 November 2011, http://www.oecd-ilibrary.org/statistics.
Trend calculated with HP filter in EViews.

countries, inflation accelerated around 1974 and 1980 and it decreased in 1986–87
more than can be explained by the output gap.

   This analysis is based on the assumption that the natural level of production is
accurately described by a smooth trend. In fact, the results give some support for
this assumption since the acceleration of inflation is quite closely correlated with

Fig. 9.10 *Trend deviation of GDP and change in inflation*

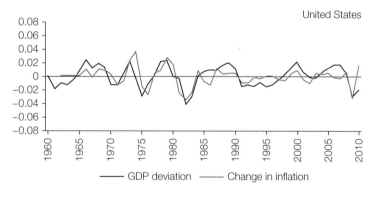

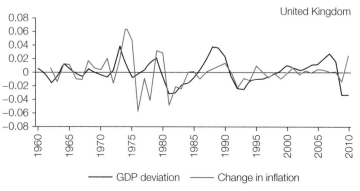

(Figure continues over the page)

Fig. 9.10 *(Continued)*

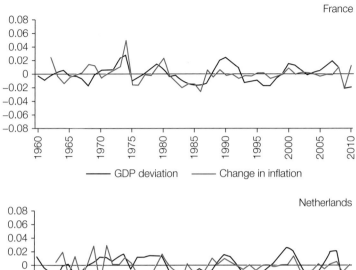

Note: Here 0.02 means two percentage units.
Source: *OECD Economic Outlook*, OECD, 4 May 2011, http://www.oecd-ilibrary.org/statistics. Calculation of HP trends made in EViews.

the trend deviation in production. Still, this is a crude approximation and it does not tell us why there were variations in trend growth, or why the natural rate of unemployment varied. According to our theory, such changes must be explained by the factors discussed in Chapters 5 and 6.

What have we learned?

With the simplified production function $Y = EN$, price is equal to a mark-up factor times wage cost per unit (W/E), and inflation equals the rate of wage increase minus the rate of productivity increase:

$$\pi = \frac{\Delta W}{W} - \frac{\Delta E}{E}.$$

In Chapter 6 we derived an equation for the desired wage change:

$$\frac{\Delta W_t^d}{W_{t-1}} = \frac{\Delta W_t}{W_{t-1}} - b(u_t - u^n).$$

If we assume that a fraction $1 - \lambda$ of the wages are set at the beginning of the period while a fraction λ adjust to the shocks in the period we get a *Phillips curve* relating wage increases to expected wage increases and unemployment:

$$\frac{\Delta W_t}{W_{t-1}} = \frac{\Delta W_t^e}{W_{t-1}} - \hat{b}(u_t - u^n) \qquad \text{where} \quad \hat{b} = \frac{\lambda b}{1 - \lambda}.$$

We also derived another version of the *Phillips curve* showing that inflation depends on three factors: the expected inflation rate π^e, the output gap $\hat{Y}$, and the cost–push shock z:

$$\pi = \pi^e + \beta \hat{Y} + z.$$

If there are no cost–push shocks and production is at the natural level, inflation equals the expected inflation rate. The higher the expected rate of inflation, the more wages increase, and the higher will inflation be.

The output gap is the deviation of production from the natural level. When production and employment are above the natural level, there is upward pressure on wages and prices.

Cost–push shocks are shocks which raise prices for given wages, e.g. unexpected increases in the prices of oil and other raw materials, increases in value added tax, and unexpectedly low productivity growth.

The position of the Phillips curve and the effects of monetary policy depend critically on how wage setters form expectations about the inflation rate. If expected inflation is zero (or some other constant) we have a stable trade-off between inflation and unemployment.

If inflation is high and variable, wage setters may expect inflation to continue at the rate observed in the past. Then, a period of expansionary monetary policy, which raises inflation, will also raise the expected inflation rate. Once a high level of inflation has come to be expected, high inflation will continue even if production returns to the natural level. Put differently, if $\pi_t^e = \pi_{t-1}$, there is a relation between the output gap and the *acceleration* (change) of inflation:

$$\Delta \pi = \beta \hat{Y} + z.$$

A strict and credible inflation target may help to stabilize the Phillips curve because it keeps the expected inflation rate stable and prevents inflation expectations from becoming self-fulfilling.

In the data, there is no stable relation between unemployment and inflation but there is a relatively strong relation between the output gap, measured as deviation from trend, and the acceleration of inflation. This is consistent with a Phillips curve where inflation expectations depend on past inflation.

Where do we go from here?

In Chapter 8 we analysed the determination of aggregate demand and production in the short run. We derived the *IS curve*, which shows how aggregate demand and production depend on the nominal interest rate. In this chapter, we have analysed wage and price adjustment in the short run. We derived the *Phillips curve*, which shows how inflation is related to the output gap. In the next chapter we use the *IS* curve and the Phillips curve to analyse the monetary policy decisions of the central bank.

Exercises

1. Assume that $\beta = 1$, $\pi_t^e = \pi_{t-1}$ and $z = 0$, so the Phillips curve is

$$\pi_t = \pi_{t-1} + \hat{Y}_t.$$

In period 0, inflation is 2 percent and the output gap is zero. In periods 1 and 2, the output gap is plus 2 percent. In periods 3 and 4 the output gap is zero. Calculate inflation for periods 1, 2, 3 and 4. Explain the results. Illustrate the results with a Phillips curve diagram. Draw the Phillips curves for each period and indicate the level of production and inflation in each period.

2. Do the same calculations as in problem 1 assuming that the expected inflation rate is constant at 2 percent. Compare the results and explain the difference.

3. The data show that many countries had higher inflation and unemployment in 1975 than in 1965.
   a) Can you suggest some possible reasons why inflation was higher in 1975 than in 1965?
   b) Can you suggest some possible reasons why unemployment was higher in 1975

than in 1965? *(Hint: Go back to Chapter 6.)*

4. We assume that $\beta = 1$, $\pi_t^e = \pi_{t-1}$, and $z_t = 0$, so the Phillips curve is

$$\pi_t = \pi_{t-1} + \hat{Y}_t.$$

Suppose that the inflation rate is 9 percent and the central bank wants to bring it down to 3 percent in the next period. What output gap should it try to achieve?

5. Suppose the situation is as above but the central bank wants to bring down inflation within three periods. What path for the output gaps would you suggest that it aims for? Why?

6. The Phillips curve is

$$\pi_t = \pi_{t-1} + \hat{Y}_t + z_t.$$

In period 0, inflation is 2 percent. In period 1 there is an unexpected increase in the oil price so $z = 0.02$. The output gap is zero all the time. Calculate inflation for periods 1, 2, and 3 and explain the results.

Answers to the exercises can be found at: **www.palgrave.com/economics/gottfries**.

Appendix

Proof that the rigid wage is equal to the expected wage

We want to find out how the average wage level is determined. To do this, we first find the flexible wage and then the rigid wage, and then we combine them. The flexible wage (relative to the lagged wage) is determined by the average wage increase and the actual rate of unemployment:

$$\frac{\Delta W_t^x}{W_{t-1}} = \frac{\Delta W_t}{W_{t-1}} - b(u_t - u^n).$$

Inserting the expression for the average wage increase in this expression, we get

$$\frac{\Delta W_t^x}{W_{t-1}} = \lambda \frac{\Delta W_t^x}{W_{t-1}} + (1-\lambda)\frac{\Delta W_t^r}{W_{t-1}} - b(u_t - u^n).$$

We now solve for the increase in the flexible wage:

$$\frac{\Delta W_t^x}{W_{t-1}} = \frac{\Delta W_t^r}{W_{t-1}} - \frac{b}{1-\lambda}(u_t - u^n).$$

The rigid wage is set according to the wage-setting equation but based on expectations at the end of the previous period about the average wage level and the unemployment rate:

$$\frac{\Delta W_t^r}{W_{t-1}} = \frac{\Delta W_t^e}{W_{t-1}} - b\left(u_t^e - u^n\right).$$

The rigid wage setters know the rigid wage and using the equation above to form expectations about the flexible wage increase we get

$$\frac{\Delta W_t^{xe}}{W_{t-1}} = \frac{\Delta W_t^r}{W_{t-1}} - \frac{b}{1-\lambda}\left(u_t^e - u^n\right).$$

Thus we get

$$\frac{\Delta W_t^r}{W_{t-1}} = \lambda \left[\frac{\Delta W_t^r}{W_{t-1}} - \frac{b}{1-\lambda}\left(u_t^e - u^n\right)\right] + (1-\lambda)\frac{\Delta W_t^r}{W_{t-1}} - b\left(u^e - u^n\right).$$

Comparing the left- and the right-hand sides, we see that the terms involving $\Delta W_t^r / W_{t-1}$ cancel out, so the only way this equality can hold is if $u^e = u^n$. Thus we see that, in this simple model, the rigid wages are set in such a way that unemployment is *expected* to be at the natural level. This result is intuitive. If wages were set so that unemployment would be expected to be lower than the natural level, firms would have incentives to raise wages. For firms to be content with their wage decision, the rigid wage must be such that unemployment is expected to be on its natural level. Then the equation for the rigid wage above implies

$$\frac{\Delta W_t^r}{W_{t-1}} = \frac{\Delta W_t^e}{W_{t-1}} - b\left(u_t^e - u^n\right) = \frac{\Delta W_t^e}{W_{t-1}}.$$

This condition is used in the text to solve for the average wage increase.

PART 3 ECONOMIC POLICY

How should the central bank react to news about the economy?

Every other month or so, the governors of the central bank meet to decide whether to raise or lower the interest rate, or to keep it unchanged. Dozens of economists are employed at the central bank to analyse the economic situation and prepare the bank's decisions. Financial market analysts listen attentively to every word that issues from the central bank in order to forecast what the central bank will do with the interest rate.

To put it simply, the central bank of a country (or monetary union) can control the short-term interest rate in that country (or that monetary union) by offering to lend money at an interest rate that is set by the governors of the central bank. Since the central bank can create new money, there is no limit to how much it can lend and hence the central bank can normally adjust its lending so as to get the short-term interest rate to the desired level.

But how do the governors of the central bank think when they set the interest rate? What are the objectives of monetary policy and what news will lead them to change the interest rate? Does the central bank look at growth, inflation, unemployment, or other factors when it sets the interest rate? Having developed theories of aggregate demand and price adjustment, we are ready to analyse monetary policy. To do this, we use the *IS-LM model* from Chapter 8 and the *Phillips curve* from Chapter 9. We will use our theory to analyse how the central bank should react to a whole series of different shocks.

We first discuss what the objectives of monetary policy should be. Then we analyse how the central bank should react to various shocks (changes in exogenous variables) assuming that the central bank can observe the shocks and react to them. Then we turn to a more realistic situation, when the central bank cannot observe the shocks themselves, so it must try to find out what the shocks are using data on production and inflation. We also discuss whether it is possible to summarize good monetary policy in the form of a simple policy rule for the central bank. In the final part of the chapter we explain in more detail what instruments the central bank can use to control the interest rate.

10.1 The objectives of monetary policy

The primary goal of most central banks is 'price stability'. In practice, this means that inflation should be low and reasonably stable. Many central banks have official inflation targets in the range of 2–4 percent per year. The central banks of New

Zealand, Chile, Canada, Israel, the UK, Sweden, and Australia have had inflation targets since the early 1990s.[1] Even if a central bank does not have an officially announced inflation target, there will often be some desired range for inflation which is more or less well known. The US has not had an officially announced inflation target but inflation in the US has been kept at around 2–3 percent for a long time.

In the following we assume that the central bank has an inflation target which is either explicit – that is, officially announced – or implicit in the bank's statements and past policy decisions. The inflation target is denoted by $\pi^{\circledast}$.

Do monetary policymakers care about anything other than price stability? Yes, they do. A common way to express the priorities of the central bank is something like the following:

> *The primary goal of monetary policy is price stability. Monetary policy should also try to achieve high and stable employment, sustainable growth, and well-functioning financial markets as long as this can be achieved without sacrificing price stability.*

In practice, this means that the central bank can allow *temporary* deviations of inflation from the target level in order to achieve other objectives, such as stability of the real economy and the financial sector, as long as the average level of inflation is kept on the desired level.

But why should price stability be seen as more important than other objectives of monetary policy? Is it not much more important that people have jobs than that we keep inflation at 2 or 3 percent? Why don't we have an employment target for monetary policy?

The reason why price stability is seen as the primary objective of *monetary* policy is that, according to standard macroeconomic theory, monetary policy cannot affect the long-run level of production and employment. We saw this in Chapters 7–9. Since the central bank cannot permanently change the levels of employment or production, it does not make sense to set targets for the central bank for those variables.

In fact, attempts to keep employment above the natural level may have very harmful effects in the long run. If the central bank tries to keep production above the natural level, inflation will increase and, sooner or later, individuals will come to expect higher inflation. Such a policy may lead to short-term gains with respect to employment, but with substantial long-term costs since inflation will increase permanently to a higher level. In order to achieve a good outcome in the long run, monetary policy should not go after temporary gains in employment that entail large long-run costs in terms of higher inflation.

Although monetary policy cannot permanently raise the *levels* of production and employment, skilful monetary policy could potentially help to *stabilize* production and employment. Therefore, a reasonable objective for monetary policy is to keep:

---

1 See Chapter 15 for a longer list of countries with inflation targets.

1. inflation close to the inflation target, and
2. production close to its natural level.

A policy with these objectives is sometimes called 'flexible inflation targeting'.[2] This means that the central bank can sometimes accept temporary deviations of inflation from the target level in order to stabilize production. In the rest of this chapter, we assume that the central bank is pursuing flexible inflation targeting in this sense.

Another central objective for central banks is stability of the financial system. This means that it should help to make the system of payments and credit supply function well. In the current chapter we will not discuss this objective. The role of the central bank in a financial crisis is analysed in Chapter 18.

10.2 How should the central bank react to shocks?

The economy is continuously affected by various shocks. Oil prices increase or decrease, consumers' expectations about future incomes change, and there are changes in the velocity of money. How should the central bank react to such shocks? To analyse this, we use the *IS-LM model* from Chapter 8 and the *Phillips curve* from Chapter 9:

$$Y = C(Y, Y^e, i - \pi^e, A) + I(i - \pi^e, Y^e, K), \qquad \textbf{\textit{IS}}$$

$$\frac{M}{P} = \frac{Y}{V(i)}, \qquad \textbf{\textit{LM}}$$

$$\pi = \pi^e + \beta \frac{Y - Y^n}{Y^n} + z, \qquad \textbf{\textit{PC}}$$

The central bank can affect demand and production via the interest rate. If production is above the natural level, unemployment will be below the natural level, and there will be upward pressure on wages, which will feed through into inflation, as seen in the Phillips curve. In order to understand how monetary policy is conducted, let us analyse how the central bank should react to the following shocks:

- an exogenous increase in money demand
- a change in expectations about future growth which affects aggregate demand
- a cost–push shock such as an increase in prices of oil or other raw materials
- an increase in productivity
- and an increase in expected inflation.

To analyse the effects of shocks, we assume that the central bank has an inflation target, $\pi^\otimes$, and that the central bank can see the shocks and react to them immediately. We start from a situation where the natural level of production is constant, so there is no growth. This makes it easier to draw diagrams but does

---

2 A central banker who cares only about inflation is called an 'inflation nut'.

not fundamentally affect our conclusions. We also assume that the money supply and prices are initially increasing at the same rate so the real money supply is constant, production is at the natural level, and the expected inflation rate is equal to the inflation target.

An exogenous increase in money demand

Suppose that there is an increase in money demand for exogenous reasons – that is, an exogenous decrease in velocity. One reason could be that there has been an increase in credit card fraud, so people become afraid of using credit cards and they use more cash for their payments. What should the central bank do?

An increase in money demand means that, for a given money supply, there is excess demand for money. Lenders want their money back, and there is upward pressure on the interest rate. For a given level of production and money supply, the equilibrium interest rate in the money market increases, so the *LM* curve shifts up. This is illustrated in Fig. 10.1. where the *LM* curve shifts up from *LM* to *LM'*.

If the central bank keeps the money supply constant, there will be an increase in the interest rate from i_0 to i_1 and production will fall from Y_0 to Y_1, which is below the natural level. Since production and employment fall, inflation will fall to π_1, which is below the target level.

Is the resulting situation a desirable outcome for the central bank? No. There is no reason to let a shock to money demand lead to instability in financial markets and in the real economy. By increasing the money supply, the central bank can keep the interest rate and production unchanged, and such a policy also serves to stabilize inflation. In terms of the *IS-LM* diagram, an increase in the money

Fig. 10.1 *A shock to money demand*

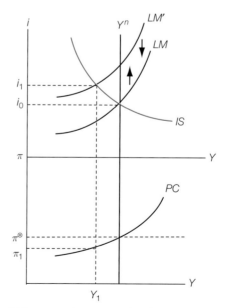

Source: ECB homepage, which contains footnotes and explanations and where data can be obtained free of charge, http://www.ecb.int/stats/monetary/rates/html/index.en.html#.

supply shifts the *LM* curve back to its original position when there is an exogenous increase in money demand.

Such a policy means that the central bank *accommodates* the shift in money demand, which is clearly better than keeping the money supply fixed. In practice, this is what central banks do. Most central banks take policy decisions about interest rates rather than money supply. By offering to buy and sell government bonds at a particular rate, the central bank keeps the short-term rate at the desired level. The basic reason why central banks decide about the interest rate rather than the quantity of money is that there are substantial shocks to the demand for money. As we saw in Chapter 7, the velocity of money is far from stable. Therefore, a policy of holding the money supply constant would lead to large fluctuations in interest rates whenever there were shocks to money demand.

Since central banks decide about interest rates rather than money supply, we focus on the interest rate rather than the money supply when analysing monetary policy in this chapter. Therefore, we will not use the *LM* curve in the rest of the chapter. Nevertheless, it is important to remember that it is because of its control of the money supply that the central bank is able to control the interest rate.

A demand shock

Suppose that consumers become more optimistic about the future, so expected future income, Y^e, increases. We assume that expected inflation does not change but remains equal to the inflation target. What should the central bank do?

When consumers become more optimistic, they consume more, so aggregate demand increases. As shown in Fig. 10.2, the *IS* curve shifts out from *IS* to *IS'*. If the interest rate is kept unchanged, production will increase to Y_1 and inflation

Fig. 10.2 *A real demand shock*

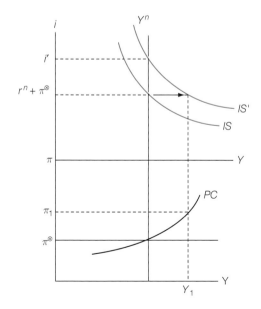

will increase to π_1, which is above the target level. In order to stabilize production and inflation, the central bank should *counteract* the aggregate demand shock by increasing the interest rate to i'. In this way, it prevents inflationary pressure from building up.

The nominal interest rate is higher in the new equilibrium, and so is the real interest rate for given inflation expectations. This is consistent with our analysis of the long run in Chapter 4. There we found that an exogenous increase in consumption raises the natural rate of interest. In fact, there is a simple interpretation of what the central bank should do when there is a demand shock:

> *In order to stabilize inflation and production, the central bank should adjust the nominal interest rate so as to keep the real interest rate equal to the natural rate of interest.*

If prices had been flexible and the money supply had been kept constant, this adjustment would have occurred through an increase in the price level, leading to a decrease in the real money supply and an increase in the interest rate. With slowly changing wages and prices, the central bank can achieve the same real adjustment by adjusting the nominal money supply so as to raise the real interest rate to the appropriate level. If the central bank does not do this, but keeps money supply or the interest rate constant, there will be a positive output gap and inflation will rise above the target.

The bottom line is that, when prices adjust slowly, the central bank can compensate by adjusting the nominal money supply so as to set the real interest rate at the appropriate level. Thereby, it can stabilize inflation as well as production. In practice, this is easier said than done because the central bank cannot observe the shocks and because monetary policy affects the economy with a considerable time lag. We discuss these practical complications later in this chapter.

A cost–push shock

Suppose, instead, that there is an unexpected cost–push shock in the form of an increase in the price of oil. Oil prices raise firms' costs and prices of petrol increase more or less immediately, so inflation will rise when the shock occurs. Let us assume that the oil price increase is perceived as a one-time permanent increase. What should the central bank do?

The situation is illustrated in Fig. 10.3. The cost–push shock shifts the Phillips curve upward so inflation will be higher for a given output gap. It is less clear how the *IS* curve and the natural level of production are affected. If oil is imported, the *IS* curve may shift inwards because an increase in the world price of oil makes an oil-importing country poorer. If oil is produced in the country, the oil price increase redistributes income, so the effect on aggregate demand is less clear. For simplicity, we assume that the natural level of production and the *IS* curve remain unchanged.

The shift of the Phillips curve creates a dilemma for the central bank. In order to stabilize inflation, it would have to raise the interest rate to i_1 in order to create a negative output gap and downward pressure on wages. Although the central bank cannot do anything about the oil price, lower wages will reduce other prices and

Fig. 10.3 *A cost–push shock*

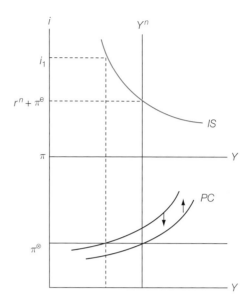

counteract the effect of the oil price on the price level. One could argue that it is better to keep production at the natural level and allow some temporary increase in inflation. It seems unnecessary to create a recession just because there was an unexpected increase in the oil price. If the *IS* curve has not shifted, this implies that the interest rate should be kept unchanged.

In this case, it is impossible to fully stabilize inflation and production at the same time, so policymakers face a dilemma and a choice has to be made. One factor that will play a role in the decision of the central bank is how wage setters form expectations about inflation. If inflation expectations are 'anchored' by the inflation target we may allow some temporary increase in inflation without the risk that inflation will remain high. But if wage setters form their expectations based on past inflation, there is a risk that a temporary cost–push shock affects inflation expectations and leads to a persistent increase in inflation. If the central bank is worried that this may happen, it may prefer to raise the interest rate even if the increase in inflation was caused by an unexpected and temporary cost–push shock.

Thus we see that a cost–push shock creates a difficult communication problem for the central bank. It can let inflation increase temporarily, but then it has to convince the public that the increase in inflation is temporary and due to a cost–push shock. The problem is that if the public perceives the increase in inflation as a shift to a more expansionary monetary policy, expected inflation may increase so that inflation persists.

Another factor is that, in practice, it may be very difficult to counteract temporary cost–push shocks because of time lags. An oil price increase or an increase in value added tax (VAT) will increase inflation more or less immediately, whereas it takes time for monetary policy to affect inflation. This means that the effects of the cost shock may very well have disappeared by the time monetary policy affects inflation. We will discuss this more below.

An unexpected and permanent increase in productivity

Now consider an unexpected increase in productivity. Suppose that a new generation of computers makes us all much more productive and that the productivity increase is perceived as permanent. What should the central bank do?

A permanent increase in productivity increases the natural level of production and expected future income will also increase. From consumption theory we know that a permanent increase in production should lead to an increase in consumption of similar magnitude, and the accelerator effect will lead to an increase in investment. As shown in Fig. 10.4, the natural level of production and the *IS* curve will both shift out. Also, an unexpected productivity increase will reduce inflation, so the Phillips curve shifts down.

Fig. 10.4 *An unexpected permanent increase in productivity*

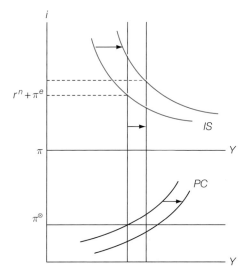

Depending on the shift in the *IS* curve and the increase in the natural level of production, either an increase or a decrease in the interest rate may be required. If demand increases more than supply, the interest rate should be increased so as to keep production at the natural level. On the other hand, the unexpected productivity increase has a direct negative effect on inflation, which calls for a lower interest rate. The appropriate monetary policy response will depend on the magnitude of the changes in supply and demand. In the case illustrated here, the *IS* curve shifts more than the natural level of production, so an increase in the interest rate is required in order to keep production at the natural level.

An increase in the expected rate of inflation

When analysing the monetary policy response to demand and productivity shocks above, we assumed that the expected rate of inflation was equal to the target rate of

Fig. 10.5 *An increase in the expected inflation rate*

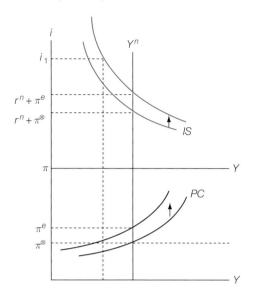

inflation. Effectively, we assumed that the inflation target of the central bank was *known and credible*, so people expected inflation to be in line with the target. But suppose that the expected inflation rate rises above the target level. What should the central bank do?

Fig. 10.5 illustrates this situation. We start from a situation when inflation expectations are in line with the target, so the *IS* curve intersects the vertical line showing the natural level of production at an interest rate equal to the natural rate of interest plus the inflation target, $r^n + \pi^\otimes$, and the Phillips curve intersects the vertical line showing the natural level of production at the target inflation rate $\pi^\otimes$. The increase in expected inflation shifts the *IS* curve as well as the Phillips curve upwards. Higher expected inflation reduces the expected real interest rate, and this has an expansionary effect on aggregate demand for a given nominal interest rate. More specifically, the interest rate has to be $r^n + \pi^e$ for production to be at the natural level, so the *IS* curve shifts up in line with the change in expected inflation. The Phillips curve also shifts up: now inflation will be π^e if the output gap is zero. We see that both *IS* and the Phillips curve shift up by an amount equal to the deviation of expected inflation from the target level.

Again, the central bank faces a dilemma. By raising the interest rate in line with expected inflation, to $r^n + \pi^e$, it can keep production at the natural level, but then inflation will be π^e, which is above the target. To bring inflation back to the target level, the central bank would have to raise the interest rate to i_1, but this would lead to a large negative output gap, which is undesirable. Although price stability is the primary target, we assume that the central bank also wants to stabilize the level of production. A reasonable response is to raise the interest rate to a level between $r^n + \pi^e$ and i_1. In this way, the central bank brings inflation some way back towards the target without creating too large a negative output gap.

Note that this policy response implies a strong reaction to expected inflation. As we see in the diagram, the central bank responds to an increase in expected inflation with an increase in the interest rate that is *larger* than the increase in expected inflation. The intuitive reason is that higher expected inflation raises actual inflation for a given output gap, so in order to bring inflation closer to the target, the central bank needs to generate a negative output gap. To do this, it has to increase the expected *real* interest rate. Therefore, the interest rate has to increase *more* than the increase in expected inflation.

This prescription for monetary policy that the interest rate should increase more than one for one when inflation deviates from the desired level is called the *Taylor principle* after the American economist John Taylor, who argued that a strong reaction to inflation was a characteristic of successful US monetary policy in the 1980s. Taylor formulated a simple rule for monetary policy, which is called the *Taylor Rule* and we will discuss this rule in Section 10.4.

10.3   Using macro data to set the interest rate

The conclusions from the analysis above can be stated simply:

1. When the expected inflation rate is in line with the inflation target, and there are no cost–push shocks, the central bank should keep production at the natural level.
2. The desired response to a cost–push shock depends on how much weight the central bank puts on stabilization of inflation versus production, and on the effect that the cost–push shock is thought to have on expected inflation in future periods.
3. If the expected inflation rate increases above the target, the central bank should bring inflation back towards the target by increasing the interest rate *more* than the increase in expected inflation.

In practice, there are several factors that complicate the task for monetary policymakers, however:

1. The central bank cannot observe the exogenous shocks, the natural levels of interest and production, or wage setters' expectations about inflation. The central bank has to assess the situation and try to infer what has happened using data for actual production and inflation and surveys of inflation expectations.
2. To make things even more difficult, data become available with a considerable time lag.
3. As we saw in Chapter 8, monetary policy affects output and inflation with a lag. The empirical evidence from vector autoregressions (VAR) shows that a change in the interest rate affects production with a lag of about six quarters and that the maximum effect on inflation appears after about two years.

Thus the art of monetary policy is to assess what the economic situation will be in one or two years from now, with data showing what the situation was several months ago. Therefore, monetary policymakers are not so much concerned about the situation today. Their focus is on what the situation will be in one or two years' time. One way to see the problems that monetary policymakers face is to consider how the central bank should react to news about production and inflation.

News about production

Suppose that new statistics come in showing that GDP has grown more quickly than previous forecasts had suggested. What will the central bank do? This will depend on how the central bank interprets the increase in production. If the increase in production is due to a demand shock, and demand is expected to remain high, the central bank should increase the interest rate so as to prevent the economy from overheating. If the increase in production is due to fast productivity growth, it is less clear what should be done with the interest rate.

To distinguish overheating from healthy growth, central banks try to estimate output gaps. Usually, the natural level of production is estimated as a trend in production, and then the output gap is calculated as the deviation from that trend. Estimates of the output gap are very uncertain, but if they indicate an increasing output gap, it is likely that the central bank will raise the interest rate.

News about inflation

Inflation is usually measured as the percentage increase in the price level this year compared with the previous year, or this month compared with the same month last year. Suppose that the latest data show that inflation is currently running above the inflation target. How should the central bank react? To analyse this, note that since inflation is determined by the Phillips curve, the deviation from target is

$$\pi - \pi^{\otimes} = \pi^e - \pi^{\otimes} + \beta \hat{Y} + z.$$

We see that there can be three reasons why inflation is above target:

- expected inflation is above target
- there is a positive output gap
- there is a cost–push shock.

How the central bank reacts to inflation being above target will depend on how the deviation from target is interpreted:

- If inflation was high because the *expected inflation* rate was above target, the central bank has a good reason to raise the interest rate so as to bring inflation down.
- High inflation may also arise because of a positive *output gap*, and if demand is expected to remain high, it is likely that the central bank will raise the interest rate.
- If inflation is the result of a temporary *cost–push shock*, there is less reason to raise the interest rate.

In order to evaluate whether the expected inflation rate deviates from the inflation target, central banks keep a close eye on survey data showing inflation expectations of business people, households, wage bargainers, and agents in financial markets. If these surveys show that the inflation expectations are drifting upwards, we can be quite sure that the central bank will raise the interest rate.

In order to gauge whether inflation is due to cost–push shocks, central banks use various alternative measures of the underlying rate of inflation, sometimes called *core inflation.* Such measures may exclude the effects of changes in energy prices and value added taxes. The effects of changes in the interest rate on housing costs may also be eliminated in such measures (housing costs are normally included in CPI). If inflation increases as measured by the consumer price index, but core inflation does not increase, this indicates that the increase in inflation is due to cost–push shocks. If these cost–push shocks are perceived as temporary, there is little reason to raise the interest rate because the effects of the cost–push shocks will have disappeared by the time a higher interest rate affects the economy.

We see that an increase in inflation may have many causes, but if there is an increase in inflation above target which cannot be attributed to temporary cost–push shocks, it is very likely that the central bank will respond by raising the interest rate.

10.4   The Taylor Rule

In 1993, the American economist John Taylor showed that US monetary policy in the period 1982–1991 could be described reasonably well by the following simple decision rule:

$$i = \bar{r} + \pi + 0.5\left(\pi - \pi^{\circledR}\right) + 0.5\hat{Y},$$

where $\bar{r}$ is an estimate of the normal real rate of interest and $\pi^{\circledR}$ is the inflation target of the central bank.[3] If we assume that expected inflation is equal to observed inflation, the implication is that the expected real rate is equal to

$$r = i - \pi = \bar{r} + 0.5\left(\pi - \pi^{\circledR}\right) + 0.5\hat{Y}.$$

The real interest rate is higher if inflation is above target. Taylor assumed that the normal real interest rate and the inflation target were both 2 percent, $\bar{r} = \pi^{\circledR} = 0.02$, leading to the decision rule

$$i = 0.02 + \pi + 0.5\left(\pi - 0.02\right) + 0.5\hat{Y} = 0.01 + 1.5\pi + 0.5\hat{Y}.$$

Fig. 10.6 illustrates how the interest rate responds to inflation if the output gap is zero. If expected inflation is equal to past inflation, the expected real rate is the difference between the interest rate and inflation. If inflation is on target – 2 percent – the nominal interest rate is 4 percent and the real interest rate is 2 percent, which is assumed to be the normal real rate. If inflation is 4 percent, the central bank sets the interest rate at 7 percent, making the expected real interest rate equal to 3 percent. For every percentage unit that inflation rises above the target, the real rate increases 0.5 percentage units.

---

3 John B. Taylor, 'Discretion versus policy rules in practice', *Carnegie-Rochester Series on Public Policy,* 39 (1999), 195–214.

Fig. 10.6 *The Taylor Rule*

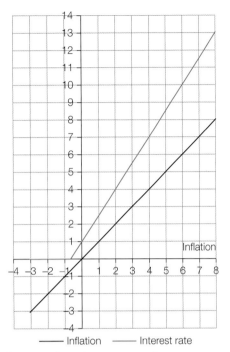

Inflation

—— Inflation   —— Interest rate

Note: Interest rate and inflation are shown in percentage units.

The basic logic of this rule is that, by a strong interest rate reaction to deviations from the target, inflation is stabilized. By reacting strongly to inflation, the central bank makes sure that high inflation leads to a high *real* interest rate and lower aggregate demand. If the central bank raises the interest rate less than one for one with inflation, *higher* inflation will lead to a *lower* real interest rate and *higher* aggregate demand, which adds to inflationary pressure. Such a policy may fuel inflation and lead to monetary instability. In fact, the Taylor Rule has been shown to describe the monetary policies of various central banks rather well.

So is it a good idea to follow a specific rule for monetary policy such as the Taylor Rule or some modification of it? In practice, no central bank has decided to follow a specific rule, and this for good reasons. First, it would put the governors of the central banks out of work. Second, the theory presented in this chapter says that the central bank's reaction to an increase in inflation should depend on the reason for the increase in inflation. If an increase in inflation is caused by a temporary cost–push shock there is less cause to raise the interest rate compared with a situation when expected inflation is above target. Most central bankers view the Taylor Rule as too mechanical. They want to maintain their freedom to interpret the data and respond to specific events in the way they find most appropriate.[4]

4 For an argument against rules that set the instrument (the interest rate) according to a pre-specified rule and suggested alternatives, see Lars Svensson, 'What is wrong with Taylor Rules? Using judgement in monetary policy through targeting rules', *Journal of Economic Literature*, 41 (2003), 426–477.

What has been generally accepted, however, is that central banks should react strongly when inflation deviates persistently from the target level. The Taylor Rule can be used as a rough description of what central banks should do and it is often used as a benchmark when evaluating monetary policy in different countries.

10.5   Rational expectations

In Chapter 9, we analysed the relation between unemployment and inflation under three different assumptions about expectations formation. First we considered a situation where the price level was expected to remain unchanged. Then we considered a situation where people expected inflation to be the same as in the previous period. Finally, we considered a situation where expected inflation was equal to the inflation target of the central bank. We argued that these different assumptions may be reasonable in different situations.

More generally, one may argue that rational individuals should form expectations in a way that is consistent with how inflation is actually determined. This means that expectations will depend on how policy is actually conducted. Such *model-consistent expectations* were originally proposed by the American economist John A. Muth in 1961, and he called them *rational expectations*.

In fact, the three expectations schemes discussed in Chapter 9 may be rational under different circumstances. In an economy where the price level is stable, the best prediction may very well be that prices will remain stable. In an economy with high, variable, and persistent inflation, the best prediction may be that inflation will remain roughly unchanged. If the central bank tries to keep inflation close to some inflation target, it is probably not a bad prediction that inflation will be close to the target.

The macroeconomic policy implications of rational expectations were formulated in the 1970s, primarily by the American economists Robert E. Lucas and Thomas J. Sargent.[5] The key policy conclusion that they derived was that, although monetary policy may be able to raise aggregate demand and employment in a particular period, any attempt to affect production by a *systematic* and therefore predictable monetary policy will be fruitless. The reason is that any predictable monetary policy will affect inflation expectations and hence it will be incorporated into wage- and price-setting. Only *unpredictable* monetary policy can affect the real economy.

This may seem to be bad news for stabilization policy. Clearly, there is no point in pursuing a random monetary policy that leads to random variations in production and employment. But even if wage setters have rational expectations, monetary policy can still play a stabilizing role in an economy with wage and

---

5   Robert E. Lucas Jr. received the Nobel Prize in 1995 'for having developed and applied the hypothesis of rational expectations, and thereby having transformed macroeconomic analysis and deepened our understanding of economic policy' and Thomas J. Sargent received the Nobel Prize in 2011 together with Christopher A. Sims 'for their empirical research on cause and effect in the macroeconomy'.

price rigidity because it can respond to unexpected shocks. As we have seen in this chapter, monetary policy can be used to ease the adjustment to shocks when wages adjust slowly. If, for example, there is a downturn in demand, and wages adjust sluggishly, a reduction in the interest rate will speed up the adjustment to the new long-run equilibrium. In this way, monetary can help to *stabilize* production and employment. Appropriate monetary policy can, at least in theory, compensate for the lack of flexibility of wages and prices.

Another important implication of rational expectations is that a clearly stated inflation target should prevent inflation expectations from drifting away from the target. A clear commitment to low inflation will help to 'anchor' inflation expectations so that the Phillips curve is stabilized. This should help to avoid situations such as that in the 1970s when expected inflation drifted upwards and high inflation became persistent. The implications of rational expectations in our model are analysed more formally in the appendix to this chapter.

10.6   The rise and fall of inflation

Fig. 10.7 shows inflation and the short-term interest rate for several countries since 1950. Let us first consider the UK and the US. In these countries (and many others) we see a strong upward trend in inflation from the 1960s until 1980, though with some swings up and down. Interest rates also increased, but less than inflation, leading to periods with low and even negative real interest rates in the 1970s. Nowadays, many economists see this as the main explanation why inflation increased in the 1970s. Nominal rates were not raised sufficiently when inflation took off, so real interest rates became very low, stimulating demand and leading to further increases in inflation.

One may object that data for real variables did not support the view that these economies were overheated in the 1970s. Real growth was low compared with the 1960s and unemployment was high in the US and the UK. Looking at the real side of the economy, monetary policymakers saw little reason to raise interest rates. But the fact is that inflation increased and this suggests that production was above the natural level. Apparently there were real factors that led to a slowdown of growth and high unemployment. Productivity growth slowed down in this period and the natural rate of unemployment seems to have increased. We discussed these developments in Chapters 5 and 6. These trends were not easy to see at the time since different indicators pointed in different directions.

Another factor was that the framework for monetary policy was changing in many countries. Until the beginning of the 1970s, most countries participated in a fixed exchange rate system (the Bretton Woods system) where the primary task of most central banks was to maintain a fixed exchange rate and where the US central bank was supposed to maintain a fixed value of the dollar in terms of gold.[6] When this system broke down, there was a period of experimentation with various exchange rate systems and the objectives of monetary policy were not clear.

6 We will analyse the history of the exchange rate system in Chapter 15.

Fig. 10.7 *Inflation and interest rates*

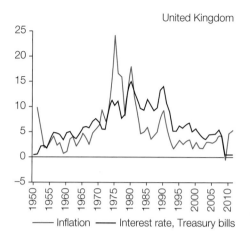

United Kingdom

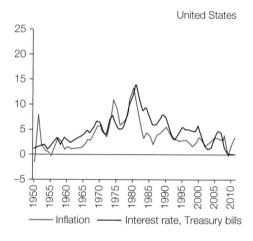

United States

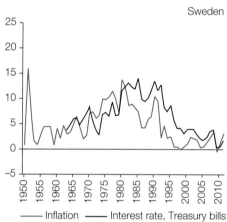

Sweden

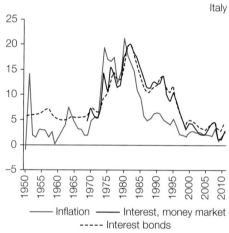

Italy

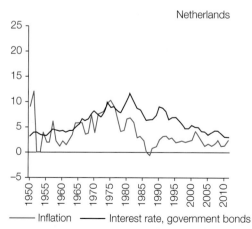

Netherlands

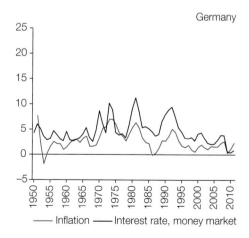

Germany

Source: International Financial Statistics, IMF, 16 July 2012.

In 1979 Paul Volcker became chairman of the Federal Reserve Board (the US central bank) and Margaret Thatcher became prime minister in the UK. Volcker and Thatcher both made low inflation the primary objective of monetary policy. Interest rates were raised and inflation came down as expected. Since then, low inflation has been the primary objective of monetary policy in both countries. As we can see in Fig. 10.7, the interest rates in the US and the UK have responded when inflation has increased and the difference between the interest rate and inflation has been positive most of the time. Initially, neither country had an explicit inflation target, but in 1992 the UK announced a target range for inflation of 1–4 percent. This was later changed to a point target of 2 percent. The US did not have an explicit inflation target but from the 1980s the Federal Reserve was generally thought to have an implicit inflation target somewhere between 2 and 3 percent.

Now consider Sweden, Italy, and the Netherlands. Sweden had a fixed exchange rate until 1992 and has had a floating exchange rate since then, Italy and the Netherlands had various kinds of fixed exchange rates throughout this period and they adopted the euro as currency in 1999. As we will see in Chapter 15, a fixed exchange rate eliminates the possibilities of pursuing an independent monetary policy. Nevertheless, we see a picture similar to that in the US and the UK. Interest rates increased less than inflation in the 1970s, leading to low real interest rates and high inflation. In the 1980s interest rates were raised and inflation was brought down. Since November 1992, Sweden has had a floating exchange rate and the Swedish central bank has an explicit inflation target of 2 percent. We see that the Swedish interest rate has responded strongly to inflation and the real interest rate has been positive after the adoption of the inflation target.

Germany has an entirely different history with respect to inflation. Because of the damaging experiences of hyperinflation in the 1920s, German monetary policy has had a strong focus on low inflation. Throughout this period, the German real interest rate was almost always positive and the German central bank, the Bundesbank, responded very strongly to inflation long before the Taylor Rule had been written down. Inflation increased to 6–7 per cent when oil prices increased in 1973 and 1979, but subsequently inflation was quickly taken down to low levels again.

10.7 The instruments of monetary policy

In our analysis of monetary policy, we have assumed that the central bank can control the money supply, and thereby the interest rate. But exactly how does the central bank go about controlling interest rates? To make a long story short, the central bank controls the short-term interest rate by offering to lend money at an interest rate which is decided by the decision-making board at the central bank. Since the central bank can create new money, or more precisely monetary base, it can always lend enough money to get the interest rate to where it wants it to be.

In practice, things are a bit more complicated, however. First, the central bank can lend and borrow in several different ways, and for different lengths of time. Second, the central bank can control the interest rate for its own short-term lending, but this is not the interest rate that is relevant for consumers and firms. This raises the question as to what influence the central bank has over the interest rates that are relevant for consumers and firms. We now study what instruments the central bank uses to control interest rates. The description refers primarily to how the European Central Bank (ECB) operates but other central banks use very similar ways of controlling short-term interest rates.[7]

The interbank market for overnight borrowing

As we saw in Chapter 7, all payments are ultimately made with monetary base. The monetary base includes currency and banks' accounts in the electronic payment system that is managed by the central bank and used to transfer money between banks. Every day, banks make a large number of transactions and people deposit and withdraw money from their bank accounts in a way that is not perfectly predictable. Depending on the amount of withdrawals and deposits that come in, a bank may end up with a deficit or a surplus on its account in the payment system. A bank can have a deficit on its account during the day, but it is not allowed to have a deficit overnight.

If a bank has a deficit as the day approaches its end, it must borrow money to balance its account. Banks borrow from each other in the *interbank market* for overnight loans. In the US, this interbank market is called the *Federal funds market*. As the day approaches its end, banks with deficits on their accounts borrow from banks with surpluses in their accounts. The overnight interest rate in the interbank market is the shortest market interest rate in the economy.

If a bank has a deficit remaining at the end of the day, it is automatically converted to overnight borrowing from the central bank, but this is usually unattractive for the bank because the interest rate on overnight loans from the central bank is normally higher than the interest rate in the interbank market. Therefore, banks avoid overnight borrowing from the central bank.

How the central bank lends and borrows to control the interbank rate

When the central bank lends money, it changes the monetary base. If the central bank lends one million to a bank, or buys treasury bills for one million from a bank, the monetary base increases by one million. Initially, this increase in monetary base ends up on the account of the bank that borrowed the money, or that sold the Treasury bill. Then the bank may use the money to make a payment to

---

7 For detailed descriptions of the procedures, see documentation from the ECB, 2011, *The Implementation of Monetary Policy in the Eurozone*, and from Bank of England, 2010, *A Framework for the Bank of England's Operations in the Sterling Money Markets*. Both documents are available at the banks' respective homepages.

another bank, lend to another bank, or it may convert it to cash that consumers and firms can withdraw from the bank.

We now describe the ways in which the central bank can lend and borrow so as to affect the monetary base and the rate of interest in the interbank market.

Banks can borrow overnight from the central bank

As mentioned above, banks that are short of cash can borrow overnight from the central bank. Since banks that participate in the payments system can borrow from the central bank, they will not borrow from another bank at an interest rate that is higher than the rate they have to pay to borrow from the central bank. Therefore, the rate at which banks can borrow from the central bank sets a *ceiling* for the interest rate in the interbank market.

Banks can deposit excess reserves in an account of the central bank

Banks with excess liquidity can deposit money overnight at the central bank. In many countries, banks get interest on such deposits. Since banks, which participate in the payments system, can deposit reserves at the central bank, and get interest on their deposits, they will not lend overnight to another bank at an interest rate that is lower than the rate they get from the central bank. Therefore, the rate that the central bank offers on overnight deposits is a *floor* for the interbank rate.

At the European Central Bank, the possibilities of borrowing from and depositing money at the central bank are called *marginal lending facility* and *deposit facility*. The Bank of England uses the term *operational standing facilities*. Together, the interest rates on these facilities define an *interest rate corridor* within which the overnight interbank rate must be.

Table 10.1 and Fig. 10.8 show the interest rates for deposits and lending offered by the European Central Bank together with the money market rate and the *refinancing rate*, which will be explained below. The Federal Reserve does not pay interest on overnight deposits, so the floor of the interest rate corridor is zero in the US.

Outright open market operations

Normally, the European Central Bank keeps the interbank rate in the middle of the interest rate corridor. To do this it uses *open market operations* – that is, it buys and sells government securities. The simplest form of open market operation is an *outright open market operation* where the central bank buys or sells government securities, thereby increasing or decreasing the monetary base. Note that if the central bank buys Treasury bills from a bank it is taking over loans from the bank to the government, so this is another form of lending by the central bank.

Repurchase agreements

Today, most central banks use a sophisticated form of open market operation called a *repurchase agreement*. A repurchase agreement is a combined sale and

Table 10.1 *The interest rate corridor and refinancing rate of the European Central Bank*

Date		Deposit facility	Main refinancing operations		Marginal lending facility
			Fixed rate tenders Fixed rate	Variable rate tenders Minimum bid rate	
With effect from		Level	Level	Level	Level
2012	11 July	0	0.75		1.50
2011	14 Dec.	0.25	1.00		1.75
	9 Nov.	0.50	1.25		2.00
	13 July	0.75	1.50		2.25
2011	13 Apr.	0.50	1.25		2.00
2009	13 May.	0.25	1.00		1.75
	8 Apr.	0.25	1.25		2.25
	11 Mar.	0.50	1.50		2.50
	21 Jan.	1.00	2.00		3.00
2008	10 Dec.	2.00	2.50		3.00
	12 Nov.	2.75	3.25		3.75
	15 Oct.	3.25	3.75		4.25
	9 Oct.	3.25			4.25
	8 Oct.	2.75			4.75
	9 July	3.25		4.25	5.25
2007	13 June	3.00		4.00	5.00
	14 Mar.	2.75		3.75	4.75
2006	13 Dec.	2.50		3.50	4.50
	11 Oct.	2.25		3.25	4.25
	9 Aug.	2.00		3.00	4.00
	15 June	1.75		2.75	3.75
	8 Mar.	1.50		2.50	3.50
2005	6 Dec.	1.25		2.25	3.25
2003	6 June	1.00		2.00	3.00
	7 Mar.	1.50		2.50	3.50
2002	6 Dec.	1.75		2.75	3.75
2001	9 Nov.	2.25		3.25	4.25
	18 Sep.	2.75		3.75	4.75
	31 Aug.	3.25		4.25	5.25
	11 May	3.50		4.50	5.50
2000	6 Oct.	3.75		4.75	5.75
	1 Sep.	3.50		4.50	5.50
	28 June	3.25		4.25	5.25
	9 June	3.25	4.25		5.25
	28 Apr.	2.75	3.75		4.75
	17 Mar.	2.50	3.50		4.50
	4 Feb.	2.25	3.25		4.25
1999	5 Nov.	2.00	3.00		4.00
	9 Apr.	1.50	2.50		3.50
	22 Jan.	2.00	3.00		4.50
	4 Jan.	2.75	3.00		3.25
	1 Jan.	2.00	3.00		4.50

Note: The distinction between fixed rate tenders and variable rate tenders has to do with how the ECB auctioned off the repurchase agreements. This is a technical detail that need not concern us here.

Source: ECB homepage, where footnotes and explanations can be found, http://www.ecb.int/stats/monetary/rates/html/index.en.html#.

Fig. 10.8 *The interest rate corridor at the European Central Bank*

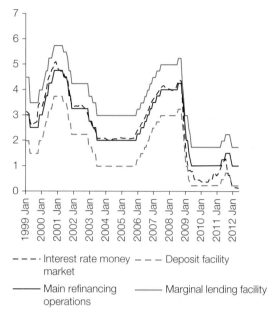

- - - · Interest rate money   – – – Deposit facility
      market

——— Main refinancing   ——— Marginal lending facility
      operations

Source: ECB homepage, which contains footnotes and explanations and where data can be obtained free of charge, http://www.ecb.int/stats/monetary/rates/html/index.en.html#.

future purchase of a government security. This means that the central bank buys a government security from a bank with a contract to resell the security at a later date, often in a week's time. During the period of the repurchase agreement, the bank has the money available to make payments. The repurchase price is some-what higher than the price at which the bank sells the security, so the bank pays for having the cash during the contract period. This cost, converted to an annual-ized rate, is called the *refinancing rate* by the ECB and the *repo rate* by the Bank of England. The central bank sets this rate by offering to make repurchase agree-ments at a specific rate of interest. The decision about the refinancing/repo rate is the main policy decision of the central bank.

We can think of a repurchase agreement as a short-term loan with the govern-ment security as collateral and the refinancing rate as the rate the bank has to pay on the loan. A main advantage of the repurchase agreement compared with direct lending is that it reduces the risk taken by the central bank. Normally, the asset bought and sold in the repurchase agreement is a government bond. If the bank goes bankrupt before the bond has been repurchased, the bank will be unable to buy back the bond, but the central bank has the bond. If there is a fiscal crisis and the bond loses some of its value, the bank still has to repurchase the bond at the price stated in the contract. It is only if the bank goes bankrupt *and* the price of the security falls at the same time that the central bank will lose some of its money.

For a bank, participating in a repurchase agreement is a close alternative to borrowing in the interbank market, so the interest rate in the interbank market is normally very close to the refinancing rate. Therefore, the central bank can control the interest rate in the interbank market by offering repurchase agreements at an interest rate determined by the central bank's decision-making board.[8]

A central bank has a board that meets about six to eight times a year to decide on the interest rate that the central bank targets. This board has different names in different countries. In the European Central Bank the *Governing Council* decides on the *refinancing rate*. In the Bank of England the *Monetary Policy Committee* decides on the *repo rate*. The Federal Reserve in the US has an *Open Market Committee* that sets a target level for the *federal funds rate* – that is, the rate on interbank loans. Once the decision has been made, the bank makes repurchasing agreements so as to keep the target interest rate on the desired level. Often, the main repurchase trade takes place on a weekly basis – banks sell government bonds and bills to the central bank with contracts to repurchase them within a week. There are also repurchase agreements of shorter duration, so-called *fine tuning operations*, which are made in order to adjust the monetary base day by day so as to keep the interbank rate on the desired level.

Normally, the central bank provides just enough liquidity to keep the interbank rate close to the officially announced refinancing rate, which is typically in the middle of the interest rate corridor. As a consequence, banks avoid using *standing facilities* to borrow from the central bank or deposit money overnight at the central bank. Banks with excess reserves prefer to lend them in the interbank market and banks with deficits on their accounts prefer to borrow from other banks rather than borrowing overnight from the central bank.

If the banking system were to end up with *excess reserves* at the end of the day, banks would have to deposit their excess reserves in the central bank and the interbank rate would fall down to the floor of the interest rate corridor. To avoid this, and to keep the interbank rate in the middle of the corridor, the central bank has yet another way to adjust the liquidity of the banking system. It can issue its own certificates (short-term bonds where the central bank is the issuer) in order to soak up liquidity and reduce the monetary base.

Control over the interest rate and the demand for money

The central bank's ability to control the short-term interest rate is based on the fact that there is a demand for monetary base for transaction purposes. Note, however, that the central bank can control the interest rate even if the demand for monetary base is unstable. Whatever the level of demand for monetary base, the central bank can adjust its lending until the short-term interest rate reaches the desired level. When people do their Christmas shopping, the demand for monetary base is high, and the central bank provides the amount of monetary base that is demanded at the interest rate set by the central bank. If the central bank were to try to keep the monetary base stable during the Christmas shopping

---

8 Repurchase agreements are made with government securities or other assets which are considered very safe. Interbank loans are made without collateral, so they are associated with credit risk. Therefore there is a risk premium on interbank loans relative to the refinancing rate. Normally, this risk premium is very small but in the financial crisis of 2008–2009, the risk premium increased. We will discuss this when we analyse financial crises in Chapter 18.

period, interest rates would rise to very high levels before Christmas Eve. Now, Christmas is a fairly predictable event, but there are many unpredictable shocks to the demand for monetary base. When monetary policy targets the interest rate in the interbank market, such shocks are accommodated by providing the amount of reserves demanded by the banks.

Reserve requirements

Some central banks, such as the Federal Reserve and the European Central Bank, require banks to hold a certain proportion of their deposits as reserves in the form of cash or deposits made with a central bank. Traditionally, reserve requirements have been seen as an instrument of monetary policy. This makes sense if we see the monetary base as exogenously determined. An increase in the reserve requirement will increase the demand for monetary base, so if the monetary base is kept unchanged, the interest rate will increase. But if the central bank targets the interest rate, reserve requirements lose their role in the implementation of monetary policy. A change in the reserve requirement has little or no effect on interest rates or broad money aggregates because banks will just borrow the amount of reserves they need. If the reserve requirement is raised and the repo rate is unchanged, banks can get the necessary reserves from the central bank by repurchase agreements and deposit the required amount of money on their accounts at the central bank. The monetary base will increase, but there will not be any direct effects on interest rates, bank lending, or deposits.

The interest rate on deposits at the central bank is normally lower than the rate on repurchase agreements, so reserve requirements are costly for banks. Therefore, reserve requirements are best seen as a form of tax on the banking system.

The interbank rate and other interest rates

Using the various instruments described above, the central bank can control the interest rate on overnight loans in the interbank market, but consumption and investment decisions depend on the interest rates on bank loans and industrial bonds (bonds issued by firms). So what is the connection between overnight rates in the interbank market and the interest rates that are relevant for consumers and firms?

The connection is that *expectations* about the interbank rate determine other market interest rates. For the bank, an alternative to lending for three months to a firm, or holding a three-month Treasury bill, is to keep lending the money overnight in the interbank market. If banks expect the interbank rate to be higher over the coming months, they will require higher returns on their loans and other assets that they hold. Therefore, the interest rate in the interbank market is a baseline interest rate, which determines the level of all the interest rates in the economy. The spreads between different interest rates depend on the credit risk, time to maturity, and other differences between the assets.

Note that it is the *expected* interbank rate over the relevant period that matters. If the central bank raises its repo rate unexpectedly, and this is interpreted

Fig. 10.9 *Repo rate, overnight interbank rate, and three-month Treasury bill rate, United Kingdom*

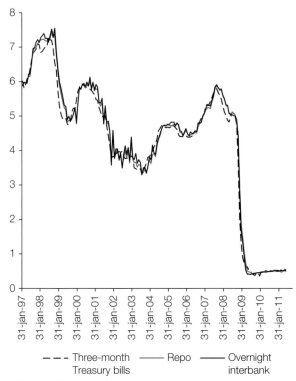

Source: The Bank of England homepage, http://www.bankofengland.co.uk.

as a signal that the repo rate will remain higher for some time to come, other interest rates will also increase. In this way, monetary policy affects all interest rates in the economy, including those that affect consumption and investment decisions. Fig. 10.9 illustrates the repo rate, the overnight interbank rate, and the three-month Treasury bill rate for the UK. We see that the three rates are very similar. In practice, the Bank of England can control the three-month Treasury bill rate.

An important implication is that the effect of an increase in the repo rate on the three- or six-month interest rate will depend on whether the change in the repo rate was expected or not. If the central bank raises the interest rate unexpectedly and financial investors expect the interest rate to remain on the higher level for a while, three- and six-month interest rates will also increase. But if the increase in the repo rate was expected by the market, three- and six-month rates have already adjusted, so there will be little effect on those rates. In fact, we see in Fig. 10.9 that the three-month rate often moved before the repo rate, which suggests that market participants were able to anticipate the decisions of the Bank of England. They can do that because they read the same news as the decision-makers in the central bank and because modern central banks are often fairly open about where monetary policy is heading.

'Long-term interest rates' are interest rates on bonds that mature in five or ten years' time, or even later. As we have seen, the central bank has almost perfect control over the three-month interest rate, but the link between the repo rate and long-term rates is much weaker. If the central bank cuts the short-term rate, the effect on long-term interest rates depends on what happens to *expected* future interest rates over the coming years. On the one hand, a reduction in the repo rate today may be taken as an indication that the central bank has a more negative view of the economy and that the interest rate will stay low for considerable time to come. On the other hand, investors in financial markets may think that a lower short-term interest rate will lead to higher inflation, which will force the central bank to raise the interest rate in the future. Depending on how expectations change, the long-term rate may respond more or less strongly to a change in short-term rates.

Central banks mainly operate on the short side of the market, buying and selling securities week by week in repurchase agreements. A central bank can also buy and sell long-term bonds in outright open market operations. This has a direct effect on the supply and demand for long-term bonds and can have a more direct effect on long-term rates. Yet long-term interest rates depend primarily on expectations about inflation and interest rates over many years, so the central bank has much less control over long-term rates than it has over short-term interest rates.

What have we learned?

According to standard macroeconomic theory, monetary policy affects the rate of inflation but cannot permanently change the levels of employment or production. Therefore, price stability is usually considered to be the main objective of monetary policy.

A central bank can have an explicit, officially announced inflation target or there may be an implicit understanding that the central bank wants to keep inflation on a certain level. Flexible inflation targeting means that the central bank also tries to stabilize production and that temporary deviations from the inflation target can be allowed.

Most central banks decide about the interest rate and adjust the supply of monetary base by buying and selling government securities so as to keep the interest rate on the level decided by the board. This means that they accommodate shocks to money demand.

The central bank can counteract a positive demand shock by raising the interest rate. In this way, the real interest rate is kept equal to the natural rate of interest and production and inflation are stabilized. In real terms, the outcome is the same as if prices had been flexible. In this way, monetary policy can compensate for the lack of wage and price flexibility.

A cost–push shock, such as an unexpected increase in the oil price or in value added tax, raises inflation and creates a dilemma for the central bank. In order to counter the increase in inflation the central bank must raise the interest rate to generate a negative output gap. Alternatively, it can stabilize production and accept a temporary increase in inflation. There may also be a concern that higher inflation will affect the expected rate of inflation, so that inflation will remain high.

An unexpected and permanent productivity shock affects both supply and demand. Depending on the relative shifts of demand and supply, the central bank may have to raise or reduce the interest rate.

If expected inflation rises above the target level, this affects the *IS* curve as well as the Phillips curve. The *IS* curve shifts up because the expected real interest rate falls for a given nominal interest rate. The Phillips curve shifts up because wage and price increases depend on expected wage and price increases. To bring inflation down, the central bank must raise the interest rate more than the increase in expected inflation.

An increase in inflation may lead to different monetary policy responses, depending on how it is interpreted. If high inflation is thought to be a result of strong demand or high expected inflation, it is likely that the central bank will raise the interest rate. If it is due to a temporary cost–push shock, there is less reason to raise the interest rate.

According to the Taylor Rule for monetary policy, the interest rate that is set by the central bank should increase 1.5 percentage points if there is a one percent increase in inflation and it should increase 0.5 percentage points if there is a one percent increase in the output gap.

When inflation increased in the 1970s, central banks raised their interest rates, but less than the increase in inflation, leading to low real rates and continued inflation. In the early 1980s, the central banks in the US and the UK raised their interest rates and brought inflation down. Other central banks followed.

The shortest market interest rate is the interest rate on overnight loans in the interbank market where banks with excess reserves lend to banks with a shortage of reserves.

Standing facilities allow banks to deposit money or borrow from the central bank overnight. The rates for such overnight borrowing and lending set a ceiling and a floor for the interest rate in the interbank market.

Through open market operations, the central bank keeps the interbank rate inside the interest rate corridor. The most common market operations are repurchase agreements where the central bank buys government securities with a contract to resell them in a short time, typically one week. We can think of repo operations as loans with collateral, whereby banks borrow money on a short-term basis. The (annualized) cost for these loans is the repo or refinancing rate.

Since repurchase agreements are close substitutes for loans in the interbank market, the overnight interest rate in the interbank market is normally very close to the repo/refinancing rate, which is set by the central bank.

Lending repeatedly in the interbank market is an alternative to holding assets with longer maturity. Therefore, other market interest rates are determined by *expectations* about the interest rate in the interbank market over the relevant period. In practice, the central bank can control the interest rate on short-term government securities, such as three-month Treasury bills, but the central bank has much less control over long-term interest rates.

Where do we go from here?

In this chapter we have analysed the role of *monetary policy*, that is, the central bank's decision about the interest rate. When wages and prices adjust slowly, skilful monetary policy can help to ease adjustment to exogenous shocks. When expected inflation is in line with the target, the central bank should try to keep the real interest rate at the natural level so as to keep production at the natural level and the output gap equal to zero. In this way, the central bank will stabilize inflation and keep production at the natural level. In the next chapter, we introduce a government in the model and we analyse the role of *fiscal policy* – that is, decisions about taxes and government expenditure. We analyse the long-run sustainability of government finances and the possibility to use fiscal policy to stabilize the economy.

Exercises

1. The latest data show that inflation, as measured by the consumer price index, is above the inflation target, but core inflation and inflation expectations seem to be in line with the target. Discuss how the central bank might interpret and react to this information.

2. Consider an economy where agriculture plays a major role. Suppose there is a poor harvest. What should the central bank do? Use the *IS* curve and the Phillips curve to analyse the problem.

3. Suppose that financial uncertainty leads to an increase in the spread between the repo rate and the interbank rate. What should the central bank do?

4. Suppose that inflation is close to the target but core inflation increases. What should the central bank do?

5. Assume that consumers and firms use the currently observed inflation rate as their best guess about inflation next year and that the central bank follows the Taylor Rule. Calculate the nominal and the expected real interest rate if inflation is zero, 2 and 4 percent.

6. Assume that consumers and firms use the currently observed inflation rate as their best guess about inflation next year. Draw the Taylor Rule in a diagram with inflation on the horizontal axis and the *real* interest rate on the vertical axis for three different levels of the output gap: zero, minus 2 and plus 2 percent.

Answers to the Exercises can be found at: **www.palgrave.com/economics/gottfries**.

Appendix

Derivation of a monetary policy rule

We have argued that when inflation increases above the target, the central bank should normally try to counteract the increase in inflation, and to do this, it has to raise the interest rate so as to create a negative output gap. The central bank should 'lean against the wind' in order to counteract high and low inflation. We can express this policy recommendation in mathematical terms:

$$\hat{Y} = -\phi \left(\pi - \pi^{\otimes} \right),$$

where ϕ is a positive coefficient. To analyse the implications of such a policy, let us assume that expected inflation is equal to the rate of inflation observed in the previous period, so the Phillips curve is

$$\pi = \pi_{-1} + \beta \hat{Y} + z.$$

Subtracting lagged inflation on both sides and substituting the policy rule into the Phillips curve we get

$$\pi - \pi_{-1} = -\beta\phi \left(\pi - \pi^{\otimes} \right) + z.$$

The coefficient in front of $(\pi - \pi^{\otimes})$ is negative. This means that if inflation is above target, it decreases, and if it is below target, it increases. Thus, our policy rule will stabilize inflation, bringing it gradually back to the target. The process of adjustment is illustrated in Fig. 10.10. Suppose that inflation in period 0 is π_0, which is above the inflation target. This inflation rate determines the position of the Phillips curve. Following the policy stated above, the central bank generates a negative output gap so $Y_1 < Y^n$ and inflation falls to π_1. Therefore, the Phillips curve shifts down in the next period and we see that inflation falls gradually towards the target.

But what interest rate does this rule imply? To see this, let us assume that consumption and investment are determined by the following simple consumption and investment functions:

$$C = c_0 + c_1 Y \qquad \text{and} \qquad I = d_0 - d_1 \left(i - \pi \right).$$

Expected inflation in the next period is assumed to be equal to current inflation. Substituting for C and I in $Y = C + I$, solving for Y, we get the output gap:

$$\hat{Y} = \frac{1}{1 - c_1} \frac{c_0 + d_0 - d_1 \left(i - \pi \right)}{Y^n} - 1.$$

Fig. 10.10 *A monetary policy rule*

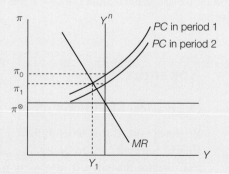

To simplify we write this equation as

$$\hat{Y} = D - b(i - \pi) \quad \text{where} \quad D = \frac{c_0 + d_0}{(1 - c_1) Y^n} - 1 \quad \text{and} \quad b = \frac{d_1}{(1 - c_1) Y^n}.$$

Here D is a variable measuring the net effects of demand and supply shocks on the output gap and b is a coefficient that measures how the real interest rate affects the output gap. In order to find out what interest rate the central bank must set, we use this equation to substitute for the output gap in the monetary policy rule (MR):

$$D - b(i - \pi) = -\phi\left(\pi - \pi^\otimes\right).$$

To solve for the interest rate we add bi and $\phi(\pi - \pi^\otimes)$ on both sides of the equation, divide by b, and switch sides:

$$i = \pi + \frac{\phi}{b}\left(\pi - \pi^\otimes\right) + \frac{1}{b}D.$$

This equation tells us how the central bank should set the interest rate. There are three terms:

1. The first term comes from the fact that an increase in inflation reduces the expected real interest rate and this increases the output gap. To counteract this effect, the nominal interest rate has to increase in line with inflation.
2. The second term captures the idea that if the inflation rate deviates from the target, the real interest rate should increase so as to bring inflation back towards the target.
3. The last term shows that the interest rate should be increased if there is a positive demand shock. As we have already discussed, monetary policy should counteract demand shocks and this is done by raising the interest rate $1/b$ units if D increases one unit.

The effect of inflation on the interest rate is found by taking the derivative:

$$\frac{di}{d\pi} = 1 + \frac{\phi}{b}.$$

We see that the interest rate will increase *more than one for one* when inflation increases. This illustrates the Taylor principle. In order to counteract high inflation, the expected real interest rate must be increased and this requires an increase in the interest rate that is larger than the increase in inflation.[9]

Rational expectations and inflation targeting

Rational expectations are model-consistent expectations. Hence they depend on how monetary policy is actually conducted. To see the implications of rational expectations in the context of our model, let us assume that monetary policy can be described by the following rule:

$$\hat{Y}_t = -\phi\left(\pi_t - \left(\pi^\otimes + v_t\right)\right),$$

---

9 For a fuller analysis along similar lines, see Wendy Carlin and David Soskice, 'The 3-equation new Keynesian model – a graphical exposition', *Contributions in Macroeconomics*, 5:1 (2005).

where $v_t = \rho v_{t-1} + \varepsilon_t$ and where ρ is a number between zero and one and ε_t is an unpredictable shock. The idea here is that the central bank has some long-run inflation target $\pi^\otimes$ but for some reason the central bank deviates from this target some of the time. In a given period, the central bank acts as if it had an inflation target which is $\pi^\otimes + v_t$. The shock v_t represents other factors that influence monetary policy.

To see what rational expectations implies in this model, recall from Chapter 9 that the rigid wages are set according to the wage-setting rule

$$\frac{\Delta W^r}{W} = \frac{\Delta W^e}{W} - b\,(u^e - u^n).$$

Now, we argued in Chapter 8 that it must be the case that the increase in the rigid wage is equal to the expected average wage increase. If this were not the case, the rigid wage setters would not act rationally since they would deliberately set a too high or a too low wage. But this means that wages are set so that unemployment is expected to be at the natural level $u^e = u^n$. Hence the *expected* output gap must also be zero. The monetary policy rule above implies that for the expected output gap to be zero we must have

$$\pi_t^e = \pi^\otimes + v_t^e.$$

Furthermore, the best prediction for v_t in period $t-1$ is ρv_{t-1}, so the model-consistent expectation is

$$\pi_t^e = \pi^\otimes + \rho v_{t-1}.$$

This is the best prediction for inflation if you can observe v_{t-1} but wage setters cannot observe v_{t-1}. Note, however, that v_{t-1} can be inferred from observations of inflation and output gaps in the previous period. Since $\hat{Y}_{t-1} = -\phi\,(\pi_{t-1} - \pi^\otimes - v_{t-1})$ we can solve for v_{t-1}:

$$v_{t-1} = \pi_{t-1} - \pi^\otimes + \frac{1}{\phi}\hat{Y}_{t-1}.$$

The intuitive interpretation of this equation is that if wage setters observe inflation above target and a positive output gap, they should conclude that the central bank has an effective inflation target which is higher than that $\pi^\otimes$. Substituting into the equation for expected inflation we get

$$\pi_t^e = \pi^\otimes + \rho\left(\pi_{t-1} - \pi^\otimes + \frac{1}{\phi}\hat{Y}_{t-1}\right) = (1-\rho)\pi^\otimes + \rho\pi_{t-1} + \frac{\rho}{\phi}\hat{Y}_{t-1}.$$

Substituting into the Phillips curve we get

$$\pi_t = (1-\rho)\pi^\otimes + \rho\pi_{t-1} + \frac{\rho}{\phi}\hat{Y}_{t-1} + \beta\hat{Y}_t + z_t.$$

This equation illustrates that expectations depend on how monetary policy is conducted. If the central bank does not deviate persistently from the long-term inflation target $\pi^\otimes$, ρ equals zero and expected inflation is equal to the target $\pi^\otimes$ (Assumption 3 in Chapter 9). If there are very persistent deviations from the inflation target, so that ρ is close to unity, lagged inflation will have a large effect on expectations and the lagged output gap will also affect expectations. In this case, high inflation and/or a high output gap are interpreted as signals of an expansionary monetary policy that will continue for some time, so inflation will remain high. With rational (model-consistent) expectations, inflation expectations depend on how monetary policy is conducted.

11 FISCAL POLICY

Are government finances sustainable? How does fiscal policy affect economic activity?

The government sector plays an important role in the economy. Government expenditure on goods and services is an important part of aggregate demand, and taxes and transfers affect the disposable incomes of the households. Governments finance their expenditure by taxes and by borrowing, issuing bonds and Treasury bills in financial markets. *Fiscal policy* is policy that affects government consumption and investment, taxes, and transfers. *Expansionary* fiscal policy is policy that is expected to increase aggregate demand such as tax reductions and increases in government consumption, investment, and transfers to the private sector. *Contractionary* fiscal policy is the opposite: tax increases and reduced expenditure.

In recent years, the merits of fiscal policy have been hotly debated. Some economists argued strongly for expansionary fiscal policy as a way to counteract the effects of the financial crisis in 2008–2009. Some favoured government expenditure on railways and other infrastructure, while others argued for tax cuts. Yet other economists argued that expansionary fiscal policy is ineffective as a way to counteract a recession and that it only leads to increased government debt.

The debate about the usefulness of fiscal policy takes place against a background of high government debt. Several countries, such as Japan and Italy, have high levels of government debt as a result of accumulated borrowing over many years. Ireland, Greece, and Portugal have been going through fiscal crises and have difficulties financing their borrowing by issuing bonds in the financial markets. The International Monetary Fund and the European Union have stepped in with support in the form of loans and guarantees.

In this chapter we analyse the role of the government from a macroeconomic point of view. We first present statistics showing the size of the public sector. Then we analyse government finances in the long run: how government debt evolves over time and what levels of public sector deficits are consistent with the long-run sustainability of government finances. Then we consider the short run. We analyse whether fiscal policy can help to stabilize the economy. Finally, we discuss lags in policymaking and *automatic stabilizer effects* that arise because tax revenue and government expenditure react automatically to economic developments in the private sector.

11.1   How large is the public sector?

The government provides *public goods* such as defence and law and order.[1] A large part of education and health care is provided by the government. Such expenditure is called *government consumption*. The government makes *investments* in schools, hospitals, fighter jets, and transport systems. A substantial part of government outlays consist of *transfers* such as pensions, child allowances, and social assistance. Governments finance their expenditure by *taxes* and by *borrowing*, and the government pays interest on the existing stock of government debt.

Often, the public sector is divided into three subsectors:

- central government
- local governments
- social security funds.

The *central government* is in charge of defence, the judicial system, higher education and research, and national transport systems, while *local governments* are in charge of local schools, roads, and transport systems. The responsibility for health care and social assistance is shared between local and central government in different ways in different countries. The *social security funds* consist primarily of the public pension system.

In federal states, there is also a distinction between the federal government and the governments of the different states.

Taken together, the different parts of government are called the 'general government' or the 'public sector'. The term *public sector deficit* refers to expenditure (consumption, investment, transfers and interest payments) minus income (mainly taxes) of the public sector. When the accounts for the whole public sector are constructed, the accounts are *consolidated*, which means that the internal transactions between the subsectors are cancelled out.[2]

How large is the public sector? The answer to this question depends on what perspective we have. As we saw in Chapter 1, we can measure economic activity from the *income side*, the *user side*, and the *production side*. Thus, we can ask the following questions:

- What share of total *income* goes through the public sector?
- What share of goods and services are *used* by the public sector?
- What share of goods and services are *produced* by the public sector?

We get different answers to the question about the size of the government depending on what perspective we take. Table 11.1 shows the size of the government sector from the income and user sides.

---

1   Public goods are goods and services that are non-excludable and non-rival. 'Non-excludable' means that it is hard to prevent someone from benefiting from production of the good. This makes it hard to charge individuals for using the good, so the market is unable to provide it. 'Non-rival' means that one individual's use of the good does not reduce another individual's utility from consuming the same good. Examples of public goods are defence and law and order.

2   Often, the term *government budget deficit* is used for the deficit in the budget of the central government. When we discuss fiscal policy in this chapter, we focus on the whole public sector.

Table 11.1 *Government income, outlays, deficit and debt, percent of GDP, 2009*

	Tax and non-tax government income	Government consumption	Government investment	Share of use	Transfers	Net interest payments	Deficit	Gross debt	Net debt
Australia	28	18	4	22	11	1	5	19	−4
Austria	49	20	1	21	30	2	4	73	39
Belgium	48	25	2	27	24	3	6	100	80
Canada	39	22	4	26	17	1	6	83	28
Czech Republic	40	22	5	27	18	1	6	42	−2
Denmark	56	30	2	32	26	0	3	52	−5
Estonia	43	22	5	27	18	0	2	12	−29
Finland	53	25	3	28	29	−1	3	52	−63
France	49	24	3	27	26	2	8	89	49
Germany	45	20	2	22	24	2	3	76	48
Greece	37						16	132	101
Hungary	46	22	3	25	21	4	4	85	59
Iceland	41	27	4	31	18	3	10	120	40
Ireland	34	20	4	24	23	1	14	72	27
Italy	47	21	3	24	24	4	5	128	100
Japan	33	20	3	23	17	1	9	194	110
Korea	32	16	6	22	12	−1	1	33	−38
Luxembourg	41	17	4	21	22	0	1	15	
Netherlands	46	28	4	32	18	1	5	68	30
New Zealand	40	21	4	25	18	0	3	34	−9
Norway	57	22	4	26	23	−2	−10	48	−156
Poland	37	18	5	23	19	2	7	58	22
Portugal	40	22	3	25	22	3	10	93	64
Slovak Republic	34	20	2	22	18	1	8	40	17
Slovenia	43	20	5	25	23	1	6	44	0
Spain	35	21	4	25	19	1	11	62	35
Sweden	54	28	4	32	24	0	1	52	−24
Switzerland	35	11	2	13	20	0	−1	41	2
United Kingdom	40	23	3	26	23	2	11	72	44
United States	31	17	4	21	20	1	11	84	60
Eurozone (15 countries)	45	22	3	25	23	2	6	87	54

Note: Data is for 'general government'. 'Tax and non-tax income' refers to total receipts. 'Transfers' is calculated as total disbursements minus consumption, investment and net interest payments, which means that it contains some other minor items.
Source: *OECD Economic Outlook*, OECD, 22 June 2011, http://www.oecd-ilibrary.org/statistics.

Income side

Let us first consider the *income side*. The income of the government consists primarily of taxes and social security fees that households and firms pay to the government. In the countries listed, the government collected between 28 and 57 percent of GDP in this way in 2009. Australia and the US had the lowest shares (28 and 31 percent) while the governments of Denmark, Finland, Norway, and Sweden collected more than 50 percent of their GDP in taxes and other income for the government. In the other countries, the government share of income was somewhere in between these figures; the Eurozone average is 45 percent.

User side

What does the government do with all this tax revenue? Turning to the *user side*, we see that a large part is used for government consumption such as health care and education. In most countries, government consumption is about 20 percent of GDP. Again, the Scandinavian countries stand out with high shares and the US is on the low side with 17 percent. A key difference is that health care and education are almost completely tax-financed in Scandinavia, while much health care and education provision are privately funded in the US. This means that a visit to a hospital, which counts as government consumption in Scandinavia, counts as private consumption in the US. A small share of GDP is used for government investment such as building of schools and roads. This share is similar, 2–4 percent of GDP, in most high-income countries, but higher in fast-growing countries such as Korea and some former communist countries, where government investment constitutes 5–6 percent of GDP.

Taken together, government consumption and government investment constitute between 20 and 30 percent of GDP in most countries. This share is lowest in Switzerland (13 percent) and the US (21 percent) and high in Sweden, Denmark, and the Netherlands (32 percent). Clearly, government expenditure on goods and services plays a more important role in the latter countries than it does in the US or in Switzerland.

Production side

Most government services are produced by the government – the government hires teachers, doctors, nurses, and judges to produce government services – but a proportion of government consumption and investment consists of goods produced by the private sector and bought by the government. Examples are buildings, roads, equipment, and other supplies, produced by private firms and bought by the government. Therefore, the proportion of GDP that is *produced* by the government is smaller than the proportion *used* by the government for consumption and investment. The production share is not shown in Table 11.1.

Transfers

As we have seen above, the government's share of income is larger than the share of use. In the Eurozone, for example, the government's share of income is 45 percent, while the share of use is 25 percent. The main difference is transfers, which constitute 23 percent of GDP in the Eurozone. The tax income of the government is used not only for government consumption and investment, but also for transfers such as pensions, social security, and child allowances. As a share of GDP, transfers are lowest in Australia (11 percent) and highest in Finland (29 percent).

Interest payments, deficits, and debt

The government pays interest on its debt but it also gets interest on its financial assets. In most countries, *government net interest payments* are less than 3 percent of GDP.

If government income is smaller than expenditure on consumption, investment, transfers, and net interest payments, the government budget shows a *deficit*. As we see in Table 11.1, most countries had a deficit in 2009, but the magnitude varied substantially between countries. Some had deficits above 10 percent of GDP while Norway had a surplus (a negative deficit) corresponding to 10 percent of GDP.

If the government budget shows a deficit, this is financed by borrowing, so the government debt will grow. The last columns in Table 11.1 show gross and net government debt as shares of GDP in 2009. Government debt takes the form of government bonds and Treasury bills that are held by households, firms, and financial institutions in the country and abroad. Net government debt is government debt minus the claims that the government has in the form of loans to households and firms, such as student loans and housing bonds held by public social security funds.

We see that Japan, Italy, and Greece had gross debts far in excess of GDP during one year and net debts that were somewhat larger than GDP. The government in Norway has a large oil fund where revenue from oil production is saved, and this is why Norway has a large surplus and the Norwegian government has large financial assets, primarily claims on foreign countries. This means that the net debt of the Norwegian government is negative.

In this chapter, we introduce a government sector into our macroeconomic model. We will not make any distinction between different parts of government, but we use the term *government* for the whole public sector and the term 'budget deficit' is used to refer to the deficit of the whole public sector. We also simplify by assuming that all production occurs in the private sector so that the government uses taxes and borrowing to buy goods and services from the private sector. We use the following notation:

G_t: government expenditure in year t on goods and services – that is, the sum of government consumption and investment.

T_t: tax income of the government minus transfers from the government to households and firms in year t.

D_t: government *net debt* at the beginning of the year in the form of bonds and Treasury bills issued by the government minus government claims on households and firms such as student loans and loans to private firms.

G, T, and D are all expressed in real terms – in units of the consumption basket. We use the term 'government debt' for D although we should remember that it is the *net* debt of the whole government sector. Note that G and T are *flows*: we take the period to be one year so these are measured as the outlays and incomes during one year. D is a *stock* at the beginning of the year and it is the result of accumulated deficits in previous years.

11.2   Sustainable government finances

We often hear about government budget deficits in the media. Should we be concerned about such deficits? How do we know if the situation is under control, or if government finances are on their way to collapse? Clearly, the answer depends on the size of the deficit, and on whether the deficit is temporary or is expected to remain. A deficit in one particular year may arise because of extraordinary expenditure, or low tax revenue because of a deep recession, and such deficits need not be a cause for concern. However, if there are continuous and large deficits, government debt will accumulate and reach a high level relative to GDP. In this section, we address the question as to what levels of deficits are consistent with government finances being *sustainable* in the long run.

To analyse this question, we must consider the relation between deficits and debt accumulation in the long run and how the level of debt grows in relation to GDP. The stock of real (net) government debt changes over time according to the equation

$$\Delta D_{t+1} = G_t - T_t + rD_t.$$

The first part on the right-hand side, $G_t - T_t$, is government expenditure on goods and services minus tax income (net of transfers) over the same period. This is called the *primary deficit*. The last part on the right-hand side of this expression is interest payments in period t in real terms. D_t is real net government debt *at the beginning of the period t* and r is the real return. To simplify, we assume that the real rate of interest is constant and implicitly we assume that the real return is the same on government claims and liabilities.[3] Thus we see that real government debt can increase for two reasons:

3

- the primary deficit adds to the stock of government debt next period
- real interest payments on the debt add to the real stock of government debt next period.

If the government has a deficit, government net debt will increase as time goes by. But in most economies GDP is also growing, so government debt can increase without growing relative to GDP, and a situation where debt is stable relative to GDP may be regarded as sustainable. Therefore, a simple and intuitive definition of sustainable government finances is that *government net debt does not grow faster than GDP*. If government debt grows faster than GDP the government must, sooner or later, raise taxes or cut expenditure relative to GDP so as to stop the growth in government debt. If such steps are not taken, government debt will eventually become many times larger than GDP and the interest payments on the debt will become astronomical.

---

3   We disregard seignorage. As we saw in Chapter 7, seignorage is a few promille of GDP in countries with low inflation rates. We could allow for seignorage by counting the central bank as part of the government and assuming that some of the government debt is monetary base, on which the government pays a lower interest rate. (The interest rate on currency is zero and the interest rate on bank reserves at the central bank is below the rate on government bonds.)

To find out when government finances are sustainable in this sense, let us consider an economy with a constant inflation rate π and a constant real growth rate g. We define the government *debt ratio*, d_t, as the amount of debt that is brought into period t relative to GDP in that period:

$$d_t = \frac{D_t}{Y_t}.$$

In order to see how the debt ratio evolves over time, we use our rule of thumb for growth rates:

$$\frac{\Delta d_{t+1}}{d_t} = \frac{\Delta D_{t+1}}{D_t} - \frac{\Delta Y_{t+1}}{Y_t},$$

where Δd_{t+1} denotes the change in the debt *ratio* from period t to period $t+1$. The growth rate of the debt *ratio* is the growth rate of the debt minus the growth rate of production. The growth rate of real GDP is g, and multiplying by D_t/Y_t on both sides we get

$$\Delta d_{t+1} = \frac{\Delta D_{t+1}}{Y_t} - g\frac{D_t}{Y_t}.$$

Using $\Delta D_{t+1} = G_t - T_t + rD_t$ to substitute for ΔD_{t+1} we get

$$\Delta d_{t+1} = \frac{G_t - T_t + rD_t}{Y_t} - g\frac{D_t}{Y_t} = \frac{G_t - T_t}{Y_t} + (r - g)\frac{D_t}{Y_t}.$$

To simplify, we omit the time index and use $\Delta\dfrac{D}{Y}$ to denote the change in the debt ratio:

$$\Delta\frac{D}{Y} = \frac{G - T}{Y} + (r - g)\frac{D}{Y}.$$

This equation is extremely useful for understanding how the government debt ratio evolves over time. In fact, most discussions about the state of government finances start from this equation. Let us therefore try to understand the different terms.

- On the left-hand side we have the change in the debt *ratio* from one year to the next.
- The first term on the right-hand side is the *primary deficit* relative to GDP, which adds to the debt ratio. If the primary deficit is one percent of GDP, one percent is added to the government debt ratio next year.
- The second term on the right-hand side shows that, if the *real interest rate exceeds the growth rate*, an amount is added to the government debt ratio and this amount depends on the government debt ratio at the beginning of the year.

To see what role the real interest rate plays, suppose that net government debt is 50 percent of GDP and the real interest rate is 4 percent. Then the real interest payment on the existing government debt is 2 percent of GDP, which will add 2 percent to the government debt ratio ($r \cdot D/Y = 0.04 \cdot 0.5 = 0.02$). Note that it is the *real* interest rate that matters because inflation reduces the real value of the debt. If the nominal interest rate is 5 percent and inflation is one percent, interest payments add 5 percent to the nominal debt but inflation reduces the real value of the debt by one percent per year. Then the real change of the debt that is due to interest and inflation is a 4 percent increase of the debt, which corresponds to 2 percent of GDP if the debt was initially 50 percent of GDP.

But why does *growth* enter this equation? The reason is simple: GDP is the *denominator* of the debt ratio, so income growth reduces the debt ratio for a given level of debt. Suppose again that government debt is 50 percent of GDP, and there is 4 percent growth. This growth will reduce the debt ratio itself by 4 percent. Since the ratio was initially 50 percent of GDP, this means that the debt ratio falls by 2 percent of GDP. This explains why growth reduces the debt ratio and why the effect of growth is proportional to the debt ratio.

To see the implications of this equation, note that if the debt ratio is to remain constant, the government needs to have a *primary surplus* equal to

$$\frac{T - G}{Y} = (r - g)\frac{D}{Y}.$$

In many developed countries, the real interest rate on government bonds and the growth rate of real GDP are both around 2–3 percent, so $r \approx g$ and the right-hand side is close to zero. This means that real interest payments increase the debt ratio at the same pace as growth reduces the debt ratio. Then the simple conclusion is that, in order to keep the debt ratio constant, the *primary* deficit needs to be close to zero. The requirement for a stable debt ratio becomes

$$G = T.$$

The numbers we hear in the media usually refer to the total deficit, in nominal terms, including nominal rather than real interest payments on the debt. To express the above equation in terms of the nominal deficit relative to GDP, we use the fact that the real interest rate is the nominal interest rate minus inflation: $r = i - \pi$. Using this to substitute for the real interest rate we get[4]

$$\Delta\frac{D}{Y} \approx \frac{G - T + iD}{Y} - (\pi + g)\frac{D}{Y}.$$

The first term constitutes the *nominal government deficit* as a share of GDP.[5] It includes the primary deficit plus net *nominal* interest payments. We see that we can have a deficit relative to GDP which is equal to $(\pi + g)D/Y$ and still keep the debt ratio constant. If, for example, inflation and growth are both 2 percent and the debt ratio is 50 percent of GDP, we can have a deficit equal to 2 percent of GDP and still keep the debt *ratio* constant $((0.02 + 0.02) \cdot 0.50 = 0.02)$. The intuitive explanation is that nominal GDP grows by 4 percent per year, so nominal debt can also increase by 4 percent per year and with an initial debt ratio of one half, this corresponds to a deficit equal to 2 percent of GDP.

The main conclusion from this analysis is that in a country with 2 percent growth and 2 percent inflation, and net debt equal to 50 percent of GDP, a deficit

---

4 The derivation is as follows:

$$\Delta\frac{D}{Y} \approx \frac{G - T}{Y} + (i - \pi - g)\frac{D}{Y} = \frac{G - T}{Y} + \frac{iD}{Y} - (\pi + g)\frac{D}{Y} = \frac{G - T + iD}{Y} - (\pi + g)\frac{D}{Y}.$$

5 G, T, Y, and D are all measured in real terms. To get nominal magnitudes we need to multiply by the price level, P, but since the condition is expressed in terms of ratios, the P's cancel out.

equal to 2 percent of GDP may be consistent with a stable debt ratio. A deficit above this level implies a growing debt ratio, so increases in taxes or cuts in government expenditure relative to GDP will be needed to prevent government debt from ballooning out of control.[6]

Whether a given deficit is sustainable or not depends on the growth rate and the inflation rate of the economy. A growing economy with high inflation can have a larger government deficit and still have government finances under control because high growth and high inflation increase the denominator of the debt ratio. Suppose, for example, that inflation is 4 percent, growth is 6 percent, and the debt ratio is 50 percent of GDP. Then we can have a deficit equal to 5 percent of GDP and still the debt ratio will remain constant $((0.04 + 0.06) \cdot 0.50 = 0.05)$. Thus, we often observe relatively high deficits in high-growth countries, but this need not be a cause of concern because the debt ratio may still be stable.

In order to judge whether the deficit is problematic, we can use our equation for the change in the debt ratio, or simply examine whether debt is on an increasing trend relative to GDP. It should be emphasized, however, that the calculations above refer to situations where the economy grows at a constant rate and where taxes and expenditures are kept at constant levels relative to income. *Temporary* shocks such as wars and natural disasters may motivate temporarily higher expenditure, which is not financed by raising taxes, and recessions lead to temporary reductions in tax revenue. Deficits that arise because of such temporary shocks may very well be consistent with long-term stability of the public finances.

Furthermore, expected *future* changes should be taken into account when evaluating the sustainability of government finances. Expected future increases in health expenditure and pension payments because of an ageing population may imply that current tax, benefit, and pension systems are unsustainable even if the debt ratio is stable today. To evaluate the long-term sustainability of government finances in such a situation, projections must be made for what future expenditures and taxes will be if the current tax, benefit, and pension systems are kept unchanged.

Are government finances under control?

Fig. 11.1 shows how the gross and net debt ratios have evolved in Japan, the US, and the UK. By definition, the level of net debt is lower than gross debt. The UK debt ratio decreased until 1990, but since then it has increased. In the US, the debt level decreased until 1980, but after 1980, there has been an upward trend, and gross debt was quickly approaching 100 percent of GDP in 2010. Government debt in Japan has increased almost continuously relative to GDP, and in 2010, gross debt in Japan was twice as large as GDP. Net debt was about 120 percent of GDP. In all three countries, there was a sharp increase in the debt ratios in connection with the financial crisis 2008–2009. This was due to falling tax revenue and expansionary fiscal policies during the crisis.

---

6 To be precise, taxes must be raised and/or expenditure reduced *relative to GDP*. Note, however, that if the government does not do anything, both *T* and *G* will increase along with GDP. If taxes are roughly proportional, tax revenue will increase at the same rate as GDP and the wages of government employees tend to rise along with the general wage level.

Fig. 11.1 *General government financial liabilities, United States, United Kingdom, and Japan, percent of GDP*

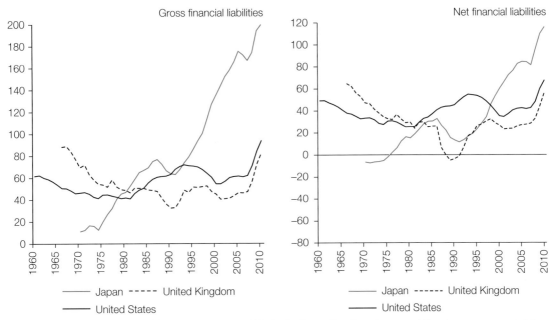

Note: Government *net financial liabilities* are government debt in the form of bonds and treasury bills minus government claims on households and firms such as student loans and loans to private firms.

Source: *OECD Economic Outlook*, OECD, 4 May 2011, http://www.oecd-ilibrary.org/statistics.

Fig. 11.2 shows that the debt ratios of France, Germany, Italy, and Spain have trended upwards for a long time.

The situation is different in the Scandinavian countries and the Netherlands (Fig. 11.3). These countries had growing debt ratios until the middle of the 1990s and serious fiscal crises led to rapidly rising debt ratios in Finland and Sweden in the early 1990s. After that time, all these countries have reduced their debt ratios. Norway (not shown) has accumulated a large negative net debt ratio because most of its oil revenue has been saved.

Thus we see that many countries are, or have been, troubled by high debt, but the situation is quite different in different countries. How serious are these problems and what measures must be taken to deal with them? To analyse this question, recall that if the debt ratio is to remain constant the government needs to have a primary *surplus* equal to

$$\frac{T - G}{Y} = (r - g)\frac{D}{Y}.$$

Fig. 11.4 illustrates the situation for some countries in 2009. The net debt ratio is on the horizontal axis and the *cyclically adjusted primary surplus* is on the vertical axis. By 'cyclically adjusted' we mean that this is the hypothetical surplus which would have occurred if production had been on the natural level. Since there was a deep recession in 2009, countries had larger deficits than shown here, but some parts of those deficits were expected to disappear once the economy recovered. Therefore, we consider the cyclically adjusted balances when analysing long-term sustainability of government finances.

Fig. 11.2 *General government financial liabilities, France, Germany, Italy, and Spain, percent of GDP*

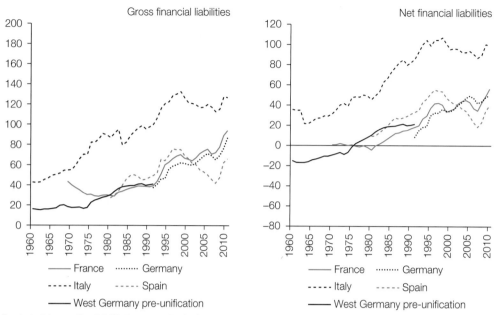

Source: Statistical Appendix, *OECD Economic Outlook*, Autumn 2010, OECD, http://www.oecd-ilibrary.org/books.

Fig. 11.3 *General government financial liabilities, Denmark, Finland, Netherlands, and Sweden, percent of GDP*

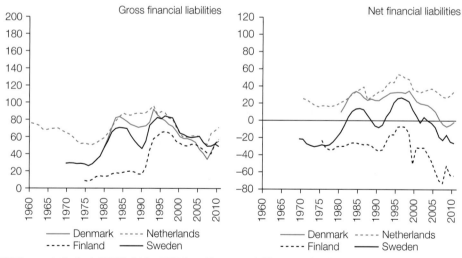

Source: *OECD Economic Outlook*, OECD, 4 May 2011, http://www.oecd-ilibrary.org/statistics.

If the real interest rate on government debt is equal to the growth rate, the right-hand side of the equation above is zero. Then the equation says that governments with primary surpluses will have falling debt ratios, and governments with primary deficits will have rising debt ratios. Thus, if the real interest rate is equal to the growth rate, the countries above the horizontal axis (Sweden, Germany,

Fig. 11.4 *Debt ratios and cyclically adjusted primary balances for some OECD countries, 2009*

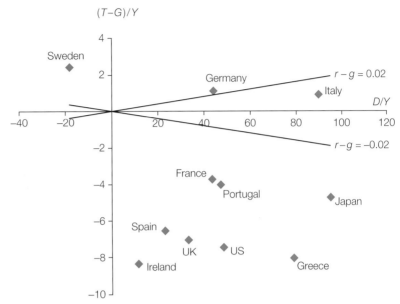

Note: D/Y is general government net financial liabilities as a percentage of GDP at the end of 2008. $(T-G)/Y$ is general government underlying balances which are adjusted for the cycle and for one-off expenditures and incomes.
Source: Statistical Appendix, *OECD Economic Outlook*, Fall 2010, OECD, http://www.oecd-ilibrary. org/books.

and Italy) will have falling debt ratios and the countries below the horizontal axis will have growing debt ratios. This means that, in order to stop the increase in the debt ratio, Greece, Ireland, Spain, the UK, and the US would need to cut their expenditure, or raise taxes, by 6–8 percent of GDP. With total government expenditure on government consumption, investment, and transfers in the order of 40–50 percent of GDP, this would mean cuts in the order of 15–20 percent of government expenditure if the adjustment was to be made only by cutting expenditure. This is an approximate calculation, but it shows that very substantial adjustments were required in order to bring the debt ratios under control in these countries.

This calculation is appropriate if the real interest rate and the real growth rate are approximately equal, and this may be a reasonable approximation in normal times. But in a fiscal crisis, the situation can easily become more difficult because interest rates increase and growth slows down. Countries that are in a serious fiscal crisis have to pay higher interest rates on their borrowing because lenders worry that they may not get their money back. Additionally, cuts in government expenditure, which are made to reduce the deficit, reduce aggregate demand and the growth rate of the economy, and this makes it harder to achieve balance. The upward-sloping line marked $r - g = 0.02$ shows what primary surplus is required to stabilize the debt ratio if the real interest rate is 2 percent higher than the growth rate. In such a situation, a country with a primary deficit and a 50 percent debt ratio needs to cut expenditure by one additional percent of GDP in order to stabilize the debt ratio.

11.3   Fiscal policy in the short run

In Chapter 10 we analysed how monetary policy can help to stabilize the economy. With rigid wages and prices, the nominal interest rate can adjust so as to ease the adjustment to shocks and keep production on the natural level. But fiscal policy can also play a role. Government consumption and investment are components of aggregate demand, and taxes and transfers affect the disposable income of the consumers. Therefore, fiscal policy decisions affect aggregate demand and production in the short run. We now analyse how changes in government consumption and investment, taxes, and transfers affect aggregate demand and production in the short run.

When we include the government in our model, production is given by

$$Y = C + I + G,$$

where C is private consumption, I is private investment, and G is government expenditure on goods and services – that is, government consumption and investment. We also have to modify our measure of the disposable income of the households. Now, disposable income of households will differ from GDP because households pay taxes and they receive interest payments from government. Real disposable income of the households is[7]

$$Y^d = Y - T + rD,$$

where T is taxes that households pay to the government minus transfers from the government to the households. To simplify the notation in this section, we assume that there is no (net) government debt initially, so we set $D = 0$. Now we must modify the consumption function that we derived in Chapter 4 to take account of taxes:

$$C = C(Y - T, Y^e - T^e, i - \pi^e, A).$$

T^e is the expected future level of the tax. In line with our analysis of monetary policy in Chapter 10, we assume that the central bank sets the interest rate. In the short run, production is determined by aggregate demand:

$$Y = C(Y - T, Y^e - T^e, i - \pi^e, A) + I(i - \pi^e, Y^e, K) + G.$$

Let us now consider how changes in government expenditure and taxes affect production in the short run. To analyse this, we should note that parliaments do not decide about the level of tax revenue but about rules and schedules for taxes and

---

7 As we saw in Chapter 1, *disposable income* is primary income, i.e. wages, interest payments, and dividends plus net secondary incomes, i.e. transfers received minus taxes paid. In the national accounts, household disposable income is reported in nominal terms, including nominal rather than real interest payments. Here we express all variables in real terms.

transfers. What tax revenue will be from a certain tax depends on what happens to the *tax base* for that tax – that is, the income, expenditure, or asset that you tax.

In a macroeconomic context, the main taxes are income taxes, indirect taxes such as VAT and sales taxes, and social security payments that are related to wage payments. To include a simple tax system in our model, we assume that the government taxes all incomes at the rate τ and at the same time it hands out a lump sum transfer Tr to the households. Then, real tax revenue minus transfers is determined by a tax (and transfer) function:

$$T = \tau Y - Tr.$$

To see more formally how production is determined, we assume that the consumption and investment functions are linear functions:

$$C = a_0 + a_1 (Y - T) + a_2 (Y^e - T^e),$$

$$I = b_0 - b_1 (i - \pi^e).$$

To simplify, we have omitted some of the factors (e.g. asset holdings, capital stock) which determine consumption and investment. Substituting into the goods market equilibrium condition we get

$$Y = a_0 + a_1 (Y - \tau Y + Tr) + a_2 (Y^e - T^e) + b_0 - b_1 (i - \pi^e) + G.$$

To solve for equilibrium production, we multiply into the parenthesis on the right,

$$Y = a_0 + a_1 Y - a_1 \tau Y + a_1 Tr + a_2 (Y^e - T^e) + b_0 - b_1 (i - \pi^e) + G.$$

Then we subtract $a_1 Y$ and add $a_1 \tau Y$ on both sides,

$$Y - a_1 Y + a_1 \tau Y = a_0 + a_1 Tr + a_2 (Y^e - T^e) + b_0 - b_1 (i - \pi^e) + G,$$

and rewrite the left-hand side,

$$(1 - a_1 + a_1 \tau) Y = a_0 + a_1 Tr + a_2 (Y^e - T^e) + b_0 - b_1 (i - \pi^e) + G.$$

Dividing by $(1 - a_1 + a_1 \tau)$ on both sides we get

$$Y = \frac{1}{1 - a_1 + a_1 \tau} [a_0 + b_0 + a_1 Tr + a_2 (Y^e - T^e) - b_1 i + b_1 \pi^e + G].$$

This shows what production will be for a given interest rate set by the central bank and given exogenous variables Tr, Y^e, π^e, G etc. Now we can calculate the short-run effect on production of an increase in government expenditure on goods and services:

$$\Delta Y = \frac{1}{1 - a_1 + a_1 \tau} \Delta G.$$

Increased government expenditure on goods and services raises aggregate demand and leads to higher production. As production increases, income increases, and this leads to further increases in consumption (the multiplier effect). The multiplier effect is smaller, than we found in Chapter 8, however, because some of the increase in income has to be paid to the government as taxes. The higher is the tax τ, the smaller is the multiplier.

We can also calculate the short-run effect on production of an increase in transfers:

$$\Delta Y = \frac{a_1}{1 - a_1 + a_1 \tau} \Delta Tr.$$

We see that an increase in transfers has a smaller effect on production compared to an increase in government expenditure on goods and services. The reason is that households save a proportion $1 - a_1$ of the increase in disposable income. Therefore, the initial effect on aggregate demand is smaller in this case. An increase in government purchases equal to 100 euros adds 100 euros directly to aggregate demand, but if the marginal propensity to consume out of a reduction in taxes is 50 percent, a tax cut of 100 euros has a direct effect on demand, which is only 50 euros. In both cases there is also a multiplier effect.

Crowding out

Above, we analysed the effects of fiscal policy for a given interest rate set by the central bank. In practice, we would not expect the interest rate to remain constant, however, when there is a change in fiscal policy. As discussed in Chapter 10, the central bank tries to stabilize inflation and production, so it reacts to shocks including changes in fiscal policy. Suppose that production is initially on the natural level and that inflation is equal to the inflation target. Now, the government increases government expenditure in an attempt to win the next election. An independent central bank will react to this by raising the interest rate so as to avoid overheating and an increase in inflation. The increase in the interest rate will have a negative effect on private investment and consumption, which counteracts the expansionary effect of fiscal policy. We say that the increase in government demand *crowds out* private demand, especially private investment. The extent of crowding out depends on how strongly the central bank reacts to the fiscal shock (Fig. 11.5).

But suppose the economy is in recession and the decision to increase government expenditure is taken in order to stimulate the economy and get back to the natural level of employment and production. Will there still be crowding out? Yes there will, in the sense that the interest rate set by the central bank will be higher than it would have been without the fiscal stimulus. Expansionary fiscal policy reduces the need to stimulate the economy with the help of monetary policy.[8]

Fig. 11.5 *Expansionary fiscal policy and crowding out*

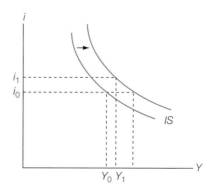

---

8   If the interest rate is at the zero lower bound, there may not be any crowding out, however.

Thus, the effects of fiscal policy on production will be smaller than the effect calculated above when we take account of the central bank reaction to the change in fiscal policy. Yet we can conclude that increased government spending and reduced taxes can stimulate aggregate demand and increase production in the short run. Potentially, fiscal policy can be used to counteract shocks to aggregate demand. If consumers become more pessimistic about the future, so private consumption falls, the government may prop up aggregate demand by increasing government investments, or reducing taxes.

The effectiveness of fiscal policy is much debated, however. Some economists argue that a tax cut will have only a very small effect on aggregate demand because rational consumers will save most of the increase in disposable income. Therefore, it is meaningless to try to use tax policy to stabilize the economy. In the next section, we explain how one can come to this conclusion.

11.4 Do lower taxes really make us richer?

According to the analysis above, a reduction in taxes increases aggregate demand because consumers spend part of the increase in their disposable income. If the marginal propensity to consume is 50 percent, a tax reduction of 100 euros will increase private consumption by 50 euros. This leads to an increase in production of 50 euros and the resulting increase in income leads to a further increase in consumption, so we get a multiplier effect.

But if the government reduces its taxes today, the government deficit will increase, and so government debt will rise. At some point, future taxes must be increased to pay back the debt, or at least to pay interest on the higher debt, so lower taxes today mean higher taxes in the future. Rational consumers should understand this, and if they do, they should be reluctant to spend more because of the tax cut.

Suppose that the Minister of Finance announces on TV that, in order to stimulate the economy, the government will give every citizen a 'stimulus cheque' worth 100 euros. This expenditure will not be financed by cutting government consumption or investment, but the government will issue bonds corresponding to 100 euros per person to finance the stimulus cheque. We all feel very happy and rush to the stores, but on the way there we start thinking. Are we really richer now? All the government has done is to borrow 100 euros per person and the interest on this loan will be financed by higher taxes in the future. We might as well have borrowed and spent 100 euros ourselves! The reason we did not do so is probably that we did not want to do so. The best we can do now is therefore to save the money. Then we will have just enough interest income to pay the higher taxes in the future. Having understood this, we all go straight to the bank with our money instead of to the store. As a result, there is no additional demand because of the stimulus cheque.

The basic point here is that, one way or another, we have to pay for government expenditure with taxes. It really does not matter whether taxes are imposed now or in the future. This result is called *Ricardian equivalence* because the argument was first made by the nineteenth-century British economist David Ricardo.

Proof of Ricardian equivalence

Let us use our theory to prove Ricardian equivalence. To do this as simply as possible, we return to the two-period model that we analysed in Chapter 4, but now with much more realism because the consumer pays taxes. A consumer lives for two periods, has no initial wealth, and does not plan to leave any bequest. His lifetime budget constraint says that the present value of consumption must be equal to the present value of his disposable labour income:

$$C_1 + \frac{C_2}{1+r} = Y_t^{\ell} - T_1 + \frac{Y_2^{\ell} - T_2}{1+r}.$$

Y_t^{ℓ} is labour income in period t and T_t is the tax in period t. Government expenditure is G_1 and G_2 in the two periods and the government sets the tax in period 2 so that the debt at the end of period 2 is zero.

Suppose now that expenditure exceeds taxes in period 1, so the government runs a deficit. To finance the deficit, the government borrows $G_1 - T_1$ in period 1. In period 2, the government has to set a tax that covers expenditure in period 2 plus repayment of the loan with interest:

$$T_2 = G_2 + (1+r)(G_1 - T_1).$$

To see what this means for the consumer, we substitute this into the expression on the right-hand side of the lifetime budget constraint:

$$Y_1 - T_1 + \frac{Y_2 - T_2}{1+r} = Y_1 - T_1 + \frac{Y_2 - G_2 - (1+r)(G_1 - T_1)}{1+r}$$

$$= Y_1 - T_1 + \frac{Y_2 - G_2}{1+r} - \frac{(1+r)(G_1 - T_1)}{1+r} = Y_1 - G_1 + \frac{Y_2 - G_2}{1+r}.$$

Thus we have:

$$C_1 + \frac{C_2}{1+r} = Y_1 - G_1 + \frac{Y_2 - G_2}{1+r}.$$

We see that the lifetime budget constraint is unaffected by the taxes. The point is that it does not matter for the consumer when taxes are paid. The lifetime budget constraint is independent of when taxes are paid, so consumption must also be independent of when taxes are paid. Rational consumers realize that they will have to pay for government expenditure by taxes, today or in the future. Therefore, consumption depends on current and expected future government consumption, but not on *when* the taxes are imposed in order to finance this government consumption.

The conclusion is that, under the conditions assumed above, lower taxes by themselves do not make us richer. A tax reduction, which is not accompanied by a spending cut, will only redistribute the tax burden over time. For private consumption possibilities to increase, the government must reduce its *expenditure*. A politician who wants a smaller government and more room for private consumption should focus on reducing government expenditure rather than taxes.

Deviations from Ricardian equivalence

Ricardian equivalence can be shown to hold in much more realistic models. In the appendix to this chapter, we show that Ricardian equivalence holds in the case of a consumer who has infinite life. But, like all arguments in economics, the argument for Ricardian equivalence builds on some critical assumptions. We have assumed that consumers

- have perfect access to the credit market
- face the same interest rate on borrowing and lending rate as the government
- expect to live to pay the future taxes
- are forward-looking,
- have full insight into the finances of the government.

One could argue that these assumptions are not fully realistic Let us see how the results are modified if we make more realistic assumptions.

Myopic and credit-constrained consumers

In Chapter 4 we argued that some consumers have very little wealth and essentially consume their current disposable income. Such consumers are not saving for the future but spending what they have. Clearly, a tax reduction will affect the consumption of such 'myopic' consumers because they spend the money when they get it.

One way to think about this is to note that these short-sighted consumers were *credit-constrained* to start with. They would have liked to borrow and spend more but the banks did not want to lend them money for consumption. If the government borrows and gives them money, the government effectively helps them to bypass the credit constraint. The government borrows on behalf of credit-constrained consumers. This is one reason why we do not have perfect Ricardian equivalence, so a tax cut increases aggregate demand, especially if it is directed to households that are more likely to be credit-constrained.

Reduced borrowing costs

Normally, the government can borrow at a lower interest rate than private individuals. If the government borrows on behalf of individuals, the cost of borrowing is reduced, which increases consumption. This effect should be small, however, since the difference is only 2–3 percent of the borrowed amount.

Finite lives

When we derived the Ricardian equivalence result we assumed that the consumer expected to live to pay the future taxes. But if consumers get the tax reduction today, some of them will think that future generations will have to pay the debt. 'When it is time to pay back those government loans I will be gone.' Reduced taxes raise the incomes of current workers at the expense of future generations. This is another reason why aggregate consumption should increase when taxes are reduced.

But this need not be the case. Many people leave bequests to their children, which suggests that they care about their children. If they care about their children, they should also care about the tax burden that is left behind when they have passed away. To see the implications of bequests, assume that we have two generations, parent and child. The child lives in the future, consumes C_c, and gets utility $U^c(C_c)$. The parent lives today, consumes C_p and gets utility from his own consumption and from the utility of the child. Then we can write the utility of the parent as

$$U\left(C_p, U^c\left(C_c\right)\right).$$

We see that if the parent cares about the utility of his child, the parent effectively gets utility from consumption in *both periods*. It is *as if* the parent lived in both periods. The argument can easily be generalized to a model with many generations. Based on this idea, the American economist Robert Barro showed that Ricardian equivalence can hold although individuals have finite lives.[9] If current workers care about future generations as specified here, and leave bequests, they will effectively try to maximize the utility of an infinite *dynasty*! In this way we get Ricardian equivalence again, even though individuals have finite lives. If taxes are reduced today, current workers save more and leave higher bequests to compensate their children for higher future taxes, so, again, a reduction in taxes has no effect on consumption.

But not everyone has children, and many people do not leave much in terms of bequests; in practice, we should expect less than full Ricardian equivalence because some of the debt is passed on to future generations. A deficit means that the government borrows on behalf of current consumers and passes on the debt to future generations.

Lack of knowledge about how the tax cut is financed

In the analysis above we analysed the effects of tax changes assuming that current and expected future government expenditure were constant and known by consumers. Clearly, this takes the idea of rational forward-looking consumers very far. In practice, consumers have only vague ideas about what the government finances look like. If they see that more money remains on their account after they have paid their taxes, they probably do not know how this was financed. A tax cut today may be financed in several different ways. There may be a reduction in government expenditure today, or in the future, or increased taxes in the future, and most consumers do not know how the future government budget will be balanced. If we think that a tax reduction today will be financed by a reduction in future government expenditure we have more money to spend on consumption.

Based on this reasoning, one might guess that the effect of a tax reduction will depend on the overall fiscal situation. If government finances seem to be in order, consumers may assume that government finances are sustainable, so taxes will

9 Robert Barrro, 'Are government bonds net wealth?', *Journal of Political Economy*, 82 (1974), 1095–1117.

remain roughly on the current level. In such a situation they may spend a large part of a tax reduction. But if there are large deficits and rumours about a coming fiscal crisis, the effect of a tax reduction is more uncertain. On the one hand, consumers get a higher disposable income, but on the other hand, the newspapers will report that the deficit has increased, raising the awareness that fiscal policy is unsustainable, and that taxes will probably increase.

The Italian economists Francesco Giavazzi and Marko Pagano have argued that, in a situation with severe fiscal imbalances, restrictive fiscal policy may actually have expansionary effects.[10] Their argument is that when the government debt grows quickly consumers worry about the finances of the government and this uncertainty makes them reluctant to spend their income. Cuts in expenditure and tax increases, which bring fiscal balance, make people more confident about the future, and may actually stimulate private consumption and investment.

Conclusion

For the reasons listed above, it is unlikely that Ricardian equivalence holds fully even if consumers are rational and forward-looking. If the government cuts taxes, consumers who are credit-constrained and those who do not care about future tax payers will increase their consumption. Further, consumers may think that at least part of the tax cut will be financed by cuts in government expenditure. If government expenditure is reduced, the present value of taxes is reduced, so consumers spend some of the increase in their disposable income.[11]

The effects of fiscal policy are hard to measure, and much debated, but one thing seems clear. When government finances are in a bad shape, tax reductions are a less reliable method of stimulating the economy.

11.5 Fiscal policy and the business cycle

Even if we believe that tax changes can be used to affect aggregate demand, there are more practical problems involved in fiscal policymaking. In this section we discuss some issues relating to short-run fiscal policy: lags in policymaking, automatic stabilizers, and structural deficits.

Policy lags

Because of time lags in policymaking, there is a considerable risk that the effects of policy arise when the business cycle situation has already changed. Expansionary measures decided in a recession may take effect when the economy is already out of the recession.

---

10 Francesco Giavazzi and Marco Pagano, 'Can severe fiscal contractions be expansionary? Tales of two small European economies', *NBER Macroeconomics Annual* 5 (1990), 75–122.

11 For a discussion of the empirical relevance of Ricardian equivalence, see Douglas Bernheim, 'Ricardian equivalence: an evaluation of theories and evidence', *NBER Macroeconomics Annual*, 2 (1987), 263–304.

There are four types of lags in economic policy:

1. *Information lag*: the time taken for policymakers to get information about what is happening in the economy.
2. *Decision lag*: the time between the observation that the economic situation has changed and the point when policymakers have analysed the situation and taken a decision.
3. *Implementation lag*: the time taken by government authorities to implement a decision.
4. *Effect lag*: the time taken for the policy action to have an *effect* on economic activity.

The longer the lags are, the less likely is it that policy can be carried out in such a way that it helps to stabilize the economy.

Clearly, there are similar lags in fiscal and monetary policy, so we may ask whether the lags involved in monetary are longer or shorter compared to the lags that are relevant to fiscal policy. Let us therefore compare the lags in monetary and fiscal policy:

1. *Information lags*: At statistical bureaus, central banks, ministries of finance, and forecasting institutes, much effort goes into the collection and analysis of data in order to find out what the economic situation is. Since central banks and government forecasting institutes have access to essentially the same information, we would expect this information lag to be similar for fiscal and monetary policy.
2. *Decision lags*: When it comes to the decision lag, monetary policy has a great advantage. There is one main monetary policy variable, the interest rate, which is decided by the board of the central bank. The board members meet, take a vote, and the decision has been made. Fiscal policy involves many different components of the government budget and all changes in taxes and expenditures have distributional consequences. Different groups gain or lose from a given change. Fiscal policy decisions are made by elected politicians who must take account of different interest groups and forthcoming elections. If there is a coalition government in power, the parties in the coalition have to reach a compromise about the policy. Therefore, fiscal policy decisions take much longer time than monetary policy decisions.
3. *Implementation lags*: This lag is also much shorter for monetary policy. A change in the repo rate is implemented within a couple of days. A tax change has to be implemented by the tax authorities, and this takes time. Increased government expenditure involves the hiring of government employees and government investments projects require a long period of planning.
4. *Effect lags*: When we come to the *effect lag*, fiscal policy has an advantage. Some fiscal policy actions have immediate and direct effects on aggregate demand. If the government builds a road or hires a nurse, this constitutes an immediate increase in demand, production, income, and employment. If pensions are increased, some of the money will be spent quickly. The effects of

monetary policy take longer time. Typically, the planning and implementation of a business investment project takes between one and two years and it is costly to stop an investment project once it has started. The evidence suggests that consumers also react with a lag. The evidence discussed in Chapter 8 suggests that a change in the interest rate has its maximum effect on output after about six quarters.

Thus we realize that there are substantial lags involved in both fiscal and monetary policymaking. These long lags mean that fiscal and monetary policy decisions must be based on a view of what the economic situation will be in a year or two's time. Governments and central banks spend considerable resources collecting and analysing data in order to make forecasts that are used as a basis for policy decisions.

Automatic stabilizers

Because of the policy lags discussed above, it is difficult to pursue active policy in such a way that the economy is stabilized. But even if there are no attempts to carry out active counter-cyclical policy, the government can have a stabilizing effect on the economy because changes in economic activity have automatic effects on tax revenue and expenditure. As noted above, the parliament decides about a *tax schedule* – that is, a function saying how taxes depend on income. Similarly, transfers are determined by rules. Individuals get social assistance if their incomes fall below a certain level. As GDP increases, there is an automatic increase in tax revenue for a given tax rate, and as more individuals get jobs, the government's expenditure on social assistance decreases. Therefore, an increase in economic activity leads to an improvement in the budget balance. *Automatic stabilizers* are automatic effects on the budget balance which occur without the government taking any new decisions.

How large are these effects? A simple calculation can give us a rough idea. Suppose that taxes and expenditures are initially 40 percent of GDP. Suppose that the tax is proportional to GDP while government expenditure is unaffected by GDP. Then, an increase in GDP by one percent raises tax revenue by an amount corresponding to *0.4 percent of GDP* and hence the budget balance improves by approximately 0.4 percent of GDP.

Another way to express this is in terms of shares of GDP. If the tax is proportional to GDP, tax revenue is a constant share of GDP. If government expenditure is constant, an increase in GDP by one percent reduces the ratio of expenditure to income by one percent, which corresponds to 0.4 percent of GDP. Clearly, this is just another way of saying the same thing.

To show this formally, assume that taxes net of transfers are

$$T = \tau Y - Tr,$$

there is no initial debt and the budget is initially balanced: $G + Tr = \tau Y$. Let b be the deficit as a fraction of GDP. Then we have

$$b = \frac{G - \tau Y + Tr}{Y} = \frac{G + Tr}{Y} - \frac{\tau Y}{Y} = (G + Tr) Y^{-1} - \tau.$$

To see how this changes with a change in production, we differentiate with respect to Y:

$$\Delta b = - (G + Tr) \, Y^{-2} \Delta Y = - \frac{G + Tr}{Y} \frac{\Delta Y}{Y} = -\tau \frac{\Delta Y}{Y},$$

where the last equality follows from the assumption that the budget was initially balanced. If $(G + Tr)/Y = \tau = 0.40$ initially, and GDP increases by one percent, the debt ratio is reduced by 0.4 percent of GDP ($0.40 \cdot 0.01 = 0.004$).

This estimate is on the low side, however, for three reasons:

1. The increase in tax revenue depends on the *marginal tax* and the income tax is progressive, so the marginal tax is higher than the average tax.
2. The revenue from taxes on capital income tends to increase with GDP because profits and capital gains increase in good times.
3. The government pays social assistance and in many countries the government pays a large share of the costs of unemployment benefits. These transfers decrease as activity improves.

For these reasons we would expect somewhat higher effects on the budget balance than indicated by tax revenue relative to GDP. Fig. 11.6 illustrates this. On the horizontal axis we have government income (i.e. mainly taxes) in percent of GDP. On the vertical axis we have estimates of the effect of a one percent increase in GDP on the budget balance, also in percent of GDP. The line shows what the effect would be according to the simple calculation above, where we assumed that tax revenue was proportional to income. The dots show the effect based on more detailed calculations for different countries, which take account of the specific tax and benefit systems in the different countries. In many countries, government income is around 40 percent of GDP but the effect of a one percent increase in GDP on the budget balance is higher, often closer to 0.5 percent

Fig. 11.6 *Government size and automatic stabilizers for 28 OECD countries*

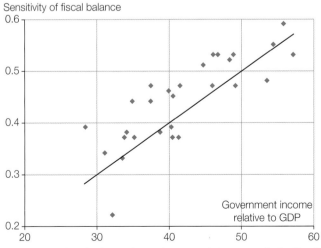

Sources: Nathalie Girouard and Christophe André, 2005, 'Measuring Cyclically-adjusted Budget Balances for OECD Countries', *OECD Economics Department Working Papers*, No. 434 and OECD.

of GDP. As expected, countries where taxes are higher have stronger automatic stabilizer effects.

The structural budget deficit

The *structural* or *cyclically adjusted deficit* for a particular year is the hypothetical deficit which we would have had if GDP had been on its natural level without any new policy decisions. This means that changes in the structural budget deficit from one year to the next are changes in the deficit that do *not* come from automatic stabilizer effects. If the structural deficit increases this indicates that expansionary policy decisions were made, which increased the deficit. Thus, the *structural deficit* can be used to measure the stance of fiscal policy. Further, the structural deficit is relevant for calculations of the long-term sustainability of government finances that we discussed at the beginning of this chapter. In order to discuss long-term sustainability, we want to consider what the deficit will be when production is on its natural level.

To see how the structural deficit is calculated, suppose that, with the current tax schedules and transfer systems, a one percent increase in GDP improves the budget balance by 0.5 percent of GDP. Suppose that we have a budget deficit equal to 4 percent of GDP and that we estimate GDP to be 4 percent below its natural level. Then we can conclude that if GDP had been on its natural level (4 percent higher) the deficit would have been 2 percent instead of 4. Then the structural (cyclically adjusted) deficit is estimated to be 2 percent.

This calculation is illustrated in Fig. 11.7. The currently observed output gap and deficit are indicated by point A and the line shows how the budget balance improves with economic activity if tax and transfer systems are kept unchanged. If the output gap were zero, the deficit would be reduced to 2 percent and if the output gap were +4 percent the deficit would be eliminated.

The calculation of the structural deficit is a hypothetical calculation which requires estimates of the effect of GDP on the government budget and also of

Fig. 11.7 *Output gap and budget balance, percent*

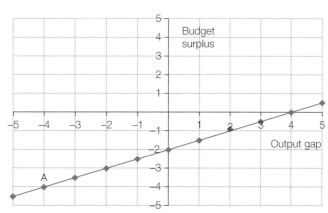

Note: The figure shows the relation between the output gap and the budget balance for a structural deficit of 2 percent.

the output gap. These estimates are uncertain, so the calculation of the structural deficit is also uncertain.

11.6   Empirical evidence on fiscal policy

Effects of fiscal policy shocks

There have been several attempts to estimate the effects of fiscal policy using statistical (econometric) techniques. As in the case of monetary policy, the basic problem is that there is two-way causality. Expansionary fiscal policy affects aggregate demand and production but, at the same time, economic activity affects tax revenue and the government's expenditure on social assistance. In fact, the effect of economic activity on fiscal variables takes two forms:

- As discussed above, there are the *automatic effects* on tax revenue and government expenditure for given tax and benefit rules
- There may also be deliberate *policy reactions* as policymakers try to counteract downturns with expansionary fiscal policy and conversely.

This means that we have to be careful when we interpret empirical correlations. In the data there is a strong positive correlation between tax revenue and economic activity but we should not jump to the conclusion that an increase in taxes stimulates economic activity. Most likely, the positive correlation arises because of reverse causality: an increase in economic activity will raise tax revenue.

The problem, then, is to identify reasonably exogenous shocks to government expenditure and taxes. To deal with this problem, alternative approaches have been used. One is to estimate VAR models as described in Chapter 8. Basically, this means that one estimates policy rules for government expenditure and taxes together with dynamic equations for production and other variables. Then one interprets the residuals from the estimated policy rules as truly exogenous policy shocks and one can use the equations to trace the effects of the shocks over time. A classic study was made by Olivier Blanchard and Roberto Perotti.[12] They found that, consistent with standard wisdom, when government spending increases, output increases; and when taxes increase, output falls. In most cases the multipliers were around one. In line with the theory presented above, private consumption increases following spending shocks, while private investment is crowded out to a considerable extent.

Some researchers have tried to deal with the problem of two-way causation by identifying specific exogenous fiscal policy shocks. Valery Ramey and Matthew Shapiro investigated the responses of the US economy to large military build-ups, which can be seen as reasonably exogenous shocks (the Korean War, the Vietnam War and the Carter–Reagan military build-up).[13] They found substantial effects on real GDP. Christina Romer and David Romer studied official documents to

---

12   Olivier J. Blanchard and Roberto Perotti, 'An empirical characterization of the dynamic effects of changes in government spending and taxes on output', *Quarterly Journal of Economics*, 117 (2002), 1329–1368.

13   Valery Ramey and Matthew Shapiro, 'Costly capital reallocation and the effects of government spending', *Carnegie-Rochester Series on Public Policy*, 48 (1998), 145–194.

identify a series of specific decisions about taxes and they also tried to identify decisions that were not reactions to business cycle developments but which could be interpreted as relatively exogenous events.[14] Then, they used statistical methods to estimate the effects of those discrete fiscal policy actions on production and other variables. They found large negative effects of tax increases on GDP: a tax increase generating a direct increase in tax revenue corresponding to one percent of GDP reduces production over the next three years by nearly 3 percent.

Thus, the predictions of the theory are confirmed. Increased government expenditure has a positive effect on GDP and tax increases have a negative effect, but the estimated magnitudes of the effects vary quite considerably, depending on the exact statistical method that is used to estimate the effect.[15]

The stabilizing role of the government

How cyclical are government income and expenditure in practice? Does the government help to stabilize the economy or does it have a destabilizing influence? Fig. 11.8 shows the output gap, government expenditure, income, and the surplus (net lending) as a percentage of GDP for some countries. As expected, the surplus is strongly pro-cyclical – that is, the budget balance improves when the output gap increases. Looking at the curves showing government expenditure and revenue we see that this is primarily due to counter-cyclicality of government expenditure relative to GDP – government expenditure falls *as a fraction of GDP* when GDP increases. Tax revenue is much more stable as a fraction of GDP. The simple model above, where tax revenue is proportional to GDP and government expenditure is more stable than GDP, seems to give a relatively good approximation of what is going on.

Note that this figure shows the results of both automatic stabilizers and active fiscal policy decisions. These data do not allow us to distinguish automatic effects from active counter-cyclical policy, so we cannot say how much is due to each factor. But whatever the reason, it seems that the government has a stabilizing effect on the economy because taxes increase with GDP while government expenditure is a stable component of aggregate demand.

Since the government appears to play a stabilizing role, we would expect countries with a larger government sector to have more stable economies. Indeed, there is some evidence that this is so. Countries with a larger government have more stable economies and the same is true if we compare states in the US.[16]

Is there any evidence of active counter-cyclical policy?

The term *discretionary fiscal policy* refers to fiscal changes that are *not* the results of automatic stabilizers. Jordi Gali and Roberto Perotti studied the cyclical pattern

---

14 Christina Romer and David Romer, 'The macroeconomic effects of tax changes: new estimates based on a new measure of fiscal shocks', *American Economic Review*, 100 (2010), 763–801.

15 For surveys of the literature on the effects of fiscal policy, see Roel Beetsma, *A Survey of the Effects of Discretionary Fiscal Policy*, Report for the Swedish Fiscal Policy Council 2008/2, and Alan Auerbach, William Gale, and Benjamin Harris, 'Activist fiscal policy', *Journal of Economic Perspectives*, 24 (2010), 141–164.

16 See Antonio Fatás and Ilian Mihov, 'Government size and the automatic stabilizers: international and intranational evidence', *Journal of International Economics*, 55 (2001), 3–28.

Fig. 11.8 *Government expenditure, income, and net lending as percent of GDP*

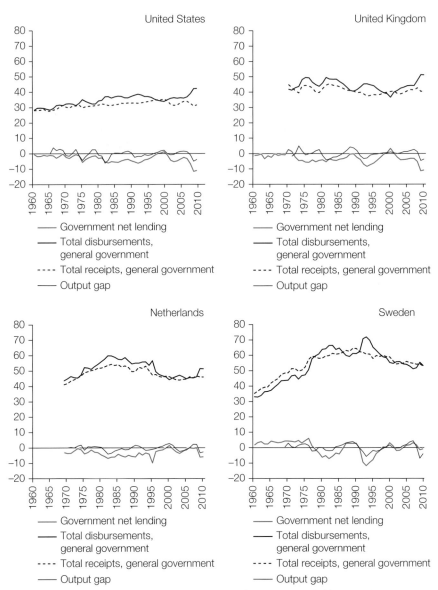

Source: *OECD Economic Outlook*, OECD, 22 June 2011, http://www.oecd-ilibrary.org/statistics.

of discretionary policy by relating the structural (cyclically adjusted) deficit to the cycle.[17] The idea is that by looking at the structural deficit we eliminate the effects of the automatic stabilizers on the deficit. If the structural deficit is higher when production is below the (estimated) natural level discretionary fiscal policy is said to be counter-cyclical. They studied countries that later adopted the euro before and after the Maastricht Treaty, which set up limits for the deficits in the

---

17 Jordi Gali and Roberto Perotti, 'Fiscal policy and monetary integration in Europe', *Economic Policy*, 37 (2003), 533–572.

Eurozone in 1992 (see Chapter 15). For these countries, they found evidence that fiscal policy was actually pro-cyclical before Maastricht – that is, the structural deficits increased when GDP increased. This means that active fiscal policy had a destabilizing effect on the economy. After Maastricht, fiscal policy was acyclical in the Eurozone. This means that active fiscal policy was less destabilizing after Maastricht but there is no evidence that active fiscal policy helped to stabilize the economies in the Eurozone. They also studied some OECD countries which did not adopt the euro. For some of those countries, especially Denmark, they found evidence of active counter-cyclical fiscal policy. Thus, the evidence on active fiscal policy is mixed and depends on which country we look at.

What have we learned?

The government spends money on government consumption and investment and on transfers. It also pays interest on the government debt. The government finances its expenditure by taxes and borrowing. If expenditure exceeds tax revenue, there is a deficit in government finances (sometimes called a budget deficit) and (net) government debt will increase.

The government share of income varies between 30 and almost 60 percent. Government consumption is typically around 20 percent, while government investment is 2–4 percent of GDP. Transfers constitute around 20 percent of GDP in most countries.

The change in the *government debt ratio* is determined by the following equation:

$$\Delta\frac{D}{Y} \approx \frac{G-T}{Y} + (r-g)\frac{D}{Y}.$$

The left-hand side is the change in the debt ratio to the next year, D/Y is the debt ratio at the beginning of the year, r is the real interest rate, and g is the growth rate.

- A higher *primary deficit*, $G - T$, raises the debt ratio.
- A higher *real interest rate*, r, raises the debt ratio and the effect is proportional to the debt ratio at the beginning of the year.
- A higher *growth rate*, g, reduces the debt ratio and the effect is proportional to the debt ratio at the beginning of the year.

Note that if the growth rate is equal to the real interest rate, a primary deficit equal to zero implies a stable debt ratio.

A debt-financed *increase in government consumption* (or investment) raises the level of demand, production, and income in the short run. There is a multiplier effect, which depends on how much of that additional income is spent by consumers and on how much of the additional income that is paid as tax.

A *tax reduction* has a smaller effect on production than an increase in government consumption of the same magnitude because consumers will save a fraction of the increase in disposable income. This makes the initial effect on demand smaller.

If consumers see through the government finances, they will realize that all government expenditure will have to be paid for by taxes, either today or in the future. Consequently, a tax reduction may have little effect on private consumption or aggregate demand. Consumption will depend on current and expected future government purchases, but not on *when* the taxes are imposed in order to finance these purchases (Ricardian equivalence).

In practice, we may expect a tax reduction to affect consumption because individuals have finite lives, some consumers are credit-constrained, and they do not know how a tax cut is financed.

Fiscal and monetary policy is associated with lags in information collection, decision-making, implementation of policy decisions, and it also takes time for the policy to have an effect on aggregate demand. For these reasons, active policy is based on forecasts for the economic situation one or two years from now.

Automatic stabilizers are effects on government income and expenditure that occur automatically, without any new policy decisions. Estimates suggest that an increase in GDP by one percent automatically improves the government balance by about 0.5 percent of GDP and that this effect is larger in countries with a large government sector.

The structural budget deficit is what the deficit would have been, for given tax and benefit rules, if production had been on the natural level.

In practice, the government sector plays a stabilizing role because expenditure is relatively stable whereas tax revenue varies with income. Put differently, government expenditure falls as a share of income when income is high, while tax revenue is a more stable proportion of income. As a result, the government balance (surplus) is positively correlated with the output gap.

Where do we go from here?

So far, we have analysed a *closed economy* – an economy that does not trade with the rest of the world. Of course, there are no such economies in the real world. Today, all countries trade extensively with other countries and there is borrowing and lending across borders. An economy that trades with other countries is called an *open economy*. Having analysed the closed economy in depth, we are ready to make the final extension of our macroeconomic model by including trade and international borrowing and lending. The next four chapters deal with the open economy.

Exercises

1. a) Why do we get different numbers if we calculate the size of the government sector from the user side and the production side? Which calculation gives the biggest share?

   b) Why do we get different numbers if we calculate the size of government from the user side and the income side? Which calculation gives the biggest share?

2. For a particular country, we have the following numbers:

   GDP: 400

   government consumption: 100

   transfers from the government to the private sector: 80

   government investment: 12

   government net interest payments: 8

   government production: 40

   tax revenue: 180

   Calculate as a share of GDP (in percent):

   a) the government use of goods and services

   b) government tax revenue

   c) government production

   d) the primary deficit

   e) the deficit of the public sector (general government).

3. Table 11.2 shows the fiscal situation in some countries in 2010. The extreme deficit for Ireland is due to the fact that the Irish government took over some debts of the banks in 2010.

   a) Which five countries had deficits of nearly 10 percent of GDP?

   b) Which three countries except Ireland had the largest primary deficits?

   c) Which two countries had the highest levels of debt and interest payments relative to GDP?

   d) Check that you can get the number in the last column by using the equation for the change in the debt ratio.

   e) Which six countries had the most rapidly rising debt ratios?

   f) In your view, which countries had the most problematic situation?

4. Consider Italy, which at the beginning of 2010 had net debt equal to GDP and a primary deficit equal to 0.3 percent of GDP. Calculate the change in the debt ratio if

   a) there is no inflation, the nominal interest rate is 2 percent and growth is 3 percent

   b) there is no inflation, the nominal interest rate is 5 percent and there is no growth.

   c) Explain the difference between a) and b).

5. A country has a budget deficit equal to 5 percent of GDP, net government debt is equal to GDP, and nominal GDP grows 10 percent per year. What happens to the debt ratio?

6. Consider the following model:

$$Y = C + I + G, \quad C = a_0 + a_1 (Y + Tr - Tx),$$
$$Tx = T^0 + \tau Y, \quad Tr = Tr^0 - hY,$$
$$I = b_0 - b_1 i.$$

Table 11.2 *Government finances, 2010*

	$(G-T+iD)/Y$	$(G-T)/Y$	iD/Y	D/Y 2009	π	g	Predicted $\Delta(D/Y)$
France	7.1	4.8	2.3	52	0.8	1.4	6.0
Germany	4.3	2.2	2.1	49	0.6	3.6	2.2
Greece	10.8	5.1	5.7	102	1.7	−3.5	12.6
Ireland	31.3	28.6	2.7	26	−2.4	−0.4	32.0
Italy	4.5	0.3	4.2	100	0.4	1.5	2.6
Portugal	9.8	6.8	3.0	65	1.1	1.4	8.2
Spain	9.3	7.8	1.5	34	0.4	−0.1	9.2
UK	10.4	7.8	2.6	44	2.8	1.8	8.4
USA	10.7	9.0	1.7	61	1.2	3.0	8.1

Note: All numbers are as percentage units of GDP. Debt ratio is beginning of year (end of 2009). $(G-T+iD)/Y$ is minus 'general government financial balances'. iD/Y is net interest payments. Primary deficit $(G-T)/Y$ is calculated from these numbers. D is net debt at the beginning of the year, and π is inflation measured by the GDP deflator.
Source: *OECD Economic Outlook*, Autumn 2011, Statistical Appendix.

Tx is the tax and Tr is the transfer from the government to the households. T^0 and Tr^0 are constants and the coefficients τ and h are positive but smaller than unity. The central bank keeps the interest rate constant. Solve for production for a given interest rate and calculate the effects of increases in G and T^0 on production. Explain the results.

7. Consider the model above and assume that the government increases government expenditure by ΔG. Suppose that production was initially on the natural level and the central bank wants to avoid overheating of the economy. By how much will the central bank raise the interest rate?

8. Suppose you get a stimulus check worth 100 euros from the government.
   a) How much would you spend? How much would you save?

   b) If you would spend some of it, can you give a rational explanation of your behaviour?

9. Assume that G is constant, and let taxes and transfers be
   $$Tx = T^0 + \tau Y, \quad Tr = Tr^0 - hY,$$
   and debt payments be iD. T^0 and Tr^0 are constants and the coefficients τ and h are positive but smaller than unity. We assume that the budget is initially in balance.
   a) Write down an expression for the deficit as a proportion of GDP.
   b) Derive an expression for how the deficit changes if GDP increases by one percent. *(Hint: Use the assumption that the budget is balanced initially.)*
   c) What is the effect on the deficit if $\tau = 0.50$ and $h = 0.10$? Explain.

Answers to the exercises can be found at:
www.palgrave.com/economics/gottfries.

Appendix

Ricardian equivalence in the infinite horizon case

In order to analyse the effects of tax changes in the infinite horizon case, we use the consumption function that we derived in Chapter 4. To make this analysis as simple as possible, we assume that:

- the real interest rate is constant and equal to the subjective discount rate: $r = \rho$
- there is no growth ($g = 0$)
- government purchases from period $t + 1$ onwards are expected to be G^e
- from period $t + 1$ on, the government sets the tax so that real debt remains constant.

These assumptions simplify the analysis but they are not important for the results. Again, we use the equation showing how government debt changes from one year to the next:

$$D_{t+1} - D_t = G_t - T_t + rD_t.$$

From period $t + 1$ onwards, the government sets the tax so that real debt remains constant, $D_{t+2} = D_{t+1}$, and thus

$$T^e = G^e + rD_{t+1}.$$

Substituting for D_{t+1} using equation above we get

$$T^e = G^e + r(G_t - T_t + rD_t + D_t).$$

We see immediately that if the government reduces the tax today by ΔT_t it has to raise the tax in all future periods by $r\Delta T_t$ so as to pay interest on the higher government debt. Now we use the consumption function that we derived in the appendix to Chapter 4:

$$C_t = \frac{r\left[Y_t^d + A_t\right] + Y^e - T^e}{1+r}.$$

Household disposable income is given by $Y_t^d = Y_t - T_t + rD_t$ and household wealth consists of the capital stock plus government debt: $A_t = K_t + D_t$. Substituting for Y_t^d, A_t and T^e in the consumption function, we get

$$C_t = \frac{r\left[Y_t - T_t + rD_t + K_t + D_t\right] + Y^e - G^e - r(G_t - T_t + rD_t + D_t)}{1+r}.$$

This is an ugly expression, but if we multiply r into the parentheses in the numerator, we see that the terms involving T and D cancel out, and we get

$$C_t = \frac{r\left[Y_t - G_t + K_t\right] + Y^e - G^e}{1+r}.$$

Neither taxes nor the level of government debt affect consumption. Consumption depends on current and expected future government consumption, but not on *when* the taxes are imposed in order to finance this government consumption – once again, we have proved Ricardian equivalence.

PART 4 THE OPEN ECONOMY

How do globalized markets for goods, services, and loans affect the economy?

Globalization has made individual countries more dependent on the world economy. All markets are affected by globalization. Trade in goods and services has increased. Many goods and services are produced in one country and used in another country. Flows of borrowing and lending between different countries continue around the clock and bonds denominated in different currencies can be bought and sold instantaneously. Workers move between countries, or live in one country and work in another.

The final step in the development of our macroeconomic model is to open up the model to take account of trade and international borrowing and lending. Once we have extended our macroeconomic model in this way, we will understand how developments in the world economy affect an individual country and we will be able to analyse growth, exchange rates, and foreign debt in the open economy.

Furthermore, our analysis of fiscal and monetary policy has to be modified. As we will see, the roles of fiscal and monetary policy are very different, depending on whether the country has a fixed or a floating exchange rate. A *fixed exchange rate* means that the central bank announces an official target level for the exchange rate and keeps the exchange rate at that level by buying and selling currency. A pure *floating exchange rate* means that the central bank does not have a target level for the exchange rate and that it does not interfere in currency markets.

In this chapter, we do the groundwork by adding exports, imports, and an international financial market to our macroeconomic model. We first analyse how exports, imports, and aggregate demand are determined in the open economy. Then we study international borrowing and lending. The *current account* shows whether the country is a net borrower or lender in international financial markets. We also study how expected returns on loans in different currencies are related to interest rates and expected changes in exchange rates. Having set up our open economy model in this chapter, we then use it in Chapters 13–15 to analyse how the open economy works in the long and the short run, and to study alternative exchange rate systems and monetary union.

12.1 The small open economy

In the macroeconomic model we have been building there are three markets: the *goods market*, the *financial market*, and the *labour market*, and interaction with other countries can take place in all three markets. In practice, however, the labour market is much less integrated with the rest of the world than the markets for goods and the financial markets. In the following, we simplify the analysis by assuming that goods and financial markets are completely integrated, while there is no international mobility in the labour market:

- Markets for goods and services are assumed to be perfectly integrated. Households and firms can trade freely without customs, import quotas, transport costs, or other trade barriers. At the same time, we assume that goods produced in different countries are *imperfect substitutes*. A Volvo is not identical to a BMW. This means that prices of goods produced in different countries will differ. The relative prices affect exports and imports; if a BMW becomes more expensive relative to the Volvo, some people will buy a Volvo instead of a BMW.
- Financial markets are also perfectly integrated in our model. Households and firms can borrow and lend freely across borders, and in different currencies, without any regulations, transaction costs, or taxes. We assume that international investors invest where they get the highest expected return. This allows us to derive the *interest parity condition*, which says that interest rates have to compensate for expected changes in exchange rates. If a currency is expected to depreciate in value, the interest rate on loans in that currency must be higher.
- Because of language differences, family ties, and cultural differences between countries, most workers are unwilling to move to another country. To simplify, we assume that all workers work and consume in the country where they were born. This means that labour markets are not integrated in our model. Hence the size of a country is determined by its population. In the long run, the level of GDP in a country is determined by the number of workers who live in the country and the available technology.

An *open economy* is an economy that interacts with the rest of the world. In the following, we analyse a *small open economy*. In this context, 'small' means that the economy is assumed to be so small relative to the rest of the world that what happens in the domestic economy has a negligible effect on the rest of the world. Thus we ignore feedback effects which arise when shocks and policies in the open economy affect economic developments abroad. We stick to the small open economy assumption because it simplifies the analysis considerably. It allows us to take production abroad, the foreign price level and the foreign interest rate as exogenous when analysing what happens in the small open economy. We can think of the foreign variables as being determined by our closed economy model in Chapters 2–11 applied to the world as a whole.

The small open economy assumption is plausible for a small country such as Finland. It is less reasonable for a large economy such as the US because economic policy in the US has significant effects on the rest of the world, so there will be feedback effects of policy actions in the US. Yet the analysis of the small open economy will give us a good indication of the *direction* of the effects of shocks on a large open economy too.

12.2 The real exchange rate

Firms in the open economy sell their goods in tough competition with foreign producers. If their costs and prices increase compared with those of their competitors, they lose market shares to foreign competitors, in export markets as well as in the home market. Therefore, competitiveness is a central concern in the open economy. One measure of competitiveness is the *real exchange rate*, which measures the price level in the country compared with the price level abroad after prices have been converted to the same currency. As we will see, the real exchange rate is an important determinant of aggregate demand in the open economy.

There are different ways of measuring the real exchange rate. In the theoretical model, we define the real exchange rate as the relative price between goods *produced* at home and abroad. We use the following notation:

P the price of the good produced at home in domestic currency
P^* the price of the good produced abroad in foreign currency
e the nominal exchange rate – the price of the domestic currency in terms of foreign currency[1]
ε the real exchange rate – the price of domestically produced goods in terms of goods produced abroad.

Consider a foreign consumer who has a choice between buying the good produced in the small open economy and the foreign good. The foreign consumer has to pay e times P in foreign currency, for one unit of the good produced in the small open economy and P^* for one unit of the foreign-produced good. Thus, the relative price of the good produced in the small open economy is

$$\varepsilon = \frac{eP}{P^*}.$$

While the *nominal* exchange rate is the price of the *currency* of the small open economy in terms of foreign currency, the *real* exchange rate is the price of the *good* produced in the small open economy in terms of the foreign good.[2] If the nominal exchange rate increases, domestic money becomes relatively more expensive. If the real exchange increases, domestic goods become relatively more expensive.

Suppose, for example, that the only goods produced are cars, the UK is the small open economy, and the US represents the rest of the world. Assume that a car produced in the UK costs 30,000 pounds, and that you have to pay 1.2 dollars for a pound. The UK car therefore costs 36,000 dollars for the US consumer

---

1   In some statistical sources, the exchange rate is defined in the opposite way.
2   The empirical counterparts to P^d and P^* are *GDP deflators* or producer price indexes.

$(1.2 \cdot 300\,00 = 36000)$. If a US car costs 27,000 dollars, the relative price of the UK car is $4/3$ $(36000/27000 = 4/3)$. Put differently, you have to give up four US cars to get three UK cars. The real exchange rate of the UK is $4/3$.

Since we ignore trade costs, the relative price for the consumer in the small open economy is the same as the relative price for the foreign consumer. The domestic consumer pays P for the domestically produced good and the price of the foreign currency is $1/e$, so the consumer pays P^*/e for the foreign-produced good. Thus, the relative price of the domestically produced good is again the real exchange rate:

$$\varepsilon = \frac{P}{P^*/e}.$$

In terms of the example above, a UK consumer pays 22,500 pounds for a US car $(27000/1.2 = 22500)$ so the relative price of the UK car is $30,000/22,500 = 4/3$.

In practice, countries produce many goods, so price levels are measured using *price indexes*. This means that the *level* of the real exchange rate has no meaning. What we are interested in is how the real exchange rate *changes* over time. If the real exchange rate increases from one year to the next, this means that goods in the country become more expensive relative to goods in other countries.

Since countries trade with many foreign countries, the question arises with which country should we compare? Normally, one tries to compare with the most important trade partners. OECD and other organizations calculate *effective real exchange rates* for different countries, which measure the price level in each country compared with a weighted average of the price levels in foreign countries. The weights are determined by the shares of imports and exports that go to and from different countries so that important trade partners have a larger weight. Typically, countries trade much more with their close neighbours than with countries on the other side of the globe, so the price levels of close neighbours have the largest weighting when the relevant competitors' price is calculated.

There are alternative measures of competitiveness. One measure is the *relative export price* – the export price of the country relative to a weighted average of the export prices of the most important trade partners. In our simplified model, we assume that domestic goods are sold at the same price at home and abroad, so the relative export price is the same as the real exchange rate.

Another concept is *terms of trade*: the ratio of export prices to import prices. Since we assume that firms charge the same price in the export market as they charge at home, the terms of trade rate is identical to the real exchange rate in our model.

Yet another measure of competitiveness is the *relative unit labour cost* (*RULC*) which is the labour cost per unit of goods produced at home compared with the labour cost per unit of goods produced abroad, again measured in the same currency. As we saw in Chapter 2, the marginal cost is proportional to the unit labour cost, *ULC*, for the Cobb–Douglas production function

$$MC = \frac{W}{MPL} = \frac{W}{(1-\alpha)\,Y/N} = \frac{WN/Y}{1-\alpha} = \frac{ULC}{1-\alpha}.$$

Thus, if the mark-ups of domestic and foreign firms are the same we have

$$\varepsilon = \frac{eP}{P^*} = \frac{e\,(1+\mu)\,ULC/\,(1-\alpha)}{(1+\mu)\,ULC^*/\,(1-\alpha)} = \frac{eULC}{ULC^*} = RULC.$$

The real exchange rate is equal to the relative unit labour cost.

In practice, the real exchange rate is often measured in terms of *consumer prices*, but there is a close relation between the real exchange rate in terms of goods *produced* in different countries and the real exchange rate in terms of the consumption bundles *consumed* in different countries. If unit labour costs in the small open economy rise, the prices of goods produced in the small open economy will also increase, and since consumers spend a large share of their income on domestically produced goods, the consumer price level in the small open economy will rise relative to consumer prices abroad. Although the *magnitude* of the fluctuations may differ between different measures, the *direction* of the changes is the same independent of which measure we use.

Fig. 12.1 shows three different measures of competitiveness: relative unit labour cost, the relative price of exports, and the real exchange rate in terms of consumer prices. All these measures are indexes compared with weighted averages of the trade partners, so the levels have no meaning. What is interesting is how they change over time. Although there are some differences in the long-term trends, the fluctuations are similar for the three series. For example, the dollar appreciated in the early 1980s, depreciated in 1986, and appreciated again in the late 1990s, and this is seen in all three measures of the real exchange rate. The Finnish currency depreciated dramatically in 1992 and this is also seen in all three measures.

12.3   Imports, exports, and aggregate demand

Imports and exports affect aggregate demand in the open economy. On the one hand, a large share of the goods and services produced in the small open economy are sold as exports to foreign countries. On the other hand, consumers in the open economy spend some of their income on imported foreign goods and this expenditure does not generate demand for production in the small open economy. This means that the goods market equilibrium condition – the *IS* equation – has to be modified when we consider an open economy.

Goods market equilibrium in the small open economy

To simplify the analysis of aggregate demand, we assume that imported goods are used only for private consumption. For government expenditure and private investment, only the domestic good is used. This assumption is reasonable for government consumption and for investments in buildings because those goods and services are mainly produced at home. It is less reasonable for investment in equipment because machines are often imported. We make this assumption because it simplifies our analysis and allowing for imported goods to be used for investments would not fundamentally change our conclusions.

Fig. 12.1 *Alternative measures of the real exchange rate*

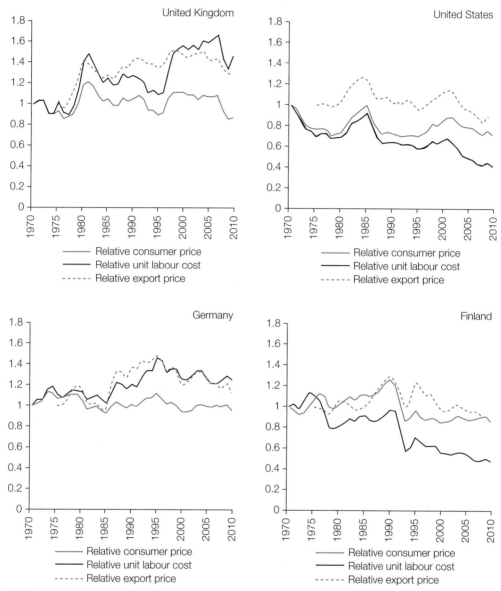

Source: *OECD Economic Outlook*, OECD, 6 October 2011, http://www.oecd-ilibrary.org/statistics.

Consumption of the domestically produced good is denoted C^d, consumption of the good produced abroad is denoted C^f and the quantity exported of the domestic good is denoted X. In order to derive demand for domestic goods, we start from the balance between sources and uses in the national accounts in *nominal* terms:

$$PY + (P^*/e)\, C^f = PC^d + (P^*/e)\, C^f + PI + PG + PX.$$

The left-hand side is the value of goods and services available: domestic production plus imports. The right-hand side is the value of goods and services used for private consumption and investment, government consumption and investment, and exports. The price of the domestically produced good is P and the price of imports expressed in domestic currency is P^*/e. Dividing by P and rearranging, we can write the demand for the domestically produced goods as

$$Y = \frac{PC^d + (P^*/e)\,C^f}{P} + I + G + X - \frac{P^*C^f}{eP}$$

or

$$Y = C + I + G + NX,$$

where C is private consumption *expressed in units of the domestic good*,

$$C = \frac{PC^d + (P^*/e)\,C^f}{P},$$

and NX is net exports (exports minus imports) also expressed in units of the domestic good,

$$NX = X - \frac{C^f}{\varepsilon}.$$

We assume that consumption and investment are determined by the same consumption and investment functions as in the closed economy. In order to complete the theory of aggregate demand, we also need to specify how imports and exports are determined. It is reasonable to assume that demand for imported goods depends on the same factors as consumption, plus the relative price between domestic and foreign goods – that is, the real exchange rate:

$$C^f = IM\left(\varepsilon, Y^d, Y^e - T^e, r, A\right).$$

The real exchange rate enters because domestic consumers can choose between consuming domestic and foreign goods and the real exchange rate is the relative price between those goods. A higher real exchange rate leads to an increase in imports, higher disposable income, Y^d, and higher expected future income, Y^e, also increase imports while a higher real interest rate, r, reduces consumption and imports. If consumers have more assets, A, they spend more on both goods. In the appendix to this chapter we show how this import function can be derived from utility maximization by the domestic consumer.

Exports from the small open economy are imports to the rest of the world. We assume that imports to the rest of the world are determined in the same way as imports to the small open economy. Therefore we have an export function:

$$X = X\left(\varepsilon, Y^{d*}, Y^{*e} - T^{*e}, r^*, A^*\right).$$

To simplify notation in the following, we define a *net export function*:

$$NX\left(\varepsilon, Y^*, Y\right) = X\left(\varepsilon, Y^{d*}, Y^{*e} - T^{*e}, r^*, A^*\right) - IM\left(\varepsilon, Y^d, Y^e - T^e, r, A\right)/\varepsilon.$$

Note that we have written out only some of the variables that affect net exports. We now have the *IS* equation that determines aggregate demand and production in the small open economy:

$$Y = C\left(Y^d, Y^e - T^e, r, A\right) + I\left(r, Y^e, K\right) + G + NX\left(\varepsilon, Y^*, Y\right).$$

4

To find real disposable income, Y^d, note that GDP is paid out to households in the form of wages, dividends, and interest payments from firms. Households also pay taxes to the government and they get interest income on their claims on the government and on foreign households. We assume that the government does not borrow abroad so domestic households hold all the government debt of the small open economy. We let F denote the net claims that households in the small open economy have on foreign households, expressed in units of the domestic good. Then, domestic households' real disposable income is

$$Y^d = Y - T + r(D + F).$$

We will often simplify by assuming that $F = D = 0$ initially, so that $Y^d = Y - T$.

Again, we can think of the *IS* equation as a standard microeconomic demand function, but now we have *two relative prices that affect aggregate demand*:

- the real interest rate (the intertemporal relative price) affects choice between consumption today and consumption in future periods
- the real exchange rate (the international relative price) affects the choice between goods produced at home and abroad.

In order to analyse the macroeconomic effects of shocks, we need to understand how the real interest rate and the real exchange rate are determined. To do this, we need to understand international financial markets, which will be analysed later in this chapter.

The effect of the real exchange rate on net exports

Compared with the closed economy, there are two new factors that affect aggregate demand in the small open economy: foreign income and the real exchange rate. Higher foreign income increases net exports and aggregate demand in the small open economy. Thus we have 'demand spill-overs' between countries: when aggregate demand increases in one country some of it spills over to neighbouring countries.

The effect of the real exchange rate is more complicated, but in order to understand how the open economy functions we must understand how the real exchange rate affects net exports and aggregate demand. Net exports, expressed in units of the domestic good, are

$$NX(\varepsilon, Y^*, Y) \equiv X(\varepsilon, Y^{d*}, Y^{*e} - T^{*e}, r^*, A^*) - IM(\varepsilon, Y^d, Y^e - T^e, r, A)/\varepsilon.$$

Note that the real exchange rate appears in three places on the right-hand side, so an appreciation (increase) in the real exchange rate has three effects on net exports:

1. As domestic goods become more expensive relative to foreign goods, foreign consumers buy more foreign goods and fewer goods produced in the small open economy, so *the quantity of exports decreases*. This substitution effect is seen in the first term on the right-hand side as X is a decreasing function of ε. This tends to *decrease* net exports.

2. As domestic goods become more expensive relative to foreign goods, domestic consumers buy more foreign goods and fewer goods produced in the small open economy, so *the quantity of imports increases*. This substitution effect is

seen in the second term on the right-hand side as *IM* is an increasing function of ε. This also tends to *decrease* net exports.

3. When imports become cheaper relative to domestic goods, this *decreases the value of imports relative to the value of exports*. This effect can be seen in the second term on the right-hand side. As ε increases, this tends to reduce the value of imports relative to exports and *increase* net exports. This valuation effect goes in the opposite direction to the first two effects.

We see that there are substitution and valuation effects on net exports. As domestic goods become relatively more expensive, foreign and domestic consumers buy less domestic goods and this tends to reduce net exports. The valuation effect goes the other way, reducing the value of imports relative to exports, and increasing net exports. If the quantities of imports and exports are sufficiently sensitive to price changes, the substitution effects dominate over the valuation effect.

The formal condition for net exports to fall with an appreciation of the real exchange rate is the *Marshall–Lerner condition*, which says that the sum of (the absolute values of) the price elasticities of import and export demand must be higher than one. To understand where this comes from, suppose that we start from a situation when net exports are zero, so the value of imports equals the value of exports. Consider now an increase in the price of exports. If there was no change in the quantities (no substitution) a one percent increase in the export price would increase the *value* of exports one percent and leave the value of imports unchanged, so net exports would increase. For net exports to decrease, the *quantity* of exports must fall one percent, or the quantity of imports must increase one percent, or there must be some combination of falling exports and rising imports. If the sum of the elasticities is greater than one, the substitution effects will dominate over the valuation effect. The Marshall–Lerner condition is derived in the appendix to this chapter.

Empirical evidence shows that, in general, demands for exports and imports are sufficiently price-sensitive so that a real appreciation leads to a decrease in net exports. Typical estimates are that the price elasticity of exports is may be around two and the price elasticity of imports is around one.[3] Also, it takes time for the full effects of price changes to materialize because established customer relationships in trade do not change overnight. Thus, the price elasticities are modest, but the Marshall–Lerner condition is fulfilled.

This means that if the pound appreciates, so goods produced in the UK become more expensive relative to goods produced in Germany, France, and other trade partners, UK net exports will decrease, which will have a negative effect on aggregate demand in the UK. In the following, we assume that the Marshall–Lerner condition holds, so an appreciation of the real exchange rate leads to a decrease in net exports and in aggregate demand. The relation between the real exchange rate and net exports is shown in Fig. 12.2.

4

---

3 For a discussion of the evidence, see Paul Krugman and Maurice Obstfeld, *International Economics: Theory and Policy*, 8th edn (Boston: Pearson, 2009). A review of estimates can be found in e.g. Morris Goldstein, and Mohsin Khan, 'Income and price effects in foreign trade', in Ronald W. Jones and Peter B. Kenen, *Handbook of International Economics*, II (Amsterdam: Elsevier, 1985), 1041–1105.

Fig. 12.2 *The real exchange rate and net exports*

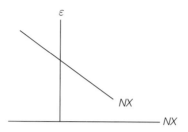

A look at the data

Our analysis implies that demand for imported goods and services should depend on the same factors as demand for domestic goods. Fig. 12.3 shows growth rates of real GDP and imports in fixed prices. As our theory predicts, there is a very close correlation. When domestic consumers and investors spend more on domestic goods and services, they also spend more on imports, so GDP and imports both increase.

We see that imports fluctuate much more than GDP. One reason is that a substantial part of imports consists of durable goods such as cars, computers and TV sets, and investment goods (machines). Demand for durable goods fluctuates more than demand for food, haircuts, and government services, which are primarily produced at home, and investment is much more volatile than GDP. Some imports are inputs into industrial production, which fluctuates more than GDP. Also, many imported goods are storable, so inventory fluctuations contribute to the volatility of imports. The same argument applies to exports, which are also much more volatile than GDP.

Our theory says that demand for exports will depend primarily on foreign income and the real exchange rate. Fig. 12.4 shows the growth rate of the volume of exports and an index of *export market growth*. The latter is constructed by the OECD as a weighted average of the growth of total real imports to the main trading partners of each country, with weights determined by the share of exports going to different countries the year before. We see that exports vary a lot, and also that fluctuations in exports are highly correlated with fluctuations in foreign demand for imports.

If the *market shares* of different exporters were constant, the growth rate of exports would be identical to the growth rate of foreign imports. In fact, the growth rates are very similar, so it seems that the market shares of different exporters change rather little from one year to the next. An important reason for this is that exporters have long term trade relations with their customers, which do not change overnight. To re-orient exports, new customer relationships have to be established, contracts must be written, and transport must be reorganized. For these reasons, market shares adjust slowly, and short-run fluctuations in exports are mainly driven by fluctuations in foreign demand for imports.

Fig. 12.3 *Growth rates of GDP and imports, percentage changes*

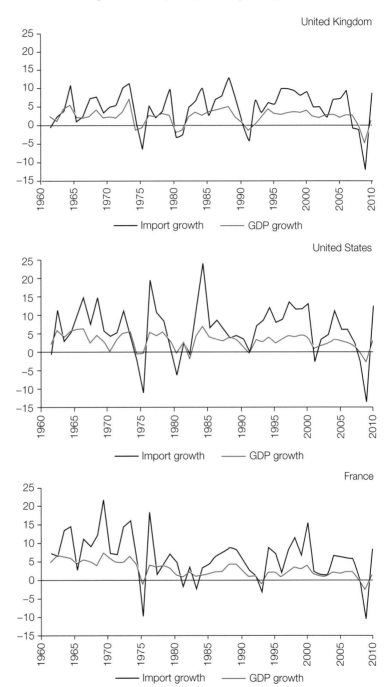

Source: *OECD Economic Outlook*, OECD, 6 October 2011, http://www.oecd-ilibrary.org/statistics.

But market shares are not constant. According to the theory presented above, one thing that affects the market share is the competitiveness of the country. Looking closely at Fig. 12.4, we see that US exports increased less than foreign imports in the periods 1982–1983 and 1999–2003, when the dollar appreciated, and that US exports increased more than foreign imports in the period 1987–1993, when the

Fig. 12.4 *Growth rates of export market demand and exports*

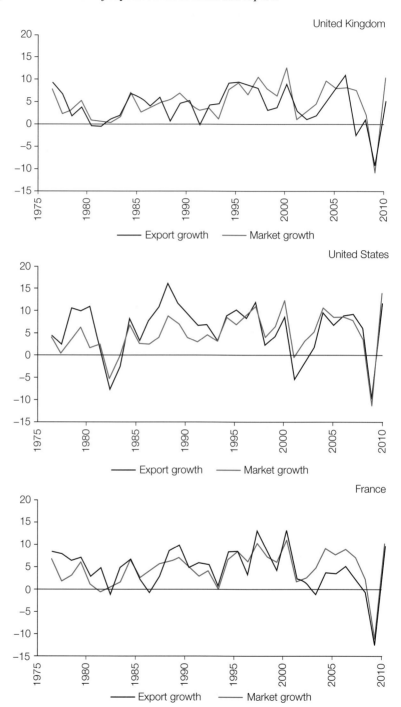

Source: *OECD Economic Outlook*, OECD, 6 October, http://www.oecd-ilibrary.org/statistics

dollar had depreciated. Thus it seems that exchange rate movements may help to explain the development of exports.

Fig. 12.5 shows the relation between the real exchange rate and the export *market share*, calculated as exports divided by a trade-weighted index of foreign imports. If we look at medium-term fluctuations, we see a relatively clear negative relation between the real exchange rate and the market share. In periods when the real exchange rate was relatively high, the market share declined. Examples are the strong pound in 1980–1982 and the strong dollar in 1983–1985 and 2000–2003. In both cases, the real appreciations were caused by nominal appreciations of the currencies, and market shares declined. Other examples are Spain and Sweden in 1989–1992. Both countries had fixed their exchange rates,

Fig. 12.5 *The real exchange rate and the export market share*

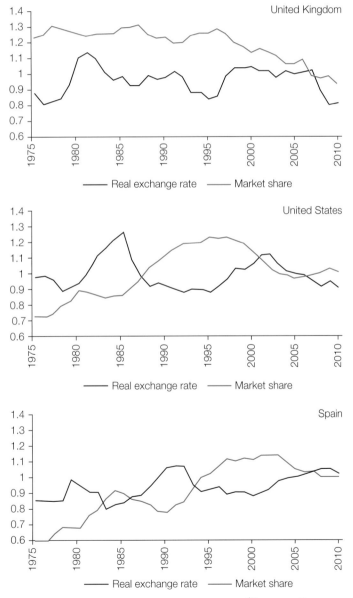

(Figure continues over the page)

Fig. 12.5 *(Continued)*

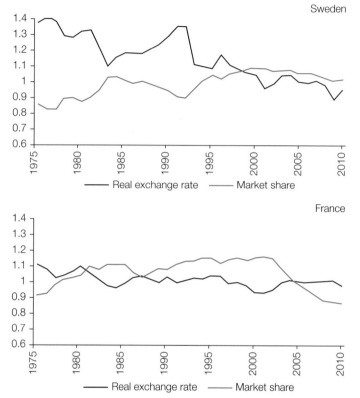

Source: *OECD Economic Outlook*, OECD, 6 October 2011, http://www.oecd-ilibrary.org/statistics.

but the real exchange rates appreciated because inflation in Spain and Sweden was high relative to these countries' trade partners. Again, we see decreases in the market shares.

In the opposite direction, the large depreciations of the dollar in 1986 and of the UK, Spanish and Swedish currencies in 1992 led to substantial increases in the market shares for those countries. Since Spain introduced the euro in 1999, inflation in Spain has been high relative to its trade partners, so there has been a real appreciation and loss of market shares for Spanish exporters.

If we look at the long-term trends, there is no clear long-term relation between real exchange rates and market shares. This may be due to changes in the composition of goods, emergence of new competition in export markets, and other long-term structural changes. For example, Spain has had a long-term increase in the real exchange rate and also in the market share. Spain has modernized its economy and now produces more high-quality goods than before, so Spanish producers can sell more goods at higher prices. Sweden, on the other hand, has experienced a long-term decrease in its real exchange rate. Reasons for long-term trends in real exchange rates are discussed in Chapter 13.

To sum up, we see quite clear evidence that imports are related to domestic demand, and that exports depend on foreign demand. The real exchange rate and the export market share seem to be negatively related in the short and medium run. These observations support the theory presented in this chapter. In the long run there seem to be other factors that drive the trends in real exchange rates and market shares.

12.4   Savings, investment, and the current account

In international financial markets, households, firms, and governments borrow and lend to foreign households, firms, and governments. Net foreign debt of a country is simply the net foreign debt of households, firms and the government in that country. It is not the 'country' that decides to borrow, or lend; it is households, firms, and the government who do that.

We now consider how financial markets work in the open economy. In this section we look at financial flows. We analyse how net claims on the rest of the world change over time and how this change is related to savings, investment, and the *current account*. In the next section, we analyse how expected returns on loans in different currencies are related to interest rates and expected changes in exchange rates. This analysis leads to the *interest parity condition* which says that countries with depreciating currencies must have higher interest rates to compensate for the expected depreciation of the currency.

In order to analyse how the accumulation of claims on, or debt to, foreign countries is related to income, savings, and investments, we assume that the government borrows only from domestic households, and that all domestic firms are owned by the domestic households.[4] Households borrow from each other in international financial markets and we use F to denote the net claims that domestic households have on foreign households. F can be positive or negative. Thus, the private sector (households and firms) has three assets: real capital, K, the government debt, D, and net claims on foreign households, F:

$$A = K + D + F.$$

Savings of the private sector – disposable income minus private consumption – can be used for real investments and to accumulate claims on the government and foreign countries:

$$Y^d - C = I + \Delta D + \Delta F.$$

As mentioned in the previous section, households' real disposable income is equal to domestic production plus the interest on government debt and on net claims on foreign households, minus the tax:[5]

$$Y^d = Y + r(D + F) - T.$$

---

4   More generally, we could have foreigners owning some of the government debt and part of the capital stock in the small open economy, but this would not change our analysis in any fundamental way.

5   To simplify, we disregard net transfers to foreign countries (e.g. development aid). Note also that income and returns on assets are measured in real terms. In the national accounts, disposable income is measured in nominal terms.

To simplify, we assume that the real return is the same on government debt and net claims on foreign households. In Chapter 10 we saw that the change in real government debt is determined by the primary surplus plus the real interest payment on the government debt:

$$\Delta D = G - T + rD.$$

Using these two equations to substitute for Y^d and ΔD in the expression above we see that

$$Y + r(D + F) - T - C = I + G - T + rD + \Delta F.$$

Several terms cancel out. Subtracting $I + G$ on both sides, we get an equation for ΔF:

$$\Delta F = Y + rF - C - G - I.$$

The change in net claims on foreign countries is equal to savings minus real investment of the country as a whole. In fact, the economy of a country is not different from the economy of an individual household. If a household saves more than its real investments, the rest of the money ends up in the bank account of the household or it is used to pay back a loan. The same applies to the country as a whole. If saving exceeds real investment, the country will increase its net claims on foreign countries.

But how is this related to exports and imports? To see this, we use $Y = C + I + G + NX$ to substitute for Y in the equation above:

$$\Delta F = \underbrace{C + I + G + NX}_{Y} + rF - C - G - I = NX + rF.$$

The change in claims on foreign countries is equal to net exports plus interest income from abroad – that is, the current account.[6] As explained in Chapter 1, the current account measures the flow of payments between a country and the rest of the world. The net inflow of payments is payment for exports minus payment for imports plus net primary income from abroad. The latter consists of net labour and capital income from abroad. In our analysis, we disregard labour income from abroad and ownership of foreign real capital, so the only primary factor income from abroad is the interest rate on net claims on foreign countries, which is positive if the country has net claims on foreign countries and negative if the country has a net foreign debt.

If there is a surplus in the current account, the country accumulates claims on foreign countries. If there is a deficit, this must be financed by net borrowing from foreign countries.[7] Thus, we have found two different ways of thinking about the

6 We should note however, that in the national accounts, the current account is reported in nominal terms, including net *nominal* interest payments on foreign assets. Since we are interested in real income, we focus here on real income and asset accumulation measured in terms of the domestically produced good. To be precise, we can think of ΔF as the *inflation-adjusted* current account. Note also that we disregard differences in returns (including capital gains) on different assets.

7 To be entirely accurate, the country could also use a surplus in the current account to buy shares or real assets abroad, but we disregard those flows here.

current account. We can think of it as national income minus consumption minus real investment:

$$\Delta F = Y + rF - C\left(Y^d, Y^e - T^e, r, A\right) - I\left(r, Y^e, K\right) - G$$

or we can think of the current account as net exports plus net primary income from abroad:

$$\Delta F = NX\left(\varepsilon, Y^*, Y\right) + rF.$$

These two expressions do not contain the same explanatory variables. The real exchange rate appears in the second expression but not in the first. A higher level of income seems to increase ΔF according to the first expression, while it seems to reduce ΔF according to the second expression. So which of these equations is the right one? The answer is that both are right, but neither equation is sufficient to determine how a specific shock affects the current account. Production and the real exchange rate are related because aggregate demand depends on the real exchange rate and most exogenous shocks will affect both production and the real exchange rate. To see how the current account is affected by a specific exogenous shock, we need to specify a complete macroeconomic model of the open economy. We now proceed to the final step in the construction of such a model, which is to analyse the relation between interest rates and exchange rates.

12.5   The interest parity condition

We now turn from the financial flows to the prices in the international financial markets: interest rates and exchange rates. We will derive the *interest parity condition*, which says that interest rates must compensate for expected changes in the exchange rates. The interest parity condition will play a central role in our analysis of the open economy.

A UK consumer who saves for retirement may put her money in a fund that invests in short-term bonds in different currencies. The managers of such a fund continuously evaluate the situation in different countries in order to get a high return on the assets. If a one-year UK government bond is bought for 1000 pounds and the interest rate is 4 percent, 1040 pounds will be paid out in one year. If a one-year German government bond is bought for 1000 euros and the interest rate is 4 percent, 1040 euros will be paid out in one year. But in the meantime, the euro may appreciate or depreciate relative to the pound. If the euro appreciates by 2 percent relative to the pound, the return on the euro loan will be approximately 6 percent measured in pounds. Therefore, the expected return on a loan in foreign currency depends on the expected *change* in the exchange rate, and investors must take account of expected changes of exchange rates when they decide where to put their money.

To simplify our macroeconomic analysis, we make a rather extreme assumption. We assume that financial investors always invest where the *expected* return is highest. This means that, for loans to be made in different currencies, interest rates and exchange rates have to adjust so that the *expected* returns are the same on loans in different currencies.

Imagine a *foreign* financial investor who considers lending one unit of her currency in period t, either in her own currency or in the currency of the small open economy. If she lends one unit of her own currency she gets an amount

$$1 + i_t^*$$

in period $t+1$ where i_t^* is the foreign interest rate. In order to lend in the currency of the small open economy, she must buy that currency. For one unit of her own currency she gets $1/e_t$ units of the currency of the small open economy, and after one period she gets an amount

$$\frac{1}{e_t}(1 + i_t)$$

in the currency of the small open economy. This money is then exchanged back to her own currency, so in the end she gets

$$\frac{1}{e_t}(1 + i_t) e_{t+1}$$

in her own currency. As mentioned above, we assume that the investor cares only about the expected return, so if loans are made in both currencies, these two alternative financial investments must give the same *expected* return. Thus, the interest rates and the expected exchange rate have to fulfil the following *interest parity condition*:[8]

$$1 + i_t^* = (1 + i_t)\frac{e_{t+1}^e}{e_t}.$$

This equation says something quite intuitive. If the currency of the small open economy is expected to depreciate, so that e_{t+1}^e/e_t is smaller than unity, the interest rate in the small open economy has to be higher than the foreign interest rate to compensate for the expected depreciation.

We can write the interest parity condition in an approximate and simpler way. To do this, we add and subtract e_t in the numerator on the right-hand side:

$$1 + i_t^* = (1 + i_t)\frac{e_t + e_{t+1}^e - e_t}{e_t} = (1 + i_t)\left(1 + \frac{\Delta e_{t+1}^e}{e_t}\right) \approx 1 + i_t + \frac{\Delta e_{t+1}^e}{e_t}.$$

To see why this approximation works, suppose that $i_t = 0.05$ and that $\Delta e_{t+1}^e/e_t = 0.02$. Then

$$(1 + i_t)\left(1 + \frac{\Delta e_{t+1}^e}{e_t}\right) = (1 + 0.05)(1 + 0.02) = 1 + 0.02 + 0.05 + 0.02 \cdot 0.05$$

$$= 1.071 \approx 1.07.$$

The approximation works well because 0.02 times 0.05 is a very small number. Rewriting the equation above we get an approximate version of the interest parity condition:

---

8 More precisely, it is the *uncovered interest parity* condition because we are considering investments that are not hedged by buying currencies forward. The forward market and *covered interest parity* are analysed in the appendix to Chapter 15.

$$i_t - i_t^* \approx -\frac{\Delta e_{t+1}^e}{e_t}.$$

The interest differential must be approximately equal to the expected depreciation of the currency in percent. If the currency of the small open economy is expected to depreciate by 3 percent over the next year, the interest rate in the small open economy has to be approximately 3 percentage units higher than the interest rate abroad.

We derived the interest parity condition assuming that investors always invest where the expected return is highest. In effect, we assumed that they do not care about risk. Financial investors are *risk neutral* and ready to put all the eggs in one basket if that basket gives the highest expected return. Obviously, this is an extreme assumption because real investors try to hold a diversified portfolio so as to reduce the risk. The interest parity condition is a simplification, but it captures an intuitively plausible idea: if a currency is expected to depreciate, lenders will require a higher interest rate in order to lend in that currency.

The implications of interest parity under fixed and floating exchange rates

The interest parity condition has different implications according to whether a country has a fixed or a floating exchange rate.

A *fixed exchange rate* means that the central bank announces an official target level for the exchange rate and keeps the exchange rate at that level by buying and selling currency. If a country has a fixed exchange rate and if financial investors believe that the central bank will keep the exchange rate fixed, the expected change of the exchange rate is zero and the implication of the interest parity condition is that the nominal interest rate in the small open economy must be the same as the interest rate abroad:

$$i_t = i_t^*.$$

More precisely, the interest rate must be the same as in the currency area to which the country has fixed its exchange rate. To see why this must be the case, suppose that the central bank in the small open economy tries to set an interest rate below the foreign interest rate. If the interest rate in the small open economy is lower than the interest rate abroad, financial investors can make a profit by borrowing in the currency of the small open economy, exchanging the money for foreign currency, and lending abroad. To keep the exchange rate fixed, the central bank has to buy its own currency and this means that the money supply decreases which puts upward pressure on the interest rate. The central bank can buy government bonds to keep the money supply unchanged.[9] At some point, however, the currency reserves of the central bank will run out, so it will be unable to buy more of its currency, and the currency will depreciate. Therefore, it is impossible to keep the interest rate below the foreign interest rate when the exchange rate is fixed.

---

9 Such an operation is called *sterilization* because the central bank counteracts the effect on the money supply of the outflow of financial capital.

Similarly, if the central bank tries to set an interest rate above the foreign interest rate, investors will exchange foreign currency for domestic currency so as to lend in the currency of the small open economy, and the central bank will have to buy extremely large quantities of foreign currency to keep the exchange rate fixed. Therefore, the only interest rate that is consistent with a fixed exchange rate is an interest rate that is equal to the interest rate abroad. With a fixed exchange rate and mobile capital, the central bank becomes unable to control the interest rate.[10]

Fig. 12.6 shows interest rates on three months' Treasury bills for some countries which are now members of the European Monetary Union (EMU). In the period before 1971 these countries were part of the Bretton Woods System, which was a fixed exchange rate system with relatively few adjustments of the exchange rates. As predicted by the interest parity condition, the interest rates were very similar in this period. In the 1970s and the 1980s, these countries tried to maintain fixed exchange rates, but there were large inflation differentials and frequent adjustments of the exchange rates, and the interest rates differed substantially between countries. The euro was introduced in 1999 and, for a decade, short-term interest rates were the same in these countries. Interest differentials increased again in 2010 because of worries that some governments might default or that some countries might leave the euro.

With a *floating exchange rate*, the situation is very different. A pure *floating exchange rate* means that the central bank does not have a target level for the

Fig. 12.6 *Interest rates in some countries that now have the euro*

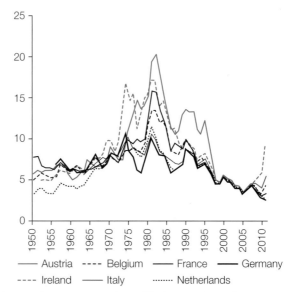

Note: Interest rates are rates on government securities in percentage points per year, but the maturities may differ.
Source: International Financial Statistics, IMF, 11 July 2012.

---

10 In this discussion we have assumed that there is no credit risk, i.e. government bonds are safe. If there are differences in the risk of government default, interest rates on government bonds may differ between countries even if the exchange rate is fixed. Also, if there is speculation that exchange rates will change, i.e. there will be a devaluation or a revaluation, interest rates may differ between countries.

exchange rate and that it does not interfere in currency markets. With a floating exchange rate, the central bank is free to set the interest rate, and we can instead think of the interest parity condition as an equation determining the level of the exchange rate. Solving the interest parity condition for the exchange rate we get

$$e_t = \frac{1+i_t}{1+i_t^*}e_{t+1}^e.$$

This equation shows that the exchange rate is determined by three variables:

1. *The domestic interest rate*: a higher interest rate makes it more interesting to invest in the currency of the small open economy, so it appreciates (increases in value).
2. *The foreign interest rate*: a higher interest rate abroad makes it less interesting to invest in currency of the small open economy, so it depreciates (decreases in value).
3. *The expected future exchange rate*: if the currency is expected to be worth more tomorrow, its price is bid up, so it is worth more today; the currency appreciates.

A key implication of the interest parity condition is that, with a floating exchange rate, monetary policy affects aggregate demand via the exchange rate. An increase in the interest rate will not only affect consumption and investment, but it also leads to appreciation of the currency, which reduces exports and aggregate demand.

As we will see, the roles of fiscal and monetary policy are very different, depending on whether the country has a fixed or a floating exchange rate. We will analyse fixed and floating exchange rates in detail when we study the open economy in the short run in Chapter 14.

12.6 Globalization in the markets for goods and services and the financial markets

Most economies have become more open in recent decades. After the Second World War, international trade agreements led to reductions in tariffs, and the elimination of import quotas and other trade barriers. The European Economic Community (EEC, now the European Union) and the European Free Trade Area (EFTA) worked to abolish trade barriers within Europe. Further, technological developments such as reduced transport costs, information technology, and increased specialization have led to increasing trade. Fig. 12.7 shows that exports and imports have increased as a proportion of GDP. Today, exports are an important component of aggregate demand in most countries. As a consequence, demand spill-overs between countries are large: what happens in one country affects demand for exports and aggregate demand in neighbouring countries.

After the Second World War, financial flows were heavily regulated. Firms and individuals could not freely borrow and lend in international financial markets. Balance in the current account, moreover, was regarded as an important goal of economic policy. As a consequence, there was little net borrowing between different countries. The current account deficits and surpluses were small relative to GDP in the 1950s and 1960s. However, most regulations of financial capital flows were abolished in the 1970s and the 1980s, and today, financial flows between the high-income countries are essentially unregulated.

Free flows of financial capital mean that countries can finance current account deficits and surpluses much more easily now than they could in the 1950s and

Fig. 12.7 *Exports, imports, net exports, and the current account, percent of GDP*

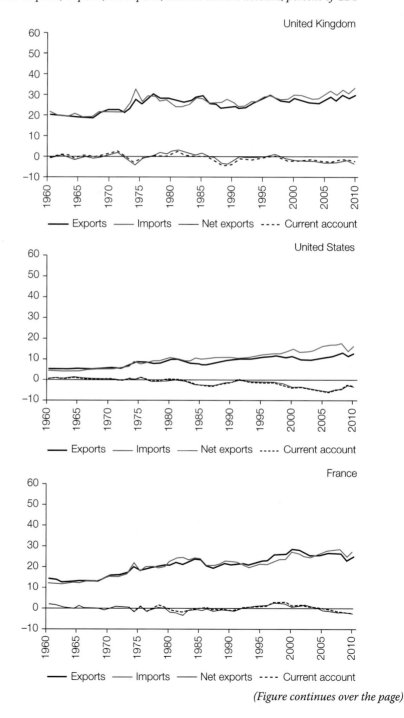

(Figure continues over the page)

Fig. 12.7 *(Continued)*

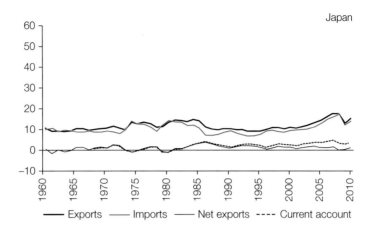

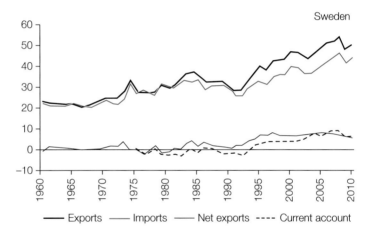

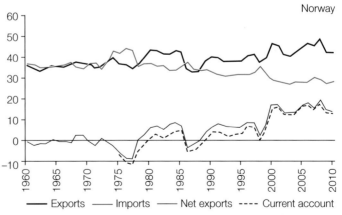

Source: *OECD Economic Outlook*, OECD, 12 October 2011, http://www.oecd-ilibrary.org/statistics.

1960s. We would expect this to lead to larger deficits and surpluses in the current accounts of different countries, and this is what we see if we look at the current account as a fraction of GDP in Fig. 12.7. The current accounts were close to zero in the 1960s, but substantial deficits and surpluses arose when regulations of capital flows were abolished.

The difference between net exports and the current account is net primary income from abroad: net labour income from working abroad and net returns on foreign assets held by domestic consumers and firms. For most of the countries shown, net primary income from abroad is small relative to GDP and the current account is essentially equal to net exports. An exception is Japan, which has had a current account surplus for a long time and accumulated large claims on foreign countries. As a result, Japan has substantial capital income from abroad.

To sum up, increased globalization has meant that exports, imports, and financial flows between countries have increased relative to GDP. Countries have become more closely integrated both in terms of trade and in terms of international borrowing and lending. Therefore, it has become more important to take account of international linkages when analysing macroeconomic developments in individual countries.

What have we learned?

In our small open economy model we assume that goods markets are perfectly integrated but goods produced in different countries are imperfect substitutes. Financial markets are perfectly integrated and financial investors invest where they get the highest expected return. Labour markets are not integrated: workers work and consume in the country where they were born.

We define the nominal exchange rate, e, as the price of domestic currency in terms of foreign currency. We define the real exchange rate, ε, as the price of domestic goods in terms of foreign goods:

$$\varepsilon = \frac{eP}{P^*}.$$

With fixed mark-ups the real exchange rate is identical to the relative unit labour cost.

In the open economy, aggregate demand consists of private consumption and investment, government consumption and investment, and net exports:

$$Y = C(Y - T, Y^e - T^e, r, A) + I(r, Y^e, K) + G + NX(\varepsilon, Y^*, Y).$$

An increase in foreign income leads to an increase in exports and therefore in net exports. An increase in domestic income leads to an increase in imports and a therefore a decrease in net exports.

An increase in the real exchange rate has a negative effect on real exports and a positive effect on real imports, but at the same time imports become cheaper. Provided that the price elasticities of import and export demand are sufficiently large, net exports will decrease when the real exchange rate appreciates (increases) and this will have a negative effect on aggregate demand.

The current account is the net lending of the country – the change in net financial claims on foreign countries. It is equal to income minus consumption (saving) minus real investment of the country as a whole. Further, the current account is equal to net exports plus net primary income from abroad, which in the model is interest income from abroad:

$$\Delta F = Y + rF - C - G - I = NX + rF.$$

The last equality follows from the fact that $Y = C + I + G + NX$.[11]

The (open) *interest parity condition* says that the *expected return* should be the same on loans in different currencies:

$$1 + i_t^* = (1 + i_t)\frac{e_{t+1}^e}{e_t}.$$

The left-hand side is the return on a loan in foreign currency. The right-hand side is the expected return, in terms of foreign currency, on a loan in the currency of the small open economy. As an approximation, we can write the interest parity condition:

$$i_t - i_t^* \approx -\frac{\Delta e_{t+1}^e}{e_t}.$$

If the exchange rate is expected to depreciate by 2 percent, the interest rate must be 2 percent higher than the foreign interest rate to compensate for the expected depreciation.

With a credibly fixed exchange rate, the expected change in the exchange rate is zero, so the nominal interest rate in the small open economy must be the same as the interest rate abroad. Thus, the central bank is unable to control the interest rate in a small open economy with a fixed exchange rate.

With a floating interest rate, the exchange rate is determined by the domestic and foreign interest rates and by expectations about the future exchange rate:

$$e_t = \frac{1 + i_t}{1 + i_t^*}e_{t+1}^e.$$

A higher interest rate leads to appreciation of the currency. A higher foreign interest rate leads to depreciation of the currency. A higher expected future value of the currency leads to an appreciation today.

In recent decades, exports and imports have increased relative to GDP and after the deregulation of capital flows in the 1970s and 1980s current account surpluses and deficits have become larger relative to GDP. This reflects globalization of markets for goods and services and financial markets.

Where do we go from here?

In this chapter we have worked hard to lay the foundations for the analysis of the open economy. We have extended our macroeconomic model by allowing for trade and international borrowing and lending. We have added exports and imports, the current account and the interest parity condition. Having extended our macroeconomic model in this way, we are ready to analyse economic developments in the open economy. In Chapter 13 we analyse the open economy in the long run: growth and foreign debt. In Chapter 14 we analyse the role of monetary

---

11 The statistics shows the nominal amounts, but this equation shows the real magnitudes.

and fiscal policy in the open economy. In Chapter 15 we study the history of the exchange rate systems and the European Monetary Union. All this analysis will be based on the theoretical foundations developed in this chapter, so you should make sure you understand the new concepts that we have introduced: the real exchange rate, net exports, the current account, and the interest parity condition.

Exercises

1) We have the following model of aggregate demand in an open economy:

$$Y = C + I + G + X - IM/\varepsilon,$$

$$C = a + b(Y - T), \qquad I = c - di,$$

$$IM = q\varepsilon Y, \qquad X = x\varepsilon^{-\sigma} Y^*.$$

a) What is the price elasticity of import demand, $\dfrac{\Delta IM}{\Delta \varepsilon} \dfrac{\varepsilon}{IM}$?

b) What is the price elasticity of export demand, $\dfrac{\Delta X}{\Delta \varepsilon} \dfrac{\varepsilon}{X}$?

c) Solve for production (Y) as a function of the interest rate and the real exchange rate. Then calculate the effect on production of an increase in government consumption (G). Interpret the parameters b and q. How do these parameters affect the multiplier? Why? Calculate the numerical value of the effect if $b = 0.6$ and $q = 0.4$.

d) Calculate the effect on imports of an increase in G. Explain the result. *(Hint: Use the answer to the previous question.)* Calculate the numerical value of the effect if $b = 0.6$, $\varepsilon = 1$ and $q = 0.4$.

e) Calculate the effect of the real exchange rate on production, i.e. $\Delta Y/\Delta \varepsilon$, then multiply by ε/Y to get the elasticity $\dfrac{\Delta Y/Y}{\Delta \varepsilon/\varepsilon}$ which measures by how many percent production changes if the real exchange rate changes by one percent. Interpret the result.

f) Suppose we have the following parameter values: $b = 0.6$, $q = 0.4$, $\sigma = 2$ and that the export share X/Y is initially 0.4. What is the value of the elasticity that you calculated above?

Answers to the exercises can be found at: **www.palgrave.com/economics/gottfries**.

Appendix

The real exchange rate in terms of prices of production and consumption

In practice the real exchange rate is often measured in terms of *consumer prices* and the consumer price index includes prices of imported goods. To see how the real exchange rate in terms of production and consumption prices are related, assume that consumers in the small open economy spend a fraction θ of their incomes on foreign goods. As noted above, P^*/e is the price of foreign goods in domestic currency. Then, a reasonable definition of the consumer price index in the small open economy is a weighted average of the prices of the two goods:

$$P^c \equiv (P^*/e)^\theta \, P^{1-\theta}.$$

This is called a geometric weighted average. In terms of logarithms of the prices, it is a standard weighted average. Since the small open economy is negligible compared to the rest of the word, the consumer price index for the rest of the world is P^*. Hence, the real exchange rate in terms of consumer prices is

$$\varepsilon^c = \frac{eP^c}{P^{c*}} = \frac{e\,(P^*)^\theta\,e^{-\theta}P^{1-\theta}}{P^*} = \frac{(eP)^{1-\theta}}{(P^*)^{1-\theta}} = \left(\frac{eP}{P^*}\right)^{1-\theta} = (\varepsilon)^{1-\theta}\,.$$

We see that there is a one-to-one relation between the real exchange rate in terms of goods *produced* in different countries and the real exchange rate in terms of the consumption bundles *consumed* in different countries. If ε increases, ε^c increases, and conversely. Although the *magnitude* of the fluctuations differs between different measures, the *direction* of the changes is the same independent of which measure we use. If unit labour costs in the small open economy rise, the prices of goods produced in the small open economy will also increase, and since consumers spend a substantial fraction of their income on domestically produced goods, the consumer price level in the small open economy will rise relative to consumer prices abroad.

The Marshall–Lerner condition

Net exports are

$$NX = X\,(\varepsilon) - IM\,(\varepsilon) \cdot \varepsilon^{-1}$$

where the quantities exported and imported are functions of the real exchange rate and other variables, which we omit because they are irrelevant here. Taking the derivative with respect to the real exchange rate and using the product rule for the last term, we get

$$\frac{dNX}{d\varepsilon} = \frac{dX}{d\varepsilon} - \frac{dIM}{d\varepsilon}\varepsilon^{-1} + IM\varepsilon^{-2} = \frac{IM}{\varepsilon^2}\left[\frac{dX}{d\varepsilon}\frac{\varepsilon^2}{IM} - \frac{dIM}{d\varepsilon}\frac{\varepsilon}{IM} + 1\right].$$

Let us now evaluate this derivative in a situation when net exports are initially equal to zero – that is, $X = IM/\varepsilon$. Substituting this into the first term in the parenthesis we get

$$\frac{\partial NX}{\partial \varepsilon} = \frac{IM}{\varepsilon^2}\left[\frac{\partial X}{\partial \varepsilon}\frac{\varepsilon}{X} - \frac{\partial IM}{\partial \varepsilon}\frac{\varepsilon}{IM} + 1\right].$$

The first two terms inside the parenthesis are the price elasticities of exports and imports. Exports decrease and imports increase if the real exchange rate increases, so both terms are negative. If the sum of these two terms is greater than unity in absolute value, the substitution effect dominates over the valuation effect, so net exports decrease when the real exchange rate appreciates. Empirical evidence suggests that the export price elasticity is in the order of 2 or 3, and the import price elasticity is around one, so the Marshall–Lerner condition seems to be fulfilled empirically. A real appreciation leads to a decrease in net exports.

Derivation of the consumption and import functions

In order to formally derive the consumption and import functions, we assume that utility is determined by a consumption index which has the 'Cobb–Douglas' form:

$$\tilde{C} = \phi \left(C^d\right)^{1-\theta} \left(C^f\right)^\theta \quad \text{where} \quad \phi = (1-\theta)^{\theta-1}\,(\theta)^{-\theta}\,.$$

Thus $U\left(\tilde{C}\right) = U\left(\phi\left(C^d\right)^{1-\theta}\left(C^f\right)^{\theta}\right)$ and, using the chain rule, we find that the marginal utility of the foreign good is

$$U'\left(\tilde{C}\right)\phi\left(C^d\right)^{1-\theta}\theta\left(C^f\right)^{\theta-1} = U'\left(\tilde{C}\right)\theta\frac{\tilde{C}}{C^f}.$$

Similarly, the marginal utility of the domestic good is

$$U'\left(\tilde{C}\right)\phi\left(1-\theta\right)\left(C^d\right)^{-\theta}\left(C^f\right)^{\theta} = U'\left(\tilde{C}\right)\left(1-\theta\right)\frac{\tilde{C}}{C^d}.$$

Let P^f be the price of the foreign good in domestic currency – that is, $P^f = P^*/e$. The consumer maximizes utility by choosing consumption of the two goods so that the ratio of the marginal utilities (the marginal rate of substitution) is equal to the relative price:

$$\frac{U'\left(\tilde{C}\right)\theta\tilde{C}/C^f}{U'\left(\tilde{C}\right)\left(1-\theta\right)\tilde{C}/C^d} = \frac{P^f}{P}.$$

Multiplying by C^f/C^d we get

$$\frac{C^f P^f}{C^d P} = \frac{\theta}{1-\theta}.$$

Suppose now that the consumer spends a sum, H, on consumption in a particular period:

$$H = C^d P + C^f P^f.$$

Using the condition above, we can write

$$H = C^d P + C^f P^f = C^d P + \frac{\theta}{1-\theta}C^d P = \frac{1-\theta+\theta}{1-\theta}C^d P = \frac{C^d P}{1-\theta}$$

which implies

$$C^d P = (1-\theta)H \quad \text{and} \quad C^f P^f = H - C^d P = H - (1-\theta)H = \theta H.$$

We see that, with the utility function specified above, the consumer spends a share θ on foreign goods and a share $1-\theta$ on domestic goods.

When the consumer allocates H optimally between the two goods, the consumption index is

$$\tilde{C} = \phi\left(C^d\right)^{1-\theta}\left(C^f\right)^{\theta} = (1-\theta)^{\theta-1}(\theta)^{-\theta}\left(\frac{(1-\theta)H}{P}\right)^{1-\theta}\left(\frac{\theta H}{P^f}\right)^{\theta}$$

$$= \frac{H}{P^{1-\theta}\left(P^f\right)^{\theta}} = \frac{H}{P^c},$$

where $P^c = P^{1-\theta}\left(P^f\right)^{\theta}$. We see that, by deflating nominal expenditure by the price index P^c we get a measure of real consumption that is relevant for utility. In this sense, P^c is the appropriate consumer price index in this model. We also see that $P^c\tilde{C} = H = C^d P + C^f P^f$.

Thus, we have shown that:

i) consumers spend a fixed share $1-\theta$ of their total consumption expenditure on the domestic good and a fixed share θ on the foreign good

ii) total consumption expenditure is $P^c \tilde{C}$ where P^c is a consumer price index $P^c = \left(P^f\right)^\theta P^{1-\theta}$.

Since Y^d and A are expressed in units of the domestic good, real disposable income and wealth *expressed in terms of the consumption index* are

$$\frac{PY^d}{P^c} \quad \text{and} \quad \frac{PA}{P^c},$$

where $Y^d = Y + r(D+F) - T$ and $A = K + F + D$. We assume that private consumption, measured in terms of the consumption index, is determined by real income and wealth according to the consumption function derived in Chapter 4:

$$\tilde{C} = \frac{r\left[\dfrac{PY^d + PA}{P^c}\right] + \dfrac{P(Y^e - T^e)}{P^c}}{\dfrac{1+r}{1+\rho} + r} = \frac{P}{P^c} \frac{r\left[Y^d + A\right] + Y^e - T^e}{\dfrac{1+r}{1+\rho} + r}$$

$$= \frac{P}{P^c} C\left(Y^d, Y^e - T^e, r, A\right),$$

where $C\left(Y^d, Y^e - T^e, r, A\right)$ is the consumption function that we used for the closed economy. P/P^c enters here because Y^d, $Y^e - T^e$ and A are expressed in units of the domestic good.[12] Aggregate consumption *measured in units of the domestic good* is therefore

$$C = \frac{P^c \tilde{C}}{P} = C\left(Y^d, Y^e - T^e, r, A\right).$$

This is the same consumption function as in the closed economy. Since $P^f C^f = \theta P^c \tilde{C}$ consumption of imported goods is

$$C^f = \theta \frac{P^c}{P^f} \tilde{C} = \theta \frac{P^c}{P^f} \frac{P}{P^c} C\left(Y^d, Y^e - T^e, r, A\right) = \theta \varepsilon C\left(Y^d, Y^e - T^e, r, A\right).$$

Thus we have the import function.

$$IM\left(\varepsilon, Y^d, Y^e - T^e, r, A\right) = \theta \varepsilon C\left(Y^d, Y^e - T^e, r, A\right).$$

The quantity of imports is determined by the same factors as domestic consumption, plus the real exchange rate. Thus we have net exports, expressed in units of the domestic good:

$$NX \equiv \underset{(-)(+)}{X\left(\varepsilon, Y^*\right)} - \underset{(+)\ (+)\ (+)(-)(+)}{IM\left(\varepsilon, Y^d, Y^e - T^e, r, A\right)} / \varepsilon = \underset{(-)(+)}{X\left(\varepsilon, Y^*\right)} - \underset{(+)\ (+)(-)(+)}{\theta C\left(Y^d, Y^e - T^e, r, A\right)}.$$

Here, the real exchange rate appears only in the first term. Expenditure on imports is independent of the real exchange rate because the substitution and valuation effects cancel out. This is a result of the constant expenditure share, which implies that the price elasticity of import demand is unity. If imported goods become more expensive, the quantity of imports decreases but the value of imports is unchanged. Provided that exports are sensitive to the real exchange rate, the

---

12 Here we have implicitly assumed that P^d/P is expected to remain constant. This is not always the case.

Marshal–Lerner condition is fulfilled, and the real exchange rate has a negative effect on net exports. Empirical evidence suggests that the price elasticity of imports is relatively close to unity, so a model with constant expenditure shares seems reasonable.

The balance of payments

The balance of payments summarizes, for a specific time period, the economic transactions of an economy with the rest of the world. Transactions consist of those involving goods, services, and income; those involving financial claims on, and liabilities to, the rest of the world; and those (such as gifts) classified as transfers. The balance of payments for the Netherlands for 2011 is shown in Table 12.1. The balance of payments consist of the *current account*, the *capital transfers account*, and the *financial account*.

Table 12.1 *Balance of payments for the Netherlands, 2011*

	Current Account			**Financial Account**	
	Goods account			*Direct investment*	
1.1.1	Exports of goods	395,370	3.1.1	Direct investment abroad	−22,924
1.1.2	Imports of goods	353,600	3.1.2	Direct investment in the Netherlands	12,322
1.1	Balance on goods	41,770	3.1	Net direct investment	−10,602
	Services account			*Portfolio investment*	
1.2.1	Exports of services	77,267	3.2.1	Foreign securities	−8,372
1.2.2	Imports of services	67,565	3.2.2	Dutch securities	24,784
1.2	Balance on services	9,702	3.2	Net portfolio investment	16,412
	Income account			*Financial derivatives*	
1.3.1	Receipts	84,619	3.3.1	Assets	493,756
1.3.2	Expenditures	74,365	3.3.2	Liabilities	−500,485
1.3	Balance on income	10,254	3.3	Net financial derivatives	−6,729
	Current transfers account			*Other investment*	
1.4.1	Receipts	13,327	3.4.1	Assets	−112,905
1.4.2	Expenditures	24,097	3.4.2	Liabilities	66,526
1.4	Net current transfers	−10,770	3.4	Net other investment	−46,380
1	*Balance on current account*	**50,956**	3	*Net financial account excluding official reserves*	**−47,299**
	Capital Transfers Account			**Increase in Official Reserves**	
2.1	Receipts	2,185	4.1	Monetary gold	0
2.2	Expenditures	4,193	4.2	Special drawing rights	218
			4.3	Reserve position in the IMF	−752
			4.4	Foreign exchange	−1281
2	*Balance on capital transfers account*	**−2008**			
			4	*Total increase (−) official reserves*	**−1,815**
			5	**Net Financial Account (3 + 4)**	**−49,113**
			6	**Errors and omissions**	**165**

Source: De Nederlansche Bank homepage, http://www.dnb.nl/statistiek/index.jsp.

The first part of the balance of payments is the *current account*. The current account shows flows of payments associated with exports and imports of goods and services, net primary incomes from abroad (e.g. wages, interest payments, dividends), and net current transfers such as foreign aid. These components were discussed in Chapter 1.

Then there is a relatively small component called the *capital transfers account*, which we have neglected in the main text.[13]

The third component of the balance of payments is the *financial account*. The financial account comprises all transactions in the external financial assets and liabilities of an economy. Direct investments typically involve a company in one country buying a company, or part of a company, or building a factory in another country. The entries portfolio investments, financial derivatives, and other investments report purchases of other types of financial assets. Finally, the central bank may increase or decrease its net claims on the rest of the world and these transactions are reported as changes in official reserves.

As we have explained in Chapters 1 and 12, a current account surplus implies that the country accumulates financial claims on the rest of the world – that is, a capital outflow. Therefore, the current account, the capital transfer account, and the financial account should sum to zero. Because data are collected from different sources, the numbers do not match perfectly. The difference is reported as *errors and omissions*.

We will not explain all the terms in the table here. Detailed explanations of the balance of payments can be found in the *IMF Balance of Payments Textbook*.[14]

---

13 For those who insist on knowing what it is, the *IMF Balance of Payments Textbook* defines capital transfers as follows: 'A *capital transfer* is transference of the ownership of a fixed asset or the forgiveness of a liability. A cash transfer (for example, an investment grant) is a *capital transfer* when the cash transfer is linked to, or conditional upon, the acquisition or disposal of a fixed asset by one or both parties to the transaction. According to BOP convention, migrants' transfers are also *capital transfers*.'

14 This text is available at http://www.imf.org/external/np/sta/bop/BOPtex.pdf.

13 THE OPEN ECONOMY IN THE LONG RUN

What factors determine the current account, the real exchange rate, and the long-run levels of income and foreign debt?

In the previous chapter we 'opened up' the economy by introducing trade in goods and services and borrowing and lending in international financial markets. We defined the *real exchange rate* as the price level in the open economy relative to the price level abroad, where price levels are converted to the same currency. We showed that the real exchange rate is an important determinant of aggregate demand in the open economy. We also showed that the *current account* is the difference between savings and real investments in the country. If there is a deficit in the current account, someone in the country is borrowing from someone abroad. Either the government or the private sector, or both, are borrowing in order to finance consumption and real investments in excess of income. We also derived the (open) *interest parity condition*, which links interest rate differentials between countries to expected changes in exchange rates.

Having formulated a model of the open economy, we are ready to analyse the macroeconomic equilibrium. How are production, consumption, investment, and the real exchange rate determined in the open economy? How are interest rates determined when households and firms can borrow abroad? Why is it that some countries have current account deficits and some have surpluses? Is it a problem to have a deficit in the current account? Why are there changes in the relative price levels between different countries?

In this chapter, we consider the open economy in the long run. As before, long-run analysis means that, when we analyse the effects of changes in exogenous variables, we assume that prices and wages have time to adjust, so employment and production are at their natural levels. We also assume that international financial markets are completely integrated, so financial capital can flow freely and that the interest parity condition holds. These are strong assumptions, but they help to clarify the difference between closed and open economies. In reality, financial markets are neither perfectly integrated nor completely separated by country borders.

We first analyse how the real interest rate is determined in the open economy. Then we analyse the determination of the current account and the real exchange rate. We also study investment and long-run growth in the open economy and we investigate what determines the long-run level of foreign debt. Finally, we also take a look at the data to better understand how integrated financial markets are in practice.

13.1   Real and nominal interest rates in the open economy

The real interest rate determines the real cost of borrowing and the required return on investment. When analysing the closed economy in Chapter 4, we found that the real interest rate was determined so as to equalize savings and investment in the country. With perfectly integrated financial markets the level of the real interest rate is instead tied to the real interest rate in the world financial market.

To understand this, we start with the interest parity condition, which says that, for foreign lenders, the expected return on loans in the currency of the small open economy must be the same as the expected return on loans in the foreign currency:

$$i + \frac{\Delta e^e}{e} = i^*.$$

The left-hand side is the interest rate in the small open economy plus the expected appreciation of the currency. The right-hand side is the return on loans in foreign currency. But what determines the rate of change of the nominal exchange rate? To see this, we use the definition of the real exchange rate:

$$\varepsilon = \frac{eP}{P^*}.$$

Solving this equation for the nominal exchange rate we get

$$e = \varepsilon \frac{P^*}{P}.$$

Let us consider an economy with constant production and a constant rate of inflation. Assume also that, in the long-run equilibrium, the real exchange rate is constant. This must be the case if there is no real growth, because all real variables are constant in the long-run equilibrium. If one country were to have a continuous increase in the price level compared with other countries, exporters in that country would become unable to compete in world markets.[1] With a constant real exchange rate, the rule of thumb for percentage changes implies that the relative change in the nominal exchange rate is equal to foreign inflation minus domestic inflation:[2]

$$\frac{\Delta e}{e} = \pi^* - \pi.$$

This equation shows the main reason why there are long-run trends in nominal exchange rates: inflation differentials between countries. A country with relatively high inflation will have a depreciating nominal exchange rate. If a country has high

4

---

1   Reasons for long-term trends in real exchange rates are discussed in the appendix to this chapter.
2   The rule of thumb for growth rates is derived in the appendix to Chapter 1. We are cheating a bit here because inflation is usually measured in terms of consumer prices and P is the price of goods *produced* at home. The consumer price index for the small open economy includes prices of both domestically produced and foreign goods. The conclusion is correct, however, because constancy of the real exchange rate in terms of prices of production implies constancy of the real exchange rate in terms of prices of consumption. See the appendix to Chapter 12 for an analysis of the relation between real exchange rates in terms of prices of consumption and production.

inflation for a number of years, and the nominal exchange rate remains constant, exporters will find it very hard to compete in world markets so the currency will have to depreciate, sooner or later.

We assume that, in a long-run equilibrium, the expected change in the exchange rate is equal to the actual change, $\Delta e^e/e = \Delta e/e$ so we can substitute for $\Delta e^e/e$ in the interest parity condition above to get

$$i + \pi^* - \pi = i^*.$$

Subtracting π^* on both sides we get

$$i - \pi = i^* - \pi^*.$$

On the left-hand side we have the real interest rate in the small open economy and on the right-hand side we have the world real interest rate. We see that the real interest rate in the open economy must be the same as abroad:

$$r = r^*.$$

This is a result of perfectly integrated financial markets. Effectively, the required *real* return on loans is determined in the world financial market. Contrary to the situation in the closed economy, the real interest rate is independent of savings and investment in the small open economy. If investment exceeds savings, the residual is borrowed in the international financial market. If savings exceed investments, the residual will be net lending to foreign countries.

Note that we can also write the above condition as

$$i - i^* = \pi - \pi^*.$$

A country with high inflation, and a depreciating currency, must have a higher *nominal* interest rate to compensate international investors so that the *real* return is the same on loans in different currencies.

Table 13.1 and Fig. 13.1 show inflation and short-term interest rates for a number of countries. The numbers are averages for the period 2005–2010. As predicted by our theory, there is a strong relation between inflation and the nominal interest rate. Higher inflation is generally compensated for by a higher nominal interest rate. The lines show what the nominal interest rates would have to be for the real interest rate to be zero and 3 percent. In most cases, the real interest rate (interest minus inflation) is between zero and 3 percent.

13.2 The current account and the real exchange rate

When we analysed the closed economy in Chapter 4, we found that the *real interest rate* adjusted in the long run so as to bring equality between aggregate demand and the natural level of production. As we have just seen, the long-run level of the real interest rate in the open economy is determined in world financial markets. Thus, it is independent of demand and supply in the small open economy. So how is equality between demand and supply brought about in the open economy?

As we saw in Chapter 12, there is another relative price that affects aggregate demand: the *real exchange rate*. What determines the real exchange rate and what

Table 13.1 *Inflation and short-term interest rates, averages, 2005–2010*

	Inflation	Interest rate	Interest minus inflation
Japan	−0.1	0.4	0.4
Switzerland	0.9	1.3	0.4
Ireland	1.4	2.7	1.3
France	1.5	2.7	1.2
Sweden	1.5	2.1	0.5
Netherlands	1.5	2.7	1.2
Germany	1.6	2.7	1.1
Canada	1.7	2.8	1.1
Portugal	1.7	2.7	1.0
Austria	1.8	2.7	0.9
Finland	1.9	2.7	0.8
Italy	1.9	2.7	0.8
Belgium	2.0	2.7	0.7
Denmark	2.1	2.8	0.7
Luxembourg	2.2	2.7	0.5
United States	2.2	3.1	0.9
Norway	2.3	3.6	1.3
New Zealand	2.8	6.2	3.4
Poland	2.9	4.8	1.9
Czech Republic	2.9	2.5	−0.4
Slovak Republic	2.9	3.0	0.1
Australia	3.0	5.6	2.6
Korea	3.0	4.0	1.0
Greece	3.2	2.7	−0.5
Mexico	4.4	7.0	2.6
Estonia	4.8	4.1	−0.7
Hungary	5.4	7.4	2.0
Iceland	8.3	11.6	3.3
Turkey	8.7	14.9	6.2
India	8.7	6.5	−2.2

Source: *OECD Economic Outlook*, OECD, 13 October 2011, http://www.oecd-ilibrary.org/statistics.

role does it play in bringing balance between demand and supply in the open economy? What is the relation between the current account and the real exchange rate? To analyse these questions, we consider supply and demand in the open economy.

The natural level of production is determined by the production function and available resources, in the same way as in the closed economy:

$$Y^n = F(K, E(1 - u^n)L).$$

Aggregate demand in the open economy is determined by the *IS* equation for the open economy, which we derived in Chapter 12:

$$Y = C\left(Y^d, Y^e - T^e, r^*, A\right) + I\left(r^*, Y^e, K\right) + G + NX\left(\varepsilon, Y^*, Y\right),$$

Fig. 13.1 *Inflation and interest rates, averages, 2005–2010*

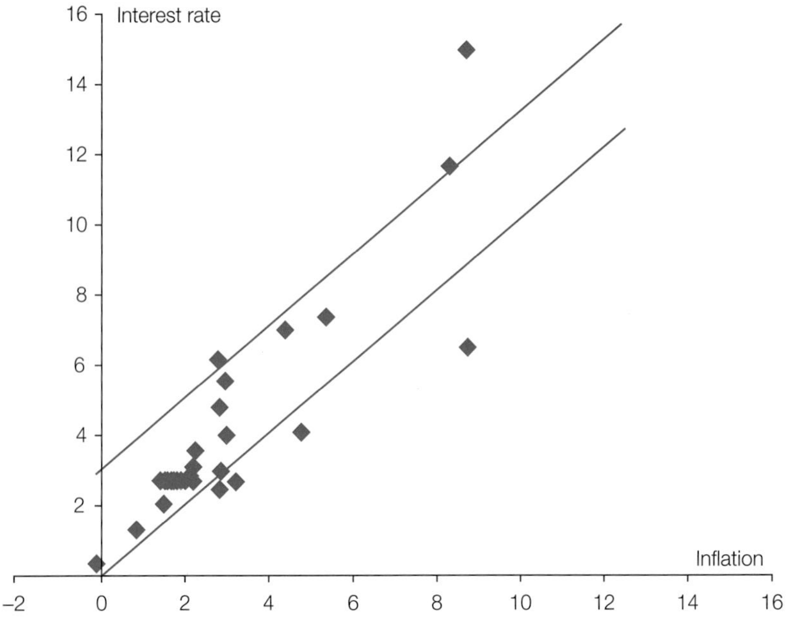

Source: *OECD Economic Outlook*, OECD, 13 October 2011, http://www.oecd-ilibrary.org/statistics.

where $Y^d = Y^n - T + r^* (D + F)$. In line with the result in the previous section we have set $r = r^*$. Since the real interest rate is determined in the world market, it cannot adjust so as to keep production at the natural level. Instead, the real exchange rate must adjust if aggregate demand is to be equal to the natural level of production in the open economy. With the *intertemporal* relative price fixed, the *international* relative price has to adjust so as to equalize supply and demand in the small open economy. For aggregate demand to be equal to the natural level of production, the real exchange rate must adjust so that firms can export the production that is not used for consumption and investment at home.

Let us try to illustrate the determination of the real exchange rate. First note that production that is not used for consumption and investment at home must be exported. For production to be at the natural level, $Y = Y^n$, we must have

$$NX\left(\varepsilon, Y^*, Y^n\right) = Y^n - C\left(Y^d, Y^e - T^e, r^*, A\right) - I\left(r^*, Y^e, K\right) - G.$$

Fig. 13.2 illustrates the determination of net exports. In a closed economy, the real interest rate would be r^a, the *autarky* interest rate. If the world real interest rate is higher than r^a, production exceeds domestic demand and the residual must be exported.

Fig. 13.3 shows the determination of the real exchange rate. In the long run, the real exchange rate must adjust so that the exporters can sell the required amount of exports in the world market. If the real exchange rate is higher, production will be below the natural level.

In fact, the relation between supply and demand for domestic goods and the real exchange rate is similar to the relation between supply and demand for any

Fig. 13.2 *Supply, domestic demand, and net exports*

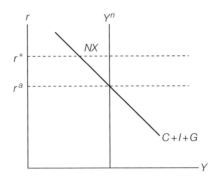

Fig. 13.3 *Net exports and the real exchange rate*

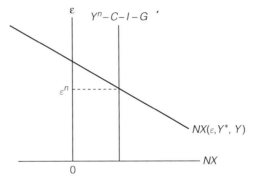

individual good and its relative price. Consider a group of farmers who grow pota-toes. They harvest the potatoes, keep some for their own consumption, and they also keep some to put back in the ground in order to grow potatoes next year. In order to sell the rest, they have to set a price so that the available supply can be sold in the market. If the price of the potatoes is too high, some potatoes will remain in the storage room. Similarly, if goods produced in the small open economy are too expensive relative to foreign goods, there will be high unemployment in the small open economy.

In the closed economy, we defined the *natural rate of interest* as the real rate that is consistent with production being at the natural level. In the open economy, we can analogously define a *natural real exchange rate*, ε'', as the real exchange rate that is consistent with production being at the natural level.

We can use these diagrams to analyse the long-run effect on the real exchange rate of various exogenous shocks. Consider, for example, an increase in invest-ment opportunities, leading to an outward shift in the investment function. This leads to an increase in domestic demand. Since the natural level of production has not changed, net exports must decrease, and this requires an apprecia-tion of the exchange rate. The effect of increased investments is illustrated in Fig. 13.4.

Fig. 13.4 *The effect on net exports and the real exchange rate of an increase in the willingness to invest*

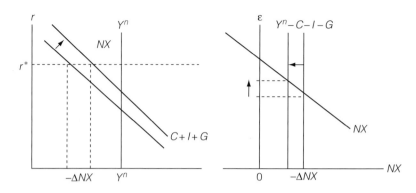

But who sets the real exchange rate? What makes the real exchange rate adjust to shocks? This will depend on the exchange rate system. Recall from Chapter 12 that the real exchange rate is the nominal exchange rate multiplied by the price level in the small open economy and divided by the world price level:

$$\varepsilon = \frac{eP}{P*}.$$

For a given price level abroad, an adjustment of the real exchange rate can be achieved by an adjustment of the price level P, or by a change in the nominal exchange rate, e. Which variable will adjust depends on the exchange rate system. Suppose, as above, that there is an increase in domestic demand:

- If the central bank keeps the nominal *exchange rate fixed*, increased investment will raise demand in the small open economy so that production will exceed the natural level of production. This will lead to inflation in the small open economy and the price level will increase until net exports have declined so much that production is back at the natural level. In this case, the real exchange rate adjustment is achieved via price adjustment.
- With a *floating exchange rate*, the nominal exchange rate will also adjust. To prevent the domestic economy from overheating, the central bank will raise the interest rate, leading to an appreciation of the currency. In this way, some of the adjustment of the real exchange rate may take place via a change in the nominal exchange rate. We will analyse this adjustment process more when we analyse the open economy in the short run in Chapter 14.

The relation between the budget deficit and the current account deficit

Two deficits are often discussed in the media: budget deficits and current account deficits. How are these deficits related? We now have a theory that allows us to answer this question in a precise way.

A budget deficit means that the *government* is borrowing, so net government debt increases. A current account deficit means that the *country* is borrowing, so net foreign debt increases. Clearly, the difference between these is net borrowing of the *private* sector. Expressing the current account in terms of surpluses (net lending) rather than deficits, we have:

$$\Delta F = NX + r^*F = Y^n - C - I - G + r^*F$$

$$= \underbrace{Y^n + r^*(F+D) - T - C(Y^n - T + r^*(F+D), Y^e - T^e, r^*, A) - I(r^*, Y^e, K)}_{\text{private sector net lending}}$$

$$+ \underbrace{T - G - r^*D}_{\substack{\text{government} \\ \text{net lending}}}.$$

An increase in the government deficit may arise because the government reduces taxes or because government expenditure is increased without an increase in taxes. Let us consider each case.

Suppose, first, that the government reduces taxes (T). If government expenditure is unchanged, government net lending falls – that is, the budget deficit increases. To determine the effect on the current account, we must consider what happens to private savings and investment. Since we are analysing the long run, we assume that production is at its natural level and our theory says that private investment will remain unchanged. The key question is what happens to private consumption. Here, the theory of Ricardian equivalence is relevant. We presented this theory in Chapter 11. With *complete* Ricardian equivalence, consumers realize that future taxes will increase, so private consumption remains unchanged. In that case, private saving will increase exactly as much as government saving was reduced by the tax cut and the current account is unaffected by the tax cut. The only result of the tax cut is a shift of national savings from the government to the private sector. The budget deficit and the current account are unrelated.

But, as we discussed in Chapter 11, there are good reasons to expect less than complete Ricardian equivalence. Some consumers will consume more when their disposable income increases, so it is unlikely that private savings increase enough to compensate for the reduction in government savings. Therefore, we would expect the savings of the country to decrease and the current account deficit to increase when taxes are reduced.

What if the increase in the budget deficit is caused by an increase in government consumption while taxes are unchanged? Again, rational consumers will realize that they will have to pay higher taxes in the future, which will reduce consumption. But consumers will not reduce consumption by as much as government consumption has increased.[3] Again, the conclusion is that there will be an increase in the current account deficit.

To sum up, our theory says that the two deficits are related. An increase in the government budget deficit will lead to a larger current account deficit, but the

---

3 Since consumers want smooth consumption over time, they will reduce current consumption less than the increase in current government expenditure if the expenditure increase is perceived as temporary. Therefore, a temporary increase in government consumption will reduce national saving even if consumers are Ricardian.

resulting change in the current account will be smaller than the change in the budget deficit.

So what do the data say? Fig. 13.5 shows government net lending and the current account for five different countries. In some cases, there seems to be a

Fig. 13.5 *Government net lending and the current account*

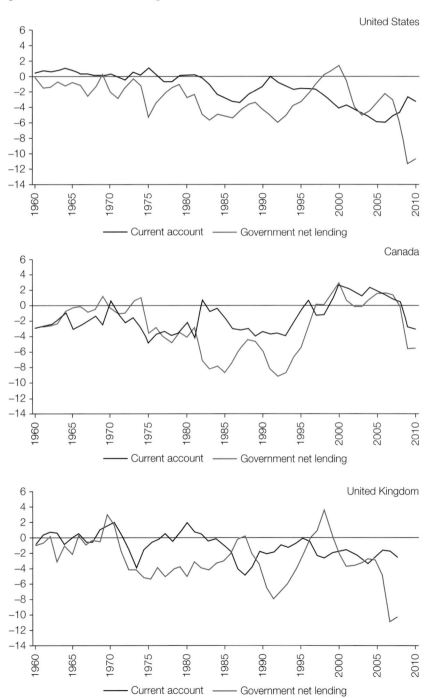

Fig. 13.5 *(Continued)*

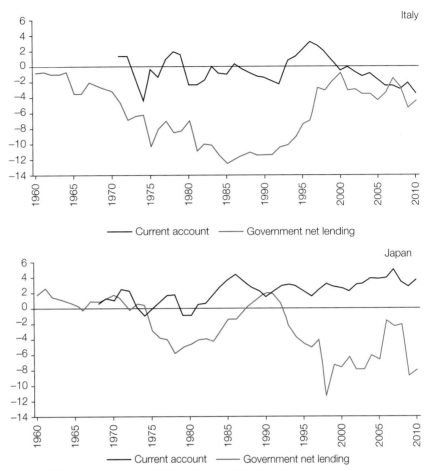

Source: *OECD Economic Outlook*, OECD, 14 October 2011, http://www.oecd-ilibrary.org/statistics.

relation. The high government deficits in the US in the 1980s and after 2001 coincided with large deficits in the current account. On the other hand, the US current account deficit remained in the 1990s although there was a dramatic improvement in government finances. For Canada, there is a clear positive relation between the two deficits. For the other countries, there is not much correlation. Japan and Italy have had large government deficits combined with surplus or balance in the current account. As a result, these countries now have very large stocks of government debt which are mainly held by domestic residents.

Our theoretical conclusion was that, unless there is complete Ricardian equivalence, shocks to taxes and government expenditure will move the two deficits in the same direction. A tax reduction, for example, will increase both deficits. In fact, there is a rather weak relation between the two deficits. How can this be? There are two possible explanations:

1. One interpretation is that Ricardian equivalence is more relevant than we may at first think, that private saving substitutes for government saving. Surely, one reason why Japanese households save so much is the poor shape of government finances in Japan.

2. Another reason is that there are other shocks to private savings and investments that drive the two deficits in opposite directions. Suppose, for example, that there is a boom arising in the private sector so that private investment and consumption both increase. This will increase the tax revenue of the government, so the government deficit decreases. At the same time, demand for imported goods will increase, so the current account deficit increases. In this way, business cycle shocks drive the two deficits in opposite directions, and this may be one reason for the low correlation between the two deficits.

Thus we see that the co-variation between the two deficits will depend on what shocks drive the variation in the data. This makes it hard to find a relation between the deficits. Yet our theory says that, *ceteris paribus* (all else being equal), a bigger government deficit should normally lead to a bigger deficit (or smaller surplus) in the current account.

Does a current account deficit lead to depreciation of the currency?

Sometimes, it is argued that a current account deficit will lead to depreciation of the currency. The US has had a current account deficit for a long time and it has sometimes been argued that this will lead to depreciation of the dollar, yet the dollar has gone up, and down, and up, and down, several times. What does macroeconomic theory say about the relation between the current account and the real exchange rate?

Consider a country where the current account is in balance ($NX = 0$) and there is initially no net foreign debt ($F = 0$). Now assume that, for a period of a few years, domestic consumers spend more, so the savings of the country are reduced, and the country runs a current account deficit. After this period, consumers stop spending and start to pay back their loans from foreign countries, resulting in a current account surplus.

Fig. 13.6 illustrates how this affects net exports and the real exchange rate. Initially, $NX = 0$ and the real exchange rate is ε_0. Now there is an increase in consumption, leading to a decrease in net exports and an appreciation of the

Fig. 13.6 *The effect on the real exchange rate of first spending and then paying back*

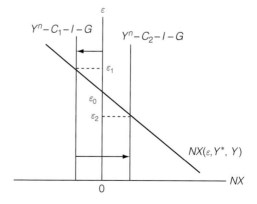

real exchange rate to ε_1. When consumers in the open economy spend more, the demand for domestic goods increases and the relative price of home goods must also increase. We see that the increase in domestic demand leads to a deficit in the current account and an appreciated exchange rate. But at some point, when consumers start to pay back their loans, the country has to increase its net exports, so the relative price of its goods must decrease. Then the real exchange rate depreciates to ε_2.

We see that if there is an increase in domestic demand we may very well see a current account deficit together with an *appreciated* real exchange rate. But when consumers stop borrowing and start to pay back their loans, there will be a real depreciation. Thus we may argue that, if a country runs a large current account deficit, it may come to a point where it has to reduce its borrowing, and then the exchange rate will depreciate. Hence, a big current account deficit may *predict* depreciation at some point in the future. Experience shows, however, that countries can run deficits and surpluses in their current accounts for a long time. It is hard to predict when a spending spree will end, so the depreciation of the real exchange rate is also hard to predict. In practice, exchange rate movements are very difficult to predict.

13.3 Investment and growth in the open economy

In the closed economy, all investment must be financed by saving inside the country. A country with a small capital stock must save a substantial share of its small income in order to build up its capital stock. With an international financial market, the possibility arises to finance investments by borrowing abroad. We now consider capital accumulation and growth in the open economy. As before, we assume that international financial markets are perfectly integrated. This is a simplification, but it is a useful starting point.

With perfectly integrated financial markets, the link between savings and investment is broken because firms and households can borrow abroad, or lend to foreign consumers and firms at a given interest rate. When firms can finance their investments by borrowing at the world real interest rate, the required return on capital is determined in the international capital market. Hence firms will invest until the net marginal revenue product of capital, minus depreciation, equals the world real interest rate. Thus the steady state capital stock per effective worker is determined by

$$\frac{f'(k^*)}{1+\mu} - \delta = r^*,$$

where $k = K/(EN)$. This condition determines the long-run capital stock per effective worker. Given this capital stock per effective worker, production is determined by the production function

$$Y = Y^n = F(K, EN^n) = F\left(\frac{K}{EN^n}, 1\right) EN^n = f(k^*) EN^n.$$

Fig. 13.7 *The required return and the steady state capital stock in the open economy*

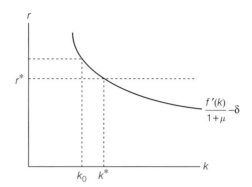

The long-run adjustment of the capital stock is illustrated in Fig. 13.7. If the capital stock is initially lower than k^*, the marginal return on capital is high, and firms will invest until the capital stock reaches k^*. If domestic savings is not sufficient to finance the desired investment, firms will borrow from foreign households to finance the investment until the capital stock reaches the optimal level. During this process, the country may run a current account deficit.

We see that, when financial markets are completely integrated, investment in the small open economy is completely disconnected from national savings. As long as the marginal return on capital is above the world real interest rate, there is no reason not to invest. With truly integrated financial markets, the required real return on investment is the same in all countries.

How quickly does the capital stock adjust? In our simple model, firms in the small open economy could just borrow in international markets so as to immediately equip their workers with the appropriate amount of capital. Taken literally, this would mean that firms in Uganda could borrow to equip their workers with the most modern sophisticated machines and then they would produce on the same level as workers in the US.

In practice, there are a number of factors that slow down this adjustment. Investment takes time and is associated with various costs. As we emphasized in Chapter 5, there are many kinds of capital, which complement each other, and if some types capital are missing, the return on investment in other types of capital will be very low. If the transport system works poorly, if the workers do not have the required education and experience, and there is no law and order, the return from investment in the most modern machines will be very low.

In practice, financial markets are neither completely separate, nor perfectly integrated. Small firms cannot borrow directly in the international financial markets. Capital can be channelled to them indirectly, through banks and investment companies, but this process is limited because of information problems. As we will discuss further in Chapter 18, the financial system is a network of relations based on trust and specific information.

Nonetheless, the main message from this analysis is that a country that has a low capital stock, but a high potential in the form of a well-educated population, can profit from borrowing to finance investments. The resulting current account deficit is not a sign of imbalance; rather, it shows that the international capital market works as it should and that capital is invested where the return is highest. By borrowing to finance its investments, and running a current account deficit, the poor country can increase its production much faster than it could if all the investment had to be financed by domestic savings. Of course, interest must be paid on the loans, but if the return on the investments is higher than the interest payment on the loan, the investment is still profitable for the country.

13.4 The current account and the long-run level of foreign debt

In the previous section we saw that, with perfectly integrated financial markets, the long-run level of the capital stock and production are independent of savings in the small open economy. Savings and investment decisions are 'separated' because investments in excess of savings can be financed by borrowing in the international financial markets at a given real interest rate. Conversely, the country can lend if savings exceed real investments.

So, if savings do not matter for investment in the open economy, what is the role of savings? Does it matter how much we save? The answer is yes, savings are important because savings determine the long-run levels of *income* and *foreign debt* of the country.

As we saw in Chapter 1, income in the open economy differs from production because of *net primary incomes from abroad*. Primary incomes from abroad consist of wage payments for working abroad, interest on loans to foreign households and firms, and returns on real assets abroad. Here, we disregard wage income from abroad and ownership of foreign real assets, so net primary income from abroad consists of net interest income from loans to foreign firms and households. This interest income depends on the stock of loans, so to understand how the long-run level of national *income* is determined, we need to determine the long-run level of net foreign debt.

At a point in time, net financial claims on foreign countries are given, determined by savings and investments decisions in the past. To understand how net claims on foreign countries evolve over time, consider, for simplicity, a small open economy with no growth, and no government debt. Assume that the capital stock and production are at the steady state level. Households have some net claims on foreign households, F. Let us assume that the consumer's subjective rate of discount is equal to the world real interest rate, which is also the real interest rate in the small open economy: $\rho = r = r^*$. Then we know from our analysis of consumption in Chapter 4 that consumption will equal income. The typical consumer will consume her labour income, dividends, and the real interest rate on her loans to firms and foreign households. This means that net claims on foreign households, F, will remain constant. Since assets remain unchanged, national income and consumption will also be constant and the current account is in balance.

4

Suppose that at some point in time, consumers become more impatient, so the subjective discount rate rises above the world real interest rate. What happens then? Since ρ is now higher than r^*, consumers will start to consume more than their income, and decrease their asset holdings over time. The capital stock and production will remain at the steady state level, but net claims on foreigners will decrease. *Domestic production* (GDP) remains unchanged but *national income* falls over time as interest income on foreign assets decreases. (Recall from the national accounts in Chapter 1 that the difference between production and income is net factor income from the rest of the world.) Since consumers in the small open economy continuously consume more than their income, their level of wealth will decrease over time, and so will national income and consumption.

This process is illustrated in Fig. 13.8. Initially, consumer spending is equal to income, and net foreign assets remain unchanged. At time $t = t_0$ consumers become more impatient and consume more than their income, so net foreign assets start to fall.

But where will this end? According to the theory presented here, there will not be a happy ending. Consumption will decrease forever, and debt will increase forever. That consumption will decrease can also be seen from the first-order condition for consumption that we derived in Chapter 4:

$$\frac{u'(C_t)}{u'(C_{t+1})} = \frac{1+r^*}{1+\rho}.$$

If ρ is larger than r^* the right-hand side is smaller than one. For the left-hand side to be smaller than one, $u'(C_{t+1})$ must be larger than $u'(C_t)$. Since the marginal utility is decreasing in consumption, this can only be the case if C_{t+1} is smaller than C_t. The consumer consumes more today than he will be able to consume in

Fig. 13.8 *The long-run effects of impatience*

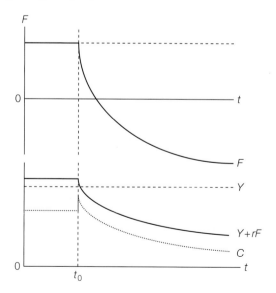

the future. Consumption falls towards zero.[4] Eventually, we end up in a situation with a very high level of foreign debt. This debt will be so high that all the income from production is used to pay interest on the foreign debt. Eventually, national *income* goes to zero and so does consumption. Not a happy ending at all.

Our model has rather extreme and depressing long-run implications. It says that if consumers in the small open economy are just a little bit more impatient than foreign consumers, they will accumulate debt until they become very poor, and use all their labour and dividend income to pay interest on their debts. In practice, the process would not go so far. Lenders would stop lending at an earlier point, worried that the highly indebted households in the small open economy would not be able to pay interest on their loans. Thus we would reach a situation where consumers have high debt and where they use a substantial share of their income to pay interest on the debt.

Our model is extreme, but it points to an important fact. Deficits and surpluses in the current account reflect the willingness and incentives to save and invest and they can persist for a long time. This is also what we have seen in Fig. 13.5. Deficits and surpluses in the current account are typically not temporary imbalances, which are reversed in the following year. Instead, they often persist for a long time. Over time, countries can accumulate substantial claims on, or debts to foreign countries.

13.5 How integrated are world financial markets?

In our analysis of the open economy, we have assumed that international financial markets are perfectly integrated so that households and firms can borrow and lend freely at a given world real interest rate. In practice, most individual households and small firms do not borrow directly in the world financial market. Although banks and other financial institutions act as intermediaries in borrowing between countries, we may wonder how integrated financial markets really are.

One indication of financial integration is the correlation between savings and investment ratios across countries. If there is no international borrowing, investment is equal to savings in each country, so there will be a perfect correlation between savings and investments relative to GDP across countries. If world financial markets are integrated, we expect less correlation between savings and investments. The American economists Martin Feldstein and Charles Horioka investigated the cross-country correlation between savings and investments in the 1960s and early 1970s.[5] They found a very close correlation and this result was interpreted as evidence that world financial markets were not very well integrated at that time. The result is not surprising; in this period, financial capital flows

---

4 If, for example we have the utility function $u(c_t) = \ln(c_t)$, we have $u'(c_t) = 1/c_t$, so if ρ exceeds r^* consumption falls forever towards zero.

5 Martin Feldstein and Charles Horioka, 'Saving and international capital flows', *Economic Journal*, 90 (1980), 314–329.

were heavily regulated and, as we saw in Chapter 12, current account deficits and surpluses were small relative to GDP.

As one would expect, the cross-country correlation between savings and investments is much weaker today. Table 13.2 and Fig. 13.9 show gross savings and gross investment relative to GDP for a number of countries in 2008. We see that savings ratios varied between 2 and 40 percent of GDP, while investment ratios varied between 17 and 32 percent of GDP, and there was only a very weak positive correlation. Clearly, some countries do finance investments by borrowing abroad and others lend excess savings in international financial markets. Interestingly, savings ratios vary much more between countries than do

Table 13.2 *Gross savings and investment, percent of GDP, 2008*

	Saving	Investment	Current account
Iceland	2	25	−22
Greece	4	21	−15
Portugal	11	23	−13
United States	12	18	−5
New Zealand	15	22	−9
United Kingdom	15	17	−2
Ireland	16	22	−6
Hungary	17	24	−7
Italy	18	21	−4
France	19	22	−2
Spain	19	29	−10
Israel	20	19	1
Estonia	21	29	8
Slovak Republic	21	28	−7
Chile	23	25	−2
Canada	23	23	0
Switzerland	24	21	1
Australia	24	28	−5
Czech Republic	24	25	−1
Denmark	25	22	3
Japan	25	24	3
Belgium	25	24	−2
Slovenia	25	32	−7
Finland	25	22	3
Germany	25	18	7
Mexico	25	27	−2
Netherlands	26	21	4
Austria	27	23	3
Sweden	29	20	9
Korea	31	31	0
Norway	40	22	18

Source: *OECD Economic Outlook*, OECD, 18 January 2012, http://www.oecd-ilibrary.org/statistics.

Fig. 13.9 *Savings and investment across countries 2008, percent of GDP*

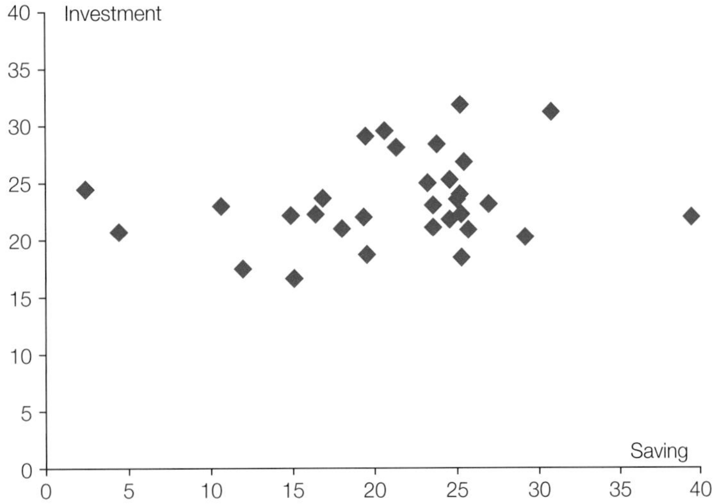

Source: *OECD Economic Outlook*, OECD, 18 January 2012, http://www.oecd-ilibrary.org/statistics.

investment ratios. Apparently, the incentives and/or willingness to save differ substantially between countries. The reasons for these differences are not well understood.

13.6 Should current account balance be an objective of policy?

Current account deficits and surpluses are often described as 'imbalances' that need to be corrected. But should we worry about the current account and should balance in the current account be an objective of economic policy?

In the 1950s and 1960s, most politicians and economists would have answered 'yes' to this question. Capital flows were regulated, so it was difficult to finance a current account deficit in international financial markets. Most countries had fixed exchange rates and could easily run into problems financing a deficit. If there was a current account deficit but no corresponding inflow of private lending, importers would come to the central bank to exchange domestic for foreign currency and the central bank would run down its foreign currency reserves. This could easily lead to an exchange rate crisis and make it impossible to maintain a fixed exchange rate.

Today, most economists take the view that balance in the current account should not be a target for economic policy.[6] International borrowing and lending

---

6 In economics, we always ask the same questions, but students should be aware that the correct answer changes as time goes by. When the author was teaching at Stockholm University in the 1970s, he taught his students that balance in the current account was a central objective of macroeconomic policy.

is no different from borrowing and lending within a country. To say that the current account should always be in balance makes no more sense than saying that a consumer should never borrow or accumulate savings in the bank. Consumers, firms, and governments can have perfectly rational reasons to borrow in some periods and accumulate financial assets in other periods, and the net borrowing of a country is just the sum of the net borrowing by consumers, firms, and the government in that country.

If a country has a low capital stock and a high return on investment, it makes sense to increase the capital stock, and to finance some of this investment by borrowing from other countries. If the return on investment, net of depreciation, is higher than the world real interest rate, firms increase their profits by borrowing and investing and these profits are handed out to the owners as dividends. Moreover, the marginal product of labour and the real wage increase as the capital stock increases. Therefore, the country with a high marginal return on investment can increase its national income by borrowing and investing.

Similarly, it makes sense to lend to other countries if the return on investment is higher abroad than it is at home. Surpluses and deficits in the current account reflect savings and investment decisions by households and firms, and if these decisions are rational there is no reason for the government to interfere. A current account deficit or surplus is not, in itself, a sign that something is wrong.

Of course, savings and investment may not always be on the optimal level from a social point of view. Taxes, pension systems, poorly functioning credit markets, and various market failures may distort the incentives to save and invest. There are very good reasons to discuss market failures and policies that affect the incentives to save and invest, but the point is that the current account is not a good measure of the possible market failures. Rather than focusing on the current account, we should to ask if the markets work properly, if the underlying incentives to save and invest are appropriate, and if government finances are sustainable.

What have we learned?

For a given real exchange rate, the rule of thumb for percentage changes implies that the relative change in the nominal exchange rate is equal to foreign inflation minus domestic inflation:

$$\frac{\Delta e}{e} = \pi^* - \pi.$$

Countries with higher inflation have depreciating exchange rates. Combining this with the interest parity condition $i + \Delta e^e/e = i^*$ and assuming that exchange rate changes are foreseen in the long run we find that

$$r = r^*.$$

In the long run, the real interest rate is determined in the international financial market – independent of savings and investment in the small open economy.

Since the real interest rate is exogenous to the small open economy, the real exchange rate has to adjust if aggregate demand is to be equal to the natural level of production.

In the long run, net exports are equal to the natural level of production minus private consumption, private investment, and government expenditure on goods and services:

$$NX\left(\varepsilon, Y^*, Y^n\right) = Y^n - C\left(Y^d, Y^e - T^e, r^*, A\right) - I\left(r^*, Y^e, K\right) - G.$$

An increase in domestic consumption or investment leads to a decrease in net exports and an appreciation of (increase in) the real exchange rate. With a fixed exchange rate, this will take the form of an increase in the price level. With a floating exchange rate, the nominal exchange rate may adjust instead.

In the long run, the stock of capital per effective worker in the open economy is determined so that the real marginal revenue product minus depreciation is equal to the real interest rate, which is determined in the international financial market:

$$\frac{f'\left(k^*\right)}{1+\mu} - \delta = r^*,$$

where $k = K/(EN)$. This condition determines the long-run capital stock per effective worker. Given this capital stock per effective worker, production is determined by the production function

$$Y = Y^n = F\left(K, EN^n\right) = F\left(\frac{K}{EN^n}, 1\right)EN^n = f\left(k^*\right)EN^n.$$

Gross national *income* is GDP plus net factor income from abroad, which includes the return on net foreign assets.

If consumers in the small open economy have a subjective rate of discount that is higher than the world real interest rate, they will consume more than their income and borrow from foreign households. GDP will remain unchanged but national income will decrease as net interest payments from abroad become negative. Eventually, they will accumulate a large foreign debt and a large part of GDP will be used to pay interest on the foreign debt.

Countries can have current account deficits or surpluses for a long time. A deficit or a surplus in the current account need not in itself be a problem. For a country with a low capital stock, and a high return on investment, it makes sense to increase the capital stock, and to finance some of this investment by borrowing abroad.

In the data there is only a weak correlation between savings and investments relative to GDP across countries. International financial markets seem to be quite well integrated.

Where do we go from here?

Having analysed how the open economy adjusts to shocks in the long run, we now try to understand how the economy responds to shocks in the short run and we analyse the role of fiscal and monetary policy in the open economy. As we will see, the exchange rate system is an important factor that determines how the economy responds to shocks. Also, the roles of monetary and fiscal policy will be very different depending on whether the country has a fixed or a flexible exchange rate.

Exercises

1. In the coming year, inflation is expected to be 3 percent, and foreign inflation is expected to be 2 percent. The foreign interest rate is 4 percent and strong demand is expected to lead to a 2 percent real appreciation of the currency. The open interest parity condition holds. What is the nominal interest rate in the country?

2. What is the effect on the current account and the real exchange rate of the following shocks?
   a) An increase in the world real interest rate
   b) A bad harvest in the small open economy
   c) A shift in export demand away from the goods exported by the small open economy.

3. Financial markets are neither perfectly integrated internationally nor are they completely separated. Which factors may limit international financial integration – that is, lending between countries?

4. How can the following institutions contribute to the integration of financial markets between countries?
   a) Banks
   b) Multinational companies
   c) Pension funds.

5. Savings ratios (savings as a proportion of GDP) vary more between countries than investment ratios. What could cause differences between countries in
   a) savings ratios
   b) investment ratios?

Answers to the Exercises can be found at: **www.palgrave.com/economics/gottfries**.

Appendix

Reasons for long-term trends in real exchange rates

In this chapter we simplified by assuming that the real exchange rate was constant in the long-run equilibrium. This must be the case if there is no real growth, so that all real variables are constant in the long-run equilibrium. Also, it is a reasonable approximation if the small open economy and the rest of the world have similar industrial structures and similar growth trends. In this case their price levels, expressed in same currency, should also follow the same trend. If the wage and price level of a country were to increase continuously compared with similar countries, the export industry in that country would find it impossible to compete in world markets. Thus, our assumption of a constant real exchange rate seems reasonable if we look at countries with similar growth and industrial structures.

If countries have very different growth trends or different industrial structures, there will typically be trends in the real exchange rates between the countries. One factor that generates long-term trends in real exchange rates is the *Balassa–Samuelson effect*, named after economists Bela Balassa and Paul Samuelson who published articles about it in 1964. This mechanism explains why price levels in low income countries are generally lower than price levels in high-income countries (expressed in the same currency) as we saw in Chapter 1. The Balassa–Samuelson effect starts from the observation that all goods and services are not traded. There are non-tradable goods and services such as haircuts or restaurant meals. Unless we live very close to a border, we cannot go to another country to get those goods and services.

To show how the Balassa–Samuelson effect works, assume that there are two types of goods in the small open economy, *traded goods* with price P_T and *non-traded goods* with price P_N. To simplify, we omit capital and we assume that labour productivity is A_T, in the tradable industry and A_N, in the non-tradable industry. This means that the marginal cost in the tradable industry is W/A_T so the price is

$$P_T = (1 + \mu) \frac{W}{A_T}.$$

Although the price of exports from the small open economy can fluctuate relative to the prices of similar goods abroad, they cannot have a completely different price trend. If cars from the small open economy become ever more expensive relative to cars from other countries, exports of cars from the small open economy will eventually fall to zero. Let us therefore assume that, *in the long run*, prices of traded goods produced in the small open economy must be equal to prices of traded goods abroad:

$$P_T = \frac{P_T^*}{e}.$$

Combining these two equations we see that this requires wages in the small open economy to adjust so that the following condition holds:

$$W = \frac{A_T}{1 + \mu} P_T = \frac{A_T}{1 + \mu} \frac{P_T^*}{e}.$$

Wages are determined by productivity in the traded goods sector and the foreign price of traded goods expressed in the domestic currency. For non-tradable goods we have a similar price equation as above, and substituting for the wage we get the price of non-tradable goods:

$$P_N = (1 + \mu) \frac{W}{A_N} = \frac{A_T}{A_N} \frac{P_T^*}{e}.$$

The main difference between rich and poor countries is that labour productivity is many times higher in rich countries. Furthermore, productivity differences are larger in the industry producing traded goods than in some of the industries producing non-traded goods. To cut someone's hair or to cook a meal in a restaurant should take approximately the same time in rich and poor countries. If we assume that A_n is the same in rich and poor countries, while A_T is higher in rich countries, we see that the prices of non-traded goods must be higher in high-income countries.

Let us finally assume that the consumer price index is a (geometric) weighted average of the prices of traded and non-traded goods:

$$P_c = P_T^\theta \cdot P_N^{1-\theta}.$$

Since prices of traded goods are the same (expressed in the same currency) while prices of non-traded goods are higher, the consumer price level is higher in high-income countries. In this way, the Balassa–Samuelson effect helps to explain why the price level is higher in high-income countries. As we discussed in Chapter 1, we need to take account of such price level differences when we compare real incomes between countries.

If a country grows quickly, labour productivity in the traded goods industry increases rapidly, so the consumer price level in that country will increase relative to the price level abroad. Thus we would expect high growth countries to have appreciating real exchange rates as measured by consumer prices. Thus, the Balassa–Samuelson effect is one reason why we see trends in real exchange rates.

There are other reasons why we see trends in real exchange rates. As a country develops it does not just produce more of the same goods. Typically, it starts to produce completely different and much more advanced goods and this means that the price level in the country can increase without negative effects on exports. Ireland had very high growth of exports in the 1990s. If this growth had consisted of more and more production of Irish whisky, the price of Irish whisky would have fallen a lot. Instead, the Irish growth was driven by new industries, especially the computer industry.

We should also note that countries export different products and price trends in world markets are different for different products. This is another reason for long term trends in exchange rates.

The Scandinavian model of inflation

Like most other developed countries, the Scandinavian countries had fixed exchange rates in the 1950s and 1960s. Competitiveness was a major concern in these very small and very open economies and a key question was how much wages could increase without loss of competitiveness and what this implied for inflation. The Norwegian economist Odd Aukrust formulated a model of inflation in a small open economy which is based on the same ideas as the Balassa–Samuelson effect. To derive the key equations of his model, consider the equation for the wage above. Assuming that the nominal exchange rate is fixed and using our rule of thumb we get

$$\frac{\Delta W}{W} = \frac{\Delta P_T^*}{P_T^*} + \frac{\Delta A_T}{A_T}.$$

In order to maintain competitiveness, wages can increase in line with the rate of growth of prices for foreign tradable goods plus productivity growth in the tradable goods industry. The right-hand side determines the 'scope' or the 'main course' for wage increases. When wages increase at this rate, prices of tradable goods will increase in line with prices of foreign tradable goods, so competitiveness is maintained. But how much do prices of non-tradable goods increase?

Applying our rule of thumb to the price equation for non-tradable goods and substituting for the wage increase we get

$$\frac{\Delta P_N}{P_N} = \frac{\Delta W}{W} - \frac{\Delta A_N}{A_N} = \frac{\Delta P_T^*}{P_T^*} + \frac{\Delta A_T}{A_T} - \frac{\Delta A_N}{A_N}.$$

Prices for non-tradable goods will increase in line with foreign price increases for tradable goods plus the difference between price productivity growth in the tradable and the non-tradable industries. Consumer price inflation will then be a weighted average of the price increases for tradable and non-tradable goods.

This model was applied to Sweden by Gösta. Edgren, Karl-Olof. Faxén, and Claes-Erik. Odhner and goes by the name of the EFO model in Sweden. The Aukrust/EFO model can be seen as a theory of inflation in a small open economy with a fixed exchange rate and it fitted the data relatively well before 1970. It has also been interpreted as a norm for how wages should be set in order to maintain competitiveness in a small open economy and this norm has played an important role in wage-bargaining in Scandinavia.

14 THE OPEN ECONOMY IN THE SHORT RUN

What roles do fiscal and monetary policies play under fixed and floating exchange rates?

We now turn to the analysis of the open economy in the short run and the roles of fiscal and monetary policy in the open economy. The exchange rate system sets the framework for macroeconomic policy in the open economy. As we saw in Chapter 12, a fixed exchange rate means that the central bank announces an official target level for the exchange rate and keeps the exchange rate at that level by buying and selling currency. A pure floating exchange rate means that the central bank does not have a target for the exchange rate and that it does not interfere in currency markets. As we will see in this chapter, the roles of fiscal and monetary policy are very different, depending on whether the country has a fixed or a floating exchange rate.

The international exchange rate system has undergone several major changes during the last half-century. Between 1945 and 1971, many countries participated in a fixed exchange rate system called the *Bretton Woods system*, where the exchange rate was tied to the dollar.[1] When the Bretton Woods system broke down, some countries opted for a floating exchange rate while others tried various kinds of fixed exchange rate arrangements. Eventually, in 1999, 11 European countries adopted a common currency, the euro, and others joined later. By 2012, 17 countries had adopted the euro while others, such as the UK, Poland, Switzerland, and Sweden had floating exchange rates.

So which exchange rate system is best? As we will see, the answer is not clear, and different countries have chosen different strategies with respect to the exchange rate. Considering this diversity, and the many changes that have occurred, it is unlikely that current exchange rate arrangements will remain as they are today. Different exchange rate systems have their advantages and disadvantages, and the debate will continue about the advantages and disadvantages of fixed and floating exchange rates, and monetary union.

In this chapter and Chapter 15, we study the role of the exchange rate system and macroeconomic policy in the open economy. In this chapter, we analyse how the open economy functions in the short run under fixed and floating exchange rates. As before, 'short run' means that prices adjust slowly, so we study the macroeconomic equilibrium taking prices as given. As we will see, the central bank is in the driving seat when the exchange rate is flexible. With a fixed exchange

---

1 We will describe this system in more detail in Chapter 15.

rate, the central bank has a much more limited role and fiscal policy becomes very important. This chapter presents the theory. In Chapter 15 we look more closely at the experiences of countries with fixed and flexible exchange rates and of those that have joined the European Monetary Union.

14.1   The Mundell–Fleming model

To analyse macroeconomic policy in the short run, we use the *IS-LM* model for an open economy. It is called the *Mundell–Fleming model* because it was developed by Robert Mundell and Ian Fleming in the early 1960s.[2] To simplify notation, we assume that net claims on foreigners and net government debt are both zero initially, that is, $F = 0$ and $D = 0$. The model consists of three equations, all of which we have seen before:

$$Y = C(Y - T, Y^e - T^e, i - \pi^e, A) + I(i - \pi^e, Y^e, K) + G + NX\left(\frac{eP}{P^*}, Y^*, Y\right), \qquad \textbf{\textit{IS}}$$

$$\frac{M}{P} = \frac{Y}{V(i)}, \qquad \textbf{\textit{LM}}$$

$$1 + i^* = (1 + i)\frac{e^e}{e}. \qquad \textbf{\textit{IP}}$$

The notation is as before: Y is production, T is taxes, Y^e is expected future income from labour and dividends, i is the nominal interest rate, π^e is expected inflation next year, A is asset holdings (wealth), K is the real capital stock, e is the nominal exchange rate (foreign currency per unit of domestic currency), P is the price level of goods produced in the small open economy, P^* is the price level of goods produced abroad, Y^* is foreign production (and income), and M is the money supply.

The open economy goods market equilibrium condition (*IS*) was derived in Chapter 12. Compared with the closed economy, the difference is that net exports have been added on the right-hand side in this equation. Since net exports depend on the real exchange rate, we also need an equation for the exchange rate and this is the interest parity equation (*IP*), which says that the expected return on loans in foreign currency and loans in domestic currency must be equal. This equation was also derived in Chapter 12. The money market equilibrium condition (*LM*) is the same as for the closed economy.

These equilibrium conditions are the same as in the long-run model of the open economy which we analysed in Chapter 13. The difference is that in the short-run analysis we take the price level P, as given. As we saw in Chapter 8, wages and prices adjust slowly and we simplify by taking the price level as given in the short run. With prices fixed, production and employment are determined by aggregate demand and production may deviate from its natural level.

With three equations, there must be three endogenous variables. Production, Y, is endogenous and determined by aggregate demand according to the first

---

2 Robert Mundell received the Nobel Prize in 1999 'for his analysis of monetary and fiscal policy under different exchange rate regimes and his analysis of optimum currency areas'.

equation. Whether the money supply, the interest rate, and the exchange rate should be treated as endogenous depends on the exchange rate system. With a credibly *fixed exchange rate*, *e* is fixed by the central bank and then the *IP* equation says that the interest rate in the small open economy must be the same as abroad: $i = i^*$. As we will see, the central bank is unable to control the money supply when the exchange rate is fixed. This means that we must treat *M* as endogenous when we consider a country with a fixed exchange rate.

If the country has a *floating exchange rate*, the central bank can control the money supply while the exchange rate is endogenous. Then production, the interest rate, and the exchange rate are jointly determined. Alternatively, the central bank can set the interest rate and adjust the money supply so as to satisfy the demand for money at the desired interest rate. This is what central banks do in practice.

Thus, the effect of an exogenous shock depends on whether the central bank holds the exchange rate, the money supply, or the interest rate constant. In the following, we first consider an economy with a fixed exchange rate. Then we analyse the more complicated case of a floating exchange rate.

14.2 A fixed exchange rate

As we saw in Chapter 12, a fixed exchange rate means that the central bank announces an official target level for the exchange rate and declares that it will keep the exchange rate at that level. The target for the exchange rate may be expressed in different ways. It may be expressed in gold as it was during the *gold standard* which was in effect from the 1870s until 1914, or in another currency as was the case during the *Bretton Woods system* which was in force from 1945 to 1971, where most major currencies were tied to the dollar. The exchange rate may also be fixed in terms of a *currency basket* – that is, an index of currencies. In all these cases, the central bank makes a promise to maintain a fixed value of the currency, although the target value is expressed in different ways.

In practice, the central bank cannot keep the value of the currency exactly constant. Instead, the central bank sets a target value, the *central parity*, and promises to keep the exchange rate within a narrow interval around this central parity. In the Bretton Woods system, this interval was ±1 percent.

To make things more complicated, fixed exchange rates are not always fixed. Sometimes the target value (the central parity) is changed. If the target value of the currency is reduced we say that the currency is *devalued*. If it is increased, we say that the currency is *revalued*. Note that the terms *devaluation and revaluation* refer to changes of the target values (parities) in a fixed exchange rate system while the more general terms *depreciation* and *appreciation* refer to the currency decreasing or increasing in value relative to another currency independent of the exchange rate system.

The possibility of devaluation, or revaluation, means that there can be speculation about exchange rate changes even if the exchange rate is fixed. To make things simple, we focus on the case of a *credibly fixed exchange rate*, meaning that there is no expectation of a future devaluation or revaluation. Speculation and exchange rate crises are discussed in Chapter 15.

How does a central bank fix the exchange rate?

In a fixed exchange rate system, the central bank uses *operations in the currency market* to keep the exchange rate close to the target value. This means that the central bank buys and sells domestic money, paying with foreign money. When the value of the home currency declines towards the lower bound of the officially declared interval for the exchange rate, the central bank buys its own currency so as to raise its value, and when the value tends to rise too high, it sells domestic currency so as to reduce its value.

In order to maintain a fixed exchange rate, the central bank needs to have *currency reserves* in the form of foreign currency with which it can buy the domestic currency when it is too weak. A simplified balance sheet for the central bank appears as follows:

Assets	*Debts*
Domestic government securities	*Monetary base*
Foreign currency reserves	

The central bank has two main assets. Domestic government securities are claims on the domestic government such as treasury bills and government bonds. The currency reserve consists of foreign currency and claims on foreign governments, such as US Treasury bills if we consider central banks outside the US. The main debt of the central bank is the monetary base: currency in circulation plus overnight deposits that private banks have in the central bank. In the open economy, the central bank can pursue two types of market operations:

- In *open market operations* the central bank buys and sells domestic government securities, typically in repurchase agreements.
- In *operations in the currency markets,* the central bank buys and sells foreign currency.

When the central bank buys bonds or foreign currency, it pays with money which it creates itself, thereby increasing the monetary base.

One may think that the central bank could use open market operations to control the interest rate and operations in the currency market to fix the exchange rate. With free capital flows this is impossible, however. To understand why, suppose that the exchange rate is on the target level and that the interest rate is equal to the interest rate abroad, but the country is in recession, so the central bank would like to reduce the domestic interest rate. The central bank buys domestic government securities so as to increase the monetary base and reduce the interest rate.

But if the fixed exchange rate is fully credible, this creates an arbitrage opportunity for investors: they can borrow in the small open economy, exchange the money to the currency of the foreign country, and lend it at a higher interest rate without risk. Therefore, international investors will sell large quantities of the currency of the small open economy. Since the central bank has promised to keep the exchange rate fixed it has to buy its own currency to maintain its value, which reduces the monetary base and counteracts the initial effect of its open market operations. The interest rate returns to the initial level. The only result of these operations is that the monetary base remains unchanged and that the central bank has exchanged foreign currency reserves for domestic government securities.

One might argue that the central bank could continue to buy government bonds so as to counteract the effect of the outflow of financial capital and keep the interest rate on the desired level. Such an operation is called *sterilization*. This might be possible if capital flows are not too large, but with free movement of capital, the possibility of profiting from interest rate arbitrage will lead to very large flows of capital and the central bank will run out of foreign currency reserves.[3]

We see that the central bank is unable to control the money supply and the interest rate in a fixed exchange rate system with free capital flows. This is also evident from the interest parity condition:

$$1 + i^* = (1 + i)\frac{e^e}{e}. \qquad\qquad IP$$

When the exchange rate is credibly fixed at some target level $e^{\otimes}$, we have $e = e^e = e^{\otimes}$ so the *IP* equation says that the interest rate has to be the same as abroad:

$$i = i^*.$$

If this condition does not hold, there will be arbitrage opportunities for financial investors.

The conclusion is that, in a small open economy with a fixed exchange rate, the central bank is unable to control the money supply and the interest rate. The only choice concerns the target level of the exchange rate. The fixed exchange rate policy *is* the monetary policy of the small open economy.

Macroeconomic equilibrium with a fixed exchange rate

Since the central bank cannot control the money supply, we treat the money supply as endogenous. It is determined by the demand for money with the interest rate equal to the interest rate abroad. Since we are not interested in the money supply per se, we can forget about the *LM* equation and concentrate on the *IS* equation. Setting $i = i^*$ we have

$$Y = C(Y - T, Y^e - T^e, i^* - \pi^e, A) + I(i^* - \pi^e, Y^e, K) + G + NX(\varepsilon, Y^*, Y) \qquad \textbf{IS}$$

where $\varepsilon = e^{\otimes}P/P^*$. The nominal exchange rate is set by the central bank and prices are taken as given in the short run, so the only endogenous variable in this equation is production. Our open economy model has boiled down to one equation

---

3 If financial investors start to think that the country will devalue its currency, the incentive to borrow in the small open economy and lend abroad becomes even stronger. Exchange rate crises are analysed in Chapter 15.

determining one variable. We can use this equation to examine how the small open economy is affected by exogenous shocks.

Let us examine how changes in fiscal policy and the foreign interest rate affect the small open economy. To see this clearly, we need to specify explicit functions for the different components of aggregate demand. We assume the following simple consumption and investment functions:

$$C = c_0 + c_1(Y - T),$$

$$I = b_0 - b_1 i,$$

where $0 < c_1 < 1$ and $b_1 > 0$. To simplify notation, we assume that consumption depends on disposable income and investment depends on the interest rate, and we omit other exogenous variables that affect consumption and investment. We also assume that taxes minus transfers are determined by

$$T = \tau Y - Tr,$$

where Tr is a fixed transfer. For imports we assume the following function:

$$IM = \varepsilon q Y,$$

where $0 < q < 1$. Note that if the real exchange rate appreciates by one percent, the quantity imported increases one percent, so the price elasticity of imports is unity. As we noted in Chapter 12, this is broadly in line with empirical estimates. Expressed in units of the domestic good, imports are $IM/\varepsilon = qY$ so the parameter q measures how much imports increase when income increases by one unit; it is the marginal propensity to import.

For exports, we assume the following export demand function:

$$X = d\varepsilon^{-\sigma} Y^*$$

where $d > 0$ and $\sigma > 0$. Note that $-\sigma$ is the price elasticity of exports:

$$\frac{dX}{d\varepsilon}\frac{\varepsilon}{X} = -d\sigma \varepsilon^{-\sigma-1} Y^* \frac{\varepsilon}{X} = -\sigma \frac{d\varepsilon^{-\sigma} Y^*}{X} = -\sigma.$$

To determine the equilibrium level of income, we use the goods market equilibrium condition from Chapter 12:

$$Y = C + I + G + X - IM/\varepsilon.$$

Substituting the equations for consumption, investments, exports, imports, and taxes into this equation we get

$$Y = c_0 + c_1 Y - c_1 \tau Y + c_1 Tr + b_0 - b_1 i^* + G + d\varepsilon^{-\sigma} Y^* - qY.$$

To solve for Y, we collect the Y-terms on the left-hand side:

$$Y - (1 - \tau)c_1 Y + qY = c_0 + c_1 Tr + b_0 - b_1 i^* + G + d\varepsilon^{-\sigma} Y^*.$$

Then we rewrite the left-hand side

$$Y(1 - (1 - \tau)c_1 + q) = c_0 + c_1 Tr + b_0 - b_1 i^* + G + d\varepsilon^{-\sigma} Y^*,$$

and divide by $(1 - (1 - \tau)c_1 + q)$ on both sides so we get the solution for Y:

$$Y = \frac{1}{1 - (1 - \tau)c_1 + q} \left[c_0 + c_1 Tr + b_0 - b_1 i^* + G + d\varepsilon^{-\sigma} Y^* \right].$$

This equation tells us how production is determined in the short run when the exchange rate is fixed. We can use it to calculate the effects of changes in exogenous variables on GDP. Consider, for example, a change in government expenditure. Differentiating with respect to G we get

$$\Delta Y = \frac{1}{1 - (1 - \tau) c_1 + q} \Delta G.$$

The increase in government demand leads to higher production and income. As in the closed economy, we have a multiplier effect as consumers spend some of the extra income, which leads to further increases in demand and production. The key difference compared with the closed economy is the presence of q in the denominator. Since this parameter has a positive value, the multiplier is *smaller* in the open economy compared with a closed economy. The reason is that, in the open economy, some of the increase in demand is directed towards imports of foreign goods and this 'leakage' of demand makes the multiplier effect smaller in the open economy.

Suppose, for example, that the marginal propensity to consume is 0.5, the marginal tax is 0.5, and the marginal propensity to import is 0.35, i.e. $c_1 = 0.5$, $\tau = 0.5$ and $q = 0.35$. The effect of government expenditure on GDP is then

$$\Delta Y = \frac{1}{1 - (1 - \tau) c_1 + q} \Delta G = \frac{1}{1 - 0.5 \cdot 0.5 + 0.35} \Delta G = \frac{1}{1.10} \Delta G \approx 0.91 \Delta G.$$

An increase in government expenditure by 1 billion will raise GDP 0.91 billion. In a closed economy, the effect would be 1.33 billion (1/0.75).

What is the effect on the current account of an increase in government consumption? To find out, we use the expression for net exports:

$$NX = d\varepsilon^{-\sigma} Y^* - qY.$$

Thus the effect on net exports is

$$\Delta NX = -q\Delta Y = -\frac{q}{1 - (1 - \tau) c_1 + q} \Delta G.$$

Net exports decrease because imports increase as some of the increase in demand is directed towards foreign goods. With the numbers assumed above, net exports decrease 0.32 billion for a one billion increase in government expenditure.

We see that fiscal policy can affect aggregate demand when the exchange rate is fixed, but part of the increase in demand is directed towards foreign goods, which reduces the multiplier effect compared with the effect that fiscal policy has in the closed economy. We will analyse the multiplier effect in more detail in Chapter 16.

Using the solution for Y above, we can examine the effects of other exogenous shocks on the small open economy. For example, the effect of an increase in the foreign interest rate is given by

$$\Delta Y = \frac{-b_1}{1 - (1 - \tau) c_1 + q} \Delta i^*.$$

If the foreign interest rate increases, the central bank in the small open economy must raise its interest rate, and the effect is a decrease in production and employment. The effect depends on the effect that the interest rate has on investment (b_1) and on the size of the multiplier effect.

The effect of the real exchange rate on aggregate demand

As we discussed in Chapter 12, competitiveness is a major concern in an open economy. If wages and prices are too high relative to the main trade partners firms in the open economy will find it hard to compete in world markets. But how important is this? In order to calculate the effect of the real exchange rate on aggregate demand and production, we use the solution for production, repeated here for convenience:

$$Y = \frac{1}{1 - (1 - \tau)c_1 + q} \left[c_0 + c_1 Tr + b_0 - b_1 i^* + G + d\varepsilon^{-\sigma} Y^* \right].$$

The effect of a change in the real exchange rate on production can be calculated by differentiating:

$$\Delta Y = -\frac{1}{1 - (1 - \tau)c_1 + q} d\sigma\varepsilon^{-\sigma-1} Y^* \Delta\varepsilon.$$

This expression is not very enlightening. To get an expression that is easier to interpret, we multiply by ε/Y so we get the elasticity of aggregate demand with respect to the real exchange rate:

$$\frac{\Delta Y}{\Delta\varepsilon}\frac{\varepsilon}{Y} = -\frac{1}{1 - (1 - \tau)c_1 + q}\sigma\frac{d\varepsilon^{-\sigma}Y^*}{Y} = -\frac{1}{1 - (1 - \tau)c_1 + q}\sigma\frac{X}{Y}.$$

In the last equality we have used the export function $X = d\varepsilon^{-\sigma}Y^*$. Assume as above that $c_1 = 0.5$, $\tau = 0.5$ and $q = 0.35$, that the price elasticity of exports is 2, and that exports are initially 35 percent of GDP. Then we have

$$\frac{\Delta Y}{\Delta\varepsilon}\frac{\varepsilon}{Y} = -\frac{1}{1 - 0.5 \cdot 0.5 + 0.35} \cdot 2 \cdot 0.35 = -0.91 \cdot 2 \cdot 0.35 = -0.64.$$

An increase in the exchange rate by one percent reduces real GDP by 0.64 percentage units. A real appreciation, or depreciation, by ten percent will reduce aggregate demand by about six percent. This is a very substantial effect on aggregate demand and production in a small open economy.

For a less open economy, exports are a smaller share of GDP, but, on the other hand, the multiplier is larger because there is less leakage of demand to imports. Suppose that imports and exports are both 15 percent of GDP while the other parameters are the same as above. Then the effect is half as large:

$$\frac{\Delta Y}{\Delta\varepsilon}\frac{\varepsilon}{Y} = -\frac{1}{1 - 0.5 \cdot 0.5 + 0.15} \cdot 2 \cdot 0.15 = -1.11 \cdot 2 \cdot 0.15 = -0.33.$$

In practice, the effect of a change in the real exchange rate on exports and aggregate demand depends on what time perspective we have in mind. As we discussed in Chapter 12, market shares change slowly when exchange rates change so it will take time for the full effect to materialise. Therefore, the short-run price elasticity is smaller than two. On the other hand, estimates suggest that the long-run price elasticity is larger than two.

Another factor is the degree to which firms let wage changes pass through into export prices. We have assumed that firms set the same price at home and abroad and that they have a fixed mark-up on marginal cost. In practice, firms adjust prices (and mark-ups) depending on the prices of their competitors in the market – so-called 'pricing to market'. This means that an increase in wages and domestic prices by ten percent will be associated with an increase in export prices which is smaller than ten percent. As a result, the effect on exports will also be smaller.

Thus we can find arguments for smaller or larger effects. Nevertheless, the calculations above tell us that changes in competitiveness have very substantial effects on aggregate demand.

Devaluation and revaluation

With a fixed exchange rate and free capital movements, the central bank cannot freely set the interest rate, but one form of monetary policy is possible, and that is to change the target value (the central parity) for the fixed exchange rate. If the domestic economy is in recession, one possibility is to devalue the currency. Since price levels adjust very sluggishly in the short run, a devaluation of the nominal exchange rate will lead to a depreciation of the real exchange rate of similar magnitude.

By reducing the value of its currency, a country can improve its competitiveness and increase demand for goods produced in the home country. Note that this is a short-run effect, however. If production is already at the natural level, demand will exceed the natural level and the result will be inflation. After a while, the gain in competitiveness will be eroded by higher wages and prices and production will return to the natural level. Thus we cannot permanently raise production by devaluing the currency, but if demand is below the natural level, devaluation can help to speed up adjustment of production back to the natural level. Put differently, a devaluation (or revaluation) may be a way to speed up the adjustment of the real exchange rate to its natural level when some real shock has occurred.[4]

So far, we have assumed that the fixed exchange rate was credible, but the *possibility* of a devaluation means that there may be speculation that devaluation will occur. If, for example, a negative shock affects the economy, and this leads to speculation that the country will devalue its currency, international investors will require a higher interest rate to compensate for the devaluation risk. This will force the central bank to set a higher interest rate, which further reduces demand in the small open economy, and this may make it too costly to defend the fixed exchange rate. We will discuss exchange rate crises in Chapter 15.

14.3   Monetary union

From the point of view of a small open economy, membership of a *monetary union* is the same as an irrevocably fixed exchange rate. The exchange rate is fixed at

---

4 As mentioned in Chapter 13, balance in the current account was considered an important objective of macroeconomic policy before the deregulation of capital flows in the 1970s. The British economist James E. Meade analysed the conflicts that can arise between the objectives of full employment and balance of the current account, and how such conflicts could be resolved by the appropriate combination of several policy instruments. The Nobel Prize was awarded jointly to James E. Meade and the Swedish economist Bertil Ohlin in 1977 'for their pathbreaking contribution to the theory of international trade and international capital movements'.

unity with respect to the other members of the monetary union. The interest rate on loans with the same risk of default must be the same as in the rest of the monetary union. Therefore, the analysis above applies also to a small country which is part of a monetary union.

The main difference between a fixed exchange rate and monetary union is that the exchange rate cannot be changed in a monetary union. There is no possibility of devaluing or revaluing the currency. Another difference is that a country that is large relative to the monetary union will have some influence on the common interest rate set by the common central bank. Moreover, a monetary union has other economic effects, such as reduced transaction costs, which should be beneficial for trade. The advantages and disadvantages of monetary union will be discussed more fully in Chapter 15.

14.4 A floating exchange rate

In its purest form, a floating exchange rate means that the central bank does not have any official or unofficial target for the exchange rate and that it does not intervene in the currency markets to influence the value of the currency. The central bank may very well react to the exchange rate but only because the exchange rate affects the ultimate objectives of the central bank, such as price stability. When representatives of the central bank are asked whether they care about the exchange rate, they typically answer something like the following:

> 'We have no target for the exchange rate, but the exchange rate affects the economy, so it is one of the things we consider when we make monetary policy decisions.'

If, for example, the currency depreciates, the central bank may think that there is increased risk of inflation, and raise the interest rate. But then it reacts to the forecast for inflation, not to the exchange rate in itself.

In order to understand the open economy with a floating exchange rate, we need to understand how the exchange rate is determined. Again, we use the interest parity condition:

$$1 + i^* = (1 + i)\, \frac{e^e}{e}. \qquad \textbf{\textit{IP}}$$

With a floating exchange rate, the central bank sets the interest rate, leaving the exchange rate to be determined in the currency market, so we rewrite the interest parity condition with the exchange rate as the dependent variable:

$$e = \frac{1 + i}{1 + i^*} e^e.$$

We see that the exchange rate depends on three variables – the interest rate, the foreign interest rate, and the expected future exchange rate:

- If the interest rate in the small open economy is raised, it becomes more attractive to lend in the small open economy so there is increased demand for the currency and the exchange rate appreciates.[5]
- If the foreign interest rate rises, it becomes less attractive to lend in the small open economy so there is reduced demand for the currency and the exchange rate depreciates.
- If the expected future value of the currency increases, the value of the currency today will increase.

The central bank controls the domestic interest rate and we take the foreign interest rate as exogenous. To make it simple, we also treat the expected future exchange rate as exogenous.[6] This is a crude assumption because the expected future exchange rate depends on expected future shocks and policies and it may very well react to shocks that happen today. We will discuss exchange rate expectations at the end of this section. In the appendix to this chapter we consider an alternative assumption: that the expected future exchange rate is equal to the current exchange rate.

We now have three endogenous variables, Y, i, and e, and three equations:

$$Y = C\,(Y - T, Y^e - T^e, i - \pi^e, A) + I\,(i - \pi^e, Y^e, K) + G + NX\left(\frac{eP}{P^*}, Y^*, Y\right), \quad \textbf{IS}$$

$$\frac{M}{P} = \frac{Y}{V\,(i)}, \quad\quad\quad \textbf{LM}$$

$$e = \frac{1+i}{1+i^*}e^e. \quad\quad\quad \textbf{IP}$$

To reduce this to two equations that we can draw in a diagram, we substitute the interest parity condition in the goods market equilibrium condition to obtain a modified *IS* equation which we call *IS**:

$$Y = C(Y - T, Y^e - T^e, i - \pi^e, A) + I(i - \pi^e, Y^e, K) + G + NX\left(\frac{1+i}{1+i^*}\frac{e^eP}{P^*}, Y^*, Y\right). \quad \textbf{IS*}$$

This equation shows how production is determined for a given interest rate set by the central bank. We see that, in the open economy, a higher interest rate affects aggregate demand through two channels:

---

5 For the interest parity condition to hold, the value of the currency must increase so much that the expected loss from depreciation of the currency is equal to the interest rate differential.
6 This means that changes in the exchange rate, which arise because of exogenous shocks, are perceived as *temporary*. In the appendix to this chapter, we consider the case where the expected future exchange rate equals the current exchange rate, so changes in the exchange rate are perceived as *permanent*.

1. There is a *direct effect* of the interest rate on domestic consumption and investment, which is the same effect as in a closed economy.
2. A higher interest rate leads to appreciation of the currency, which reduces net exports. We can call this the *exchange rate channel*.

The difference between IS and IS* is illustrated in Fig. 14.1. The IS curve is drawn for a fixed exchange rate equal to e^e. The IS^* curve takes account of the fact that the interest rate affects the exchange rate via the IP equation. The IS and IS* curves intersect at the point where $i=i^*$ so that $e=e^e$ according to the interest parity condition. The IS^* curve is flatter than the IS curve because an increase in the interest rate has a bigger effect on production when we take account of the exchange rate channel. The reduction in the interest rate from i^* to i_1 increases production to Y_1 for a given exchange rate but to Y_2 if we take account of the exchange rate channel.

Comparing IS^* with the IS curve for the closed economy, we see that there are three things that are different in the open economy:

- We have more exogenous variables that affect aggregate demand: the expected future exchange rate, e^e, the foreign interest rate i^*, and the foreign level of income, Y^*.
- Some demand is directed towards imports, so net exports fall as income increases, and this makes the multiplier effect smaller in the open economy.
- The interest rate affects aggregate demand both directly and via the exchange rate channel.

The macroeconomic equilibrium is illustrated in Fig. 14.2, which has two quadrants. The quadrant to the right is the usual *IS-LM* diagram, but we now use the IS^* curve instead of IS. In the left quadrant we draw the IP relation with the exchange rate on the horizontal axis. Note that a point further to the left means a higher exchange rate. The IP slopes up to the left because a higher interest rate implies a higher exchange rate – that is, the value of the currency increases.

The model we have just presented is the Mundell–Fleming model of an open economy with a floating exchange rate. It allows us to analyse the effects of many types of shocks on many different variables. To analyse the effects of shocks, and economic policy, we follow the same steps as for the closed economy. Let us consider monetary and fiscal policy.

Fig. 14.1 *The relation between the IS curve for given exchange rate and IS**

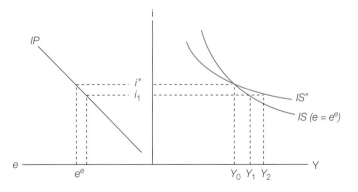

Fig. 14.2 *The Mundell–Fleming model*

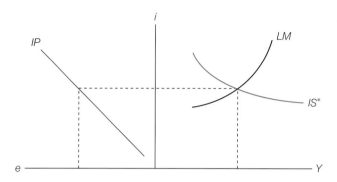

Monetary policy with a floating exchange rate

Consider an increase in the money supply.

1. *Which curves shift and why? LM* that shifts *down* because the interest rate will be lower in the money market for a given level of production.
2. *What is the effect on production, the interest rate, and the exchange rate?* As we see in Fig. 14.3, the interest rate falls, production increases, and the currency depreciates.
3. *What is the economic explanation?* The central bank buys bonds, or lends to banks, so as to increase the money supply and reduce the interest rate. This stimulates consumption and investment. Also, the reduction in the interest rate makes it less attractive to hold the currency, so the currency depreciates, and this stimulates exports. Aggregate demand and production increase and there is a multiplier effect as increased income leads to a further increase in consumption.
4. *What is the effect on other variables?* Since income increases and the interest rate falls, consumption increases, as does investment. The weaker currency stimulates exports but higher demand increases imports, so the effect on net exports is ambiguous.

Fig. 14.3 *The effect of an increase in the money supply in the Mundell–Fleming model*

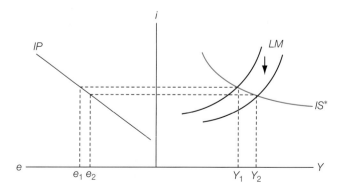

We see that monetary policy is powerful when we have floating exchange rate. It affects not only consumption and investment but also net exports via the exchange rate channel.

Fiscal policy with a constant money supply

Consider an increase in government expenditure, G. As in the closed economy, the effect of fiscal policy depends on whether the central bank holds the money supply or the interest rate fixed. Let us first assume that the money supply is held constant. What is the effect on production and other variables?

1. *Which curves shift and why?* The IS^* curve shifts to the right because higher government expenditure increases demand for a given interest rate.
2. *What is the effect on production, the interest rate, and the exchange rate?* As we see in Fig. 14.4, production increases, the interest rate goes up, and the exchange rate appreciates.
3. *What is the economic explanation?* Since aggregate demand increases, production increases, which leads to higher income and increased consumption. As the volume of transactions increases, demand for money increases, there is a shortage of liquidity, and the interest rate increases. The increase in the interest rate counteracts the increase in aggregate demand because investment is reduced. Also, the higher interest rate makes it more attractive to buy the currency of the small open economy, so the currency appreciates, leading to a reduction in exports.
4. *What is the effect on other variables?* Income increases but the interest rate also increases, so the effect on consumption is ambiguous. The increase in the interest rate has a negative effect on investment. There is also an appreciation of the currency which leads to reduced competitiveness and falling exports. Also, higher income implies higher imports, so net exports will decrease. Expansionary fiscal policy crowds out private investment and net exports.

Fig. 14.4 *The effect of increased government expenditure in the Mundell–Fleming model*

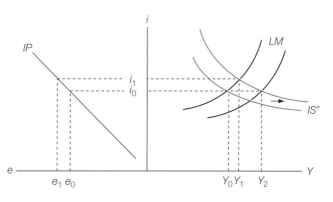

Fiscal policy and the central bank reaction to the shock

The analysis above is based on the assumption that the central bank holds the money supply fixed. As we discussed in Chapter 10, central banks usually set the interest rate rather than the money supply. If the central bank keeps the interest rate unchanged, there need not be any appreciation of the currency, or any crowding out of investments and exports. The effect of fiscal policy will then be similar to what it is when the exchange rate is fixed. In Fig. 14.4, production will increase to Y_1 if the money supply is kept constant but to Y_2 if the interest rate is kept constant.

In practice, though, we would expect the central bank to react to a more expansionary fiscal policy by setting a higher interest rate than it would otherwise have set, so there will be some crowding out of private demand. There will be a negative effect on investment because the interest rate increases and a negative effect on net exports via the exchange rate. Such 'crowding out' of private demand does not occur with a fixed exchange rate since both the interest rate and the exchange rate remain fixed. Because of the crowding out of investment and exports, the effect of fiscal policy on production is smaller with a floating rate compared to the case of a fixed exchange rate.

Exchange rate expectations and the importance of the exchange rate channel

The effect of monetary policy depends on the slope of the *IS** curve. For a given expected future exchange rate e^e, the slope of *IS** depends on how consumption and investment are affected by the interest rate but also on how changes in the exchange rate affect net exports. But how important is the exchange rate channel? To get a rough estimate, note that for a given expected exchange rate next year, the exchange rate is

$$e = \frac{1+i}{1+i^*}e^e. \qquad \qquad \textbf{IP}$$

This equation says that an increase in the interest rate by one percentage unit, e.g. from 0.03 to 0.04, will lead to an increase in the exchange rate of approximately one percent.[7] Since prices change little in the short run, the change in the real exchange rate is of the same magnitude. In the section above about fixed exchange rates, we derived a rough estimate that a one percent appreciation of the real exchange rate leads to a 0.6 percent decrease in production. Hence, an increase in the interest rate by one percent will reduce GDP by roughly 0.6 percent via the exchange rate channel. This is a substantial effect.

This calculation was made assuming that the expected exchange rate next year is unchanged. However, tight monetary policy may very well affect the

---

7 Suppose, for example, that both interest rates are initially 3 percent. Then we have $e = \dfrac{1.03}{1.03}e^e = e^e$.

With an interest rate equal to 4 percent we get $e = \dfrac{1.04}{1.03}e^e \approx 1.01\,e^e$.

expected exchange rate in future periods. A high interest rate today may generate expectations that future monetary policy will also be tight, so inflation will be low in the small open economy. Then, the expected future exchange rate will also increase, and this will lead to a further appreciation of the exchange rate today, and a further decline in demand. Hence, the effect via the exchange rate channel will be even stronger.

We can formalize this by assuming that the expected future exchange rate is an increasing function of the current exchange rate. Then, the interest rate will have a bigger effect on aggregate demand – that is, the IS^* curve will be flatter. In fact, changes in exchange rates are more or less impossible to predict, so the best prediction of next year's exchange rate may very well be the current exchange rate. Suppose we assume that investors expect the exchange rate next year to be the same as this year:

$$e^e = e.$$

This assumption makes the IS^* curve completely flat at $i = i^*$, so production is determined by the intersection of the LM curve with the flat IS^* curve. In this case, we get very extreme conclusions about the roles of monetary and fiscal policy. Monetary policy has powerful effects on aggregate demand but the effect goes via the exchange rate rather than via the interest rate. Any attempt to set an interest rate below the interest rate in the rest of the world leads to a large depreciation of the currency. Fiscal policy, on the other hand, has no effect on production because expansionary fiscal policy leads to an appreciation of the exchange rate and crowding out of net exports that completely counteracts the effect of increased government expenditure. This case is analysed more thoroughly in the appendix to this chapter.

The roles of monetary and fiscal policy under fixed and floating exchange rates

The conclusions concerning the short-run effects of monetary and fiscal policy under fixed and floating exchange rates are summarized in Table 14.1. The conclusions concerning monetary policy are clear:

- With a *fixed exchange rate* there is no monetary policy except the possibility to change the target level (parity) of the exchange rate.
- With a *floating exchange rate*, monetary policy is powerful, working both directly via the interest rate effects on consumption and investment and indirectly via the exchange rate channel.

Table 14.1 *The role of monetary and fiscal policy under fixed and floating exchange rates*

	Fixed exchange rate	Floating exchange rate
Monetary policy	No control over interest rate. Devaluation/revaluation.	Direct effect on C and I and effect via exchange rate channel on NX.
Fiscal policy	No crowding out of I and X, but leakage via imports reduces multiplier effect.	Crowding out of I and NX depends on monetary policy and exchange rate expectations.

What about fiscal policy?

- With a fixed exchange rate fiscal policy is effective although some demand 'leaks' abroad via imports.
- The role of fiscal policy in the case of a floating exchange rate is less clear. There may be 'crowding out' of domestic demand and of net exports, but this is not necessarily the case. The effect of fiscal policy depends on whether the central bank keeps the interest rate or the money supply constant, and on the way exchange rate expectations are formed.

Thus we see that monetary policy can be used only if we have a floating exchange rate, but the picture with respect to fiscal policy is less clear. In practice, countries with floating exchange rates do use fiscal policy. For example, the US and the UK governments pursued expansionary fiscal policies to counteract the effects of the financial crisis in 2008–2009. Apparently, leading economists and policymakers believed that fiscal policy would be effective although these countries had floating exchange rates.

14.5 Long-run adjustment with fixed and floating exchange rates

In the previous section, we analysed the effects of exogenous shocks in the short run, holding prices fixed. Let us now try to relate the analysis of short-run adjustment to the long-run analysis in Chapter 13.

Suppose that production is initially at the natural level. Consumers now become less optimistic about the future, savings increase and the consumption function shifts down. Using again the diagram that we used in Chapter 13, we find that this will lead to a real depreciation. Fig. 14.5 shows the long-run effect on net exports and the real exchange rate. As C falls, $Y^n - C - I - G$ increase, so net exports must increase. The relative price of home goods needs to fall so that domestic goods become cheaper relative to foreign goods and exporters can increase their market shares. Let us now consider how this

Fig. 14.5 *The long-run effect of increased savings propensity on the real exchange rate*

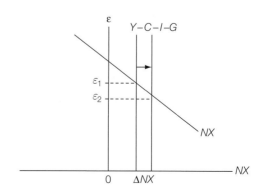

adjustment is achieved depending on whether the country has a fixed or a floating exchange rate.

With a *fixed exchange rate*, production is determined by

$$Y = C(Y - T, Y^e - T^e, i^* - \pi^e, A) + I(i^* - \pi^e, Y^e, K) + G + NX\left(\frac{e^\otimes P}{P^*}, Y^*, Y\right),$$

where $e^\otimes$ is fixed. We start from a situation where domestic inflation is equal to foreign inflation so the real exchange rate remains unchanged. Further, we assume that expected inflation is equal to foreign inflation, π^*. Falling consumption leads to an inward shift in the *IS* curve as illustrated in Fig. 14.6. Production falls to Y_1 in the short run.[8] Since production is now below the natural level, inflation will now be lower than that abroad, and the real exchange rate will decrease. Net exports will increase and the *IS* curve will shift out again until production is back at the natural level. The real depreciation is achieved through a period of low demand and low inflation relative to inflation abroad.

The adjustment with a *floating exchange rate* is illustrated in Fig. 14.7. Again, we have an inward shift in the *IS* curve, which leads to falling output. If the money supply is held constant, there will be a decrease in the interest rate which leads to a decrease in the value of the currency. The lower interest rate and the depreciated exchange rate help to counteract the decrease in production. Nevertheless, there will be a decrease in production if the money supply is kept unchanged. However, the central bank can increase the money supply

Fig. 14.6 *Real exchange rate adjustment with a fixed exchange rate*

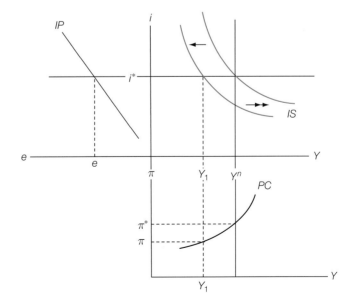

---

8 In the background, the money supply decreases endogenously so the *LM* curve shifts along with the *IS* curve.

Fig. 14.7 *Real exchange rate adjustment with a floating exchange rate*

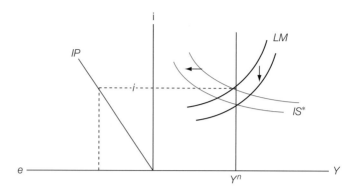

so as to reduce the interest rate further and keep production at the natural level. Depending on how the central bank reacts, the real depreciation is achieved by a combination of nominal depreciation of the exchange rate and lower inflation.

The main conclusion from this analysis is that if the central bank reacts in a sensible way to shocks, a floating exchange rate will act as a *shock absorber* that speeds up the necessary real exchange rate adjustment to shocks, thereby dampening the effects of the shocks on aggregate demand and production. Whether exchange rates do this in practice is another matter, which we will discuss in the next chapter.

14.6   Evidence on the exchange rate channel

A key implication of the above analysis is that, with floating exchange rates, monetary policy affects the economy not only because the interest rate affects investment and consumption, but also because an increase in the interest rate leads to appreciation (increase in value) of the currency which has a negative effect on exports. The empirical effects of monetary policy in open economies have been studied with statistical methods. As in the closed economy, the problem is that monetary policy makers react to what happens in the economy, so it is hard to isolate truly exogenous changes in monetary policy.

Clearly, there is two-way causation between monetary policy and the exchange rate:

- On the one hand, our theory says that an exogenous increase in the interest rate will lead to an immediate appreciation of the exchange rate. A higher interest rate makes it more profitable to lend in the currency of the small open economy so there is increased demand for the currency and the value of the currency is bid up.
- On the other hand, a shock that causes the exchange rate to depreciate will, most likely cause the central bank to increase the interest rate. Suppose, for example, that there is an increase in expected future inflation, causing investors

to believe that the currency will have a lower value in the future. According to the interest parity condition, this will lead to depreciation of the currency already today and, since a weaker currency will raise inflation, the central bank will raise the interest rate.

If there is a monetary policy shock, the interest rate and the exchange rate move in the same direction. If there is a change in expectations, the exchange rate and the interest rate move in opposite directions. Thus we can see a positive or negative correlation between interest rate changes and exchange rate changes depending on which underlying shocks that occur.

Because of this problem, sophisticated statistical methods are used to isolate supposedly exogenous monetary policy shocks and to identify their effects. One approach is to use so-called VAR-models, which we described briefly in Chapter 8.[9] Fig. 14.8 shows the effects of a monetary policy shock in Norway and Sweden according to two such studies. The figure shows the effects on the interest rate, production, employment, and inflation 0, 1, 2, 3, and more quarters after the shock. We see that monetary policy has the expected effects on production and inflation. A one percentage point increase in the interest rate causes a decline in

Fig. 14.8 *Effects of a monetary policy shock on GDP, inflation and the exchange rate*

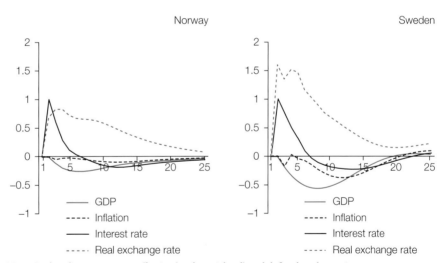

Note: Real exchange rates are effective (trade-weighted) and defined so that an increase represents an increase in the value of the currency. Real GDP and exchange rate are measured in percent, interest rate (three-month) and inflation are measured in percentage points. Periods are quarters.

Sources: Hilde Bjørnland, 'Monetary policy and exchange rate interactions in a small open economy', *Scandinavian Journal of Economics*, 110 (2009), 197–221; and Hilde Bjørnland, 'Monetary policy and exchange rate overshooting: Dornbusch was right after all', *Journal of International Economics*, 79 (2008), 64–77.

---

9 To be precise they are called structural VAR models (SVAR) because economic assumptions are needed in order to identify the effects. The identifying assumption made in the studies reported below is that a monetary policy shock should not affect the real exchange rate, in the long run – i.e. monetary neutrality holds in the long run.

production of 0.2 percent in Norway and 0.6 percent in Sweden and the maximum effect occurs after one and a half to two years. Inflation also declines but only after a long lag. These effects are similar to what we found for the US in Chapter 8 and they support the view that prices adjust slowly, so monetary policy does affect real economic activity.

According to these studies, there are substantial effects of monetary policy shocks on the real exchange rates of these small open economies. A one percentage point increase in the interest rate raises the real exchange rate by about 0.8 percent in Norway and by about 1.5 percent in Sweden. Such a change in the real exchange rate will have a significant effect on net exports. Thus there is evidence that monetary policy works via the exchange rate channel, as predicted by the Mundell-Fleming model.[10]

What have we learned?

The *Mundell–Fleming model* consists of three equations:

$$Y = C(Y-T, Y^e-T^e, i-\pi^e, A) + I(i-\pi^e, Y^e, K) + G + NX\left(\frac{eP}{P^*}, Y^*, Y\right), \qquad \textbf{IS}$$

$$\frac{M}{P} = \frac{Y}{V(i)}, \qquad \textbf{LM}$$

$$1+i^* = (1+i)\,\frac{e^e}{e}. \qquad \textbf{IP}$$

If the exchange rate is *fixed and credible*, the expected change in the exchange rate is zero. Then the interest rate on assets with the same default risk must be the same as abroad. The central bank cannot control the money supply or the interest rate.

Since some part of demand is directed towards foreign goods, the multiplier effect of fiscal policy is reduced compared to the closed economy. Fiscal policy and devaluation/revaluation are the only tools left for stabilization policy.

Membership of a *monetary union* has the same implications for macroeconomic policy in the open economy as an irrevocably fixed exchange rate.

With a *floating exchange rate*, monetary policy affects not only consumption and investment, but also net exports via the exchange rate. Therefore, monetary policy is powerful when a country has a floating exchange rate. If we combine the IS equation and the interest parity condition we get the IS^* equation:

$$Y = C(Y-T, Y^e-T^e, i-\pi^e, A) + I(i-\pi^e, Y^e, K) + G + NX\left(\frac{1+i}{1+i^*}\,\frac{e^eP}{P^*}, Y^*, Y\right), \qquad \textbf{IS}^*$$

The IS^* curve is more flat than the IS curve because it incorporates the effect of the interest rate via the exchange rate channel.

---

10 The results vary between studies, however, and they are sensitive to the exact specification of the VAR model.

If the money supply is kept unchanged, fiscal policy is less effective because there is crowding out of net exports via the exchange rate. The effect of fiscal policy depends on whether the central bank keeps the interest rate or the money supply unchanged.

A persistent demand shock requires adjustment of the real exchange rate. With a fixed exchange rate, this adjustment will be achieved through *inflation or deflation*. With a floating exchange rate, the adjustment can be eased by an adjustment of the nominal exchange rate.

Provided that the central bank acts in a reasonable way, the exchange rate will move in such a way as to counteract shocks to aggregate demand. A floating exchange will work as a shock absorber according to the Mundell–Fleming model. Since inflation depends on the output gap, exchange rate movements will also help to avoid inflationary pressures and deflation in the small open economy.

Where do we go from here?

We have completed our macroeconomic model of the open economy. In Chapter 15 we use this model to analyse the experiences with alternative exchange rate systems and monetary union.

Exercises

1. We have a small open economy with a credibly fixed exchange rate, or a member of a monetary union. The economy is described by the equations below:

$$Y = C + I + G + X - C^f/\varepsilon \quad \text{market equilibrium}$$
$$C = 3 + 0.60\,(Y - T) \quad \text{consumption function}$$
$$T = 0.5Y - 20 \quad \text{tax schedule}$$
$$C^f = 0.25\varepsilon Y \quad \text{import function}$$
$$X = (0.9 - 0.6\varepsilon)\,Y^* \quad \text{export function}$$

a) How large is the marginal tax? Draw the tax function graphically. (*Hint: What will T be if Y = 0? At what income will the tax be zero?*)

b) What is the price elasticity of imports, that is $\dfrac{dC^f}{d\varepsilon}\dfrac{\varepsilon}{C^f}$?

c) Find an expression for the price elasticity of exports $\dfrac{dX}{d\varepsilon}\dfrac{\varepsilon}{X}$. Evaluate what the elasticity is when $\varepsilon = 1$.

d) Write down the equation for net exports. How do Y, Y^*, and ε affect net exports? (We assume that exports are initially positive.)

e) Solve for production as a function of I, G, Y^* and ε.

f) Calculate the increase in production if investment increases by ΔI. The multiplier is close to unity. Why?

g) Assume that $I = 20$, $G = 30$, $\varepsilon = 1$ and $Y^* = 100$. Calculate the level of production.

h) Suppose that there is a financial collapse and investment falls by 20 percent, from 20 to 16. Calculate the new level of production and compare with the answer above. How much does GDP decrease in percent? Explain the result.

i) We assume that the government net debt is zero. Calculate the budget deficit before and after the decrease in investment. Does the country pass the rule of the stability and growth pact that $G - T + iD$ should be a maximum 3 percent of GDP after the shock?

j) Suppose that production was initially at the natural level $Y = Y^n = 100$. If investment remains on the lower level after the shock, how can the economy adjust to the shock so that production returns to the natural level?

k) What change in the real exchange rate is required to bring production back to the natural level? (*Hint: Use the solution for production above to find the real exchange rate that is consistent with production being at the natural level.*)

2. Consider an economy with a floating exchange rate. The interest parity condition says that a foreign investor must have the same expected return if she lends in foreign currency or the currency of the small open economy:

$$1 + i_t^* = \frac{1}{e_t} (1 + i_t) e_{t+1}^e.$$

a) Explain this condition.

b) Solve the interest parity condition for the current exchange rate e_t and explain the relation between the interest rate and the exchange rate.

c) We take the time period to be one year. Assume that $e_{t+1}^e = 2$ and $i^* = 0.05$. Use the interest parity condition to calculate the current exchange rate if the interest rate in the small open economy is 4, 5, and 6 percent. Fill in the second column in the table below. You can round to three decimals. Plot the relation between the interest rate and the exchange rate with the interest rate on the vertical axis.

	$e_{t+1}^e = 2.00$	$e_{t+1}^e = 2.20$
$i = 0.04$		
$i = 0.05$		
$i = 0.06$		

d) Suppose that the expected future exchange rate rises to $e_{t+1}^e = 2.20$. Fill in the last column in the table below. Plot the new relation between the interest rate and the exchange rate with the interest rate on the vertical axis. Explain the difference between the graphs.

e) In what direction will the graph shift if the foreign interest rate increases? Why?

3. Consider a small open economy with a floating exchange rate. To simplify notation, we assume that net government and foreign debt are both zero. We take the expected future exchange rate, e_{t+1}^e, as given (exogenous). The following relations describe the economy:

$$Y = C \left(Y^d, Y^e - T^e, i - \pi^e, A \right)$$
$$+ I \left(i - \pi^e, Y^e, K \right)$$
$$+ G + NX \left(\frac{1+i}{1+i^*} \frac{e_{t+1}^e P}{P^*}, Y^*, Y \right) \qquad IS^*$$

$$\frac{M}{P} = \frac{Y}{V(i)} \qquad LM$$

$$e = \frac{1+i}{1+i^*} e_{t+1}^e. \qquad IP$$

Suppose that foreign consumers become more optimistic, and the foreign central bank raises the interest rate so as to keep foreign production at the natural level $Y^* = Y^{*n}$. There is no corresponding demand shock in the small open economy. Let us now analyse how Y, i, e, C, I, and NX are affected *if the foreign interest rate increases*. We initially assume that the central bank keeps the money supply constant.

a) Draw the IS^*, LM, and IP curves. Which curves shift and why?

b) Use the diagram to determine the effects on Y, i, and e.

c) Explain in economic terms what happens in the currency, goods, and money markets.

d) How will C, I, and NX be affected?

e) Suppose that, instead of keeping the money supply constant, that the central bank keeps the interest rate unchanged, and adjusts money supply to satisfy demand. Will the effect on the exchange rate and production be larger or smaller compared to the case when the money supply is kept constant? Why?

f) Suppose that production was initially at the natural level $Y = Y^n$ and that inflation was in line with the target. What should the central bank do with the interest rate when the foreign interest rate increases?

g) Suppose that the ECB raises its interest rate. How does this affect the likelihood that the Bank of Norway raises its interest rate at the next board meeting? Why?

4. Again we consider a small open economy with a floating exchange rate. We assume that the central bank sets the interest rate so we do not need the *LM* curve.

$$Y = C\left(Y^d, Y^e - T^e, i - \pi^e, A\right)$$
$$+ I\left(i - \pi^e, Y^e, K\right)$$
$$+ G + NX\left(\frac{1+i}{1+i^*}e^e_{t+1}, Y^*, Y\right) \quad \textit{IS}^*$$

$$e = \frac{1+i}{1+i^*}e^e_{t+1}. \quad \textit{IP}$$

Assume that a member of the board of the central bank suddenly decides to leave and a new board member is appointed. The new board member is known to be very 'hawkish' compared with the previous board member, who was a real 'dove'. The financial markets become convinced that future monetary policy will be less expansionary. This means that future inflation will be lower than previously expected.

The new board has not yet taken any decisions and the interest rate is kept unchanged. The question is how the economy will be affected by the *news* that there is a new board member.

a) How will this news affect expected future inflation and the expected future exchange rate?

b) Draw the *IS** and *IP* curves and show how they shift because of the news.

c) What happens to the exchange rate and production?

d) Explain in economic terms what happens in the currency and goods markets.

e) Suppose that production was initially at the natural level and that the majority of the board wants to keep production on this level. What will the central bank do with the interest rate? Explain why.

5. A country has a floating exchange rate. Suppose that there is a discovery of oil or some other natural resource in a country. This will increase future incomes in the country and investments need to be made to extract the resource. Compare the following policy responses:

a) an increase in taxes

b) a reduction in government expenditure

c) an increase in the interest rate.

Which, in your view, is the best way to deal with the shock?

Answers to the exercises can be found at: **www.palgrave.com/economics/gottfries**.

Appendix

The case when the expected future exchange rate is equal to the current exchange rate

In the main text we took the expected future exchange rate as exogenous and unaffected by the shocks that we analysed. Effectively, this meant that any changes in the exchange rate were perceived as *temporary*. This was a simplification since the expected future exchange rate will change with changing expectations about future shocks and policy. In practice, changes in exchange rates are extremely hard to predict, so an equally plausible assumption may be that investors expect the exchange rate to remain on the current level:

$$e^e = e.$$

This means that all changes in the exchange rate are perceived as *permanent*. In this case, we see immediately from the interest parity condition

$$1 + i^* = (1 + i)\frac{e^e}{e} \qquad \textbf{IP}$$

that the interest rate must be the same as abroad:

$$i = i^*.$$

This is just the same condition that we had for the fixed exchange rate case, but there is a very important difference. With a fixed exchange rate, the exchange rate is determined by the central bank and the money supply is endogenous. With a floating exchange rate, the money supply is controlled by the central bank and the exchange rate is endogenous. As soon as the domestic interest rate rises above the international level, the exchange rate appreciates and production falls. Production and the exchange rate are determined by the following *IS* and *LM* equations:

$$Y = C(Y - T, Y^e - T^e, i^* - \pi^e, A) + I(i^* - \pi^e, Y^e, K) + G + NX\left(\frac{eP}{P^*}, Y^*, Y\right) \qquad \textbf{IS*}$$

$$\frac{M}{P} = \frac{Y}{V(i^*)}. \qquad \textbf{LM}$$

Note that since *M*, *P*, and i^* are exogenous, production is determined by the position of the *LM* curve. In terms of our diagram, the *IS** curve becomes completely flat. The reason is that as soon as the interest rate tends to increase above the world level, the currency appreciates, and production falls.

The effect of an increase in government expenditure is illustrated in Fig. 14.9. The increase in *G* shifts out the *IS* curve (without an asterisk), that is, demand increases at the original exchange rate, but the currency appreciates, so *IS* shifts to the left until production is back at its original level (Y_0). Fiscal policy is completely ineffective.

Similarly, an increase in savings shifts the *IS* curve inwards, but the exchange rate falls immediately, leading to increased exports and returning production to its original level. All the adjustment to the shock is done via the nominal exchange rate even if there is no change in the money supply and production remains at the natural level. Real demand shocks are completely absorbed by movements in the exchange rate.

In this case, monetary policy, which shifts the *LM* curve, has a big effect on production, and the effect works entirely via the exchange rate. Any attempt to reduce the domestic interest rate below the international level leads to a large depreciation of the exchange rate and increased net exports.

Fig. 14.9 *The effect of increased government expenditure in the Mundell–Fleming model when $e_{t+1}^e = e_t$*

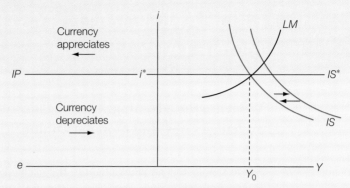

Source: Hilde Bjørnland, 'Monetary policy and exchange rate interactions in a small open economy', *Scandinavian Journal of Economics*, 110 (2009), 197–221, and Hilde Bjørnland, 'Monetary policy and exchange rate overshooting: Dornbusch was right after all', *Journal of International Economics*, 79 (2008), 64–77.

EXCHANGE RATE SYSTEMS AND MONETARY UNION

What are the advantages and disadvantages of fixed and floating exchange rates, and monetary union?

As we saw in the previous chapter, the exchange rate system sets the stage for macroeconomic policy. But what is the most preferable exchange rate system? This question is far from settled. There is a striking diversity in the way countries have dealt with the question of the exchange rate. Some countries have floating exchange rates, others have a common currency, and a few have a fixed exchange rate.

In this chapter we review the history of the exchange rate system and experiences with fixed and floating exchange rates. We also present the main arguments for and against monetary union and the fiscal framework in the European Monetary Union (EMU). At the end of the chapter, we review developments within the EMU.

15.1   Fixed exchange rate systems

The history of the exchange rate system is long and complicated, and characterized by trial and error. Many different approaches have been tried.[1]

The gold standard

From the 1870s until 1914 most major currencies were on the *gold standard*, which meant that the currencies were convertible to gold at fixed prices. The participating central banks had *gold reserves* and promised to buy and sell gold at a fixed price. Since the different currencies had fixed prices in gold, the values of the different currencies were fixed relative to each other. Hence, it was a fixed exchange rate system.

As in any fixed exchange rate system, the gold standard determined the monetary policy of the participating countries. If a central bank printed too much money, pushing the interest rate below the level abroad, there was an outflow of financial capital. Investors would exchange the currency for gold in order to buy

---

1 For more thorough reviews than the one provided here, see Paul Krugman and Maurice Obstfeld, *International Economics Theory and Policy* (Boston: Pearson, 2009), and Barry Eichengreen, *Globalizing Capital: A History of the International Monetary System* (Princeton: Princeton University Press, 1996).

another currency. As people exchanged money for gold, the money supply would decrease, counteracting the initial increase in the money supply.

In the short run, the central bank could continue to print money so as to keep the money supply unchanged. Such an operation was called *sterilization* because the effect on the money supply of the capital outflow was counteracted (sterilized). But as time went by, the gold reserves of the central bank would be depleted and eventually the bank would become unable to keep the interest rate below the level abroad.

Thus, the gold standard imposed strict limits on the monetary policy of the participating central banks. Monetary policy was geared to exchange rate stability and could not be used to stabilize production or employment. The period of the gold standard was a period with low average inflation, stable exchange rates, and high economic growth, but there were rather large fluctuations in production and prices from year to year and unemployment was relatively high. Capital flows were relatively free in this period, and countries had substantial surpluses and deficits in their current accounts. Britain was a big exporter of capital, with a current account surplus around 5 percent of GDP.

When the First World War broke out in 1914, many countries financed their war expenditure by increasing the money supply, inflation increased, and it became impossible to maintain a stable price of gold. Most countries had to leave the gold standard.

After the war had ended, price levels were higher than they had been before the war. Despite this, several major countries decided to return to the gold standard.[2] As a result, the price levels had to come down and this led to deflation and high unemployment in the early 1920s.

When the Great Depression started in 1929, most major economies were on the gold standard, which prevented them from pursuing expansionary monetary policy to counter the depression. Instead, some countries were forced to raise interest rates so as to defend their gold stocks. Britain left the gold standard in 1931, but several countries adhered to the gold standard until 1936. One result of the depression was that countries tried to protect their own industries by raising trade barriers and regulating capital flows. This exacerbated the problems in other countries and contributed to further deepening of the worldwide depression in the 1930s.

The Bretton Woods system

Towards the end of the Second World War, representatives from a number of countries came together in Bretton Woods in New Hampshire, US. The participants wanted to encourage free trade between their countries and they were convinced that unstable exchange rates would have negative effects on trade. They

---

2 In fact, this was a new version of the gold standard called the *gold exchange standard*. As opposed to the classic gold standard, where all central banks had to be ready to exchange their currency for gold, smaller countries could now guarantee the value in terms of a major currency instead. Major currencies were still on the gold standard. This was similar to the Bretton Woods system (see below) where currencies had a fixed value in dollars and dollars had a fixed value in gold.

agreed to set up a system of fixed exchange rates, which came to be called the *Bretton Woods system*. In this system, most major currencies had a fixed exchange rate relative to the dollar. Each currency had a target value, which was called the *central parity*, with respect to the dollar and each participating central bank was obliged to keep the value of the currency within an interval of ± 1 percent compared with the central parity by buying and selling dollars. Furthermore, the dollar could be exchanged for gold at a fixed value of 35 dollars per ounce. In this way, the currencies of all the participating countries were indirectly tied to gold.[3]

The Bretton Woods system was in effect from 1946 to 1971. It was similar to the gold standard in that all currencies effectively had a fixed value in gold, but one difference was that all currencies were not directly convertible to gold. Central banks needed fewer gold reserves since they could hold dollar reserves instead. In theory, the dollar was 'as good as gold' or even better since American Treasury bills yield interest. As a result, the dollar became the primary reserve currency.

Financial capital flows had become heavily regulated in the 1930s and these regulations remained after the Second World War. The regulations made it hard for countries to finance large current account deficits. If there was a deficit in the current account, importers would buy more foreign currency from the central bank than exporters would sell to it, and there was a risk that the currency reserves of the central bank would run out. The creators of the Bretton Woods system foresaw that countries could run into difficulties. The *International Monetary Fund* (*IMF*) was created at the same time and endowed with contributions from the participating countries. The IMF could lend money to countries which had current account deficits so as to give them time to sort out their problems. Such loans were to be paid back within five years. A country with a 'fundamental disequilibrium' could be allowed to devalue – that is, to reduce the value of its currency – but only after approval by the IMF. Exactly what a 'fundamental disequilibrium' meant was never precisely defined, however.

After some adjustments in the 1940s, the exchange rates between most currencies remained fixed through the 1950s and 1960s. This was a period of low inflation and high and stable economic growth. Towards the end of the 1960s there were increasing imbalances, however, and some exchange rate adjustments were made. After a period of speculation, the British pound was devalued in 1967. The franc was devalued in 1969 and the German mark was revalued the same year – that is, its value was raised.

Eventually, the Bretton Woods system was brought down by developments in the US. The US was supposed to keep the value of the dollar fixed relative to gold, but monetary and fiscal policies in the US led to inflation, which rose to 4–5 percent by the end of the 1960s. Obviously, this inflation also increased the market price of gold, so it became profitable to buy gold from the Federal Reserve at 35 dollars per ounce and sell it in the private market. There were attempts to prevent

---

3 For a collection of essays on the gold standard, see Tamim Bayoumi, Barry Eichengreen, and Mark Taylor, *Economic Perspectives on the Classical Gold Standard* (New York: Cambridge University Press, 1996).

such trade by separating 'reserve gold' from the gold that was traded in the private market, but such a system was hard to maintain. The gold reserves of the Federal Reserve were depleted and eventually it became impossible to keep the gold price fixed. In 1971, the USA unilaterally declared that the dollar was no longer convertible to gold. This marked the end of the Bretton Woods system. After some attempts to save the fixed exchange rate system, the dollar became a floating currency in 1973, and it has been floating since then.

The EMS, the ERM, currency baskets, and target zones

When the Bretton Woods system broke down, most of the countries in the *European Economic Community* (the predecessor of the European Union) agreed to maintain stable exchange rates between them, but with somewhat wider bands of ± 2.25 percent around the central parities. Inflation increased, however, and diverging inflation rates led to several adjustments of the parities. Expectations about devaluation or revaluation led to substantial interest rate differentials between these countries (see Fig. 12.6).

After a rather chaotic period in the 1970s, monetary cooperation between the European countries was strengthened in the *European Monetary System* (*EMS*) that was created in 1979. The key element in the EMS was the *European Exchange Rate Mechanism* (*ERM*) which stipulated that all participating central banks should keep the exchange rates with respect to the other currencies in the system within narrow bounds by buying and selling currencies. Most of the countries that participated in the ERM are now members of the European Monetary Union. Denmark remains in the ERM, however, with a currency of its own, and a fixed exchange rate with respect to the euro. The ERM also serves as a 'waiting room' for aspiring euro members: countries which plan to adopt the euro must first tie their currencies to the euro by participating in the ERM.[4]

Some countries have instead chosen to maintain fixed exchange rates relative to a *currency basket* – that is, an index of foreign currencies, where the weights in the index reflect the importance of different currencies in the foreign trade of the country. Sweden implemented such an exchange rate policy in the 1980s, but went to a floating exchange rate in 1992.

Sometimes, countries have broader bands for the exchange rate, called *target zones*. A target zone means that the exchange rate is kept within a band of ± 15 percent, for example, relative to some target value. Target zones are somewhere between fixed and floating exchange rates, but from the point of view of monetary policy, they are best seen as a form of fixed exchange rate. When the central bank has a band for the exchange rate, the main objective of monetary policy is to keep the exchange rate within the band, and this prevents the central bank from using monetary policy to achieve other objectives.

---

4 For reviews of how the EMS worked in the 1980s see Francesco Giavazzi and Alberto Giovannini, *Limiting Exchange Rate Flexibility: The European Monetary System* (Cambridge, MA: The MIT Press, 1989).

Speculation, exchange rate crises, and devaluation cycles

As mentioned above, fixed exchange rates are not always fixed. A fixed exchange rate means that the central bank has a target value (parity) for the exchange rate, but this target value may be changed. As we saw in our analysis of the open economy in the long run in Chapter 13, weak domestic demand means that a real depreciation is needed and a devaluation of the currency is one way to achieve this. A devaluation is a quicker way to improve competitiveness, and increase exports and aggregate demand than to go through a period of recession and low inflation, or even deflation. Sometimes countries have used this option as a way out of recession.

Thus, devaluation may be seen as a good way to deal with a serious imbalance, but there is another side of the coin. The *possibility* of devaluation means that there may be *speculation* in the financial markets about a future change in the exchange rate. Even if the central bank has declared that the exchange rate will not be changed, the fixed exchange rate may not be credible. If a country goes into a deep recession this may lead to speculation that the country will devalue its currency. If investors (lenders) think that there is a risk that a country will devalue its currency, the expected return on loans in that currency is reduced, so, in order to defend the fixed exchange rate, the central bank must raise the interest rate. We can see this from the approximate interest parity condition, which says that the interest rate must be set so that the expected return is the same on loans at home and abroad:

$$i_t + \frac{\Delta e^e_{t+1}}{e_t} = i^*_t.$$

Suppose, for example, that financial investors think that there is a 10 percent probability that the currency will be devalued by 20 percent within the coming year. Then the interest parity condition says that

$$i_t - i^*_t = -\frac{\Delta e^e_{t+1}}{e_t} = -0.10 \cdot (-0.20) = 0.02.$$

To defend the exchange rate, the central bank has to set an interest rate that is 2 percentage units higher than the foreign interest rate. But a high interest rate will push the country further into recession, which will add to the speculation that the currency will eventually be devalued.

This situation is illustrated in Fig. 15.1. Initially, the exchange rate is on the target level, denoted $e^\otimes$, production is on the natural level, and since the exchange rate is credible, the interest rate in the small open economy is the same as abroad. Now suppose that a negative demand shock hits the economy, so the *IS* curve shifts inwards. If the fixed exchange rate is credible, the interest rate can be kept unchanged, and production will fall to Y_1. But suppose that the weak economic situation leads to speculation that the currency will be devalued in the future. This reduces the expected future exchange rate to e^e_{+1} and shifts the *IP* curve inwards: if the interest rate is kept unchanged, the currency will depreciate to e^e_{+1}. In order to keep the exchange rate on the target level, the interest rate must be raised to i_1,

Fig. 15.1 *Recession and speculation against a currency*

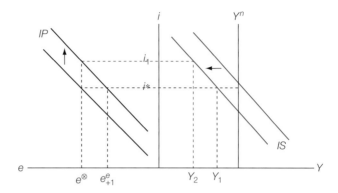

which leads to a further decrease in production to Y_2. Speculation about a possible devaluation forces the central bank to raise the interest rate, and this makes the macroeconomic imbalance even worse.

Speculation against a currency creates a serious dilemma for the central bank. In some cases, it may be possible to defend the exchange rate, but if the economy is in very bad shape, it becomes too costly to defend the exchange rate and the central bank is forced to devalue the currency. *Currency crises* involving speculation against currencies with officially fixed exchange rates have occurred many times, and they have often ended with a devaluation.

In several countries, attempts to maintain a fixed exchange rate have led to *devaluation cycles*. Such cycles occur when the exchange rate is officially fixed, but the country fails to bring down inflation to the level in the countries to which it has tied its currency. With higher inflation, the competitiveness of the export industry is gradually undermined and this leads, sooner or later, to an exchange rate crisis, which forces the country to devalue its currency. The devaluation restores competitiveness for a while, but then the process starts again. Sweden and Finland went through several such devaluation cycles when they tried to maintain fixed exchange rates.

Note that the basic problem behind a devaluation cycle is not monetary policy. With a fixed exchange rate, the central bank cannot do much more than to set the interest rate that is required in order to defend the fixed exchange rate. The basic reason behind a devaluation cycle is that fiscal policy is not sufficiently tight to bring down inflation in line with the countries to which the currency is tied. After a number of years with high inflation, competitiveness is eroded to such an extent that it becomes impossible for the central bank to defend the exchange rate.

A major exchange rate crisis occurred in 1992, the *ERM crisis*. During the latter part of the 1980s, the countries participating in the *European Exchange Rate Mechanism* kept their mutual exchange rates fixed, but inflation rates differed between the participating countries, and this led to changes in competitiveness. In the early 1990s, the unification of East and West Germany led to large fiscal spending in Germany, and in order to avoid inflation the Bundesbank raised the interest

4

Fig. 15.2 *Real effective exchange rates before and after the ERM crisis*

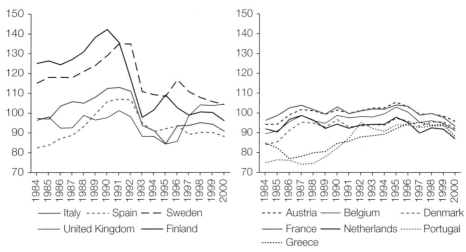

Italy ----- Spain — — Sweden   ---- Austria —— Belgium ---- Denmark
—— United Kingdom —— Finland   —— France —— Netherlands ······· Portugal
······· Greece

Note: The real effective exchange rate is a weighted average of real exchange rates relative to the most important trade partners. It is an index so the level has no meaning. It is the changes over time that are interesting.
Source: Statistical Appendix, *OECD Economic Outlook*, Spring 2011, OECD, http://www.oecd-ilibrary.org/books.

rate (see Fig. 10.7). The problem was that a higher interest rate was undesirable for most other countries in the ERM, which were in recession. The exchange rate crisis broke out in the summer and autumn of 1992 and several countries had to devalue their currencies, or let them float. Some countries switched from narrow bands to wider target zones for their exchange rates.

The ERM crisis is illustrated in Fig. 15.2, which shows the development of the effective *real* exchange rates during the crisis. In the left-hand panel we see the developments of the real exchange rates of Spain, Italy, Sweden, Finland, and the UK. These countries saw their currencies depreciate by 15–30 percent, and with slowly changing price levels this also led to real depreciations of similar magnitudes. Most of these countries had suffered serious losses of competitiveness in the years before the ERM crisis. This is seen from the increase in the real exchange rate before the crisis, which was caused by relatively high inflation in these countries. The exception to this pattern is the UK, which had a large depreciation although it had not suffered much loss of competitiveness.

The countries shown in the right-hand panel of Fig. 15.2 managed to keep their exchange rates roughly unchanged during the ERM crisis, although some of them were also subject to speculative attacks. Most of these countries had not suffered large losses of competitiveness. An exception is Portugal, which managed to keep its exchange rate roughly unchanged, although it had suffered a substantial loss of competitiveness in the years before the ERM crisis.[5]

---

5 For an analysis of the possibilities to maintain fixed exchange rates, see Maurice Obstfeld and Kenneth Rogoff, 'The mirage of fixed exchange rates', *Journal of Economic Perspectives*, 4 (1995), 73–96.

Deregulation of capital flows and the sustainability of fixed exchange rates

Deregulation of capital flows has made it harder to maintain a fixed exchange rate. From the 1930s until the mid 1970s, there were heavy regulations of capital flows in most countries. Individuals were not allowed to exchange currencies to buy foreign bonds or shares, or to borrow from foreign countries. Firms could exchange currencies, but only to make payments for imports and exports and for foreign direct investment such as purchases and sales of production facilities abroad. Of course, firms and individuals always find ways to exchange currencies, so speculation against currencies was still possible, but not on the scale that is possible today.

Most regulations of capital flows were abolished in the 1970s and 1980s. With free movement of financial capital, and modern IT technology, speculation against currencies can occur faster and on a larger scale. Some economists have argued that free movement of financial capital makes it impossible to maintain a fixed exchange rate today. In fact, few countries have a fixed exchange rate, but there are some exceptions. Denmark and some countries that are waiting to introduce the euro have fixed exchange rates against the euro. The Baltic countries went through extremely deep recessions around 2008 but still they managed to defend their fixed exchange rates against attacks. These examples show that it is possible to maintain a fixed exchange rate if the political will is strong and fiscal policy is conducted in such a way that it supports the fixed exchange rate.

15.2 Floating exchange rates and inflation targeting

Some countries have chosen to let their exchange rates float. A strict floating exchange rate regime means that the central bank does not have any target value for the exchange rate and that it does not intervene in the currency markets in order to influence the exchange rate. In practice, central banks with floating exchange rates sometimes do intervene in currency markets, but most of the time, such interventions have played little role.

As we saw in Chapter 14, a floating exchange rate can, in theory, help to ease the adjustment to real macroeconomic shocks. With a floating exchange rate, required changes of the real exchange rate can take place by changes of the nominal exchange rate, without any need for changes of the nominal price levels in different countries. But how do floating exchange rates work in practice? Obviously, this depends on how monetary policy is conducted. A floating exchange rate allows the central bank to pursue other objectives than to stabilize the exchange rate, but the consequences of a floating exchange rate depend on what other objectives the central bank is trying to achieve.

A fixed exchange rate regime defines monetary policy of the country: the central bank has to set the interest rate that is required in order to defend the exchange

Table 15.1 *Countries with inflation targeting regimes*

	Adoption of inflation target	Current target (2010)
New Zealand	March 1990	1–3%
Chile	September 1990	3%
Canada	February 1991	1–3%
Israel	January 1992	1–3%
United Kingdom	October 1992	2%
Sweden	January 1993	2%
Australia	April 1993	2–3%
Czech Republic	January 1998	3%
Korea	April 1998	3%
Poland	January 1999	2.5%
Norway	March 2001	2.5%

Source: Pia Fromlet, 'Rational expectations and inflation targeting – an analysis for ten countries', Working Paper 2010:17, Department of Economics, Uppsala University.

rate. But to say that a country has a floating exchange rate does not, in itself, define the monetary policy of that country. Countries with floating exchange rates can have many different kinds of monetary policies and there is no reason to expect countries with floating exchange rates to have similar economic developments unless they pursue similar monetary policies.

With a floating exchange rate, the exchange rate is determined by the interest parity condition

$$e = \frac{1+i}{1+i^*}e^e.$$

The exchange rate depends on the expected future exchange rate, and hence on expected future monetary policy. Therefore, uncertainty about future monetary policy will translate into uncertainty and volatility of the exchange rate. When exchange rate stability is not an objective of monetary policy, it is important to have some other clear objective so as to anchor expectations about monetary policy and inflation, and this should also help to stabilize the value of the currency.

Today, many countries with floating exchange rates have announced explicit inflation targets. The first country to do this was New Zealand in 1990, and many others have followed since. Some countries with floating exchange rates and inflation targets are listed in Table 15.1. The US has not had an explicit inflation target, but the Federal Reserve seems to have had an implicit inflation target somewhere between 2 and 3 percent.

So what are the experiences of countries, with floating exchange rates and (explicit or implicit) inflation targets? Fig. 15.3 shows exchange rates and output gaps for the US and some countries that have had floating exchange rates and inflation targets for some time. The output gap is the deviation of production from a smooth trend. Nominal and real effective exchange rates are weighted averages of nominal and real exchange rates versus the main trade partners of each country.

Fig. 15.3 *Exchange rates and output gaps for countries with floating exchange rates*

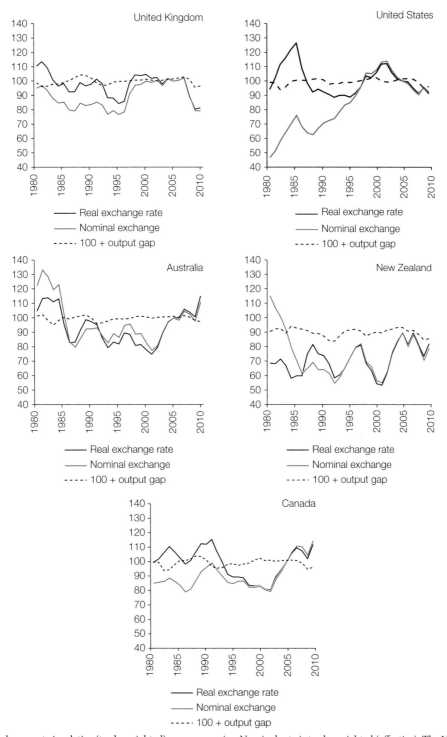

Note: Real exchange rate is relative (trade weighted) consumer price. Nominal rate is trade-weighted (effective). The UK was part of the ERM from October 1990 to September 1992.

Source: *OECD Economic Outlook*, OECD, 4 November 2011, http://www.oecd-ilibrary.org/statistics.

Looking at the diagrams we can note three things:

1. There have been large fluctuations in nominal and real exchange rates. Changes in the order of 10 or 20 percent from one year to the next are not uncommon. Prominent examples are the dollar cycles in 1980–1986 and 1995–2007, where the dollar first appreciated by 20–30 percent and then depreciated by a similar amount.

2. Short-run changes in nominal and real exchange rates are very highly correlated. This is not surprising since inflation targeting has led to low and stable inflation rates, especially in the latter part of the period. With large movements in nominal exchange rates, and stable prices, real exchange rates must move together with nominal exchange rates.

3. There is no obvious correlation between real exchange rate and the output gap.

Nominal and real exchange rates fluctuate a lot, but why? If the exchange rate moved so as to stabilize aggregate demand and production, we would expect the currency to depreciate when the economy was in recession, and appreciate when there was a boom, but this is not evident in the data. Exchange rate fluctuations seem to be 'disconnected' from real economic developments.

This evidence has led economists to draw different conclusions. Some argue that, in line with the Mundell–Fleming model, exchange rates help to stabilize shocks, at least some of the time, and that, overall, countries with floating rates and inflation targeting have had relatively stable economies. Others argue that exchange rate movements are largely disconnected from macroeconomic developments and that the large fluctuations in exchange rates that we see are just a nuisance for business and an impediment to trade. By joining a monetary union, we can eliminate this uncertainty without losing much in terms of macroeconomic stability.

15.3 The pros and cons of monetary union

The plan for the European Monetary Union was formulated in the *Maastricht Treaty*, which was formally signed in 1992. In January 1999, 11 countries introduced the *euro*. These were Belgium, Finland, France, Ireland, Italy, Luxemburg, the Netherlands, Portugal, Spain, Germany, and Austria. Greece joined in 2001. Later, Slovenia, Cyprus, Malta, Slovakia, and Estonia adopted the euro, and by 2012, 17 of the 27 member states of the EU were using the euro. The EU countries that had not introduced the euro in 2012 were Bulgaria, the Czech Republic, Denmark, Hungary, Latvia, Lithuania, Poland, Romania, Sweden, and the UK. Fig. 15.4 shows the current extension of the Eurozone.[6]

Monetary union means that countries have the same currency, the same exchange rate against foreign currencies, and a common monetary policy that

---

6 For a review of the process leading up to the monetary union, see Daniel Gros and Niels Thygesen, *European Monetary Integration: From the European Monetary System to European Monetary Union* (London: Longman, 1997).

Fig. 15.4 *The Eurozone, 2012*

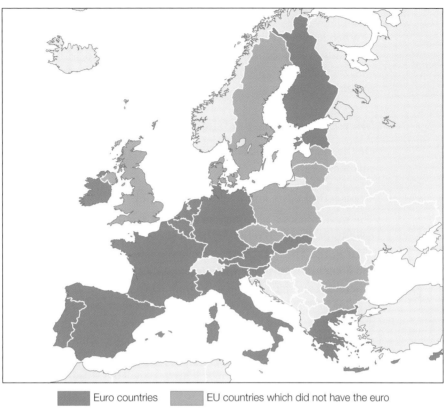

Euro countries   EU countries which did not have the euro

Note: Eurozone countries are marked in dark blue and EU countries that did not have the euro in 2012 are marked in light blue.
Euro countries: Belgium Finland, France, Ireland, Italy, Luxemburg, Netherlands, Portugal, Spain, Germany, Austria, Greece, Slovenia, Cyprus, Malta, Slovakia and Estonia.
EU countries which did not have the euro: Bulgaria, Czech Republic, Denmark, Hungary, Latvia, Lithuania, Poland, Romania, Sweden, and the UK.

is decided by the common central bank. From a macroeconomic point of view, membership in a monetary union has the same implications as taking part in a fixed exchange rate system with an irrevocably fixed exchange rate. In terms of our model, membership of a monetary union with the rest of the world simply means that we set $e = 1$.[7]

What are the advantages and disadvantages of monetary union? Below we review the arguments for and against monetary union, focusing on the case of the European Monetary Union (EMU). In order to discuss membership of a monetary union, we need to make clear what alternative we are comparing with. Here we take the alternative to be a floating exchange rate regime with an inflation target as the main objective of monetary policy. This is the policy pursued by many

---

7 In our theoretical model we have only two countries: the small open economy and the rest of the world. In reality, there is also trade with countries outside the monetary union, and the common currency will fluctuate in value relative to other currencies.

countries that are not members of a monetary union. To fix the exchange rate, as Denmark has done, is similar to being a member of the monetary union, except that it is easier to leave the fixed exchange rate than to leave the monetary union.

When looking at the economic effects of monetary union, it is useful to divide them into microeconomic effects, which have to do with trade and economic efficiency, and macroeconomic effects, which have to do with macroeconomic stability.[8]

Microeconomic aspects: efficiency and trade

On the microeconomic level, we can see several advantages of having a common currency.

Transaction costs and price transparency

The most obvious advantage of having a common currency is that there is no need to deal with different currencies. We pay a fee for exchanging currencies, often in the form of different exchange rates for buying and selling currencies, and a common currency will eliminate these transaction costs. This is the most concrete economic effect of a common currency and it can be estimated by considering how much revenue banks and other financial institutions make on these transactions. This is a real cost to society because the people who trade with currencies could spend their time producing other goods and services. The reduction in transaction costs from introducing the euro has been estimated to be in the order of 0.2–0.3 percent of GDP. This is a small but steady gain from membership of a monetary union.

Another advantage is increased price transparency. When prices are quoted in the same currency, it is easier to compare prices. Of course, prices in different currencies can be compared quite easily by multiplying by the exchange rate, but prices are easier to remember and compare when they are in the same currency. This should have a positive effect on competition and simplify trade, but the magnitude of the effect is hard to judge.

Short-term exchange rate fluctuations

An important consequence of monetary union is that exchange rate fluctuations are eliminated within a monetary union. As we saw in the previous section, floating exchange rates do vary considerably, and, from the point of view of an individual firm, these fluctuations can be quite disturbing. Membership in a monetary union does not completely eliminate exchange rate uncertainty, however, because there is also trade with countries outside the monetary union. For countries in the EMU, 30–50 percent of foreign trade is trade with countries outside

---

8 For the most part, the presentation below follows that of *EMU: A Swedish Perspective* by Lars Calmfors, Harry Flam, Nils Gottfries, Matlary Haaland, Janne Jerneck, Magnus Lindahl, Rutger Nordh Berntsson, Christina Rabinowicz, and Anders Vredin (Amsterdam: Kluwer, 1997). This book contains a broad analysis of the arguments and contains references to the literature on which the analysis is based. See also the report by the EU Commission: 'One Market, one money – An evaluation of the potential Costs and Benefits of Forming an Economic and Monetary Union', *European Economy*, 44 (1990), Brussels.

the monetary union and this trade is still subject to exchange rate uncertainty. Nevertheless, we would expect overall exchange rate uncertainty to decrease if a country joins a large monetary union such as the EMU.

When discussing the effects of exchange rate fluctuations it is important to distinguish between the short-run effects on the values of existing contracts and medium and longer-term fluctuations in competitiveness.

In the short run, fluctuations in exchange rates change the values of existing contracts. Consider a UK firm that orders a machine from a German firm, to be delivered in three months' time and to be paid at the time of delivery in euros. If the pound depreciates, the cost of the machine will increase in terms of pounds, and this increase in the cost may eliminate a substantial proportion of the profits from the investment. In the end the investment may turn out to be unprofitable. If, on the other hand, the pound appreciates, the machine becomes cheaper than was expected when the contract was made. Obviously, the managers of the firm dislike this uncertainty.

Unpleasant as it is, this uncertainty about payments on existing contracts can easily be avoided, however. A simple way is that the UK firm can change the required amount of money into euros immediately and put the money into a euro account so as to be sure to have the required amount when it is time to pay. Another alternative is to buy foreign currency in the forward market. This means that the firm writes a contract with a bank stating that it will buy a specific amount of euros at a specific price at a specific future date. The bank will charge a fee for this, but the cost is small. The forward market is analysed in the appendix to this chapter.

In practice, firms choose different strategies. Some firms eliminate the currency risk by buying and selling currency in the forward market. Some firms have foreign currency accounts that they use for incoming and outgoing payments in foreign currency. Some do not hedge (guard against) the currency risk, taking the view that gains and losses from exchange rate fluctuations will even out in the long run. Since it is cheap to eliminate the effects of short-run exchange rate uncertainty, this uncertainty cannot be a major problem for firms.

Medium-term exchange rate fluctuations

Medium-term fluctuations in exchange rates are more difficult to deal with. As seen in Fig. 15.3, changes in exchange rates tend to be persistent. In fact, exchange rate *changes* are very hard to predict, so if a currency increases in value, the best prediction is that it will remain on a higher value. Exchange rate fluctuations imply persistent changes in the competitiveness of countries, and of individual firms. If the domestic currency appreciates, exporters can either keep their foreign currency prices unchanged, and reduce their mark-ups, or raise their prices in foreign currency, and lose market shares. Either way, profits will decrease. This medium-term exchange rate uncertainty is harder to deal with because it concerns contracts that have not yet been written. If the domestic currency remains strong, it will affect the profits of the firm, sooner or later.

What are the effects of exchange rate uncertainty on trade and investments? To analyse this question, consider a firm that has successfully developed a new product, which it sells in the domestic market. Now the firm considers entering the export market. In order to do this, the firm has to invest in production capacity, establish a sales network, and market the product abroad. If the company makes these investments and the home currency appreciates, the profit margin on exports may be eliminated. If, on the other hand, the home currency depreciates, exports will turn out to be more profitable than expected. We might expect exchange rate uncertainty to have a negative effect on the firm's willingness to undertake the investment. In this way, exchange rate uncertainty may have negative effects of on investment and trade.

Somewhat surprisingly, however, economic theory does not offer clear predictions concerning the effect of exchange rate uncertainty on investment. From the point of view of an exporting firm, exchange rate uncertainty can be seen as uncertainty about the price levels in foreign countries. But economic theory says that price uncertainty will generally increase the expected return on an investment. The intuitive reason is that a firm can benefit from selling a lot when the price is high and selling less when the price is low. For this reason, the *expected* profit from an investment will generally be higher when prices fluctuate compared with when prices are constant.

On the other hand, companies have good reasons to dislike uncertainty. Shocks that cause the firm to make losses may lead to financial problems and even the bankruptcy of the firm. So, even if price variation makes exports more profitable on average, it also increases the risk that the company will get into financial difficulties. This risk is particularly important for small firms, which are less diversified and have limited access to finance. Thus, it appears plausible that exchange rate uncertainty is particularly troublesome for small firms, and that it makes them reluctant to enter foreign markets.

Yet another aspect must be considered when we discuss the effects of exchange rate uncertainty on investment and trade. We must ask the question *why* the exchange rate varies. If exchange rate variation is due to irrational speculation, then it is clearly a good thing to eliminate it. But if there is some truth to the Mundell–Fleming model, exchange rate fluctuations may actually help to stabilize demand, for the whole economy and for the individual firm. According to this model, the exchange rate will appreciate when domestic demand is strong and depreciate when domestic demand is weak. For a firm that sells its products in domestic as well as foreign markets, this should *reduce* the uncertainty about the *total* demand for the firm's products. Thus, when judging whether exchange rate uncertainty is good or bad for investment and trade, a crucial question is *why* the exchange rate varies in the first place. As discussed above, we have too little understanding of exchange rate movements to give a clear answer to this question.

Financial integration

A common currency may help financial integration. Firms and individuals will find it easier to borrow in one country and lend in another when there is no currency risk. This should make it easier for banks and other financial institutions to operate across borders. That said, the large current account surpluses and deficits of countries with floating exchange rates, for example, Japan and the US, show that countries with floating exchange rates do have access to the international financial markets. We do not need a common currency in order to borrow and lend across borders.

Summary of microeconomic effects: increased gains from trade

To sum up the effects on efficiency, we would expect a monetary union to bring benefits by reducing transaction costs, simplifying trade, and improving competition. We should expect increased gains from trade, but the effects on investment and growth are less clear.

Macroeconomic aspects: stability

What are the macroeconomic implications of a common currency? To analyse this question, we use the standard model for analyzing macroeconomic stability in the open economy, the Mundell–Fleming model. This model, which was presented in Chapter 14, is based on some key assumptions.

1. Financial markets are assumed to be well integrated. In our theoretical analysis, we assumed interest parity – that the expected return must be the same on loans in different currencies. This represents a high degree of integration of financial markets.
2. There is free trade but demand curves for exports and imports are *not* perfectly elastic. To sell more in the export market, exporters must reduce their relative prices.
3. Nominal wages and prices are set in domestic currency and change slowly.

Demand in the open economy consists of private consumption, C, and investment, I, government consumption and investment, G, and net exports, NX. If production is to be on the natural level, the following equality must hold:

$$Y^n = C\,(Y^n - T, Y^e - T^e, i - \pi^e, A) + I\,(i - \pi^e, Y^e, K) + G + NX\,(eP/P^*, Y^*, Y)\,.$$

The Mundell–Fleming model has clear implications. When there are shocks to demand or supply, relative price changes are needed if production is to remain on the natural level. Changes in the real exchange rate can be achieved either by a change in the nominal exchange rate or by a change in the price level. According to the Mundell–Fleming model, an adjustment of the nominal exchange rate can *ease the adjustment* of the real exchange rate. But a country that is member of a monetary union cannot adjust its nominal exchange rate or the nominal interest rate. How will the economy adjust in this case?

This depends on whether the shock is country-specific (*asymmetric*) or common to most countries in the monetary union (*symmetric*). If the shock is *symmetric*, affecting all countries in the monetary union in a similar way, the central bank of the monetary union will adjust its interest rate and the exchange rate of the common currency will also be affected. The common central bank will react much like a national central bank would have done and the effect of the shock on the small open economy will be similar to what it would have been with a floating exchange rate. But if the shock is *asymmetric*, affecting only one small country in the monetary union, the situation is different. In this case, the nominal interest rate and the exchange rate of the small open economy will be unaffected by the shock.

Sometimes it is argued that asymmetric shocks are unlikely because it is hard to imagine a major shock that affects one country but not the others. But 'shocks' are all the things we take as exogenous in our very stylized theoretical models, and they can arise for many reasons. Shocks can arise because of technological developments, structural change, emergence of new competition in world markets, changes in laws and institutions, differences in economic policies, changes in moods and expectations, and so on. Much of the time, the business cycles of the individual European countries are highly correlated, but there are also situations where the economic developments in individual countries diverge significantly from the average in the monetary union.

Macroeconomic adjustment inside a monetary union

So what adjustment mechanisms are available when an asymmetric shock affects an individual country in a monetary union? One possibility is to achieve a real exchange rate adjustment via *wage and price adjustment*. If there is a persistent negative demand shock, production will fall below the natural level and inflation will be lower. As time goes by, competitiveness improves, net exports increase, and the level of production is restored. This process was analysed in Chapter 14. The evidence suggests that this process will take considerable time because wages and prices change slowly.

Another adjustment mechanism is *labour mobility*. If one country is in recession and another is in a boom, workers may move to where the jobs are. In Europe, such movements are limited by language differences, cultural factors, and regulations. For some very small countries such as the Baltic countries, labour mobility plays an important role, but for most countries in the EMU, labour mobility is too small to play an important role on the macroeconomic level.

Looking at the equation above, we see yet another potential adjustment mechanism: fiscal policy. Changes in government expenditure (G) and taxes (T) can be used to stabilize aggregate demand. Since countries do not have their own monetary policy, fiscal policy is of central importance in a monetary union. Fiscal policy can be carried on the union level – federal fiscal policy – and on the national level. Let us consider these two types of fiscal policy.

Federal fiscal policy: In theory, federal fiscal policy could help to stabilize developments in individual countries. The EU could tax countries which are in boom and transfer money to countries which are in recession. In practice, the possibilities of doing this in the European Union are very limited because the EU budget constitutes a small fraction of GDP. The EU collects about one percent of GDP in membership fees from the member countries and most of this money is used for agricultural subsidies and regional support. The purpose of this expenditure is to give continuous support to agriculture and regional development and it would not be efficient to vary those programmes in a cyclical fashion. Whether federal fiscal policy will become more important in the future depends on the degree of political integration, but, so far, voters and politicians have been reluctant to hand over a large share of their tax revenue to the European Union.

National fiscal policy: With very limited fiscal policy on the federal level, the main way to deal with asymmetric shocks inside a monetary union is to use fiscal policy on the national level. As discussed in Chapter 11, the government does play a stabilizing role because of the operation of automatic stabilizers. When economic activity increases, tax revenue increases and payments of social assistance and government-subsidized unemployment benefits decrease, and this has a stabilizing effect on the economy. Most EU countries are welfare states with relatively large government sectors, so the automatic stabilizers can be relied upon to play an important stabilizing role. In theory, governments could also carry out actively countercyclical fiscal policy, raising taxes and reducing expenditure when the economy is in a boom and reducing taxes and raising expenditure when the economy is in recession. As discussed in Chapter 11, the empirical evidence does not indicate that governments generally succeed in pursuing an active countercyclical fiscal policy, however.

There is a specific variant of fiscal policy that can be used to affect competitiveness. An *internal devaluation* is a policy package consisting of a reduction in the pay-roll tax and a simultaneous increase in other taxes such as the income tax or the value added tax. Since firms do not pay value added tax on exports, such a policy improves the competitiveness of the export industry. An internal devaluation shifts taxes from firms to consumers and it can be designed in such a way that the government budget balance remains roughly unaffected. To some extent, it can substitute for a nominal exchange rate adjustment, but the magnitude of the effect will be much more limited than if the currency depreciates by 20 or 30 percent. Nevertheless, it can help to improve competitiveness.

In theory, an active fiscal policy can at least partially substitute for the absence of national monetary policy in a monetary union. That it does so in practice is more doubtful.

Monetary policy and exchange rate fluctuations outside the monetary union

In order to evaluate the arguments for and against monetary union, one must form a view of what the alternative – non-membership – is like. Sometimes, it is argued that membership of a monetary union leads to lower interest rates because it is seen as a way of achieving a credible low-inflation monetary policy. But theory does not suggest any reason why the credibility of monetary policy should have anything to do with monetary union. The credibility of the European Central Bank derives from its independence and commitment to low inflation, and there is no reason why the central bank of an individual country should not be able to achieve the same credibility as the European Central Bank. If the (implicit or explicit) inflation targets are the same, we can expect the average levels of the interest rate and inflation to be the same inside and outside the monetary union. There will be periods when a country outside the monetary union has a higher or a lower interest rate, but, on average, the levels should be similar. In fact, Switzerland, Canada, and New Zealand had all established low inflation regimes before the EMU was established, and other countries have subsequently followed the same path.

One lesson from the Mundell–Fleming model is that, if the central bank pursues a sensible monetary policy, the exchange rate will move in a way that helps to stabilize the economy. In theory, this is the main advantage of a floating exchange rate. But as discussed in the previous section, it has been hard to show that exchange rates really play the stabilizing role predicted by the Mundell–Fleming model. Floating exchange rates often vary substantially and we do not know whether these movements are stabilizing fundamental economic shocks or they represent irrational speculation and moods in the market. Because of our poor understanding of exchange rate movements, serious economists have very different views on the merits of floating exchange rates, and this affects their attitudes towards membership of a monetary union.

Summary of macroeconomic effects: increased risk of macroeconomic instability

If there is high economic integration between the countries participating in a monetary union the business cycles will be highly correlated. This means that, most of the time, the common monetary policy will be appropriate for the individual member states. Sometimes, however, the economic situation in an individual country will deviate substantially from the average within the union, and such a situation may be difficult to deal with within a monetary union. Economists tend to agree that the loss of an independent monetary policy may involve a cost in terms of macroeconomic stability, but they disagree on how important this loss will be.

Optimum currency areas

To sum up, there are efficiency gains from a monetary union in terms of reduced transaction costs, reduced exchange rate uncertainty, and increased gains from trade, but also increased risks of macroeconomic instability. The choice as to whether to join a monetary union or not involves a comparison of benefits and costs. The more integrated countries are, economically and politically, the greater the benefits from monetary union and the smaller the costs:

- If countries trade a great deal with each other, there are larger efficiency gains from reductions in transaction costs and exchange rate uncertainty.
- High economic integration also means that business cycles will be similar, so there will be less risk of asymmetric developments. If the labour market is well integrated, workers can move to where the jobs are, and if there is high political integration, federal involvement in fiscal policy is more acceptable.

Thus, countries that are well integrated should have greater benefits and lower costs if they form a monetary union, and we would expect such countries to be more likely to form a monetary union. The reasoning outlined above is called the *theory of optimal currency areas* and was proposed by the American economist Robert Mundell as an explanation for why some countries form a monetary union and others do not. Regions characterized by high economic and political integration will choose a common currency while others are better off with separate currencies.[9]

But what does this mean in practice? Sometimes, different regions within Germany and the US have divergent economic developments. Does that mean that it is optimal for each region to have its own currency? Should Bavaria have its own currency that can increase in value when there is a boom in Bavaria? Michigan has been severely affected by the troubles of the US automobile industry. Would it have been better if there had been a separate Michigan dollar that could be devalued in order to stimulate economic growth in Michigan?

Unfortunately, it is very difficult to quantify the different benefits and costs of monetary union and this makes it hard to judge whether a particular area is an optimal currency area. One thing we can say, however, is that there is a stronger case for a common currency in the US than in Europe. The degree of economic integration between US states is higher than between European countries, so there are larger efficiency gains from a common currency and the business cycles in the different states are more highly correlated. Also, labour mobility is much higher between US states. Studies show that much of the adjustment to regional shocks in the US takes place via labour mobility. When the jobs disappear in a particular state, many workers leave that state.[10]

Moreover, the federal government is more important in federal states such as the US, Canada, and Germany than it is in the European Union. In these countries, the federal budget constitutes between 15 and 30 percent of GDP. If the federal tax were proportional to income, this would imply that 15 to 30 percent of a change in income in an individual state would be channelled into the federal government. In practice, taxes are progressive, so they increase more than proportionally when income increases. For the US, estimates show that when income in a US state increases by one dollar, tax payments from the state to the federal budget increase by 34 cents.[11] Since federal tax money is spent across the federation, this has an equalizing influence on economic developments within the federation. As we have already noted, the EU budget is only one percent of GDP so it cannot play much of an equalizing role. Clearly, this difference reflects a difference in the degree of political integration between the US and the EU.

15.4   The fiscal framework in EMU

From the arguments made above we realize that fiscal policy is very important in a monetary union. When countries cannot use monetary policy, a heavier

---

9   Robert Mundell, 'A theory of optimum currrency areas', *American Economic Review*, 51 (1961), 657–665.

10 See Olivier J. Blanchard and Lawrence F. Katz, 'Regional evolutions', *Brookings Papers on Economic Activity* 1992:1.

11 See Xavier Sala-i-Martin and Jeffrey Sachs, 'Fiscal federalism and optimum currency areas: evidence for Europe from the United States', in Matthew Canzoneri *et al.* (eds), *Establishing a Central Bank: Issues in Europe and Lessons from the US* (Cambridge: Cambridge University Press, 1992).

burden falls on fiscal policy. Further, fiscal imbalances in individual countries can create very serious problems in a monetary union. If a country accumulates large government debt it may end up in a fiscal crisis where it becomes unable to finance its borrowing in the financial markets. Then there will be huge pressure on the common central bank to bail out the country by buying its government debt.

In view of the importance of fiscal policy in a monetary union, the degree of EU involvement in fiscal policy has been intensely debated ever since the monetary union was first planned. There were three major plans for monetary union in Europe:

1. The first plan for a monetary union, the *Werner plan* in 1970, argued that a high degree of fiscal coordination should be part of the monetary union. The plan stated that the *ECOFIN*, the council of finance ministers in the EU, should have the power to impose changes in fiscal policy in individual member states, and that the ECOFIN should not only be concerned with the overall budget deficit but it should also be able to require changes in individual taxes and expenditures. However, such a high degree of EU involvement in fiscal policy was not acceptable to some member countries, and the Werner plan was never implemented.

2. A second plan for European monetary union was formulated in the *McDougall report* in 1977. The McDougall report argued instead that the EU should carry out stabilization policy itself with the help of a substantially increased federal budget. Again, this was not an idea that received wide political support.

3. A third plan for monetary union was put forward in the *Delors report* in 1989. This report contained the basic ideas that were incorporated into the *Treaty of the European Union*, which was signed in Maastricht in 1992, and which is often called the *Maastricht Treaty*. This treaty laid out the plans for the introduction of the euro. It has been revised several times.

The Maastricht Treaty required neither an extensive coordination of fiscal policy, nor a dramatic expansion of the EU budget. Instead, the philosophy was that each individual country could manage its own fiscal policy, provided that it did not seriously mismanage its government finances. The Maastricht Treaty stated that member states should avoid *excessive government deficits* and criteria were set up for what was meant by an excessive government deficit. A member state was considered to have an excessive deficit if

i) the government deficit (public sector net borrowing) exceeded a reference value of 3 percent of GDP, or

ii) the gross consolidated government debt (i.e. the consolidated debt of the central government, local governments, and social security funds) exceeded a reference value of 60 percent of GDP.

There were, however, some escape clauses. The deficit would not be judged to be excessive if it had 'declined substantially and continuously' and reached a level that came close to the reference value, or if it was 'exceptional and temporary' and remained close to the reference value. Also, a level of debt over 60 percent would not be regarded as excessive if it were 'diminishing and approaching the reference value at a satisfactory pace'.

If a member state did not fulfil the above requirements, and was therefore considered to have an excessive deficit, the European Commission should prepare a report and the ECOFIN would then issue recommendations on fiscal policy measures to be implemented by the country. If the member state failed to comply with the recommendations, the ECOFIN council could apply certain sanctions. These could involve forcing the member state concerned to make non-interest-bearing deposits of an appropriate size with the Community until the deficit had been corrected. Ultimately, the ECOFIN could 'impose a fine of an appropriate size'. Note, however, that there was *no requirement* in the Maastricht Treaty that these sanctions would be imposed. Ultimately, any imposition of sanctions was (and remains) a political decision by the ministers of finance.

Another central element in the Maastricht Treaty was the so-called *no bail-out clause*, which prohibits the European Central Bank from taking over liability for payment of a member state's debt. The principal idea in the Maastricht Treaty was that each member state should be responsible for its own government debt.

On the initiative of Germany, in 1997 the rules of the excessive deficit procedure were further tightened in the *Stability and Growth Pact*. This pact stated that each member state should aim for a medium-term budgetary position 'close to balance or in surplus' and that members of the monetary union should have *stability programmes* that should be updated annually. These stability programmes should state the medium-term budgetary objectives, explain what was being done to achieve these objectives, and outline the expected adjustment path. Moreover, the Stability and Growth Pact set time deadlines for the various steps in the excessive deficit procedure outlined above. If a member state failed to comply with the ECOFIN council's recommendations, a decision to impose sanctions should be taken within ten months. Initially, the sanctions would involve non-interest-bearing deposits with the EU, which would be converted into a fine after two years if the deficit continued to be excessive.

The Stability and Growth Pact also tried to define more precisely when a deficit above 3 percent of GDP should be considered 'exceptional'. As a rule, a deficit should be considered exceptional if there was an annual fall in real GDP of at least 2 percent. In such a situation, the deficit should not lead to sanctions. If GDP were to fall by between 0.75 and 2 percent, an exception could also be made.

The aim of the Stability and Growth Pact was to ensure that the member countries pursued a prudent fiscal policy and that they would not accumulate such large public debts that the other countries would have to bail them out. The Stability and Growth Pact is part of the Maastricht Treaty. The current versions of the no bail-out clause and the excessive deficit procedure are presented in the appendix to this chapter. So, how have these rules worked in practice? We will explore this in the next section, where we review the first decade with the euro.

15.5   Ten years with the euro

The euro has existed since 1999, for more than a decade. How has it worked? We now have enough data for a preliminary evaluation. We can compare economic developments inside and outside the Eurozone. Of course, we can never be sure whether observed differences between insiders and outsiders are due to the euro, or caused by other factors, but it is interesting to see if there are any marked differences.[12]

Trade

As discussed above, we would expect the euro to have a positive effect on trade *within* the Eurozone. The effect on trade between the Eurozone and countries *outside* the monetary union is ambiguous. On the one hand, trade with outside countries is also facilitated by a common currency since an exporter outside has only one currency to deal with. On the other hand there may also be *trade diversion*: when trade is made easier within the monetary union, firms in the euro countries may chose to trade between themselves instead of trading with firms in other countries.

In order to evaluate the effects of the euro on trade we can examine how trade within the Eurozone has evolved compared with trade outside the Eurozone. Such a comparison is made in Fig. 15.5 where exports within, to, and from the Eurozone are compared with exports between similar countries outside the Eurozone.[13] The comparison is made by constructing a volume index for each category of exports and setting it to 100 in 1995. This index is then divided by an index of exports between countries that have not adopted the euro. Fig. 15.5 shows that exports within the Eurozone have increased by about 30 percent relative to exports between countries outside and that most of this increase occurred around the time when the euro was introduced in January 1999. Exports from the Eurozone have also increased relative to exports between countries outside the Eurozone.

But this comparison does not tell us anything about the *effect* of the euro on trade. There may be other factors that caused these differences. Trade may have increased because general growth was higher in some countries, or there may have been exchange rate movements that affected competitiveness and trade. To address this problem, researchers have estimated statistical regression equations for exports where they include other explanatory variables that may affect exports, primarily the real exchange rate and GDP in the exporting and the importing country. In these equations they include *dummy variables* to capture the effects

---

12   This chapter draws heavily on the report *EMU at Ten: Should Denmark, Sweden, and the UK Join?* by Harry Flam, Antonio Fatas, Steinar Holden, Tullio Jappelli, Ilian Mihov, Marco Pagano, and Charles Wyploszis (Stockholm: SNS, 2009). Many references to the literature can be found in this book.

13   The results reported below are taken from Harry Flam and Håkan Nordström, 'Euro effects on the intensive and extensive margins of trade', working paper, Institute for International Economic Studies, Stockholm University, 2007. See also Richard Baldwin, 'The euro's effects on trade', ECB working paper 594.

Fig. 15.5 *Exports within, to, and from the Eurozone relative to exports between ten countries outside the Eurozone (volume index)*

Source: Harry Flam and Håkan Nordström, 'Euro effects on the intensive and extensive margins of trade', working paper, Stockholm University, 2007.

of the euro. One dummy variable takes the value one when the exporting and the importing country has the euro and zero when this is not the case, and the coefficient on the dummy variable is interpreted as a causal effect of the euro on trade. Basically, this means that we are comparing trade between euro countries with trade between non-euro countries, but controlling for other factors that affect exports. Similarly, another dummy variable can be included, which is one when the exporting country has the euro but not the importing country.

Fig. 15.6 shows estimated effects of the euro on trade when other factors are taken into account using the statistical approach described above. The estimated effect on trade rises to about 35 percent by 2005. This is a very substantial effect. The estimates also indicate that the euro has had positive effects on trade with countries outside the Eurozone. Exports to the Eurozone and exports from the Eurozone both increased by some 10–15 percent compared with trade between countries outside the Eurozone. The trade-stimulating effect of the common currency seems to dominate the trade diversion effect discussed above.

The method described above can be used to estimate the causal effects of the euro on trade, and most studies of this issue have concluded that the euro has had positive effects on trade. A couple of studies have questioned this conclusion, however, arguing that much of the increase in trade may be caused by other factors. Before the introduction of the euro, there was already a long-term trend of increased trade within Europe, and this trend continued when the euro was introduced. Thus we cannot exclude the possibility that much of this increase in trade would have occurred without the euro. On the other hand, it can be argued that this long-term trend is in large part due to policies that have facilitated trade, such

Fig. 15.6 *Effects of the EMU on trade: a comparison with ten countries outside the OECD*

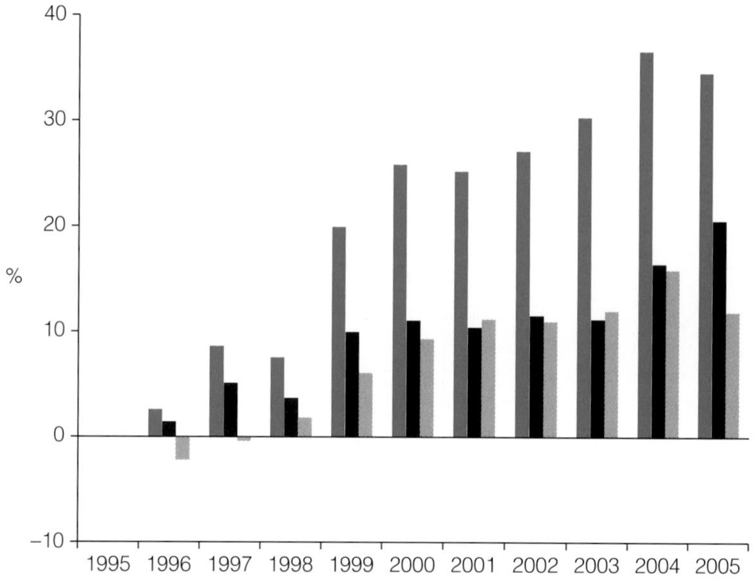

Note: Blue columns are estimated year-dummies for trade within the Eurozone. Black columns are dummies for exports from euro countries to ten countries outside the OECD. Grey columns are dummies for exports from ten countries outside the OECD to euro countries. Comparison is trade between ten countries outside the OECD. The estimation controls for other factors such as GDP and real exchange rates.

Source: Harry Flam and Håkan Nordström, 'Euro effects on the intensive and extensive margins of trade', working paper, Stockholm University, 2007.

as the elimination of tariffs in the 1960s, the creation of the internal market in the late 1980s, and the introduction of a common currency in 1999. Without further steps to facilitate trade, the trend might well have stopped.

Thus, there are indications that the euro has had a substantial positive effect on trade. The benefits from increased trade arise because comparative advantages and scale economies are better exploited and consumers gain from a wider selection of goods and services that they can buy. How large is this gain? This is hard to judge. As a simple example, suppose that the production cost is reduced by 10 percent for the goods that are traded because of the common currency. Suppose that trade constitutes 25 percent of GDP in value-added terms and that trade increases 30 percent. Then the cost savings from this additional trade is about 0.75 percent of GDP ($0.25 \cdot 0.30 \cdot 0.10 = 0.0075$). This may appear rather limited, but we should note that this gain is obtained every year and also that the full effects of the common currency may not yet have materialized.

Macroeconomic performance on the union level

To evaluate macroeconomic developments in the Eurozone we need some countries to compare with. Since we take a floating exchange rate with inflation targeting as the main alternative to monetary union, it seems natural to compare with industrialized countries that have had an inflation-targeting regime for a

Table 15.2 *Comparison of the Eurozone with five inflation-targeting countries*

Inflation	1999–2004	2005–2010	1999–2010
Australia	3.1	2.9	3.0
Canada	2.3	1.8	2.0
New Zealand	2.0	2.9	2.4
Sweden	1.4	1.4	1.4
United Kingdom	1.2	2.6	1.9
Inflation-targeting countries	2.0	2.3	2.2
Eurozone	2.1	2.0	2.0
Difference	0.1	−0.4	−0.1
Real GDP growth	**1999–2004**	**2005–2010**	**1999–2010**
Australia	3.5	2.8	3.2
Canada	3.4	1.5	2.5
New Zealand	4.0	1.7	2.9
Sweden	3.2	1.7	2.5
United Kingdom	3.0	0.7	1.8
Inflation-targeting countries	3.4	1.7	2.6
Eurozone	2.1	1.0	1.5
Difference	−1.3	−0.7	−1.0
Short-term interest	**1999–2004**	**2005–2010**	**1999–2010**
Australia	5.2	5.6	5.4
Canada	3.8	2.8	3.3
New Zealand	5.7	6.2	5.9
Sweden	3.4	2.1	2.7
United Kingdom	4.8	3.8	4.3
Inflation-targeting countries	4.6	4.1	4.3
Eurozone	3.3	2.7	3.0
Difference	−1.3	−1.4	−1.3

Note: The average for the inflation targeting countries is not weighted by country size.
Source: *OECD Economic Outlook*, statistical appendix, http://www.oecd-ilibrary.org/books.

substantial time. In Table 15.2 we compare the Eurozone with Australia, Canada, New Zealand, Sweden, and the UK.

The main objective of monetary policy in the EMU is low *inflation*. The inflation objective of the ECB has been formulated as 'close to but not above two percent'. In fact, the average inflation rate in 1999–2010 was 2 percent, so the ECB was successful in reaching this objective. The average inflation rate of the inflation targeting countries has been very similar, 2.2 percent. This is not surprising since the countries have similar inflation targets. There is no need to join a monetary union in order to get low inflation.

As discussed in the previous section, it is not clear how a monetary union will affect growth. Exchange rate stability may stimulate trade and competition, leading to increased gains from trade and increased economic efficiency, so we may have a positive effect on growth. On the other hand, a monetary union may lead to macroeconomic instability, which may have a negative effect on investment and growth. In fact, the growth performance of the Eurozone has been relatively poor.

During the period 1999–2010, average growth in the Eurozone was one percent lower than the average for the inflation-targeting countries. However, it is hard to say whether this difference should be attributed to the euro or to other factors.

The average of the short-term *interest rates* has been 3 percent in the Eurozone as against 4.3 percent in the inflation-targeting countries. Since the inflation rates have been very similar, it is unlikely that this difference reflects a difference in the credibility of monetary policy. More likely, it is explained by the higher rate of growth in the inflation-targeting countries. If financial markets are less than perfectly integrated, a country with higher growth will have a higher real interest rate (see Chapter 5).

Macroeconomic developments in individual countries

Table 15.3 shows the inflation rates in the original 11 euro countries plus Greece, which introduced the euro in 2001. Most of the euro members had inflation rates close to the average for the Eurozone, but some had diverging inflation rates. Over the period 1999–2010, Greece and Spain had the highest inflation rates, while Germany had the lowest inflation rate. Fig. 15.7 shows the price levels of some of the countries relative to the euro average.

Inflation differentials are to be expected in a monetary union. Sometimes, real exchange rates need to change, and with the nominal exchange rate fixed at unity, necessary adjustments of the real exchange rate will take the form of inflation differentials between countries. Such inflation differentials need not be a problem if they represent equilibrium adjustments of the real exchange rates. On the contrary, differing developments of aggregate demand and supply in different countries imply that inflation differentials are necessary if production is to remain on the natural level in the different countries.

Table 15.3 *Inflation differences in the Eurozone*

	Inflation 1999–2010	Difference
Germany	1.6	−0.5
Finland	1.8	−0.3
Austria	1.9	−0.2
France	1.9	−0.2
Belgium	2.1	0.0
Eurozone (14 countries)	2.1	0.0
Netherlands	2.2	0.1
Italy	2.3	0.2
Ireland	2.5	0.4
Portugal	2.5	0.4
Luxembourg	2.7	0.6
Spain	2.9	0.8
Greece	3.4	1.3

Note: Inflation is measured by the percentage change of harmonized consumer price indexes.
Source: *OECD Economic Outlook*, OECD, 10 October 2011,
http://www.oecd-ilibrary.org/statistics.

Fig. 15.7 *Relative consumer prices in some Eurozone countries*

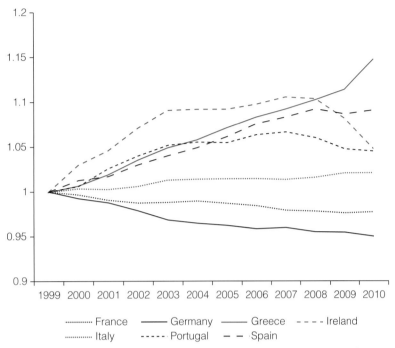

Note: The figure shows harmonized consumer price indexes relative to the average of 14 Eurozone countries. All indexes have been set to 1 in 1999.

Source: *OECD Economic Outlook*, OECD, 19 October 2011, http://www.oecd-ilibrary.org/statistics.

However, there are signs that the inflation differentials in the Eurozone are not only equilibrium adjustments. Partly, they seem to be caused by overheating and recessions in different member countries – that is, deviations of production from the natural level. These cycles may be amplified because interest rates cannot be adjusted to the situation in individual countries.

Fig. 15.8 shows inflation, the ECB interest rate, and interest rate minus inflation for some countries. Inflation is measured using the GDP deflator, which is the price that is relevant for domestic producers. Ireland, Greece, and Spain, have gone through boom–bust cycles where a period of high growth and investment, and increasing in property values, was followed by a deep recession. In the early years of the euro, Ireland, Greece, and Spain had relatively high inflation and negative real interest rates, which stimulated domestic demand in those countries. As these countries went into recession in 2007–2008, inflation dropped and real interest rates increased.

Germany experienced the opposite cycle. Since nominal interest rates had to be equalized when the euro was introduced, Germany had to accept a higher interest rate although domestic inflation was near zero in 1999. The result was a very high real interest rate in the first years with the euro and a period of weak growth in Germany. By 2010, many years of low inflation had improved the competitiveness of German industry, and the German economy was doing well compared with other countries in the Eurozone.

Fig. 15.8 *Nominal and real interest rates in some countries in the EMU*

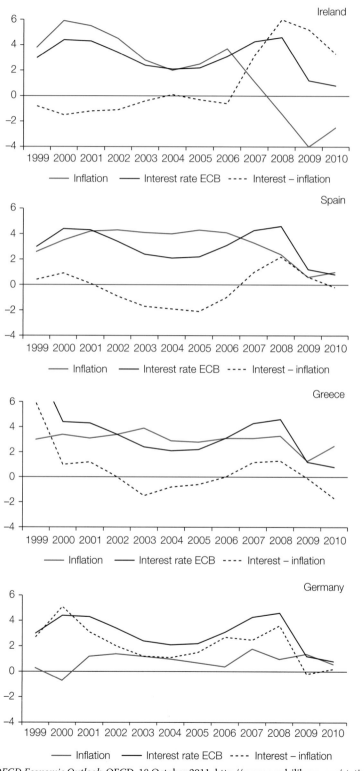

Source: *OECD Economic Outlook*, OECD, 18 October 2011, http://www.oecd-ilibrary.org/statistics

In our discussion about the Taylor rule in Chapter 10, we argued that a strong interest rate response to inflation helps to stabilize production and inflation. The Taylor principle says that, when inflation increases, the central bank should raise its interest rate more than the increase in inflation so as to raise the *real* interest rate and reduce aggregate demand. But as a member of a monetary union, an individual country cannot raise the interest rate. Instead, an increase in inflation in one country will *reduce* the real interest rate in that country. As a result, real interest rates may amplify the fluctuations. When there is an upsurge in demand, inflation increases, and the real interest rate is reduced, further fuelling the high demand so that inflation continues. With relatively high inflation, competitiveness is gradually eroded. In the short run, weakening exports may be compensated for by strong domestic demand, but at some point, the boom ends, inflation drops, and the real interest rate increases.[14]

Fiscal policy

When it comes to fiscal policy, the evidence for the first ten years suggests that, in general, imbalances in individual countries have not been countered by active fiscal policy.[15] On the other hand, the relatively high tax levels in most European countries imply that the *automatic stabilizers* are strong in Europe and this should help to stabilize the European economies. Another side of this coin is that budget balances are sensitive to general economic developments. With a marginal tax equal to 50 percent, 2 percent lower growth leads to an increase in the budget deficit corresponding to one percent of GDP if expenditure remains unchanged (see the calculations in Chapter 11).

A European debt crisis broke out in 2010 and it was still going on in 2012. To understand the background of this debt crisis, we must consider fiscal developments and the application of the Stability and Growth Pact in the decade leading up to the debt crisis.

As discussed in Section 15.4, the Maastricht Treaty in 1992 set up rules that the public sector deficit should not be larger than 3 percent of GDP and that gross consolidated government debt should not be larger than 60 percent of GDP, and these rules were reiterated in the Stability and Growth Pact in 1997. The idea was that countries should fulfil these criteria in order to become members of the euro club and that they should also adhere to these rules after the introduction of the common currency. In fact, many countries made serious efforts to improve their government finances in the 1990s. They were helped by the economic recovery in the latter half of the 1990s and most countries were below, or at least close to, the stipulated levels when the euro was introduced in 1999. Apparently, the threat that a country might not be able to join had a disciplining effect on fiscal policymakers.

---

14 This instability problem was pointed out in the context of fixed exchange rates by the British economist Alan Walters and is known as the *Walters critique* of fixed exchange rates. It seems to have some relevance also for monetary unions.

15 See Harry Flam, Antonio Fatas, Steinar Holden, Tullio Jappelli, Ilian Mihov, Marco Pagano, and Charles Wyploszis, *EMU at Ten: Should Denmark, Sweden, and the UK Join?* (Stockholm: SNS, 2009).

When the monetary union was formed in1999, the rules were not applied very strictly, however. As we saw in Section 15.4, there are some loopholes in the treaty, and these were used. Belgium, for example, was allowed to join although it had a level of debt that was far above 60 percent of GDP.

As we mentioned above, Germany experienced a period of weak growth in the beginning of the new millennium. As a result, German government finances deteriorated, and by 2003 Germany did not fulfil the rules of the Stability and Growth Pact. Nor did France fulfil the criteria. A strict application of the rules would have meant that Germany and France would be fined by the European Union, but this did not happen. Ultimately, the application of the rules was a political decision and ministers from the other countries did not want to make life difficult for their colleagues. Thus, a precedent was set: countries could break the rules of the Stability and Growth Pact without any sanctions from the European Union. The pact lost much of its credibility.

By the end of the first decade, there were fiscal crises in several euro countries: Portugal, Italy, Ireland, Greece, and Spain. The background was different in the different countries. Portugal and Italy had experienced weak growth and high government debt for many years. Ireland, Greece, and Spain had gone through boom–bust cycles as described in the previous section. Ireland and Spain had strong government finances before they went into recession and their problems were primary a result of banking crises caused by booms and busts in the property market. Greece had high debt and large deficits when the economy was doing well and things got completely out of hand when the boom ended.

It is important to realize that the seriousness of the crises in these countries was due to a combination of two problems:

1. High government debt and a large government deficit, so the debt continued to grow.
2. Weak competitiveness because of several years with inflation above the euro average.

High government debt and large government deficits are in no way unique for the Eurozone countries. In fact, the fiscal situation of the Eurozone as a whole is better than that of the US. In 2009, the fiscal situation of the US and the UK was similar to that of Spain, Ireland, and Portugal (see Fig. 11.4 in Chapter 11). House price bubbles and financial crises occurred in the US and the UK which had floating exchange rates. Thus, the fiscal problems were not due to the euro.

The key difference between a country that has a floating exchange rate and one that is member of a monetary union has to do with competitiveness. If a country with a floating exchange rate goes into a deep crisis, the value of its currency will normally depreciate. The weaker currency stimulates exports, which helps to pull the economy out of the recession. A combination of weak government finances and weak competitiveness is harder to deal with for a country that participates in a monetary union. When the country cannot adjust its exchange rate, there is a risk that it enters a negative spiral. High debt and deficits lead to high interest rates and force the government to cut expenditure, which has negative effects on aggregate demand, so production falls and this leads to a further reduction in tax revenue and a further increase in the deficit. This can happen outside a monetary union, but the risk that the situation becomes unmanageable is higher when exports do poorly because of weak competitiveness.

In fact, this is what happened in some euro countries. The most extreme case is that of Greece, which had weak government finances for a long time. In 2005, the interest rate on Greek ten-year government bonds was a couple of tenths of a percentage unit above the German rate, and this difference increased to half a percentage unit in 2007 and two percentage units in 2008. In 2010, it was revealed that the Greek government had not given correct information about its fiscal balances, and that the situation was even worse than had been previously reported. Lenders realized that Greece would probably default on its debt and the interest rate that Greece had to pay to issue new debt increased dramatically. Greece could no longer finance its borrowing in the private financial markets.

Similarly, lenders started to worry that Ireland, Portugal, Spain, and Italy would default on their debt, and the difference between the interest rates that these governments had to pay and the German interest rate increased dramatically. With higher interest rates, it became even harder to prevent the debt ratio from rising (see the analysis of fiscal sustainability in Chapter 11).

The response to the debt crisis by the European Union[16]

As discussed in Section 15.4, the spirit of the Maastricht Treaty was that each country should be responsible for its own government finances. Countries with fiscal problems should not be bailed out. As of March 2010, the Treaty of the European Union says that:

> 'Overdraft facilities or any other type of credit facility with the European Central Bank ... in favour of Union institutions, bodies, offices or agencies, central governments, regional, local or other public authorities ... shall be prohibited, as shall the purchase directly from them by the European Central Bank or national central banks of debt instruments.'

> 'The Union shall not be liable for or assume the commitments of central governments, regional, local or other public authorities ... of any Member State .... A Member State shall not be liable for or assume the commitments of central governments, regional, local or other public authorities ... of another Member State ....'

Only if a member state is in 'severe difficulties caused by natural disasters or exceptional occurrences beyond its control' can the European Union grant financial assistance to the member state concerned.

In fact, however, countries with fiscal problems were bailed out. The EU created two large funds, the European Financial Stability Facility (EFSF) and the European

---

16 Some information in this section is taken from Mats Persson, *The European Debt Crisis* (Stockholm, SNS, 2012) (in Swedish).

Financial Stability Mechanism (EFSM). These funds raise money by borrowing in the financial markets and give loans to troubled member countries with guarantees from the euro countries. By the beginning of 2012, these funds had been lending about 175 billion euros to Greece and about 146 billion euros to Portugal and Ireland. Also, the European Central Bank has bought government bonds from the troubled countries.

As a result of this, euro countries with fiscal problems can borrow at a lower interest rate than they could do in private financial markets. The lower interest rate is due to the guarantee that is given by the other euro countries, which have a better fiscal situation – that is, mainly Germany.

Even at this lower interest rate, the Greek government finances were out of control, and in March 2012, Greece defaulted on part of its government debt. But by this time, the EFSF, EFSM and ECB had taken over almost half the Greek government debt from banks and others who had held Greek bonds. The default was partial in the sense that the private holders of Greek bonds had their bonds replaced with bonds with longer maturity and a lower interest rate, which in effect reduced their value to about one quarter of the original bonds. Greece did not default on its debts to the EFSF, EFSM and ECB, however.

The end result was that a large part of the Greek debt was moved from banks, insurance companies, and other private investors to the EU. Legally, these actions were defended by referring to loopholes in the treaty, but the decisions were hardly in the spirit of the Maastricht Treaty. What started as a pure monetary union has now rapidly turned into a fiscal union where the euro countries take joint responsibility for each other's debts. Where this process will end remains to be seen.[17]

Conclusion

After more than ten years experience of the euro there is fairly clear evidence that the main arguments for and against monetary union are both relevant. The euro appears to have substantial positive effects on trade. On the other hand, serious macroeconomic imbalances have developed in *some* countries within the monetary union, and these imbalances are very difficult to deal with.

What have we learned?

From the 1870s until 1914 most major currencies were on the *gold standard*, which meant that the currencies were convertible to gold at fixed prices.

---

17 Interesting analyses of economic developments in Europe can be found in the *EEAG report on the European Economy*, which is published annually by CESifo: see www.cesifo-group.de, and reports from the Centre for Economic Policy Research: see www.cepr.org. See also Franklin Allen, Elena Carletti, and Giancarlo Corsetti, eds., 'Life within the Eurozone with or without sovereign default', report published by the European University Institute and Wharton Financial Institutions Center, 2011, available at http://cadmus.eui.eu/handle/1814/17716.

In the *Bretton Woods system* 1946–1971 most major currencies had a fixed exchange rate relative to the dollar while the dollar was convertible to gold at a fixed price.

The US dollar has been floating since the breakdown of the Bretton Woods system. The European countries tried to maintain fixed exchange rate arrangements in the 1970s but there were large inflation differentials and many exchange rate adjustments. The European Exchange Rate Mechanism (ERM), which was introduced in 1979, stipulated that all participating central banks should keep the exchange rates with respect to the other currencies within narrow intervals. ERM lead to greater exchange rate stability.

The *possibility* of devaluation means that there may be *speculation* in the financial markets about a future change in the exchange rate. Speculation against a currency creates a serious dilemma for the central bank. In order to defend the exchange rate it has to set a high interest rate, which has a negative effect on the economy, leading to further speculation that the currency will be devalued. At some point, it may become too costly to defend the exchange rate and the central bank may be forced to devalue the currency. In the ERM crisis in 1992, several countries had to let their currencies depreciate.

Today, few countries have fixed exchange rates but Denmark and some other countries have fixed exchange rates with respect to the euro within the ERM system.

Many countries with floating exchange rates adopted explicit inflation targets in the 1990s and they have been quite successful in keeping their inflation rates near the target. Sometimes they have experienced large fluctuations in real and nominal exchange rates which appear to be unrelated to the level of activity.

In 1999, 11 countries introduced the euro and by 2012, 17 of the member states in the European Union had introduced the euro.

Advantages of monetary union are that transaction costs are reduced, it becomes easier to compare prices, and there is less exchange rate uncertainty in the short and medium run. A common currency should facilitate trade but the effects on investment and growth are less clear theoretically.

The main cost of membership is that the country cannot adjust the interest rate and the exchange rate to economic conditions in the home country. This is a problem if economic developments in the country diverge substantially from the euro average. Normally, this should not be a problem but sometimes countries may end up with serious imbalances.

According to the Mundell–Fleming model, a floating exchange rate can ease the adjustment to shocks and imbalances. Within a monetary union, wage and price adjustment, labour mobility, and federal and national fiscal policy are the main adjustment mechanisms. Within the European Monetary Union, the former adjustment mechanisms are weak so national fiscal policy has a central role.

According to the theory of optimum currency areas, the choice as to whether to join a monetary union or not involves a comparison of benefits and costs. The more integrated countries are, economically and politically, the greater the benefits from monetary union and the smaller the costs.

The Maastricht Treaty in 1992 and the Stability and Growth Pact in 1997 stated that the government deficit (public sector net borrowing) should not exceeded a reference value of 3 percent of GDP and the gross consolidated government debt (i.e. the consolidated debt of the central government, local governments, and social security funds) should not exceeded a reference value of 60 percent of GDP. There are some escape clauses, however.

Statistical estimates indicate that the euro may have increased trade within the Eurozone by about 35 percent and trade between euro countries and countries outside the euro area has also increased because of the euro.

Inflation in the Eurozone has been 2 percent which is not very different from the average inflation rate for similar countries with floating exchange rates and explicit inflation targets. Growth in the Eurozone has been weak and the interest rate has been somewhat lower compared to similar countries with floating exchange rates and explicit inflation targets.

There have been substantial inflation differentials within the Eurozone. Some inflation differentials are to be expected since this is the way that real exchange rates can adjust when the nominal exchange rate is fixed and equal to unity.

Some countries in the Eurozone have experienced boom–bust cycles during the first decade. In the bust, their fiscal balances have deteriorated. Fiscal problems are in no way unique to the Eurozone but they may be harder to deal with when the country cannot use monetary policy, especially if there is also a problem of competitiveness.

Exercises

1. Compare the Bretton Woods system, the gold standard, a currency basket, and a target zone. What are the similarities and differences?

2. In Chapters 12 and 14 we showed that the following three objectives cannot be achieved at the same time:
   - a stable exchange rate
   - free capital flows
   - monetary policy independence.
   a) Explain why this is impossible.
   b) Is it possible to achieve two of these objectives while sacrificing one? If so, explain how this can be done for each pair.

3. Consider a small open economy with a large deficit in the government budget. Production is on the natural level and inflation is in line with the inflation target. A new government comes into power and, in order to eliminate the deficit, the government raises taxes. We assume that there is not full Ricardian equivalence.
   a) Assume that the country has a floating exchange rate. Analyse the adjustment process using the IS^*, Phillips and IP curves.
   b) Assume that the country is member of a monetary union. Analyse the adjustment process using the IS, Phillips and IP curves.
   c) What happens in each case above if there is full Ricardian equivalence?

4. Denmark has a fixed exchange rate with respect to the euro.
   a) Does this mean that interest rates in Denmark will be the same, higher, or lower compared with the interest rate in the Eurozone?

b) If the difference may vary over time, when will the Danish interest rate be higher/lower?

5. Fig. 15.3 shows that the dollar appreciated more than 20 percent, in real and nominal terms, between 1995 and 2001. In Chapters 3 and 4 you find diagrams showing US interest rates, inflation, and growth rates for GDP, consumption, and investment during this period. Discuss the following questions:
   a) How would inflation and growth have been affected if the dollar had not appreciated?
   b) Did the appreciation harm the US economy?

6. Fig. 15.3 shows that the pound appreciated by about 20 percent, in real and nominal terms, between 1995 and 1999. In Chapters 3 and 4 you find diagrams showing UK interest rates, inflation, and growth rates for GDP, consumption, and investment during this period. Discuss the following questions:
   a) How would inflation and growth have been affected if the pound had not appreciated?
   b) Did the appreciation harm the UK economy?

7. In 2012, the euro countries decided to keep a closer look at the current accounts of the countries in the Eurozone. Does this make sense? In what sense may a current account deficit signal problems/imbalances? Should balance in the current account be an objective of policy? (Before answering this question, repeat the discussion of the current account in Chapters 12 and 13.)

8. Consider a country with a fixed exchange rate, which is subject to an exchange rate crisis as described in this chapter. The country is in recession and there is speculation that the country will devalue its currency. What are the policy options for the government? Discuss the alternative options and their advantages and drawbacks. What can go wrong in each case?

9. 'Monetary union means that you have a common monetary policy. It should have nothing to do with fiscal policy.' Do you agree? Explain your answer.

10. 'Exports and imports have increased continuously relative to GDP. If this process continues, the case for joining the European Monetary Union will become stronger.' Do you agree? Explain your answer.

Answers to the exercises can be found at: **www.palgrave.com/economics/gottfries**.

Appendix

The forward market and covered interest parity

Consider a UK firm, which has ordered a machine from a German firm. The machine costs 1 million euros. It will be delivered in one year and paid for at the time of delivery. From the point of view of the UK firm, the payment for the machine is uncertain in terms of pounds. If the euro appreciates by 5 percent before the payment is made, the machine will cost 5 percent more in pounds. There are several ways in which the firm can guard against (hedge) the currency risk associated with the payment.

If the UK firm has the money to pay for the machine today, a simple way in which it can eliminate the uncertainty is to buy an appropriate amount of euros today and put the money in a euro account. This way, the firm is sure to have 1 million euros when it is time to pay and the cost in terms of pounds is no longer uncertain. But how does that affect the cost of buying the machine?

- In order to have an amount X in foreign currency in one year, the firm must deposit $X/(1+i^*)$ today in foreign currency, where i^* is the interest rate on an account in foreign currency, so the cost of the machine in domestic currency is $\dfrac{X/e}{1+i^*}$.

- If, instead, the firm exchanges to euros when it is time to pay, the actual cost is uncertain but the expected cost of the machine is $\dfrac{X/e^e}{1+i}$. We divide by one plus the domestic interest rate in order to express the cost in present value terms.

We see that the cost of insuring against exchange rate uncertainty depends on the interest rate differential. Note that if the uncovered interest parity condition holds – that is, $1+i^* = (1+i)\,e^e/e$ – the *expected* cost is the same, but by transferring the money to euros today, the firm avoids the uncertainty.

The above argument presupposes that the firm already has enough money to pay for the machine. If it does not, it can borrow a sufficient amount of pounds, exchange it for euros, and put it in a euro account. But since the interest rate on borrowing is higher that the interest rate on deposits, this will entail an extra cost for the firm. If it borrows pounds at 6 percent interest and puts the money in a euro account at 2 percent interest there will be an extra cost equal to 4 percent of the amount that is deposited.

Yet another way in which the firm can avoid the uncertainty is to buy 1 million euros in the *forward market*. This means that the firm makes a contract with a bank that it will buy 1 million euros in one year's time at a fixed price in pounds. This way, the firm knows what it will pay in pounds after one year. But what will the exchange rate be on such a contract? To ascertain this, note that the bank can hedge the uncertainty in the same way as we described above. If the bank signs a contract to sell 1 million euros for pounds in one year, it can move the corresponding amount of money from pounds to euros so as to be sure to have the money. The cost for the bank is the difference between the interest rates. To see this more precisely, assume that the bank offers to sell pounds in one year at the rate $f_{t,t+1}$. To hedge its risk, it buys euros today. For one pound it gets e_t euros and it lends the euros at the rate i_t^*. After one year it sells the euros at the price given in the forward contract, that is, $1/f_{t,t+1}$. The return to the bank in pounds is

$$e_t\left(1+i_t^*\right)\frac{1}{f_{t,t+1}}.$$

If the bank instead kept the money in pounds it would have received $1+i_t$. For the bank not to make a loss or profit on this contract, the two returns must be equal:

$$1+i_t = e_t\left(1+i_t^*\right)\frac{1}{f_{t,t+1}},$$

so the forward rate must be equal to $\left(1+i_t^*\right)e_t/\left(1+i_t\right)$. This arbitrage condition is called *covered interest parity* condition because it says that the return must be the same on holding assets in one currency as it is on buying assets in another currency, holding them, and exchanging the money back at the known forward rate. In practice, this condition holds almost perfectly for currencies that are traded in well-developed markets. It does not hold exactly, however, because there are transaction costs and banks charge a small fee for helping their customers to hedge the currency risk.

If we disregard transaction costs, the covered interest parity condition should hold independent of how investors value risk. The *uncovered interest parity* condition was derived in Chapter 12, assuming that lenders do not care about risk and simply invest where the expected return is highest:

$$1 + i_i^* = (1 + i_t) \frac{e_{t+1}^e}{e_t}.$$

The two conditions are closely related, however: if the uncovered interest parity condition holds, the forward exchange rate is equal to the expected future exchange rate. This is easily seen by comparing the two interest parity conditions.

Another way in which the bank can hedge the risk associated with the forward contract to sell euros is to buy euros forward from someone else. There may be a German firm that has ordered a machine from a UK firm and this machine is to be paid for in pounds. To guard against its currency risk, the German firm wants to buy pounds, and sell euros, in the forward market. Thus the banks can make a profit by selling and buying euros in the forward market without taking any risk themselves. By this form of intermediation, the currency risk is reduced for both buyers and sellers of euros.

In practice, there are many payments to be made at different points in time and in different currencies, so the matching of these positions is a complicated process. A particular bank may end up having sold more euros forward than it has bought and then it may buy euros forward from another bank so as to avoid currency risk. This matching process involves a large volume of transactions in the financial markets. Often, these transactions are described as 'speculation'. In fact, a large share of these financial transactions have exactly the opposite purpose: to hedge risks associated with fluctuations in exchange rates.

The no bail out clause and the excessive deficit procedure

The paragraphs below are taken from *Consolidated versions of the Treaty on European Union* and the *Treaty on the Functioning of the European Union* 30 March 2010, available at http://eur-lex.europa.eu/en/index.htm. The paragraphs below can be found in the latter part of the Treaty on the Functioning of the European Union.[18] 'The Commission' refers to the *European Commission*, which has one commissioner per member state, though members are bound to represent the interests of the EU as a whole rather than their home state. 'The Council'

---

18 The text is lightly edited. Some cross-references to other paragraphs have been omitted.

refs to the *Council of the European Union*. The Council consists of the relevant ministers representing the different member states.[19]

Article 122

1. Without prejudice to any other procedures provided for in the Treaties, the Council, on a proposal from the Commission, may decide, in a spirit of solidarity between Member States, upon the measures appropriate to the economic situation, in particular if severe difficulties arise in the supply of certain products, notably in the area of energy.
2. Where a Member State is in difficulties or is seriously threatened with severe difficulties caused by natural disasters or exceptional occurrences beyond its control, the Council, on a proposal from the Commission, may grant, under certain conditions, Union financial assistance to the Member State concerned. The President of the Council shall inform the European Parliament of the decision taken.

Article 123

1. Overdraft facilities or any other type of credit facility with the European Central Bank or with the central banks of the Member States (hereinafter referred to as 'national central banks') in favour of Union institutions, bodies, offices or agencies, central governments, regional, local or other public authorities, other bodies governed by public law, or public undertakings of Member States shall be prohibited, as shall the purchase directly from them by the European Central Bank or national central banks of debt instruments.
2. Paragraph 1 shall not apply to publicly owned credit institutions which, in the context of the supply of reserves by central banks, shall be given the same treatment by national central banks and the European Central Bank as private credit institutions.

Article 124

Any measure, not based on prudential considerations, establishing privileged access by Union institutions, bodies, offices or agencies, central governments, regional, local or other public authorities, other bodies governed by public law, or public undertakings of Member States to financial institutions, shall be prohibited.

Article 125

1. The Union shall not be liable for or assume the commitments of central governments, regional, local or other public authorities, other bodies governed by public law, or public undertakings of any Member State, without prejudice to mutual financial guarantees for the joint execution of a specific project. A Member State shall not be liable for or assume the commitments of central governments, regional, local or other public authorities, other bodies governed by public law, or public undertakings of another Member State, without

---

19　The *Council of the European Union* should not be confused with the *Council of Europe*, which is not an EU institution.

prejudice to mutual financial guarantees for the joint execution of a specific project.

2. The Council, on a proposal from the Commission and after consulting the European Parliament, may, as required, specify definitions for the application of the prohibitions referred to in Articles 123 and 124 and in this Article.

Article 126

1. Member States shall avoid excessive government deficits.
2. The Commission shall monitor the development of the budgetary situation and of the stock of government debt in the Member States with a view to identifying gross errors. In particular it shall examine compliance with budgetary discipline on the basis of the following two criteria:
   (a) whether the ratio of the planned or actual government deficit to gross domestic product exceeds a reference value, unless:
      – either the ratio has declined substantially and continuously and reached a level that comes close to the reference value,
      – or, alternatively, the excess over the reference value is only exceptional and temporary and the ratio remains close to the reference value;
   (b) whether the ratio of government debt to gross domestic product exceeds a reference value, unless the ratio is sufficiently diminishing and approaching the reference value at a satisfactory pace.
      The reference values are specified in the Protocol on the excessive deficit procedure annexed to the Treaties.
3. If a Member State does not fulfil the requirements under one or both of these criteria, the Commission shall prepare a report. The report of the Commission shall also take into account whether the government deficit exceeds government investment expenditure and take into account all other relevant factors, including the medium-term economic and budgetary position of the Member State.

   The Commission may also prepare a report if, notwithstanding the fulfilment of the requirements under the criteria, it is of the opinion that there is a risk of an excessive deficit in a Member State.
4. The Economic and Financial Committee shall formulate an opinion on the report of the Commission.
5. If the Commission considers that an excessive deficit in a Member State exists or may occur, it shall address an opinion to the Member State concerned and shall inform the Council accordingly.
6. The Council shall, on a proposal from the Commission, and having considered any observations which the Member State concerned may wish to make, decide after an overall assessment whether an excessive deficit exists.
7. Where the Council decides, in accordance with paragraph 6, that an excessive deficit exists, it shall adopt, without undue delay, on a recommendation from the Commission, recommendations addressed to the Member State concerned with a view to bringing that situation to an end within a given period. Subject to the provisions of paragraph 8, these recommendations shall not be made public.

8. Where it establishes that there has been no effective action in response to its recommendations within the period laid down, the Council may make its recommendations public.

9. If a Member State persists in failing to put into practice the recommendations of the Council, the Council may decide to give notice to the Member State to take, within a specified time limit, measures for the deficit reduction which is judged necessary by the Council in order to remedy the situation.

   In such a case, the Council may request the Member State concerned to submit reports in accordance with a specific timetable in order to examine the adjustment efforts of that Member State.

10. The rights to bring actions provided for in Articles 258 and 259 may not be exercised within the framework of paragraphs 1 to 9 of this Article.

11. As long as a Member State fails to comply with a decision taken in accordance with paragraph 9, the Council may decide to apply or, as the case may be, intensify one or more of the following measures:
    – to require the Member State concerned to publish additional information, to be specified by the Council, before issuing bonds and securities,
    – to invite the European Investment Bank to reconsider its lending policy towards the Member State concerned,
    – to require the Member State concerned to make a non-interest-bearing deposit of an appropriate size with the Union until the excessive deficit has, in the view of the Council, been corrected,
    – to impose fines of an appropriate size.
    The President of the Council shall inform the European Parliament of the decisions taken.

12. The Council shall abrogate some or all of its decisions or recommendations referred to in paragraphs 6 to 9 and 11 to the extent that the excessive deficit in the Member State concerned has, in the view of the Council, been corrected. If the Council has previously made public recommendations, it shall, as soon as the decision under paragraph 8 has been abrogated, make a public statement that an excessive deficit in the Member State concerned no longer exists.

13. When taking the decisions or recommendations referred to in paragraphs 8, 9, 11 and 12, the Council shall act on a recommendation from the Commission.

   When the Council adopts the measures referred to in paragraphs 6 to 9, 11 and 12, it shall act without taking into account the vote of the member of the Council representing the Member State concerned.

PART 5 BUSINESS CYCLES, POLICYMAKING, FINANCIAL MARKETS

What are business cycles and why do they occur?

Most of the time, real GDP grows from one year to the next, but it does not grow at a constant rate. Boom periods with high growth are followed by periods of low growth or even declines in GDP. Periods of negative income growth are called *recessions*. In the US, the National Bureau of Economic Research defines recessions as occurring if there are at least two consecutive quarters with negative growth of real GDP.

It is not just production that fluctuates. Consumption, investment, and employment fluctuate together with GDP in a way that is very similar over time and in different countries. It is this common pattern of co-variation that we refer to when we talk about the business cycle.

But what do these fluctuations look like and why do they arise? In this chapter we describe the business cycle and we discuss why business cycles occur. We first consider different methods that are used to decompose GDP into a trend and a cyclical component. Then we examine the co-movement of consumption, investment, government consumption, imports, and exports over the business cycle. We also discuss why there are business cycles and how problematic they are for society.

16.1 The trend and the cycle

Economists often divide real GDP into a *trend* and a *cyclical* component. The terms 'trend' and 'cycle' are used differently by different authors, but usually the idea is that changes in the trend component represent *permanent* changes in GDP, while changes in the cyclical component represent *temporary* deviations from the trend. This is the way we will use the terms trend and cycle in this chapter. Denoting the log of real GDP by y_t, we can write the decomposition into trend and cycle as follows:

$$y_t = y_t^T + y_t^C,$$

where y_t^T is the trend component, and y_t^C is the cyclical component.

What factors drive the trend and the cyclical fluctuations? According to the theory presented in Chapter 5, the factors driving the trend component are those that permanently change the natural level of production. Permanent changes in production may be caused by permanent changes in

- technology
- capital stock
- human capital (the education and experience of the workforce)
- population
- labour force participation
- the natural level of unemployment.

What causes cyclical fluctuations? As we saw in Chapter 8, demand shocks can cause production to deviate temporarily from the natural level, and such shocks may cause cyclical fluctuations.

Note, however, that there may also be *temporary* changes in production possibilities, which cause temporary variations in the natural level of production. A crop failure will cause a deviation from trend in production even if production is continuously on the natural level. Structural change, leading to the closing down of a major industry, may also cause a temporarily low natural level of production. Thus, cyclical fluctuations may be caused by shocks emanating from the demand as well as the supply side.

Thus, the distinction between the trend and the cyclical component is not the same as that between the *natural level of production* and the *output gap*. According to the theory presented in Chapters 2–9, the natural level of production is what production would have been if prices had been completely flexible. Production can only temporarily deviate from the natural level. This means that the trend must be driven by permanent changes in the natural level of production, but temporary variations in the natural level of production are part of the cycle as we have defined it above. Table 16.1 shows the relation between the shocks, the trend, the cycle, and the natural level of production.

The question arises how to divide production into a temporary and a permanent part. Several different methods are used for this purpose, and they yield somewhat different results. Here we will present these approaches briefly without going into the details of how different statistical models are estimated.

A linear trend

The simplest approach is to assume that the trend is linear:

$$y_t^T = a + bt.$$

Here t is a variable that increases by one unit every year, so it can take values 1, 2, 3, 4, ... This means that y_t^T increases b units every year. As was explained in Chapter 1, the change in the log of a variable is approximately equal to the relative change of that variable, so if $b = 0.03$ trend GDP increases by 3 percent each year. Substituting for y_t^T in the equation above we get

Table 16.1 *Factors causing permanent and temporary variations in production*

	Natural level of production	Output gap
Trend	Permanent changes in production possibilities	–
Cycle	Temporary changes in production possibilities	Demand shocks

$$y_t = a + bt + y_t^C.$$

If we run a statistical regression of GDP on a constant and time, we get estimates of the coefficients a and b. The trend component can then be calculated as

$$\hat{y}_t^T = \hat{a} + \hat{b}t.$$

where circumflexes denote the estimated values of the coefficients a and b. Furthermore, an estimate of the cyclical component of log of GDP can be calculated as the deviation from the trend line:

$$\hat{y}_t^C = y_t - \hat{a} - \hat{b}t.$$

We can make the trend somewhat more flexible by including a break in the trend at some point. Many countries experienced a slowdown of economic growth around 1970, so we could allow for a break at that point. This is easily done by specifying the trend as

$$y_t^T = a + b \cdot t + c \cdot t70,$$

where $t70$ is a variable that is zero until 1970 and then increases one unit every year, and a, b, and c are coefficients to be estimated.

Fig. 16.1 shows actual GDP, trend and the trend deviation for some countries. A break in the trend is assumed to occur in 1970. We see that the cyclical component of GDP is itself very persistent. Production tends to stay above or below the trend for many years. When production rises above trend, the best prediction is that it will stay above the trend for several years.

The same point can be seen if we look at growth rates of GDP in Fig. 16.2. If production were to quickly return to trend, we would expect growth rates to be negatively correlated over time. A period of high growth would be quickly followed by a period of low growth. This is not at all what we see. Instead, high growth continues for several years, followed by a number of years with low growth. This again shows that GDP does not quickly revert to some stable trend line.

If we think of the problem in terms of economic theory, we realize that a linear trend is very rigid. It says that, except for the break in 1970, the percentage change in the permanent part of income is the same each year. But this is not very plausible. The main factor driving the trend is technological change in a broad sense, including changes in organization and institutions which affect the natural level of production. An important part of economic development is restructuring, which involves closure of production units that are no longer profitable and creation of new ones, which may produce completely new goods and services. There is no reason to believe that the pace at which this development takes place has been constant between 1970 and 2010. Clearly, there are years with faster and slower rates of technological change and restructuring. Put differently, the permanent change in GDP is probably not exactly the same from year to year, so a linear trend is probably too rigid.

The Hodrick–Prescott filter

A more flexible way to construct a trend line is to use the *Hodrick–Prescott* filter. Without going into the technicalities, we can think of this method as a technique for drawing a smooth curve through a rocky graph where the researcher himself

Fig. 16.1 *Log of real GDP and linear trend with a break in 1970*

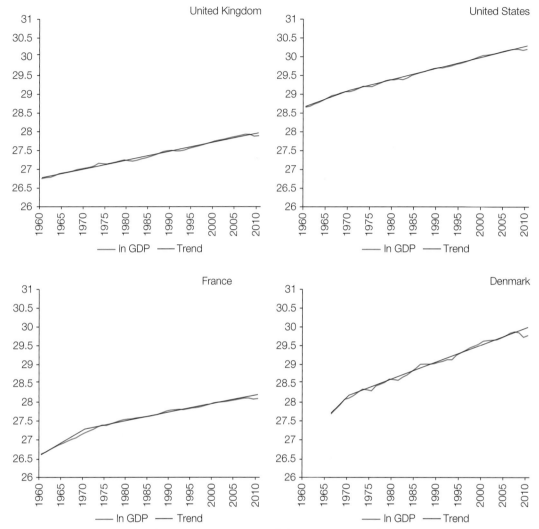

Source: Calculations based on data from *OECD Economic Outlook*, OECD, 4 November 2011, http://www.oecd-ilibrary.org/statistics.

decides how smooth the curve should be. By choosing a parameter that governs the smoothness of the trend, the researcher can force the trend to be very smooth or more varying. If a high degree of smoothness is imposed, the trend will be very similar to the linear trend discussed above. If the trend is made very flexible, the trend will be close to the series itself. For an intermediate level of smoothness, the trend will be in-between these two extremes. Normally, the smoothness parameter is chosen so that the trend becomes very smooth, yet more flexible than a linear trend. The Hodrick–Prescott filter is described in the appendix to this chapter.

An advantage of the Hodrick–Prescott filter is that it allows trend growth to vary instead of being constant for 40 years. A disadvantage is that the division between trend and cycle is arbitrary since it depends on the smoothing parameter chosen by the person who constructs the trend.

Fig. 16.2 *GDP growth*

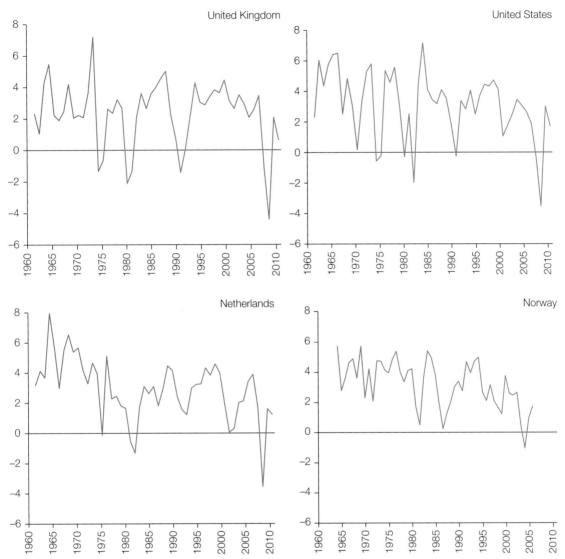

Source: *OECD Economic Outlook*, OECD, 4 November 2011, http://www.oecd-ilibrary.org/statistics.

A stochastic trend

As we have seen, fluctuations in GDP are very persistent. If GDP rises above the linear trend, the best prediction is that GDP will remain high. If there is a recession – if GDP declines – the best prediction is that GDP will remain low for some time. In fact, we cannot be sure that GDP will ever return to the original trend line after a shock. An alternative way to think of the trend is to assume that the trend itself is stochastic. This means that there are random shocks both to the cyclical and to the trend component of GDP. The following statistical model includes a *stochastic trend*:

$$y_t = y_t^T + y_t^C,$$
$$y_t^T = g + y_{t-1}^T + \varepsilon_t^T,$$
$$y_t^C = \varepsilon_t^C + b_1 \varepsilon_{t-1}^C + b_2 \varepsilon_{t-2}^C.$$

Here, the trend component y_t^T is what it was in the previous period plus a constant g plus a random shock ε_t^T. Such a process is called a *random walk with drift*. The constant g captures the average growth rate and ε_t^T is a random shock. This specification implies that the shock ε_t^T has a permanent effect on GDP. This is most easily seen by taking the equation for y_t^T in the next period, and substituting the equation for y_t^T to get

$$y_{t+1}^T = g + y_t^T + \varepsilon_{t+1}^T = g + \left(g + y_{t-1}^T + \varepsilon_t^T\right) + \varepsilon_{t+1}^T = y_{t-1}^T + 2g + \varepsilon_t^T + \varepsilon_{t+1}^T.$$

We see that a shock in period t raises production in periods t and $t + 1$ by the same amount. The same applies to future periods, so a shock in one period raises the whole expected future path of production.

The shock ε_t^C is a cyclical shock that has a temporary effect on GDP. In this case, the effect of the cyclical shock is assumed to last for three years. The coefficients g, b_1, and b_2 are unknown and the variables y_t^T and y_t^C are unobserved. The only thing we can observe is y_t. This model can be estimated with a sophisticated statistical technique called the Kalman filter.[1] Actual and estimated trend GDP is shown in Fig. 16.3. This specification of the trend is more flexible, so a larger part of the fluctuations in GDP are ascribed to the trend component.

Compared with the model with a linear trend, this model has very different implications for long-run forecasts of GDP. In the model with a linear trend, GDP always returns to the linear trend, independent of what shocks have occurred. In the stochastic trend specification, shocks to the trend component have permanent effects on GDP.

Comparison of alternative measures

Fig. 16.4 shows three measures of the cyclical component of GDP for the US. These are obtained by linear de-trending with a break in 1970, by de-trending with the Hodrick–Prescott filter, and by estimating the stochastic trend by the Kalman filter. The three measures of the cyclical component of GDP are fairly similar, but the measures diverge considerably towards the end when there was an exceptionally large decline in GDP because of the financial crisis.

The size of the cyclical variation depends on how flexible we make the trend. The Hodrick–Prescott trend is more flexible than the linear trend, so the cyclical variations become somewhat smaller with this method compared to the linear trend. The stochastic trend is even more flexible, so the cyclical fluctuations

---

1 Another name for this type of model is a state-space model. The variables y_t^T and y_t^C are unobserved state variables which determine the observable variable y_t (GDP) and which follow specific laws of motion.

Fig. 16.3 *Log GDP and stochastic trend, United States*

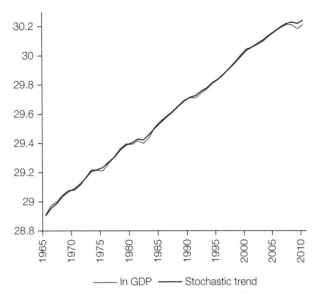

———— ln GDP ———— Stochastic trend

Note: The figure shows the natural log of GDP and the estimated stochastic trend.
Source: Calculations based on data from *OECD Economic Outlook*, OECD, 11 November 2011,
http://www.oecd-ilibrary.org/statistics. Trend estimated in EViews.

Fig. 16.4 *Cyclical component of GDP using three different detrending methods,*
United States

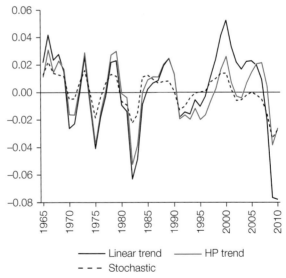

———— Linear trend ———— HP trend
– – – Stochastic

Source: Calculations based on data from *OECD Economic Outlook*, OECD, 11 November 2011,
http://www.oecd-ilibrary.org/statistics.

become smallest when we assume the trend to be stochastic. Statistical tests do
not give a clear answer as to which of these models of the trend fits the data best,
and different economists use different methods to decompose GDP, and other
variables, into trends and cycles.

How long do business cycles last?

Looking at the different measures of the cyclical component, we see that peaks in production occurred in 1966, 1973, 1979, 1989, 2000, and around 2006, and that troughs occurred in 1970, 1975, 1982, 1991, 2002, and 2009–2010. This means that the time from one peak to the next varied between 6 and 11 years. Thus we see that business cycles have quite variable length and that fluctuations in GDP are quite persistent. If GDP increases unexpectedly, our forecasts for future GDP should normally be revised upwards, and when GDP declines, it may take considerable time before it recovers.

16.2   Co-movement of macroeconomic variables

How do the different components of demand fluctuate over the business cycle? To analyse this question, we need to look at the cyclical fluctuations in the variables. There are different ways of describing business cycle fluctuations. One way is to look at the growth rates of GDP and the main components of aggregate demand. By looking at growth rates, we bypass the problem of defining the trend. This is what we did when we first looked at the data for consumption and investment in Chapters 3 and 4. There we saw that the growth rates of consumption and investment are positively correlated with the growth rate of GDP and that investment is much more volatile than GDP while private consumption fluctuates about as much as GDP.

The same thing can be illustrated by looking at the cyclical components of these variables. Fig. 16.5 shows the cyclical components of consumption, investment, and production. The cyclical components have been estimated by fitting a Hodrick–Prescott trend for the log of each variable and calculating the cyclical component as the deviation from the trend. We see that investment and consumption are highly correlated with GDP. In fact, the trend deviations in private consumption are strikingly similar to the trend deviations in production. Investment is much more volatile than private consumption but it constitutes a smaller component of aggregate demand. Therefore it is not obvious whether fluctuations in investment or consumption are most important for fluctuations in aggregate demand.

How much do the different components of demand contribute to the business cycle? One way of establishing this is to start from the GDP identity:

$$Y = C + I + G + X - IM$$

and differentiate:

$$\Delta Y = \Delta C + \Delta I + \Delta G + \Delta X - \Delta IM.$$

Dividing by Y we can rewrite this:

$$\frac{\Delta Y}{Y} = \frac{\Delta C}{Y} + \frac{\Delta I}{Y} + \frac{\Delta G}{Y} + \frac{\Delta X}{Y} - \frac{\Delta IM}{Y},$$

Fig. 16.5 *Cyclical variations in private consumption, total investment, and production*

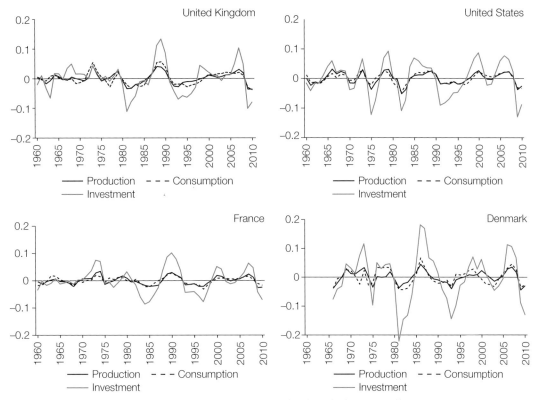

Note: All variables are measured as deviations from trend constructed with Hodrick–Prescott filter.
Source: *OECD Economic Outlook*, OECD, 4 November 2011, http://www.oecd-ilibrary.org/statistics. Hodrick–Prescott trend calculated in EViews.

and

$$\frac{\Delta Y}{Y} = \frac{\Delta C}{C}\frac{C}{Y} + \frac{\Delta I}{I}\frac{I}{Y} + \frac{\Delta G}{G}\frac{G}{Y} + \frac{\Delta X}{X}\frac{X}{Y} - \frac{\Delta IM}{IM}\frac{IM}{Y}.$$

In the first term we have multiplied and divided by C and similarly for the other terms. As we see from this equation, the importance of each component for aggregate demand depends on two factors:

1. how volatile it is, as measured by percentage changes of the variable itself, and
2. how large the demand component is compared with GDP.

Investment seems to be two or three times as volatile as private consumption. In Chapter 1 we saw that private consumption constitutes 50–60 percent of aggregate demand in most countries, while investment constitutes 20–30 percent.

Thus, private consumption is about twice as large as investment, but more stable, so the contributions to fluctuations in aggregate demand from private consumption and investment are of similar magnitude.

Clearly, the positive correlation between private consumption, investment, and GDP is a result of two-way causation. Private consumption and investment are the main components of aggregate demand, so if consumers and investors spend more because they become more optimistic about the future, GDP will increase. But the causation goes also in the other direction, from GDP to consumption and investment. As we have just seen, changes in GDP are generally quite persistent, so if GDP increases, consumers should revise their expectations about future incomes and spend a substantial part of the increase in income. A persistent increase in income also means that firms need more capital to satisfy future demand, so investment will increase. Therefore we should expect both consumption and investment to increase if there is an increase in GDP for some exogenous reason.

Thus we have two-way causation. Independent of whether the shocks originate on the supply side or the demand side, we would expect consumption and investment to be positively correlated with GDP. Therefore, the high correlation between production, consumption, and investment is not surprising.

Fig. 16.6 shows cyclical fluctuations in government consumption and GDP. Overall, there is no clear cyclical pattern. We see no evidence of countercyclical fiscal policy when it comes to government consumption. Still, one may argue that the government plays a stabilizing role because government consumption is more stable than GDP. This is largely due to the fact that expenditure on services such as education, health care, and defence is not very cyclical. As discussed in Chapter 11, government tax revenue fluctuates automatically with GDP and this, in combination with stable government consumption, leads to the automatic stabilizing effect of government that we analysed in Chapter 11.

Fig. 16.7 shows cyclical variation in imports, exports, and production. As we noted in Chapter 12, imports are strongly correlated with GDP. The reason, of course, is that an increase in consumption and investment leads to increased demand for goods produced domestically as well as abroad, so domestic production and imports both increase. As discussed in Chapter 12, imports vary more than GDP because a substantial part of imports consist of durable goods, investment goods, and raw materials and demand for such goods is more volatile than demand for domestically produced services such as haircuts or health care.

Exports are also positively correlated with GDP, but less so than imports. Exports are not driven by domestic demand but by foreign demand, and although business cycles in different countries are correlated, they are not perfectly correlated. There are periods when foreign demand increases although the domestic economy is weak, and vice versa.

Fig. 16.6 *Cyclical variations in government consumption and production*

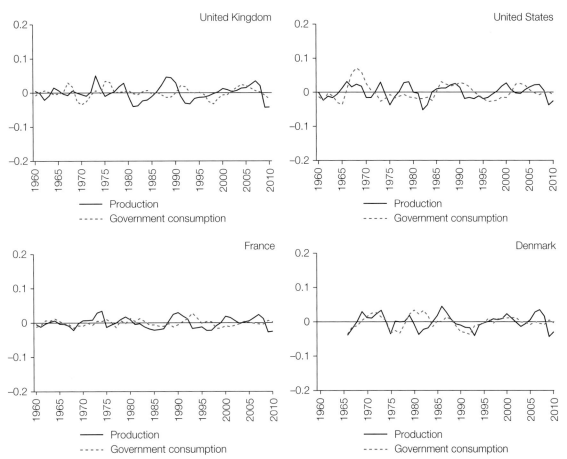

Note: All variables are measured as deviations from trend constructed with Hodrick–Prescott filter.
Source: *OECD Economic Outlook*, OECD, 4 November 2001, http://www.oecd-ilibrary.org/statistics. Hodrick–Prescott trend calculated in EViews.

To sum up, we see that consumption, investment, and imports are positively correlated with GDP. Exports are less well correlated with the cycle and government consumption has no strong cyclical pattern.

16.3   What drives the business cycles?

But why are there business cycles in the first place? Going back to our macroeconomic model, we realize that the endogenous variables in our macroeconomic model can only fluctuate if there is some variation in the exogenous variables. We use the term 'shocks' to denote changes in the exogenous variables. But what are those exogenous shocks and what shocks are large enough to generate the business cycle fluctuations that we observe? By what mechanisms do exogenous shocks lead to business cycles?

Fig. 16.7 *Cyclical variations in exports, imports, and production*

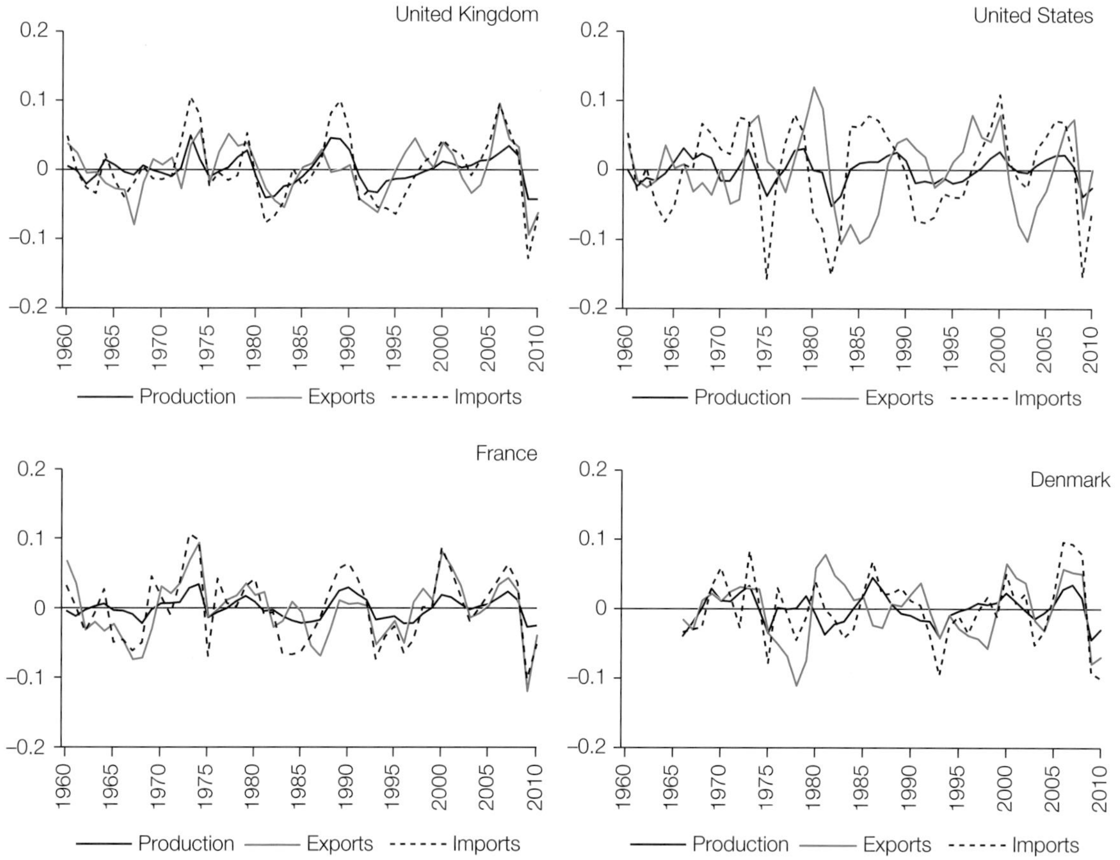

Note: All variables are measured as deviations from trend constructed with Hodrick–Prescott filter.
Source: *OECD Economic Outlook*, OECD, 4 November 2011, http://www.oecd-ilibrary.org/statistics. HP trend calculated in EViews.

Shocks can emanate from the supply and the demand side, and various amplification mechanisms can magnify the effects of exogenous shocks.

Shocks

Technology shocks

One obvious candidate shock is a change in production possibilities. As discussed above, the pace of technological change, in a wide sense of the word, is hardly constant. One line of research, called *real business cycle theory*, tries to explain business cycles as a result of changes in production possibilities, for short called 'technology shocks'. The basic real business cycle model was developed by economists Finn Kydland from Norway and Edward Prescott from the United States. It is a closed economy model which is based on competitive markets and flexible prices.[2] Production is always on the natural level so the output gap is zero.

---

2 The Nobel Prize 2004 was awarded jointly to Finn E. Kydland and Edward C. Prescott 'for their contributions to dynamic macroeconomics: the time consistency of economic policy and the driving forces behind business cycles'.

There is no unemployment but workers vary their labour supply and they work more when the real wage is high. There are exogenous changes in factor productivity (E in the production function). These 'technology shocks' are assumed to be persistent but not permanent. This means that an improvement in productivity in one period can be expected to remain in future periods, but eventually it dies off.

In fact, this simple theory can explain several of the basic facts of the business cycle. A positive and persistent technology shock raises production possibilities and the marginal product of labour. With a higher marginal product of labour, the real wage increases, and workers increase their labour supply. Since the technology shock is persistent, investment becomes more profitable and, since consumers feel richer, they increase their consumption. Hence aggregate supply and demand both increase and there is a simultaneous increase in production, hours worked, consumption, and investment. Since the shock is persistent, but not completely permanent, consumers want to smooth their consumption over time, so consumption will increase less than income. In a closed economy, all production that is not consumed will be invested, so investment varies more than GDP. Therefore, the model can explain a high volatility of investment, as we observe in the data.

The real business cycle model fares less well in explaining prices. According to the real business cycle theory, real wages and real interest rates both increase when there is a positive technology shock, but this is not apparent in the data. Looking across countries there is no clear evidence that real wages and real interest rates move in a systematic way over the cycle.[3]

Another weakness of the real business cycle model is that it disregards unemployment and explains variations in hours worked as variations in works hours supplied by the typical worker. But most of the fluctuations that we see in hours worked are due to movements of workers between employment and unemployment, rather than changes in labour supply by those workers who have jobs. As we saw in Chapter 6, most of the workers who get jobs in a boom are workers who were unemployed in the recession – that is, they were willing to work, able to work, and searching actively for work.

Another common critique of real business cycle theory is that it is unlikely that there are sufficiently large changes in technology to generate business cycles. Technological progress is the result of thousands of inventions, which are gradually developed and implemented, and it is hard to believe that individual innovations lead to large jumps in aggregate productivity. But if we interpret 'technology' more broadly, to include reorganization and restructuring, and closures of major industries, we realize that there are indeed changes in the pace of technological development. One example is the slow-down of growth that occurred around 1970, and which is sometimes blamed on government regulations and strong

5

---

3 In the US, the real wage has been found to be slightly pro-cyclical, but not sufficiently to explain employment fluctuations as movements along the labour supply function. To do that, one would have to have an implausibly large elasticity of labour supply; see Gary Solon, Robert Barsky, and Jonathan Parker, 'Measuring the cyclicality of real wages: how important is composition bias', *Quarterly Journal of Economics*, 109 (1994), 1–25.

unions. Another example is the acceleration in growth in the 1990s, which is often attributed to the wide adoption of information technology that occurred in this period. Thus, it is undeniable that there are changes in the pace of technological progress – in the broad sense of the term.

Nevertheless, many economists find it implausible to explain large recessions by technology shocks. Was the recent crisis, where GDP decreased by 5 per-cent in many countries, a result of a negative technology shock? This seems unlikely.

Animal spirits

If technology shocks are not the only cause of business cycles, what are the other shocks? The conventional answer from economists with a 'Keynesian' view of the world would be 'demand shocks'. As we saw in Chapter 8, demand shocks can cause temporary deviations of production from its natural level when wages and prices adjust slowly. But where do demand shocks come from? Why would con-sumers suddenly decide to consume more, or less? Why would firms decide to invest more if there is not some fundamental change in production possibilities that motivates higher investment?

John Maynard Keynes used the term *animal spirits* to point to the importance of confidence and changes in moods; sometimes, there are periods when people are very optimistic, and sometimes this optimism is replaced by pessimism and fear. Keynes wrote:

> '*Even apart from the instability due to speculation, there is the instability due to the characteristic of human nature that a large proportion of our positive activities depend on spontaneous optimism rather than mathematical expectations, whether moral or hedonistic or economic. Most, probably, of our decisions to do something positive, the full consequences of which will be drawn out over many days to come, can only be taken as the result of animal spirits – of a spontaneous urge to action rather than inaction, and not as the outcome of a weighted average of quantitative benefits multiplied by quantitative probabilities.*'[4]

We see changes in moods in the stock market, which may shift within a couple of months from being an optimistic 'bull market' to a pessimistic 'bear market'. Changes of moods affect the stock market, but also firms' willingness to invest, and households' willingness to buy new cars and houses. But where do these changes in moods come from? Throughout this book we have emphasized the idea that consumers and firms make rational decisions so as to maximize utility and prof-its. To simply add some exogenous changes in moods is not very satisfactory as an explanation.

---

4 John Maynard Keynes, *The General Theory of Employment, Interest and Money* (London: Macmillan, 1973 [first edn 1936], p. 161.

What we can say, however, is that expectations play an extremely important role in economic decision-making. As we saw in Chapters 3 and 4, decisions about consumption and investment are inherently forward-looking decisions. Consumption and investment decisions are not primarily determined by what happens today, but by what consumers and firms *expect* to happen tomorrow. Therefore, expected future income is the single most important factor that determines the level of demand for goods and services today.

There are often reasons for expectations to change. Unexpected events happen all the time and when they do happen it is often hard to evaluate their consequences. The US stock market crash in October 1987, the collapse of the Soviet Union in 1991, the ERM crisis in 1992, the Asian financial crisis in 1997, Russia's default on government debt in 1998, the emergence of the dot-com bubble in the late 1990s and its collapse in 2000, the al-Qaeda attack in 2001, the financial crisis in 2008, and the Arab spring and the earthquake in Japan in 2011 were all largely unforeseen events whose consequences were hard to evaluate when they happened, and which affected the expectations of firms and households.

Note also that changes in expectations are partly self-fulfilling. If consumers and managers become more pessimistic about the future, consumption, investment, and aggregate demand will fall, and this in itself will lead to a reduction in demand and production. As we saw earlier in this chapter, changes in the level of production are generally quite persistent, so if production falls, it is rational to expect economic activity to remain low for some time.

The worldwide financial crisis, which broke out in the autumn of 2008, is a dramatic example of how expectations can change very rapidly. This crisis started because some financial institutions (primarily banks and investment banks) had made large losses and some of them even went bankrupt. Since financial institutions have claims on each other in a complicated network, there were worries that these problems would spread and that other financial institutions would collapse. Expectations changed dramatically within a few months in the autumn of 2008. Across the world, investment plans were put on hold, and orders for machines, cars, and lorries were cancelled. Workers were threatened by redundancy. Consumers became worried and reduced their consumption. Consumption, investment, demand, and production decreased substantially within a few months.

Was this a rational reaction on the part of firms and consumers? Even with hindsight, this is hard to say. There was indeed a deep recession, so, to a large extent, the change in expectations became self-fulfilling. In the end, there was no worldwide collapse of banks, but when the financial crisis started, nobody knew how deep the crisis would be. In fact, a worldwide collapse of banks was avoided only because governments and central banks stepped in with massive support to troubled banks. If the authorities had been less successful in doing this, the outcome could have been much worse.

5

The financial crisis in 2008–2009 is an extreme example, but it illustrates in a clear way that expectations can change quickly and have large effects on aggregate demand. The same thing happens, but on a smaller scale, in normal business cycles. When we look at historical data, it is easy to draw a smooth trend line that captures the long-run development of GDP, but when we look into the future, we are genuinely uncertain about future growth, and our expectations may change from one year to the next.

Today, there is generally wide agreement among economists that both supply and demand shocks contribute to the business cycle, but there is disagreement about the relative importance of supply and demand shocks.

Amplification mechanisms

Whatever the underlying shocks are, the effects of shocks can be increased by mechanisms that amplify the effects of the shocks. Three such amplification mechanisms are the *multiplier effect*, the *accelerator effect*, and the *financial accelerator effect*.

The multiplier effect

The *multiplier effect* was explained in Chapter 8. It is based on the assumption that wages and prices change slowly, so, in the short run, production is determined by aggregate demand. If demand increases for some reason, production increases, workers get jobs, and households see their incomes increase. As a result, private consumption increases, and this leads to a further increase in aggregate demand. The size of the multiplier effect depends on how consumers' expectations are affected. As we have just seen, changes in income are typically persistent, so it would normally make sense to revise expectations about future income when current income increases. Consumption theory tells us that, if an increase in income is perceived as permanent, consumption should increase by as much as the increase in income (see Chapter 4).

There are two factors that reduce the size of the multiplier, however:

- Since tax revenue is a function of income, a substantial fraction of an increase in income will go to taxes rather than to consumption.
- In an open economy, a substantial share of consumption expenditure is directed towards goods produced abroad.

What is a realistic number for the multiplier effect when we take account of these factors? To find out, consider the multiplier for an exogenous increase in investment in the open economy. Let private consumption be determined by disposable income according to

$$C = c_0 + c_1 (Y - T).$$

Let the tax schedule be $T = \tau Y - Tr$ and assume also that imports are proportional to GDP:

$$IM = qY.$$

Then we have

$$Y = C + I + G + X - IM = c_0 + c_1 (Y + Tr - \tau Y) + I + G + X - qY.$$

We can calculate the multiplier for an exogenous increase in investment in the same way as we did in Chapter 14:

$$\frac{\Delta Y}{\Delta I} = \frac{1}{1 - (1 - \tau)\, c_1 + q}.$$

We see that a high marginal tax (τ) and a high marginal propensity to import (q) reduce the size of the multiplier. Let us calculate the multiplier for a large economy with a small government sector, such as the US, and a small open economy with a large government sector, such as Sweden. To do this, we need numbers for the marginal propensity to consume, the marginal tax rate, and the marginal propensity to import:

- In line with the arguments made above, we assume that the increase in income is perceived as persistent, so the marginal propensity to consume is close to unity; we set $c_1 = 0.8$.
- In Chapter 11 we reported the government share of income to be 31 percent in the US and 54 percent in Sweden. To simplify, we assume that taxes are proportional to income so we set $\tau = 0.31$ for the US and $\tau = 0.54$ for Sweden.
- In Chapter 1 we saw that imports are 18 percent of GDP in the US and 46 percent of GDP in Sweden. Thus we set $q = 0.18$ for the US and $q = 0.46$ for Sweden.

For the US we get

$$\frac{\Delta Y}{\Delta I} = \frac{1}{1 - (1 - 0.31) \cdot 0.8 + 0.18} \approx 1.59.$$

An exogenous increase in investment leads to an increase in GDP which is more than 50 percent larger than the initial shock. For the Sweden we get

$$\frac{\Delta Y}{\Delta I} = \frac{1}{1 - (1 - 0.54) \cdot 0.8 + 0.46} \approx 0.92.$$

The multiplier is somewhat lower than unity. The reason, of course is that much of the increase in demand is directed towards imports and the multiplier effect is reduced by a high marginal tax rate. Thus we can conclude that the multiplier effect is much more important in a large economy than it is in a small economy. We should remember, however, that the imports of one country are the exports of another country, so on the international level, we still have substantial multiplier effects.

What about the empirical evidence on multiplier effects? In Chapter 11, we discussed the evidence on effects of fiscal policy in the US. We found that the direction of the effect was as expected although different studies produced quite different estimates of the multiplier. Focusing on open economies, Roel Beetsma, Massimo Giuliodori, and Frank Klassen studied the effects of shocks to government purchases in the European economies using the VAR methodology described in Chapter 8.[5] They found that an increase in government purchases

---

5 See Roel Beetsma, Massimo Giuliodori, and Frank Klassen, 'The effects of public spending shocks on trade balances and budget deficits in the EU', *Journal of the European Economic Association*, 6 (2007), 414-423.

equal to 1 percent of GDP increases GDP by 1.2 percent in the same year and the effect reaches a maximum of 1.6 percent in the next year. As predicted by the theory, imports increase and exports fall and there is a decrease in net exports equal to 0.5 percent of GDP. They also divided the countries into more open and less open economies where openness is measured by exports and imports relative to GDP. For the more open economies (Austria, Belgium, Denmark, Ireland, Netherlands, Portugal, and Sweden) they found a first-year effect of only 0.8 percent. For the less open economies (i.e. mainly the large European countries) the first-year effect was 1.4 percent. These results are well in line with the calculations made above.

The accelerator effect

The *accelerator effect* on investment, which was explained in Chapter 3, plays an important role in the business cycle. It arises because firms want to increase their production capacity when expected demand increases. The capital stock is about twice as large as GDP, and with constant returns to scale, firms want to have equipment in proportion to how much they produce. A permanent increase in production by 1 percent leads to an increase in the desired capital stock by 1 percent, which corresponds to roughly 2 percent of GDP. The resulting increase in investment demand amplifies the effects of shocks, regardless of whether they arise on the demand or the supply side.

The logic of the accelerator effect applies also to property and consumer durables. Consumers' demand for houses, cars, and other consumer durables is related to their level of income. If income increases, and this change is perceived as permanent, consumers buy newer, larger, and better cars, houses, and TVs. If prospects about future income become worse, purchases of consumer durables are postponed, so demand for such items collapses. Therefore, purchases of durable goods fluctuate much more than purchases of nondurable goods, such as food and haircuts.[6]

The financial accelerator

In our analysis of investment in Chapter 3, we assumed that firms could always finance all investments that are profitable – that is, where the expected marginal revenue product of capital minus depreciation exceeds the required return. This analysis builds on an idealized model of the credit market, however, which disregards uncertainty and imperfect information. In reality, potential lenders often have imperfect information about the prospects of the firm, and this may make them unwilling to lend. As a consequence, firms often find it difficult to borrow in order to finance investments, so they have to rely on their own resources in order to finance investments. In practice, a large proportion of investments are financed by profits which are not paid out to the shareholders but reinvested by the firms (retained earnings).

The heavy reliance on internal funds creates a link between current profits and investment. If production increases, firms make more profits, and this makes it

---

6   A haircut can also be seen as an investment, but it depreciates quite fast.

easier for them to finance investments. When investment increases, this leads to a further increase in aggregate demand. Conversely, if demand decreases, profits decrease, and investments are constrained by available earnings, leading to a further contraction of aggregate demand. This amplification mechanism is called the *financial accelerator.* We will discuss it further in Chapter 18.

In many ways, the implications of the financial accelerator are similar to those of the standard accelerator. Both effects imply that higher demand leads to higher investment, but there is a subtle difference. The accelerator effect arises because higher *future* demand makes investment more profitable. The financial accelerator effect arises because high *current* demand leads to high profits, which make it easier to finance investments. Since expected future demand is closely correlated with current demand, the two accelerator mechanisms are hard to distinguish empirically.

These three amplification mechanisms help to explain why the total effects of exogenous shocks can be larger than the shocks themselves. Through the multiplier, accelerator, and financial accelerator effects, the effects of exogenous shocks are amplified. An initial change in the moods of investors and consumers will become at least partially self-fulfilling through these mechanisms.

16.4   Should we care about business cycles?

Every day, there are reports in the media about the business cycle outlook. Forecasting institutes, banks, the government, and international organizations make regular forecasts for the business cycle.[7] Many individuals have good reasons to follow these reports. Business managers need to follow the news in order to make the right decisions about investments, hiring, production plans, and other strategic issues. Financial investors know that news about the business cycle will affect interest rates and asset prices. For individuals who are considering whether to buy a house or a car, or to switch jobs, the economic outlook is also important.

But how problematic are business cycles for society? Is it important that the government tries to counteract business cycles? The answer is not obvious. Real business cycle theory tells us that economic fluctuations may be perfectly rational and efficient. If production possibilities change because of poor harvests, new technology being introduced on a wide scale, or restructuring of industries, production will change and it would be foolish to try to counteract such fluctuations by fiscal or monetary policy.

Deviations of production from the natural level are more problematic. If production falls below the natural level we will have lower production and employment than we could have had. If production rises above the natural level, inflation may increase.

5

---

7 Important international forecasts are *World Economic Outlook* from IMF and *OECD Economic Outlook* from the OECD. The OECD also makes specific reports about the situation in individual countries. Both organizations also give recommendations concerning economic policy in individual countries. Their reports are available at www.imf.org and www.oecd.org.

Yet it is not obvious that fluctuations in the output gap are very costly for society. Consider two economies that are similar in all respects except the stability of production and employment. The average levels of production and employment are the same in the two economies. In one economy, unemployment is always 5 percent. In the other economy, unemployment is 7 percent half the time and 3 percent half the time. In which of these economies would you prefer to live? On average, your risk of being unemployed will be the same. Since you have decreasing marginal utility of consumption, a more stable level of consumption is preferred to unstable consumption, but this gain cannot be very large. We are talking about fluctuations in production and consumption of a couple of percent around the trend. Thus, it seems unlikely that modest fluctuations in production are very costly.[8]

Major economic crises might be more costly because they lead to disruptions in production that may have negative long-term effects on production and employment. A deep recession leads to closure of firms that could have thrived in a better environment. Long periods with very high unemployment mean that some people remain unemployed for a long time and perhaps never get back to work.

In fact, we know very little about the real costs of business cycles. Clearly, these issues cannot be analysed with a simple macromodel where all firms and workers are identical. One can argue that the cost of normal business cycles is small, so the main purpose of stabilization policy should be to avoid major economic crises.

What have we learned?

Production is sometimes decomposed into a *trend* and a *cyclical* component. The trend part represents permanent changes in production, while the cyclical part represents temporary deviations from the trend.

The trend can be estimated as a linear trend for the log of GDP. This means that the trend value is assumed to grow at a constant rate for the whole data period and that GDP always returns to the trend independent of the shocks. A linear trend with breaks allows for changes in trend growth.

The *Hodrick–Prescott* filter fits a smooth curve through the time series for (log) GDP.

A *stochastic trend* allows random shocks to have permanent effects on GDP.

Different estimates of the trend lead to different decompositions into trend and cycle. The more flexible the trend, the lower is the amplitude of the cycle. All methods lead to the conclusion that variations in GDP are very persistent.

Other variables can also be decomposed into trend and cycle. Deviations from trend in private consumption, investment, exports and imports are all positively correlated with deviations from trend of real GDP.

---

8   This argument is based on Robert Lucas, *Models of Business Cycles* (Oxford: Basil Blackwell, 1987). For a more extensive discussion of the costs of business cycles, see David Romer, *Advanced Macroeconomics*, 4th edn. (New York: McGraw-Hill Irwin, 2012).

Investment, exports, and imports are more volatile than GDP, while private consumption fluctuates about as much as GDP.

Government consumption is more stable than GDP and not strongly correlated with GDP.

Real business cycle theory explains the business cycle as a result of changes in production possibilities. When technology improves, it becomes more profitable to work and invest and consumers feel richer so they consume more. This theory can explain some of the basic facts of the business cycle. It implies a positive correlation between production, investment, consumption, and hours worked and that investment should be more volatile than consumption, as seen in the data.

John Maynard Keynes emphasized changes in moods – *animal spirits* – as a key factor driving fluctuations.

Three amplification mechanisms magnify the effects of shocks:

The multiplier effect: When production and income increase, consumers increase their consumption, which leads to a further increase in aggregate demand. In the US, the multiplier may be around 1.6. In a small open economy with a large government sector, such as Sweden, the multiplier may be around 0.9 because a large part of demand is directed towards foreign goods and increases in income are taxed to a high degree.

The accelerator effect: When aggregate demand increases and demand is expected to remain high, it becomes more profitable to invest and higher investment leads to a further increase in aggregate demand.

The financial accelerator: When production increases, firms make more profits, so it becomes easier to finance investments by retained earnings. This leads to a further boost of aggregate demand.

If business cycles are driven by changes in production possibilities, there is little reason for the government to try to counteract business cycles.

Deviations of production from the natural level are costly but the costs of modest business cycles are probably low. Large cycles may be more costly, because deep economic crises may have lasting effects on production and employment.

Exercises

1. Repeat the definitions of trend, cycle, and the natural level of production. Then analyse how the following shocks affect the trend, the cycle, and the natural level of production:
   a) a permanent improvement in technology
   b) an earthquake that destroys some factories
   c) a labour market reform that reduces the natural rate of unemployment.

2. For the shocks above, discuss how the output gap may be affected and how this depends on the reactions of the central bank. *(Hint: Draw the IS curve and the line marking the natural level of production and analyse the shocks and the central bank reaction to the shocks.)*

3. Suppose that, on average over the cycle, private consumption is 60 percent of GDP and private investment is 20 percent of GDP. A normal trend deviation for private consumption is 1.5 percent and a normal trend deviation for private investment is 6 percent. Which variable contributes most to the volatility of aggregate demand in this economy?

4. What are the similarities and what are the differences between:
   a) the multiplier effect and the accelerator effect
   b) the accelerator effect and the financial accelerator effect
   c) the multiplier effect and the financial accelerator effect?
   Discuss specifically how demand is affected by the level and the change of production.

5. Consider two economies where economy A has more fluctuations than economy B.
   a) Which one would you prefer to live in if the average levels of income, employment, and inflation were the same?
   b) Discuss how fluctuations might affect the average levels of income and employment.

6. Different parts of expenditure have different import shares. For Sweden, we had the following approximate import shares in 2008:

private consumption	35 percent
public consumption	12 percent
investment	43 percent
exports	40 percent.

   Expressed as shares of GDP, private consumption was 47 percent of GDP, public consumption was 26 percent, investment was 20 percent of GDP and exports were 53 percent of GDP. Calculate imports as a share of GDP and compare this with the number reported in Chapter 1.

7. A more careful calculation of the multiplier effect should take account of the different import shares for different parts of aggregate demand. To make such a calculation, we specify imports as follows:

   $$IM = q_C C + q_G G + q_I I + q_X X,$$

   where the q's represent import shares. We assume a consumption function and a tax function:

   $$C = c_0 + c_1(Y - T) \quad \text{and} \quad T = T_0 + \tau Y.$$

   a) Find an expression for the equilibrium level of production for given $G, T_0, I,$ and X.
   b) Calculate the multipliers for $G, T_0, I,$ and X and evaluate them numerically using the import shares from the previous exercise and assuming $c_1 = 0.8$ and $\tau = 0.54$. Compare to the multiplier calculated in this chapter and explain the differences.

Answers to the exercises can be found at: **www.palgrave.com/economics/gottfries**.

Appendix

The Hodrick–Prescott filter

This is a method for constructing a smooth curve which was originally proposed by E. T. Whittaker in 1923 and introduced to economics by Edward Prescott and Robert Hodrick. For a given sample period, here assumed to be $t = 1, 2, 3, \ldots, T$, the sequence of trend values $y_1^T, y_2^T, y_3^T, \ldots, y_T^T$ is chosen to *minimize* the following expression:

$$\sum_{t=1}^{T}\left(y_t - y_t^T\right)^2 + \lambda \sum_{t=2}^{T-1}\left(\Delta y_{t+1}^T - \Delta y_t^T\right)^2.$$

Thus the minimization is made over *all* the values of y_t^T. The first term is a penalty for deviations of the trend value from the actual series and the second term is a penalty for large changes in trend growth. The idea is that, on the one hand, we want the trend to be reasonably close to the actual value y_t, and on the other hand, we want the trend to be smooth, so there should be small changes in trend growth. By minimizing the above expression, we strike a balance between these two objectives. Standard statistical programmes contain routines for fitting a trend in this way. With a high value of λ, the trend will be very smooth and similar to a linear trend. With a low value of λ, the trend will be very close to the actual series. Thus the division between trend and cycle depends on how we set lambda.

17 INSTITUTIONS AND ECONOMIC POLICY

How do institutions shape economic policy?

So far, we have analysed the effects of monetary and fiscal policy, taking policy as exogenous. We have analysed how changes in the interest rate, taxes, and government expenditure affect the economy in the short and the long run. This analysis was based on a thorough analysis of the behaviour of consumers and firms. Throughout, we have assumed that consumers and firms act in a rational way, maximizing utility and profits.

We found that the short-run effects of policy are quite different from the long-run effects. As we saw in Chapters 8–10, monetary and fiscal policies affect aggregate demand and the level of activity in the short run because wages and prices adjust slowly, but in the long run, a continuous expansion of the money supply leads to inflation. Moderate inflation should have little effect on real variables but high inflation will lead to distortions of the price system which have negative effects on the allocation of resources (see Chapter 7).

As we saw in Chapter 11, expansionary fiscal policy can increase demand in the short run, but a government deficit raises the level of government debt, and a high level of government debt may lead to a fiscal crisis.

To take policy as exogenous is reasonable if the purpose of the analysis is to understand the *effects* of a given policy. But we may also ask *why* certain policy decisions are made. Why do countries sometimes have very high inflation? Why have so many countries accumulated high levels of government debt?

In this chapter we analyse how policy decisions are made, and this means that we treat policy as endogenous. To make policy endogenous we need to ask who makes decisions about policy and what objectives the policymakers have. Our analysis of policy decisions can help us to understand policy failures – that is, situations in which policy leads to undesirable outcomes for society such as high inflation and fiscal crises. To understand how policy decisions are made may also help us to design institutions for policymaking in such a way that better policy decisions are made.

As we will see in this chapter, a central concern is that policy decisions may be short-sighted (myopic), giving priority to short-run gains and winning the next election. As they say in politics:

> *'To win is not everything but to lose is not anything.'*

In monetary policy, there may be a temptation to reduce the interest rate so as to stimulate the economy in the short run, although such a policy will increase inflation in the long run. In fiscal policy, there is a temptation to spend more and cut taxes today, although this leads to an increase in government debt and large interest payments in the future. Thus, short-sighted policies may lead to high inflation and large budget deficits: there may be an *inflation bias* in monetary policy and a *deficit bias* in fiscal policy.

In the last two decades, many countries have implemented institutional reforms in order to deal with these biases and achieve better policy decisions. A large number of countries have delegated monetary policy decisions to independent central banks. There have also been changes in the institutional framework for fiscal policymaking.

We first consider monetary policy. In this area, many countries have already implemented institutional reforms, and these reforms seem to have been quite successful in bringing down inflation. We then discuss fiscal policy, where fewer reforms have been made and success has been more limited.[1]

17.1   Inflation bias

According to the theory presented in Chapters 8 and 9, wages and prices change slowly, and more expansionary monetary policy leads to higher production and employment. Inflation also increases, but the evidence suggests that the short-run Phillips curve is quite flat, so the short-run effect on inflation is small. This means that, in the short run, policymakers face a trade-off: higher employment can be bought at the price of somewhat higher inflation. A policymaker who cares a good deal about employment may prefer to expand output even if this raises the level of inflation. Somewhat higher inflation may be considered a price worth paying for higher employment.

At the same time, we know that money is neutral in the long run. Constantly high money growth will lead to high inflation, but, according to the theory that we presented in Chapters 7 and 9, a higher rate of money growth will have no effect on employment in the long run. Monetary policy should be ineffective as a policy for raising the level of employment because employment will return to the natural level independent of inflation.

But suppose policymakers are short-sighted and attempt to achieve short-run increases in employment? What will happen then?

We can analyse this problem with the help of our macroeconomic model. Let us assume that expected inflation is equal to the inflation rate in the previous period: $\pi_t^e = \pi_{t-1}$, so the Phillips curve is

$$\pi_t = \pi_{t-1} - \hat{b}\left(u_t - u_t^n\right) + z_t, \text{ where } \hat{b} = \frac{\lambda b}{1 - \lambda}.$$

5

1 More advanced books on economic policymaking are Allan Drazen, *Political Economy in Macroeconomics* (Princeton: Princeton University Press, 2001), and Torsten Person and Guido Tabellini, *Political Economics: Explaining Economic Policy* (Cambridge, MA: The MIT Press, 2002).

Fig. 17.1 *The short-run trade-off between inflation and unemployment*

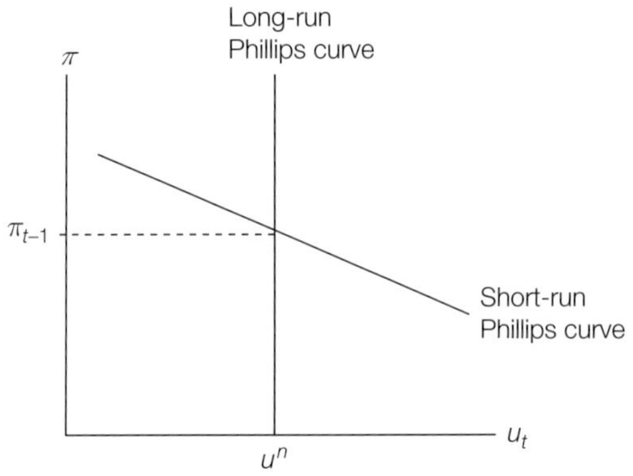

This Phillips curve, which was derived in Chapter 9, implies a short-run trade-off between unemployment and inflation, as shown in Fig. 17.1. According to the theory presented in Chapter 9, the slope of the Phillips curve depends on the slope of the wage-setting function, b, and the fraction of wages that are flexible, λ.

Now consider a simple theory of economic policy. To simplify, we assume that there are no shocks to the Phillips curve ($z_t = 0$) or to demand and that, through its control of the interest rate, the central bank can control aggregate demand and the level of unemployment. Thus we can think of monetary policy choice as choosing the level of unemployment.

Let us assume that monetary policy is controlled by short-sighted politicians who do not care at all about the future. Their goal is to win the next election and they know that the voters care about inflation and unemployment today. The objective of the policymakers is to *minimize* the following loss function:

$$L(\pi_t, u_t) = \pi_t^2 + \lambda u_t^2.$$

This loss function is minimized, and equal to zero, if both inflation and unemployment are zero. The further away we are from that point, the bigger are the losses from unemployment and inflation. From the point of view of policymakers, we can think of this loss as the probability of losing the next election. From the point of view of society, this loss function is also reasonable: unemployment means that production is lower than necessary and high inflation is associated with costs, particularly distortions of the price system. The costs of inflation were discussed in Chapter 7.

We can illustrate this loss function with indifference curves, or rather rings, as in Fig. 17.2. Each curve shows combinations of inflation and unemployment, which lead to a certain level of loss. These curves are like level curves on a map. The map shows a bowl and the policymaker wants to get down to the bottom of the bowl, where $\pi = u = 0$ so that the loss is zero.[2]

To find the policy decision, we combine the Phillips curve with the loss function of the policymaker as in Fig 17.3. Suppose that inflation was zero in period zero so expected inflation is zero in period 1. Then the short-run Phillips curve cuts the long-run Phillips curve in the point $(u^n, 0)$ in period 1. If unemployment is kept

---

2 In practice, unemployment cannot be negative, but such trivialities need not concern us here.

Fig. 17.2 *Policymaker loss function*

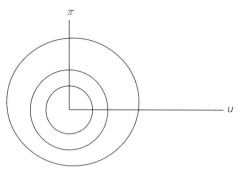

Note: The figure shows the level curves for the loss function. The loss is zero if inflation (π) and unemployment (u) are both zero, and the loss rises as you move away from this point.

Fig. 17.3 *Equilibrium inflation and unemployment in the short and the long run*

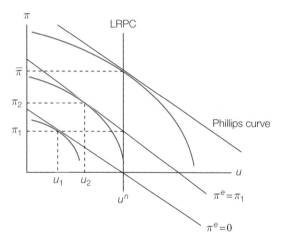

at the natural level, inflation will remain at zero. In fact, this is the best we can achieve in the long run. However, it is not an equilibrium situation when we treat policy as endogenous.

Facing the trade-off given by this short-run Phillips curve, the policymaker will choose the point on the short-run Phillips curve where the loss is lowest. This is the point along the Phillips curve where the level curve of the loss function is tangent to the Phillips curve. As we see in the figure, this implies a positive rate of inflation equal to π_1 in period 1. Faced with a trade-off between inflation and unemployment the policymaker decides to reduce unemployment below the natural level, although this leads to some increase in inflation.

But the point (u_1, π_1) is not a stable equilibrium either. In period 2, the expected inflation rate will be π_1. Therefore, the Phillips curve shifts up and intersects the long-run Phillips curve at $\pi = \pi_1$. Now, the policymaker faces a more difficult trade-off and the preferred point is where inflation is π_2 and unemployment is increased to u_2. But as people discover that inflation has increased even more in period 2, they raise their expectations about inflation, and the Phillips curve shifts up further.

Where will this process end? The long-run equilibrium point is where inflation is $\bar{\pi}$ and unemployment is back at the natural level. At this point, the short-run Phillips curve is tangent to the level curve of the loss function. Since inflation is already high, the marginal cost of further inflation is so high that the policymaker does not want to increase inflation further. In the long run, we end up in a situation with high inflation without achieving any reduction in unemployment. The self-defeating attempts to achieve a higher level of employment have led to a situation with high inflation without any gains in employment.

This is clearly an undesirable situation. If we had kept inflation at zero, we would have been better off. In fact, the point where we started, with $\pi = 0$ and $u = u^n$ was the best point we could achieve in the long run. It is the point where a level curve of the loss function is tangent to the *long-run* Phillips curve, so it is the point along the long-run Phillips curve that is associated with the lowest value of the loss function. In the long run, unemployment must be at the natural level and the best we can do is to keep inflation at the preferred level, which we assume to be zero.[3] But how can we return to this point?

Note that, if the policymakers make a promise that they will keep inflation at zero, and if people believe this promise, expected inflation will be zero, and the Phillips curve will shift down and cut the long-run Phillips curve at zero inflation. But the problem is that if people do believe this promise, the policymaker has the incentive to deviate and pursue a more inflationary policy; the promise to keep zero inflation is not credible. This *credibility problem* was analysed in a famous article by Finn Kydland and Edward Prescott in 1977.[4] Another name for this problem is *inflation bias*, which captures the idea that policy leads to a long-run level of inflation that is higher than desired.

Solutions to the inflation bias problem

Several different solutions to the inflation bias problem have been suggested. These include *norms* and *rules* for monetary policy, *delegation* of monetary policy to an independent central bank, and a *contract* for the central bank that gives it the incentive to keep inflation on a low level.

A fixed norm for inflation

One way to avoid the equilibrium with high inflation is to pass a law whereby inflation should be zero, or some other low number, and make the central bank obliged to follow that law. Such a strict norm has some problems, however. First, there are shocks to the Phillips curve, so the central bank does not have perfect control over inflation. One would have to set a range for inflation and decide what

3 If the preferred rate of inflation is somewhat higher than zero, the analysis can easily be modified to take account of that.
4 As mentioned on page 459, the Nobel Prize 2004 was awarded jointly to Finn E. Kydland and Edward C. Prescott 'for their contributions to dynamic macroeconomics: the time consistency of economic policy and the driving forces behind business cycles'. To be precise, Kydland and Prescott made a somewhat different analysis because they assumed rational expectations instead of assuming that expected inflation is equal to last year's inflation, but the policy conclusions are approximately the same. The case of perfect foresight about inflation is analysed in an exercise.

would happen if inflation fell outside that range. Also, a strict norm for inflation would eliminate all possibilities for the central bank to help in short-run stabilization of output. If there is a supply side shock, such as an increase in the oil price, it may be better to allow some temporary increase in inflation than to push the economy into a recession so as to keep inflation constant (see the discussion in Chapter 10).

A rule for monetary policy

In theory, we could allow more flexibility if we pass a law whereby the central bank should follow a specific decision rule for monetary policy. Such a rule would prescribe how the central bank should react to different disturbances, and assure low average inflation while at the same time allowing the central bank to react in a reasonable way to shocks. For example, the rule could stipulate that if there is an increase (decrease) in oil prices or the value added tax, inflation should be allowed to be temporarily higher (lower) than the target. This is an ideal solution in the model, but it would be difficult to implement in practice. There are so many different things that can happen that the optimal rule would be very complicated, and a simple rule will not work well if an unexpected shock occurs.

Delegation to a 'conservative' central banker

One way to reduce long-run inflation is to delegate monetary policy to the central bank, and to elect a board, or head of the central bank, that puts a lot of weight on low inflation and little weight on employment. This can be seen in our model. If we choose a 'conservative' head of the central bank who dislikes inflation but does not care about employment – that is, a person with $\lambda = 0$ – we make sure that inflation is zero. Such a person has horizontal level curves in the loss function and so will always keep inflation at zero.

But, again, this would mean that the central bank does not try to stabilize employment. Thus we may want to choose a central banker who puts low, but not zero, weight on employment. We should select a leader (or board) of the central bank who is conservative, but not too conservative. Thus we face a *credibility–flexibility trade-off*: the less weight the central bank puts on employment, the more we reduce the inflation bias, but at the same time the central bank will be less flexible in allowing temporary variations in inflation.[5]

Long-term contracts

By giving the board members of the central bank long-term contracts, we can ensure that they care about the long-run effects of their policies. This will make them less inclined to pursue a monetary policy that raises the rate of inflation in the future.

A contract for the central bank

Another idea is to delegate monetary policy to an independent board, or head of the central bank, and to set up a contract for the leaders of the central bank

---

5   This problem was first analysed by Kenneth Rogoff in a paper published in 1985.

Fig. 17.4 *A contract for the central bank*

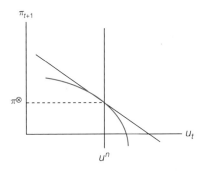

that gives them incentives to pursue a low inflation policy. Such a contract could punish the leaders of the central bank if inflation is too high. In theory, this is a very elegant solution. As shown in Fig. 17.4, the contract tilts the indifference curves so that the inflation bias problem is eliminated while still allowing a flexible response to shocks.[6]

Reforms of the institutional framework for monetary policy

These ideas have had substantial influence on how monetary policy is organized. In recent decades, many countries have implemented reforms along the lines suggested by this theory. These include:

- *Inflation targets*: Many countries have made the price stability objective more explicit by announcing an explicit inflation target and saying that the primary objective of monetary policy is to keep average inflation on the target level.
- *Delegation and independence*: In several countries, the independence of the central bank has been strengthened. Monetary policy decisions are made by a board or policy committee in the central bank which does not take instructions from elected politicians.
- *Long-term contracts*: Board members are elected for long periods (e.g. six years) in an overlapping system.

In most countries with inflation targets and independent central banks, inflation has been low for decades; it seems that these countries have managed to solve the inflation bias problem.

17.2   Deficit bias

As we saw in Chapter 11, many countries have high public sector deficits and high government debt. That a country has a deficit in a particular year need not be a cause of concern, but, over time, deficits accumulate, leading to high levels of

---

6   This solution was suggested by Torsten Persson, Guido Tabellini and Carl Walsh in papers published between 1993 and 1995.

government debt. In the following we first analyse the effects of high government debt and the reasons why countries tend to accumulate high government debt. Then we discuss institutional reforms that may help to reduce the deficit bias.

How serious is the problem of high government debt?

In a world with full Ricardian equivalence and non-distortionary taxes, the level of government debt does not matter. Individuals take account of the utility of future generations, so it is effectively as if they lived forever, and they know that they have to pay for government expenditure sooner or later. If the government cuts taxes, people will save more to compensate their children for the higher taxes that they will have to pay. As a consequence, aggregate consumption, saving, and production are unaffected by the level of debt, and so is the utility of current and future generations. But in reality we can think of at least three types of effect of deficits and high debt.

Intergenerational redistribution

As we discussed in Chapter 11, it is unlikely that Ricardian equivalence holds fully. Two main reasons are that individuals do not fully take into account the utility of future generations and that they are credit constrained. For these reasons, people will spend some of the increase in disposable income that they get from a tax reduction. This means that aggregate saving is reduced by a tax cut. In a closed economy, this leads to lower capital accumulation. With fully integrated financial markets, the capital stock will be unaffected, but net foreign assets will decline. In reality, we would expect some combination – there will be some decline in the capital stock and some decline in foreign assets, and both effects make future generations poorer. By running a deficit, the government allows individuals living today to borrow at the expense of future generations. There is a *redistribution of income* from future to current generations.

Is this necessarily a bad thing? This is a matter of judgement. Since productivity increases over time, future generations will probably be better off than those currently living and paying taxes. From this point of view, we may view some government borrowing as justified. As individuals, we are unable to borrow on account of future generations, but we can use the government to do that for us.

If we are more pessimistic about future growth, we may think that we should not pass on a large debt to future generations. Further, we may expect future working generations to face difficulties because of environmental problems and a large number of old-age people that they have to support. In the final analysis, the desired amount of intergenerational redistribution is a political issue, which should be decided on the basis of political preferences and projections about future incomes and demographic changes.

5

Distortions and tax smoothing

Another aspect is that taxes have distortionary effects. To simplify our macroeconomic analysis, we have assumed labour supply to be completely inelastic in our basic macroeconomic model, but in reality we expect taxes to have negative effects on labour supply. Because of taxes, labour supply is below the socially efficient level, and the distortion will increase more than proportion-ally with the level of taxes. Thus, we want to avoid a situation where taxes are very high. A stable level of taxes is preferred to a tax that is sometimes high and sometimes low.

This *tax smoothing* argument is an argument for temporary deficits if gov-ernment consumption varies over time. By running a deficit when government consumption is temporarily high, and repaying in future periods, the tax level is kept relatively stable and the distortionary effects of taxes are reduced. This can explain why countries engaged in a war will typically finance a large part of the increased military expenditure by borrowing. The same argument applies if there is some major natural catastrophe.

One argument against high government debt may be that a high level of debt will force the government to impose high taxes in order to pay interest on the debt. Does a higher steady state level of debt imply much higher taxes? To see what tax is consistent with a stable debt ratio, we use the equation for the change in the debt ratio from Chapter 11. Setting the change in the debt ratio equal to zero and solving for the tax as a fraction of GDP we get

$$\frac{T}{Y} = \frac{G}{Y} + (r - g)\frac{D}{Y}.$$

The relation between the debt level and taxes depends on the relation between the real interest rate and the growth rate. If the real interest rate is higher than the growth rate, a higher debt ratio does indeed lead to a higher required tax rate in steady state. But if the real interest rate on government debt and the growth rate are equal, a higher level of steady state debt does not imply higher taxes relative to GDP. The reason is that real growth counteracts the effect of the interest rate on the debt ratio, so, to keep the ratio of debt to GDP constant, it is enough to keep the *primary* deficit equal to zero. Thus, the tax distortions associated with a higher level of debt do not seem to be a major concern.

Sustainability and fiscal crisis

An important argument against high debt is that it may become unsustainable. If lenders start to worry that the debt will not be paid back, they will require a higher interest rate to compensate for the risk of default. This means that the next time the government debt is rolled over – that is, when governments bonds expire and new ones have to be issued – the government will have to offer a higher interest rate, and this makes the fiscal deficit even higher. As a result, the country may end up in a fiscal crisis.

To see how serious this problem can become, suppose that a country has gross debt that is 100 percent of GDP and, for simplicity, the government has no finan-cial claims on the private sector. Government expenditure is 40 percent of GDP, the real interest rate on safe loans is 2 percent and the real growth rate is also 2 percent.[7] Suppose that lenders are risk neutral and that government debt is ini-

---

7   Here we include transfers in government expenditure.

tially considered to be safe. Then the equation above tells us that the government needs to collect 40 percent of GDP in taxes in order to keep the debt ratio constant:

$$\frac{T}{Y} = \frac{G}{Y} + (r - g)\frac{D}{Y} = 0.40 + (0.02 - 0.02) \cdot 1.00 = 0.40.$$

Suppose now that, for some reason, lenders become worried that the government will default on its debt; they perceive a 10 percent risk that the government will default within the next year. If lenders are risk neutral, the government has to pay a 10 percent higher interest rate to compensate for the risk of default, so the total real interest on the debt rises to 12 percent $(10 + 2$ percent$)$. What level of taxes is required in order to keep the debt ratio from growing? Using the equation above we get

$$\frac{T}{Y} = \frac{G}{Y} + (r - g)\frac{D}{Y} = 0.40 + (0.12 - 0.02) \cdot 1.00 = 0.40 + 0.10 = 0.50.$$

For a given level of expenditure, we find that taxes must be raised from 40 to 50 percent of GDP in order to stabilize the debt ratio. This is a dramatic increase in the tax rate.[8]

If the government is unable to raise the tax, or cut expenditure, the debt ratio will grow, and lenders will become even more worried about default. Then, the interest rate will rise even higher, the required tax increase will become even higher. In this way, a country can enter into a negative spiral which is hard to escape from.

When the debt ratio is on an unsustainable path, some adjustment must occur. Sooner or later, one of the following things will happen, or perhaps a combination of these:

- the primary deficit is reduced by increased taxes or reduced government expenditure
- the government defaults on the debt, or part of it
- the central bank monetizes the debt – that is, it buys government bonds, financed by an increase in the monetary base.

Each of these outcomes is associated with problems.

An increase in taxes or a reduction in transfers can be implemented quickly but such actions will encounter fierce political resistance. To cut government consumption takes time. Most of this expenditure is wage payments for government employees, so it involves firing government employees. In many countries, the unemployment insurance system is publicly funded to a large extent, so if the persons who are laid off by the government do not find new jobs, the government still has to support them via unemployment insurance and social assistance.

An outright default on government debt means that the government stops paying interest on the debt and does not repay bonds that mature. The advantage is that the existing debt is wiped out, but lenders will lose trust in the government,

---

8   This calculation exaggerates the problem because the higher interest rate applies only to new bond issues. If a large part of the bonds are long-term bonds, it takes time before the higher interest rate must be paid on a large part of the debt.

so it will be unable to borrow again. From the day it defaults, the government has to finance all expenditure by taxes. This means that the primary balance has to be zero from the day of default and onwards. Furthermore, government default may lead to bankruptcies of banks and other institutions that hold large quantities of government bonds.

An indirect way to default is that the central bank buys large amounts of government bonds, and finances this by increasing the monetary base. We say that the debt is 'monetized' – that is, converted from government bonds to monetary base. This will lead to an increase in inflation so that the real value of the existing debt is reduced. For a *given nominal interest rate*, higher inflation reduces the real interest rate on the debt, which helps to reduce the debt ratio. At any point in time, there is a stock of bonds of various maturities which are held by financial investors. On most of these bonds, the interest payments and the repayment are fixed in nominal terms, so unexpectedly high inflation will reduce the realized real return on the existing bonds below what the lenders expected when they bought the bonds. This means that by *unexpected* inflation, some of the existing debt is inflated away. But if inflation is increased, expectations about future inflation will be raised, so when bonds mature, and new bonds are issued, investors will require a higher nominal interest rate to compensate for higher inflation. For new loans, the real interest rate is not reduced. Thus it is only by unexpected inflation that the government can reduce the real value of the existing government debt.[9]

To sum up, there is no easy way out of a debt crisis.

Reasons for deficit bias

As we saw above, a high and rising debt ratio can cause huge problems and there is good reason to try to avoid such a situation. This notwithstanding, several countries have had large deficits for a long time and accumulated dangerously high levels of government debt. This tendency to run deficits is sometimes called a *deficit bias* in fiscal policy. In many ways, it is similar to the *inflation bias* in monetary policy, but while the inflation bias problem has been solved in many countries, the deficit bias seems harder to deal with. What are the reasons for the deficit bias? Some possible reasons are listed below.

Myopia

By allowing a deficit, the government can raise expenditure and reduce taxes today. The costs come later. In this sense, running a large deficit can be seen as a myopic policy. The government in power may gain votes from such a policy, but only if voters themselves do not care about the future costs of this policy. One reason may be that voters do not understand the future consequences of the policy. They see the current benefits in the form of lower taxes and better government services but they do not understand the implications for future government finances. Alternatively, the voters may understand the consequences, but do not

---

9 Up to a point, higher inflation will increase the seignorage revenue for the central bank. As discussed in Chapter 7, revenue from seignorage makes up a small proportion of GDP, however.

care about them. If voters are themselves myopic, and credit-constrained, they may rationally vote for a government that borrows on their behalf and passes on the costs to future generations.

Political fragmentation and the common pool problem

Another factor is political fragmentation. When there are many political parties that have to compromise, they may all push for their specific interests without taking responsibility for the overall consequences for the economy as a whole. This is a version of the common pool problem, similar to the problem of overfishing when many countries fish in the sea without taking account of the negative effects on reproduction of fish stocks.

In a system with division of power, it may be difficult to reach a compromise. When a country has a deficit, there will typically be strong disagreement about how the deficit should be reduced. Conservative parties will argue for reduced expenditure and left-wing parties will argue for higher taxes, and the two sides may block each other. If a compromise cannot be reached, the deficit reduction may be postponed even though it is obvious to everyone that the current policy is unsustainable. Such a situation has existed for some years in the US, where Democrats and Republicans have controlled different parts of government and they have been unable to agree on how the deficit is to be reduced.

Strategic deficits

More sophisticated political reasons for high deficits have also been suggested. A party does not stay in power forever; at some point in time, other parties will come to power. If the politicians in power today think that a future government will waste the resources of the government, they may think that it is better to spend money today on things that they like, or to cut taxes, rather than leaving the money to be spent by future governments.[10]

Reforms of the framework for fiscal policymaking

The question arises whether it is possible to implement institutional reforms of the framework for fiscal policymaking so as to reduce the deficit bias. Some different approaches have been proposed, and reforms have been implemented in some countries.[11]

Targets and ceilings

One way to attack the deficit bias problem is to set up targets and/or ceilings for deficits and debt. The aim is that these targets and ceilings should be relatively permanent commitments and thus act as constraints on day-to-day policy decisions. In practice, such limits may be more or less permanent and more or less

5

---

10 These ideas were developed by Torsten Persson, Lars E. O. Svensson, Guido Tabellini and Alberto Alesina in papers published between 1989 and 1990.

11 For a discussion of reforms in a European perspective, see L. Calmfors, 'Fiscal policy coordination in Europe, report for the European Parliament' (2010). An empirical study of how different institutional factors affect government balances is Stefania Fabrizio and Ashoka Mody, 'Can budget institutions counteract political indiscipline?', *Economic Policy*, 21 (2006), 690–739.

binding. Many countries have balanced budget rules for local governments which are established in law. On the central level, the target may be set in a long-term policy decision that is hard to renege on without losing reputation. It may also be a multiparty agreement that is meant to hold even if there is a shift of government.[12]

Should targets be set for the deficit, for the level of debt relative to GDP, or for both? As discussed above, it is not primarily deficits (government borrowing) in individual years that we should worry about, but high levels of government debt. From an economic point of view it would make more sense to set a target for the long-run level of debt than for the deficit. But the problem with such a target is that it will have little effect on day-to-day policy decisions. Politicians can easily argue that they have a long-term plan to stabilize the debt, but right now there are special reasons to spend more.

However, there is a close relation between the deficit and the steady state debt ratio, so we can set a target level for the deficit in order to achieve some desired long-run target level for the net debt ratio. To see the relation between the deficit and the long-run level of debt, we can use the equation that we derived in Chapter 11, and which shows how the debt ratio changes over time:

$$\Delta\left(\frac{D}{Y}\right) = \frac{G-T}{Y} + (r-g)\frac{D}{Y}.$$

Here D/Y is the ratio of net government debt to GDP, G is government consumption and investment, T is tax revenue minus government transfers to the private sector. $G-T$ is the primary deficit – the deficit before net interest payments – and $(G-T)/Y$ is the primary deficit as a fraction of GDP. The real interest rate is r and the growth rate of real GDP is g. As explained in Chapter 11, the primary deficit and real interest payments add to the debt ratio while high growth reduces the debt ratio because GDP is in the denominator of the debt ratio.

In order to express the change of the debt ratio in terms of the government deficit (including interest payments on the debt) we use the fact that the real interest rate is the nominal rate minus inflation, $r = i - \pi$, so we can write

$$\Delta\left(\frac{D}{Y}\right) = \frac{G-T+iD}{Y} - (\pi+g)\frac{D}{Y}.$$

The first term on the right-hand side is the government deficit as a fraction of GDP and $\pi+g$ is the growth rate of nominal GDP.[13] Suppose that the rates of growth and inflation are constant and that the deficit is a fixed fraction of GDP. Will the debt ratio stabilize and, if so, at what level? To find the long-run debt ratio we set the change in the debt ratio (the left-hand side) equal to zero and add $(\pi+g)D/Y$ on both sides:

$$(\pi+g)\frac{D}{Y} = \frac{G-T+iD}{Y}.$$

---

12 The rules set up in the Maastricht Treaty of the European Union are examples of such rules. These rules are discussed in Chapter 15.

13 Here, expenditure, taxes, and production are all expressed in real terms, but if we multiply by the price level in the nominator and the denominator of the first term we get the nominal deficit relative to nominal GDP.

Fig. 17.5 *The relation between the deficit and the long-run debt ratio when nominal GDP grows by 4 percent per year*

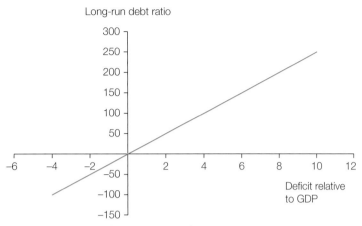

Note: Both variables are expressed as a percentage of GDP.

Dividing by $(\pi + g)$ we find the long-run (steady state) debt ratio:[14]

$$\frac{D}{Y} = \frac{(G - T + iD)/Y}{\pi + g} = \frac{\text{deficit/GDP}}{\text{growth rate of nominal GDP}}.$$

Suppose that the real interest rate and the real growth rate are both 2 percent. Then the growth rate of nominal GDP is 4 percent. For this case, the relation between the deficit and the long-run debt ratio is illustrated in Fig. 17.5. If the deficit is 4 percent of GDP net government debt will eventually stabilize at 100 percent of GDP.

If the deficit is constant at one percent of GDP, net government debt will eventually stabilize at 25 percent of GDP:

$$\frac{D}{Y} = \frac{\text{nominal deficit/GDP}}{\text{growth rate of nominal GDP}} = \frac{0.01}{0.04} = 0.25.$$

Note that this number refers to net debt. In 2009, the countries in the Eurozone had financial claims equal to 1/3 of GDP on average, so a net debt ratio equal to 25 percent of GDP would correspond to a gross debt equal to 58 percent of GDP (25 + 33 percent).[15] Thus, if we do not want the debt to exceed this level in the long run, the deficit should not be more than one percent of GDP on average. Thus we can achieve some long-run debt target by setting a target for the deficit.

---

14 Why does the debt ratio stabilize rather than grow forever when a country has a deficit? The reason is that nominal growth of GDP tends to reduce the debt ratio, and this effect is stronger the higher the debt ratio is. For a given level of deficit relative to GDP, there is a level of the debt ratio where the effect of the deficit on the debt ratio is exactly offset by the effect of growing nominal GDP.

15 Here we are using the OECD definitions, which are not exactly the same as those used by the EU, to evaluate whether countries fulfil the rules of the Stability and Growth Pact.

A problem, though, is that a target level for the deficit is associated with a credibility–flexibility trade-off which is similar to that in monetary policy. A very strict rule for the deficit is undesirable because it eliminates flexibility. As discussed above, a deficit in a particular year need not be a matter of concern. On the contrary, it may be well motivated by tax-smoothing considerations, or be the result of countercyclical fiscal policy. Also we should let the automatic stabilizers do their job: in a recession, taxes will decrease relative to government expenditure, which will help to stabilize aggregate demand.

Some countries have set the targets for the *average deficit over the cycle* or for the cyclically adjusted deficit. The advantage of such a target is that it allows some flexibility in dealing with business cycles and other temporary shocks, but, on the other hand, cyclical adjustments of the deficit are very uncertain, so this flexibility can be misused by politicians who want to postpone unpleasant policy actions. Thus, the credibility–flexibility trade-off is not easy to deal with.

Budgetary procedures

Reforms of budgetary procedures have been implemented to make sure that the total effect of fiscal policy is given a good deal of consideration in the political decision process. With this aim, some countries have changed the order of decision-making, so that the total size of spending is decided first, and then this spending is divided between different departments. This top-down approach is meant to bring more discipline than a situation where decisions are made about different individual expenditures without anyone thinking about what the total sum will be.

Delegation

A radical suggestion is to delegate some aspects of fiscal policy to an independent body analogous to the central bank. In practice, delegation of fiscal policy is much more controversial than delegation of monetary policy. Delegation to independent experts requires that there is wide agreement on what the *objective* of the policy should be. There is wide agreement that low average inflation should be the primary aim of monetary policy, and the task of achieving low inflation can be seen as a technical problem that can be delegated to independent experts. As concerns fiscal policy, it is much less clear what levels of deficits and debt we should aim for: this choice depends on how we weigh the utility of future generations compared with the utility of the current generation.

Another problem is that all the *instruments* of fiscal policy have very clear distributional consequences. Each specific tax and each type of expenditure affects some groups more than others. This makes fiscal decisions inherently political, and for this reason it is less appealing to delegate fiscal decisions to independent experts, who are not elected by the voters. The effects of a change in the interest rate are more widespread and diffuse, and hard to identify, so monetary policy decisions are less controversial from a political point of view.

Fiscal policy councils

For the reasons discussed above, delegation of fiscal policy to independent experts may be seen as problematic from a democratic point of view. Some countries have instead set up independent fiscal policy councils, which evaluate and give advice about fiscal policy. These councils, which consist mainly of independent experts, function as watchdogs that can protest when they think that fiscal policy is mismanaged, but they have no power to decide about fiscal policy. Denmark has had such a council since 1962 and Sweden introduced a fiscal policy council in 2007.[16]

Myopia and public investments

If the government is acting in a myopic way, it will favour expenditure that gives immediate payoff over expenditure that gives future payoffs. This means that public investments in infrastructure such as schools and transport systems will be too low. This is a consequence of myopia, not of deficit limits, but one way to reduce the underinvestment is to exclude net public investments when setting a rule for the deficit. In fact, many state governments in the US have such rules, prohibiting deficits for government consumption, but allowing deficits for financing public investments.

Another reason to exclude net public investments is that governments may make negative real investments – that is, they sell off assets – so as to meet a deficit target. If the government sells an office building to a private company, and then rents it back from the same company, there will be a reduction in the deficit in the year when the building is sold, but there is no real improvement in government finances. If the revenue from the sale is equal to the present value of the future rent payments, government finances are effectively unchanged.

Gross debt or net debt?

When we analysed the dynamics of government debt we focused on *net government debt*. If the interest rate on government debt and financial assets is the same, it is net debt rather than gross debt that is relevant for the sustainability of government finances. As we saw above, a deficit target can be seen as an implicit target for the long-run net government debt ratio.

In much of the public discussion, the focus is instead on *gross government debt* relative to GDP. One reason may be that it is an easier concept to understand. Another reason may be that this is the debt that is actually held by the lenders and which has to be rolled over in the financial market.

A more detailed analysis should take account of government gross debt and financial assets. In practice, the financial assets of the government may be harder to evaluate and they may also yield a lower rate of interest than the rate at which the government borrows. This will affect the evaluation of the fiscal situation.

Dealing with an ageing population

Many countries are experiencing large demographic changes. The proportion of the population that is over 64 years of age is expected to rise dramatically over the coming decades. If the pension age does not rise, and pensions are publicly

---

16 For a discussion of the role of fiscal councils, see Lars Calmfors and Simon Wren-Lewis, 'What should fiscal councils do?', CESifo working paper 3382 (2011). For information about fiscal councils, see the webpage created by Simon Wren-Lewis: http://www.economics.ox.ac.uk/members/simon.wren-lewis/fc/fiscal_councils.htm.

funded and kept at a fixed level relative to the wages of those who work, there will be a need to raise tax rates so as to finance higher pension payments relative to GDP. Another factor is increased medical expenditure, which is publicly financed in many countries. As people grow older and new medical treatment possibilities emerge, the pressure for increased medical expenditure will rise.

To some extent, these effects are countered because people not only live longer, they are also healthier. Many countries have increased the pension age and the incentives to continue working past the traditional retirement ages. Nonetheless, projections show that an ageing population will put a strain on public finances. In terms of our debt accumulation equation we can see this as an expected *future* increase in government consumption and transfers. This means that even if the debt ratio is stable today, the current level of taxes is not sustainable because G/Y will increase. To keep the debt ratio constant, taxes will have to increase relative to GDP. This leads to a tax-smoothing argument for running a surplus today so as to reduce the required future tax increase.

What have we learned?

Attempts to achieve a higher level of employment by expansionary monetary policy will be self-defeating and lead to a situation with high inflation without any gains in employment. Yet a promise to keep inflation low may not be credible. If people believe this promise, the short-sighted policymaker has an incentive to deviate and pursue a more inflationary policy.

A strict norm for inflation limits the possibilities for the central bank to help in the short-run stabilization of output.

In theory, we could adopt a policy rule that ensures low average inflation while at the same time allowing the central bank to react in a reasonable way to shocks. In practice, there are many different shocks that can occur, so it is hard to formulate an effective rule in advance.

If we delegate monetary policy to a 'conservative' central banker, we face a *credibility–flexibility trade-off*. The less weight the leader of the central bank puts on employment, the more we reduce the inflation bias, but at the same time the central bank will be less flexible in allowing temporary variations in inflation. Thus we may want to choose a central banker who puts low, but not zero, weight on employment.

Many countries have implemented reforms of the monetary policy framework that include explicit inflation targets, delegation of monetary policy to an independent central bank, and long-term contracts for the board members.

In a world with full *Ricardian equivalence* and non-distortionary taxes, the level of government debt does not matter. The current generation will save to compensate future generations for increased future tax payments. With less than full Ricardian equivalence, a deficit will *redistribute income* from future to current generations.

Tax distortions increase with the level of taxes, so we want to avoid a situation when taxes are very high. From an efficiency point of view, a stable level of taxes is preferred to a tax that is sometimes high and sometimes low.

High debt can easily become unsustainable as lenders require higher interest rates to compensate for the risk of default. When the debt ratio is on an unsustainable path, at least one of the following things will happen:

- taxes are increased, transfers are reduced, and/or government expenditure is reduced relative to GDP,
- the government defaults on (some part of) the debt, or
- the central bank monetizes the debt.

One reason for deficit bias may be that voters do not understand the future consequences of the policy. Alternatively, voters may themselves be myopic, and credit-constrained, so they rationally vote for a government that borrows on their behalf and passes on the cost to future generations.

If politicians think that a future government will waste government resources in some way, they may think that it is better to spend the money today, that is, run a deficit.

When there are many political parties that have to compromise, they may all push for their specific interests without taking responsibility for the consequences for the economy as a whole.

One way to deal with the deficit bias is to set up targets or ceiling for deficits and debt. These are meant to be relatively permanent commitments which act as constraints on day-to-day policy decisions. There is a close relation between the deficit and the steady state debt ratio:

$$\text{long run debt ratio} = \frac{\text{deficit/GDP}}{\text{growth rate of nominal GDP}}.$$

This means that a target level for the deficit can be seen as an implicit target for the long-run net debt ratio.

Reforms of budgetary procedures have involved a top-down approach where the total size of spending is decided first, and then this spending is divided between different departments.

A radical solution to the deficit bias problem is to delegate some aspects of fiscal policy to an independent body similar to the central bank. In practice, delegation of fiscal policy is more controversial than delegation of monetary policy because fiscal policy decisions are inherently more political.

If the government is acting in a myopic way, public investment in infrastructure will be too low. This may be a reason exclude net public investments when setting a limit or a target for the deficit.

Because of an ageing population, current tax and expenditure levels may be unsustainable in some countries.

Exercises

1. We have the loss function and the Phillips curve:

   $$L = \pi^2 + \lambda u^2 \quad \text{and} \quad \pi = \pi_{-1} - a(u - u^n) + z,$$

   where π_{-1} is inflation in the previous period. The policymaker can see the cost–push shock z and react to it. Let us do the loss minimization to find the inflation rate. In order to do that, it is convenient to express the loss as a function of inflation.

a) Rewrite the Phillips curve so that you have unemployment on the left-hand side.

b) Use the result in a) to substitute for u in the objective function of the central bank.

c) Calculate the rate of inflation that minimizes the loss function. *(Hint: It is convenient to multiply the first order condition by a^2.)*

d) How do π_{-1}, u^n and z affect the rate of inflation chosen by the policymaker? Why?

e) In the long run, inflation must be constant. Set $\pi = \pi_{-1}$ and $z = 0$ to calculate the long-run rate of inflation and explain the result.

f) How do the parameters λ and a affect the long-run inflation rate? Why?

2. We have the loss function and the Phillips curve:

$$L = \pi^2 + \lambda u^2 \quad \text{and} \quad \pi = \pi^e - a(u - u^n),$$

where π^e is the expected inflation rate. The policymaker can see the cost–push shock z and react to it.

a) Follow the same steps as above to calculate inflation as a function of π^e, and u^n.

b) Assume that wage setters can perfectly foresee the shock and the inflation rate chosen by the policymaker. What will the inflation rate be?

c) Compare this case to the case where expected inflation is equal to inflation in the previous period.

3. Use the diagram with the Phillips curve and the level curves of the loss function to illustrate what happens if we get a new chairman of the central bank who is more inflation adverse.

4. Who gains and loses from a more expansionary monetary policy
a) in the short run?
b) in the long run?

5. As before, we have the Phillips curve:

$$\pi = \pi_{-1} - a(u - u^n) + z$$

but now the loss function is

$$L = \frac{1}{2}\pi^2 + \lambda u.$$

The policymaker can see the cost–push shock z and react to it.

a) Use the Phillips curve to substitute for inflation in the loss function and calculate the inflation rate that minimizes the loss function.

b) How does the inflation rate depend on the parameters λ and a?

c) Does the policymaker stabilize cost–push shocks in this case?

6. A country has an average deficit over the cycle which is equal to 2 percent of GDP. The real growth rate is 3 percent and inflation is 2 percent.

a) What will the debt ratio be in the long run?

b) How does the result change if growth falls to 2 percent?

c) How does the result change if the deficit is instead 4 percent of GDP?

d) How does the result change if inflation increases to 3 percent?

Explain your results.

7. In country A the government deficit is 10 percent of GDP, inflation is 5 percent, and the real growth rate is 7 percent. In country B the government deficit is 3 percent of GDP, inflation is 2 percent, and the real growth rate is one percent. In both countries, debt relative to GDP is stable. Which country has the highest debt ratio? Explain the result.

8. The citizens of a certain country refuse to pay more than 31 percent of GDP in taxes. What level of expenditure relative to GDP is compatible with net government debt being 50 percent of GDP in the long run? Answer the question for cases a) and b):

a) The real interest rate is 4 percent and the real growth rate is 2 percent.

b) The real interest rate is 2 percent and the real growth rate is 4 percent.

c) Explain the difference between a) and b).

d) Do the same calculations allowing net government debt to be 100 percent of GDP and explain the difference.

9. Citizens sometimes vote for politicians who pursue short-sighted policies.

a) Why do citizens sometimes vote for politicians who pursue short-sighted policies?

b) Given your answer to a), what can be done in order for policymakers to pursue policies that are beneficial in the long run?

10. The government in a country has financial claims on the private sector equal to 30 percent of GDP. It views a long-run gross debt ratio equal to 60 percent of GDP as the maximum acceptable level. Nominal GDP is expected to grow by 5 percent per year. What is the maximum average level of the deficit over the cycle that is consistent with this level of debt?

11. If government finances are unsustainable at least one of the following things will happen:

- the primary deficit is reduced by increased taxes, reduced transfers, and/or reduced government consumption and investment relative to GDP
- the government defaults on the debt, or part of it
- the central bank monetizes the debt – that is, it buys government bonds, financed by an increase in the monetary base.

Discuss the advantages and disadvantages of each possible line of action.

Answers to the exercises can be found at: **www.palgrave.com/economics/gottfries**.

What roles do financial markets and institutions play?

In our basic macroeconomic model, we assumed that firms financed their investments by borrowing from the households, who were also the owners of the firms, and that firms handed out all profits to households in the form of dividends. This is a very simplified picture of the financial markets, however. In practice, firms finance their investments by borrowing, by issuing shares, and by reinvesting profits (so-called retained earnings). Shares represent ownership of the firm and entitle the owners to a share of the dividends – that is, the part of the profits that is paid out to the shareholders. Shares are traded in the stock market and share prices reflect expectations about future profits. The stock market is therefore an important indicator of future economic developments.

A typical firm may have debt in the order of 60–70 percent of total assets, while 30–40 percent of the financing has come from share issues and retained profits (earnings). The level of debt finance varies, however, depending on the type of firm.

Another important aspect of financial markets is that households do not normally lend directly to firms, but most lending is channelled through banks and other financial institutions, which borrow funds from savers and lend them to firms and households who need money to invest, or to consume. Institutions that intermediate credit in this way are called *financial intermediaries*. Banks and other financial intermediaries play an important role channelling funds from savers to investors. They can also be a source of instability, as seen in the recent financial crisis.

In this chapter we take a close look at financial markets. We first analyse the difference between debt and equity and the role played by the stock market as a predictor of future economic developments. Then we analyse what role of financial intermediaries play, the possibilities of *bank runs*, and banking regulation, which aims to reduce the risk of bank runs and financial crises. Finally, we discuss the recent financial crisis, which led to a dramatic recession across the world. As we will see, the financial markets reflect current and expected future macroeconomic developments, and what happens in financial markets can have big effects on the macro economy.

18.1   Debt and equity

Firms finance their operations in two ways: by debt and equity. A simplified balance sheet of a firm looks as follows:

Assets	**Liabilities and owner's equity**
Financial assets	Liabilities
Real assets (machines and buildings)	Equity
Total	Total

'Equity' is simply the difference between total assets and liabilities, so the total sum is always the same on both sides of the balance sheet. If assets exceed liabilities, so that the firm has positive equity, we say that the firm is *solvent*. The composition of debt and equity is called *capital structure*.

But where does the equity come from? It comes from money that shareholders (owners) have originally invested in the firm, and from retained earnings – profits that were not handed out as dividends but reinvested in the firm. Let us take a simple example. Suppose we set up a firm. The shareholders invest 4000 euros and the firm borrows 6000 euros, 3000 euros are kept by the firm in the form of bank deposits, and 7000 are used to buy machines. Then the balance sheet of the firm will look as follows:

Assets		**Liabilities and owner's equity**	
Financial assets	3000	Liabilities	6000
Real assets	7000	Equity	4000
Total	10,000	Total	1000

Suppose that, over the first year, the firm makes a profit after tax of 1000 after paying interest and replacing depreciated capital. If this profit is paid out as dividends, the balance sheet remains unchanged. If the profit is instead used to buy more machines, the balance sheet of the firm will look as follows at the end of the first year:

Assets		**Liabilities and owner's equity**	
Financial assets	3000	Liabilities	6000
Real assets	8000	Equity	5000
Total	11,000	Total	11,000

The equity has now increased to 5000, of which 4000 was originally invested by the shareholders and 1000 comes from retained earnings. Earnings are a flow, while the balance sheet reports stocks at the end of the year. If earnings are retained – that is, not paid out as dividends – the stocks on the balance sheet will change. Retained earnings may be used to buy real or financial assets, or to pay off debt, and in either case, the amount of equity will increase.

The shareholders own the firm and thereby the equity of the firm. Assets such as machines and buildings are initially registered in the books at the price that the firm pays for them, and then some given proportion is written off each year as depreciation.[1] Shareholders have the right to receive future dividends, so the value of the firm's stocks in the stock market is based on expected future profits and dividends, which may be higher or lower than the book value of the equity. Any retained earnings that are reinvested will normally increase expected future profits and the value of the company. Thus we see that profits can generate a return to shareholders in two ways, either in the form of direct dividend payments, or in the form of an increase in the value of the firm.

Suppose now that, over the second year, the firm makes a loss of 2000 after paying interest and replacing depreciated capital. In this case, the firm could go to the shareholders and ask them to put in more money. If it does not do that, there must again be some changes in the stocks on the balance sheet. Suppose that the loss is financed by a reduction of financial assets by 1000 and sale of real assets of 1000. Then the balance sheet of the firm will look as follows at the end of the second year:

Assets		Liabilities and owner's equity	
Financial assets	2000	Liabilities	6000
Real assets	7000	Equity	3000
Total	9000	Total	9000

The equity has now decreased to 3000. We see that profits and losses lead to changes in the level of equity, while the claims of the debt holders are unchanged.

But what happens if there are larger losses? Suppose that, in the third year, the firm makes a loss of 4000. Many of the investments turned out to be unprofitable and many of the machines are sold off at a loss. As a result, there is a further reduction in real assets of 3000 and a further reduction in financial assets of 1000. At the end of the third year, the balance sheet looks as follows:

Assets		Liabilities and owner's equity	
Financial assets	1000	Liabilities	6000
Real assets	4000	Equity	−1000
Total	5000	Total	5000

Now we see that the firm has negative equity. It is *insolvent* and cannot continue operating. In this situation, one possibility is that the shareholders invest more money in the firm, paying off debt so the equity again becomes positive. To raise more capital, the firm issues new shares which are bought by old or new shareholders. If the shareholders put in another 2000 and this money is used to pay off debt, debts are reduced to 4000 and the firm again has positive equity equal to 1000.

If the shareholders do not put in more money, the firm will go bankrupt. If the firm goes bankrupt, those who have lent money to the firm have the right to any

---

1 Liquid assets, e.g. government bonds, which are held temporarily and traded in organized markets, may instead be registered at the market, a practice called *mark-to-market*. With mark-to-market, changes in the market prices of the assets will generate profits and losses and changes in the balance sheet of the firm.

proceeds that can be obtained by selling off the assets of the firm. The shareholders get nothing, but nor are they responsible for the losses. *Limited liability* means that the shareholders are not required to pay back the loans that were taken by the firm. The shareholders lose their investments, but they can walk away from the losses.

Bankruptcy does not necessarily mean that the operations of the firm will be aborted. If the firm has a viable business it may be sold off as a going concern and the proceeds of the sale can then be shared among the debt holders. In such a case, bankruptcy means that there are new owners and that the original debt holders lose some of their money. If it is impossible to find a buyer for the firm, the operations of the firm may be discontinued, so the workers are fired and remaining equipment and property are sold off.

In practice, there are substantial real costs that arise when a firm goes bankrupt or is close to bankruptcy. Often, the existing owners play an active leadership role, so it is hard to replace them. As the firm approaches bankruptcy, there will be disruptions as customers and key personnel leave the firm. Lawyers have to be paid and assets (e.g. machines) which are sold after a bankruptcy may have a much lower value in the secondary market than the price originally paid for them and registered in the books.

In the case above, we can imagine different scenarios. On paper, the debt holders have claims of 6000, but the book value of the assets is 5000. If the assets are sold off at this price, and there are no other costs of bankruptcy, the debt holders get 5000, so they lose 1/6 of what they originally lent to the firm. But suppose that the assets are worth only 3000 in the secondary market and the costs of the bankruptcy are 1000. Then the debt holders recover only 2000, so they lose two thirds of their money. If, on the other hand, they find someone who is willing to pay 4000 for the firm, it is better to sell the firm as it is than to cancel the operations and sell the assets. In that case the debt holders lose only one third of their money.

Debt, equity, and risk

There are two fundamental differences between shareholders and debt holders:

1. Shareholders control the firm, at least indirectly. They appoint the board of the company at the shareholders' meeting and the board appoints the managing director. Debt-holders have no direct control although they may set up restrictions on what the firm can and cannot do with the money.
2. Debt-holders are promised a fixed repayment i.e. the loan plus interest. It is only in the case of bankruptcy that the debt-holders get less than what they were promised. Shareholders are not promised a fixed return on their investment. What shareholders get depends entirely on how well the company does so the return to the shareholders is very uncertain.

In order to illustrate the difference between debt and equity in a simple way, consider an entrepreneur who invests in a project with a cost X. The project has an uncertain future (gross) return V, with expected value $\bar{V}$. To simplify, we take the size (and cost) of the investment project as fixed. Assume that the entrepreneur

Fig. 18.1 *Gross returns on investment, debt, and equity*

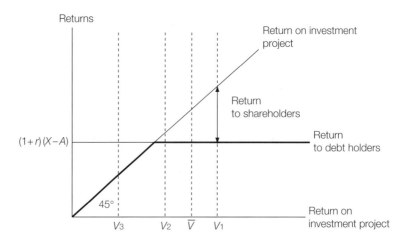

can put up an amount A and that X is larger than A, so the entrepreneur has to borrow $X - A$ in order to carry out the project. If the interest rate is r, the promised repayment of the loan is $(1+r)(X-A)$.

Fig. 18.1 illustrates how the returns on debt and equity depend on the return on the project. On the horizontal axis we have the gross return on the investment project, V, and on the vertical axis we have the return to the debt holders. The horizontal line at $(1+r)(X-A)$ shows the promised repayment to the debt holders – that is, what they get if the firm does not go bankrupt.

If the return turns out to be equal to the expected value $\bar{V}$, the debt holders get $(1+r)(X-A)$ and the shareholders get $\bar{V} - (1+r)(X-A)$. But what happens if the value turns out to be higher or lower? If the return is V_1 or V_2 the debt holders still get $(1+r)(X-A)$ but the shareholders get either $V_1 - (1+r)(X-A)$ or $V_2 - (1+r)(X-A)$, depending on the outcome. Under normal conditions, it is the shareholders who bear the risk, while debt holders get what they were promised.

But suppose that things go really bad so the gross return on the project is only V_3. What happens then? Now the firm defaults and the lenders get V_3 and make a loss on their investments. The (gross) return for the debt holders as a function of the gross return on the investment is given by the thick line in Fig. 18.1.

Thus we see that investment in shares is normally more risky than lending. In normal times, it is the shareholders who bear the risk. Equity is a buffer that absorbs shocks so that debt holders are protected. But if there are big losses, they will eat through the equity buffer and lenders will lose some of their money.

Note that the distribution of risk between debt and shareholders depends on how the firm is financed. If the firm has financed a larger proportion of the investment by borrowing, and less by equity, the promised repayment is higher, so the line $(1+r)(X-A)$ is higher up, and the likelihood of default will be higher. The higher the proportion of the investment that is financed by debt, the more risky is the debt. Therefore, lenders will typically require that a large part of an investment is financed by equity so that there is a sufficient buffer that can absorb losses without the company becoming insolvent.

Why debt finance?

As we discussed above, there are real costs of bankruptcy. Therefore one could ask why there is debt financing in the first place. If firms financed all their investments by issuing shares, we would never have any bankruptcies. In good times, shareholders would get a high return and in bad times they would get a low return, but we would never have to worry about firms going bankrupt and the associated costs of financial distress.

There are several reasons why firms issue debt. One is taxation. The money that is handed out to shareholders comes from profits, which are subject to corporate income tax, and then the individuals who receive the dividends have to pay personal income tax on the dividends. Interest payments, on the other hand, are only subject to personal income tax.

A more fundamental reason why there are different forms of finance has to do with information. Different investors are more or less well informed about the prospects of the firm. If we consider a small or medium-sized firm, there may only be a small group of owners and managers who have any idea what the future profits of the firm might be. In such a situation it is impossible to sell shares in the company to outside (uninformed) investors at a reasonable price because they cannot value them. On the other hand, the firm may be able to borrow a limited amount, especially if it is able to use some of its assets as collateral.[2]

To understand this, consider Fig. 18.1. Suppose that outside (i.e. less well-informed) investors know that the return will be somewhere between V_1 and V_2 but they have no idea what the probability distribution is between the outcomes in this interval. Then it is impossible for them to know what a share in the company is worth. However, they will still be willing to lend $X - A$ to the firm because they do know that the return will be sufficient for the firm to pay back the loan. Thus the firm may be able to borrow a limited amount from outside (less informed) investors although it cannot sell shares to them for a reasonable price. This example illustrates that it is normally harder to say what the shares are worth than to judge the risk of a loan. To estimate the value of a share, one has to have an idea about the whole probability distribution of the return. To evaluate a loan, one needs to know the probability of default and how much of the money can be recovered in the case of default.

Lenders often reduce the uncertainty by requiring collateral for their loans. *Collateral* means that if the firm does not pay the debt, the lender gets ownership of certain assets. This puts a lower bound on the losses. If lenders require collateral, the amount that the firm can borrow is constrained. More generally, the information problems discussed here will limit firms' access to debt finance.

---

2 The American economist Robert Townsend developed a model of 'costly state verification' which points to imperfect (asymmetric) information as the key reason for debt contracts. In his model, it is costly for the outside investor to verify the outcome (state) of the project. The advantage of the debt contract compared with financing only by shares is that, most of the time, the investor gets his money without any need to know the exact outcome of the project. For a good presentation of the Townsend model, see David Romer, *Advanced Macroeconomics*, 4th edn (New York: McGraw Hill Irwin, 2012).

The lenders will require that a substantial share of the investment is financed by equity – that is, retained earnings or issues of shares.

In practice, a company may have equity in the order of 30–40 percent of its total assets while 60–70 percent of the investments are financed by debt, but the division between debt and equity depends on the type of company we are considering. In volatile industries, companies have lower levels of debt relative to total assets because the risks of big losses are larger. Companies with assets that are easy to sell in case of default can have higher debt ratios because the assets can be used as collateral. Banks have diversified portfolios, so losses tend to cancel out. This reduces the risk, so banks operate with lower levels of equity, around 10 percent of the assets of the bank.

Debt, equity, and incentives to take risk

The capital structure affects the risk of bankruptcy but it may also affect the decisions taken by the firm, especially with respect to risk taking. The reason is that investment projects with a high return and high variance may be attractive for the shareholders. Although they risk losing their money, they also have a chance of getting a very high return. If there is a large loss, most of the loss will be borne by the debt holders.

To illustrate this, we can again use Fig. 18.1. Suppose that the firm has borrowed an amount $X - A$ but now the firm has a choice between two projects with the same expected return. One project yields V_2 with certainty. The other project yields either $\bar{V}$ or V_3 with equal probabilities – that is, 50 percent. If the return is V_3 the shareholders get nothing and the debt holders lose a large part of what they have lent to the firm; they only recover V_3. Since the return when $V = \bar{V}$ is more than twice the return when $V = V_2$, it is better for the shareholders to get $\bar{V} - (1+r)(X - A)$ with 50 percent probability than to get $V_2 - (1+r)(X - A)$ with certainty. Thus the shareholders (owners) prefer to gamble, and take the risky project although there is a 50 percent of a large loss for the debt holders. The debt holders, on the other hand, would clearly prefer the project that gives V_2 with certainty. It is the shareholders and their appointed managers who control the firm, so they will decide to take the risky project. If debt holders are poorly informed about the riskiness of alternative projects, they may be unable to prevent the firm from gambling with their money.

This problem becomes particularly serious when the level of equity is low. In such a situation, the shareholders have little to lose, but by investing in the risky project, they gamble with the money of the debt holders and get a share of the return if things go well. This incentive to gamble when the level of equity is low is another reason why lenders will typically require the shareholders to put in a substantial portion of the funding for the investments.

18.2 The financial accelerator

In our analysis of investment in Chapter 3, we assumed that firms could always finance all profitable investments. All investments where the expected marginal revenue product of capital minus depreciation exceeded the rate of return in the credit market were carried out. But this is an idealized model of the credit market. As we have just seen, uncertainty and imperfect information limit access to funds for investments. For reasons explained above, lenders will require owners to put in a substantial share of the funds, so firms have to rely on their own resources in order to finance a substantial part of their investments. If shareholders' funds are limited, this will be a constraint on investments.

As a simple example, suppose that lenders (e.g. banks) have very little information about the prospects of the firm. To safeguard their lending, they ask for collateral in order to lend to the firm. Suppose, further, that only 60 percent of the investments can be used as collateral. Then, 40 percent of the investments must be financed by retained earnings or issues of new shares. Now suppose that the owners have no more money to invest and that, again because of information problems, they cannot sell shares to new shareholders at a reasonable price.[3] Then the investments will be constrained by the availability of retained earnings. When profits are low, the firm will be unable to invest even if there are profitable investment opportunities available. When profits are high, all profitable investment opportunities can be exploited.

This leads to a link between current profits and investment. If there is an increase in aggregate demand, production increases, and firms make more profits. This makes it easier to finance investments, which leads to a further increase in aggregate demand. If demand decreases, profits decrease, and investments will be constrained by available earnings, leading to a further contraction of aggregate demand. This feedback effect from aggregate demand to profits, investment, and aggregate demand is called the *financial accelerator*. We have already discussed it in Chapter 16. As we noted there, the implications of the financial accelerator are similar to those of the standard accelerator effect in that downturns and upturns in aggregate demand are reinforced.

18.3 The stock market and Tobin's *q*

The stock market as a predictor of future economic developments

Stocks represent the ownership shares of a company and give the right to receive a share of the dividends paid out by the firm. If a company has issued 1000 shares, the owner of a share has the right to receive 1/1000 of the dividends paid out by that company. This means that the value of a share is determined by the expected present value of future dividends. If households discount future dividends with a real interest rate r, the value of the shares is

$$S_t = \frac{d^e_{t+1}}{1+r} + \frac{d^e_{t+2}}{(1+r)^2} + \frac{d^e_{t+3}}{(1+r)^3} + \frac{d^e_{t+4}}{(1+r)^4} + \cdots$$

---

3 Another reason why they may be unwilling to bring in new shareholders is that this would reduce their control over the firm.

where d^e_{t+j} is the expected dividend in period $t+j$. This formula may be applied to an individual company, or to the stock market as a whole. As a simple example, suppose that dividends are expected to be equal to d in the next period and that they are expected to increase at the rate g from $t+1$ onwards. Then $d_{t+2} = (1+g)\,d$, $d_{t+3} = (1+g)\,(1+g)\,d$, and so on. So we have

$$S = \frac{d}{1+r} + \frac{(1+g)\,d}{(1+r)^2} + \frac{(1+g)^2\,d}{(1+r)^3} + \frac{(1+g)^3\,d}{(1+r)^4} + \ldots$$

$$= \frac{d}{1+r}\left(1 + \frac{1+g}{1+r} + \left(\frac{1+g}{1+r}\right)^2 + \left(\frac{1+g}{1+r}\right)^3 + \ldots\right)$$

$$= \frac{d}{1+r}\frac{1}{1 - \dfrac{1+g}{1+r}} = \frac{d}{r-g}.$$

Here we have used the formula for a geometric sum: $1 + b + b^2 + b^3 + \ldots = 1/(1-b)$. We see that the value of the shares is determined by three factors:

- expected dividends in the next period
- the relevant real discount rate
- the expected growth of dividends.

Uncertainty concerning future dividends affects the value of the shares. Stock prices are volatile, and investors want compensation for this risk. To compensate for risk, investors require a higher expected rate of return on shares than the interest rate on government bonds, which are normally considered as a safe investment. Suppose that the required real return on shares is 7 percent and that dividends are expected to grow along with GDP at 2 percent per year. Then we have

$$\frac{S}{d} = \frac{1}{r-g} = \frac{1}{0.07 - 0.02} = \frac{1}{0.05} = \frac{100}{5} = 20.$$

In this case, the value of the shares is 20 times the value of dividends. The direct return on shares in the form of dividends is 5 percent and shares are expected to increase by 2 percent per year in real terms, resulting in a total real return of 7 percent.

Future dividends come from future profits, which will either be handed out to shareholders directly or reinvested into the company, generating future dividend growth. Fig. 18.2 shows the ratio of stock prices to earnings (profits) for the US.

If expectations about future production and profits increase, share prices will increase. Therefore, we expect the stock market to predict future economic developments. Fig. 18.3 shows that there is a strong correlation between changes in share prices and GDP growth, and at least some of the time, the stock market leads relative to GDP.

Movements in stock prices are far from perfect predictors of future economic developments, however. The American economist Paul Samuelson pointed to this fact when he said that the stock market had predicted 'nine of the last five recessions'. In fact, the stock market seems to have a life of its own, with very

Fig. 18.2 *Price to earnings ratio, US*

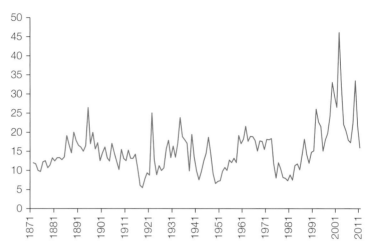

Note: Stock price to earnings ratio, one year earnings, Standard & Poor 500.
Sources: Stock market data from Standard & Poor, used in Robert Shiller, *Irrational Exuberance* (Princeton: Princeton University Press, 2000, 2005). Updated data available at Robert Shiller's webpage, http://www.econ.yale.edu/~shiller/data.htm.

Fig. 18.3 *Stock price growth and GDP growth*

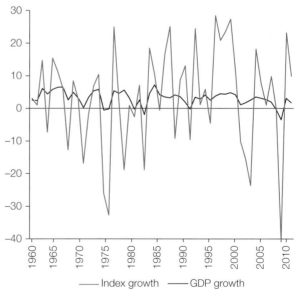

——— Index growth ——— GDP growth

Sources: Stock market data from Standard & Poor, used in Robert Shiller, *Irrational Exuberance* (Princeton: Princeton University Press, 2000, 2005). Updated data available at Robert Shiller's webpage, http://www.econ.yale.edu/~shiller/data.htm. Real GDP from *OECD Economic Outlook*, OECD, 8 March 2012; http://www.oecd-ilibrary.org/statistics.

high volatility. Stock prices often increase or decrease 10–20 percent in a year. In theory, stock prices movements should reflect news about future dividends, but dividends are much more stable than stock prices. In fact, stock prices vary more than can be explained by changes in expected future dividends. In this sense, there is *excess volatility* in the stock market, as shown by the American economist Robert Shiller.[4]

Tobin's q theory of investment

High future profits imply high future dividends and when expected future profits are high, firms have strong incentives to increase the capital stock. Therefore, we should expect share prices to be closely related to investment. The relation between share prices and investment was formalized by the American economist James Tobin. Tobin argued that investment should be a function of the market value of the capital stock relative to the replacement value of the capital stock, a ratio which is called 'Tobin's q'. His argument was that if existing capital assets are worth more than the costs of producing new ones, there should be incentives to increase the capital stock, and conversely.

Tobin's theory is broadly consistent with the theory of investment that we presented in Chapter 3. To see this, assume, for simplicity, that firms finance all their investments by issuing shares, that they hand out all profits as dividends, and that shares of all firms are traded in the stock market. To simplify, we also assume that there is perfect competition in the product market.[5] Then we can measure Tobin's q as the value of the companies in the stock market relative to the existing capital stock:

$$q = \frac{S}{K},$$

where S is the real value of all the firms in the economy. We saw in the previous section, that if profits (and dividends) are expected to remain constant, the real value of the shares is π/r. With a Cobb–Douglas production function, the share of gross income going to capital is α so real profits after depreciation of capital are given by $\pi = \alpha Y - \delta K$. Thus we get Tobin's q as:

$$q = \frac{S}{K} = \frac{\pi/r}{K} = \frac{\alpha Y - \delta K}{Kr} = \frac{\alpha Y/K - \delta}{r}.$$

But what determines investment? With perfect competition in the product market, the theory in Chapter 3 implies that, in the long run, the capital stock is chosen so that the real marginal product of capital minus depreciation is equal to the real interest rate. If we assume that investment is associated with adjustment costs, which slow down adjustment of the capital stock, we may think of investment as being determined by the ratio between the marginal product minus depreciation and the real interest rate:

$$I = I\left(\frac{MPK - \delta}{r}\right).$$

4 Robert Shiller, 'Do stock prices move too much to be justified by subsequent changes in dividends?', *American Economic Review*, 71 (1981), 421–436.

5 The assumption that firms finance all their investments by issuing shares is the opposite assumption to what we assumed in Chapter 3: that firms finance all their investments by borrowing. In the appendix to this chapter we analyse a more realistic case with debt and equity finance and monopolistic competition. We reach a similar but slightly modified conclusion.

Fig. 18.4 *Stock price growth and investment growth*

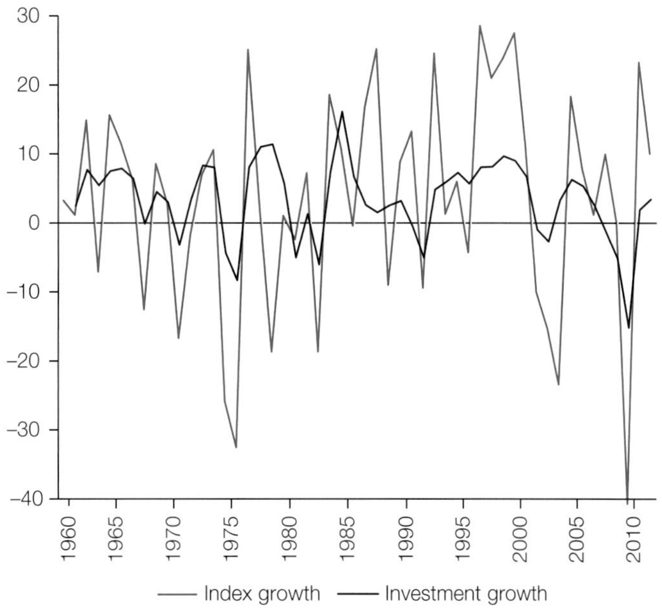

Sources: Stock market data from Standard & Poor, used in Robert Shiller, *Irrational Exuberance* (Princeton: Princeton University Press, 2000, 2005). Updated data available at Robert Shiller's web-page, http://www.econ.yale.edu/~shiller/data.htm. Real investment from *OECD Economic Outlook*, OECD, 8 March 2012; http://www.oecd-ilibrary.org/statistics.

With a Cobb–Douglas production function, the marginal product of capital is $\alpha Y/K$, so we see that investment is a function of Tobin's q.[6] The intuition behind the result is that Tobin's q is high when the expected future total return on capital is high, and then the marginal return on investment is also high.

Fig. 18.4 illustrates that there is indeed a strong correlation between changes in stock prices and changes in investment. When investors become more optimistic about the future, share prices increase, and firms also invest so as to increase their production capacity.

18.4 Banks and other financial intermediaries

Having analysed the role of the stock market, we now consider the other source of finance: debt. We take a closer look at the credit market. As mentioned above, more than 50 percent of the financing of firms comes from debt. Also, households may borrow in order to buy a house or a car, or by using their credit card for everyday consumption purchases.

---

6 The argument made here is somewhat inconsistent because a situation where $q > 1$ is a disequilibrium situation, so profits per unit of capital would not be expected to remain unchanged. As the capital stock increases, profits per unit of capital will decrease. Taking account of this does not change the result that high value of q is associated with high investment, and conversely. A precise formulation of Tobin's q theory of investment was developed by Fumio Hayashi and Lawrence Summers in articles published in 1981–1982. For a rigorous presentation, see e.g. David Romer, *Advanced Macroeconomics*, 4th edn (New York: McGraw Hill Irwin, 2012).

So far we have discussed the credit market as if households were lending directly to firms. In practice, however, households seldom do this. Instead, most of the lending goes through banks, which borrow from the households in the form of deposits and lend in the form of bank loans and by purchasing bonds and other financial assets. There are also other financial intermediaries which perform roles similar to those of banks.

So why do we need banks? To understand the role of banks, note two problems that occur when households lend directly to the firms, or to other households.

1. *Trust and information*: The credit market differs from markets for goods and services in that, once the loan has been made, the transaction is not over. The lender wants to see the borrower again: the loan should be paid back with interest. Therefore, the lender will only make the loan if he trusts the borrower to pay back the loans. But for a normal household, it is difficult to judge the credit worthiness of potential borrowers. This is a problem of trust and information.

2. *Maturity mismatch*: Another problem is that the length of the period, for which a borrower wants to borrow, will typically not coincide with the period for which a lender wants to lend. A firm that makes a major investment in a plant may have a time horizon of many years, while a household that saves for a holiday has a time horizon of a few months. In general there is a maturity mismatch in that lenders want to have access to their funds at short notice, while borrowers want to invest the funds in long-term investment projects. An asset is said to be *liquid* if it is easy to sell when you need the money. Households want their assets to be liquid, but bank loans are often illiquid, tied up in long-term investment projects.

This is where banks come in, playing two very important roles:

1. *Credit management*: Banks provide households with an essentially safe way to save, although the repayments of bank loans are uncertain.

2. *Liquidity provision*: Banks allow households to withdraw their deposits at any time, although much of the assets of the bank consist of long-term lending.

On their asset side, banks have uncertain and illiquid lending; on their debt side they have liquid and (normally) safe deposits. This sounds like magic! How can they manage this? As we will see, this 'magic' is based on the *law of large numbers*, and on the fact that banks have *buffers* in the form of equity and liquid assets that they can use when credit losses or withdrawals of deposits are particularly large.

Let us look more closely at the two main functions of banks: management of credit and provision of liquidity. For the sake of simplicity, we focus the discussion on regular commercial banks. As we will see later, there are other financial institutions which perform similar roles without being standard commercial banks.[7]

---

7 Formal models of banking have been developed by Franklin Allen and Douglas Gale, Douglas Diamond and Philip H. Dybvig, Bengt Holmström and Jean Tirole, Hayne E. Leland and David H. Pyle, and others. These models are fairly complicated. A useful book on banking is Xavier Freixas and Jean-Charles Rochet, *Microeconomics of Banking* (Cambridge, MA: The MIT Press, 2008).

Banks as managers of credit

Banks receive deposits from households and firms and lend the money in various forms. Some money is lent directly to firms. For small firms, bank lending is a very important source of finance. Banks can also hold industrial bonds – bonds issued by firms – which is another way of lending to firms. Some lending goes to households who want to buy cars or houses. When households borrow to buy houses, they often borrow from special mortgage institutions, which finance their lending by issuing housing bonds. These housing bonds are often held by banks, so a substantial share of housing loans are ultimately financed by the banks.

As discussed above, lending can take place only if the lender believes that the borrower will pay back the loan, and banks play an important role in this process, monitoring credit. This involves both evaluating the credit worthiness of the borrowers before lending, and taking actions to recover as much as possible of the loan if the borrower gets into financial difficulties. Banking is based on trust and specific information. People deposit money in the bank because they trust the bank. A bank that lends to a firm will typically have specific information about that firm that other banks do not have. There is a long-term *lending relationship* between the bank and the firm. Banks often require collateral in order to lend to a firm or a household.

Even if banks are cautious in their evaluation of credit worthiness, lending is never risk-free, and banks make credit losses on their lending. Nevertheless, we normally regard our bank deposits as essentially safe. How is this possible? The conversion of uncertain lending to safe deposits is based on two conditions.

1. *The law of large numbers*: The bank makes a large number of loans, and although the repayment of each individual loan is uncertain, the proportion of losses for the whole portfolio may be fairly predictable. For example, the bank may know from experience that credit losses on particular types of loans are normally one percent of the total amount that they lend and the bank will then set a one percent higher interest rate on such loans to compensate for expected credit losses.

2. *The equity capital buffer*: The second key condition is that the assets of the bank exceed the liabilities by a sufficient amount so that equity remains positive even if there are unexpectedly large defaults on the loans. As in any firm, equity is a buffer that protects the lenders. In the case of a bank, the lenders are you and me, who have deposits in the bank.

A stylized balance sheet of a bank is shown in Fig. 18.5. Large losses on the lending portfolio will wipe out some of the equity of the bank, but provided that the equity of the bank is sufficient, it will be a sufficient buffer to absorb the losses.

Banks as liquidity providers

As mentioned above, another important role of banks is provision of liquidity. An asset is said to be liquid if it is easy to sell when you need the money. Cash is the most liquid asset because you can pay with it directly. Government bonds and

Fig. 18.5 *A stylized bank balance sheet*

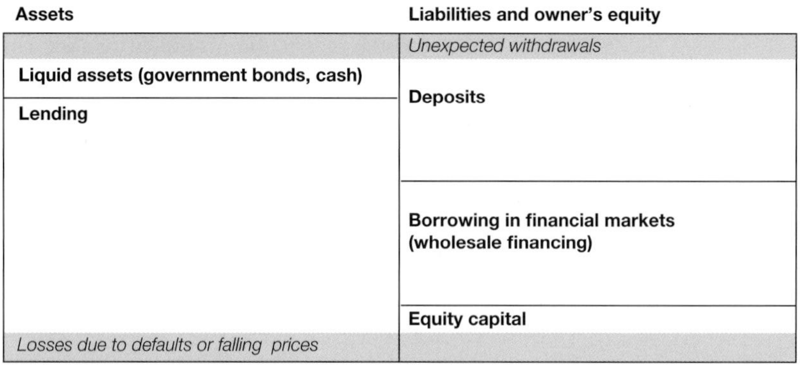

Assets	Liabilities and owner's equity
Unexpected withdrawals	
Liquid assets (government bonds, cash)	**Deposits**
Lending	
	Borrowing in financial markets (wholesale financing)
	Equity capital
Losses due to defaults or falling prices	

Treasury bills are normally very liquid because they can be sold quickly in well-functioning markets. Transaction accounts in banks are very liquid because the money can be withdrawn whenever you want, for example by using a payment card in a shop.

Because of the information problems described above, a loan to a small or medium-size firm or a household is not a liquid asset. The borrower will typically be unable to pay back the loan immediately. Suppose, for example, that a firm has borrowed a large sum of money to build a new factory building and the building is halfway through construction. If the bank asks the firm to pay back the money, the firm will be unable to pay back because a half-finished factory building will not be worth much if you sell it. Also, since the loan is based on relation-specific information, it may be very hard to convince another bank to take over the loan. Other banks have less information about the firm and if the firm's regular bank denies credit, this may be taken as a signal that there may be some problem with the firm. Therefore, denial of credit may lead to financial problems and even bankruptcy of the firm that is denied credit. For this reason, the bank cannot easily convert its outstanding loans to cash.

So a large part of the assets of a bank are illiquid, while the debts (deposits) are very liquid. How is this possible? Again, there are two conditions that make this work:

1. *The law of large numbers*: The bank has many customers and, in each period, many households withdraw money and many households make new deposits. Most of these transactions cancel each other out.
2. *A buffer of liquid assets*: The bank holds enough liquid assets, such as government bonds and Treasury bills, on the balance sheet that can be sold if withdrawals of deposits exceed the inflow of new deposits in a particular period.

Again we can illustrate this using the stylized balance sheet of the bank shown above. If there are unexpectedly large withdrawals of deposits, the bank can handle the situation provided that it has a sufficient buffer of liquid assets. Thus, banks provide liquidity to households. Economists say that banks are involved in *maturity transformation*, converting illiquid long-term loans to liquid, short-term deposits.

We see that banks perform important roles intermediating and monitoring credit and providing liquidity to households and firms. Of course, they do not do this for free. A very important source of income for the bank is the *interest differential* between the deposit and lending rates. This interest differential compensates for expected defaults on the loans, administrative and other costs that the bank has, and banks also get much of their profits from this interest differential. The more the bank borrows and lends for a given level of equity capital, the higher the return to the shareholders of the bank. But the more the bank borrows and lends for a given level of equity, the higher also the risk that unexpected large losses wipe out the equity of the bank.

18.5 Bank runs and banking regulation

As explained above, banks perform a magic trick converting uncertain and illiquid lending to safe and liquid deposits. But, as with all magic tricks, there is a risk that something goes wrong if the gods are not on your side. The combination of liquid deposits and illiquid lending can be a source of instability, for the individual bank and for the financial system as a whole.

Bank runs

If a large proportion of the depositors come to withdraw their money at the same time, the bank will be in serious trouble. With much of its money tied up in long-term lending, it will not have the money to pay all deposit holders. A *bank run*, where a large proportion of the depositors try to withdraw their money at the same time, can drive a bank out of business even if the bank was in good shape before the bank run. There is thus an inherent instability in the banking system. In fact, for any bank with positive equity, there are two equilibria:

- In the good equilibrium, depositors trust the bank, only some of them take out their money, the bank's liquid assets are sufficient to cover withdrawals, and the bank can continue its operations.
- In the bad equilibrium, people lose trust in the bank and withdraw a large amount of deposits. Unless the bank is able to borrow from other banks, or from the central bank, it becomes unable to fulfil its commitments with regard to the deposit holders.

Thus, a sufficiently large *bank run* can topple a bank even if it has substantial buffers of liquidity and equity. In practice, however, we would expect a bank run to be triggered when a bank has made large losses, or is feared to have made large losses. Since deposit holders are poorly informed, rumours about losses may be sufficient to induce people to withdraw their money. Since the first deposit holders who withdraw their money will get their money back, people may withdraw their money just to be on the safe side. Even a person who knows for sure that the losses of the bank are manageable will rationally withdraw his money if he thinks that many other deposit holders will try to withdraw their deposits. Therefore, the mere suspicion that the bank has made substantial credit losses can lead to a bank run that destroys the bank. The magic trick can go seriously wrong.

Note the key ingredients in a bank run:

1. There is a suspicion that the bank has made *losses* which are large relative to the initial amount of equity.
2. There are many deposit holders who have *imperfect information* about the magnitude of the losses and about what other deposit holders do.
3. Deposits are *liquid* – that is, they can be withdrawn at short notice, and those who withdraw their deposits first will get their money back, while a substantial part of the lending of the bank is *illiquid*, tied up in long-term loans which cannot be liquidated without substantial losses.

It is this combination of leverage, losses, lack of information, and maturity mismatch that generates the possibility of a run on a bank.

Contagion and financial crises

The collapse of a bank leads to losses for those who have deposits in the bank (if they are not insured – see below). It will also create problems for the firms that depend on the bank for their financing. The effects may also spread to other parts of the financial system. Banks are like spiders in a large web of financial relations, based on trust, and the default of some banks may lead to runs on other banks and financial institutions – that is, to a financial crisis. There are several ways in which problems in a few banks can spread to other banks:

1. Banks and other financial institutions have substantial claims on each other, so default in one institution leads to losses in other institutions, potentially leading to runs on those institutions.
2. The default of one bank may lead to a loss of trust in other institutions that have similar assets on their balance sheet as people fear that they have made similar losses.
3. Banks that have seen their equity being drastically reduced by losses need to restore a reasonable level of equity relative to total assets. If they are unable to raise new capital by issuing new shares, they must instead reduce the total balance sheet by selling off assets and reducing their liabilities. Such 'fire sales' reduce the prices of the assets, and this creates losses for other banks that hold similar assets, wiping out some of their equity.

The initial losses, which trigger a financial crisis, may be large defaults on loans to a particular sector. Often, loans to real estate have played a key role initiating financial crises because investments in real estate rely heavily on debt and sometimes property prices become inflated and collapse.

Losses need not be caused by defaults; they can also be caused by declines in asset prices. One source of risk for banks is *interest rate risk*, which is associated with changes in the level of interest rates. Maturity mismatch means that the bank borrows short term and lends long term, for example by buying housing bonds. If the interest rate rises quickly, the prices of long-term bonds will fall, which reduces the value of the assets. This may wipe out a large part of the equity of the bank. This was an important factor behind the crisis in the American savings banks (so-called savings and loans associations) in the 1980s.

Banking regulation

In order to avoid bank runs, and to protect deposit holders, commercial banks are heavily regulated. Two important regulations are *capital requirements* and *deposit insurance*.

Capital requirements require banks to have equity corresponding to a certain proportion of the assets of the bank. Thus, capital requirements are not requirements that the bank has money set aside on some specific account, but that liabilities are not too large relative to assets. As we explained at the beginning of this chapter, equity is the difference between assets and liabilities, and the idea behind capital requirements is that equity should be a sufficiently large buffer to absorb credit losses that may occur. If, because of large losses, equity threatens to fall below the required level, the bank must issue shares to raise new equity in order to continue its operations, or reduce its volume of lending.

In fact, capital requirements serve several functions:

1. With more equity capital, there is a larger buffer that can absorb losses. If losses occur, there is a better chance that assets will still exceed liabilities and this makes it easier for the bank to raise new equity capital in order to restore the level of equity relative to assets.
2. Capital requirements mean that the owners invest more of their own money and this should make the owners more cautious when formulating the bank's lending policy. As discussed in Section 18.1, the owners may have strong incentives to take risks when they are not risking much of their own money.
3. If the government has to take over the bank, the losses that must be covered by the tax payers will be smaller if equity is still positive. We will explain below why the government may have to take over the bank.

A large number of countries agreed on minimum capital requirements and other types of banking regulation in the so-called Basel accords in 1988 (Basel I) and 2004 (Basel II). A further refinement, Basel III, is on its way to being implemented. One change in the Basel II agreement was that capital requirements became *risk-adjusted*. This means that assets are classified into risk classes, so banks have to hold more equity for more risky assets. The basic requirement in Basel II is that equity should be at least 4 percent of total risk-adjusted assets. This is a minimum requirement; commercial banks often have equity in the order of 10 percent of their assets.

Capital requirements reduce the risk that credit losses wipe out the equity of the bank, but, as discussed above, a bank run can destroy a bank even if the bank has positive equity initially. Another important element of banking regulation is *deposit insurance*, which is meant to protect deposit holders and prevent bank runs. Individuals holding deposits in commercial banks are guaranteed to get their money back. Deposit insurance covers deposits up to a certain maximum amount, and banks pay a fee for this insurance.

Since the default of a large bank may lead to losses that spread through the whole financial system, and cause a general loss of trust, governments and central banks typically try to prevent the default of a large bank. If the main problem is liquidity, they can do that by lending to the bank. If the bank has made large losses, the government may inject equity capital by buying newly issued shares of the bank. If necessary, the government takes over the whole bank.

18.6   Recent developments in the financial industry

In recent decades, several changes have occurred in the financial industry. Three important developments will be described below: increased reliance on *wholesale financing*, development of a *shadow banking system (quasi-banks)*, and *securitization*. These are complicated matters and our description of these phenomena will be very brief.

Wholesale financing

Regular deposits are only one source of funding for the banks. Today, banks rely heavily on other types of borrowing. Banks issue various types of securities (e.g. bank certificates) that are bought by pension funds and other institutions. Often, this is short-term borrowing that is 'rolled over' every three months or so. When it is time to repay the loans, the bank must issue new securities in order to finance its lending. Note that this borrowing is not covered by deposit insurance.

Quasi-banks

In the decades before the financial crisis in 2008, so-called quasi-banks increased in importance. These are institutions that perform similar roles to banks, but which are not commercial banks and hence they are not subject to the same regulations as commercial banks. Such institutions are sometimes said to make up a *shadow banking system*. Before the financial crisis in 2008, a large industry of quasi-banks had developed outside the regular banking system, especially in the US.

Prominent examples of such institutions were the American investment banks, which have now either gone bankrupt, merged with commercial banks, or become commercial banks. Investment banks do not take regular deposits. They are involved in issuing, buying and selling housing bonds and other securities, and when doing so they hold inventories of securities. For their funding, they rely heavily on short-term borrowing. Before the crisis, they had lower capital requirements than regular banks and they operated with equity in the order of 4–5 percent of total assets.

Securitization

Securitization means that various types of loans, which would traditionally be held on the balance sheet of the bank, are packaged and sold off as securities to other institutions. Loans on houses, cars, and credit card debt may be packaged and sold in this way. For the borrower, there is no difference. She goes to the bank and takes a loan, promising to pay back with interest some time in the future. But then the bank makes a package with a large number of such loans and sells off these claims as a security to another bank, a fund, an insurance company, or some other investor. The buyer of the security has the right to receive the interest and the repayment of the loans. If borrowers default, the buyer of the security will make losses, but often the originating institution (bank) is guaranteeing the loan in some way, explicitly or implicitly.

These assets can be transformed in various ways to make them more attractive to investors. One common approach is to divide the security into 'tranches' with different priorities if borrowers default. Let us consider a simplified example. Suppose the bank has 10 million dollars of housing loans. Statistical estimates suggest an expected default rate of 2–3 percent and that it is extremely unlikely that more than 10 percent of the money will be lost. Suppose now that we finance these loans by issuing two types of securities, 9 million of security A and 1 million of security B. The difference between A and B is that any credit losses below 1 million will be borne by the holders of security B. The point of this transformation is that, although the repayment of each underlying loan is uncertain, security A can be seen as almost perfectly safe. This means that we can sell securities of type A to pension funds and other institutions that have a policy of only buying very safe assets. The buyers of security A do not need to bother about the details of the risk because essentially all the risk is borne by those who hold security B. In fact, security B is a buffer that absorbs risk in much the same way as the bank's equity would do if the loans were kept on the balance sheet of the bank.

Rating agencies play an important role in the securitization process, making supposedly objective evaluations of the riskiness of various securities. In the above case, a rating agency would classify security A as AAA, a very safe investment. Other three-letter acronyms associated with securitization and the recent financial crisis are listed in Table 18.1.

Ingenious as it appears to be, this 'financial engineering' relies on the presumption that the estimates of the risk are reasonably correct. If we have misjudged the risk, and the losses exceed 10 percent of the loans, the holders of security A will suffer losses. In fact, it is very difficult to evaluate the risk because there are sometimes unexpected events that break previously observed statistical patterns. If we estimate risk of default on housing loans over a 20-year period, when house prices were continuously increasing, those estimates tell us nothing about what will happen if there is a major collapse of house prices, and the risk of a major decline in house prices is also very hard to estimate.

18.7   The financial crisis in 2007–2009

As discussed above, a financial crisis typically starts with large losses somewhere in the system. The 2008 financial crisis started in 2007 with losses on loans for housing and other property investments.

Table 18.1 *The alphabet soup: various acronyms associated with securitization*

SIV	A bank that originates mortgage loans may sell the cash flow from these loans to a special entity, a *structured investment vehicle*, which is set up for this purpose. To finance this purchase, the SIV issues *mortgage backed securities (MBS)*.
SPV, SPE	*Special purpose vehicles* and *special purpose enterprises* are institutions similar to *structured investment vehicles*.
MBS	A *mortgage-backed security* is backed by a bundle of mortgage loans with houses as collateral. This means that the interest income and payment at maturity come from these loans (via the SIV). From the 1990s MBSs were created with subprime debt.
CDS	A *credit default swap* is a contract that gives X the right to sell asset Y to Z for a fixed price if the borrowers, who took the loans which are securitized in asset Y, default. Effectively, X buys insurance from Z and pays a fee. Provided the borrowers do not default, Z gets a nice flow of income, but if they do default, Z has to buy the asset for more than it is worth. CDSs are assets that are traded. They can be traded for insurance or to speculate.
CDO	A *collateralized debt obligation* is a bundle of securities such as MBSs and other securities consisting of car loans, credit card debt, corporate loans. It may also contain CDSs that serve as insurance against defaults on the underlying debt. A CDO is often split into tranches, as explained in the chapter text.
OTC	Many complicated securities were traded *over the counter* so there were no public market prices. This made it hard to evaluate how large the losses were.
AAA	*Triple A rating* is the highest credit rating. Assets rated AAA should be a very safe investments.
GSE	Fannie Mae and Freddie Mac are *government-sponsored entities* in the US, which finance housing loans. They made large losses on subprime lending and were taken over by the government during the financial crisis.
AIG	*American International Group* is a large insurance company that sold large quantities of credit default swaps and therefore suffered large losses during the subprime crisis. The US government became the main shareholder.
MBA, PHD	The people behind all this financial engineering.
OWS	*Occupy Wall Street*, a political protest starting in 2011 that originated at Zucotti Park in New York City.

Sources: This information is partly taken from Adrian Buckley, *Financial Crisis*, FT Prentice Hall, 2001 and the EEAG Report *The European Economy*. Both sources contain interesting reviews of the financial crisis.

In the US, house prices had been increasing for a long time. Housing loans are made with the house as collateral and financial institutions were lending to households with low incomes on the assumption that, if the household were not able to pay the interest, the bank would take over the house and recover the money by selling the house. With steadily rising house prices, this would not be a problem. Loans to borrowers with low credit worthiness are called *subprime* loans.[8] As house prices started to fall in 2007, loans on housing turned out to be much more risky than initially estimated. Fig. 18.6 shows the house price bubble in the US.

Loans to real estate also played an important role in several European countries. After the introduction of the euro in 1999, some European countries (especially Ireland, Greece, and Spain) had booming economies and high inflation. Since they

---

8 A 'prime borrower' is a borrower with high credit worthiness, so 'subprime' means that the borrower has lower credit worthiness. In the popular debate another term has been used for subprime loans: NINJA loans (No Income, No Job, and No Assets).

Fig. 18.6 *Real house price index, United States*

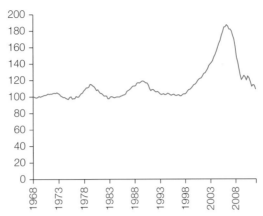

Note: The figure shows the S&P/Case-Shiller nominal house price index deflated by the consumer price index. The index is set to 100 at the first quarter of 1968.
Source: Data from Robert Shiller, *Irrational Exuberance* (Princeton: Princeton University Press, 2005, 2009; Broadway Books, 2006, also Subprime Solution, 2008, as updated by author). Available at http://www.econ.yale.edu/~shiller/data.htm.

were members of the Eurozone, high inflation meant that real interest rates were low, property prices were going up, and property appeared to be a very good investment. The property booms lasted for quite a few years, but, as time went by, competitiveness was eroded and eventually there were sharp recessions in these countries. Property prices fell, borrowers defaulted, and banks made large losses.

The Baltic countries had tied their currencies to the euro and a similar process went on in those countries around 2005. When their economies collapsed around 2008, there was speculation that they would leave the fixed exchange rate to the euro, so the central banks had to set high interest rates to compensate for the depreciation risk. This further reduced asset prices and exacerbated the problems in the financial sector. Booms and busts in the real estate market have triggered many financial crises and they played a central role in the recent crisis, in the US as well as in Europe. The risk in loans to real estate had been grossly underestimated.

In September 2008, the American investment bank Lehman Brothers went bankrupt. A key contributing factor was its large exposure to housing loans. Lehman Brothers was one of four big investment banks in the US, and as it went bankrupt a shock wave was sent through the world financial system. There was a general loss of trust. No one was sure who had claims on Lehman, or whether other institutions with similar assets would also go bankrupt. Nobody knew for certain who had those 'toxic assets' or who might be affected by the crisis, directly or indirectly. As financial investors realized that major financial institutions could actually go bankrupt, they stopped lending to those institutions. Banks and other financial intermediaries found it hard, sometimes impossible, to roll over their short-term debt. The markets froze and the financial crisis spread quickly across the world.

Fig. 18.7 *Interest rates in the United Kingdom*

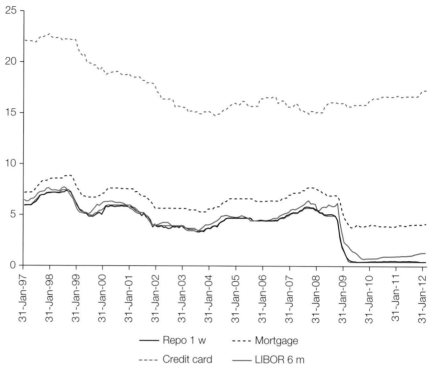

Source: Bank of England webpage, http://www.bankofengland.co.uk.

Even banks which seemed to have their house in order found it difficult to roll over their debt. Furthermore, the interbank market ceased to function properly. One measure of the loss of trust is the difference between the interest rates in the interbank market and the repo rate – that is, the rate on repurchase agreements with the central bank (see Chapter 10). Fig. 18.7 shows that the spread between the UK six-month interbank rate (LIBOR) and the repo rate increased substantially during the crisis.

As mentioned in Section 18.5, banking regulations are meant to guarantee that the financial system is stable. Capital requirements are supposed to reduce the risk that banks go bankrupt and deposit insurance should prevent bank runs and protect deposit holders. So why did these regulations not prevent the worldwide financial crisis that culminated in 2008–2009? The following factors appear to be important:

- Some of the most severe problems appeared in the *shadow banking system,* which was mentioned in the previous section. Institutions such as the American investment banks had much lower equity capital than commercial banks and they were not covered by deposit insurance. This made them particularly sensitive to large losses and bank runs.
- Only in a few instances did deposit holders actually queue up outside the bank in order to withdraw their money. Yet it could be argued that a bank run

occurred since those who were lending short term to banks refused to renew their lending. As we have mentioned above, banks rely to a considerable extent on *wholesale financing* – short-term borrowing in the financial markets – which is not covered by deposit insurance. The general loss of confidence made it difficult, sometimes even impossible for banks to roll over the debt – to emit new securities as the old ones matured. In this sense, we can think of the 2008 financial crisis as a worldwide bank run.

- *Securitization* contributed to the crisis by creating complicated linkages between institutions and making it hard to evaluate the risks and losses of individual institutions. Securitization helps to spread risks, but it also spreads the losses in a complicated way. As the financial crises broke out, there was a lot of uncertainty about who had 'toxic assets' on their portfolios and how large the losses would be.[9]
- *Fire sales* also contributed to the crisis. Financial institutions that had made losses, and could not raise new equity during the crisis, were forced to sell their assets, which led to sharply reduced prices of those assets. As asset prices decreased, other banks saw their equity capital being reduced, so they were forced to also sell assets in a vicious circle of falling asset prices and forced sales of assets.

Short-run crisis management

In order to limit the extent of the crisis, central banks and governments stepped in to rescue banks and other financial institutions. These rescue operations were often described as 'pumping money into the banks'. To be more precise, the support to banks took several different forms: *short-term lending, medium-term lending, guarantees*, and provision of *equity*. In some cases, banks were *nationalized*.

Short-term lending

As discussed in Chapter 10, central banks regularly lend money to banks. This is nothing new. What was new was the scale of the lending. When the markets froze, some banks were unable to roll over debt, so the central bank had to step in as *lender of last resort* on a big scale.

Normally, banks that have excess liquidity lend to banks that have a shortage of liquidity in the interbank market. During the financial crisis, banks were unwilling to lend to each other in the interbank market. Instead of lending directly to other banks, banks with excess liquidity left their excess balances overnight on their accounts at the central bank. As a result, banks that needed liquidity had to borrow from the central bank and this led to an explosion of the balance sheets of the central banks as both assets and debts increased. As explained in Chapter 7, the monetary base consists of currency and the claims that banks have on the central bank, so the monetary base also increased.

5

---

9 Another factor was that investment banks, which had sold securities to other investors, had made commitments and guarantees that made them responsible for losses even if the assets were not on their balance sheets.

From a macroeconomic point of view, we can think of this as a shift in the demand for monetary base. Normally, banks economize on their holdings of monetary base by lending to each other in the interbank market. When lending in the interbank market was reduced, demand for monetary base increased, and this increased demand was satisfied by short-term borrowing from the central bank. From this point of view, one could argue that this was business as usual for the central banks, but on a larger scale. The central banks were just doing what they normally do: accommodating a shock to the demand for monetary base.

The effect of a shock that increases the demand for monetary base is illustrated in Fig. 18.8. Demand for monetary base increases for a given level of production, so if the monetary base is held constant, the interest rate will increase. The *LM* curve shifts up. Since the central bank does not want the interest rate to increase, it has to increase the monetary base so the *LM* curve is shifted downwards again. We have already discussed how the central bank should react to shocks to the demand for money in Chapter 10.

Fig. 18.8 *Increased demand for monetary base due to freezing of the interbank market*

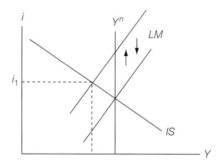

Another way to think of this is as insurance provided by the central bank. Loans in the interbank market are made without collateral, so if a bank goes bankrupt, other banks will lose their money. When one bank lends to the central bank and another bank borrows from the central bank, the lending bank avoids the risk of losses if the borrowing bank defaults. Banks pay for this insurance because the overnight deposit rate at the central bank is lower than the rate in the interbank market. (Recall the discussion of the interest rate corridor in Chapter 10.) The difference can be seen as an insurance fee that the central bank charges for taking on the credit risk.

Medium-term loans

As discussed above, banks are dependent on wholesale financing and they need to roll over their short-term debt. But many banks had difficulties issuing securities during the financial crisis. In many cases, central banks stepped in with short- and medium-term lending to banks, rather than overnight loans only.

Guarantees

In some cases, governments issued guarantees for the short-term lending of the banks. This means that those who were lending money to the bank were guaranteed to get their money back even if the bank defaulted. Effectively, we can think of this as a widening of the deposit insurance, which made it easier for the banks to borrow in the markets. Banks were charged a fee for these guarantees.

Equity and nationalization

Banks that had made large losses and risked not satisfying the capital requirements had to raise new capital, or reduce their lending, so as to satisfy the capital requirements. But raising new capital was difficult when there was uncertainty about the bank's situation. In several cases, governments stepped in with new equity capital and became major shareholders of the banks. In some cases, governments took over the banks. By taking over banks, partially or fully, and honouring the debts of those banks, the government prevented the systemic effects of losses spreading through the financial system.

Purchase of assets

In the autumn of 2008 the *Troubled Assets Relief Program* (TARP) was introduced in the US. The aim was that the government would relieve the banks by buying some of their 'toxic' assets. An obvious problem with such a programme is to determine the purchase prices of those assets. The eventual losses are unknown and in a crisis situation the market prices of the assets might be distorted. If the government were to pay too high a price for an asset it would effectively be subsidizing the bank that sold the asset; if the government offered a low price, the bank might prefer to hold on to the asset in the hope that it would recover some of its value. In the end, only some of the money allocated to TARP was used to buy assets from the banks.

Stress tests

As we have seen, lack of information is a key element in bank runs and financial crises. Uncertainty about the size of the losses may cause a general loss of trust, so the markets freeze. To reduce the uncertainty, several governments and the European Union conducted *stress tests* where they tried to evaluate the size of the losses each bank would suffer under different scenarios. The purpose was that the stress tests would reduce the uncertainty by clarifying which banks were in trouble and which were not.

'Throw money at the problem and then mop it up'

These were the main elements of short-term crisis management. Fortunately, the money that was 'pumped' into the banks did not go into a black hole. Most of it will be recovered. Most of it was loans that will be paid back or have already been paid back. When a government takes over a bank, or part of it, the shares can eventually be sold if the bank recovers. The American economist Charles Kindleberger summarized the principles of financial crisis management by saying that economists think that they know how to handle financial crises: 'throw money at them, and after the crisis is over, mop the money up'.[10]

---

10 Charles P. Kindleberger, *Manias, Panics, and Crashes*, 3rd edn (New York: John Wiley and Sons, 1996).

Measures to avoid future financial crises

One way to reduce the likelihood of future financial crisis is to reduce the level of debt in the banking sector. As we mentioned above, an increase in capital requirements is a main element of the new agreement on banking regulation, Basel III.

Another possibility is to regulate liquidity. Some countries have sharpened the regulation of the maturity structure of the debt, requiring that a certain proportion of the borrowing must have a longer maturity than one year. If more of the borrowing is long term, fewer bonds will mature in a given time interval. This will leave more time for the banks, and for the government, to deal with the situation if a new crisis unfolds.

Higher equity capital and less dependence on short-term borrowing should make the banking system more robust. At the same time, we should note that credit intermediation and maturity transformation are key services produced by banks. Very strict regulation will limit their ability to provide these services and this may restrict financing available to firms. There is also a risk that, if commercial banks are too heavily regulated, credit intermediation and maturity transformation will be taken over by non-bank institutions which are less strictly regulated. The shadow banking system may grow. Many observers have argued that the scope of regulation must be broadened to cover institutions that are not formally banks but perform functions similar to those of banks: 'If it looks like a bank, regulate it as a bank.'[11]

Lack of transparency is another problem. As discussed above, securitization contributed to the crisis because many assets were so complicated that it was hard to evaluate the risks. Moreover, many of these assets are not traded in organized exchanges but 'over the counter', directly between sellers and buyers. One way to increase transparency is to standardize assets so they can be traded in organized exchanges at publicly known market prices. When the assets are priced in the market, it is easier to evaluate the financial situation of a bank and to know if it is in trouble or not.

As discussed above, financial crises are often caused by booms and busts in the real estate market. A much debated issue is whether monetary policymakers should take account of asset prices and try to counteract bubbles in asset prices. To what extent did monetary policy, with very low interest rates in the period 2002–2005, contribute to inflated prices of real estate before the crisis? Would it have been better to keep interest rates in the US and the UK higher between 2002 and 2005 in order to cool down the housing market? Many economists would argue that the primary job of the central bank is to stabilize the macroeconomy and that policymakers should only take account of asset prices if they affect aggregate demand and inflation. Higher interest rates in 2002 would have weakened the economy in a situation where growth was relatively weak. At the same time, it is clear that movements in asset prices play a very important role in boom–bust

---

11 This is an application of the general principle: 'If it walks like a duck, and quacks like a duck, it is a duck.'

cycles. Alternative ways of dealing with such fluctuations are to use property taxes or to regulate the level of lending, for example, by not allowing banks to lend above a certain proportion of the market value of a house.

Conclusion

The future is hard to predict; unforeseen events happen, risks will be misjudged, and asset prices will continue to fluctuate. But asset price movements by themselves are not sufficient to create a financial crisis. Neither the stock market crash in 1987, nor the collapse of the IT bubble in 2000 caused financial crises. What turns losses into a financial crisis is the fact that the losses occur in financial institutions with high levels of debt, which are dependent on short-term borrowing, and therefore susceptible to bank runs. Increased capital requirements for banks should improve the ability of those banks to handle losses, but that is hardly sufficient to eliminate the possibility of future financial crises. There is still the possibility of runs in the wholesale financing market and against less regulated institutions. The debate about financial regulations to prevent future financial crises will continue.[12]

18.8   Macroeconomic management of financial crises

As the financial crisis culminated in 2008–2009, the outlook for the future became very pessimistic, and this had big effects on consumption and especially on investment (see Fig. 1.1 in Chapter 1). In terms of the *IS-LM* model, increased pessimism implied a big leftward shift of the *IS* curve. What the central bank should do in such a situation is obvious: reduce the interest rate. Unfortunately, there are two complications that limit the power of monetary policy in a severe crisis. First, increased uncertainty leads to increased margins between the interest rates set by the central bank and the rates relevant to consumers and firms. Second, there is a zero lower bound on the interest rate which limits the monetary policy response when there is a severe negative shock.

Increases in margins charged by the banks

In our macroeconomic model, we assumed that there was only one interest rate for all kinds of loans. In practice, there are of course different interest rates for different types of credit. The interest rate that banks charge firms and households is

---

12 Recent issues of *Journal of Economic Perspectives* and the *EEAG Report on the European Economy* contain interesting articles about these issues and references to the relevant literature. On the websites of central banks you can find speeches and documents describing how the central banks handled the crisis. How the crisis evolved can be studied by reading the *World Economic Outlook* from the IMF, available online at www.imf.org. A classic review of historical experiences is Charles P. Kindleberger, *Manias, Panics, and Crashes*, 3rd edn (New York: John Wiley and Sons, 1996). A review of the financial crisis in Finland and Sweden in 1991–1992 can be found in Lars Jonung, Jaakko Kiander, and Pentti Vartia (eds), *The Great Financial Crisis in Finland and Sweden: The Nordic Experience of Financial Liberalization* (Cheltenham: Edward Elgar, 2009).

higher than the interest rate on government debt. In terms of our macroeconomic model, let i denote the interest rate on short-term government debt. As explained in Chapter 10, this interest rate is effectively controlled by the central bank. Assume that all credit is intermediated through the banking system and let m be the margin between the bank lending rate and the short-term interest rate on government debt. Then the interest rate that is relevant for the borrowers is $i + m$ and we get the modified *IS* equation:

$$Y = C(Y{-}T, Y^e - T^e, i + m{-}\pi^e, A) + I(i + m{-}\pi^e, Y^e, K) + G + NX(\varepsilon, Y^*, Y). \qquad \textit{IS}$$

In a financial crisis, increased uncertainty will lead to an increased margin between the lending rate and the rate on government debt, and this shifts the *IS* curve to the left. The policy conclusion is obvious: the central bank should reduce the interest rate to counteract the effect of the increase in the margin. In addition, a financial crisis closes down the flow of credit in some parts of the financial system and firms and households become more pessimistic about the future. All these factors have negative effects on investment, consumption, and aggregate demand, which call for further reductions in the interest rate. In fact, central banks reduced interest rates dramatically in the autumn of 2008, but the effect was partly counteracted by increasing margins (see Fig. 18.7 above).

The zero lower bound on the interest rate

When the economy is slowing down the central bank will normally counter the downturn by reducing the interest rate. The central bank is able to reduce the interest rate because it can offer to lend money at a lower rate. However, there is a limit to how low far the interest rate can be reduced: it cannot become negative. If the interest rate on Treasury bills were negative, firms and households would prefer to hold coins and notes instead of Treasury bills, so the demand for cash would be very large. If the interest rate is exactly zero, the return on Treasury bills and cash is the same, so people can as well hold cash as Treasury bills. Fig. 18.9 shows the demand for money as a function of the interest rate. For a positive interest rate, there is an opportunity cost of holding cash and people hold as much currency as they need for their transactions. As the interest rate falls, the demand for money increases, but as the interest rate falls to zero, demand for money becomes

Fig. 18.9 *The effect of an increase in the money supply when the interest rate falls to zero*

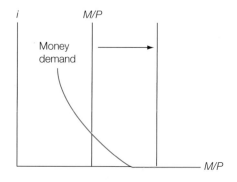

infinitely elastic – the demand curve becomes flat. Once people have enough cash to cover their transactions, currency and Treasury bills are perfect substitutes.

What does this imply for monetary policy? It means that increases in the money supply beyond a certain point will not reduce the interest rate. All that will happen if the central bank buys Treasury bills is that people exchange one piece of paper, which does not yield interest, with another piece of paper, which does not yield interest. In the words of John Maynard Keynes, the increase in the money supply falls into a *liquidity trap*.

The zero lower bound can have serious consequences for stabilization policy. To see this, note that for low levels of income, money demand is low relative to money supply and the interest rate falls to zero. This means that the *LM* curve becomes horizontal as the interest rate goes to zero. An *LM* curve with a zero lower bound is illustrated in Fig 18.10. Assume that the *IS* curve is initially IS_0, the interest rate is i_0, production is on its natural level, and expected inflation is equal to the inflation target. Now there is a large negative demand shock so the *IS* curve shifts to IS_1. The central bank increases the money supply so *LM* shifts from LM_0 to LM_1. The interest rate falls to zero, but this is not sufficient to counteract the shock, so production is still below the natural level.

The central bank appears to be powerless in this situation. Beyond the point where the interest rate hits the zero lower bound, the central bank becomes unable to counter negative demand shocks with a cut in the interest rate. Furthermore, the low level of production means that inflation will fall, and if people expect production to remain low, expectations about future inflation will fall. This means that the expected real interest rate will rise, which will shift the *IS* curve further to the left because consumption and investment depend on the expected real interest rate. (Note that expected inflation is one of the variables in the *IS* equation above.)

Fig. 18.10 *A large negative demand shock and the zero lower bound*

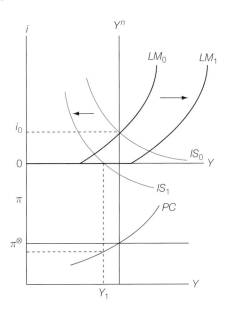

Thus we get a further reduction in production and we may end up in a vicious circle of deflation and weak demand.

Another way to look at this is to consider our discussion of the Taylor principle in Chapter 10. There we argued that when actual and expected inflation rise above target, the central bank should raise the interest rate more than the increase in inflation so as to raise the expected real interest rate and cool down the economy. Of course, a similar argument holds if inflation falls below the target level. But what happens when an economy has fallen into the liquidity trap is that actual and expected inflation fall but the central bank is unable to reduce the nominal interest rate, so the real interest rate increases, and this leads to a further fall in aggregate demand.

Some economists have argued that the situation is not as serious as it may appear. The central bank could use other measures in this situation. In principle, the central bank could print money (or, more precisely, increase the monetary base) to buy anything. It can buy long-term government bonds, housing bonds, corporate bonds, and real assets. It can buy foreign currency so as to reduce the value of its own currency and stimulate exports. If the money supply is increased considerably, it is hard to believe that the real value of the money will not fall. At some point, inflation should increase so that the real interest rate is reduced.[13]

What have we learned?

Firms finance their real and financial investments with debt and equity. Equity arises from money invested by shareholders and retained earnings being reinvested.

Debt holders are promised a fixed repayment – the loan plus interest; it is only in the case of bankruptcy that the debt holders get less than what they were promised. Shareholders are not promised a fixed return on their investment.

In normal times, it is the shareholders who bear the risk. Equity is a buffer that absorbs shocks.

The higher the share of the investment that is financed by debt, the more risky is the debt. Lenders will typically require that a substantial share of the investments are financed by equity so that there is a sufficient buffer that can absorb losses without the company becoming insolvent.

In practice, a company may have equity in the order of 30–40 percent of its total assets while 60–70 percent of the investments are financed by debt, but the division between debt and equity differs between industries and countries. Banks may have around 10 percent equity.

13 For writings about the liquidity trap, and how to deal with it, see e.g. Paul R. Krugman, 'It's baaack: Japan's slump and the return of the liquidity trap', *Brookings Papers on Economic Activity*, 1998:2, 137–205, and Lars E. O. Svensson, 'Escaping from a liquidity trap and deflation: the foolproof way and others', *Journal of Economic Perspectives*, 17 (2003), 145–166.

When firms have to finance a share of their investments by retained earnings, there is a link between current profits and investment. If there is an increase in aggregate demand, firms produce more and make more profits, and this makes it easier to finance investments, leading to a further increase in aggregate demand. This mechanism is called the financial accelerator.

If expectations about future production and profits increase, share prices should increase. Therefore, we expect the stock market to predict future economic developments, but stock prices vary more than can be explained by changes in expected future dividends. There is *excess volatility* in the stock market.

Under certain conditions, investment is a function of *Tobin's q*, the market value of the capital stock relative to the replacement value of the capital stock.

Direct lending from households to firms, or other households, is usually not possible because of lack of trust and information and maturity mismatch.

Normally, banks provide households with a safe way to save although the repayments of the bank loans are uncertain. Banks monitor credit and establish long-term lending relationships with firms. The law of large numbers means that the share of credit losses in the loan portfolio can be estimated rather well and the bank's equity acts as a buffer that absorbs unusually large losses on the loans.

Banks provide liquidity by allowing deposit holders to withdraw their deposits at any time although a large part of the assets of the bank consist of long-term lending. The law of large numbers means that withdrawals and new deposits tend to cancel out and banks have some liquid assets, such as government bonds, which can be sold at short notice.

In theory, a *bank run* can topple a bank even if it has substantial buffers of liquidity and equity. In practice, however, we would expect a bank run to be triggered when a bank has made large losses, or is feared to have made large losses.

Problems in some financial institutions can spread and lead to a financial crisis because financial institutions have claims on each other, people fear that other institutions have made similar losses, and *fire sales* reduce the value of the assets on the balance sheets.

Capital requirements require banks to have a certain amount of equity relative to assets so there is a buffer that can absorb losses. *Deposit insurance* is meant to protect deposit holders and prevent bank runs.

Banks finance a large part of their investments by short term borrowing (wholesale financing) which is not covered by deposit insurance. The shadow banking system is not as tightly regulated as regular commercial banks. Securitization has created very complicated links between financial institutions. These factors played a role in the spread of the financial crisis in 2007–2009.

Like many other financial crises, the 2008 financial crises started with large losses on loans to real estate when house price bubbles collapsed in several countries.

Central banks and governments managed to prevent a general collapse of the financial system by supporting banks with liquidity in the form of short and medium term lending. They also offered guarantees for loans taken by banks to help them roll over their short-term debt. In some cases, the government injected equity and took over the bank or a large part of it. Stress tests were meant to restore confidence by improving the information about the situation of various financial institutions.

A main element in the Basel III agreement is that capital requirements are increased.

When a financial crisis arises, the central bank should reduce the interest rate, but two factors limit the power of monetary policy. Increased uncertainty leads to rising margins between the repo rate, which is controlled by the central bank, and the rates at which households and firms can borrow. Also, the interest rate set by the central bank may hit the zero lower bound.

Weak demand may lead to very low expected inflation, or even deflation, which raises the expected real interest rate, leading to a further weakening of aggregate demand.

Exercises

1. A company has the following balance sheet:

Assets		Liabilities and owner's equity	
Financial assets	3000	Liabilities	6000
Real assets	7000	Equity	4000
Total	*10000*	*Total*	*1000*

How does the balance sheet change if:
   a) new shares are issued to shareholders and sold for 2000 and 50 percent of the money is used for real investments?
   b) the company makes a profit of 2000; half of it is used for real investments and half is used to pay off loans?

2. An entrepreneur wants to invest in a project that costs 100,000 euros. The return on the project is very uncertain but it is known that, in the worst case, the equipment can be sold to recover 60,000 euros. There is only one potential investor other than the entrepreneur. This investor has a lot of money but refuses to take any risk and requires a 20 percent return on her investment.
   a) What contract would you suggest between the entrepreneur and the investor?

   b) How much money does the entrepreneur have to invest in order to carry through the project?

3. The return on an investment is known to be either +50 percent or −30 percent with equal probabilities. Outside lenders lend at zero interest rate but they refuse to take risk. Owners try to finance as large a share as possible of the project by debt and the rest is financed with equity.
   a) What is the expected return, in percent, on the investment project?
   b) How large a share of the investment can be financed by loans?
   c) What is the expected return to the shareholders?
   d) What is the maximum and minimum return (in percent) for the shareholders?

4. A company pays out 10 million in dividends. Investors are risk neutral and require an expected return on shares of 5 percent. What is the value of the company if:
   a) dividends are expected to remain constant?
   b) dividends are expected to grow 3 percent per year?

c) dividends are expected to grow 3 percent per year but there is also a risk that the company goes bankrupt, so dividends fall to zero from then on? The risk of bankruptcy is one percent each year?

5. Is banking regulation sufficient to prevent a major financial crisis in the future? Discuss.

6. What are the main tasks of the central bank when there is a financial crisis?

7. The Taylor rule refers to the interest rate set by the central bank (see Chapter 10). Discuss how the Taylor rule might be modified to take account of changes in the margins between different interest rates.

8. Assume that the output gap is minus 4 percent. Consider the Taylor rule that was presented in Chapter 10.

a) What interest rate does it prescribe if there is zero inflation?

b) What interest rate does it prescribe if there is deflation, so prices fall by one percent per year?

c) Why are these prescriptions impossible to implement?

9. 'Lower nominal wage increases will always lead to higher employment.' Is this true?

10. Suppose that there is 2 percent productivity growth and the central bank follows the Taylor rule. What level of wage growth will minimize the real interest rate?
(Hint: Use the relation between wage growth and inflation that we derived in Chapter 9.)

Answers to the exercises can be found at:
www.palgrave.com/economics/gottfries.

Appendix

Tobin's q theory of investment with debt and equity, and monopolistic competition

Suppose that firms finance a share θ of their investments by borrowing. All profits are handed out as dividends to the shareholders and a share $1 - \theta$ of the investment is financed by new issues of shares. Then the real profit (dividend) of the typical firm is

$$\pi = Y - \frac{W}{P}N - \delta K - \theta r K.$$

Assume that, for a given capital stock, the firm hires the profit-maximizing number of workers, so that

$$\frac{MPL}{1+\mu} = \frac{W}{P}.$$

With Cobb–Douglas production function we have $MPL = (1 - \alpha) Y/N$ and substituting into the expression for profits above, we get

$$\pi = Y - \frac{1-\alpha}{1+\mu}Y - \delta K - \theta r K = \frac{\mu+\alpha}{1+\mu}Y - \delta K - \theta r K.$$

To simplify, we assume that there is no growth, real profits (dividends) are expected to remain unchanged, and that shareholders discount future profits by r. Then the value of the shares is

$$S = \frac{1}{r}\left(\frac{\mu+\alpha}{1+\mu}Y - (\delta + \theta r) K\right).$$

With debt and equity, we must calculate Tobin's q as the value of the shares *and the borrowing* of the firms relative to the replacement value of the capital stock:

$$q = \frac{S + \theta K}{K} = \frac{S}{K} + \theta = \frac{1}{r}\left(\frac{\mu + \alpha}{1 + \mu}\frac{Y}{K} - \delta - \theta r\right) + \theta = \frac{1}{r}\left(\frac{\mu + \alpha}{1 + \mu}\frac{Y}{K} - \delta\right).$$

In this case, we can assume that investment is determined by the ratio between the real marginal revenue product minus depreciation and the real interest rate:

$$\frac{MPK/(1 + \mu) - \delta}{r}.$$

With a Cobb–Douglas production function, the marginal product of capital is $\alpha Y/K$. Thus, we see that investment is a function of

$$\frac{1}{r}\left[\frac{\alpha}{1 + \mu}\frac{Y}{K} - \delta\right].$$

With a positive mark-up, the relation between Tobin's q and investment is modified. Monopoly power raises the value of the firms in the economy because the capital share increases, but it has a negative effect on the incentives to invest.

KEY EQUATIONS

This section summarizes the key equations that describe our macroeconomic model.

Production and prices

The production function shows how production, Y, depends on the inputs of capital, K, and labour, N, and the technology factor, E:

$$Y = F(K, EN).$$

A specific production function is the Cobb–Douglas production function:

$$Y = K^{\alpha} (EN)^{1-\alpha}.$$

By taking the derivative with respect to N we get the marginal product of labour:

$$MPL = (1 - \alpha) E^{1-\alpha} \left(\frac{K}{N} \right)^{\alpha}.$$

With monopolistic competition, firms set prices with a mark-up, μ, on marginal cost:

$$P = (1 + \mu) MC.$$

The marginal cost is the wage divided by the marginal product of labour, so we have

$$P = (1 + \mu) \frac{W}{MPL}$$

and thus

$$\frac{W}{P} = \frac{MPL}{1 + \mu}.$$

With the Cobb–Douglas production function we have

$$MPL = K^{\alpha} (1 - \alpha) E^{1-\alpha} N^{-\alpha} = (1 - \alpha) \frac{Y}{N}$$

and thus

$$\frac{WN}{PY} = \frac{1 - \alpha}{1 + \mu}.$$

The real interest rate, investment, and consumption

Inflation is the rate of growth of the price level: $\pi_t = \Delta P_t / P_{t-1}$. One plus the real interest rate is the price of goods today divided by the discounted price of goods next year:

$$1 + r_{t+1} = \frac{P_t}{P_{t+1}/(1 + i_t)} = \frac{1 + i_t}{P_{t+1}/P_t} = \frac{1 + i_t}{1 + \pi_{t+1}}$$

or, approximately

$$r_{t+1} \approx i_t - \pi_{t+1}.$$

Firms invest in order to increase the capital stock and to replace depreciated capital:

$$I_t = K_{t+1}^d - K_t + \delta K_t.$$

K_{t+1}^d is the desired capital stock next period and δ is depreciation. The profit-maximizing investment level is such that the real marginal revenue product minus depreciation is equal to the real interest rate:

$$\frac{MPK}{1+\mu} - \delta = r.$$

According to the investment function, investment depends on the real interest rate, r, expected future income, Y^e, and the existing capital stock at the beginning of the period, K:

$$I = I(r, Y^e, K).$$

The utility-maximizing consumption/savings decision is such that the ratio of marginal utility of consuming today divided by the discounted marginal utility next year is equal to one plus the real interest rate:

$$\frac{u'(C_t)}{u'(C_{t+1})/(1+\rho)} = 1 + r_{t+1},$$

where ρ is the subjective discount rate. Real disposable income is production minus tax payments plus the real interest rate on net claims on the government and foreign households and firms:

$$Y^d = Y - T + r(D+F).$$

According to the consumption function, consumption depends on income today, expected future income, the real interest rate and the level of assets (wealth):

$$C = C(Y^d, Y^e - T^e, r, A).$$

Long-run growth

With constant returns to scale, production per effective worker depends on the capital stock per effective worker:

$$\frac{Y}{EN} = F\left(\frac{K}{EN}, 1\right) = f(k) \qquad \text{where} \quad k = \frac{K}{EN}.$$

On the steady state growth path the capital stock per effective worker is determined by

$$\frac{f'(k^*)}{1+\mu} - \delta = \bar{r}.$$

With constant capital per effective worker on the steady state growth path, the capital stock and production grow at the same rate as the effective number of workers:

$$K = k^* EN, \qquad Y = f(k^*) EN, \qquad \frac{\Delta K}{K} = \frac{\Delta Y}{Y} = g + n.$$

In a closed economy, the long-run level of the real interest rate is equal to the subjective discount rate plus the technological growth rate: $\bar{r} \approx \rho + g$.

The labour market and the Phillips curve

The unemployment rate is the fraction of the labour force that is not employed:

$$u = \frac{U}{L} = \frac{L-N}{L}.$$

The wage-setting equation says that if unemployment is above the natural level, firms want to raise wages less than the average wage increase, and conversely:

$$\frac{\Delta W_t^d}{W_{t-1}} = \frac{\Delta W_t}{W_{t-1}} - b\left(u_t - u_t^n\right).$$

In the long run, desired wage increases must be equal to actual wage increases, so unemployment must be on the natural level. This means that employment is on the natural level given by

$$N^n = (1 - u^n)\,L.$$

Assuming that a share $1 - \lambda$ of the wages are set in advance we can derive a Phillips curve:

$$\frac{\Delta W}{W} = \frac{\Delta W^e}{W} - \hat{b}\,(u - u^n); \qquad \hat{b} = \frac{\lambda b}{1 - \lambda}.$$

The rate of wage increase depends on the expected wage increase and unemployment. In the short-run analysis we disregard capital, so inflation is the rate of wage increase minus productivity growth:

$$\pi = \frac{\Delta W}{W} - \frac{\Delta E}{E}.$$

Another version of the Phillips curve relates inflation to expected inflation π^e, the output gap $\hat{Y}$, and a cost–push shock z:

$$\pi = \pi^e + \beta\hat{Y} + z.$$

Government debt

The change in real government debt is equal to the primary deficit, $G - T$, plus the real interest rate, r, times net government debt, D:

$$\Delta D = G - T + rD.$$

The change in the ratio of net government debt to GDP is determined by

$$\Delta \frac{D}{Y} = \frac{G - T}{Y} + (r - g)\frac{D}{Y},$$

where g is now the growth rate of real GDP.

The open economy

The real exchange rate is the price of domestic goods relative to foreign goods:

$$\varepsilon = \frac{eP}{P*}.$$

Net exports depend primarily on the real exchange rate and domestic and foreign income:

$$NX = NX\,(\varepsilon, Y^*, Y).$$

The interest parity condition says that the expected return on loans in the foreign currency should be equal to the expected return on loans in the currency of the small open economy:

$$1 + i^* = (1 + i)\,\frac{e^e}{e} \qquad \text{or approximately} \qquad i^* = i + \frac{\Delta e^e}{e}.$$

With a constant real exchange rate in the long run we have

$$\frac{\Delta e}{e} = \pi^* - \pi \qquad \text{and} \qquad r = r^*.$$

The current account, net exports plus the return on net claims on foreign countries, determines the change in net claims on foreign countries. It is equal to savings minus investment for the country as a whole:[1]

$$\Delta F = NX + rF = \underbrace{Y + rF - C - G - I}_{\text{saving minus investment}}$$

$$= \underbrace{Y + r(D+F) - T - C - I}_{\text{private net lending}} + \underbrace{T - G - rD}_{\text{government net lending}}.$$

Production and the interest rate in the short run

In the short run, product demand is determined by the IS equation:

$$Y = C(Y - T, Y^e - T^e, i - \pi^e, A) + I(i - \pi^e, Y^e, K) + G + NX(eP/P^*, Y^*, Y).$$

The interest rate is determined in the money market:

$$\frac{M}{P} = \frac{Y}{V(i)}.$$

With a credibly fixed exchange rate, e is fixed and the interest parity condition says that the interest rate must be the same as abroad. With a floating exchange rate, we instead combine IS and the interest parity condition, so we get the IS^* equation:

$$Y = C(Y - T, Y^e - T^e, i - \pi^e, A) + I(i - \pi^e, Y^e, K) + G + NX\left(\frac{1+i}{1+i^*}\frac{e^e P}{P^*}, Y^*, Y\right).$$

---

1 In the statistics the current account is reported in nominal terms while here we express the change in real net claims on the rest of the world. In reality, there are also other primary incomes from the rest of the world, such as wage income, and international transfers.

INDEX

Printed and bound in China